ONLINE DISTANCE EDUCATION

Issues in Distance Education
Series editors: Terry Anderson and David Wiley

Distance education is the fastest-growing mode of both formal and informal teaching, training, and learning. It is multi-faceted in nature, encompassing e-learning and mobile learning, as well as immersive learning environments. Issues in Distance Education presents recent research results and offers informative and accessible overviews, analyses, and explorations of current topics and concerns and the technologies employed in distance education. Each volume focuses on critical questions and emerging trends, while also situating these developments within the historical evolution of distance education as a specialized mode of instruction. The series is aimed at a wide group of readers, including teachers, trainers, administrators, researchers, and students.

Series Titles

The Theory and Practice of Online Learning, Second Edition
Edited by Terry Anderson

Mobile Learning: Transforming the Delivery of Education and Training
Edited by Mohamed Ally

A Designer's Log: Case Studies in Instructional Design
Michael Power

Accessible Elements: Teaching Science Online and at a Distance
Edited by Dietmar Kennepohl and Lawton Shaw

Emerging Technologies in Distance Education
Edited by George Veletsianos

Flexible Pedagogy, Flexible Practice: Notes from the Trenches of Distance Education
Edited by Elizabeth Burge, Chère Campbell Gibson, and Terry Gibson

Online Distance Education: Towards a Research Agenda
Edited by Olaf Zawacki-Richter and Terry Anderson

ONLINE DISTANCE EDUCATION

Towards a Research Agenda

Edited by
OLAF ZAWACKI-RICHTER
AND TERRY ANDERSON

AU PRESS

Published by AU Press, Athabasca University
1200, 10011 – 109 Street, Edmonton, AB T5J 3S8

ISBN (print) 978-1-927356-62-3   (PDF) 978-1-927356-63-0   (epub) 978-1-927356-64-7
doi: 10.15215/aupress/9781927356623.01

Cover design by Marvin Harder
Interior design by Sergiy Kozakov
Printed and bound in Canada by Marquis Book Printers

Library and Archives Canada Cataloguing in Publication
    Online distance education : towards a research agenda / Olaf Zawacki-Richter and Terry
Anderson, eds.

(Issues in distance education series, 1919-4382 ; 8)
Includes bibliographical references and index. Issued in print and electronic formats.
. ISBN 978-1-927356-62-3 (pbk.). – ISBN 978-1-927356-63-0 (pdf). –
ISBN 978-1-927356-64-7 (epub)

    1. Distance education–Computer-assisted instruction–Research. I. Anderson, Terry, 1950-,
editor of compilation II. Zawacki-Richter, Olaf, 1972-, editor of compilation III. Series: Issues
in distance education series ; 8

LC5803.C65O55 2013   371.35'8072   C2013-905413-8
C2013-905414-6

We acknowledge the financial support of the Government of Canada through
the Canada Book Fund (CFB) for our publishing activities.

Canadian   Patrimoine
Heritage   canadien

Assistance provided by the Government of Alberta, Alberta Multimedia
Development Fund.

Contents

Figures and Tables

Foreword

Research in the emerging field of online distance education has, so far, evolved in a somewhat haphazard fashion, consisting largely of an assemblage of contributions made by researchers working on different topics, often in isolation from one another. Olaf Zawacki-Richter and Terry Anderson's proposal that research in the field should instead be guided by a systematic agenda is therefore both timely and richly deserving praise. This much-needed volume provides practitioners, theorists, and researchers with a comprehensive survey of the state of online distance education as an independent field of inquiry, while also offering a clear orientation for future research. Like early explorers, Zawacki-Richter and Anderson have succeeded in mapping territory that, while not unknown, has remained uncharted. This is a remarkable achievement in a field so very new. Educators are already aware that online distance education is the way of tomorrow, and this book will help to ensure that research in this area becomes a priority.

Readers may be surprised to see that, even in relatively short span of time, research in online distance education has grown to be so multifaceted that the editors have subdivided it into three levels: macro-, meso-, and micro-. In this way, three frames of reference are established that call for different theoretical justifications and research methods. Each frame is characterized by a number of significant typical research themes. These themes were not developed in the abstract, with specific pedagogical goals in mind, but were instead empirically derived from the existing literature by applying the Delphi method.

The achievements of the volume can be understood from a number of perspectives:

(1) Not only does the book present a detailed structure of the field of online distance education and a respective research agenda, but its chapters also demonstrate why the proposed structure is justified.

(2) The volume mirrors the ongoing globalization of education. By incorporating ideas and practical achievements drawn from various institutional settings throughout the world, it facilitates the international collaboration of online distance education researchers.

(3) A volume like this one could only become possible in an era of advanced digitalization. Digitalization facilitated the Delphi study immensely. Using social network analysis techniques, the editors were quickly able to identify research experts in the field of distance education all across the globe and invite them to participate in this project. Digital communications media expedited the exchange of relevant research ideas, issues, approaches, theoretical interpretations, and findings. The research agenda that the editors present in this volume is the result of a collaborative process that occurred at a pace never before experienced.

(4) The essays in the volume stand as proof that distance education can no longer be considered a one-dimensional phenomenon. In the past, laypersons, practitioners, and even specialists in the field often described distance education simply as an approach in which proximity is replaced by distance and spoken dialogue by mediated communication. This overly simple definition lingers in the memory of many people. In contrast, this volume convincingly demonstrates that online distance education is a comprehensive, many-sided process and a multifunctional system. This is a major step forward.

(5) In the same way that, during the 1970s and 1980s, the founding of open universities enhanced the image of distance education, in part through the establishment of centres for the study of educational technology, this book will enhance status of distance education as a legitimate topic of research. No longer will distance education be defined principally in terms of practice; rather, it will be regarded as a field of activity that can be empirically explored, critically analyzed, and theoretically interpreted, as well as one that continues to be fundamentally transformed by the powerful impact of digitalization.

(6) The volume will help to raise the level of professionalism in the field of online distance education, as it will enable practitioners to become familiar with specific research results and research methods. More and more, those working in the field will come to consider their

own activities as teachers, media experts, tutors, and counsellors as akin to scientific processes, which can (and should) be carefully and systematically planned, tested, implemented, and evaluated. This emerging area of educational practice, once represented exclusively by exceptional practitioners, is now also the domain of scholars who are able to subject this practice to scientific scrutiny. Specific theoretical models and hypotheses have already been developed, and, in this volume, empirical research areas are identified.

Perhaps the overriding value of this volume lies, however, in its authors, all of them noted academics who were carefully selected to contribute to the discussion. The chapters they have written, which are often the product of considerable reflection on experience, fit nicely into the described framework, but they also prove that research in the field of online distance education has entered an exciting phase of development. Topics that have too long been neglected—such as costs and other economic considerations, student dropout rates, issues of social justice, the influence of cultural factors and the need for sensitivity to those factors, provisions for faculty professional development, and the role of learner communities—are here given close and thoughtful attention.

In addition, the research agenda outlined in this book reminds researchers, who are still in the habit of putting technology first, of the significant pedagogical, social, psychological, economic, and political influences on distance education. Not only should researchers be fully aware of these influences, but they should in fact give them priority. The proposed agenda recognizes that obvious gaps in the existing research must be filled.

Together, the scholarly contributions collected in this volume offer an open and thorough assessment of the present state of the art of online distance education research. For that reason, they are bound to provoke international discussion. At the same time, they set an international standard and set of objectives that present and future distance education researchers will need to meet.

* * *

A few personal concluding remarks may be added. As a pedagogue with no experience in distance education whatsoever, I became aware of and interested in correspondence education, which was already going on in the late 1950s. Since then, I have witnessed four periods in the evolution of distance education research. The first was characterized by the *complete absence of research*. As an educational format, correspondence education was unknown both to my colleagues and within my academic discipline, and pedagogical compendia were silent on the subject, apparently unaware even of its existence. And, indeed, no scholarly research was devoted to this form of education—with the unique and praiseworthy exception of Charles A. Wedemeyer, an outstanding distance education expert and a shining visionary and pioneer.

The second period was characterized by the *dominance of comparative studies*. As someone who has been attending the conferences of the International Council for Correspondence Education (ICCE) since 1965, I often had the chance to listen to Gayle Childs, who frequently reported on studies that compared conventional, face-to-face classroom instruction to correspondence education. At that time, the leading practitioners of correspondence education were preoccupied, if not obsessed, with the idea that it was absolutely necessary to prove that the two formats were *equal* with regard to student performance. This was methodically questionable and pedagogically impossible, as these two formats are structurally very different and should therefore be expected to produce different outcomes. However, these comparative studies were the modest beginning of distance education research—without a guiding theory and without deeper insights into its specific educational possibilities.

Then, in the 1970s, a third period emerged, which was characterized by a focus on educational technology. During this period, technological frameworks and methods dominated distance education research, to the clear disadvantage of significant pedagogical issues. The fourth period was marked by the advent of online education. Only now, after having experienced these developmental phases, have distance education experts become conscious of the full complexity of the format and its multifarious aspects.

Looking back at the stark absence of academic research in the 1950s and at its modest beginning in the 1960s, we become keenly aware of the enormous progress achieved in online distance education in a relatively short time. The research agenda presented by Olaf Zawacki-Richter and Terry Anderson reminds us of this remarkable development and outstanding accomplishment.

Otto Peters
Hagen, Germany

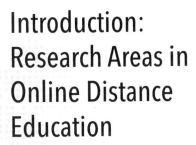

Introduction: Research Areas in Online Distance Education

Olaf Zawacki-Richter and
Terry Anderson

THE STRUCTURE OF RESEARCH AREAS

Research questions should be posed within a theoretical framework and, most commonly, quality research is embedded within a holistic structure of research areas within a discipline. Furthermore, the structure, culture, history, and past accomplishments of a research discipline form the foundation for identifying gaps and priority areas for researchers. Thus, with regard to distance education, Mishra (1998) made a plea for "a comprehensive and cohesive structure internationally to provide a strong foundation to the discipline" (p. 281).

Over the years a number of reviews of distance education literature have been published in which the authors developed categorization schemes of research topics that they mapped onto the articles under review (e.g., Holmberg, 1985; Sherry, 1996; Koble & Bunker, 1997; Mishra, 1997; Berge & Mrozowski, 2001; Rourke & Szabo, 2002; Lee, Driscoll, & Nelson, 2004; or Oviatt, Burdis, & West, 2012). However, the various attempts to describe the broad and interdisciplinary field of distance education showed a disparate picture. In contrast to unsystematic and often arbitrary selection and aggregation of research topics, Zawacki-Richter (2009) carried out an international Delphi study (cf. Charlton, 2004) to develop a validated framework of research topics that would help organize the knowledge in the field and identify research gaps and opportunities.

Three broad categories of research were described in the Delphi study:

- macro-level: distance education systems and theories
- meso-level: management, organization, and technology
- micro-level: teaching and learning in distance education

Under these three levels, the research issues were further categorized into the following 15 research areas:

Macro-level: Distance Education Systems and Theories

(1) Access, equity, and ethics: the democratization of access to distance education afforded by new media and finding ways to deliver high quality education to those who have limited resources and poor infrastructure. Issues that refer to the (sustainable) provision of distance education in developing areas. For example, what is the impact of distance education (e.g., via mobile learning) on narrowing (or broadening) the digital divide? What is the role of ICT (information and communication technologies) and/or OER (open educational resources) in terms of access to education? Should distance education have an inherent and explicit goal to reduce inequality and promote both high quality and affordable educational opportunity?

(2) Globalization of education and cross-cultural aspects: aspects that refer to the global external environment and drivers; the development of the global distance education market; teaching and learning in mediated and multicultural environments; and the implications for professional development and curriculum development.

(3) Distance teaching systems and institutions: distance education delivery systems, the role of institutional partnerships in developing transnational programs and the impact of ICT on the convergence of conventional education and distance education institutions (hybrid or mixed-mode).

(4) Theories and models: theoretical frameworks for and foundations of distance education, e.g., the theoretical basis of instructional

models, knowledge construction, interaction between learners, and the impact of social constructivism, connectivism, and new learning theories on distance education practice.

(5) Research methods in distance education and knowledge transfer: methodological considerations, the impact of distance education research and writing on practice, and the role of professional associations and higher education institutions in improving practice. Literature reviews and works on the history of distance education are also subsumed within this area.

Meso-level: Management, Organization and Technology

(6) Management and organization: strategies, administration, and organizational infrastructures and frameworks for the development, implementation, and sustainable delivery of distance education programs. What is required for successful leadership in distance education? Distance education and policies relating to continuing education, lifelong learning, and the impact of online learning on institutional policies, as well as legal issues (copyright and intellectual property).

(7) Costs and benefits: aspects that refer to financial management, costing, pricing, and business models in distance education. Efficiency: What is the return on investment or impact of distance education programs? What is the impact of ICT on the costing models and the scalability of distance education delivery? How can cost-effective but meaningful learner support be provided?

(8) Educational technology: new trends in educational technology for distance education (e.g., Web 2.0 applications or mobile learning) and the benefits and challenges of using OERS, media selection (e.g., synchronous versus asynchronous media), technical infrastructure, and equipment for online learning environments, and their affordances for teaching and learning.

(9) Innovation and change: issues that refer to educational innovation with new media and measures to support and facilitate change in institutions (e.g., incentive systems for faculty, aspects referring to staff workloads, promotion and tenure).

(10) Professional development and faculty support: professional development and faculty support services as a prerequisite for innovation and change. What are the competencies of online teachers, counsellors and support service staff, and how can they be developed?

(11) Learner support services: the infrastructure for and organization of learner support systems (from information and counselling for prospective students to library services and technical support, to career services and alumni networks).

(12) Quality assurance: issues that refer to accreditation and quality standards in distance education. The impact of quality assurance requirements and regulation and the impact of quality learner support on enrolments and drop-out/retention, as well as reputation and acceptance of distance education as a valid form of educational provision.

Micro-level: Teaching and Learning in Distance Education

(13) Instructional or learning design: issues that refer to the stages of the instructional design process for curriculum and course development. Special emphasis is placed on pedagogical approaches for tutoring online (scaffolding), the design of (culturally appropriate) study material, opportunities provided by new developments in educational technology for teaching and learning (e.g., Web 2.0 applications and mobile devices), as well as assessment practices in distance education.

(14) Interaction and communication in learning communities: closely related to instructional design considerations is course design that fosters (online) articulation, interaction, reflection, and collaboration throughout the learning and teaching process. Special areas include the development of online communities, gender differences, and cross-cultural aspects in online communication.

(15) Learner characteristics: the aims and goals of adult and younger students studying at a distance, the socio-economic background of distance education students, their different approaches to learning, critical thinking dispositions, media literacies, and special needs. How do students learn online (learner behaviour patterns, learning

styles) and what competencies are needed for distance learning (e.g., *digital literacy*)?

The Delphi study initiated a fruitful discussion about the structure of research areas in distance education. Later literature reviews have referred to and build upon this framework (cf. Simonson, Schlosser, & Orellana, 2011; Guri-Rosenblit & Gros, 2011). In 2009 a research consortium in Australia between the University of New England (UNE), Charles Sturt University (CSU), Central Queensland University (CQU), the University of Southern Queensland (USQ), and Massey University in New Zealand was established and funded by the Australian government– the Distance Education Hub (DEHub). In this project the universities developed a research program for 2011–2021 with research themes categorized by the main research levels (macro-, meso-, micro-) and by the 15 research areas identified in the Delphi study (http://wikieducator.org/DEHub/Research_Themes).

This structure was the starting point for a number of further bibliographic studies into the field of distance education research. The next step in our research program was a large-scale literature review to investigate and quantify research trends and gaps, methods, and authorship patterns in distance education research published in scholarly journals (Zawacki-Richter, Bäcker and Vogt, 2009). Five of the major peer-reviewed journals were reviewed for this study: *Open Learning* (OL), *Distance Education* (DE), the *American Journal of Distance Education* (AJDE), the *Journal of Distance Education* (JDE) and the *International Review of Research in Open and Distance Learning* (IRRODL). The sample comprised of 695 full papers that were published in the five journals between 2000 and 2008. The major outcome of this study was a frequency tabulation of the research areas covered in the publications revealing a strong imbalance: The micro-perspective (teaching and learning in distance education) is highly over-represented. Over 50% of all papers deal with the top three issues, i.e., interaction and communication in learning communities (17.6%), instructional design (17.4%), and learner characteristics (16.3%), whereas other important areas (e.g., costs and benefits, innovation and change management, or intercultural aspects of distance learning) are dreadfully neglected.

Table i.1 Ranking of research areas by number of published articles (N=695).

Rank	Research Area	Level[a]	Frequency	%	Cumulative %
1	Interaction and communication in learning	3	122	17.6	17.6
2	Instructional design	3	121	17.4	35.0
3	Learner characteristics	3	113	16.3	51.2
4	Distance teaching systems and institutions	1	62	8.9	60.1
5	Educational technology	2	48	6.9	67.1
6	Quality assurance	2	41	5.9	42.9
6	Professional development and faculty support	2	41	5.9	78.8
7	Access, equity, and ethics	1	31	4.5	83.3
8	Theories and models	1	24	3.5	86.8
9	Learner support services	2	23	3.3	90.1
10	Management and organization	2	18	2.6	92.7
11	Research methods in DE and knowledge	1	13	1.9	94.5
11	Globalization of education and cross-cultural	1	13	1.9	96.4
11	Innovation and change	2	13	1.9	98.3
12	Costs and benefits	2	12	1.7	100.0
	Total		**695**	**100**	

[a]Level: 1=macro, 2=meso, 3=micro

Based on the same sample of research publications, Zawacki-Richter and von Prümmer (2010) explored gender and collaboration patterns in distance education research. Following a bibliometric approach, collaboration was operationalized through co-author relationships. The study revealed a significant trend over the nine years of this study towards collaborative research in distance education. There are no significant gender differences regarding the number of co-authors of collaborative papers. However, female researchers significantly choose different research topics than their male colleagues. Women are over-represented in research areas such as learner characteristics, learner support or interaction, and communication in learning communities, while men are more concerned with topics stereotypically associated with them: technology and management. There is a significant propensity for female researchers to apply more qualitative methods or to triangulate qualitative and quantitative methods than males. Research methods also affect collaboration. On average, research teams on quantitative projects are significantly bigger than those who produce articles that are qualitative in nature.

A third set of studies investigated the impact of distance education journals in terms of citations and the perceived value of journals by experts in the field and the structure of the scholarly journal network to investigate relationships and patterns of scientific information exchange. The sample was extended to 12 journals (6 open access and 6 published in closed/proprietary format by commercial publishers) and 1,123 full articles published between 2003 and 2008 (Zawacki-Richter, Anderson, & Tuncay, 2010).

Open access dissemination resonates with many distance education researchers and practitioners because it aligns with their fundamental mission of extending access to learning opportunities. However, there remains lingering doubt whether this increase in access comes at a cost of reducing prestige, value (often determined in promotion and tenure hearings), or reference to the work by other authors. Using an online survey completed by members of the editorial boards of the 12 journals and a systematic review of the number of citations per article (N=1,123) and per journal issue between 2003 and 2008, the impact and the perceived value of the 12 journals were investigated. The results showed that distance education editors do not perceive the open access journals as significantly more or less prestigious than their closed counterparts. The number of citations per journal and per article also indicates no significant difference. However, a trend towards more citations per article in open access journals was observed. Articles in open access journals are also cited earlier than in non-open access journals. The most prestigious journals in terms of citations and perceived value are IRRODL, DE, AJDE, JDE and OL.

Publication of research results in peer-reviewed journals is the most important means of dissemination, discourse, and arguably to application and practice in the discipline of distance education. However there has been little work analyzing the relationships and influence among these journals. Our fourth study (Zawacki-Richter & Anderson, 2011) applied social network analysis techniques in which the nodes in the network are the journals and the links between them are the citations by one author to the works of another. The bibliographic description and analysis helps to investigate the intellectual structure and patterns of information exchange within the field of distance education research. The analysis of this citation network and the similarities in citation patterns revealed a clear core-periphery structure among distance education journals with regard to the centrality and prestige of the journals, network congruence, sending/receiving, and self-feeding ratios (see figure i.1). The vertical and horizontal scales in the figure show the relative distances between the journals based on citations (Multidimensional Scaling, cf. Borg & Groenen, 2005; Kruscal, Wish, & Uslaner, 1978).

Figure i.1 Core-periphery structure of the distance education journal network (Zawacki-Richter & Anderson, 2011, p. 451).

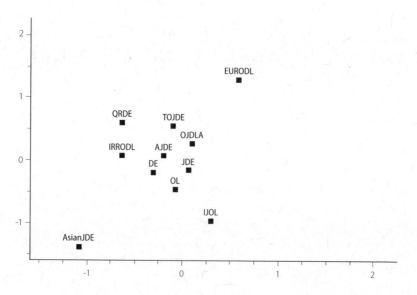

The goal of this volume is to create a comprehensive overview of distance education research and the disciplines from which it emerged that could be a primary reference and guide to distance educators, researchers, and policy makers. We also wanted to synthesize the issues, opportunities, questions, and challenges associated with each of these major focus areas to create an empirically driven research agenda. To achieve these goals, the editors of this volume invited an international expert or, occasionally, a team of experts with international reputations for research and leadership in each of the 15 research areas identified in the 2009 Delphi study. We asked each author to create an overview of the respective issue and its relevance, the major theoretical insights that guide and have arisen from the research on this topic, a short summary/review of the major research articles/authors/controversies and empirical data relative to the issue, open questions and directions for future research, as well as implications for distance education practice that arise from this research. Of course, being academics they did not all follow precisely our directions, but each did produce a quality piece that frames the challenge and opportunities associated with a research area in which they have had many years of experience and which they bring world-class expertise. Distance education scholars and students will no doubt recognize many of the names of the chapter authors, as we sought and in most cases were successful in recruiting the scholars whom we believe had not only the greatest expertise, but who have a reputation for looking beyond the obvious and being able to map out a research agenda in the particular area of their special expertise.

As shown in table i.1, the majority of published research deals with topics and issues with regard to teaching and learning processes in online distance education. The very broad field of instructional design could be taken as the overall umbrella term for this kind of research with learner characteristics and interaction and communication in learning communities as sub-fields. Given the richness of topics and issues addressed in this wide area, it was decided to further differentiate the micro-level by two additional chapters. The broadest area of interaction and communication in learning communities is covered by a chapter that emphasizes quantitative methods to investigate online interaction patterns; whereas, another chapter deals with this topic with a focus on theoretical and qualitative considerations. Two chapters in this volume also cover the broad field of research into distance learners and learner characteristics. One chapter deals with the changing profiles and characteristics of both traditional adult distance education students and so-called *net generation* students who are coming in increasing numbers to online education opportunities. We also realize that issues around persistence and high dropout rates have long been associated with distance education and continue to be debated with newer forms of online learning. Thus, we integrated an additional chapter to provide an overview of research into dropout and retention in distance education.

As distance education research develops, it will continue to address new themes by enlarging its scope of research areas. The editors hope that this volume is an important step towards a research agenda to develop a clear-cut profile of the discipline.

* * *

As a form of executive summary, we have overviewed the main ideas, content, and approaches of the chapters for all research areas on the macro-level (distance education systems and theories), meso-level (management, organization and technology), and micro-level (learning and teaching in distance education) in the following section.

MACRO-LEVEL RESEARCH: DISTANCE EDUCATION SYSTEMS AND THEORIES

Access, Equity, and Ethics

Alan Tait and Jennifer O'Rourke combine their experience (as distance education administrators, consultants, and academics in the UK and Canada) and talents to create a compelling and very practical chapter on the challenging issues associated with social justice. Social justice, especially as it is manifest in the provision of access to education to those groups to whom such opportunity has traditionally been denied, has always been a major driving force for individual educators and distance educational institutions. However, distance education historically and online education today has also been seen as an opportunity for business and for profit and for exploitation by so-called degree mills. Thus there is a need to understand thoroughly the components of social justice and to have a clear rationale for thoughtful inclusion of social justice concerns in the policy and the practice of all online programming. Tait and O'Rourke meet this challenge in an engaging chapter that not only defines social justice in this context but, more practically, offers a framework for a social justice audit to measure it. They provide a path towards both recognizing and improving effective social justice policy and practice within online education development and delivery.

In the first part of the chapter, Tait and O'Rourke cover the historical and political roots of the basic ideas that ground ideals of social justice— namely, that "our concept of social justice for each individual encompasses both the notion of equality rights as a 'level playing field,'" and the "right to opportunities and support that enable each person to fully participate in all aspects of society—to get to the playing field in the first place."

The chapter then turns to the particular role of online distance education and social justice. No particular technology, institution, or discipline need bear the total responsibility for maintaining and building social justice, but distance education has a long and proud tradition of working towards these goals. The increasingly powerful and costly technologies used in online forms of education offer possibility of exclusion as well as of inclusion. Thus, there is an increased need for vigilance and for a formalized process to analyze social justice impact and to create polices for any open and distance learning program. To meet this agenda Tait and O'Rourke introduce an audit by which institutions, teachers, and learners can insure—through measurement, external and self-evaluation, participatory dialogue, and reflection—that their programming does, in fact, promote a social justice and equity agenda. They provide guidelines for looking at various components of online distance systems from a social justice perspective. These components include not only the familiar accessibility issues, but they expand to the choice of curriculum and pedagogy; to the operations and administration of ODE systems; and to the provision of quality assurance, adequate student support services, and effective institutional administration. They do not exclude social justice issues that are related to the costs and sustainability of ODE programs.

This chapter, like others in this volume, illustrates the complexity of ODL systems, but it also makes a clear and compelling argument to insure that all forms of distance education are challenged to think carefully and plan effectively to insure that they are used as positive tools in the continuing effort to insure social justice for each individual and all societies.

Globalization and Cross-cultural Aspects

Charlotte Gunawardena, a scholar from the University of New Mexico originally from Sri Lanka, writes about ODL's increasing global impact and effect and response to cultural change. Gunawardena has researched and published many articles on the implications of these educational models on both distance education exporting and importing countries. Gunawardena begins her chapter by positioning ODL within the larger context of globalization with its wide focus on mobility, international transportation, and marketing, and the emergence of global cultures, memes, and economies. She directly confronts the question: Does ODL merely represent another example of Western hegemony and an attempt to export (for profit) a homogenizing Western culture? Such questions are challenging if not impossible to answer definitively; however, sensitivity to the biases inbuilt in all cultural artifacts—including formal education content and institutions—cannot and should not be ignored. Gunawardena notes the deficiencies of static description of whole cultures such as those developed by Hofstede (1986) and instead argues for a change from an *essentialist* to a *negotiated* perspective, to conceptualize culture as being negotiated within the ODL course.

Gunawardena next turns to a challenge experienced by any teacher (or student) involved in educational activities with students from other cultures, languages, and geographic locales. Educational behaviour and expectation are not homogeneous, with many cultures promoting and discouraging different types of activity, work ethics, respect for authority, and other activities that define much of formal education experience. When participants from different cultures engage in the same context of learning, misunderstanding and unmet expectations are likely. When these occur online, with limited opportunities for personal intervention or even awareness of concerns, the results can be devastating. However, such cultural encounters can also be very powerful learning experiences as we learn to live with each other and steward our single, global ecosystem.

The chapter then focusses on major issues that surface when teaching and learning across multiple cultures and geographies, including issues of language and of silence, of unequal wealth distribution, differences in expectations, and initiation of help-seeking behaviours. The chapter concludes with reflections on Gunawardena's own research in cross-cultural contexts. She, like other researchers who conduct research in multiple contexts, writes from her first-hand experience of the challenges of finding comparison groups, given global diversity and the necessity of collaborating with local educational researchers to insure both validity of research outcomes and the engagement and support of local researchers.

Distance Education Systems and Institutions

In the next chapter, distinguished Israeli researcher and author Sarah Guri-Rosenblit addresses the effects on distance education institutions induced by the rapid and disruptive changes of technological development and delivery platforms that define online education. Ironically, the single-mode distance education institutions, especially those large enough to be considered as mega-universities (Daniel, 1996), that led the innovation to distance education as "open universities" in the 1970s, are faced with some of the greatest challenges in moving to online delivery. Lest we be accused of being technologically driven and assume that online education makes obsolete all previous modes of distance delivery, we repeat Guri-Rosenblit's contention that the traditional (often text or mass media) modes of delivery common at the open universities "are able to enrol large numbers of students at a lower cost, and as such contribute greatly to the broadening of access to higher education and to social equity" (p. 4). Little evidence to date indicates that institutions employing typical small classes and interactive and constructivist models of online learning show the per-student costs are not significantly lower than traditional campus-based education.

Guri-Rosenblit concludes the first part of this chapter by reviewing the type of macro- research usually related to the innovations, costs, and affordances of the then-new industrial models of distance education. Given the affordances of the online environment, and especially the capacity to increase modes of student–student and student–teacher interaction in distance education, Guri-Rosenblit points out the shift in research away from the macro- issues related to increasing access and reducing, to those focussing on micro- issues such as interaction and instructional designs. Then moving to blended learning, she notes that it is easy in both online and blended learning to keep adding on features, toys, and tools, without analysis of the costs, usage, and accessibility issues involved. These are especially challenging for the large, single-mode open universities that for many years dominated research in distance education. Now they are left wondering if their delivery model is hopelessly out of date—even though it has proven to be cost- and learning- effective.

The chapter then notes both the national culture and perspective that influence educational intuitions and the technologies and pedagogies they employ. Further, Guri-Rosenblit notes the emergence of global culture and the challenges it represents as institutions attempt to exploit the "anywhere" capacity of distance education, while still insuring that it is relevant and effective for students across the globe.

She next turns to the opportunities afforded by new tools to increase the collaborations and the cost-effectiveness of distance education institutions by sharing resources and services. The open scholarship and open education movements are prime examples of the potential of sharing, but in these early years, we are finding less adoption than expected—both by individuals and by institutions—including those charged with open and distance mandates (Ngimwa & Wilson, 2012). It seems that the success of these early distance providers in the past is slowing rather than accelerating an appetite (perhaps wisely) for change and adoption of online learning by these dedicated distance education institutions.

Guri-Rosenblit concludes her chapter by noting the extra challenge of researching distance education systems and institutions when there is such diversity and lack of consensus about what online learning is and what (if any) are its special mandates (especially related to costs, access, and accessibility). She notes how important it is for researchers to study the multiple modes and models of distance education, without losing sight of the still valued contribution, accessibility, and cost-effectiveness of traditional models of distance education.

Distance Education Theories and Models

Margaret Haughey and Terry Evans do an excellent job of moving beyond the theories and models of distance education based on earlier technologies (postal communications, mass production, and big media) and earlier pedagogies to focus on the social technologies of Web 2.0 and the net-informed pedagogies of connectivism. The chapter chronicles developments of online education, from its first mass use in the earlier 1990s when access to online resources was a major issue, to 2012 when the use of multi-forms of text, data, audio, video, and immersive communications has become ubiquitous. However, they also point out that universal use does not imply universal social homogeneity or effectiveness in educational use. They note in their summary, "there is a need to extend research to be of a socially critical kind that takes into account, local, regional, and global circumstances and diversities." Such research demands the active participation of both researchers and, especially, practitioners as prescribed in design-based and action research.

Haughey and Evans also provide an overview of new theories developed mostly in social activity and media studies such as actor–network theory and activity theory. They argue for the necessity to get beyond a focus on the technology prescribed for delivery by institutions, to the interactions and actual use and adaptation of these tools by active participants. Finally, the extraordinary speed with which new information and communications are introduced and the rapid decrease in their costs compel researchers to pay attention to effects of change—adoption issues, obsolescence, literacy, training, and support systems.

Research Methods in Distance Education

American scholar Farhad Saba notes in his chapter on research methods that distance education research has been subject to harsh and consistent critique (e.g., Berge & Mrozowski, 2001; Bernard et al., 2004; Perraton, 2000; Saba, 2000). Moore (1985) stated that there is "a massive volume of amateur, unsystematic and badly designed research producing information of very little value" (p. 36). After a review of the Indian distance education literature, Panda (1992) concluded that "most of the studies are either descriptive status surveys or experimental studies with poor methodological footing" (p. 322).

In 2000 Saba criticised the lack of theoretical underpinnings in distance education research: "Research questions are rarely posed within a theoretical framework or based on its fundamental concepts and constructs" (Saba, 2000, p. 2), and he was supported by Perraton (2000): "An examination of existing research shows that it is often atheoretical and predominantly descriptive" (p. 1). Have things improved?

In his chapter, Saba remarks on having seen early signs of maturity in the scholarship of distance education. In a recent article, Simonson, Schlosser and Orellana (2011) come to similar conclusion: "the literature of the field has matured, and research has improved" (p. 124). For them, "scientific inquiry, conducted with rigorous attention to correct procedures, is the key to success of this field. Research and theory are at the foundation of credibility and quality" (p. 125).

Distance education in particular and the teaching and learning process in general are complex matters. Many variables are involved in instructional settings, not to mention other elements involved in distance education, such as social, organizational, technical, and global issues affecting the theory and practice in the field. Therefore, Saba and other experts advocate for mixed methods research: "Researchers are realizing that in practice the methodologies can be viewed as complementary. . . . Researchers who advocate combining quantitative and qualitative methods are thus on solid epistemological ground" (Garrison & Shale, 1994, p. 25). This approach, also termed *triangulation* (cf. Neumann, 2007, p. 149), has the advantage that a complex research field such as distance education can be explored from different ontological and episitomological perspectives (or angles), utilizing different instruments and methods, and the data gathered can be used to triangulate or mutually validate the results. Furthermore, Saba describes the ascendance of qualitative methods such as phenomenological research, and he emphasizes the need for further exploratory studies, which are important sources for formulating hypotheses that can be tested in rigorous quantitative investigations.

The notion that qualitative or interpretive studies serve mainly to guide the development of later quantitative work has been hotly contested by warriors on both sides of the paradigm wars between qualitative and quantitative social science research over the past two decades. Our position is that exploratory studies (of all paradigms) are necessary but that they do not necessarily lead to the development of any particular methodology as a climax species, to use a biological methaphor. Rather, each research paradigm answers important questions and opens understanding and insights for online distance education research and practice that are not often seen, or conceived of, through the lens of alternative research paradigms.

Management and Organization of the Distance Education Enterprise

Ross Paul brings his scholarship and experience to the critical research issues associated with management and leadership in distance education. Paul has served as president or vice-president off both single-mode open universities and of dual-mode, campus-based universities. Thus, he brings in his considerable experience as both a senior administrator and as a scholar to the two dominant educational systems for delivering post-secondary distance education. Paul addresses the common and the unique challenges of leadership, planning, and administration in both and, more importantly for this text, clearly outlines the research imperatives.

As in other industries, Paul notes the increase in focus on consumers (in this case, students) and the, sometimes, related speed of technology-induced change. These changes force and often conflict with existing university culture, and Paul notes the need for researchers and change agents to acknowledge and work with these powerful sociological and psychological forces, which have defined university culture and context for hundreds of years.

Paul also examines the impact of *openness*, which goes far beyond that envisioned in the last century with the founding of the open universities. Open courseware, open textbooks, open research publications, and access to a wealth of non-institutional knowledge resources (such as Wikipedia, Google books, and so on) force universities not only to lose their exclusive roles of knowledge repositories but also that of exclusive providers of credited courses. This presents challenges, of course, but also provides great research opportunities as different economic and pedagogical models are tested in the real world. Finally, the cost of entry to post-secondary education has plummeted, leaving opportunities for organizations with different models and cultures to develop online distance education programs. These may provide different models to meet their student, staff, and institutional resource capacity and opportunity—but many of the same challenges that have confronted the earliest providers of distance education programming remain.

Finally, as also noted by other writers in this book, Paul regrets the two solitudes that separate scholarship in research in classroom and campus contexts to those forms of education offered at a distance and online. At a practical level, online tools unite in delivery and learning resources these two modes of teaching and learning, and certainly the number of learners alternating between the two, in either blended courses or a mix of on-campus and online courses, continues to grow. Yet as Paul shows, the crossover in authorship and citations of research articles is minimal with neither group benefitting from the past and current research conducted by the other.

Any research agenda proposed for this book and other suggestions for the future needs to maximize not only the past expertise and knowledge of researchers from all modes of education, but also to ensure that future research takes account of and partners with the growing number of researchers using any mode of education development and delivery at any age and sector.

Costs and Funding of Distance Education

Greville Rumble, formerly professor of distance education management at the OUUK, and one of the very few researchers and scholars in this area of expertise, authors the chapter on the costs and funding of online distance education. Cost effectiveness is one of the most important research areas and yet one the most neglected. The literature review carried out by Zawacki-Richter, Bäcker, and Vogt (2009) revealed that this area is at the bottom of the list in terms of the number of studies conducted in the field of distance education.

Rumble laments the dearth of (comparative) case studies to explore the costs of distance teaching institutions and the application of educational technology in distance, online, and face-to-face settings. A possible explanation for the lack of study in this area is that the data is simply not available. It is not surprising that educational institutions, as competitors in the global education market, are unwilling freely to share business models and data on their budgets and costs.

The issue of costs and funding of distance education is closely related to access to education as a human right. Rumble emphasizes the problem of introducing online distance education courses priced at developed country levels "into a developing world country where the costs of imported technologies are high, and labour costs are low." He criticizes the gap between rhethoric and reality in developing countries: many students who would benefit most from access to online distance education simply cannot afford it.

However, in the developed countries the fees are continuously rising due in large part to budget cuts in the educational systems. For example at the OUUK, the modular fees will rise from GBP 1.300 to 5.000 per full-time, full-year study for resident students in England in September 2012. This increase will likely affect the take-up rate of higher education studies as students will consider more than before their return on investment: "What someone is prepared to pay may, of course, depend on the benefits that they think they will attain in terms of employment, pay, and future job security. Here no research has been done comparing the private and social costs and benefits of distance and online education on the one hand, and face-to-face education on the other."

In this context, Rumble raises the question of the credentialling power of distance teaching compared with campus-based universities, i.e., the intangible value and reputation of a degree. Is a degree taken online less prestigious and will thus generate lower income benefits than those of a person from a conventional university? Which factors have an impact on the private and social rates of return? Rumble suspects notions that resonate with authors studying the hidden curriculum of higher education (Ahola, 2000) that it is not so important what and where one learns but "who one gets to know in the process."

Educational Technology

Research into educational technology is an important cross-cutting area and interdisciplinary topic. It has a wide impact on all levels of distance education research: The development of educational technology accelerated the globalization of education and has shaped educational institutions and systems. Media characteristics have to be considered in the instructional design process with regard to access, media literacies of teachers and learners, and the subject matter to be learned. The application of educational media implies a process of change in institutions, influences the quality of instruction and programs, and affects the costs and economics of distance education.

In her chapter on the application of technology in distance education, Gráinne Conole from Leicester University explores the enormous potential of educational technologies and media and the opportunities they afford for innovative teaching and learning in formal, informal, and non-formal contexts. She places a special emphasis on Web 2.0 tools and social media and the potential for open practice and a paradigm shift from expository teaching and receptive, passive learning to participatory, active, and social learner engagement.

Conole outlines three major challenges in the field: institutional and organizational barriers to the uptake of technologies (e.g., lack of faculty training, limited budgets), the lack of studies that are adequately grounded in theory, and a disconnect between research results and their impact on policy and practice.

Finally, the chapter highlights a number of open research questions and ideas for further research projects that will help us to better harness the potential and opportunities of educational media for teaching and learning. With the emergence of Web 2.0 tools and social online communities, a very relevant and hot topic is the tension between open and closed, formal and non-formal learning environments, especially as instantiated in OERs and MOOCs. How can we design a *social learning management system,* and what are the implications of open educational resources and courses for formal institutions and their business models?

Innovation and Change Management

In perhaps one of the most far-reaching and visionary chapters in this book, Jon Dron from Athabasca University, Alberta, looks at the large, recursive, and rapidly evolving relationship between distance education and technology. Jon does not directly advocate for or against any particular technology or the pedagogies that have become associated and that most thoroughly resonate with particular technologies. However, he articulates the ways in which past, current, and future technologies need to become more directly responsive to the needs of those closest to the coalface of teaching and learning. However, simply adding capacity for or requiring deep customization and assembly of technologies (softening them) by end users can often lead to increasing complexity, sense of disconnection, frustration, and lack of ownership and integration within educational systems. Alternatively, technologies that are too hard cannot be adapted to the cultural, political, and personal agendas of learners, teachers, and educational administrators. Thus, there is the need for balance, even in times of rapid technological change.

Dron also notes the challenges of change within component systems. Formal distance education is composed of many subsystems (most of which are detailed in chapters of this book). Each of the subsystems has technologies and cultural norms deeply embedded within their current practice. Changing one such system often sends ripples through others, or, as too often happens, attempted change in one subsystem fails as it is dashed against adjacent systems. Thus, the early research from systems perspective related to distance education (notably that of Otto Peters) need not be abandoned, but rather needs to evolve to theorize and generate solutions for vastly more complex systems and networks that define current and next-generation education institutions.

Questions of technology thus must be integrated into all of the research agendas that emerge from the research overviewed in this book and from the practice of distance education. We can assume that technology will become more pervasive, embedded into our learning objects, relationships and tools, will be cheaper and, as Dron points out most emphatically, will give rise to adjacent possibilities that we cannot plan for, but to which we must react and exploit for their educational affordances as they emerge.

Although technology has capacity and is changing at exponential speeds, it is becoming apparent that humans, as biological creatures, are not genetically equipped for the same speed of change. So the capacity to manage change and use emerging technologies effectively becomes as great or greater a research question than the use of the technology itself. We need to research how to best adapt and what type of formal educational institution needs to emerge to support this rapidly changing context. Such change process needs to be understood at the institutional level, but, as importantly, it needs to be understood as individual choices as well. How much and how radical a change in technology-enhanced systems can and should be our goal? At what point is the cost of change higher than the benefits it promises? And more fundamentally, why are some innovations (e.g., the iPad or iPhone) successful while others lead only to bankruptcy and failure?

Professional Development and Faculty Support

In this chapter, Australian scholar Margaret Hicks tackles the research issues and accumulating knowledge from research related to faculty development. It is readily apparent that effective teaching demands effective teachers. Ironically many teachers in higher education and especially those teaching at a distance are themselves inexperienced network navigators who bring many of the fears, inhibitions, and bewilderment of students when first exposed to the very different context of teaching in mediated and networked contexts. This, of course, provides opportunity as well as challenges as teachers experience the disruptive impact of these new tools simultaneously with students. However, this inherent "fellow traveller" role is not a familiar one for many teachers, whose considerable effort and time spent acquiring and producing discipline-based knowledge, equips them with an attitude more akin to an esteemed expert than to a new initiate.

Hicks begins the chapter by reminding us that the term and the activities known as *distance education* are continually changing. The recent arrival of blended learning contexts, in which parts of a learning sequence are facilitated online and parts in face-to-face classrooms, demonstrate that all teachers—even those who don't see themselves as distance educators—are compelled to acquire many, if not most of the skills of a dedicated distance educator. Thus there is need for in-depth qualitative study of what it means to one's professional image and personal efficacy as one transitions from a classroom to a blended or fully distance educator.

Despite the emphasis on change and transition that marks the profession and this chapter, Hicks is careful to unpack the historical function and results of faculty development as it has matured as a professional support feature in many educational institutions. Despite the expanse of formal programs, assessments, and even associations to support professional faculty developers and employees of teaching development centres, Hicks notes there is very little systematic research on the effectiveness of these interventions and support services. Hicks overviews the first large-scale study of faculty attitude and experience of teaching online and notes the results from this survey point to a number of important but unanswered questions. These include the need to better understand the characteristics, backgrounds, and skill sets of those who are in the front lines of online teaching (many as part-time sessional employees); of their professional competencies and needs; of the various types, costs, and delivery modes of training and support initiatives that are made available to them; and the cost and time effectiveness of these interventions. Finally, of perhaps greatest importance (but equally challenging to answer), is the question of whether formal professional development activities actually affect student learning.

Despite the increase in established centres that employ dedicated professional development staff, there is growing evidence that most professional learning happens informally within a community of practice in which teachers share, critique, learn from, and help each other while engaged in their daily work lives. Opportunities for such community involvement are, however, often diminished when faculty are distributed over a large area and when large numbers are part-time employees with perhaps limited access to services and integration with the online education institution by whom they are employed. Will new Web 2.0 and social networking tools such as public services (e.g., LinkedIn and Facebook, or institutional equivalents such as ELGG or WordPress Buddy) be able to support communities of practice among these widely dispersed, but highly networked teachers?

Learner Support Services

Canadian distance education teacher and researcher Jane Brindley overviews the research agenda and issues related to student support. Student support in all forms of education, including online distance education, is like the proverbial motherhood and apple pie: one can never get enough of any of these, but they come at a cost! However the stakes are higher and in many cases the challenges greater for all forms of distance education. As Brindley points out in her opening paragraph, the skills sets, dedication, time management, and motivation levels required of distance students often exceed that required of campus students who have the ability to immerse themselves in the pace, expectations, and culture of campus living. She notes, "Studying at a distance requires maturity, a high level of motivation, capacity to multi-task, goal directedness, and the ability to work both independently and cooperatively."

Since many new students to distance education courses and programs lack at least some component of these skills and attitudes, it falls on the education delivery institution to provide support for students as they gain these critical skills—or risk the high costs to both students and institutions of student drop out (see chapter 17 in this text). Fortunately, the online world itself affords new tools for communication, knowledge and skill acquisition, and peer and group support that were not available to earlier generations of distance students. Thus, opportunity grows, but the evidence for effectiveness and especially cost effectiveness is hard to find.

In her chapter, Brindley covers the three major sources that guide the development and design of learner support services. These are theoretical models of learning theory that have evolved within the distance education tradition, the ideas from customer management and support literature, and predictive models developed by testing support interventions (as independent variables) and, largely, student persistence as outcomes or dependent variables.

The chapter then describes the models of good practice that have emerged from practice and the research literature—exposing a rich history of effective case study provision and general principles of high-quality student service provision. Next, Brindley provides an overview of the major types of empirical research in this domain. These include studies of student satisfaction and met and unmet needs analysis, the need for institutions to understand the type of learners and their general characteristics before implementing expensive services, and more recent studies of effective use of new online technologies—especially in regard to peer and community support that were not possible in earlier, independent study modes of distance education.

Brindley aptly sets a tentative research agenda for learner support services by concluding with four broad areas filled with research questions and as yet meagre answers. These include more study on interventions: which are most cost effective and which result in genuine value added to all students, including marginal groups? Secondly, she notes the need to think about effective ways for institutions to provide these services and underlines the need for cost effectiveness and the study of collaborative or even outsourced provision of student support. Turning to the competencies of individual professionals in this area, she asks: What are the types of training and support needed for those responsible for effective student support? Finally, in an era of social networks she asks how these tools and environments can be used to allow online distance education students to create and sustain their own support networks and communities.

This chapter highlights the need for effective student services and the even greater need to make certain these services are provided or made available at costs that are affordable to students and to institutions.

Quality Assurance in Distance Education

The neo-capitalist agenda that seeks to induce accountability, student fee for service, competition from private enterprise and other components of a free market economy into what originated as a public service is creating tension and challenges throughout higher education systems in the West (Altbach, Gumport, & Berdahl, 1988). Regardless of whether individual students (or their parents) pay for services or if these services are provided from the public wealth, there is an ever-increasing call for accountability and assurances that online and campus education systems are producing quality product. Unfortunately, as the chapter on quality assistance by Australian Colin Latchem states in its opening paragraph, quality depends on your definition of quality and how you choose to measure it. There is very little consensus over what constitutes quality in campus-based education systems, much less in innovative and new online systems. Yet, there is great pressure to insure that both public and private systems are operating at peak efficiency and producing quality outputs. Thus Latchem's chapter and this issue are of critical importance to researchers, funders, students, and faculty.

Latchem first notes the continuing discrimination by a host of governments, teachers unions, accrediting agencies, and even students against all forms of distance education, including those offered at a distance. It seems the 30 years of no significant difference in learning outcomes research still has not convinced all of the fact that students can and do learn equally as well on campus or a distance. However Latchem is quick to point out that not all online systems are operating at levels of quality process, or outputs, and indeed cyberspace is home to a disproportionately high number of fraudulent degree mills offering degrees for purchase, with no attempt to hide their vacuous credibility.

Latchem next provides an overview of the function and focus of the typical quality assurance agency that most governments have established—or at least support—to regulate and certify accredited higher education institutions in their domain. He also notes the growing number of multinational organizations and treaties that have been struck to try to regulate and accredit learning systems internationally thus supporting increasing mobility of students, graduates, and faculty. Turning to the distinct challenges of accreditation for online education systems, Latchem overviews the debate on whether online systems should be judged by exactly the same criteria as campus based, or if the technological mediation, common disaggregation of services, and the often-seen "innovative" administrative hiring and service provisions that define some online institutions, demand higher levels of scrutiny and extra burdens of assuring quality. Despite the challenges, Latchem then provides references to the many national and international quality standards that have been developed and the quality models that underpin many of their operating systems. The chapter demonstrates that quality standards are being systematically applied to institutions globally— even if many academics choose to believe that only they can define quality learning within their own online or campus classroom. Thus, the opportunity for research—not only on nature, focus, and intent of quality systems themselves, but on their acceptance, adherence, effectiveness, return on investment, and impact on innovation—are all important and largely unstudied terrain.

Finally, Latchem notes the increasing capacity and growth of online systems that span geographic and cultural boundaries and create challenges and increased demand for quality standards that reflect differing conceptions of quality. Latchem concludes the chapter with references from many of the international quality groups and the different perspectives that these groups adopt when developing quality standards. The mere number of such agencies and documents reminds us of the old joke: "I love standards, because there are so many of them." This chapter provides an excellent overview and summary of the work that has been done and is ongoing among quality agencies around the world to insure that online education does meet quality guidelines—even if the nature of these guidelines are not standardized themselves. Latchem demonstrates that the costs of determining and then measuring and insuring quality in education systems are not insignificant. Thus, there is room for research on ways in which technology and communications tools can be harnessed to reduce these costs. The chapter ends with challenging research questions related to the nature of quality controls, their cultural underpinnings, and challenges of measuring outputs that may take years to be fully recognized in the highly skilled, engaged, and motivated citizens of tomorrow.

MICRO-LEVEL RESEARCH: LEARNING AND TEACHING IN DISTANCE EDUCATION

Instructional Design

In this insightful journey through the historical development of instructional design, Canadian scholars Katy Campbell and Rick Schwier uncover the connections between psychological theories, social epistemologies, and the cultural contexts that create and shape the designs that teachers and professional designers use to create distance education content and communications. Distance education has had a special focus on the construction of learning content—it was developed to be consumed by individual learners. This focus on the individual and the objective reality of the behavioural learning objectives that framed the instructional designs of early distance education marked a similar understanding of social as well as mechanical and technical "truths." Thus, distance education tended to be constructed as if it sat outside of cultural and economic classes and distinctions. However, as chronicled in this chapter, we see that such one-dimensional thinking and design fails to meet the unique and the social construction of knowledge that defines more modern constructivist instructional designs. Such designs take into account—and allow—learners as individuals or especially in groups to co-create the knowledge, rather than to merely assimilate it. Such an analysis begs the question: Are there various types of knowledge extending beyond the simple procedural and declarative distinctions that best lend themselves to learning using older cognitive behaviour designs? Are there other skills, learning designs, and knowledge that can only be acquired in an active social community of learning? The chapter does not provide definitive answers to these questions, but it is obvious that effective distance education designers must be able to operate in both contexts and, perhaps most importantly, must be able to identify and react appropriately to the culture, gender, and economic gestalt in which all forms of formal learning are engulfed.

Campbell and Schwier also focus briefly on the newest and most emergent learning theory coined by George Siemens (Siemens, 2005) as *connectivism*. They describe the massive open online courses (MOOCs) and other forms of very open education that have attracted both students and designers using connectivist theories. However in these early days it is hard to see if connectivism can find a home in either the objective outcome world of online training or the more constructivist groups that are created using the ubiquitous learning management systems (LMS) of formal education.

The chapter ends with an excellent set of questions that will drive instruction and learning design into the future, but they also add a wise and cautionary note. "In order to be effective, instructional designers need to develop a connoisseur's appreciation for the broad cultural forces in play when instructional design is done, the ways in which instructional design work interacts with sweeping societal change, and the social ramifications of new communication technologies and the affordances they offer." There are no easy, or formulaic, solutions. Rather, designers need to be equipped with a connoisseur's eye for quality, while always searching for innovation and improvement.

Interaction and Communication in Learning Communities

Learning is a social activity that is immersed in social context and understanding, even if carried out by individual learners. Therefore, interaction and communication between members or actors who collaborate in a learning community are at the core of the learning process. The popular community of inquiry model reinforces this social nature of learning and assumes that learning occurs through the interaction of three core elements: social, cognitive, and teaching presence (Garrison, Anderson, & Archer, 2000). The educational experience is constituted through sustained interaction and communication between and among learners, teachers, and learning objects embedded in a social context. In distance education this process is facilitated through asynchronous and synchronous communication media and technologies.

Given the centrality of interaction and communication, it is no wonder that this research area gained great attention in the scientific and, particularly, in the education community. In contrast to the ephemeral communication in face-to-face classrooms, the speech acts in computer-mediated communication are text-based, saved on a server, and therefore much more readily available for the analysis of interaction patterns in online learning communities. Thus, the availability of text-based communication data from computer conferences might be another practical reason for the high number of studies in this area. The era of totally text-based online learning is coming to end, with the increasing use of voice, video, and immersive technologies. However, interactions mediated through the Internet create distinct trails and traces that can and are being gathered and analyzed in the exploding area often referred to as *learning analytics* (Siemens & Long, 2011)

Canadian scholar Dianne Conrad (Chapter 14) and American Allan Jeong (Chapter 15) are leading researchers and scholars with considerable expertise in the field of interaction and communication in online learning communities. Dianne Conrad follows a qualitative approach to explore the nature of interaction in online learning communities in relation to issues of control, autonomy, content, learning styles, culture, and gender. She discusses current trends in educational technology such as the availability of open educational resources, social media as engagement tools, and the move to ubiquitous mobile learning. How these developments affect the nature of interaction and communication behaviour in online distance learning is still an open question.

Allan Jeong advocates for quantitative approaches to analyze online discourse that go beyond content analysis based on mere frequencies of students' speech acts and utterances in order to explain and predict how online learners respond to given messages and how particular communication patterns influence the quality of interaction and the success or failure of the learning experience. A central methodological question here is how to code the students' utterances and how to analyze the discourse data. In his chapter, Jeong describes the advantages and disadvantages of quantitative methods to analyze online discourse: quantitative content analysis, social network analysis, Markov chain analysis, quantitative sequential analysis, structural equation modelling and path analysis. The author has developed a software suite to carry out quantitative sequential analysis, which is freely available (cf. Jeong, 2005). Further, a group of Australian researchers from the University of Wollongong released the SNAPP (Social Networks Adapting Pedagogical Practice) tool that works as a plugin for major learning management systems, such as Moodle, to apply social network analysis to investigate asynchronous computer conferences.

Jeong reminds us that each learning community is unique and situated in a social context. Quantitative interaction models have to be applied carefully: "As a result, it may not be theoretically possible or even desireable to develop interaction models that can be generalized across multiple contexts." Therefore, a mixed-methods approach, i.e., a combination, or *triangulation*, of qualitative and quantitative methods, might be appropriate and desirable in many cases to investigate interaction and communication patterns in online learning communities.

Learner Characteristics and Profiles of Distance Learners

The study of learning characteristics has long attracted researchers in distance education. Perhaps borrowing from distance education's psychological roots, there has been continuing interest on individual characteristics such as gender, age, previous experiences and more distinct psychological variables such as learning styles, approaches to learning, locus of control, and so on. Typically, studies sought to determine relationships between these independent variables and critical distance education output or dependent variables such as learning outcomes, persistence and satisfaction, or intent to enrol in continuing studies.

In this chapter, Joachim Stöter, Mark Bullen, Olaf Zawacki-Richter, and Christine von Prümmer discuss the changing demographics of the "average" online distance education student. Traditionally, distance education has attracted older students, with a high proportion of female learners and those from socio-economic groups that had little previous participation in higher education. This group of "second chance" and fully engaged working adults, many with families, is still a large component of online distance learning. However, increasingly younger students, many enrolled as full-time learners in traditional campus or dual mode institutions, are also enrolling in ODL. Thus, the population can at minimum be described as very eclectic. They might all be classified though as life-long learners—some just beginning their lifetime learning as full-time students, but the majority returning or completing programs that their life work demands and that the flexibility of ODL supports.

From descriptions of online learners' demographic characteristics, the chapter moves to a discussion of how these interact with institutional variables such as services to support institutional integration and academic resources and activities to engage and motivate academic integration.

A chapter on learner characteristics in ODL can not hope to avoid the controversy swirling around ideas of *digital natives* or *net generations*. Some authors, such as Tapscott, Prensky, or Palfrey and Gassner, argue that members of the so called net-generation have been immersed in a networked world of digital technology; they behave differently, have different social characteristics, different ways of using and making sense of information, different ways of learning, and different expectations about life and learning. These assumptions are mostly anecdotal, however, and not based on empirical evidence. In a recent study, Mark Bullen concluded: "Generation is not the issue" (Bullen, 2011). However, we do need to understand what kind of technical devices students own and use today, how students use various media and ICTs for academic activities, and what tools they find are most effective to support their learning. Based on this knowledge we can make better informed decisions in the ID process with regard to the selection of media and online learning activities in the online learning environment.

There may indeed be a shifting of the skills sets and attitudes of learners as they experience and live with the tools and within the merging culture of the online world. However, it is also apparent that there are very high levels of variability of experience and adoption that make age-based generalizations hard to support. Nonetheless, it is equally unlikely that students with many years of experience with educational models that feature multimedia, multiforms and genre of interaction, and support of learning agents will be satisfied with modes of distance education that are reliant on a single medium (such as printed text) and very slow or outdated communications infrastructure and pedagogies.

Yet, the authors also note that because a new technology is available does not mean it meets individual or collective needs of learners, teachers, or institutions. Rather, research needs to continue into supporting adoption of tools that meet criteria for effectiveness and efficiency in learning experience and outcome.

Drop-out and Retention

This chapter on drop-out and retention is a slight departure from the format of a scholarly book chapter and the other chapters in this book, but it very succinctly captures the wealth of knowledge from two of the world's most experienced distance education researchers. Alan Woodley and Ormond Simpson (both recently retired from the Open University, UK) engage in a conversation focussed on the "elephant in the distance education room": student dropout, or the low rates of successful completion or persistence. The conversation reveals the brutal facts (hidden as they often are by reluctant institutions), reasons for the regrettable complacency of all actors—including students themselves. The chapter ends with suggestions for interventions—some of which have been tried, but none of which has resulted in the completion rates commonly achieved with campus-based teaching and learning. As always, complicated problems have multiple and complicated causes; Woodley and Simpson do not suggest that there are easy silver bullet solutions, but they are equally adamant that complacency and acceptance is neither economically nor morally justified or acceptable.

In particular they argue for research focussed on interventions. It is not enough to understand the causes, the context, or the circumstances of individuals or aggregates. Rather, we need to focus on things we can do change, measure, and improve student success with distance education programming. The authors wisely point out the necessity for action but equally note the importance of cost effectiveness in these interventions. Thus the research challenge might best take a design-based research approach in which serious study is made of the 50 years or more of research on causes and the successful and unsuccessful interventions that have been tried and tested and, secondly, on working with teachers, tutors, student support staff, and administrators to devise interventions that are cost effective and that can be integrated into institutional practice. Third, we need to monitor the results of these interventions effectively—possibly using the many new tools of learning analytics and data mining that are becoming available as student learning interactions go online. Finally, we need to articulate the design principles of effective interventions, such that they can be scaled, replicated, and re-created in other distance education teaching and learning contexts.

This chapter also points to the factors that allow the elephant in the room to remain hidden. In an era of increasing institutional accountability, both the ease of hiding and the acceptance of personal and instructional cost of high attrition is ending. Governments and students as consumers are becoming more demanding of policies and record keeping that allow us to measure the effectiveness of our educational programming. This provides an ideal opening for policy research that shows the impact and effect of changes in government policy, funding formulas, and student support programs. What impact does higher personal cost of higher education have on completion? As Woodley and Simpson show, higher tuition may be a very effective way to increase completion rates, but will it at the same decrease the capacity for inclusion that has been a defining feature of distance education systems? There is high potential for very productive policy research that grows from the complex interaction among institutions, government and employer funding, and individual students and their advocacy organizations.

ACKNOWLEDGEMENTS

Many of the readers of this text will likely be familiar with some, or even most, of the authors of the various chapters. We selected these authors based upon our awareness of their work acquired as students, practicing distance educators, authors, researchers, and journal reviewers and editors. We supplemented this personal knowledge with Google Scholar searches to determine those researchers who have had the greatest impact on the broader distance education research community. In many cases the authors are generally acknowledged as the foremost experts in the world in the research topic that is the focus of their chapters within a distance education context. To our delight, most of these very well-known (but not coincidently, very busy) authors and researchers agreed to contribute to this important text. We thank them for the time and energy they have freely given to the project and now offer their contributions to our readers in open access format.

REFERENCES

Ahola, S. (2000). *Hidden curriculum in higher education: Something to fear for or comply to?* Paper presented at the Innovations in Higher Education, Helsinki. Retrieved from http://ruse.utu.fi/pdfrepo/HCarticle.pdf.

Altbach, P. G., Gumport, P., & Berdahl, R. (1988). *American higher education in the twenty-first century: Social, political, and economic challenges.* Baltimore, MD: Johns Hopkins University Press.

Berge, Z., & Mrozowski, S. (2001). Review of research in distance education. *American Journal of Distance Education, 15*(3), 5–19.

Bernard, R. M., Abrami, P., Lou, Y., Borokhovski, E., Wade, A., Wozney, L. W. P. A., . . . Huang, B. (2004). How Does Distance Education Compare to Classroom Instruction? A Meta-Analysis of the Empirical Literature. *Review of Educational Research, 74*, 379.

Borg, I., & Groenen, P. J. F. (2005). *Modern multidimensional scaling: Theory and applications.* Berlin: Springer.

Bullen, M., Morgan, T. & Qayyum, A. (2011). Digital learners in higher education: Generation is not the issue. *Canadian Journal of Learning Technology, 37*(1).

Charlton, J. R. H. (2004). Delphi technique. In M. S. Lewis-Beck, A. Bryman, & T. F. Liao (Eds.), *The SAGE encyclopedia of social science research methods (Vol. 1).* Thousand Oaks, CA: Sage.

Daniel, J. S. (1996). *Mega-universities and knowledge media: Technology strategies for higher education.* London: Kogan Page.

Fini, A. (2009). The technological dimension of a massive open online course: The case of the CCK08 course tools. *International Review of Research in Open and Distance Learning, 10*(5). Retrieved from http://www.irrodl.org/index.php/irrodl/article/view/643/1402

Garrison, D. R., Anderson, T., & Archer, W. (2000). Critical inquiry in a text-based environment: Computer conferencing in higher education. *The Internet and Higher Education, 2*(2–3), 87–105.

Garrison, D. R., & Shale, D. (1994). Methodological issues: Philosophical differences and complementary methodologies. In D. R. Garrison (Ed.), *Research perspectives in adult education* (pp. 17–37). Florida: Krieger

Guri-Rosenblit, S., & Gros, B. (2011). E-Learning: Confusing terminology, research gaps and inherent challenges. *Journal of Distance Education/Revue de l'enseignement à distance, 25*(1).

Hofstede, G. (1986). Cultural differences in teaching and learning. *International Journal of Intercultural Relations, 10*(3), 301-20.

Holmberg, B. (1985). *Status and trends of distance education.* Lund, Sweden: Lector Publishing.

Jeong, A. (2005). A guide to analyzing message–response sequences and group interaction patterns in computer-mediated communication. *Distance Education, 26*(3), 367–83.

Koble, M. A., & Bunker, E. L. (1997). Trends in research and practice: An examination of *The American Journal of Distance Education* 1987–1995. *American Journal of Distance Education, 11*(2), 19–38.

Kruskal, J. B., Wish, M., & Uslaner, E. M. (1978). *Multidimensional scaling: Quantitative applications in the social sciences.* Thousand Oaks, CA: Sage.

Lee, Y., Driscoll, M. P., & Nelson, D. W. (2004). The past, present, and future of research in distance education: Results of a content analysis. *American Journal of Distance Education, 18*(4), 225–41.

Martin, J. N., & Nakayama, T. K. (2004). *Intercultural communication in contexts (3rd ed.),* New York, NY: McGraw-Hill.

Mishra, S. (1997). A critical analysis of periodical literature in distance education. *Indian Journal of Open Learning, 6*(1–2), 39–54.

Mishra, S. (1998). Distance education research: A review of its structure, methodological issues and priority areas. *Indian Journal of Open Learning, 7*(3), 267–82.

Moore, M. G. (1985). Some observations on current research in distance education. *Epistolodidaktika,1,* 35–62.

Neumann, W. L. (2007). *Social research methods: Qualitative and quantitative approaches.* Boston: Pearson.

Ngimwa, P., & Wilson, T. (2012). An empirical investigation of the emergent issues around OER adoption in Sub-Saharan Africa. *Learning, Media and Technology,* 1–16.

Oviatt, D., Burdis, J., & West, R. E. (2012). Educational technology research journals. *Distance Education,* 2000–2010. *Educational Technology, 52*(1), 44–48.

Panda, S. (1992). Distance educational research in India: Stock-taking, concerns and prospects. *Distance Education, 13*(2), 309–26.

Perraton, H. (2000). Rethinking the research agenda. *International Review of Research in Open and Distance Learning, 1*(1). Retrieved from Abgerufen von internal-pdf://perraton2000-3038331659/perraton2000.pdf

Peters, O. (2001). *Learning and teaching in distance education.* London: Kogan Page.

Rourke, L., & Szabo, M. (2002). A content analysis of the *Journal of Distance Education* 1986–2001. *Journal of Distance Education, 17*(1), 63–74.

Saba, F. (2000). Research in Distance Education: A Status Report. *The International Review of Research in Open and Distance Learning, 1*(1).

Scriven, B. (1991). Ten years of "distance education." *Distance Education, 12*(1), 137–53.

Sherry, L. (1996). Issues in distance learning. *International Journal of Educational Telecommunications, 1*(4), 337–65.

Siemens, G. (2005). A Learning theory for the digital age. *Instructional Technology and Distance Education, 2*(1), 3–10. Retrieved 2010 from http://www.elearnspace.org/Articles/connectivism.htm

Siemens, G., & Long, P. (2011). Penetrating the fog: Analytics in learning and education. *Educause Review, 46*(5). Retrieved from http://www.educause.edu/EDUCAUSE+Review/EDUCAUSEReviewMagazineVolume46/PenetratingtheFogAnalyticsinLe/235017

Simonson, M., Schlosser, C., & Orellana, A. (2011). Distance education research: A review of the literature. *Journal of Computing in Higher Education,* (23), 124–42. doi:10.1007/s12528-011-9045-8.

Zawacki-Richter, O. (2009). Research areas in distance education: A Delphi study. *International Review of Research in Open and Distance Learning, 10*(3), 1–17.

Zawacki-Richter, O., & Anderson, T. (2011). The geography of distance education: Bibliographic characteristics of a journal network. *Distance Education, 32*(3).

Zawacki-Richter, O., Anderson, T., & Tuncay, N. (2010). The growing impact of open access distance education journals: A bibliometric analysis. *Journal of Distance Education, 24*(3). Retrieved from http://www.jofde.ca/index.php/jde/article/view/661

Zawacki-Richter, O., Bäcker, E. M., & Vogt, S. (2009). Review of distance education research (2000 to 2008): Analysis of research areas, methods, and authorship patterns. *International Review of Research in Open and Distance Learning, 10*(6), 21–50.

Zawacki-Richter, O., & von Prümmer, C. (2010). Gender and collaboration patterns in distance education research. *Open Learning, 25*(2), 95–114.

Part I

MACRO-LEVEL RESEARCH: DISTANCE EDUCATION SYSTEMS AND THEORIES

Internationalization and Concepts of Social Justice: What Is to Be Done?

Alan Tait and Jennifer O'Rourke

Introducing the concept of social justice into discussions of open, distance, and e-learning immediately creates tension. At its core is the question as to whether ODEL contributes to or detracts from social justice, given its facility for supporting the development of formal education on an international basis and the complexity of intentions, inputs, and outcomes in any educational provision.

Let us first consider what we mean by social justice. Clear, agreed-upon concepts of this term are essential underpinnings for robust support for strategies to remedy *social injustice*. Without this clarity, there is a risk that those who claim it as a goal but have no intention or capacity to deliver it will appropriate the term.

CONCEPTS OF SOCIAL JUSTICE

Social Justice for Individuals

The central concept of social justice is a conviction that human beings have some core characteristics of equality. Philosophical and religious traditions developed this concept long before English priest John Ball asked the following of rebel peasants in 1381:

> When Adam delved and Eve span, Who was then the gentleman? From the beginning all men by nature were created alike, and our bondage or servitude came in by the unjust oppression of naughty men. For if God would have had any bondmen from the beginning, he would have appointed who should be bond, and who free. (Chisholm, 1911, p. 263)

The concept of equality was also developed in the secular tradition of Universal Human Rights, articulated in the *Egalité* of the French Revolution, then adopted in the UN Declaration of Human Rights in 1948, and subsequently embodied in UN institutions. Both religious and secular concepts of the value of each person underlie an ideological commitment to the fundamental equality of status of all human beings regardless of the lived reality of privilege and social hierarchy. Indeed, John Ball's support for the Peasants' Revolt might be seen as a very early attempt to bring these concepts together.

Rawls' account (2001) of a social contract begins with a commitment to equality of worth of human beings and demands that entitlements be proposed by representatives of the population, especially those with responsibilities for government, on a "blind" basis, i.e., as if they had no knowledge of their own entitlement and acted for all rather than as advocates of their own interests. Rumble's discussion of education and social justice elaborates Rawls' contribution and, following Honderich, dismisses Rawls' liberalism as too permissive of gross inequalities (Rumble, 2007, pp. 171-72).

The social justice concepts listed above tend to portray social justice as enabling individuals to access their fair share of social and economic benefits. In contrast, Sen and Nussbaum identify much broader and universal human rights as integral to social justice.

Sen's human development theory (1999, 2009) contributes another dimension to the concept of social justice by focussing on what he terms the *Capability Approach*—the support of positive freedoms to be or do something "to choose a life one has reason to value" (Sen, 1999, p. 74). These freedoms depend on *functionings* or, "the various things a person may value being or doing" (Sen, 1999, p. 75). Sen's perspective is significantly different from equality provisions because it regards material benefits or services not as social justice indicators in themselves, but as the basis for the freedom to deploy capabilities that represent the real social justice outcomes. Sen does not propose a set of universal capabilities, suggesting instead that they must be elaborated in specific contexts.

Nussbaum (2003) builds on Sen's work by stipulating a list of essential capabilities for social justice. This step is crucial, Nussbaum argues, because there is no benefit in having rights without the underlying capabilities that make it possible to exercise those rights: "Thinking in terms of capability gives us a benchmark as we think about what it is really to secure a right to someone. It makes clear that this involves affirmative material and institutional support, not simply a failure to impede" (Nussbaum, 2008, p. 38).

Of the ten capabilities that Nussbaum (2003) identifies, three have direct relevance to education and learning, and two others have significant supporting roles. Those directly related to education and learning are:

> 4. Senses, Imagination, and Thought. Being able to use the senses, to imagine, think, and reason—and to do these things in a "truly human" way, a way informed and cultivated by an adequate education, including, but by no means limited to, literacy and basic mathematical and scientific training. Being able to use imagination and thought in connection with experiencing and producing works and events of one's own choice, religious, literary, musical, and so forth. Being able to use one's mind in ways protected by guarantees of freedom of expression with respect to both political and artistic speech, and freedom of religious exercise. . . . 5. Emotions. Being able to have attachments to things and people outside ourselves . . . not having one's emotional development blighted by fear and anxiety. (Supporting this capability means supporting forms of human association that can be shown to be crucial in their development.) 6. Practical Reason. Being able to form a conception of the good and to engage in critical reflection about the planning of one's life. (This entails protection for the liberty of conscience and religious observance.) (p. 41)

Nussbaum (2003) describes capabilities that support education and learning as follows:

> 7. Affiliation. A. Being able to live with and toward others, to recognize and show concern for other human beings, to engage in various forms of social interaction; to be able to imagine the situation of another.

(Protecting this capability means protecting institutions that constitute and nourish such forms of affiliation, and also protecting the freedom of assembly and political speech.) B. Having the social bases of self-respect and non-humiliation; being able to be treated as a dignified being whose worth is equal to that of others. This entails provisions of non-discrimination on the basis of race, sex, sexual orientation, ethnicity, caste, religion, or national origin. (pp. 41–42)

Also relevant is Nussbaum's capability 10:

Control Over One's Environment. A. Political. Being able to participate effectively in political choices that govern one's life; having the right of political participation, protections of free speech and association. B. Material. Being able to hold property (both land and movable goods), and having property rights on an equal basis with others; having the right to seek employment on an equal basis with others; having the freedom from unwarranted search and seizure. In work, being able to work as a human being, exercising practical reason and entering into meaningful relationships of mutual recognition with other workers. (2003, p. 42)

This concept of social justice as capabilities to which every human is entitled is consistent with Article 26 of the UN Declaration of Human Rights (1948) on the right to education:

(1) Everyone has the right to education. Education shall be free, at least in the elementary and fundamental stages. Elementary education shall be compulsory. Technical and professional education shall be made generally available and higher education shall be equally accessible to all on the basis of merit.

(2) Education shall be directed to the full development of the human personality and to the strengthening of respect for human rights and fundamental freedoms. It shall promote understanding, tolerance, and friendship among all nations, racial or religious groups.

(3) Parents have a prior right to choose the kind of education that shall be given to their children.

In summary, our concept of social justice for each individual encompasses both the notion of equality rights as a level playing field and the right to opportunities and support that enable each person to fully participate in all aspects of society—to get to the playing field in the first place. These include affordable education, housing, access to decent work with sufficient pay to sustain a family—rights that go far beyond access to participate in the economy.

SOCIAL JUSTICE AMONG SOCIETIES AND WITHIN DEFINED SECTORS OF SOCIETY

But there is more to social justice than the cumulative human rights of each individual. As Judt (2010, p. 131) points out, despite the current "cult of the private" that emphasizes enterprise over justice, an underlying concept of the common good is essential for democratic governance.

Both Judt (2010, p. 67) and Franklin (1990, p. 42) identify trust and reciprocity as essential components of social justice and as elements that convey social values. Franklin distinguishes divisible and indivisible benefits and the social and economic implications of both. Sharing a crop among all farm workers is an example of divisible benefits among a specified group. Indivisible benefits are inclusive and for everyone and include justice, peace, clean air, equal access to education, public institutions. Some significant indivisible benefits that, until recently, were supported by the public domain are being increasingly shifted into the private sector, for example, transportation, utilities, health care, and education (Judt, 2010; Franklin, 2006). Moreover, although the public purse has sustained the infrastructure that makes private divisible benefits possible, there is increasingly less political support and protection for the sources of indivisible benefits, such as the global environment (Franklin, 1999). Education provides both indivisible and divisible benefits, and it is difficult to isolate the benefits of education to the individual from the benefits to society.

As Franklin (2006) notes, the process of establishing social justice should be systemic rather than case-specific, so that the onus is on society rather than the individual to change structural, institutional, and cultural barriers that impede equal access to human rights, rather than on "putting the primary burden of change on the disadvantaged" (p. 345).

The ILO's Declaration on Social Justice for a Fair Globalization summarizes the links between individual and social aspects of social justice in Article A1, which supports the following objectives:

promoting employment by creating a sustainable institutional and economic environment in which:

- individuals can develop and update the necessary capacities and skills they need to enable them to be productively occupied for their personal fulfilment and the common well-being
- all enterprises, public or private, are sustainable to enable growth and the generation of greater employment and income opportunities and prospects for all
- societies can achieve their goals of economic development, good living standards and social progress (ILO, 2008, p. 4)

WHY THERE ARE NO SIMPLE LINKS BETWEEN SOCIAL JUSTICE AND ONLINE DISTANCE EDUCATION AND LEARNING

On the face of it, it would seem that educational provision that is consciously intended to be more accessible to more people would make a contribution to social justice. But each of ODEL's main attributes brings with it a caveat:

- ODEL's capacity to disaggregate the constitutive elements of classroom learning offers freedom from place and time, providing the ability to offer flexibility and to support educational systems across national boundaries. However, flexibility brings with it the potential for disconnection from the learners' contexts and from direct association with others engaged in learning. ODEL's capacity to traverse national and regional boundaries also enables it to displace local or national provisions, and to disseminate ideologies that are incompatible with local beliefs or cultures.

- National governments, inter-governmental organizations, and NGOs have, as part of development of the Third World, or the Global South, promoted ODEL's flexibility and scalability as an opportunity to fulfil the moral obligation to create urgently needed educational provision.

However, as McLuhan (1964) pointed out, no technology is neutral; all technologies affect both the creator and the user. Each technology includes underlying concepts and assumptions that may not always be evident to planners or practitioners. As well, the capacities and limitations of hardware and software affect how pedagogies are applied. For example, broadcast radio assumes a functional network, access to electricity, learners who can listen attentively at the broadcast time, and learners who can learn effectively from a transitory auditory medium. Radio can convey a voice of authority that is not easy to challenge, or a conversational tone that invites participatory learning.

Transplanting any technology along with its ideological roots brings the risk of imposing an inappropriate set of assumptions and values on the users, thus detracting from, rather than supporting, intended goals.

ODEL's history includes the commercial provision of accessible accreditation both locally and internationally (for example, for-profit correspondence schools, or University of London External Studies). Online learning has greatly expanded opportunities to offer education and accreditation across international boundaries, making it possible for learners around the world to access the specific programs they need.

However, even with ready availability of online communication in some locations, learners are not always in the best position to assess the quality and appropriateness of a specific program that is on offer, given the lack of clear international standards for ODEL provision and the limited access to the kind of collegial local knowledge that is available in face-to-face learning settings. As well, ODEL that relies on advanced technologies can (intentionally or not) reinforce inequality by providing access only to those on the "have" side of the digital divide.

WHAT IS TO BE DONE, PART 1: SHOULD ODEL EMBED SOCIAL JUSTICE PRINCIPLES?

Many ODEL providers began with a stated commitment to provide greater access to education for those who were previously excluded. However, there are questions about the effectiveness of access to education as a route to social justice and about the success rate of ODEL institutions in enabling disadvantaged people to attain their educational goals. (Prinsloo, 2011, summarizes these arguments.)

Moreover, times have changed since contemporary forms of ODEL emerged in the early 1980s with the promise of reaching underserved learners at all levels of education throughout the globe. Short-term economic goals have displaced social justice from policy agendas, along with a shift in societal expectations that supported publicly-funded access to affordable education.

These factors prompt the question: Should all ODEL provisions be required to follow social justice principles, and if so, what would this look like? Can a society or government require an educational provider to adopt a social justice mandate? Oversight bodies that represent government and/ or society can require educational providers to meet specific standards— why not include social justice? Exploring this question involves considering different concepts of social justice in education: access, curriculum, pedagogy, and management.

Social Justice as Improved Access

Many distance education providers include social justice in their mission or values statements. For example, the Open University of the United Kingdom (OUUK) current website states, "We promote educational opportunity and social justice by providing high-quality university education to all who wish to realise their ambitions and fulfil their potential. . . . The OU was founded to open up higher education to all, regardless of their circumstances or where they live." Athabasca University in Canada "dedicated to the removal of barriers that restrict access to and success in university-level study and to increasing equality of educational opportunity for adult learners worldwide" (AUP, 2009). These statements associate social justice with providing greater access to learning.

But Woodley (2011) points out the social justice disconnect in most distance learning models intended to improve access to learning: the provider benefits financially when learners do not continue in courses because the provider has received payment, but the learner does not use all the services paid for (such as counselling or tutoring). ODEL's economics, like that of health care provision, rely on funding for a larger population than is directly served. Woodley also cites 2009 HEFCE data showing that the OUUK's graduation rate is 20%, and that just 40% of first-year students proceed to take a second-year course. However, given OUUK's student population of 250,000, one could also argue that the 50,000 students that graduate each year from OUUK, representing a significant number of graduates who might otherwise not achieve this goal. While there have been 382,000 graduates at bachelor's and master's levels since start of teaching in 1971, at the time of writing, the graduation rate is difficult to assess and may in fact be less than the percentages identified by Woodley.

By comparison, the online for-profit University of Phoenix has a six-year graduation rate of 5.1%, but this "measures fewer than 1% of its more than 253,000 students" (Waddington, qtd. in Blumenstyk, 2012).

The flexibility of ODEL may be one factor in lower graduation rates, given the higher participation rate of working adults, the percentage of learners who study at several institutions to obtain transferable credits, and ODEL's accessibility for personal interest studies. So a proportion of ODEL students may be accomplishing personal goals without completing full programs.

Given these considerations, it is possible to argue that ODEL can benefit society as a whole, even if not all learners are able to achieve their individual goals. However, this argument requires recognizing every individual's right to learning which is appropriate to his or her needs, and acknowledging that strengthening society's capacity requires responding to both individual and societal needs.

Social Justice as Curriculum and Pedagogy

As Freire (1983) and many others have pointed out, curriculum and pedagogy are not value-neutral: content and methods that enable learners to think for themselves and engage in dialogue with resources, instructors, and other learners are more likely to support social justice goals. Prinsloo (2011a, para. 10) argues that learning must "empower graduates to critique, to formulate their own opinions, to question accepted ways of seeing the world (ontologies) and accepted canons of market-dominated knowledge (epistemologies)." He also cites Giroux's critical commentary about higher education becoming the "handmaiden" of corporations in an

> age of money and profit, [where] academic disciplines gain stature
> almost exclusively through their exchange value on the market, and
> students now rush to take courses and receive professional credentials
> that provide them with the cache they need to sell themselves to the
> higher bidder. (2003, p. 182)

Freire's concept of social justice in learning proposes that discussion, interaction, and problem solving can enable learners to develop a critical consciousness that is "integrated with reality" and prepares learners to act in response to challenges (Freire, 1983, p. 44). But distance education practice can itself limit this kind of engagement. Previous generations of distance educators were concerned about the tendency of then-current technologies, such as print, radio, and television, to emphasize the authority of the message, rather than enabling learners to engage with the content and discuss concepts. Although multiple technologies can now accommodate discussion and collaboration among ODEL learners and instructors, there are questions about whether these strategies support genuine engagement for all learners, rather than a pro forma interaction that meets assessment requirements (Harris, 2011). Writing about South Africa, Daweti and Mitchell (2011) observe that "third-generation ODL usually suggests a greater reliance on electronic media, but in our context, it suggests once again the need for more student support, more contact, and more flexibility of access to technology than ever before"(p. 63). Moreover, without ready and affordable access to the Internet or required bandwidth, the promise of active engagement is empty.

Without denying the realities of dominant ideologies influencing both curriculum and pedagogy, it is also important to recognize the capacity of committed educators to enable learners to think outside these dominant forces, whether it is a professor teaching "a hidden curriculum" that challenges the prevailing totalitarian mantra in pre-1989 Poland (Potulicka, 1991), or a facilitator enabling Kenyan women with limited literacy to develop skills in managing businesses in a male-dominated occupation (Kere, 2006). Moreover, as Derounian (2012) explains, distance-learning assessment that enables learners to deal with genuine workplace issues can actually support rather than undermine personal integrity.

Social Justice in ODEL Management and Operations

Curriculum and pedagogy are both particular and situational, linked to an academic and cultural context and governed by academic freedom. Given these considerations, society can, at best, strongly encourage the inclusion of social justice principles in these aspects of ODEL provision.

However, social justice is also relevant to many of the most common operational elements of ODEL provision, notably access and support, as well as management, financing, and staffing. Despite cultural, social, and economic differences, there is evidence of widespread acceptance of social justice principles, especially those related to work and education. For example,

182 countries signed the 2008 ILO Declaration on Social Justice for a Fair Globalization, which provides a broad framework for applying social justice principles in specific sectors and affirms that "the fundamental values of freedom, human dignity, social justice, security and non-discrimination are essential for sustainable economic and social development and efficiency."

The issue is how to reconcile a social justice mandate with all the other pressures that affect policy and practice. How can an ODEL provider make social justice an integral part of all levels of its operations and provision?

WHAT IS TO BE DONE, PART 2: IMPLICATIONS FOR EMBEDDING SOCIAL JUSTICE IN ODEL

In accepting the case for social justice, there is the embedded *a priori* assumption that the world is not structured fairly enough, and that something should be done about it. This assumption does not gain universal assent, especially from those who regard the market as the most simple and effective mechanism for distributing goods. Even where the abstract principle is supported, it is likely to strike the rock of self-interest as soon as it demands the shifting of resources from some of the haves to some of the have-less or have not groups.

Implementing Social Justice

There are relatively passive approaches to social justice, for example, those that restrict themselves to making opportunity more equally available, alongside the much harder task whose objective is to make achievement more equally accessible. Attempting to implement the latter concept into practice soon begins to affect the distribution of resources and meets resistance fairly early in its development. In the creation of institutions and organizations for ODEL, this interpretation would lead to policies and practices of equal opportunity, with remedial support given to those who needed it.

Consideration of the extent to which ODEL contributes to or detracts from social justice when working on an international basis requires a deep understanding of how an institution or a program contributes to the freedoms that its learners might deploy in their lives (Sen, 2009). In more concrete terms this might include:

- ensuring, or seeking to ensure, the admission of students to programs according to their need and not to their capacity to pay
- ensuring the alignment of curricula with the skills and knowledge that students need to function in their individual, family, and economic lives
- ensuring the commitment to student success, and thus to a range of support services on a differentiated basis
- ensuring the validity and credibility of qualifications in terms of societal acceptance and value.

This approach moves away from abstract commitment to equality but demands practical outcomes, within which we can place commitments to ethics and to equal opportunity practices. Following this approach, ODEL can contribute to social justice, whether nationally or internationally, in its ability to support development of the activities needed to live a free, fully human, life.

Let us return therefore to the question as to whether ODEL on an international basis contributes to or detracts from social justice. Are we restricted to asserting that all for-profit educational initiatives are educationally suspect? It is certainly the case that for-profit educational organizations would need, logically speaking, to serve the market, which in a fundamental way suggests accepting the world as it is rather than identifying its structural inequalities. Both publicly funded and private for-profit educational institutions are designed to serve market needs, and both include learners and their employers as their markets. Public institutions are more likely to include their primary funder, that is, the government and the people it represents, as one of the markets they serve, and to take these broader needs into consideration in planning, policy, and operations.

However, private sector institutions can do two things that could be regarded as valuable contributions to a society committed to social justice. Firstly, the private sector can serve established audiences that do not need the support of the state or other not-for-profit sources; and secondly, the private sector can invent markets and through innovation provide products and services that users have not asked for but take up, sometimes with great enthusiasm, when first offered. This can apply in educational contexts as well as in more familiar product-led sectors. An issue for both public and private sector ODEL is whether financial considerations outweigh social justice principles. We will expand on this question in the next section.

Therefore, rather than starting from one of the ideological positions that are frequently proposed (for example, that all institutions working internationally in ODEL are involved in cultural imperialism, or that all private sector institutions are more interested in shareholder returns than educational missions, or that public sector institutions are likely to serve staff interests rather than client interests), we can assess the contribution to social justice for our own or other organizations through the construction of characteristics that support or detract from social justice, developing these principles within our own contexts, and sharing these in order to construct larger order understandings.

To that end, the following is a proposed framework for a social justice audit of ODEL.

WHAT IS TO BE DONE, PART 3: FRAMEWORK FOR AN ODEL SOCIAL JUSTICE AUDIT

We propose a social justice audit as a method for assessing how well an ODEL organization's policies and practices support its identified social justice goals. Both the process and outcomes of a social justice audit can guide a reorientation of policies and practices, or potentially, a rethinking of social justice goals. A social justice audit can emerge from the overarching question: What characteristics should ODEL have in order to achieve social justice, or to have an impact towards social justice? In other words, what should social justice look like, in terms of goals, policies, and practices? An audit also needs to consider a practical question: What dimensions of social justice are actually identifiable and measurable through the appropriate and available research methods? At an organizational level, a social justice audit can examine the clarity of its social justice goals and the extent to which the organization is meeting its stated social justice goals at each level of its operation.

Using a participatory process is consistent with social justice principles because it engages those who are directly involved and affected by the organization's management and services, providing multiple perspectives and greater depth of information than selective research. Moreover, a participatory process among those directly involved in ODEL, as learners, staff, funders, government, and representatives of society, can strengthen both the organization and its links with stakeholders.

A Participatory Approach to Examining Social Justice in Practice

A participatory approach to a social justice audit builds on the concept of participatory evaluation, a method that engages those directly affected by a process or project. Participatory evaluation originally developed in the 1970s as a response to concerns about externally managed project evaluation that did not involve project participants, beneficiaries, or their communities, and has since evolved into a widely used practice.

Participatory evaluation is a process of self-assessment, collective knowledge production, and cooperative action in which stakeholders in a development intervention participate substantively in the identification of the evaluation issues, the design of the evaluation, the collection and analysis of data, and the action taken as a result of the evaluation findings. By participating in the process, the stakeholders also build their own capacity and skills to undertake research and evaluation in other areas (Jackson & Hassam, 1998).

There are now many variations of participatory evaluation, such as participatory action research, cooperative inquiry, and others however, it is beyond the scope of this chapter to consider each of these threads. Variations of participatory evaluation meet different needs, and organizations are in the best position to identify a variation or combination of approaches that is most appropriate for their situation. Considerations include the goals of the inquiry, who is included, and their level of decision making in planning, gathering, and interpreting information; timing and extent of participation; choices of inquiry processes; methods for sharing outcomes, and developing action plans based on the outcomes and the extent to which each part of the process can contribute to organizational learning.

A literature review indicates that the term *social justice audit* is not used extensively in educational contexts. However, the application of the concept in enterprise monitoring and in development initiatives indicates its potential for education, especially ODEL, because it examines the extent to which organizational practice at each level is consistent with agreed principles. Examples of social audits in enterprise monitoring and in development programs provide useful lessons for a social justice audit in ODEL.

A participatory approach can strengthen the reliability and impact of social audits that monitor compliance with international labour standards, compared to a "snapshot" audit by an external evaluator who relies solely on management input and pro forma checklists (Auret & Barrientos, 2004). A genuinely participatory approach to a social audit of an enterprise involves:

> companies, trade unions, NGOs and government in local initiatives that provide independent forms of monitoring and verification of (labour) codes. Local multi-stakeholder initiatives require active engagement by all relevant actors that have knowledge of employment issues on the ground. This helps to provide space for the interests of more vulnerable unorganized groups, such as women, to be articulated. The process of (labour) code implementation by multi-stakeholder initiatives, rather than external governance, is sustainable locally as an ongoing process of improvement—it encourages active involvement of workers and managers, enables discussion, creates awareness, and enables people to identify problems and priorities. (Auret & Barrientos, 2004, p. 1)

This participatory approach contrasts with some corporations' self-monitoring reports on their corporate social responsibility (CSR) commitments, which may provide extensive quantitative information but without contextual or other information that would enable society as a whole to assess the corporation's compliance with CSR goals (Owen, 2003).

Participatory approaches to assessing effectiveness of development projects can redress imbalances of power among funders, implementing agencies, and beneficiaries and strengthen accountability and results. As Jackson and Kassam (1998) note, "no one has a greater stake in optimizing results than project beneficiaries on the ground" (p. 13).

In summary, a social justice audit engages those who are directly and indirectly affected by the organization by looking within the organization, outwards to its immediate clientele, and beyond to society as a whole. However, as with other methods of assessing progress towards goals, the process must be much more meaningful and engaging than a pro forma exercise of ticking boxes and filling in forms. Several proponents of participatory process describe it as a *conversation* (Williamson et al., 2000).

With the appropriate intentions, engagement, support, and resources, a participatory social justice audit of ODEL can enable all those involved in provision to:

- identify social justice as it applies to ODEL, by contributing their perspective based on their role or involvement with an ODEL provider
- focus on social justice dimensions that are most relevant for the

specific ODEL context, in terms of policy, strategies, operations, and impact on society

- create and implement appropriate strategies for clarifying how well the ODEL organization is supporting its own social justice goals
- develop action plans to strengthen practical support for agreed social justice goals for the ODEL organization.

We propose a social justice audit that can serve as an instrument for assessing whether ODEL is meeting identified social justice goals, the following section outlines steps in the process.

Explicit Social Justice Goals

Clearly identified social justice goals set the tone and framework for an organization's mandate. Without an explicit statement of goals for social justice, it is difficult to establish policies that will support achievement of social justice goals, or to identify practices that are consistent with social justice policies. To have a real impact, social justice needs to be adopted and applied at every level of the organization.

Examining an organization's social justice goals can explore the clarity, depth, and scope of these goals in relation to its mission, those it serves, and members of the organization.

POLICIES THAT SUPPORT SOCIAL JUSTICE GOALS

Policies articulate principles that demonstrate commitment to specific areas of social justice and provide a framework for developing the organization's strategies for meeting its responsibilities to learners. Without policies that are clearly based on social justice goals, it is difficult to ensure that social justice principles are the formulation of procedures and day-to-day practice. Policy areas most relevant to social justice govern access, quality, consistency, and sustainability, and the social contract implications of providing learning opportunities that benefit both the individual and society.

Policies Related to Access

Access, the *sine qua non* of ODEL, may be defined as the removal of barriers (geographic, social, economic, gender) and/or as the enabling of learners to overcome potential barriers (disability, incomplete prior education, social exclusion, and so on). Access may be defined differently in different contexts, depending on the barriers to learning. For example, providing genuine access to basic literacy programs requires resources that non-readers can use. Clear access policies put the onus on the provider rather than on the learner to ensure accessibility.

A review of policies related to access could consider the organization's definition of barriers to access, and assess how effectively its policies address these barriers, such as support, flexibility, and responsiveness.

Policies Related to Quality

ODEL literature frequently refers to learners' reluctance to question poor quality learning materials, resources, or services. Providing genuine access to learning opportunities entails a commitment to quality provision that is fair to all learners and accompanied by appropriate instructional and administrative support. Policies related to quality should guide appropriate strategies that consistently enable learning materials, resources, services, and administrative systems to meet acceptable standards.

A review of policies related to quality can consider the extent to which policies define standards, quality assessment, and quality improvement guidelines for each aspect of provision.

Policies Related to Consistency and Sustainability

Many ODEL initiatives begin on a trial basis, often with dedicated funding for a limited duration. However, many ODEL learners, who typically study part-time, require a fairly long time frame to complete their qualifications. Courses or programs that are a limited time offer are unlikely to meet most learners' needs. Learners who are working towards a specific qualification, such as a university degree, rely on all the required courses in a program to be available when they need to take them. ODEL providers that cancel required courses due to lack of funding or other resources (such as instructional staff or technical support) are not meeting learners' needs for continued access.

A review of policies related to consistency and sustainability can consider the extent to which policies specify standards for ensuring continuity of funding and support for programs and for communicating time limits on availability of specific programs.

Policies Related to Social Contract Aspects of ODEL Provision

Both publicly and privately funded education fulfill an implied social contract based on the benefits of education and training for both the individual and society. Society provides funding for public education and oversight and accreditation for both public and private education. In turn, education and training enable an individual to have a livelihood and contribute to society, to the benefit of both the individual and society. Several African countries make this social contract explicit in practical terms by providing free university education to qualified students, and in turn, requiring graduates to complete a year of free national service in their field (Idogho, 2011, personal communication). The global reach of ODEL offers learners the opportunity to acquire internationally recognized qualifications: This is potentially a mixed benefit for society, if it accelerates the loss of its well-educated citizens to other countries where their skills command a higher income. (For example, about one third of African-trained health professionals relocate to Europe or North America, representing a net loss to their countries of origin, even when considering remittances from expatriates.) Moreover, initiatives to use open educational resources (OER) in ODEL increase the possibility that ODEL learning materials will include resources developed in contexts and cultures that are different from those of the learners.

A review of an organization's social contract policies could consider the extent to which policies identify social contract commitments to society, to learners, and to specific stakeholders.

OPERATIONAL STRATEGIES THAT SUPPORT SOCIAL JUSTICE POLICIES

Policies provide the rationale and conceptual framework for supporting social justice; strategies identify practical ways of realizing these goals in each area of ODEL practice. While policies are relatively stable, strategies require regular review and recalibration to ensure they are appropriate for the organizational and learners' contexts and consistent with policy objectives.

A broad consideration of strategies that support social justice could examine the consistency between stated policies on each aspect of social justice and the operational strategies that implement these policies, the effectiveness of the strategies for implementing these policies, and the organization's capacity to improve or revise strategies to respond to social justice needs. More specific strategies address the issues of access, quality, consistency, and sustainability, and the social contract for learning.

Strategies that Address Accessibility

Strategies that Address Accessibility of Entry to Learning
In situations where social justice is a guiding principle for ODEL provision, accessibility involves more than putting access strategies in place. Ensuring accessibility requires viewing the organization through the eyes of prospective learners, identifying barriers as they perceive them, developing strategies to minimize or eliminate barriers, and anticipating learners' needs at each stage: enrolment, participation, and completion. Accessibility can be described as passive, simply allowing learners who are familiar with the organization to enrol in programs, or active, proactively reaching out to communities and providing prospective learners with enough information to enable them to make an informed choice and to guide them through the enrolment process.

A review of access strategies can consider whether there are effective strategies to minimize or remove barriers to access and to support at-risk learners, and adequate resources to implement these strategies.

Strategies that Address Continuity of Access to Learning
After making the first step to enter a learning program, learners are still vulnerable to individual and social factors that can impede or stop their progress. As well, organizational decisions (such as course availability, technologies, and support systems) can make it difficult or impossible for learners to continue to their goal. Genuine access includes the opportunity to continue learning towards a specific goal.

A review of strategies that support sustained learning can consider the scope and effectiveness of its support services, of strategies for ensuring adequate communication with learners and for monitoring accessibility of its technologies for learners.

Strategies for Maintaining Quality

Every element of ODEL provision has quality requirements and implications: management, administration, learning resources, services that support students directly and indirectly.

Quality in Management Strategies

The quality of management strategies of ODEL impacts all levels of society and provision of services:

- decision makers who rely on ODEL to broaden access to education and to prepare people for a livelihood that contributes to society
- professions and occupations that depend on ODEL programs to help meet the demand for well-trained staff
- learners for whom ODEL is the only chance for access to education or training
- staff who rely on good management to enable them to meet their commitments to learners

Quality in management strategies implies supporting continuity and consistency in all aspects of provision that affect the learning experience. The longer time frame for many ODEL learning experiences has an impact on decisions that could change priorities, funding, or instruction, which can affect learners' ability to achieve goals successfully. Moreover, ODEL learners often have difficulty overcoming physical and social distance so they can communicate their views to management.

A review of quality in management strategies could examine the extent to which decisions about management strategies consider consistency with policy and with learner and societal needs, and could help determine whether adequate resources are in place to support agreed-upon strategies.

Quality in Administrative Services

Quality in administrative services is an essential link between policy and provision. Unfortunately, it can be the weak link in ODEL, especially in situations where administrative systems are modelled on those used for face-to-face provision. ODEL learners can be discouraged or defeated by administrative delays that prevent them from meeting administrative or academic deadlines. Quality in administrative services includes responsiveness, timeliness, and accuracy, and it requires adequate staff resources that have appropriate guidance, training, and support.

A review of quality in administrative services can consider the responsiveness and timeliness of administrative systems and services and the adequacy of resources to ensure effective administrative services.

Quality in Instructional Support and Services

In social justice terms, fairness is an important attribute of instruction and entails providing the type of instructional support that is appropriate to the content, to learners' needs, and to the expected learning outcomes. Short-changing instructional services is unfair to learners and to supporters and funders of the learning program because it reduces the likelihood that it will achieve its goals. Moreover, a lack of quality instruction can impede learners' capacity to apply their learning in work or life situations.

A review of quality in instructional services could examine the suitability of instructional services for the specific characteristics of a program and the needs of learners and the adequacy of resources to support appropriate instruction.

Quality in Instructional Resources

In social justice terms, quality instructional resources are appropriate for the intended learning outcomes, content, context, learners, and instructional strategies. Instructional resources that are incomplete, or designed for a different context, or are not consistent with the level or focus of the program or course, present a disadvantage to learners. Moreover, because learning materials seem authoritative, learners can assume that their difficulties in using the materials are their fault, rather than that of the materials, and can lose confidence as a result.

A review of quality in instructional resources can examine the strategies that ensure instructional resources are appropriate for the instructional content, learners, and context.

Strategies for Maintaining Consistency and Sustainability

ODEL learners are particularly vulnerable to changes in provision because ODEL is often the only option that will enable them to meet their learning goals. However, there are many examples of short-term ODEL initiatives that showed promise but ended due to lack of funding, leaving many learners without alternatives for completing their program. While pilot projects can provide an opportunity to demonstrate the viability of an ODEL program, pilot learners need realistic information about the likelihood of longer-term provision. As well, initiating pilot projects that are not representative of the core mandate of the ODEL provider can be unfair to funders, staff, and learners, because of the reduced possibility of continued support and possible diversion of resources from core programs.

A review of strategies to ensure consistency and sustainability can examine provisions that govern planning and implementing new programs, especially those dependent on short-term or contingent funding.

Strategies for Sustaining the Social Contract Aspects of ODEL Provision

Clearly defined strategies can govern some, but not all, social contract aspects of ODEL provision. By *social contract*, we mean a society's agreed mutual obligations that support equity. The factors that can balance or outweigh social contract elements include learners' freedom of choice, academic freedom as related to instructors' choices of curriculum content and pedagogy, and prevailing values and expectations in the social and political context. However, clearly articulated strategies can help to ensure consistency between stated policy on social contract elements and day-to-day provision.

A review of the ODEL's strategies that support social contract policies can examine the degree of meaningful consultation with communities it serves, about aspects of provision and the impact of its programs, and the extent of its engagement in community service initiatives.

WHAT ABOUT MEASURING OUTCOMES?

One reviewer of this chapter recommended that a social justice audit should also consider outcomes. However, we argue that paying attention to social justice in all ODEL processes serves as a counterweight to the current focus (obsession) on outcomes as the primary strategy for external assessments of the effectiveness of learning provision. Moreover, a social justice audit initiated from within an organization can provide insights into the underlying reasons for the organization's effectiveness, and identify areas it can improve in order to strengthen effectiveness. External assessment that focusses only on outcomes provides information without a great deal of context. For example, readers will not know whether a high program completion rate is due to selective intake of high achievers, effective teaching, or less stringent standards. A study of processes provides contextual information that enables an organization to focus on strengthening areas that can improve outcomes.

For example, in the UK, league tables rank universities according to a set of measures that include student satisfaction, student outcomes, and job placements after graduation. However, one commentator notes that it's quite possible to focus on strategies that improve league table outcomes, and quotes a marketing director at one university that improved its league table standing significantly.

It's not rocket science, according to Stuart Franklin, director of marketing and communications at Exeter: "We took the trouble to understand how the league tables worked and then implemented a deliberate policy of using the metrics to drive institutional performance." In effect, Exeter designed its policy around the demands of the league tables, but Stuart Franklin rejects the charge that this was a subversion of institutional strategy "student outcomes, research, student satisfaction—league tables measure the sorts of things that any well run organisation should be focussing on" (Catcheside, 2012).

In Canada, a national magazine's annual ranking of universities measures student success in obtaining national academic awards; student access to instructors; the proportion of faculty who win major awards and research grants; resources allocated to research, teaching, student support, library holdings; and the institutions' reputation. The outcomes are focussed on exceptional achievement rather than on the general student and faculty population; the inputs are identified in physical terms, investments, numbers of books, journals, and so on, rather than in terms of the nature of the interaction and engagement of instructors and learners.

Typically, outcomes are based on program completion rates and, in some cases, on post-graduation employment (Dwyer, 2011). However, outcomes on graduation or shortly thereafter may not be a predictor of the long-term viability of students' education. Some surveys follow up students five years after graduation, but with diminishing data returns from students and less relevant input for current programs.

One potential rationale for capturing outcomes is to assess if an educational provider is meeting an objective of enabling learners to achieve their goals despite a disadvantage—social, economic, and others. However, numbers alone are not enough to answer this question, because they do not answer the qualitative questions: Typical data collected indicates whether learners are employed, but not the kind of work they are doing. However, an educational provider that actively engages with its alumni would be able to include former students in participatory social justice audits, thereby putting in practice the concept of a community of learners—past, current, and future.

CONCLUSION

This chapter presents more questions than answers, for several reasons. The topic of social justice is not easily confined within one category of experience or study: It imbues everyday life decision-making at all levels of work, society, and governance. It engages many disciplines, ranging from philosophy and theology to environmental studies, medicine, political science, and management. By its nature, social justice does not lend itself to prescriptions or road maps that "experts" recommend to others. Moreover, raising questions is in keeping with the book's theme of building towards a research agenda.

For many philosophical, social, and practical reasons, a commitment to social justice can be considered an essential element rather than an optional extra for ODEL provision. A social justice audit should protect against the easy use of rhetoric about social justice that does not and, in worst cases is never intended, to drive practice. The proposed framework for a social justice audit is intended to serve as an initial step in the process of demonstrating the viability of a social justice orientation and its effectiveness in meeting both a social and economic mandate, in the face of increasing pressures to operate in a competitive business model rather than a public service model.

In contrast to the prevailing competitive model of education, Finnish educator Pasi Sahlberg (Sahlberg & Hargreaves, 2011) provides strong evidence of the strength of an educational system based on equity rather than competition, focussed more on process than on measuring outcomes, and on social justice rather than market values. Sahlberg's work documents the transformation of the Finnish public education system, which has achieved "academic excellence through its particular policy focus on equity" (Partanen, 2012 p. 31).

Further work is needed to map the application of this social justice audit approach to particular institutions, organizations, and systems that deploy

ODEL. A range of valuable studies could be constructed that compare, for example, learner support strategies of private for-profit providers with those of public sector institutions, or of dual-mode organizations with the major open universities. These studies could inform the development of benchmarks that could guide more effective practice.

We hope that readers will adapt the proposed social justice audit framework to meet the specific needs of their organizations and share their reflections and comments on the concept of a social justice audit for ODEL. We hope to provide an impetus for practical explorations of the implications of social justice in specific ODEL contexts and for continued conversations about how commitments to social justice can be embodied in ODEL practice. Ideally, the result will be the embedding of social justice in practical outcomes and its removal from the anodyne or rhetorical.

A SAMPLE OF GUIDING QUESTIONS FOR A SOCIAL JUSTICE AUDIT IN ODEL

Social Justice Goals

- To what extent does the organization identify social justice goals within its mandate that will support success (for example, access to learning and resources)?

- How does the organization define individual and societal social justice goals? How are goals defined in terms of specific stakeholders, for example?

- What are individuals entitled to as learners? How does the organization define equity in access, provision, support?

- What is society entitled to as part of the social contract; given that society's collective investment in education is for the benefit of both the individual and society?

- What is the role of staff members in supporting social justice goals, in their interactions with learners and with other staff?

Policies Related to Access

- To what extent does the organization have policies that demonstrate a genuine commitment to identify and remove barriers that impede entry to learning (financial, geographic, social—lack of equity for specific groups, lack of gender equity)?

- To what extent does the organization have policies that demonstrate a commitment to identify and remove barriers to learners' continuing participation in learning and proceeding towards a successful outcome? Indicators can include policies that identify learners' entitlement to accessible, appropriate support and policies that enable staff to identify and recommend removal of institutional barriers that can curtail learners' continuing participation.

- To what extent are there policies that identify accessible, appropriate institutional support and that define how to remedy institutional barriers that are inconsistent with accessible, supportive learning (e.g., specific academic regulations imposing time limits on completing a program, use of technologies that are not widely available or affordable)?

- To what extent are there policies that indicate commitment to organizational flexibility and adaptability when required to ensure accessibility to entry and continuing learning? An example would be administrative policies that accommodate learners who may not be able to participate continually in learning (i.e., policies about completing programs within a specified time frame, or policies that enable learners to obtain accreditation based on requirements when learner began a program, rather than having to meet changed requirements).

General Policies Related to Quality

- To what extent are there organizational policies that identify acceptable standards in key aspects of management, administration, and provision of all components of the ODEL experience for learners?
- To what extent are there organizational policies that govern quality assessment and remedies for inadequate quality?

Policies Related to Consistency/Sustainability

- To what extent are there policies that govern the proportion of programs that must be fully supported by base funding, and the proportion that can be supported by contingent funding?
- To what extent are there policies that govern the proportion of the learner population that must be in fully funded programs and the proportion that can be in programs supported by contingent funding?
- To what extent are there policies that govern the lifespan of courses and programs and require strategies for maintaining uninterrupted provision of courses and programs?
- To what extent are there policies governing short-term initiatives, such as specially funded pilot programs, in terms of commitments to learners as well as to funders?

Policies Related to Social Contract

- To what extent are there policies that support engagement with society by senior management, instructional and administrative staff, and learners, about such topics as community learning needs, curriculum, applied learning opportunities?

- To what extent are there policies that require curriculum and pedagogy to be appropriate and relevant for the learners that the organization serves?

- To what extent are there policies that support arrangements that enable linkages between learning and practice, e.g., through workplace learning, internships, work terms, etc.?

Strategies that Support Social Justice Goals and Policies

- To what extent do the general operational strategies support the organization's stated goals and policies for social justice?

- What are the indicators of the effectiveness of these strategies?

- What are the provisions for assessing the effectiveness of these strategies using appropriate, consistent measures and tools?

- What is the outcome of these assessments? Does assessment guide changes that improve practice?

Strategies that Support Access to Entry to Learning

- To what extent are there effective strategies to reach out to specific groups that are now or were previously restricted from access to learning, for example, due to economic circumstances, gender, social class, or ethnicity?

- To what extent are there clear strategies to inform prospective learners about study opportunities, explain how they can access these opportunities, and provide guidance at each stage of the process (enquiry, program choices, registration, and starting the course or program)?

- To what extent are there clear strategies to actively inform prospective learners about accessibility policies and practices that are relevant to the learners' situation?

- To what extent are there adequate financial and staff resources in place to support these strategies?
- What are the indicators that the organization's access strategies are effective and are applied effectively?

Strategies that Support Access to Sustained Learning

- To what extent does the organization provide support services, such as academic and individual counselling, that can help learners deal with personal or social factors that affect their learning?
- To what extent does the organization assess its provision to ensure that administration, instruction, and technologies are accessible to all its current and prospective learners?
- To what extent are there effective strategies to inform learners of any changes in administration, instruction, or technologies that could affect accessibility to learning?
- If changes have an impact on learners, to what extent does the organization take steps to remedy the situation? (Changes could include a change to a courier that does not serve some learners' communities, a change that makes phone calls to the institution more costly for learners, and so on.)
- To what extent are there academic provisions to accommodate learners who may not be able to participate consistently in a learning program over a period of time and may need to take time out from learning (for example, catch-up materials, extra tutoring support, assurances that academic credits will not expire after a specific time)?
- What are the indicators that these strategies help learners to continue learning and achieve their expected outcome (for example, programs for housebound learners or for learners dealing with health problems)?

Technology Access

While new technologies can bring additional dimensions to the learning process, introducing a technology that is not readily available or affordable is unfair to learners and defeats goals of inclusiveness and access.

- To what extent does the organization assess availability of a technology to learners before incorporating that technology into programs?

- What are the organization's requirements for the percentage of learners who have assured access to a technology before that technology is included as an essential element of a program?

- To what extent does the organization make provisions for learners who do not have reliable, affordable access to the technology?

Quality in Management Strategies

- To what extent are management strategies consistent with agreed social justice goals and policies?

- To what extent do proposed changes in management strategies consider agreed policies and input from all relevant stakeholders and take into account the impact on learners and the learning experience over the long term?

- To what extent do proposed changes in management strategies provide appropriate resources for implementation, including finances and staffing?

- To what extent do management strategies ensure that staff have adequate job security training, support, and financial compensation to enable them to use their skills effectively and dedicate the required time for responding appropriately to learners, whether for administrative or academic needs?

Quality in Administrative Services

- To what extent are there clear guidelines about the expected response time to routine administrative enquiries from learners?

- What are the indicators that these guidelines are met for a specific proportion of enquiries?

- What are the indicators that the first administrative response met the enquirer's need, or that there were follow-up enquiries?

- Resources

- To what extent are there adequate staffing and other resources (e.g., financial, communications systems) to support responsive administrative services? What are the indicators of the adequacy of these resources?

Quality in Instructional Services

- To what extent is there consistency between the types of instructional services provided for a specific program or course (e.g., tutoring, help line, assessment) and the requirements of that program or course?

- To what extent is there consistency between the instructional strategies for a course or program and agreed learning outcomes?

- To what extent is there adequate staffing, financial and technical resources to support quality in instructional services (e.g., enabling appropriate response times for learner questions and assessment so that learners can proceed according to the program or course schedule)?

Quality in Instructional Resources

- To what extent are the instructional resources designed, chosen, or modified specifically for the program or course on offer, by staff knowledgeable about ODEL, learners' needs, and the subject matter?

- To what extent have the instructional resources been pilot-tested with typical learners before using them for full-scale provision?

- To what extent are the instructional resources complete, including assessment, guidance for learners, and guidance for instructors?

- How frequently are the instructional resources updated, and how does this time frame correspond to expected changes in the subject matter?

- To what extent are staff that develop or modify instructional resources provided adequate time and compensation for their work?

Strategies that maintain consistency and sustainability

- To what extent are there strategies for assessing the viability of proposed pilot initiatives for a new ODEL course or program?

- What are the common characteristics of pilot initiatives that have received long-term funding, and what proportion of pilot initiatives are eventually sustainable?

- To what extent are staff and learners provided adequate information about proposed pilot initiatives to enable them to make an informed decision about committing time to studying or instructing the course or program?

Strategies that Support a Social Contract

- To what extent does the organization actively engage in meaningful consultation with representatives of the communities it serves (students, society, employers) when identifying needs and planning programs, delivery methods, curriculum?

- To what extent does the organization research the impact of its activities on the communities it serves, for example, the proportion of graduates who obtain employment in a field related to their studies, or the longer-term roles of graduates in social, environmental, and economic initiatives?

- To what extent does the organization actively identify sectors of society that could benefit from the organization's expertise, and provide that expertise as a community service?

REFERENCES

Athabasca University. (2009). Mission statement. Retrieved from http://www. athabascau.ca/aboutau/mission.php

Auret, D., & Barrientos, S. (2004). *Participatory social auditing : A practical guide to developing a gender-sensitive approach.* Brighton, Sussex: Institute of Development Studies. Retrieved from http://www.ids.ac.uk/files/dmfile/Wp237. pdf

Blumenstyk, G. (2012). For-profit colleges compute their own graduation rates. *Chronicle of Higher Education.* Retrieved from http://chronicle.com/article/For-Profits-Develop/131048/

Catcheside, K. (2012, March 16). What do universities actually gain by improving league table performance? *The Guardian.* Retrieved from http://www.guardian. co.uk/higher-education-network/blog/2012/mar/16/league-table-performance

Chisholm, H. (Ed.). (1911). Ball, John (priest). *Encyclopædia Britannica 3* (11th ed.), p. 263. Cambridge, UK: Cambridge University Press.

Daweti, M., & Mitchell, J. (2011). Flexible distance education for social transformation. In E. J. Burge, C. C. Gibson, & T. Gibson (Eds.), *Flexible pedagogy, flexible practice: Notes from the trenches of distance education* (pp. 55–66). Edmonton, AB: AU Press.

Derounian, J. (2012). Exploring the part-time learning experience: Assessment and value. *The Guardian.* Retrieved from http://www.guardian.co.uk/higher-education-network/blog/2012/jan/03/value-part-time-university-students

Dwyer, M. (2010). Measuring excellence. *On Campus.* Retrieved from http:// oncampus.macleans.ca/education/2010/11/11/measuring-excellence/

Franklin, U. M. (1995). Looking forward, looking back. In *The Ursula Franklin reader: Pacifism as a map.* Toronto: Between the Lines Press.

Freire, P. (1983). *Education for critical consciousness.* New York: Continuum.

Giroux, H.A. (2003). Selling out higher education. *Policy Futures in Education, 1*(1), 179–200.

Harris, D. (2011). The paradoxes of flexible learning. In E. J. Burge, C. C. Gibson, & T. Gibson (Eds.), *Flexible pedagogy, flexible practice: Notes from the trenches of distance education* (pp. 275–84). Edmonton: AU Press. Retrieved from http://www. aupress.ca/index.php/books/120203

Idogho, P. (2011). Personal communication about Nigeria's provisions for supporting university students in return for national service.

International Labour Conference. (2008). *Declaration on social justice for a fair globalization.* Retrieved from http://www.ilo.org/public/english/bureau/dgo/ download/dg_announce_en.pdf

Jackson, E. T., & Kassam, Y. (Eds.). (1998). *Knowledge shared: Participatory evaluation in development cooperation.* Retrieved from http://web.idrc.ca/ openebooks/868-6/

Judt, T. (2010). *Ill fares the land.* New York, NY: Penguin.

Kere, J. (2006). A livelihood enhancement community based distance learning program. Retrieved from http://pcf4.dec.uwi.edu/viewpaper.php?id=107&print=1

McLuhan, M. (1964). *Understanding media: The extensions of man*. New York, NY: McGraw-Hill.

Nussbaum, M. C. (2003). Capabilities as fundamental entitlements: Sen and social justice. *Feminist Economics*, 9(2–3), 33–59.

Nussbaum, M. C. (2011). *Creating capabilities: The human development approach*. Cambridge, MA: Belknap.

Owen, D. L. (2003). Recent developments in European social and environmental reporting and auditing practices: A critical evaluation and tentative prognosis. *International Centre for Corporate Social Responsibility*. Retrieved from http://www.nottingham.ac.uk/business/ICCSR/research

Partanen, A. (2012). Finland's superior schools focus on cooperation, equity. *CCPA Monitor*, 18(9).

Potulicka, E. (1991). The student, community and curriculum: Their integration. Polish perspectives and the case of comparative education course. *The Student, Community and Curriculum: International Perspectives on Open and Distance Learning*. Presented at the 4th Cambridge International Conference on Open and Distance Learning.

Prinsloo, P. (2011a). Slow learning in a fast-changing and increasingly unequal world. Retrieved from http://opendistanceteachingandlearning.wordpress.com/2011/12/07/slow-learning-in-a-fast-changing-and-increasingly-unequal-world-change11/

Prinsloo, P. (2011b). Towards a social justice architecture for open, distance and e-learning. In *Internationalisation and social justice: The role of open, distance and e-learning. Collected Conference Papers of the 14th Cambridge International Conference on Open, Distance and E-Learning*. Retrieved on Dec. 20, 2012 from http://www.cambridgedistanceeducation.org.uk/ciconference2011ou/authorsmtor.pdf

Ramkumar, V., & Krafchik, W. (2006). The role of civil society organizations in auditing and public finance management. In *Auditing for social change: A Strategy for citizen engagement in public sector accountability*. UN department of economic and social affairs. p. 21ff. Retrieved from http://www.unpan.org/Portals/0/60yrhistory/documents/Publications/Auditing%20for%20Social%20Change.2007.pdf

Rawls, J., & Kelly, E. (2001). *Justice as fairness: A restatement*. Cambridge, MA: Harvard University Press.

Rumble, G. (2007). Social justice, economics and distance education. *Open Learning*, 2(22), 167–176.

Sahlberg, P., & Hargreaves, A. (2011). *Finnish lessons: What can the world learn from educational change in Finland?* New York: Teachers College Press.

Sen, A. (1999). *Development as freedom*. New York: Knopf.

Sen, A. (2009). *The idea of justice*. London: Allen Lane.

United Nations. (1948). *The universal declaration of human rights*. Retrieved from http://www.un.org/en/documents/udhr/

Walker, M., & Unterhalter, E. (Eds.). (2007). *Amartya Sen's capability approach and social justice in education*. New York: Palgrave Macmillan.

Williamson, J., Ranyard, R., and Cuthbert, L. (2000). A conversation-based process tracing method for use with naturalistic decisions. *British Journal of Psychology, 2*, 203–221.

Woodley, A. (2011). "Plenty of saps". In E. J. Burge, C. C. Gibson, & T. Gibson (Eds.), *Flexible pedagogy, flexible practice: Notes from the trenches of distance education* (pp. 299–312). Edmonton, AB: AU Press. Retrieved from http://www.aupress.ca/index.php/books/120203

Globalization, Culture, and Online Distance Learning

2

Charlotte N. Gunawardena

Globalization, the Internet, and access to telecommunication networks have increased the demand for education and educational quality across the globe. The reasons for this demand explains Carnoy (2005) are two-fold: The first is economic, the rising payoffs to higher education in a global, science-based, knowledge intensive economy make university training more of a "necessity" to get "good" jobs, which in turn, changes the stakes at lower levels of schooling and the demand for high-quality secondary schools. The second reason is socio-political: Demographics and democratic ideals increase pressure on universities to provide access to groups that traditionally have not attended university. In this context, online distance learning (ODL), which can transcend local, state, and national borders, has the potential to reach out internationally to enhance learning for diverse learners in varied geographical and socio-cultural contexts and increase intercultural awareness and communication. In addition, demand is propelled by rising awareness of the potential for online education to provide services to nearly any location on the planet.

Although distance learning can transcend geographical boundaries, differences in sociocultural contexts, values, and expectations of diverse educational systems and learners may prove to be its greatest challenge (Hanna,

2000). While distance educators proclaim an international focus with international content and learners, instructional design, teaching methods, and learning activities frequently carry Western bias (defined for this chapter as Eurocentric and North American). Moore, Shattuck, and Al-Harthi (2005) point out that American and European distance education is guided by certain theories, which are derived from American and European culture, and that it is important to raise questions about how the views of teaching and learning based on these theories might come into conflict with the values that underpin the cultures of students taking courses from or in other countries. They further note that the potential of online distance education to become a global phenomenon will be frustrated as long as educators in more technologically developed countries fail to understand the needs and perspectives of students in other countries, and that the potential to learn from the perspectives of people in other countries will be lost for students in more technologically developed countries. The promise of a global e-learning system, they observe, can only be realized by better understanding the views of learning in different cultural contexts. Therefore, in order to provide quality education to diverse audiences, distance educators should be sensitive to hegemonic perspectives, "the imposition of cultural values and practices" (Latchem, 2005, p. 189), educational differences, and the social, cultural and language assumptions embedded in courses.

This chapter explores issues related to the impact of globalization and culture on online distance learning. It is organized into four parts. In Part I, I begin by taking a closer look at what *globalization* means and then explore some of the debates that surround this term and the impact of globalization for online distance learning design. In Part II, I attempt to define *culture*, specifically culture for the online context, and explore several theoretical dimensions that can be used to explain cultural variability. Part III is focussed on examining research on how culture influences online education related to four selected areas: diverse educational expectations; learners and preferred ways of learning; the sociocultural environment and online interaction; and language and issues related to second language speakers. Part IV concludes with a discussion of issues related to researching cultural factors in online distance learning. I address issues of culture from a review of literature, as well as from my own previous discussion of the topic (Gunawardena, in press; Gunawardena & La Pointe, 2007; Gunawardena & La Pointe, 2008), and research conducted in China, Mexico, Morocco, Spain, Sri Lanka, Turkey, and the United States.

Globalization is a difficult concept to define. Generally, it means global interconnectedness and interdependence, but there are many interpretations about what this really means. Block and Cameron (2002) define *globalization* by citing Giddens's (1990, p. 64) definition: "the intensification of worldwide social relations which link distance localities in such a way that local happenings are shaped by events occurring many miles away and vice versa." Held, McGrew, Goldblatt, and Perraton (2003) after discussing many concepts related to globalization, define it as:

> a process (or set of processes) which embodies a transformation in
> the spatial organization of social relations and transactions—assessed
> in terms of their extensity, intensity, velocity and impact—generating
> transcontinental or interregional flows and networks of activity, inter-
> action, and the exercise of power. (p. 68)

In this context *flows* refer to the movements of physical artifacts, people, symbols, tokens, and information across space and time, while *networks* refer to regularized or patterned interactions between independent agents, nodes of activity, or sites of power. Held, McGrew, Goldblatt, and Perraton (2003) emphasize that globalization is not conceived as in opposition to localization, regionalism, or nationalism, which are more spatially limited processes, but on the contrary, as standing in a complex and dynamic relationship with them. For example, processes such as regionalization can create the necessary kinds of economic, social, and physical infrastructures, which facilitate and complement the deepening of globalization. This definition, therefore, affords us the opportunity to see the complex and dynamic interplay between localization and globalization.

While the concept of globalization is debated from many perspectives related to economics, culture, identity, politics, and technology, one debate in particular is relevant here. According to Block and Cameron (2002) this debate concerns the extent to which globalization is a homogenizing process. While some view it as promoting standardization and uniformity, others discuss concepts such as *hybridization* (Pieterse, 1995) and *globalization* (Robertson, 1995) to make the point that globalization involves a synergetic relationship between the global and local as opposed to any necessary dominance of the former over the latter. They further point out that while some see globalization as hegemonically Western, and above all an extension of American imperialism, others make the point that the process is more dispersed and that it is unhelpful to frame the discussion in terms of Western dominance over "the rest." "Arising from such debates about Western hegemony and the relative strength of the local is the question of whether globalization is on balance a 'positive' or a 'negative' phenomenon" (p. 3). For those who consider globalization as an unfortunate (or fortunate) fact of life, it is better to engage with the present, forging new identities, organizations and ways of life, rather than dreaming of a return to the past.

"Globalization lies at the heart of modern culture; cultural practices lie at the heart of globalization" (Tomlinson, 1999, p. 1). The reciprocal relationship between these two is an important one; globalization needs to be understood through the lens of culture and cultural identity. While nationally shaped cultures such as those in the USA, India, and Japan still exist, the global flow of information and migration of people make it possible for persons to construct their own identities. Block and Cameron (2002) point out that the continuing and relatively intense interaction between diaspora communities and ancestral communities elsewhere in the world made easier by the communication technologies that accompany globalization, spur the development of plural or hybrid identities, challenging the assumption that people must identify with a single imagined community or geographic region.

Demographics change as technologies and transportation connect people. Cultural migration influences the formation of new communities as people cross borders, creating multiple cultures. We are becoming members of a planetary community as evidenced by transnational cultures that are not wholly based in any single place (Heaton, 2001, p. 221). International distance education caters to those individuals who are unable or unwilling to reside in one single location.

From an economic perspective, educational systems are judged by their contributions to the development of goods and services, quality human resources, and national development goals (Panda, 2005). The need for education extends beyond the individual's desire to learn serving as an economic resource for national growth, competitiveness, poverty reduction, and quality of life (The World Bank, 2005). Nations look for education to assist with the development of socially and economically useful skills (Day,

2005; Badat, 2005), addressing the needs of those at the margins (Panda, 2005), addressing the whole person (Visser, 2005), and contributing to a peaceful globe. Since all nations can potentially gain from incorporating the knowledge of other countries and cultures into their thinking and actions, international learning networks should be conceived as horizontal (localized), vertical (globalized), and bottom-up as well as hub-periphery (Afele, 2003).

While the new information and communication technologies that connect us in a globalized world have their advantages and attractiveness, the problems of education are always more complex than solutions provided by technology alone. Technology connects us but it is not culturally neutral. Solely focussing on the technology and the view of learning that it facilitates influences the designer and instructor to look at learning in prescribed ways, usually ignoring alternative, cultural views (Visser, 2005). With technology, come the questions of who will use it and what meanings the users will assign to it (Heaton, 2001).

The affordances of the technologies are constrained by the traditional forms of expression people use. Thorne (2003), after analyzing three case studies, observes that Internet communication (like other technologies) is not neutral media. She notes, "The cultures-of-use of Internet communication tools, their perceived existence and on-going construction as distinctive cultural artifacts, differs interculturally just as communicative genre, pragmatics, and institutional context would be expected to differ interculturally" (Thorne, 2003, p. 38).

One of the main criticisms of globalization is the perception of an underlying tendency to colonize and import dominant paradigms into contexts that are either unfriendly to those paradigms or that can be harmed by those solutions (Carr-Chellman, 2005). Inherent within what some naively perceive as a value neutral tool—the Internet-based technologies used for online learning—are culturally biased amplifications that have their roots in the Industrial Revolution, which according to Bowers (cited in Carr-Chellman, 2005, p. 9) are: (1) context-free forms of knowledge; (2) conduit view of language; (3) Western view of autonomous individuals; (4) Western ways of experiencing time; (5) Western value of anthropocentrism; and (6) subjectively determined moral values. Carr-Chellman (2005) argues that making a single online course that is available worldwide is efficient but culturally and contextually bankrupt. In order to make a product truly marketable globally it is necessary to homogenize it, or to allow for its radical customization by end users. Carr-Chellman argues, "Isn't learning necessarily contextualized in our own cultures and contexts?" (pp. 9–10). Globalization should not blind us to the need to help individuals and groups build on their own cultural traditions and unique strengths (Mintzberg, 2003).

Block and Cameron (2002) point out that distance is not an issue in a globalized world with advanced telecommunication systems, but language remains an issue of practical importance. Global communication not only requires a shared communications channel such as the Internet but also a shared linguistic code. For many who engage in global communication, the relevant linguistic codes will have been learned rather than natively acquired. This means that members of global networks need to develop competence in one or more additional languages and/or master new ways of using languages they know already. "Globalization changes the conditions in which language learning and language teaching takes place" (p. 2). The new technologies demand new literacies and new communication skills.

One of the most important reasons for understanding cultural factors is the awareness it raises of our own cultural identity (Martin & Nakayama, 2004). "The reason man does not experience his true cultural self is that until he experiences another self as valid, he has little basis for validating his own self" (Hall, 1973, p. 213). A better understanding of one's own self as well as alternative approaches to learning lies in exposure and study of new ideas, techniques, strategies, and methodologies (Muirhead, 2005).

In discussing the implications of globalization for distance learning in the United States, Boubsil, Carabajal, and Vidal (2011) ask two fundamental questions: Will the academic programs of American-model institutions reflect American cultures and values or will they adapt to reflect local culture? And "what does adaptation mean?" (p. 10). They note that there is no quick and easy solution to these issues. While face-to-face programs have to reflect the host country culture, values, and customs to be successful, international students and host country governments that sponsor students insist on getting the same programs and content as in the United States. Finding such a balance requires effort and capital outlays that universities may not be ready or willing to embark on. While online distance learning expands curriculum and delivery opportunities for improving the quality of the learning experience, these curricular choices also present a host of challenges when considering international distance education programs.

According to Boubsil, Carabajal, and Vidal (2011) these include several factors: (1) Linguistic plurality: To what extent do English-dominated learning platforms disadvantage those for whom English is the second language and how does one address instructional examples, idioms, writing style, and so on that does not easily transfer across cultures? (2) Innovations in pedagogical methods: To what extent should online curriculum continue to impose Western approaches to learning on students from other cultures for whom debate, critical questioning, collaboration, and discussion may prove alien and difficult? (3) Localized cultural character of online programs: To what extent does the curriculum encourage local initiatives, which value local culture and promote national, regional beliefs, skills, and knowledge? (4) Relevant content: Does the content of online courses fit local needs in terms of applicability and job-related skills? and (5) Teaching models of faculty: Who will teach what to whom and with what effect? Some of these factors are also echoed in Sadykova and Dautermann's (2009) four domains that are critical to address in international online distance education: (1) host institution, (2) technology, (3) learning models of students, and (4) teaching models of faculty.

Mason (1998) recommends three approaches to globalizing education: beginning in areas of curriculum that have global content so all participants have an equal status and an equal contribution to make; trans-border consortia, where each partner contributes courses to the pool to avoid the trap of the dominant provider and the dependent receiver; and focussing on developing resources and international contacts to enable one's own students to become global citizens and not focussing at all on exporting courses.

Developing international distance education also presents ethical challenges. Very often ethical principles are culture-bound, and intercultural conflicts arise from different perspectives of ethical behaviour. Understanding the sociocultural context helps us to distinguish ethical from unethical behaviours given differences in cultural priorities and to develop guidelines for ethical behaviour within our courses. Boubsil, Carabajal, and Vidal (2011) conclude that these issues will shape the dialogue of transnational curriculum delivery in an era when cultural and linguistic plurality could well become a hallmark of transnational distance education. Recent interest in the development of massive online open courses (MOOCs) will provide fertile ground for addressing some of these issues related to globalization.

Many of the studies that have examined the role of culture in ODL (Gunawardena, et al., 2001; Moore, Shattuck, and Al-Harthi, 2005; Uzuner, 2009) have defined *culture* by employing the four dimensions of nationally held cultural values: individualism–collectivism, power distance, uncertainty avoidance, and masculinity–femininity, developed by Hofstede (1980, 1986) based on a factor analysis of business-oriented cultural values; and dimensions of contextual information, high- and low-context communication styles advanced by Hall (1973, 1990).

Ess (2009) provides a considered critique of the applicability of Hofstede's framework to the online context and notes that what interests CMC researchers is how national as well as other cultural identities, such as ethnicity, youth culture, and gender, and so forth, interact with intercultural communication online, which is already removed from the face-to-face setting. Very often those who communicate online identify with multiple frames of reference. They note that Hofstede's framework (1980) and to a lesser extent Hall's (1973, 1990) conceptualization of culture appear to be limited to national cultural differences and thus less well-suited for understanding and researching the multiple cultural differences within nation-states, including the third or hybrid identities that are themselves fostered by the cultural flows facilitated by the Internet and the Web.

Our research (Gunawardena, Idrissi Alami, Jayatilleke, & Bouacharine, 2009) supports this view by showing that, although Sri Lankan and Moroccan societies would be classified in Hofstede's framework as high-power distance societies, participants from these countries look to the online medium as a liberating medium that equalizes status differences, thereby providing them with a level playing field. Therefore, their interactions online will not necessarily reflect high-power distance communication, even though their culture would be classified as high-power distance. On the other hand, we found Hall's (1973,1990) conceptualization of high-context and low-context communication styles, and implied indirect and direct communication styles, useful for analyzing cultural differences in communication online. Context is important to understanding a message and its connotations in both Moroccan and Sri Lankan cultures. Many Moroccans and Sri Lankans adopt indirect communication styles in face-to-face communication. Therefore, Hall's conceptualization helped us to analyze if there were changes in communication styles when participants interacted online, or whether they were using the same communication styles online as they would use face-to-face (Gunawardena et al., 2009).

Goodfellow and Hewling (2005), and Goodfellow and Lamy (2009), like Ess (2009) critique the essentialist frameworks developed by Hofstede and Hall to describe national cultural characteristics as inappropriate for understanding culture in transnational online learning contexts. Goodfellow and Hewling (2005) move from an essentialist to a *negotiated* perspective to conceptualize culture as being negotiated in online discussions. This stance on seeing culture as negotiated is similar to Hall's definition of *culture* as communication: "Culture is communication and communication is culture" (Hall, 1990, p. 186). Raffaghelli and Richieri (2012) note that "Networked learning should emphasize Bruner's idea about education as *forum* where culture is not transmitted but generated through interaction" (pp. 102–103) leading to new learning cultures.

Goodfellow and Lamy (2009) undertake the task of problematizing the very notion of culture in connection with online learning environments and move on to develop the concept of *learning cultures*, which takes account of the emergence of new cultural and social identities in virtual learning communities that draw on cybercultures of the Internet as well as from systems of cultural relations inherited from conventional educational or corporate settings. They note that the emergence of learning cultures might transcend both the institutional cultures of learning in which the resources originated and the cultural learning styles predominant in the sites where they were taken up:

> It is characteristic of online learning cultures that the negotiation of personal and social identities is integral to learning, just as a critical awareness of culture is integral to a nonhegemonic model of online learning. . . . The identities of participants become part of the knowledge constructed as well as the means of construction. (Goodfellow and Lamy, 2009, p. 176)

Therefore, one can come to terms with the complexity of culture in online courses by defining it from the perspective of the Internet as a culture in its own right, blurring the boundaries between the real and virtual worlds. Creating and participating in new communities is one of the primary pleasures people have interacting online, and these communities develop their own conventions for interaction and for what is acceptable and not acceptable behaviour online (Baym, 1995). "This web of verbal and textual significances that are substitutes for and yet distinct from the networks of meaning of the wider community binds users into a common culture whose specialized meanings allow the sharing of imagined realities" (Reid 1995, p. 183). Ess (2009) expands this line of thought further by exploring the notion that technology itself is culturally produced and thus is also a culturally shaped artifact, in contrast to the notion that technology is culturally neutral or just a tool and hence its design and implementation requires no attention to its cultural origin. He discusses how digital environments can create *third cultures* where identity can be constructed and negotiated through interaction with other participants.

Thus, subscribing to a view of culture as negotiated online, I have adopted the definition of *culture* as an "idioculture," a concept developed by Gary Alan Fine and cited by Cole and Engestrom (2007), in my own work (Gunawardena et al., 2009) as an appropriate definition of culture online:

> An idioculture is a system of knowledge, beliefs, behaviours, and customs shared by members of an interacting group to which members can refer and that serve as the basis of further interaction. Members recognize that they share experiences, and these experiences can be referred to with the expectation they will be understood by other members, thus being used to construct a reality for the participants. (Fine, 1987, p. 125)

This definition accommodates the idea of culture as a locally emerging activity system involving a briefer stretch of history (Cole & Engestrom, 2007), and it includes multiple cultural selves and hybrid identities on the Internet that interact with each other cross-culturally to form unique cultures of their own. The definition allows for the development of culture through dialogue, negotiation, and the sharing of experiences. The definition fits well with the ephemeral, fluid nature of the Internet, which fuels the development of cybercultures, cultures that emerge among those who use the Internet to communicate, developing its own etiquette, norms, customs, ethics and mythology, just as an idioculture does.

With this definition of culture online, I next explore a selection of research studies on culture and online distance learning.

Several researchers (Edmundson, 2007; Rogers, Graham, & Mayes, 2007; Uzuner, 2009; Wang & Reeves, 2007) have noted the dearth of research in the field of culture and online learning. This could be partly because developing definitions of *culture* for the online context, framing questions related to culture, and conducting cross-cultural research studies is challenging. Zawacki-Richter (2009), in his Delphi study of research areas in distance education, noted that the role of culture and cultural differences in global distance learning programs should receive much more attention. In this study, globalization of education and cross-cultural aspects were deemed by distance education experts to be important areas for distance education research. In this light, an editorial in the *American Journal of Distance Education* by Moore (2006) and the research review by Uzuner (2009) addressing questions of culture in distance education are noteworthy.

Discussing recent research that addressed issues of culture, Moore develops a list of questions on cultural factors in cross-border distance education that future researchers should address. Uzuner reviewed 27 studies (qualitative, quantitative, and mixed methods) that addressed questions of culture and distance education and called for continued research that is grounded in sound methodology. Other areas of hope for research addressing culture and online distance education are recent international conferences that have begun to address the issue, and noteworthy among them is the Cultural Attitudes towards Technology and Communication (CATaC) conference held biennially (http://www.catacconference.org/) since 1998.

In the following section I address research studies on selected factors, such as diverse educational expectations, preferred ways of learning, the sociocultural environment, and language, where cultural differences can affect online education.

DIVERSE EDUCATIONAL EXPECTATIONS

Different cultures bring different attitudes toward education and its purpose. In Uzuner's (2009) review of studies on questions of culture, researchers express broad agreement that the diverse cultural assumptions students bring to online learning concerning how teaching and learning should be done bring about conflicts, disagreements, and frustrations. Consider the philosophical differences reflected in the following two statements by learners whom La Pointe and Barrett (2005) interviewed: "I don't know what I'll do with my education; I'm basically purposing my degree to meet a personal goal I set for myself" (Joan, an American student). "The purpose of my education is to learn as much as I can and share that knowledge with others, so our nation can become great" (Luming, a Taiwanese student). The American student chose to pursue education for self-benefit while the Taiwanese student's purpose focussed on economic well-being and serving the nation. One could doubtlessly find many other distance students who are studying for purely instrumental or vocational reasons. Students have very different motives, and likely they are culturally as well as individually linked.

Traditionally, teaching in Mainland China and many other countries involved the teacher standing on a raised platform lecturing and interrogating from the front of the room to large groups of students. Choral responses in teacher-led recitations reflected the traditional value on the collective, the community consensus, and the uniform conduct in social interaction (Hu, 2004). Memorization is the most reliable and desirable attribute a student can have to ensure school success, for "The Chinese cultural tradition has always stressed memorization in education to ensure the transmission of culture from one generation to the next" (p. 637).

Today in Asia e-learning is used to explore innovative strategies to promote engagement through active and independent learning, self-assessment, digital libraries, and just-in-time learning. There is emphasis on (a) designing authentic learning tasks to facilitate learning engagement and (b) providing support and media-rich resources (Hedberg & Ping, 2005). This model is, of course, markedly different than the pedagogical model described earlier, leaving room for challenging adoption and potential confusion.

Many online courses being offered in Mainland China, Hong Kong, Taiwan, and India offer video lectures online and on demand, so learners can continue to "see and hear" their instructors giving lectures. Eye movement, gestures, gaze, and the human voice provide the contextual information learners from high-context cultures rely upon to interpret meaning. Thus ODL is sustaining rather than challenging traditional understanding of formal education.

Turkey's culture and oral traditions have emphasized the sacredness of the text, honour the responsibility of the professor to interpret the text, and expect students to memorize the professor's words (Gursoy, 2005). In many developing countries, the quality of education is not seen as a property of the system or the intelligibility of materials but as a property of the students measured by their performance on examinations. In such environments, assessment of student performance by group work presents a challenge. The paradigm of flexibility, openness, and the self-paced, independent learner is not a value-free, neutral idea. Likewise, a teacher who functions primarily as facilitator, learning designer, organizer, and friendly critic (Jin & Cortazzi, 1998) is not a global ideal. The cultural values of individualism, secularism, and feminism are not recognized as desirable in many cultures that place higher value on religion, group efforts, and well-defined gender roles (McIsaac, 1993).

Most Western learners and instructors, believe that each learner (a) is a distinct individual, (b) controls his or her behaviour, (c) is responsible for outcomes of behaviour, (d) is oriented toward personal achievement, and (e) frequently believes group membership compromises goal achievement (Nisbett, 2003). Many learners from Asian countries, on the other hand, believe success is a group goal as well as a national goal. Attaining group goals is tied to maintaining harmonious social relations. These differences in expectations have implications for designing the online learning environment and learner support systems to meet the needs of these diverse learners.

LEARNERS AND PREFERRED WAYS OF LEARNING

People reared in different cultures learn to learn differently (Merriam, 2007). Some do so by following behaviourist theory—pattern drill, memory, and rote; some work in groups by learning through interaction with others to cross the zone of proximal development (Vygotsky, 1978). In today's learning environments, whether face-to-face or distance, one will encounter diverse learners and preferred ways of learning. As Moore (2006, p. 4) asks, "how to set up a course and manage it so as to induce the different forms of understanding that lie in the culture represented by each student, to the greater benefit of the whole class?"

Facilitating learning for diverse learners requires putting learner needs first rather than institutional or national needs. Generally, the primary theory of knowledge construction underlying most emerging online course designs emphasizes the exchange of ideas, expressions of agreement and disagreement to construct meaning. Biesenbach-Lucas (2003), in her survey of the differences between native and non-native students in their perceptions of asynchronous discussions, found that both groups of students tended to avoid challenge-and-explain cycles where they had to do more than demonstrate knowledge by also agreeing and disagreeing in non-abrasive ways. She notes that non-native speakers, particularly students from Asian countries, consider it far less appropriate to challenge and criticize the ideas of others. In addition, they may not know how to express disagreement appropriately in English. She cites similar findings of the absence of challenge to the input of others in Wegerif's (1998) study and in Curtis and Lawson's study of asynchronous discussions (2001), attributed to lack of sufficient exchanges among students, but which is likely linked to culturally induced reluctance to debate.

Biesenbach-Lucas notes that this lack of challenge and disagreement of ideas is troubling as it is the "resolution of such areas of agreement and disagreement that 'results in higher forms of reasoning' because 'cognitive development requires that individuals encounter others who contradict their own intuitively derived ideas.'" (p. 37). The point we need to consider here is whether such challenges to ideas expressed by others and discussion of disagreement at the level of ideas in online discussions is a necessary condition for higher forms of reasoning or knowledge construction, or whether it is merely an expectation from a Western point of view, particularly American. Going further, we need to consider whether higher cognitive reasoning and knowledge construction can happen without such open disagreement of ideas. The following discussion of studies from Mexico and Sri Lanka provides a different perspective from two different cultural contexts.

Lopez-Islas (2001) analyzed knowledge construction in online discussion forums at Monterrey Tech-Virtual University in Mexico using the Gunawardena, Lowe and Anderson (1997) Interaction Analysis Model (IAM). The IAM describes five stages in the process of knowledge construction: 1) sharing, comparing, and agreement; 2) cognitive dissonance or disagreement of ideas; 3) negotiation of meaning and co-construction of knowledge; 4) testing and modification of proposed co-construction; and 5) application of newly constructed meaning. Lopez-Islas observed that open disagreement with ideas expressed by others is not appropriate in the Mexican cultural context; therefore, participants moved to knowledge construction without moving through the cognitive dissonance phase as described in the IAM model.

We found a similar result in our studies, which employed the IAM model to examine the impact of cross-cultural e-mentoring on social construction of knowledge in asynchronous discussion forums between American e-mentors and Sri Lankan protégés (Gunawardena et al., 2008; and Gunawardena et al., 2011). The Sri Lankan participants did not openly disagree at the level of ideas but moved to negotiation of meaning and co-construction of new knowledge based on consensus building. Therefore, we had to redefine *dissonance* as specified in the IAM model in cultural terms. Sri Lankan learners were often very polite before discussing and disagreeing about a point with another learner. In the following quote, a learner acknowledges the work done by another person before providing a suggestion to make it better:

> The suggested outline seems to be ok. I think, if possible it's better if we all can contribute to all the topics because different persons will look at an issue in different point of views. So we will be able to gather more information and later we can decide what to include in the final report. (Gunawardena et al., 2008, p. 7)

This quote exemplified the way in which Sri Lankan participants built consensus online as they interacted with each other and an international e-mentor. In further exploration of the online asynchronous interactions, we found that while the academic discussion was very polite and lacked open disagreement of ideas, strong opinions and disagreements were expressed by the same participants in the informal online virtual cafe, where they engaged in a heated debate about gender issues. This finding made us reflect on the role of culture in academic online discussions. It is possible that collectivist traits in both the Sri Lankan and Mexican cultural contexts may have transferred to online group interaction in an academic setting where open disagreement of ideas would make the participants uncomfortable. Yet, it also shows that these very same participants as noted in the Sri Lankan context would engage in a heated debate in an informal discussion space. So, the context of the discussion, whether it was formal or informal, is key in the expression of open disagreement. This is an interesting cultural difference that should be explored further in online cross-cultural communication contexts.

From his study of a global e-mail debate on intercultural communication, Chen (2000) showed that differences in thinking patterns and expression styles influence student reactions to teaching methods. The debate format caused orientation problems for some participants, as the debate is a product of low-context culture that requires a direct expression of one's argument by using logical reasoning. Many students who come from high-context cultures in Asia and Latin America find an argumentative format uncomfortable in an academic context, and this discomfort is exacerbated when the debate is facilitated through a medium devoid of non-verbal cues. Further insight into this cultural difference is provided in Covey's DVD (2005), *The 7 Habits of Highly Effective People*, when an interviewee who identifies himself as predominantly Anglo-Saxon and American makes a comparison between Western and Asian ways of looking at life in the context of Mauritius, a predominantly Asian society. He observes:

> I have a very Anglo Saxon upbringing and which I think is also very
> American. And we have a confrontational system in the West. Two
> ideas confront, they fight it out, and the best one wins. Now, what I have
> learned here where the majority of the population is Asiatic, now the
> Asiatics have a completely different way of looking at life. Their way of
> looking at it is you look at what your opponent's, what his position is,
> and you try to get as close to his position as possible. (2005, no. 6)

In this same video, another interviewee, discussing the Asian perspective, points out the importance of listening to others, considering their opinions, and accepting them. The idea is to take a little bit of everything to get a better end result.

Fahy and Ally (2005), in their study of online students at Athabasca University, point out that when students are not permitted to participate in CMC in accordance with their individual styles and preferences, the requirement for online interaction ironically becomes a potential learning barrier rather than a liberating opportunity for self-expression.

Kim and Bonk (2002), in their cross-cultural comparisons of online collaboration between Korean, Finnish, and US students using the Curtis and Lawson's (2001) coding scheme, found differences in online collaborative behaviours: Korean students were more social and contextually driven online; Finnish students were more group-focussed as well as reflective and, at times, theoretically driven; and US students more action-oriented and pragmatic in seeking results or giving solutions.

In Shattuck's (2005) attempt to understand how non-American students perceive the values related to study in an American distance learning program through in-depth online interviews primarily with Asian students, she found that these students felt marginalized within the e-learning environment. She notes that online learning designs based on constructivist pedagogy and a high level of interaction can be a lonely and uncomfortable place for an international online learner whose cultural experiences are different than the dominant educational culture (cited in Moore, Shattuck, & Al-Harthi, 2005).

In our study using nine instruments to analyze Hispanic learning styles (Sanchez & Gunawardena, 1998), we found that Hispanic adult learners in a Northern New Mexico community college showed a preference for collaborative over competitive activities; reflectivity in task engagement; and a preference for an action-based, active approach to learning. For these learners, we recommend designing real world problem solving or case-based reasoning tasks in asynchronous learning environments that provide opportunities for reflection and active collaborative learning. In general, it is best to design alternative activities to reach the same objective and give students the option of selecting activities that best meet their culturally adapted ways of learning.

As we design, it is important to consider that within cultural groups individuals differ significantly from each other, and therefore, it is equally important to identify and respond to an individual's learning preference. While matching teaching and learning styles may yield higher achievement in test scores, providing learners with activities that require them to broaden their repertoire of preferred learning styles and approaches more fully prepares them to function in our diverse and global society. There is a need to provide a delicate balance of activities that give opportunities to learn in preferred ways and activities that challenge the learner to learn in new or less preferred ways. Gibson (1998) makes a plea for understanding the distance learner in context (for example, in relation to classroom, peer group, workplace, family, culture, and society) and the impact of their learning on those who share their lives in the multiple interacting contexts that contain them. "Our challenge as educators is to consider how the context might be seen as a partner in teaching and learner support," (p. 121), a point of view also supported by Rye & Stokken (2012).

SOCIOCULTURAL ENVIRONMENT AND ONLINE INTERACTION

Wegerif (1998) argues that the social dimension—especially how students relate to each other—is important to the effectiveness of discussions and student learning. He provides evidence to support this view from an ethnographic study of a computer-mediated course at the British Open University. His study found that individual success or failure in the course depended upon the extent to which students were able to cross a threshold from feeling like outsiders to feeling like insiders.

We undertook a study in Morocco and Sri Lanka (Gunawardena, Idrissi Alami, Jayatilleke, & Bouacharine, 2009) to explore what happens when individuals whose self-images are characterized by a sense of group identity based on factors such as nationality, ethnicity, religion, gender, language, and socioeconomic status, use the culturally heterogeneous and technically ephemeral forums of the Internet to pursue personal communication goals. Through a qualitative ethnographic perspective and an inductive theory-generation process, we identified three major themes that constitute a conceptual framework to explain the sociocultural context of Internet chat users in Morocco and Sri Lanka. The three themes were identity, gender, and language, interacting with each other in their expression in synchronous chat. Identity is expressed through language reflecting the gender roles either real or assumed in the online sociocultural context. Three properties also emerged related to the expression of identity: trust-building, self-disclosure, and face negotiation. Gender differences were observed in the expression of identity, trust-building, self-disclosure, and face negotiation. These findings enabled us to suggest implications for the role of learning cultures and provide insight into how we can design online environments, which encourage the types of communication we are striving to support, especially when we may be addressing participants from high-context and/ or multi-lingual cultures.

In the following section, I explore from a cultural perspective three factors that have an impact on the social environment in online distance education: social presence, help-seeking behaviours, and silence.

Social presence is the degree to which a person is perceived as a "real person" in mediated communication (Short, Williams, & Christie, 1976). One of our studies established that social presence is a strong predictor of learner satisfaction in a computer conference (Gunawardena & Zittle, 1997). Richardson and Swan (2003), adapting this survey, replicated and extended these findings. They determined that students' overall perception of social presence was a predictor of their perceived learning in 17 different online courses.

Studies have begun to examine cultural perceptions of social presence. Tu (2001) conducted a study of how Chinese students perceive social presence in an online environment and found that three dimensions affected student perceptions of social presence—social context (subjective perceptions of others), online communication (technological attributes), and interactivity (how we engage students in interaction). He noted that engaging Chinese students in a more interactive online learning environment would increase social presence. In addition, online privacy and public/private issues impacted the level of social presence. Chinese students perceived online communication as a more comfortable medium to express their thoughts due to lack of confrontation and face-saving concerns, but they were concerned that their messages may appear in public areas that may cause them to lose face and privacy.

In a cross-cultural study of group process and development in online conferences in the United States (us) and Mexico, we (Gunawardena et al., 2001) found that social presence emerged as a theme addressed by both us and Mexican focus group participants. us participants felt that social presence is necessary to the smooth functioning of a group, to provide a sense that the group members are real people. Social presence built trust and led to self-disclosure. Building relationships enhanced online civility. The Mexican focus group participants, however, felt that having personal information about the participants was unimportant. For these participants, how peers contribute to the conference is more important than knowing their personal information. The differences in the way that us participants and Mexican participants perceived social presence could be attributed to cultural differences related to power distance (Hofstede, 1980) in the two societies. In a high-power distance society like Mexico, computer-mediated communication was seen as equalizing power and status differences present in society. Therefore, participants did not want their peers to interject social context cues that would take away the equalizing power of the online environment.

To further examine social presence from a cultural perspective, we undertook a study (Gunawardena, Idrissi Alami, & Jayatilleke, 2006) that generated a theoretical model of social presence from the perspective of two sociocultural contexts—Morocco and Sri Lanka—by examining the communication conventions and processes employed by Internet chat users who develop online relationships with people they do not know. Employing qualitative ethnographic analysis and grounded theory building, this study explored cultural perspectives on social presence and properties related to the construct of social presence in online communication. Preliminary results showed that social presence played a key role in the communication patterns of Internet chat users. Properties associated with social presence in both cultural contexts include: self-disclosure, building trust, expression of identity, conflict resolution, interpretation of silence, and the innovation of language forms to generate immediacy.

Al-Harthi (2005) conducted in-depth telephone interviews with Arab students in order to understand how they perceived the values related to study in an American distance learning program, and found that for them the lack of physical presence in the online environment was seen as a positive feature because, in addition to accessibility advantages, it provided a reduced risk of social embarrassment. Female Arab students in particular felt more comfortable studying online as it allowed for an easy conformity with the separation of genders that is traditional in Muslim culture. Moore (2006) notes that this sensitivity to what other people think is more foreign to American students, but for people of more collectivist (as contrasted with individualist) cultures, a form of communication that gives ways of saving face has value that may outweigh some of what the Western student might consider drawbacks. Al-Harthi's study identified several ways in which Arab students dealt with problems differently than their American colleagues. These findings provide insight into the social dynamic of online education and the factors we need to keep in mind as we design.

Cultures differ in help-seeking behaviours. Help-seeking is a learning strategy that combines cognition and social interaction (Ryan, Gheen, & Midgley, 1998) and involves the ability to use others as a resource to cope with difficulty encountered in the learning process. When learners do not seek help, performance and learning can suffer. In formal education contexts that emphasize competition and normative evaluation, students from other cultures are unwilling to seek help because they fear others will perceive they lack ability (Ryan, Gheen, & Midgley, 1998). Where the socio-emotional needs of students and learning for intrinsic reasons are emphasized over performance and competition, learners seek help.

The socio-emotional needs of students are recognized as part of the classroom design in other cultures. Chinese students communicate with their teachers outside of class for guidance with personal problems (Zhang, 2006). Teachers in China assume responsibility for educating the whole person instructionally, cognitively, affectively, and morally and are expected to care about students' behaviours and problems inside and outside the classroom. The collaborative strength of home and school, of parents and teachers, works harmoniously toward the mutual goal of preparing learners (Hu, 2004) for rigorous national examinations and the country's economic development. In contrast, Western teachers are expected to perform academic duties and generally are unconcerned about or at least not responsible for students' behaviours and problems outside of school. Westerns students are advised not to bring personal problems to the classroom. Western students do not expect the warm interaction many Asian learners expect outside the classroom with their instructors.

In our study of e-mentoring across cultures (Gunawardena et al., 2008), we found differences in facilitation styles between US and Sri Lankan e-mentors in the way they provided guidance and help to their protégés. US e-mentors encouraged protégés and put them on track by asking questions to deliver the necessary message indirectly, while the Sri Lankan e-mentors appeared to provide more direct advice to solve a problem. This could also be related to the style and approach to teaching and learning adopted by individual e-mentors. Often, US e-mentors used indirect coaching to get the protégés to think through the problem and come up with their own solutions. Sri Lankan protégés often expected more direct guidance on how to go about solving the problem. Feedback received from the e-mentors was always welcomed and helped reduce feelings of isolation. This helps us to be more cognizant of the expectations of diverse learners related to help-seeking behaviours and of the need to make our teaching and learning philosophies, procedures, and practices explicit in course design, the syllabus, and course outlines.

SILENCE

Silence, while frustrating for American and Western Europeans, is quite comfortable for Asian and Pacific Island cultures (Brislin, 2000). For Americans, silence indicates rudeness, inattention, or uncertainty. However, in other cultures, silence indicates respect (Matthewson & Thaman, 1998). Silence allows people time to collect thoughts, think carefully, listen to others, and provide opportunity for reflection, integration, and consensus of many diverse perspectives into a workable solution. LaPointe and Barrett's (2005) experience teaching English via Voice Over Internet Protocol (VOIP) to Chinese students showed that, initially, American instructors and Chinese learners were both uncomfortable in the classroom. The American instructors expected the Chinese learners to speak at will as students do in American classrooms. American instructors were initially uncomfortable with the long, reflective pauses in the synchronous voice communication. The Chinese respect for authority conditioned learners to wait for an explicit invitation to speak rather than make the impolite gesture of raising a question or criticizing someone else's (and especially an instructor's) thoughts.

LANGUAGE LEARNING

Language represents a different way of thinking and speaking, and cognition is mediated by language (Gudykunst & Asante, 1989; Pincas, 2001). Language also reinforces cultural values and worldviews. The grammar of each language voices and shapes ideas, serving as a guide for people's mental activity, for analysis of impressions, and for synthesis of their mental stock in trade (Whorf, 1998). Those from oral cultures may not embrace written communication (Burniske, 2003) and the abstract discussions that permeate Western discourse. Learners from oral traditions such as the Maori desire intimate connections with the instructor and a way to apply knowledge according to Maori customs (Anderson, 2005). Malaysia, strong in oral culture, uses storytelling while teaching history, culture, and moral values (Norhayati & Siew, 2004). Learners from visual and oral cultures expect that learning resources will be offered in media beyond mere text (Jiang, 2005) and prefer a great deal of detail and visual stimulation (Zhenhui, 2001). Chat may provide an outlet for interaction that more closely resembles spoken language (Sotillo, 2000). Learners from collectivist countries may refrain from contributing critical comments in text conferencing to avoid tension and disagreement in order to maintain interpersonal harmony (Hu, 2005). Limiting online learning to text-based expression restricts the voices and the richness that can be a part of the online class.

Although English is increasingly recognized as the international lingua franca, using English to learn rather than using one's native language puts learners at a disadvantage. Often English is a learner's third or fourth language with little opportunity to actually use English daily. Communicating in English requires Asian and Arabic speakers to enter individual letters, one stroke at a time, on a keyboard while frequently referring to online dictionaries. English as a Second Language (ESL) learners need additional time for reading and need content provided in a variety of formats—written lectures, audio recordings, and concept maps.

Goodfellow and Lamy (2009) note that research into telecollaborative projects for language learning carries many stories of full or partial failure, not in the use of code (French, Spanish or Japanese, and so on) but in the partners' understandings of each other's cultural styles and genres. When computer users from different cultures communicate with each other they may not be aware of each other's genre (discourse type or discourse style) that is appropriate for the exchange. Kramsch and Thorne's study (2002) offers a good example of how miscommunication in an intercultural asynchronous online dialogue between American and French students was caused, not so much by deficient individual linguistic styles, but mostly by a lack of understanding "cultural genres" in each other's discourse.

In our study of informal synchronous chatting in Morocco and Sri Lanka, (Gunawardena et al., 2009), one of the most interesting findings was the innovations in language forms to adapt to communication via chat. While the predominant language of chat in Morocco was French and in Sri Lanka, English, participants interjected the native language using the Latin keyboard to increases their level of social presence and connectedness when they were chatting with people who understood the native language. One participant in our study noted that he examines the English used by chatters and the amount of mistakes made, especially if the person claims to be from an English-speaking country such as the UK or US. In this case, the level and type of language use can be a factor in creating credibility. In analyzing online communication conventions in this study (Gunawardena et al., 2009), it is evident that chatters have developed unique forms of textual language and visual expressions to communicate their ideas and feelings through a new medium. Users bring with them the conventions of their native language, which embody cultural traits as well as their prior use of the second language, English or French. This implies that as online learning cultures develop, students and facilitators have to adjust to new modes of communication and interaction.

Smith (2005) found that a lack of awareness of cultural differences and generalizations about others who use English as a second language may enable learners from dominant cultures to *deauthorize* group members unknowingly with group coping strategies that, although well intended, limit opportunities for discussion. Groups assigned minimal responsibilities to their non-native English-speaking members because they felt these learners face unusual challenges of adapting to the United States and completing their studies. These non-native-English speakers then felt uncomfortable and unproductive. This crystallized the recognition of difference among group members: Non-native speakers were perceived as "others" and treated as a threat to the group in ways that mirror hierarchical structures within larger society, thereby creating unsafe learning spaces (Smith, 2005).

Bilingual teaching assistants and staff of the *Speak2Me* program (Ladder Publishing of Taipei's web-based ESL program, which uses an *iTalk* synchronous platform), and La Pointe and Barrett (2005), who taught English at a distance, travelled to Taiwan and Mainland China to conduct face-to-face interviews with Taiwanese and Mainland China ESL learners in order to learn about their perceptions. They found that, although students recognize the need to study English through materials from the target culture, when they have no prior experience with the content of the materials they cannot participate. Students pointed out that, if neither they nor their families have prior knowledge about a topic, they find engaging in a conversation difficult—they cannot participate when the "topic is too far away." Such topics do not produce the intended level of critical thinking as much as topics that more directly affect students' lives.

Many individuals have a fear of speaking English with native speakers. One student in their study observed, "We Taiwanese—if we can't speak English very nice, very fluent—we want to learn English and speak, but we are afraid. We are afraid to talk with foreigners because we are afraid if I can't speak the proper words or listen to it." Students, particularly adults, seek a safe place to speak. The Internet provides that safe space through the removal of visual cues; informants have reported that they are more willing to try to speak English when they cannot see either other students whom they perceive to be better English speakers or the teacher's dismay as they are speaking. They also feel safer participating from their homes.

Given the issues that emerged in this discussion, we as online learning designers need to pay special attention to cultural differences in communication conventions, which may be manifested differently in this unique space for communication devoid of non-verbal cues.

RESEARCHING CULTURE AND ONLINE DISTANCE LEARNING

Bhawuk and Triandis' (1996) review and critique of methodology for studying culture is a good starting point for the beginning researcher. They note that *emics* and *etics* are perhaps the two most crucial constructs in the study of culture because they emphasize two perspectives. Emics focus on the native's point of view; etics focus on the cross-cultural scientist's point of view. Goodfellow and Lamy (2009) observe that projects intending to research online learning cultures should not be conducted entirely from an etic perspective, which is by researchers who share a particular cultural perspective and who look at culture from the outside. They advocate that the emic perspective, or the insider view, should be adequately represented and recommend that future research be conducted by teams of researchers that are themselves culturally diverse "for whom the construction of their own learning culture would be an acknowledged outcome of the research" (p. 182).

Our own experience conducting collaborative cross-cultural research with teams of researchers (Gunawardena et al., 2001; Gunawardena et al.,

2008 March; Gunawardena et al., 2009, 2011) taught us a great deal about the research process, the value of emic over etic approaches for studying phenomena related to culture, and the challenges of conducting reliable and valid cross-cultural research studies. Reflecting on our research process, I feel that the greatest challenge to conducting cross-cultural research is finding equivalent samples for comparison in quantitative studies. This problem is echoed by van de Vijver and Leung (1997), who noted. "Cross-cultural studies often involve highly dissimilar groups. Consequently, groups can differ in many background characteristics, only some of which are relevant to the topic studied" (p. 32). Further, individual differences in cultural groups need to be accounted for so that we do not subscribe to the fallacy of homogeneity (that terms such as *American* or *Western* connote internal sameness) or the fallacy of monolithic identity (the assumption that individuals in groups have no differential identities) (Stanfield II, 1993). Therefore we recommend that future researchers use a more comprehensive model for comparison such as the one developed by Shaw and Barrett-Power (1998) to understand cultural differences. Future researchers need to conceptualize identity in cross-cultural studies to go beyond simplistic stereotyping or assigning a group identity, and use qualitative methods to understand how people define themselves.

We believe we were able to design our studies and interpret the results better because we collaborated with teams of researchers from the countries and cultural contexts we studied and would recommend this approach to future researchers. The research strategy was determined jointly. The research team simultaneously developed the instruments with the first version developed in English and then translated. One problem we encountered in spite of this was construct equivalence. For example, the construct "conflict" was perceived differently in the two national contexts we studied: American and Mexican (Gunawardena, 2001). The use of a mixed-method approach: employing both quantitative and qualitative data in one study (Gunawardena et al., 2001), and a qualitative design that used grounded theory in another (Gunawardena et al., 2009), helped us to avoid some of the pitfalls in analysis and interpretation of the data.

Bhawuk and Triandis (1996) advocate subjective cultural studies, which maximize the advantages of both emic and etic approaches and the use of many methods that converge. They noted that each culture is likely to have its own way of reacting to each method (each method has a unique meaning in each culture), and therefore, a multimethod approach is preferable. They point out the difficulty of conducting experiments in cross-cultural settings as well as the difficulty of using tests such as ability, personality, and attitude, because a test usually measures one or, at most, a few variables out of context. Gradually, cross-cultural researchers are recognizing the value of interpretive and critical approaches to the study of cultural phenomena over logical empiricist approaches (Martin & Nakayama, 2004.)

"We have seen that with regard to intercultural communication online in general, and intercultural learning online in particular, the role of culture is both central (contrary to ethnocentric assumptions that one's own views, principles, etc., may be universal) and profoundly challenging" (Ess, 2009, p. 26). We would like to encourage distance-learning researchers to take up the challenge of conducting sound theoretical research and empirical studies examining cultural issues in the online environment to guide our future practice.

ACKNOWLEDGEMENT

It is with deep gratitude that I acknowledge the significant contributions made by Deborah K. LaPointe (1952–2009) to collaborative writing on issues of culture in previous publications.

REFERENCES

Afele, J. S. C. (2003). *Digital bridges: Developing countries in the knowledge economy.* Hershey, PA: Idea Group.

Al-Harthi, A. S. (2005). Distance higher education experiences of Arab Gulf students in the United States: A cultural perspective. *The International Review of Research in Open and Distance Learning, 6*(3). Retrieved from http://www.irrodl.org/index. php/irrodl

Anderson, B. (2005). New Zealand: Is online education a highway to the future? In A. A. Carr-Chellman (Ed.), *Global perspectives on e-learning: Rhetoric and realities* (pp. 163–178). Thousand Oaks, CA: Sage.

Badat, S. (2005). South Africa: Distance higher education policies for access, social equity, quality, and social and economic responsiveness in a context of the diversity of provision. *Distance Education, 26,* 183–204.

Baym, N. K. (1995). The emergence of community in computer-mediated communication. In S. G. Jones (Ed.), *CyberSociety: Computer-mediated communication and community* (pp. 138–163). Thousand Oaks, CA: Sage.

Bhawuk, D. P. S., & Triandis, H. C. (1996). The role of culture theory in the study of culture and intercultural training. In D. Landis & R. S. Bhagat (Eds.), *Handbook of intercultural training* (2nd. ed.) (pp. 17-34). Thousand Oaks, CA: Sage.

Biesenbach-Lucas, S. (2003). Asynchronous discussion groups in teacher training classes: Perceptions of native and non-native students. *Journal of Asynchronous Learning Networks, 7*(3), 24-46. Retrieved from http://sloanconsortium.org/publications/jaln_main

Block, D., & Cameron, D. (Eds.). (2002). *Globalization and language teaching.* London: Routledge.

Boubsil, O., Carabajal, K., & Vidal, M. (2011). Implications of globalization for distance education in the United States. *American Journal of Distance Education 25,* 5-20.

Brislin, R. (2000). *Understanding culture's influence on behavior* (2nd ed.). Fort Worth, TX: Harcourt.

Burniske, R. W. (2003). East Africa meets West Africa: Fostering an online community of inquiry for educators in Ghana and Uganda. *Educational Technology Research and Development, 51*(4), 105-113.

Carnoy, M. (2005, July). *Globalization, educational trends and the open society.* Paper presented at the Open Society Institute Education Conference, Palo Alto, CA, Stanford University.

Carr-Chellman, A. A. (Ed.). (2005). Introduction. In *Global perspectives on e-learning: Rhetoric and reality* (pp. 1-16). Thousand Oaks, CA: Sage.

Chen, G. M. (2000). Global communication via Internet: An educational application. In G. M. Chen & W. J. Starosta (Eds.), *Communication and global society* (pp. 143-157). New York, NY: Peter Lang.

Cole, M., & Engestrom, Y. (2007). Cultural-historical approaches to designing for development. In J. Valsiner & A. Rosa (Eds.), *The Cambridge handbook of sociocultural psychology* (pp. 484-507). New York: Cambridge University Press.

Covey, S. R. (2008). *The 7 habits of highly effective people: Foundational principles.* [DVD]. Salt Lake City, UT: Franklin Covey.

Curtis, D. D., & Lawson, M. J., (2001). Exploring collaborative online learning. *Journal of Asynchronous Learning Networks, 5*(1), 21-34. Retrieved from http://sloanconsortium.org/publications/jaln_main

Day, B. (2005). Open and distance learning enhanced through ICTs: A toy for Africa's elite or an essential tool for sustainable development? In Y. L. Visser, L. Visser, M. Simonson, & R. Armirault (Eds.), *Trends and issues in distance education: International perspectives* (pp. 183-204). Greenwich, CT: Information Age.

Edmundson, A. (Ed.). (2007). *Globalized eLearning cultural challenges.* Hershey, PA: Information Science.

Ess, C. (2009). When the solution becomes the problem: Cultures and individuals as obstacles to online learning. In R. Goodfellow & M. N. Lamy (Eds.), *Learning cultures in online education* (pp.15-29). London, UK: Continuum.

Ess, C., & Sudweeks, F. (2006). Culture and computer-mediated communication: Toward new understandings. *Journal of Computer-Mediated Communication*, 11(1), 179–191. doi:10.1111/j.1083-6101.2006.tb00309.x.

Fahy, P. J., & Ally, M. (2005). Student learning style and asynchronous computer-mediated conferencing. *American Journal of Distance Education*, 19, 5–22.

Fine, G. A. (1987). *With the boys: Little league baseball and preadolescent culture*. Chicago, IL: University of Chicago Press.

Gibson, C. C. (1998). The distance learner in context. In *Distance learners in higher education: Institutional responses for quality outcomes* (pp. 113–125). Madison, WI: Atwood.

Goodfellow, R., & Hewling, A. (2005). Reconceptualising culture in virtual learning environments: From an "essentialist" to a "negotiated" perspective. *E-Learning*, 2(4), 355–367. doi:10.2304/elea.2005.2.4.355.

Goodfellow, R., & Lamy, M. N. (Eds.). (2009). *Learning cultures in online education*. London, UK: Continuum.

Gudykunst, W., & Asante, M. (1989). *Handbook of international and intercultural communication*. Newbury Park, CA: Sage.

Gunawardena, C. N. (in press). Culture and online distance learning. In M. G. Moore (Ed.), *Handbook of distance education*. (3rd ed.). New York, NY: Routledge.

Gunawardena, C. N., Bouacharine, F., Idrissi Alami, A., & Jayatilleke, G. (2006, April). *Cultural perspectives on social presence: A study of online chatting in Morocco and Sri Lanka*. Paper presented at the Annual Meeting of the American Educational Research Association, San Francisco, CA.

Gunawardena, C. N., Idrissi Alami, A., Jayatilleke, G., & Bouacharine, F. (2009). Identity, gender, and language in synchronous cybercultures: A cross-cultural study. In R. Goodfellow & M. N. Lamy (Eds.), *Learning cultures in online education* (pp. 30–51). London, UK: Continuum.

Gunawardena, C. N., Keller, P. S., Garcia, F., Faustino, G. L., Barrett, K., Skinner, J. K., & Fernando, S. (2011, December). Transformative education through technology: Facilitating social construction of knowledge online through cross-cultural e-mentoring. In V. Edirisinghe (Ed.), *Abstracts of The 1st International Conference on the Social Sciences and the Humanities*, 1, 114–118. Peradeniya, Sri Lanka: Faculty of Arts, University of Peradeniya.

Gunawardena, C. N., & LaPointe, D. (2007). Cultural dynamics of online learning. In M. G. Moore (Ed.), *Handbook of distance education* (2nd ed.) (pp. 593–607). Mahwah, NJ: Lawrence Erlbaum.

Gunawardena, C. N., & LaPointe, D. (2008). Social and cultural diversity in distance education. In T. Evans, M. Haughey, & D. Murphy (Eds.), *International handbook of distance education* (pp. 51–70). Bingley, UK: Emerald.

Gunawardena, C. N., Lowe, C. A., & Anderson, T. (1997). Analysis of a global online debate and the development of an interaction analysis model for examining social construction of knowledge in computer conferencing. *Journal of Educational Computing Research*, 17(4), 395–429.

Gunawardena, C. N., Nolla, A. C., Wilson, P.L., López-Islas, J. R., Ramírez-Angel, N., & Megchun-Alpízar, R. M. (2001). A cross-cultural study of group process and development in online conferences, *Distance Education, 22*, 85-121.

Gunawardena, C. N., Skinner, J. K., Richmond, C., Linder-Van Berschot, J., LaPointe, D., Barrett, K., & Padmaperuma, G. (2008, March). *Cross-cultural e-mentoring to develop problem-solving online learning communities*. Paper presented at the 2008 Annual Meeting of the American Educational Research Association, New York.

Gunawardena, C. N., & Zittle, F. (1997). Social presence as a predictor of satisfaction within a computer mediated conferencing environment. *The American Journal of Distance Education, 11*, 8-25.

Gursoy, H. (2005). A critical look at distance education in Turkey. In A. A. Carr-Chellman (Ed), *Global perspectives on e-learning: Rhetoric and realities* (pp. 35-51). Thousand Oaks, CA: Sage.

Hall, E. T. (1973). *The silent language*. New York, NY: Anchor Book Editions.

Hall, E. T., & Hall, M. R. (1990). *Understanding cultural differences: Germans, French, and Americans*. Yarmouth, ME: Intercultural.

Heaton, L. (2001). Preserving communication context. In C. Ess (Ed.), *Culture, technology, communication: Towards an intercultural global village* (pp. 213-240). Albany: State University of New York.

Hedberg, J. G., & Ping, L. C. (2005). Charting trends for e-learning in Asian schools. *Distance Education, 26*, 199-213.

Held, D., McGrew, A., Goldblatt, D., & Perraton, J. (2003). Rethinking globalization. In D. Held & A. G. McGrew (Eds.), *The global transformations reader: An introduction to the globalization debate* (2nd ed.) (pp. 67-70). Cambridge, U.K.: Polity.

Hofstede, G. (1980). *Culture's consequences: International differences in work-related values*. Beverly Hills, CA: Sage.

Hofstede, G. (1986). Cultural differences in teaching and learning. *International Journal of Intercultural Relations, 10*(3), 301-320.

Hu, G. (2005). Using peer review with Chinese ESL student writers. *Language Teaching Research, 9*(3), 321-342.

Hu, Y. (2004). The cultural significance of reading instruction in China. *The Reading Teacher, 57*(7), 632-639.

Jiang, J. Q. (2005). The gap between e-learning availability and e-learning industry development in Taiwan. In A. A. Carr-Chellman (Ed.), *Global perspectives on e-learning: Rhetoric and reality* (pp. 35-51). Thousand Oaks, CA: Sage.

Jin, L., & Cortazzi, M. (1998). Dimensions of dialogue: Large classes in China. *International Journal of Educational Research, 29*, 739-761.

Kim, K., & Bonk, C. J. (2002). Cross-cultural comparisons of online collaboration. *Journal of Computer Mediated Communication, 8*(1). doi:10.1111/j.1083-6101.2002.tb00163.

Kramsch, C., & Thorne, S. (2002). Foreign language learning as global communicative practice. In D. Block & D. Cameron (Eds.), *Globalization and language teaching* (pp. 83-100). London, UK: Routledge.

LaPointe, D., & Barrett, K. (2005, May). *Language learning in a virtual classroom: Synchronous methods, cultural exchanges*. Paper presented at the meeting of Computer-Supported Collaborative Learning, Taipei, Taiwan.

Latchem, C. (2005). Towards borderless virtual learning in higher education. In A. A. Carr-Chellman (Ed.), *Global Perspectives on e-learning: Rhetoric and reality* (pp. 179–198). Thousand Oaks, CA: Sage.

Lopez-Islas, J. R. (2001, December). *Collaborative learning at Monterrey Tech-Virtual University*. Paper presented at the Symposium on Web-based Learning Environments to Support Learning at a Distance: Design and Evaluation. Asilomar, Pacific Grove, CA.

Martin, J. N., & Nakayama, T. K. (2004). *Intercultural communication in contexts* (3rd ed.), New York, NY: McGraw-Hill.

Mason, R. (1998). *Globalising education: Trends and applications*. London, UK: Routledge.

Matthewson, C., & Thaman, K. H. (1998). Designing the rebbelib: Staff development in a Pacific multicultural environment. In C. Latchem & F. Lockwood (Eds.), *Staff development in open and flexible Learning* (pp.115–126). New York, NY: Routledge.

McIsaac, M. S. (1993). Economic, political, and social considerations in the use of global computer-based distance education. In R. Muffoletto & N. Knupfer (Eds.), *Computers in education: Social, political, and historical perspectives* (pp. 219–232). Cresskill, NJ: Hampton.

Merriam, S. B., & Associates (2007). *Non-Western perspectives on learning and knowing*. Malabar, FL: Krieger.

Mintzberg, H. (2003, October 27). *Africa's "best practices"* [Online forum comment]. Retrieved from http://www.project-syndicate.org/commentary/mintzberg1/English

Moore, M. G. (2006). Questions of culture [Editorial]. *The American Journal of Distance Education, 20*, 1–5.

Moore, M. G., Shattuck, K., & Al-Harthi, A. (2005). Cultures meeting cultures in online distance education. *Journal of e-Learning and Knowledge Society, 2*(2). Retrieved from http://je-lks.maieutiche.economia.unitn.it/index.php/Je-LKS/index

Muirhead, B. (2005). A Canadian perspective on the uncertain future of distance education. *Distance Education, 26*, 239–254.

Nisbett, R. E. (2003). *The geography of thoughts: How Asians and Westerners think differently . . . and why*. New York: Free Press.

Norhayati, A. M., & Siew, P. H. (2004). Malaysian perspective: Designing interactive multimedia learning environment for moral values education. *Educational Technology & Society, 7*(4), 143–152.

Panda, S. (2005). Higher education at a distance and national development: Reflections on the Indian experience. *Distance Education, 26*, 205–225.

Pieterse, J. N. (1995). *Globalization as hybridization*. In M. Featherstone, S. Lash, & R. Robertson (Eds.), Global modernities (pp. 45–68). London, UK: Sage.

Pincas, A. (2001). Culture, cognition, and communication in global education. *Distance Education, 22*(30).

Raffaghelli, J. E., & Richieri, C. (2012). A classroom with a view: Networked learning strategies to promote intercultural education. In L. Dirckinck-Holmfeld, V. Hodgson, & D. McConnell (Eds.), *Exploring the theory, pedagogy and practice of networked learning* (pp. 99–119). New York: Springer.

Richardson, J., & Swan, K. (2003). Examining social presence in online courses in relation to students' perceived learning and satisfaction. *Journal of Asynchronous Learning Networks, 7*(1). Retrieved from http://sloanconsortium.org/publications/jaln_main

Reid, E. (1995). Virtual worlds: culture and imagination. In S. G. Jones (Ed.), *CyberSociety: Computer-mediated communication and community* (pp. 164–183). Thousand Oaks, CA: Sage.

Robertson, R. (1995). Glocalization: Time-space and homogeneity-heterogeneity. In M. Featherstone, S. Lash, & R. Robertson (Eds.), *Global modernities* (pp. 25–44). Thousand Oaks, CA: Sage.

Rogers, C., Graham, C. R., & Mayes, C. T. (2007). Cultural competence and instructional design: Exploration research into the delivery of online instruction cross-culturally. *Educational Technology Research and Development, 55*, 197–217.

Ryan, A. M., Gheen, M. H., & Midgley, C. (1998). Why do some students avoid asking for help? An examination of the interplay among students' academic efficacy, teachers' social-emotional role, and the classroom goal structure. *Journal of Educational Psychology, 90*, 528–35.

Rye, S. A., & Støkken, A. M. (2012). The implications of the local context in global online education. *International Review of Research in Open and Distance Learning, 13*(1), 191–206. Retrieved from http://www.irrodl.org/index.php/irrodl

Sadykova, G., & Dautermann, J. (2009). Crossing cultures and borders in international online distance higher education. *Journal of Asynchronous Learning Networks, 13*(2), 89–114. Retrieved from http://sloanconsortium.org/publications/jaln_main

Sanchez, I., & Gunawardena, C. N. (1998). Understanding and supporting the culturally diverse distance learner. In C. Campbell Gibson (Ed.), *Distance learners in higher education: Institutional responses for quality outcomes* (pp. 47–64). Madison, WI: Atwood.

Shattuck, K. (2005) *Cultures meeting cultures in online distance education: Perceptions of international adult learners of the impact of culture when taking online distance education courses designed and delivered by an American university.* Unpublished doctoral dissertation, Pennsylvania State University, University Park.

Shaw, J. B., & Barrett-Power, E. (1998). The effects of diversity on small work group process and performance. *Human Relations, 5*(10), 1307–1325.

Short, J., Williams, E., & Christie, B. (1976). *The social psychology of telecommunications.* London, UK: John Wiley.

Shuter, R. (1990). The centrality of culture. *The Southern Communication Journal, 55*, 237–249.

Smith, R. O. (2005). Working with difference in online collaborative groups. *Adult Education Quarterly, 55*(3), 182–99.

Sotillo, S. (2000). Discourse functions and syntactic complexity in synchronous and asynchronous communication. *Language Learning and Technology, 4*(1), 82–119. Retrieved from http://llt.msu.edu/

Stanfield II, J. H. (1993). Epistemological considerations. In J. H. Stanfield II, & R. M. Dennis (Eds.), *Race and ethnicity in research methods* (pp. 16–36). Newbury Park, CA: Sage.

Thorne, S. L. (2003). Artifacts and cultures-of-use in intercultural communication. *Language Learning and Technology, 7*(2), 38–67. Retrieved from http://llt.msu.edu/

Tomlinson, J. (1999). *Globalization and culture*. Illinois: The University of Chicago Press.

Tu, C. H. (2001). How Chinese perceive social presence: An examination of interaction in online learning environment. *Education Media International, 38*(1), 45–60. doi:10.1080/09523980010021235.

Uzuner, S. (2009). Questions of culture in distance learning: A research review. *International Review of Research in Open and Distance Learning, 10*(3), 1–19. Retrieved from http://www.irrodl.org/index.php/irrodl

Van de Vijver, F., & Leung, K. (1997). *Methods and data analysis for cross-cultural research*. Thousand Oaks, CA: Sage.

Visser, J. (2005). The long and short of distance education: Trends and issues from a planetary human development perspective. In Y. L. Visser, L. Visser, M. Simonson, & R. Armirault (Eds.), *Trends and issues in distance education: International perspectives* (pp. 35–50). Greenwich, CT: Information Age.

Vygotsky, L. S. (1978). *Mind in society: The development of higher psychological processes*. Cambridge, MA: Harvard University.

Wang, C., & Reeves, T. C. (2007). The meaning of culture in online education: Implications for teaching, learning and design. In A. Edmundson (Ed.), *Globalized e-learning cultural challenges* (pp. 1–17). Hershey, PA: Idea Group.

Wegerif, R., (1998). The social dimension of asynchronous learning networks. *Journal of Asynchronous Learning Networks, 2*(1), 34–49. Retrieved from http://sloanconsortium.org/publications/jaln_main

Whorf, B. (1998). Science and linguistics. In M. J. Bennett (Ed.), *Basic concepts of intercultural communication: Selected readings* (pp. 85–95). Yarmouth, ME: Intercultural Press.

World Bank (2005). *Central America education strategy: An agenda for action*. Washington, DC: The World Bank. Retrieved from http://www.worldbank.org/

Zhang, Q. (2006). Immediacy and out-of-class communication: A cross-cultural comparison. *International Journal of Intercultural Relations, 30*, 33–50.

Zawacki-Richter, O. (2009). Research areas in distance education: A delphi study. *International Review of Research in Open and Distance Learning, 10*(3), pp. 1–17. Retrieved from http://www.irrodl.org/index.php/irrodl

Zhenhui, R. (2001). Matching teaching styles with learning styles in East Asian contexts. *The Internet TESL Journal, 7*(7). Retrieved from http://iteslj.org/

3 Distance Education Systems and Institutions in the Online Era: An Identity Crisis

Sarah Guri-Rosenblit

The discourse and research on distance education in the online era suffers from inherent problems: the immense confusion as to what today constitutes distance education and a common misleading tendency to refer to *online* education as a synonym for *distance* education. The reality is that many distance education institutions, particularly the large-scale distance teaching universities, do not yet employ the electronic media as their main delivery medium, and most of the online education takes place at mainstream campus universities (Guri-Rosenblit, 2009). Many of the online learning technologies are used today to enrich and support lectures, seminar meetings, and face-to-face tutorials. During 2004–2005 the OECD conducted an in-depth survey of e-learning practices in 19 tertiary education institutions in 13 countries in the Asia-Pacific region, Europe, Latin America, and North America (OECD, 2005). One of the main conclusions of the OECD study was that most higher education institutions use the online teaching to enhance classroom encounters rather than to adopt a distance teaching pedagogy.

For over 150 years the distinction between mainstream campus education and distance education was clear. By its very nature distance teaching at higher education level was different from teaching at mainstream institutions. Instead of assembling students from dispersed destinations onto one campus, distance-teaching institutions have reached out to individual students wherever they live or wish to study. The early correspondence institutions that started to operate in the 19th century offered academic or professional studies mainly for profit purposes. The establishment of the Open University of the United Kingdom (OUUK) in 1969 and the founding of the large-scale distance teaching universities in many national jurisdictions have marked the beginning of a new era of distance education. Many heralded the new large-scale distance teaching universities as the most conspicuous development in higher education systems in recent decades, as a radical challenge to the concept of a university, and as a new species of university (Garcia-Garrido, 1988; Keegan & Rumble, 1982; Perry, 1976, 1977, 1996; Peters, 1983, 1992). The main role of the autonomous large-scale distance teaching universities has been to broaden access to higher education by offering high-quality education at a lower cost.

The clear and distinct function of distance education providers for over 150 years is not clear and distinct anymore. The new digital technologies enable any campus university to reach out to students outside its residential campus and offer online courses to both off-campus and on-campus students. Many policy makers, scholars, and practitioners in higher education tend to use the terms *distance education* and *online learning* interchangeably, as synonyms, and refer to online learning as *the new generation of distance education*. Just a few examples: A comprehensive report issued by the Pew Learning and Technology Program in the US stated that, "The terms 'distance learning', 'distance education', 'distributed learning' and 'online learning' are used more or less interchangeably" (Twigg, 2001, p. 4). Mackintosh (2006), in describing alternative models of implementing the digital technologies in higher education, used the term *distance education technologies* as a synonym for the term *information and communication technologies* (ICT).

Bates (2005) stressed that the strong advocates of e-learning "who see e-learning as an educational paradigm shift, making obsolete all forms of distance education that preceded it make a fundamental mistake, since distance learning can exist without online learning, and online learning is not necessarily distance learning" (pp. 14–15). In a recent international seminar devoted to examining the impact of ranking tables on online and distance education, it was argued that, so far, online providers and distance teaching institutions are not included in most ranking tables since there exists a confusion among higher education experts as to what constitutes *distance education* and *online learning* (Bengoetxea, 2011; Guri-Rosenblit, 2011). The result of this confusion is that the discourse and research on distance education suffer currently from an identity crisis and are characterized by blurred and confusing research questions, contexts, and outcomes.

TRADITIONAL DISTANCE EDUCATION INSTITUTIONS: RESEARCH FOCI

The most prominent modes of distance teaching institutions until the last decade were the single-mode distance teaching universities, the dual-mode universities (most notably in Australia and Canada), and the extensions in US universities. The distinct status of distance teaching providers had also shaped the nature of research, which was conducted by many academics on distance education. Typical research themes dealt with impact studies comparing students' outcomes in distance education frameworks with those of students in conventional settings; perseverance in studies (most particularly, trying to explain the relative high drop-out rates in distance education); the use of diverse technologies in distance teaching environments; the importance of various support systems in distance teaching; the economies of scale provided by distance teaching; and so on. Until the last decade, most of the researchers of distance education at the macro-level purported to prove two major things: that educational outcomes of distance teaching at university level can be considered on a par with conventional teaching at a campus university, and that the operation of distance teaching universities, most particularly, the large-scale distance teaching universities, provides economies of scale and is considerably cheaper than conventional university teaching. Thus, distance-teaching universities are able to enrol large numbers of students at a lower cost and, as such, contribute greatly to the broadening of access to higher education and to social equity.

Most of the books and articles on distance education in the 1970s, 1980s, and 1990s were devoted to the analysis of the unique nature of the industrial mode of distance education, pioneered by the OUUK (Bell & Tight,

1993; Daniel, 1996, 1997; Holmberg, 1986, 1989; Keegan, 1980, 1986; Keegan & Rumble, 1982; Mugridge, 1997; Perraton, 1981; Perry, 1976, 1977, 1996; Peters, 1983, 1992, 1994; Reddy, 1988; Rumble, 1992, 1993; Rumble & Harry, 1982). Many of these publications aimed to highlight the fact that not only have the new autonomous large-scale distance teaching universities presented a revolutionary and innovative idea of a university as compared to campus universities, but they have also departed from the conceptual framework and operating practices of the first generation of correspondence and extension institutions. Daniel asserted that the large distance-teaching universities were established "with the express purpose of breaking the perceived link between quality of education and exclusivity of access" (Daniel, 1997, p. 10). These universities have demonstrated that wider access, high quality, and lower costs can go together.

The unique operation of the large-scale distance teaching universities has been achieved through the industrial mode of their operation, which was extensively explained and elaborated by Otto Peters (1983, 1992, 1994). Peters stressed that the salient feature of the large distance-education institutions was their high degree of industrialization. As in industrial production, the processes of developing materials for learning and teaching at a distance-teaching university were modelled by the principles of rationalization, the most important of which were the division and subdivision of labour, specialization, objectification, and automation. Since instructional materials of quality are expensive to produce, large numbers of students must use them before the cost per head becomes reasonable and provides economies of scale. It means that distance-teaching universities have to be established as large-scale organizations, otherwise their operation and quality may be compromised. Indeed, many of the distance teaching universities teach hundreds of thousands, and even millions, of students. John Daniel has introduced the notion of *mega-universities* that teach over 100,000 students, and their infrastructure and operation differ significantly from smaller-scale institutions (Daniel, 1996).

The search for less expensive ways of providing higher education to large numbers of students was one of the main considerations behind the establishment of the distance-teaching universities by national governments in the 1970s and 1980s. However, comparison of costs between mainstream conventional universities and distance-teaching universities turned out to be most difficult to conduct, since their cost structures differ immensely

(Perraton, 1993) and many institutions are reluctant or unable to share comparable cost data. Distance-teaching universities do not support campuses or residential facilities; in this respect, they are significantly cheaper to maintain as compared to campus universities. On the other hand, they require heavy investments to set up the infrastructure for the production of high-quality study materials even before a single student is enrolled. The capital costs of distance-teaching universities is also altered by the choice of media, the number of subjects taught, and the number of courses provided (Rumble, 1993). A handful of studies have helped to establish a methodology for estimating costs and have demonstrated the cost advantage of some distance-teaching universities (Mugridge 1994; Perraton, 1993, 2000; Rumble, 1993; Wagner, 1977).

The themes that were dealt with extensively in the relevant literature on distance education in the industrial era were of a theoretical nature, highlighting the uniqueness of the new species of universities by analyzing their innovative features. The macro-level analysis was of tremendous importance in depicting the underlying premises of the industrial mode of large-scale distance teaching universities, since it has been the responsibility of the institution as a whole to design appropriate mechanisms for developing materials, setting support systems, coordinating a complex network of study centres within national boundaries—and beyond—and monitoring the quality of the learning and teaching process.

EMERGING DISTANCE EDUCATION PROVIDERS

The new digital technologies have altered meaningfully the operation of campus-based and distance teaching universities worldwide and have offered exciting opportunities to enrich learning environments. Quite clearly, the new technologies are most attractive for distance teaching. They have the potential to overcome three major shortcomings of traditional distance education: to rescue the isolated students from their loneliness by providing interaction with teachers, professors and tutors, as well as with other peer students throughout the study process; to provide easy access to libraries and other information resources, which was nearly impossible in the past; and to update, share, and reuse the self-study materials on an ongoing basis. No wonder that research on distance education in the online era has shifted strongly to studies dealing with interactivity, constructivism, and flexibility (Anderson & Elloumi, 2004; Andrew & Haythornthwaite, 2009; Moore, 2006; Rovai, 2004; Woo & Reeves, 2007).

The preoccupation with a variety of themes related to student–student, student–teacher, and student–content interaction in distance education settings is natural in the online era. However, most of these studies are conducted at the micro-level and focus on the impact of the technologies in small settings. Zawacki-Richter (2009) and Zawacki-Richter, Bäcker, & Vogt (2009) conducted two interesting `studies on research themes in the leading distance-education literature. They related in these studies to three broad areas of research at the macro-, meso-, and micro-levels. Their studies revealed a strong imbalance in the three research levels. Issues that refer to the micro-perspectives dominate research on distance education. Over 50% of the examined papers dealt with issues of interaction and communication of learning communities (17.6%), instructional design (17.4%), and learner characteristics (16.3%). Only 8.9% of the examined studies by Zawacki-Richter, Bäcker, & Vogt (2009) were dedicated to the examination of distance-teaching systems and institutions. Obviously, there are noticeable research lacunas on online distance education at the macro-level.

It is important to stress that the online era is still very young and has not established itself yet as a well-defined field of study and research (Bates, 2005; Guri-Rosenblit & Gros, 2011). Part of the obscurity as to the potential and actual uses of the new technologies is reflected in a plethora of different terms in the relevant literature that attempts to depict their various functions. Even the modest exploration of the growing number of articles and publications describing technology applications in study and training settings yields a long list of hard-to-distinguish terminology. Donohue and Howe-Steiger (2005) claimed that the marketplace of ideas that once related to the applications of the new technologies has become a cacophony of jargon.

An important impact of online learning has been the initiation of the blended mode, in which face-to-face encounters are combined with online teaching, and new consortia-type ventures coordinated by several universities (or other parties from the corporate world) using online teaching. These new modes of teaching are offered both to on-campus and off-campus students, and they have contributed to the blurring of boundaries between conventional and distance education. Many conventional campus-based universities offer online professional and academic programs, and many partnerships between universities and the corporate world, as well as private and corporate universities, have been formed in the last decade offering for-profit online education.

For instance, the Open University System of China combines former China Central Radio and TV University, which was established in 1979, with other radio and TV universities across China. It was the sole distance education provider in China until 1998. Between 1998 and 2003, the Ministry of Education licensed 68 colleges operating from within conventional universities and other institutions to become online providers. By 2008, 2,250,000 students were studying through the Open University System, whereas 1,310,000 were enrolled at the online colleges (Jung, Wong, Li, Baigaltugs, & Belawati, 2011, p. 66). Obviously, such a trend enhances competition between single-mode distance teaching universities and new providers of distance education. Some of the new emerging distance-education institutions in many countries suffer from poor practices and resulting bad reputation; an urgent need exists to establish national and international quality assurance mechanisms, as will be discussed further.

A noticeable absence in the discourse and research on distance education in the online era relates to the inherent difficulty of the large-scale distance-teaching universities to fully adopt the advantages of the new technologies. The reason is that most of these universities lack the appropriate infrastructure and human capital to utilize the new technologies broadly and efficiently (Bernath & Hülsmann, 2004; Guri-Rosenblit, 2009).

Efficient online communication is, by its very nature, labour intensive. The industrial model is based on the notion of a small number of academics who are responsible for developing high-quality materials for large numbers of students. Obviously, small numbers of academic faculty are unable to interact with thousands or even with hundreds of students. Most, if not all, large distance-teaching universities cannot afford to hire many more academics in order to facilitate student–professor interaction in most of their large courses, often taken by thousands of students. In many distance-teaching universities, the faculty members who developed the courses are not involved at all in their actual teaching (Guri-Rosenblit, 1999). Furthermore, the extensive course contents that in large part defined the quality of these industrial model institutions is not designed to support learning community interaction. In addition, the production model is threated by the general decrease in value of content and from the growing number of open (and free) educational content being released by campus universities. The adoption of the interactive technologies requires a total overhaul of the very basic characteristics of the industrial mode of distance education.

An additional difficulty embedded in the adoption of the digital technologies by large- scale distance-teaching universities relates to cost-effectiveness considerations. Many e-learning applications are human intensive, require expensive technical support, and are most effective when conducted in small online classes. Rumble, for instance, demonstrated that online education is more costly than traditional distance education delivery and suggested, "it may prove to be more costly than traditional education" (2001, p. 230). The lack of reliable costs data in virtually all areas related to the application of electronic media is quite striking, most particularly at the institutional level. Few good, rigorous cost studies on the applications of technologies in higher education settings exist in developing countries, and very few such studies have been conducted in OECD countries (Arafeh, 2004; Perraton, 2000; Trucano, 2005). Obviously, many more studies should be conducted in the future on the costs, as well as on other implications, entailed in the adoption of the digital technologies in distance education systems and institutions.

NATIONAL AND CULTURAL CONTEXTS

Clearly, each national higher education system has its own peculiar features and qualities. As Burton Clark put it: "National systems of higher education vary in their organization and structure. . . . Different national structures then produce different responses to common trends and demands. The structure of a national system is generally the primary determinant of the direction and intensity of change within it, and the degree of success in deliberate reforms" (1986, p. 259).

When the large distance-teaching universities were established in the early 1970s, they adopted different policies in relation to open access and the utilization of available technologies, taking into consideration the prevalent academic culture of each national higher education system in which they were embedded. The OUUK, the Israeli Open University, and the Canadian Athabasca University adopted an open admission policy, whereas FernUniversität in Germany and UNED in Spain decided to require the same entry requirements as the conventional universities. They did so because they feared that their counterparts would look down on them if they practiced an open access policy (Guri-Rosenblit, 1999). In countries with smaller populations, distance education systems had to further differentiate themselves from and be more flexible than campus systems in order to attract students. For instance, NKI in Norway and Athabasca University developed continuous enrolment models, rather than the semester enrolment.

The large-scale distance-teaching universities also related differently to the utilization of mass communication technologies. Television in the 1970s was the queen of the media, and the new distance-teaching universities were expected to harness the technology of mass communication to the purpose of widening access to higher education. Interestingly, though Germany was a leader in mass communication technologies in the 1970s, the FernUniversität decided from the outset not to broadcast on television or radio, but rather to stay mainly with print technology, in order to be as similar as possible to other German universities (Bartels & Peters, 1986). FernUniversität adopted this policy deliberately in order to be acknowledged as a respectable new university adhering to the existing cultural norms in the German higher education, and not to endanger its reputation through collaboration with television broadcasts, which were associated in those days mainly with entertainment.

Academic cultures and national settings affect immensely the implementation of online education in various national jurisdictions. The complexity of cultural and political differences between nations is of tremendous importance in explaining and predicting the success or failure of implementing innovations, such as online education. A successful university in one country can turn to be a total failure in a different cultural context. For instance, Phoenix University, the largest for-profit distance-teaching university in the US, pulled out in 2005 of the UK market because of a lack of enrolment demand. Its ethos of operation and the structure of its courses have not been attractive in the British context. And vice versa: the OUUK, the most successful distance-teaching university in Britain, attempted to develop a system serving the US market, only to find that its style of teaching and curriculum structure did not appeal to the American market. It pulled out this venture in 2003 (Douglass, 2005; Garret, 2004).

Evidently there are significant differences in the effect that the advanced technologies are having in different countries, related in large to their economic wealth. Advanced economies have advanced systems of higher education and the appropriate infrastructure needed for the technologies' implementation. In all OECD countries, both state and national governments play a significant role in the strategic direction and funding of higher education in general and e-learning in particular (OECD, 2005; UNESCO, 2005; World Bank, 2002).

Major challenges in the implementation process of online education, mainly in developed countries, is to achieve the appropriate integration of the digital technologies into the education systems and institutions and to ensure that the new technologies become agents of expanded access and equity and increase educational opportunities for all, not just for the wealthy and the technologically privileged. Digital technologies are of great importance to tertiary education in developing countries. They have the potential to expand access, speed interactions, and improve the quality of instruction and learning at all levels; they might vastly broaden access to information and data resources, and greatly assist in professional training. However, most of the developing countries do not possess the appropriate infrastructure for utilizing the wide spectrum of the digital technologies' capabilities. Many scholars relate to the danger of the digital divide, which has introduced increasing reliance on digital information and advanced communication technologies (Mackintosh, 2006; Warschauer, 2003).

The emerging mobile technologies are thought to hold more promise for providing connectivity to remote areas, particularly in developing countries. Motlik (2008) argued that reliance on e-learning methods does not appear to work well in most developing countries so far, and that the Internet applications seem to be a poor fit for most of the Asian and African countries. Even in the emerging and successful economies of Korea and China, recent reports show that the adoption of Internet-based learning has been fraught with problems: lack of necessary technology, lack of Internet accessibility, lack of online resources, high costs, and lack of credibility for online degrees (Baggaley & Belawati, 2007). Visser & West (2005) believe that there is great promise for the use of mobile phones in education in Africa. However, projects utilizing mobile technologies today are for the most part in pilot or planning stages and face many regulatory hurdles (Attewell, 2005; Trucano, 2005; Visser & West, 2005). It should be noted that many of the most successful applications of mobile learning in developing countries have been to augment, speed up, and alert students but they do not replace industrial models of distance education (Barker, Krull, & Mallinson, 2005). Many more studies are needed to investigate the effective utilization of mobile technologies, mainly in developing countries.

FROM NATIONAL SYSTEMS TO A GLOBAL LANDSCAPE

Globalization is perceived as a key reality in the 21st century, profoundly influencing higher education (Altbach, Reisberg, & Rumbley, 2009). Many scholars of globalization claim that the process of globalization "is a force more powerful than industrialization, urbanization, and secularization combined" (Douglass, King, & Feller, 2009, p. 7). Universities have operated for hundreds of years, mainly in national contexts, and are challenged today to be attentive to both local and global needs and opportunities. Many universities and colleges are torn between the growing pressure to operate in the global higher education market in order to diversify their funding base by various mechanisms, enhance their traditional roles of serving national priorities, and mainly accommodate the needs of their local surrounding environments.

For many higher education institutions, the potential of globalization offers exciting new opportunities no longer limited by national boundaries, but for some others it still seems a threatening phenomenon that forces them to change drastically their policies and search for innovative ways of engaging in a totally new world, whose rules depart sharply from old and well-known conventions.

Distance teaching providers by their very nature can easily transcend national borders and admit huge numbers of students situated in different countries. According to a rough estimate, around 15 million students, out of a total of over 150 million students, currently study in various types of distance teaching institutions and online programs, and these numbers are likely to grow in the future (Boyd, 2006; Guri-Rosenblit, 2009, 2011; Zawacki-Richter & Kourotchkina, 2012). Naturally, each distance-teaching university needs to design the appropriate strategies for operating in diverse international markets by translating and contextualizing study materials, finding suitable academic staff, and establishing appropriate support networks.

Broadening the operation beyond the national borders carries advantages and promises, but also encounters inevitable obstacles and problems. The broader the operation of any given university, the more difficult it is to assure the quality of the studies which it offers, particularly if the international students have not mastered the English language (or any other taught language), and if the academic cultures in the foreign countries differ meaningfully from that of the teaching institution. The University of Maryland University College (UMUC) is the largest public distance-teaching university in the US. Quite obviously, it has to employ different logistics when it reaches out beyond its traditional market, which is to serve American soldiers scattered all over the world, as compared to teaching non-English speaking populations in countries that lack an appropriate technological infrastructure.

The decision of any distance-teaching university to broaden its operation to international markets has a huge impact on the composition of its student population, the scope of its curricula, the role of its academic faculty, the nature of the support systems it is able to provide, its overall budget, the language of instruction, and the setting of appropriate quality assurance mechanisms. With many new providers offering options for higher education, it is sometimes difficult to distinguish legitimate institutions from diploma and degree mills (Levy, 2008). This increases the urgency of international mechanisms for quality assurance. UNESCO has launched an online portal to guide individuals to sources of information that will help them distinguish legitimate from bogus institutions (Guri-Rosenblit, 2011), but many more efforts should be invested in this domain.

INTER-INSTITUTIONAL COLLABORATIONS

In the past, distance-teaching universities emphasized being stand-alone and autonomous universities. It has been of immense importance to establish their autonomous status vis-à-vis traditional campus universities. But the rules of the game have changed dramatically in the higher education market in the last two decades. Universities are required to operate in a global market, in which means to combine forces with other higher education institutions— and the corporate world offers compelling advantages to all partners.

Partnerships, if they are successful, create synergetic strengths. The basic underlying idea behind cooperation is that the *whole* may be greater than the *sum of its parts*. Failure to collaborate often results in an unnecessary duplication of efforts and in ineffective investments of scarce resources. But successful collaborations are immensely difficult to achieve and sustain.

Many collaborative ventures turn to be more fanfare than reality, others fail in short order, and those that have been implemented successfully do not always turn out as intended.

Successful inter-institutional collaborations of distance-education providers have the potential to attract new student clienteles, reduce costs for course development, enhance flexibility, support higher quality mechanisms and infrastructure, provide richer and better programs, and strengthen the financial basis of the distance-teaching institutions. Finding appropriate partners and maintaining a fruitful collaboration constitute the most challenging but critical tasks for the future of distance education providers. Two important areas in which cooperation is an imperative for distance-teaching institutions relate to the open access movement, and the need to establish regional and international quality assurance mechanisms for the various modes of distance education provision.

The open access movement, which is based on the technological infrastructure of the Internet, provides an illuminating example of collaboration among a growing number of higher education institutions. Clearly, easier and more cost-effective access to sources of scholarly information, libraries, courseware, and software code can benefit all participants in higher education, but most particularly it benefits teaching and research in those countries that suffer from severe shortages in adequate academic staff and research facilities. Within the academic community there are currently many initiatives widening open educational resource usage all over the world (Altbach, Reisberg, & Rumbley, 2009; Vest, 2007). The open access movement holds special promise for distance-teaching providers: It has the potential to reduce costs of developing high quality materials, to bridge over the digital gap between developing and developed countries and between poor and rich, and assist in assuring quality. No wonder two UNESCO chairs initiated in 2010 on OER (Open Educational Resources) are led by Fred Mulder, the former president of the Dutch open university, and by Rory McGreal from Athabasca University, the Canadian open university. Naturally, research on the open access movement should address critical issues relating to language barriers, cultural and national obstacles, and accreditation mechanisms.

An additional important area in which inter-institutional collaboration is an imperative relates to establishing quality assurance guidelines. The new technologies gave rise to a large number of diploma mills, which Daniel

Levy called "fly by night institutions" (Levy, 2008). The industrial mode of distance education and the founding of the large-scale distance-teaching universities have given distance education a new legitimacy and established their high-quality standards. The emergence of many new distance education providers in the online era, some of poor quality, threatens the status and reputation of distance education in the global higher education landscape. Only efficient quality control mechanisms can guard against the destructive effects of many diploma mills and false academic institutions (Stella & Gnanam, 2004; Jung, Wong, Li, Baigaltugs, & Belawati, 2011). In a comprehensive study by Jung et al. on quality assurance in ten Asian countries (China, India, Indonesia, Japan, South Korea, Malaysia, Mongolia, Philippines, Singapore, and Sri Lanka) and one territory (Hong Kong), they highlighted the crucial importance of defining quality assurance mechanisms for distance education providers, as well as outlining the obstacles embedded in such an effort. Their final conclusions were:

> These policy directions should be further elaborated in strong research evidence. Future research is needed to investigate culturally considerate QA guidelines and key performance indicators, understand learners' perceptions of distance education quality, look into different QA issues in various forms of distance education, examine the flexibility of a regional or cross-border QA mechanism for Asian distance education, and explore possibilities of linking with other regions' QA frameworks. (Jung, et al., 2011, p. 81)

Inter-institutional and inter-regional collaboration is essential for conducting such research and for defining clear indicators for assuring quality of the operation of distance education providers.

RESEARCH ON DISTANCE EDUCATION IN THE ONLINE ERA: MAJOR CHALLENGES

This chapter aimed at portraying the major theoretical insights that have guided research on distance-teaching institutions and systems since the 1970s. Many publications and studies on the industrial mode of distance education that characterized the nature of the large-scale distance-teaching universities dealt with macro-level issues. These universities were by and large a product of governmental planning as large-scale higher education institutions set to fulfill national missions. Their operation entailed a well-coordinated and orchestrated institutional planning and monitoring. The new electronic technologies gave birth to many new distance education providers, some of which are operated by conventional universities, and many are new type ventures. The blurring of boundaries between conventional and distance education has created an identity crisis as to what constitutes distance education. The category of *online distance education* excludes most large-scale distance teaching universities that do not use the electronic media as their main delivery system. The broad category of *online education* encompasses a wide range of institutions and programs that are not targeted to distant students. The blurring of boundaries between distance and residential institutions and a confusing terminology in the relevant literature dealing with the many applications of the new technologies are responsible for much confusing and non-conclusive research findings.

Furthermore, the interactivity enabled by digital technologies between students and teachers, among students, and between students and content has strongly shifted the research foci on online education to the micro-level, presenting a huge amount of studies dealing with the impact of various new applications of the technologies, mainly in small settings. There are currently thousands of scattered studies at the micro-level that present contradictory results, suffer from various biases and methodological errors, and mostly do not yield robust conclusions that enable policy makers and practitioners at the institutional and systems level to use them in an intelligible way.

The research on online education, both at campus-based universities and distance teaching providers, is marked today by large lacunas, notably at the institutional and wide systems levels. Four major areas particularly need to be treated in the relevant research on systems and institutions of distance education in the online era: the cultural and national and international context of distance education operation; the search for a golden triangle offering high-quality online distance education to large numbers of students at a lower cost; the variables responsible for successful inter-institutional collaborations; and the optimal ways to overcome the digital and literacy divides.

There is a noticeable lack of comparative studies dealing with the cultural and national and international contexts related to the operation of distance-teaching institutions and systems, particularly in the online era.

Neither the single-mode distance teaching universities nor the blended mode provision should be treated as representing homogeneous-type institutions. One of the most important lessons retained from the comparative research of the large-scale distance-teaching universities has been that vast and profound differences exist between them (Guri-Rosenblit, 1999, 2009). Distance-teaching institutions provide more than one grand model of an innovative university. Some are national universities; others are regional. Some encompass a wide international scale and scope, while others are more locally oriented. Some are mega-universities teaching hundreds of thousands, and even millions of students, compared to relatively small-scale distance-teaching universities. Few distance-teaching universities exercise an open admission policy, while most others adhere to conventional admission procedures, and other conventional practices. The cultural and the national and international contexts have an immense impact on the missions, potential student clienteles, range of programs, and the nature of support systems of any higher education institutions. Particular attention should be devoted in the relevant literature dealing with online distance education with a clear portrayal of their online dimensions.

An additional challenge for researchers on distance education institutions in the online era is to find the golden triangle between wide access to higher education, high-quality learning, and economies of scale. The industrial mode of distance education has demonstrated that it succeeded in creating an admirable equilibrium between being able to absorb very large numbers of students while still monitoring tightly the quality of the study materials and study process at a lower cost as compared to conventional campus universities. Such a balance has not been demonstrated yet for the operation of distance education institutions and systems using online learning technologies and pedagogies.

The gradual move among higher education institutions from operating mainly within national boundaries to an international landscape constitutes both an opportunity and a challenge. Universities are required to adopt their structure and operations to the needs of the knowledge society. Besides the obvious challenge of competing for students with increased numbers of international competitors, operating in a global and networked landscape has a crucial impact on shaping the missions, strategic planning, and operational practices of higher education institutions. Distance-teaching providers by their very nature can easily transcend national borders and admit students situated in different countries. With the emergence of many providers of distance education in the last decades it is currently difficult to distinguish between legitimate and respectable institutions from diploma and degree mills. This increases the urgency of establishing international mechanisms for quality assurance and of conducting appropriate research following the definition and operation of such mechanisms. The successful operation of distance education institutions and systems in the global arena depends highly on insuring their reputation as providing high-quality education by launching inter-institutional and inter-regional alliances, and by wisely utilizing the open resources.

And last but not least, the digital divide between the developed and developing countries, and between rich and poor in any given country, is still huge—creating immense gaps in existing technological infrastructures and personal access. Some advanced technologies hold the potential to decrease the digital gap, whereas others contribute to its widening. International bodies and distance education providers should play a prominent role in planning strategies on how to diminish the existing gaps and should follow these efforts by insightful studies. Particular attention should be devoted in the relevant research on distance education institutions and systems in the online era to the potential of mobile technologies to bridge over the digital divide.

REFERENCES

Altbach, P. G., Reisberg, L. & Rumbley, L. E. (2009). *Trends in global higher education: Tracking an academic revolution.* Chestnut Hill, MA: Centre for International Higher Education, Boston College.

Anderson, T. (Ed.). (2008). *The theory and practice of online learning* (2nd ed.). Edmonton, AB: Athabasca University Press.

Andrew, R., & Haythornthwaite, C. (Eds.). (2009). *Handbook of e-learning research.* Los Angeles: Sage.

Arafeh, S. (2004). *The implications of information and communications technologies for distance education: Looking toward the future.* Final Report, P11913. Arlington, VA: SRI International.

Attewell, J. (2005). *Mobile technologies and learning: A technology update and M-learning project summary.* London, UK: Learning and Skills Development Agency.

Baggaley, B. & Belawati, T. (Eds.). (2007). *Distance education technology in Asia.* Lahore: Virtual University of Pakistan.

Barker, A., Krull, G., & Mallinson, B. (2005). *A proposed theoretical model for m-learning adoption in developing countries*. Paper presented at the mLearn 2005, Capetown. Retrieved February 2008 from www.mlearn.org.za/CD/BOA_p.14.pdf

Bartels, J. & Peters, O. (1986). The German FernUniversität: Its main features and function. In G. van Enckevort, K. Harry, & H. G. Schutze (Eds.), *Distance education and the adult learner*, 97-110. Herleen, NL: Dutch Open University.

Bates, A. W. (2005). *Technology, e-learning and distance education* (2nd ed.) London: RoutledgeFalmer.

Bell, R. & Tight, M. (1993). *Open universities: A British tradition?* Buckingham, UK: The Society of Research into Higher Education, The Open University Press.

Bengoetxea, E. (2011). *Academic rankings: New developments*. Paper presented at the 1st International Seminar on Higher Education Rankings and E-Learning, 22–23 September, Barcelona.

Bernath, U. & Hulsmann, T. (2004). Low cost/high outcome approaches in open, distance and e-learning. In U. Bernath & A. Szcus (Eds.), *Supporting the learner in distance education and e-learning: Proceedings of the Third EDEN Research Workshop*, 485-491. Oldenburg: Bibliotheks-und-Informationssytem der Universitat Oldenburg.

Boyd, D. (2006). *Glocalization: When global information and local interaction collide*. Paper presented at the O'Reilly Emerging Technology Conference. Retrieved March 2006 from http://www.danah.org/papers/Etech2006.html

Clark, B. R. (1986). Implementation in the US: A comparison with European higher education. In L. Cerych & P. Sabatier (Eds.), *Great expectations and mixed performances: The implementation of higher education reforms in Europe*. Stoke-on-Trent, UK: Trentham Books.

Daniel, J. S. (1996). *The mega-universities and the knowledge media*. London: Kogan Page.

Daniel, J. S. (1997). *Reflections of a scholar gypsy*. Paper presented at the 'What Kind of University?' International Conference, June 1997, London.

Donohue, B. & Howe-Steiger, L. (2005). Faculty and administrators collaborating for e-learning courseware. *EDUCAUSE Quarterly, 28*(1), 20-32.

Douglass, J. A. (2005). *All globalization is local: Countervailing forces and the influence on higher education markets*. Research and Occasional Paper Series, 1.05. Berkeley, CA: UC Berkeley.

Douglass, J. A., King, C. J., & Feller, I. (2009). The room with a view: Globalization, universities and the imperative of a broader US perspective. In J. D. A. Douglass, C. J. King, & Feller, I. (Eds.), *Globalization's muse: Universities and higher education systems in a changing world* (pp. 1–11). Berkeley, CA: Berkeley Public Policy Press.

Garcia-Garrido, J. L. (1988). The Spanish UNED: One way to a new future. In G. R. Reddy (Ed.), *Open universities: The ivory towers thrown open* (pp. 200–214). New Delhi: Sterling.

Garret, R. (2004). The real story behind the failure of the UK eUniversity. *EDUCAUSE Quarterly, 27*(4).

Guri-Rosenblit, S. (1999). *Distance and campus universities: Tensions and interactions – A comparative study of five countries*. Oxford: Pergamon Press & International Association of Universities.

Guri-Rosenblit, S. (2009). *Digital technologies in higher education: Sweeping expectations and actual effects*. New York: Nova Science.

Guri-Rosenblit, S. (2011). Universities: From a national system to a glocal network policy. In I. Tubella & B. Gros (Eds.), *Turning the university upside down: Actions for the near future*. Barcelona: Editorial UOC.

Guri-Rosenblit, S. (2011). Online universities: What parameters should be used for ranking? A lecture presented at the 1st International Seminar on Higher Education Rankings and E-Learning, 22-23 September, Barcelona.

Guri-Rosenblit, S. & Gros, B. (2011). E-Learning: Confusing terminology, research gaps and inherent challenges. *Journal of Distance Education, 23*(20), 105-122.

Holmberg, B. (1986). *Growth and structure of distance education*. Beckenham, UK: Croom Helm.

Holmberg, B. (1989). *Theory and practice of distance education*. London: Routledge.

Jung, I., Wong, T.M., Li, C., Baigaltugs, S., Belawati, T. (2011). Quality assurance in Asian distance education: Diverse approaches and common culture. *International Review of Research in Open and Distance Learning, 12*(6), 63-83.

Keegan, D. (1980). On defining distance education. *Distance Education, 1*(1), 44-55.

Keegan, D. (1986). *The foundations of distance education*. Beckenham, UK: Croom Helm.

Keegan, D., & Rumble, G. (1982). Distance teaching universities at university level. In G. Rumble & K. Harry (Eds.), *The distance teaching universities* (pp. 15-31) London: Croom Helm.

Levy, D. (2008). *Private higher education's global surge: Emulating US patterns?* Paper presented at the Conference on Privatization in Higher Education, Haifa. Samuel Neaman Institute.

Mackintosh, W. (2006). Modelling alternatives for tomorrow's university: Has the future already happened? In M. F. Beaudoin (Ed.), *Perspectives on higher education in the digital age* (pp. 111-136). New York: Nova Science.

Moore, D. (2006). E-learning and the science of instruction: Proven guidelines for consumers and designers of multimedia learning. *Educational Technology Research & Development, 54*(2), 197-200.

Motlik, S. (2008). Mobile learning in developing nations. *International Review in Open and Distance learning, 9*(2).

Mugridge, I. (Ed.). (1994). *The funding of open universities: Perspectives on distance education*. Vancouver, BC: The Commonwealth of Learning.

Mugridge, I. (Ed.). (1997). *Founding the open universities*. New Delhi: Sterling.

OECD. (2005). *E-learning in tertiary education: Where do we stand?* Paris: Centre for Educational Research and Innovation.

Perraton, H. (1981). A theory for distance education, *Prospects, 11*(1), 381-390.

Perraton, H. (1993). The costs. In H. Perraton (Ed.), *Distance education for teacher education* (pp. 381-390). London, UK: Routledge.

Perraton, H. (2000). *Open and distance learning in the developing world*. London, UK: Routledge.

Perry, W. (1976). *Open university: A personal account of the first vice-chancellor*. Milton Keynes, UK: The Open University Press.

Perry, W. (1977). *The open university*. San Francisco, CA: Jossey Bass.

Perry, W. (1996). Distance systems in Europe. In A. Burgen (Ed.), *Goals and purposes of higher education in the 21st century* (pp. 62-68). London, UK: Jessica Kingsley Publications.

Peters, O. (1983). Distance teaching and industrial production. In D. Sewart, D. Keegan, & B. Holmberg (Eds.), *Distance education: International perspectives* (pp. 95-113). London, UK: Croom Helm.

Peters, O. (1992). Distance education: A revolutionary concept. In G. E. Ortner, K. Graff & H. Wilmersdoerfer (Eds.), *Distance education as two-way-communication* (pp. 28-34). Frankfurt: Peter Lang.

Peters, O. (1994). Distance education and industrial production: A comparative interpretation in outline. In M. Keegan (Ed.), *Otto Peters on distance education* (pp. 107-127). London: Routledge.

Reddy, G. R. (Ed.). (1988). *Open universities: The ivory towers thrown open*. New Delhi: Sterling.

Rovai, A. P. (2004). A constructivist approach to online college learning. *Internet and Higher Education, 7*(2), 79-83.

Rumble, G. (1992). The competitive vulnerability of distance teaching universities. *Open Learning, 7*(2), 31-45.

Rumble, G. (1993). The economics of mass distance education. In K. Harry, J. Magnus, & D. Keegan (Eds.), *Distance education: New perspectives* (pp. 94-107). London: Routledge.

Rumble, G. (2001). Just how relevant is e-education to global education needs? *Open Learning, 16*(3), 223-232.

Rumble, G., & Harry, K. (Eds.). (1982). *The distance teaching universities*. London: Croom Helm.

Stella, A., & Gnanam, A. (2004). Quality assurance in distance education: The challenges to be addressed. *Journal of Higher Education, 47*(2), 143-160.

Trucano, M. (2005). *Knowledge maps: ICTs in education*. Washington D.C.: The Information for Development Program.

Twigg, C. (2001). *Innovations in online learning: Moving beyond the no significant difference*. Troy, NY: Rensselaer Polytechnic Institute, Centre For Academic Transformation, Pew Learning & Technology Program.

UNESCO. (2005). *ICT in education: Policy makers' toolkit*. Bangkok: Author.

Vest, C. M. (2007). *The American research university from World War II to World Wide Web*. Berkeley: University of California Press.

Visser, L., & West, P. (2005). The promise of M-learning for distance education in South Africa and other developing nations. In Y. Visser, L. Visser, M. Simonson, & R. Amirault (Eds.), *Trends and issues in distance education: International perspectives* (pp. 117-129). Greenwich, CT: Information Age Publishing.

Wagner, L. (1977). The economics of the open university revisited. *Higher Education, 6*, 359-381.

Warschauer, M. (2003). *Technology and social inclusion: Rethinking the digital divide.* Cambridge, MA: MIT Press.

Woo, Y., & Reeves, T. C. (2007). Meaningful interaction in web-based learning: A social constructivist interpretation. *Internet and Higher Education, 10*(1), 15-25.

World Bank. (2002). *Constructing knowledge societies: New challenges for tertiary education.* Washington D.C.: Directions in Development.

Zawacki-Richter, O. (2009). Research areas in distance education: A Delphi study. *International Review of Research in Open and Distance Learning, 10*(3), 1-17.

Zawacki-Richter, O., Bäcker, E. M., & Vogt, S. (2009). Review of distance education research (2000 to 2008): Analysis of research areas, methods and authorship patterns. *International Review of Research in Open and Distance Learning, 10*(6), 21-49.

Zawacki-Richter, O., & Kourotchkina, A. (2012). The Russian higher education system and the development of distance education in the Russian Federation and the former Soviet Union. *International Review of Research in Open and Distance Learning, 13*(3), 165-184.

Online Distance Education Models and Research Implications

4

Terry D. Evans and
Margaret Haughey

As a form of education, distance education is influenced by educational theories and ideologies. Hence, over time its various theoretical models have reflected varying emphases on students, both individually and in groups, on content and process, and on administration and costs, and its guiding philosophies have ranged from knowledge replication to knowledge creation, and from teacher direction to learner engagement. Its founding purpose was the provision of education to populations who were not able to access available residential education. The reasons were not only based on the individual situation, such as, geographic location, family commitments, work commitments, or cost factors, but also included state issues such as insufficient institutions or a lack of enrolment places, full-time funding, or sufficient staff. These factors have contributed in various ways to the growth of distance education, both historically as when distance education was a major focus in many European countries after WWII, and as a current imperative in many countries where the need and desire for education outstrips the supply through residential institutions, regardless of their fiscal capacities. Education is seen by both individuals and states as essential for the development of a better socio-economic environment, hence, distance education has become the cost-affordable means of provision for millions worldwide.

Distance education, then, is framed within larger socio-economic and political contexts. These are not only reflective of societal characteristics like those identified by Keegan (2000): immediacy, globalization, privatization, and industrialization, to which we added professional learning, but also reflective of current social, political, and economic circumstances, such as the sequence of global economic crises this century.

Within these contexts then, the provision of distance education seldom arises from the desire of an institution alone; rather there are likely to be complex national, local, and individual aspirations where distance education is seen as the best solution. The realization of this provision depends on the issues being addressed and the various influences on the particular configuration of design and provision. It may be publicly or privately funded; it may seek to emulate or extend educational provision in residential institutions; its focus may be on increasing access or openness or convenience. Models or designs for distance education, then, have generally arisen from consideration of these instances, in part to provide a framework for researchers and in part to provide a means to reflect on issues that the models themselves have tried to resolve and sometimes inadvertently create.

ONLINE DISTANCE EDUCATION

Growing involvement of the Internet and digital media are shaping the present context of distance education. Garrison (2000) proposed that the concern with overcoming distance as a geographical reality, a strong focus of earlier distance education models, would be replaced by a greater focus on the teaching and learning process itself; a review of recent literature readily supports this point. But it is not so much the realization of an absence of distance in contemporary discussion of online distance education as the recognition that we are increasingly focussed on models of learning and their application to distance education that signal the change of emphasis in this digital age. We have moved from models *of* distance education to models *for* distance education.

In reviewing recent work on online distance education we found a number of authors who provided frameworks for theories of learning and linked them to pedagogical models to create a model of learning design for online learning, most frequently referred to as *e-learning*. The emphasis on e-learning, rather than on distance education, reflects a change from serving those with difficulty accessing education, to the use of technologies in learning. The more ubiquitous the Web, the less need to focus on the penalties of distance. Furthermore, the recognition that digital literacy is an important attribute for all school students makes it unsurprising that increasing numbers of institutions are including aspects of technology within classroom settings (Casey & Evans, 2011). Currently, providing opportunities for students without coming on campus is less about providing access to disadvantaged learners than it is about providing flexibility and convenience. Consequently, models of distance education, which examined aspects of where learning was to be encouraged and supported without a teacher's presence, have been replaced by e-learning models of how learning can be best enabled with technologies.

Dabbagh (2005) contends that the Internet has redefined the "boundaries and pedagogies of distance learning by stretching its scope and deepening its interconnectedness," to the extent that "new learning interactions that were not perceived possible before can now be facilitated" (p. 25). She sees such activities as prompting a redefinition of distance learning as "the deliberate organization and coordination of distributed forms of interaction and learning activities to achieve a shared goal" (p. 25). Bean and Yao (2010) similarly sought to revise the UK Open University (OUUK) open learning model, which focussed on the intersection of individual learning activities, resources, and systematic support, to a model that placed greater emphasis on technology. It involved a balance of three components: ideas, people, and technologies, which in turn were linked to the relationships among trust, open sharing, and community. However, Mayes and de Freitas (2004), in a review of e-learning theories, models and frameworks, stated it even more bluntly:

> There are really no models of e-learning *per se*—only enhancements
> of models of learning. That is to say, using technology to achieve better
> outcomes, or more effective assessment of these outcomes, or a more
> cost-efficient way of bringing the learning environment to the learners.
> (p. 4)

Despite this contention, and developments of models since 2004, the focus of distance education and the concern of distance educators remain: how to ensure that the learner in the virtual environment is given quality educational experiences and the best opportunities for success.

A model with wide support from both practitioners and researchers is the Community of Inquiry framework (Garrison, Anderson, & Archer, 2000). Its publication coincided with the growing acceptance of computer conferencing to enable student interaction in groups, while retaining the options for asynchronous participation denied by video- and audio-conferencing, for example. It also built upon earlier work of Anderson and Garrison (1998), which saw dialogue and debate as essential for establishing and supporting learning. The model defines three major components of a virtual learning environment as aspects of a community of inquiry: teaching presence (instructional activities required to facilitate learning), social presence (activities that support discussion and dialogue for learning), and cognitive presence (the learning resulting from the interactions in the community).[1]

The model has been the basis for many research studies. Most recently, Shea and colleagues at SUNY (Albany) (2011) reviewed current research on the model and added the Structure of Observed Learning Outcomes (SOLO) taxonomy in an attempt to examine some of the anomalies identified by previous researchers. In their analysis, they found that much of the "teaching presence occurs outside the threaded discussions that are the traditional object of research on the COL framework" (Shea et al., 2011, p. 109), and noted in particular was the amount of teaching presence in feedback on assignments. They found support for the relationship among the various forms of presence and noted:

> These results are significant in that they lend additional support to the validity of the model but employ more direct measures of learning processes reflected by cognitive presence residing in learning artifacts. Additional research investigating the relationship between the presences is recommended. (Shea et al., 2011, p. 109)

Complementing other studies, they found little evidence of student engagement at the higher levels of cognitive presence, irrespective of their grades.

---

1 A copy of the model is available at https://coi.athabascau.ca/

They propose various explanations for this including a failure to develop measures of assessment of learning that are meaningful to both students and instructors and recommend more research exploring correlations between cognitive presence and instructor assessment.

Other community models have also influenced how we think about online learning. In literature on professional learning in organizations, the notion of a community of practice was similarly outlined by Lave and Wenger (1998) as involving groups of people interacting for a shared goal or topic and producing communal resources for the members. Wenger defined three dimensions: the domain (the topic), the community (the members), and the practice (mutual engagement). For Wenger and his colleagues (2002) these formed a "knowledge structure" (p. 29). This model has informed online models where the focus is on learner-directed activities. Similarly, Jonassen, Peck, and Wilson (1999), in delineating the aspects of constructivist learning environments, focussed on learners' activities. They argued that active engagement was an essential component of meaning making. The major premise was the importance of interaction with the environment through manipulation and observation, construction, and reflection, within an authentic, goal-directed activity requiring social negotiation with others to build and reshape knowledge.

The notion of interaction as an important activity within online environments was also addressed by Salmon (2000, 2002) whose five-stage model focussed on the role of the moderator in developing and supporting effective online forums. She saw the role of the e-moderator as involving "online teaching and facilitating roles" (2000, p. 169), in particular, building community through assisting with socialization, information exchange, knowledge construction, and development. She identified not only the technical tasks that were required of the moderator but also the specific activities that increased interactivity. For example, in the knowledge construction stage, she described the skills of the best e-moderators as:

> "weaving": they pull together the participants' contributions by, for example, collecting up statements and relating them to concepts and theories from the course. They enable development of ideas through discussion and collaborations. They summarize from time to time, span wide-ranging views and provide new topics when discussions go off track. They stimulate fresh strands of thought, introduce new themes

and suggest alternative approaches. In doing all this work, their techniques for sharing good practice and for facilitating the process become
critical. (2000, p. 33)

Salmon's e-moderating model and its e-activities provided a framework
for instructors who were using computer conferencing as their main interactive strategy.

Research on the implementation of Salmon's model (Vlachopoulos &
Cowan, 2010) shows it is more successful in the training than the instructional setting. Despite their own expectations that they would behave in a
learner-focussed way, some tutors found it too difficult to step away from
the role of academic expert. Others saw the five-stage model as too prescriptive. Thomas, Jones, Packman, and Miller (2004), in a study of effective
e-moderation, concluded that students' preconceived expectations of the
role of the e-moderator were shaped by their previous classroom experiences. Similarly, the students' silence or non-response tended to encourage
the e-moderator to be authoritative. Garrison and Anderson (2003), who
use a similar model in their "teaching presence" component, stress the possibility of the roles being shared among students and e-moderator, a point
also raised by Salmon and one most likely to reduce the academic expert
role.

Simultaneously, web-based course tools were being explored, resulting
in the development of learning management systems (LMSs), one of the first
being WebCT created by a University of British Columbia professor in 1997.
The success of WebCT encouraged the development of other systems, some
based on open source production and support models. There is extensive
literature about the various models embedded in LMSs, the critiques they
engendered and about the experiences of instructors and students who
used them (see, for example, Lane, 2009).

The focus on learning management systems gave way to a focus on information access. Yahoo and Google began to index web accessible information so that access to scholarly materials online is commonplace in many
fields. In 2001, MIT (Massachusetts Institute of Technology) began to provide open access to the online components of its courses. In the same year
Laurence Lessig and his associates established the Creative Commons
licencing initiative that encouraged the sharing of digital material by creating licenses that allowed rights for use, copying, and modification. This

helped propel the open educational resources (OER) movement. All of these events reflect new affordances the Internet made available to distance educators and learners.

The development of Web 2.0 tools with their emphasis on social software encouraged the next generation of models for online learning. In an earlier publication (Haughey, Evans, & Murphy, 2008) we commented that learners' engagement with computers is unlike their involvement with other pedagogical forums. They "have a sense of immediacy and responsiveness, of control and choice, and of the opportunity to browse and search" (p. 15). They employ a wide variety of skills—from composing and editing, to messaging and responding, from browsing and searching, to evaluating and integrating, and from imagination and creation in multimedia environments, to the metacognition required to assess and integrate these activities within their own sense of knowing. In this we were highlighting the changes from working "on the computer" to working within virtual learning environments. Koper (2000) defined these environments as "advanced, flexible, social systems, supported with ICT" (p. 2) and identified five characteristics of such environments: representation, personalization, integration, cooperation, and process management. These reflect an aspect of the computer–Web interface that provides a sense of seamless flow, immediacy, and choice.

Characteristics of recent Web tools (Alexander, 2006) include increased possibilities for collaboration among multiple users; micro-content, from Twitter feeds to video clips, has replaced extended text posts; both the variety of tools and amount of user-generated content are increasingly rapidly; and sophisticated interfaces allow us to create more dynamic, semantic, and pleasing Web designs. How then do we respond to this bounty of options in these learner spaces in designing online distance education?

In a model focussed on the connected nature of this networked world, Siemens (2005) used the metaphor of a learning ecology to elucidate his theory of connectivism. Basing his work on principles derived from an analysis of chaos theory, networks, complexity theory, and self-organization, he proposed that:

> Learning is a process that occurs within nebulous environments of
> shifting core elements—not entirely under the control of the individual.
> Learning (defined as actionable knowledge) can reside outside of

> ourselves (within an organization or a database), is focussed on con-
> necting specialized information sets, and the connections that enable
> us to learn more are more important than our current state of knowing;
> (Siemens, 2005, Connectivism section, para. 1)

> Personal knowledge is comprised of a network, which feeds into organ-
> izations and institutions, which in turn feed back into the network,
> and then continue to provide learning to individuals. This cycle of
> knowledge development (personal to network to organization) allows
> learners to remain current in their field through the connections they
> have formed. (Connectivism section, para. 7)

In such a fluid environment, then, where information may be in human and non-human sources, the learner needs to be able to facilitate and nurture connections which will encourage further learning, to be able to recognize the connections between others' contributions and the dissonance or resonance with the learner's own knowledge, and to be open enough to examine these contributions and, where accepted, recognize their tenuousness. For Siemens, connectivism provides insight into "the learning skills and tasks needed for learners to flourish in a digital era" (Conclusion, para. 2).

The recognition of non-human objects in learning was raised earlier by Anderson (2003). He explored relationships between learners, with content, with designated instructors, and with the computer and other digital objects. Siemens has pushed this further to include not only physical objects, but also digital media and virtual learning objects, as well as interior memories and other ephemera. Actor-Network Theory (ANT) (Latour, 2005), which examines activities that involve interaction with such objects, provides a means of exploring the conventions and associations embedded in the interaction and its place in a larger system of knowledge creation. Connectivism has three major concepts: learner-directed, actionable learning and digital technologies. It does not refer to distance education or e-learning, nor does it separate informal learning from formal learning activities. These three concepts underlie the current writing on virtual learning environments, where the focus is on the use of social software and networking tools in designing learning opportunities in a digital environment.

Running parallel to theories of learning are models for teaching. Each model reflects a particular theoretical orientation to learning, states identified outcomes, has underlying concepts of engagement, and employs a variety of strategies. Joyce and Weil's (2009) well-known compendium of models included over 24 approaches based on four learning theory families, or groups. The authors outline their goal as primarily to increase students' capacities for personal growth, social growth, and academic learning, to help liberate students' learning capacity, and to build learning communities. They cluster the 24 approaches into inquiry models using concept attainment and advanced organizers; cooperative learning approaches based on the group work models of Slavin, and Johnson and Johnson; the personal or learner-directed models, which are based on the work of Rogers; and the behavioural models emanating from Skinner's work and involving direct instruction and mastery learning. These approaches highlight different goals and the means to achieve them. They are not meant to reduce the importance of the discipline or the teacher's individual creativity, but to provide a language to assist teachers in describing their role in learner development. Recent writing on pedagogical designs for e-learning work reflects this foundation (Dabbagh, 2005; Bower, Hedberg, & Kuswara, 2010).

A different grounding for learning designs derives from the work of the IMS Learning Design specification http://www.imsglobal.org/learning-design/ which focuses on methods for identifying the decisions involved in design as a way to create a language among designers that is also machine readable. The initial emphasis on learning sequences, a form of learning objects, has been followed by one on learning activities. Conole (2010) views learning design as "the set of methods associated with creating and representing practice" (p. 190) where the goal is to create the descriptions and to adapt and reuse them in future activities. She refers to these descriptions as "mediating artifacts" (2008, p. 187). These can range from models and vocabularies to diagrams and cases and can be specific or generic (FAQs, planning guides, guidelines, toolkits).

Activity theory (Cole & Engeström, 1993) reveals the relationships that influence the actions between the intention and achievement of the activity. It has been used to frame the context and relationships involved in the design of such artifacts. It is not a predictive theory, but instead documents the context, constraints, dialogic options, and roles of those involved in the process. In exploring how people created mediating artifacts, Conole and her team (Conole, Galley, & Culver, 2011), discovered the pre-eminent value of dialogue with peers in this process. Basing their framework on Engeström's (2005) social objects and Bouman and colleagues' (2007) notion of mediation in designing social software, Conole and Culver (2009) describe the basis for the creation of a design-based, object-oriented, research methodology that focussed on (1) the development of conceptual tools to guide the design process and provide a means of representing designs; (2) the development of visual tools to enable the digital visualization of concepts for adapting and sharing; and (3) the development of collaborative tools to aid the dialogue. The methodology and tools are available on Cloudworks (http://cloudworks.ac.uk/cloudscape/view/1882). Conole (Conole & Oliver, 2007) raised other research questions about the role of openness in design, provision, evaluation, and research, and provided an overview of various activity patterns within the Cloudworks site using Goffman's (1955) notion of *face work* and *ritual performance* and Levy's (1997) shared collective intelligence; these theorists encourage more situated research to explore the connections and associations generated by the activity of the participants (Alevizou, Conole, Culver), & Galley, 2010; Conole, 2010).

Anderson and Dron (2011) suggest that, "it is not so much a question of building and sustaining networks as of finding the appropriate set of things, people and activities" (p. 90). Cloudworks may be one example of such a network for those involved in learning design but it is not a model that translates easily into a course design. There has been substantial critique of learning management systems as confining the possibilities of instructors to the formats embedded in the system. What Anderson and Dron speculate may well be possible within an LMS (Lane, 2009), but increasingly people are looking at Web 2.0 technologies for student support, either in addition, or as a Web alternative, to LMS designs. Dyke, Conole, Ravenscourt, and De Freitas (2007) concluded that the dynamic social-cultural and communicative context makes it difficult to design e-learning environments and suggested that, "the adoption of the principles of the open source movement might lead to a better model for evolution of e-learning" (p. 94). Wenger's community of practice model has provided an alternative approach used by Gundawardena, et al. (2009). They propose a social networking spiral employing social software tools to build an environment that has five phases from context and discourse, through action and reflection, to reorganization and eventually to socially mediated metacognition.

Over the past 20 years, the orientation to distance education has changed significantly, from a focus on interaction and community afforded by the use of computer conferencing, through the issues associated with designing for learning management systems, to designing learning activities, that encourage more learner involvement with user-created content, OERs, and a greater variety of software tools.

IMPLICATIONS AND IDEAS FOR RESEARCH

The contemporary socio-economic circumstances are characterized by uncertainty and complex interconnectedness between local, regional, and global forces (Marginson & Rhoades, 2002). Contemporary models of online distance education, therefore, are both a feature of the times and partly constitute the contemporary circumstances and how people (learners) understand and work within such circumstances. In our view, the contemporary circumstances represent rich opportunities for research in online distance education, but there are also responsibilities for scholars in online distance education to apply a socially critical lens to their research. A perusal of the journals in open and distance education shows that there are increasing numbers of articles on online learning over the past two decades (Koble & Bunker, 1997; Rourke & Szabo, 2002; Smith, 2005). The majority of these articles are based on evaluative research or descriptive case-studies of particular practices of a particular course within a particular institution. In most cases they tend to be descriptive, rather than critical, and relate to particular local circumstances, rather than relate critically to, for example, national policy or global inequalities. Oliver et al. (2005) show it is possible to produce informative meta-analyses of aggregated smaller empirical studies that may inform critiques of educational policy and practice. Some major studies concern the broader social and economic potential of online distance education (for example, Bacsich, Ash & Heginbotham,2001; Cunningham, et al., 2000; Cunningham,, et al., 1997; Ryan & Stedman, 2002) in advanced economies. Others have noted the tension between conceptualized learning undertaken and constructed by individuals for themselves within an educational setting and learning in higher educational settings created and located in large corporate educational facilities in the service of the economy (see Barnett, 1997; McNay, 2006).

Furthermore, research is needed to study the application and consequences of online distance education models and practices beyond the advanced democratic nations. Daniel (2010) argues for the necessary use of online distance education approaches in helping to achieve universal basic education for grades 8 to 10 children in poorer nations. Such ventures would be worthy of significant comparative research across nations and regions. In a different way, researching the socio-political implications of accessibility to OER-based online educational approaches in national and cultural contexts where people and ideas are repressed may be potentially significant for the future of humanity. Finally, the impact of many new models and technologies on existing educational systems can have both disruptive and sustaining components that require both short- and long-term strategies. We make these points to illustrate that there are important considerations beyond researching models of online distance education within advanced democratic societies, circumstances to which we shall now return.

In the case of online forms of distance education, the matter of scale assumes a fluidity and invisibility due to the virtual nature of the educational settings. In "conventional" higher education, problems of scale are manifest in crowded classrooms, complex timetables, extended teaching periods, and even in the architecture and construction of new "classrooms." The *liquid modernity* (Bauman, 2000) of contemporary mediated forms of learning creates possibilities, opportunities, and problems for researchers (and others). However, the technology (the knowledge, values, and meanings associated with tools) is contested terrain in the sense that tools, such as proprietary learning management systems, are created with particular ideological and corporate economic interests at the fore; the teacher and, especially, the learner are relegated to the role of mere users. This contrasts markedly with the relative fluidity and unpredictability of social media that occupy and exploit the same Internet and telecommunications resources.

One of the major developments in online distance education has been the institutional adoption of learning management systems (LMSs) as a way to manage and coordinate online activities, organize materials on the Web, and provide for some interactivity. They have become ubiquitous in many distance education operations. As identified by a number of writers (Siemens, 2010), such systems were designed with a focus on management and control, rather than on learning and pedagogy. As such, they lacked many of the tools that instructors required; as the systems are centrally controlled and managed, their parameters have become the limits of teaching and learning. Once in place, further expansion of an institution's enrolments may require expanding the software's capabilities and its servers.

Arguably, these LMSs shape significantly the practices of the teachers and the experiences of the learners. Followers of actor-network-theory (Latour, 2005) attribute *agency* to such machines in social life. That is, in terms of online education, LMS are not passive tools used by educators (actors) to create teaching experiences as they wish, but rather there is a complex interplay (network) of meaning and action between them. It may be questionable to invest machines with agency in the sense of conscious deliberative action, but if one recognizes that LMS software is the product (embodiment) of peoples' conscious deliberative action in their own interests and according to their particular understanding of teaching and learning, then the actors-educators have to deal with their LMSs' embedded meanings and understandings of what constitutes the accepted range of educational activities and how they may be deployed.

This seems to be an immensely fruitful field for research that could benefit from different studies applying various theoretical and critical approaches to design, analyze, and explain the consequences of current online distance education and/or explore and develop the possibilities and potential of the media for more creative and liberatory purposes. Such research would need approaches that can investigate and interrogate LMSs' embedded meanings and understandings of their "permitted" range of educational activities and, perhaps, the variations that can be accommodated and under what circumstances and authority. Furthermore, qualitative analyses of the activities that occur between learners and their teachers within the learning contexts afforded by LMSs and what these mean to the parties involved is also worthy of investigation, in particular to explore the tensions, contradictions, and contests that may occur in the local teacher's development within these learning contexts and the students' uses thereof (Sharpe, Beetham, & de Freitas, 2010; Conole, Galley, & Culver, 2011).

Beyond the Web 1.0 LMSs are the new Web 2.0 social media and the other related media enabled by 3G and 4G mobile phone telephony and other devices. Again, theoretical approaches such as actor-network-theory have potential here to explore, critique, and explain the human and technological interplay that occurs in, for example, m-learning or Web 2.0 media used for educational purposes. However, Activity Theory and Transaction Theory are other approaches that are usefully deployed to research online learning communities and their participation (see, for example, Jaldemark, 2008; Jameson, 2011). Likewise, community of practice theory (see Lave & Wenger,

1991) has proven worthwhile to study and analyze particular learning communities, especially where professional interests are in the foreground (see, for example, Mackey & Evans, 2011). This is not limited to online distance education. Haggis (2009) argues that there is much to be done in these respects in higher education in general:

> In more general terms, there are many aspects of learning that are still not well understood, which currently dominant ontologies and epistemologies struggle to investigate and represent. For example, research into learning is still not able to deal well with "the fleeting", "the distributed," "the multiple," and "the complex" (Law & Urry, 2003, p. 10). To my knowledge, there is as yet little research that attempts to document different types of dynamic interaction and process through time in relation to "learning" situations in higher education. (Haggis, 2009, p. 389)

What each of the theoretical approaches noted above requires is detailed qualitative data and analyses. The online systems and telecommunications media often facilitate this in that the messages and other written texts occur in forms that are able to be collected, searched, and analyzed both manually and by using software. It may also be possible for visual and audio texts to be collected and stored for subsequent analyses. This is a significant advantage over classroom research where "talk" has to be recorded and transcribed, that is, transferred into a form for analysis that is different from that which was spoken and heard, with all its nuances and gestures, in the classroom. There are traps here, though.

The "data" in the online form, especially those collected and archived routinely by LMSs, were not collected as research data. Their authenticity as teaching and learning texts, for example, may be invaluable, but they were not systematically selected and collected with specific research questions in mind. Likewise the quantitative data (log-in times and durations, numbers of messages read, and so on) are not collected with research in mind; therefore, additional or other data may be required to address the research required. It must be emphasized also that the participants in these learning contexts are not research participants, but students. In university contexts in most democratic nations, human research ethics codes of practice generally require that students give informed consent for their teaching and learning conversations or activity data, for example, to be used for academic research purposes leading to publication. Educational institutions outside these university contexts often have no such requirements; we suggest, however, that behaving ethically in these respects is also good educational practice.

Once the above matters are considered, it is important that research in online distance education develops beyond replicating topics, research designs, and approaches used in earlier forms of distance education. For example, studies of dropout and retention were very popular in the early days of distance education when distance education was justifying its existence. Subsequently, media comparison studies and those comparing classroom and distance study flourished. It is doubtful if replicating such research and its theoretical considerations within online education is as important now. The new media enable forms of collaborative and participatory research, such as action research (see Kemmis & McTaggart, 2005; Noffke & Somekh, 2005) and design-based research (see Wang & Hannafin, 2005) to be practised "at a distance" as part of virtual teams. Furthermore, such forms of research lend themselves to analysis drawn from the models of learning discussed above and the research methodologies outlined in this section. The challenge is to be creative researchers who are receptive to the possibilities of the new media and respectful of the existing values and standards of scholarship.

CONCLUSION

This chapter discusses a selection of the theoretical models for online distance education that arose in the past 20 years to inform contemporary policy and practice. We applied a critical lens to this discussion based on our work in distance education spanning 30 years. We argue that this is a good time, indeed a necessary time, to undertake research on the consequences and implications of these models of online distance education. Some valuable research has been conducted in the field, which has informed educational practices of a more socially constructionist kind; we suggest in this chapter that there is a need to extend research to be of a socially critical kind that takes into account, local, regional, and global circumstances and diversities.

REFERENCES

Alevizou, P., Conole, G., Culver, J., & Galley, R. (2010). *Ritual performances and collective intelligence: Theoretical frameworks for analysing activity patterns in Cloudworks*. Symposium paper presented at 7th International Conference in Networked Learning, 3-5 May, Aalborg, Denmark.

Alexander, B. (2006). *Web 2.0: A new wave of innovation for teaching and learning? EDUCAUSE Review, 41*. Retrieved from http://www.educause.edu/ EDUCAUSE+Review/EDUCAUSE

Anderson T. (2003). Getting the mixture right again: An update and theoretical rationale for interaction. *International Review of Research in Open and Distance Education, 4*(2).

Anderson, T., and Dron, J. (2011). Three generations of distance education pedagogy. International Review of Research in Open and Distance Learning, *12*(3), 80-97.

Anderson, T., & Garrison, R. (1998). Learning in a networked world: New roles and responsibilities. In C. Gibson (Ed.), *Distance learning in higher education* (pp. 97-112). Madison, WI: Atwood.

Bacsich, P., Ash, C., & Heginbotham, S. (2001). *The cost of networked learning, phase two*. Sheffield, UK: Sheffield Hallam University.

Barnett, R. (1997). *Higher education: A critical business*. Buckingham, UK: Society for Research into Higher Education, Open University Press.

Bauman, Z. (2000). *Liquid modernity*. Malden, MS: Polity Press.

Bouman, W., Hoogenbloom,T., Jansen, R., Schoondorp, M., de bruin, B., & Huizing, A. (2007). *The realm of sociality: Notes on the design of social sofware*. PrimaVera Working Paper Series. Amsterdam: Universitiet Van Amsterdam. Retrieved from http://choo.fis.utoronto.ca/fis/courses/lis2176/Readings/bouman.pdf

Bower, M., Hedberg, J. G., & Kuswara, A. (2010). A framework for Web 2.0 learning design. *Educational Media International, 47*(3), 177-183.

Casey, G., & Evans, T. D. (2011). Designing for learning: Online social networks as a classroom environment. *International Review of Research in Open and Distance Learning, 12*(7), 1-26.

Cole, M., & Engeström, Y. (1993). A cultural-historical approach to distributed cognition. In G. Salomon (Ed.), *Distributed cognition: Psychological and educational considerations* (pp. 1-16). Cambridge, UK: Cambridge University Press.

Conole, G. (2008). The role of mediating artifacts in learning design. In L. Lockyer, S. Bennett, S. Agostinho, & B. Harper (Eds.), *Handbook of research on learning design and learning objects: Issues, applications and technologies* (pp. 187-207). Hershey, PA: IGI Global.

Conole, G. (2010). *Learning design: Making practice explicit*. Paper presented at the ConnectEd Conference, Sydney, Australia, June 28. Retrieved from http:// cloudworks.ac.uk/cloud/view/4011

Conole, G., & Culver, J. (2009). Cloudworks: Social networking for learning design. *Australasian Journal of Educational Technology, 25*(5), 763-82.

Conole, G., Galley, R., & Culver, J. (2011). Frameworks for understanding the nature of interactions, networking and community in a social network site for academic practice. *International Review of Research in Open and Distance Learning, 12*(2),119–38.

Conole, G., & Oliver, M. (Eds.). (2007). *Contemporary perspectives in e-learning research: Themes, methods and impact on practice*. London, UK: Routledge Falmer.

Cunningham, S., L. Ryan, Y., Stedman L., Tapsall, S., Bagdon, K., Flew, T., & Coldrake, P. (2000). *The business of borderless education*. Canberra, AU:Department of Education, Training and Youth Affairs.

Cunningham, S., Tapsall, S., Ryan, Y., Steadman, L., Bagdon, K., & Flew, T. (1998). *New media and borderless education: A review of the convergence between global media networks and higher education provision*. Canberra: Australian Goverment Publishing Service.

Dabbagh, N. (2005). Pedagogical models for e-learning: A theory-based framework. *International Journal of Technology in Teaching and Learning, 1*(1), 25–44.

Daniel, J. S. (2010). *Mega schools, technology and teachers: Achieving education for all*. New York: Routledge.

Dyke, M., Conole, G., Ravenscourt, A., & de Freitas, S. (2007). Learning theory and its application to e-learning. In G. Conole & M. Oliver, *Contemporary perspectives in e-learning research: Themes, methods and impact on practice* (pp. 82–97). Abingdon, UK: Routledge.

Engstrom, Y. (2005, 13 April). *Why some social network services work and others don't—Or the case for object-oriented sociality*. [Blog]. Retrieved from http://www.zengstrom.com/blog/2005/04/why_some_social.html

Garrison, R. (1989). *Understanding distance education*. London, UK: Routledge.

Garrison, R. (2000). Theoretical challenges for distance education in the 21st century: A shift from structural to transactional issues. International Review of Research in Open and Distance Learning, *1*(1), 1–17.

Garrison, R., Anderson, T., & Archer, W. (2000). Critical thinking in a text-based environment: Computer conferencing in higher education. *The Internet and Higher Education, 2*(2), 87–105. (See also: http://communityofinquirymodel.com)

Goffman, E. (1981). *Forms of talk*. Philadelphia, PA: University of Phildelphia Press.

Gunawardena, C., Hermans, M. B., Sanchez, D., Richmond, C., Bohley, M., & Tuttle, R. (2009). A theoretical framework for building online communities of practice with social networking tools. *Educational Media International, 46*(1) 3–16.

Haggis, T. (2009). What have we been thinking of? A critical overview of 40 years of student learning research in higher education. *Studies in Higher Education, 34*(4), 377–390.

Haughey, M., Evans, T., & Murphy, D. (2008). Introduction: From correspondence to virtual learning environments. In T. Evans, M. Haughey, & D. Murphy, (Eds.), *International Handbook of Distance Education* (pp.1–23). Bingley, UK: Emerald.

Jaldemark, J. (2008). Participation and genres of communication in online settings of higher education. *Education and Information Technologies, 13*(2), 129–146.

Jameson, J. (2011). Leadership of shared spaces in online learning communities. *International Journal of Web Based Communities, 7*(4), 463–477.

Jonassen, D. H., Peck, K. L., & Wilson. B. G. (1999). *Learning with technology: A constructivist perspective.* Upper Saddle River, NJ: Merrill.

Joyce, B., & Weil, M. (2009). *Models of teaching 8/E.* London, UK: Allyn & Bacon/ Pearson.

Keegan, D. (2000). *Distance training: Taking stock at a time of change.* London, UK: RoutledgeFalmer.

Kemmis, S., & McTaggart, R. (2005). Participatory action research: Communicative action and the public sphere. In N. K. Denzin & Y. S. Lincoln (Eds.), *Handbook of qualitative research* (3rd ed.), (pp. 559–603). Thousand Oaks, CA: Sage.

Koble, M. A., & Bunker, E. L. (1997). Trends in research and practice: An examination of *The American Journal of Distance Education* 1987 to 1995. *American Journal of Distance Education, 11*(2), 19–38.

Koper, R. (2000). *From change to renewal: Educational technology foundations of electronic environments.* Inaugural address, Educational Technology Expertise Centre, OU, Netherlands. Retrieved from http://dspace.ou.nl/handle/1820/38

Lane, L. (2009). Insidious pedagogy: How course management systems affect teaching. *First Monday, 14*(10). Retrieved from http://firstmonday.org/htbin/ cgiwrap/bin/ojs/index.php/fm/article/view/2530/2303

Latour, B. (2005). *Reassembling the social: An introduction to actor-network-theory.* Oxford, UK: Oxford University Press.

Lave, J., & Wenger, E. (1991). *Situated learning: Legitimate peripheral participation.* Cambridge, UK: Cambridge University Press.

Mackey, J., & Evans T. D. (2011). Interconnecting networks of practice for professional learning. *International Review of Research in Open and Distance Learning, 12*(3) 1–18.

Marginson, S., & Rhoades, G. (2002). Beyond national states, markets, and systems of higher education: A glonacal agency heuristic. *Higher Education 43,* 281–309.

Mayes, T., & de Freitas, S. (2004). *JISC e-learning models desk study.* Available from http://www.jisc.ac.uk/epedagogy/.

McNay, I. (Ed.). (2006). *From mass to universal education.* Buckingham, UK: Society for Research in Higher Education & Open University Press.

Meilun, S., Feng, J., & Tsai, C. (2008, September). Research and trends in the field of e-learning from 2001 to 2005: A content analysis of cognitive studies in selected journals. *Computers & Education, 51*(2), 955–996.

Noffke, S., & Somekh, B. (2005). Action research. In B. Somekh & C. Lewin (Eds.), *Research methods in the social sciences* (pp. 89–96). London: Sage.

Oliver, R., Price, P., Boycheva, S., Wake, J. D., Jones, C., Mjlestad, S., Kepmp, B., Nikolov, R., & van der Meij, H. (2005). *Empirical studies of the impact of technology-enhanced learning on roles and practices in higher education* Kaleidoscope Project Report D 30-03-01-F London, UK. Retrieved from Knowledge Lab http://www.lkl. ac.uk/research/oliver_impact.html.

Rourke, L., & Szabo, M. (2002). A content analysis of the Journal of Distance Education 1986–2001. *Journal of Distance Education, 17*(1), 63–74.

Ryan, Y., & Stedman, L. (2002). *The business of borderless education: 2001 update.* Canberra, AU: Evaluation and Investigations Program, Department of Education Science and Training.

Salmon, G. (2000). *E-moderating: The key to teaching and learning online.* London, UK: Kogan Page.

Salmon, G. (2002). *E-tivities: The key to active online learning.* London, UK: Kogan Page.

Sharpe, R., Beetham, H., & de Freitas, S. (2010). *Rethinking learning for the digital age: How learners shape their experiences.* London, UK: RoutledgeFalmer.

Shea, P., Gozza-Cohen, M., Uzuner, S., Mehta, R., Valtcheva, A.V., Hayes, S., & Vickers, J. (2011). The Community of Inquiry framework meets the SOLO taxonomy: A process-product model of online learning. *Educational Media International, 48*(2), 101–113.

Siemens, G. (2005, December 12). *A learning theory for the digital age.* [Blog]. Retrieved from http://www.elearningspace.org/Articles/connectivism.htm

Siemens, G. (2010, March 12). *Learning or management systems.* [Blog]. Retrieved from http://www.elearningspace.org/Articles/connectivism.htm. Originally posted Oct 6, 2006 Learning Technologies Centre, University of Manitoba.

Smith, P. J. B. (2005). Changing times in research? A speculative analysis of refereed contributions to *Distance Education* from 1980 to 2003. In T. D. Evans, P. J. B. Smith. & E. A. Stacey, (Eds.), *Research in Distance Education 6.* Geelong, AU: Deakin University. Retrieved October 16, 2011, from http://www.deakin.edu.au/arts-ed/education/research/conferences/publications/ride/2004/index.php

Thomas, B., Jones, P., Packman, G., & Miller, C. (2004). *Student perceptions of effective e-moderation: A qualitative investigative of E-College Wales.* Paper presented at the Networked Learning Conference. Retrieved from http://www.networkedlearningconference.org.uk/past/nlc2004/proceedings/individual_papers/thomas_et_al.htm

Vlachopoulos, P., & Cowan, J. (2010). Reconceptualizing moderation in asynchronous online discussions using grounded theory. *Distance Education, 31*(1), 23–26.

Wang, F., & Hannafin, J. (2005). Design-based research and technology-enhanced learning environments. *Educational Technology Research and Development, 53,* (4)5–23.

Wenger, E. (1998). *Communities of practice: Learning, meaning and identity.* Cambridge, UK: Cambridge University Press.

Wenger, E., McDermott, R., & Snyder, W. M. (2002). *Cultivating communities of practice: A guide to managing knowledge.* Cambridge, MA: Harvard Business School.

Methods of Study in Distance Education: A Critical Review of Selected Recent Literature

Farhad Saba

The field of distance education is complex in nature because it is composed of constructs from a variety of academic fields in addition to its own foundational concepts, constructs, and theories. Although research in distance education can be traced back to the 1930s when researchers were examining the effectiveness of educational radio, it is only now that inquiry in distance education is beginning to show the maturity that is required for such a complex and multifaceted phenomenon.

Evidence of this maturity can be found in rigorous quantitative and qualitative methods of inquiry that researchers have begun to apply in their studies in recent years. Simple descriptive articles about how distance education is being implemented in a specific institution have all but disappeared in scholarly journals. In addition, the number of comparative statistical analyses between two methods or modes of instruction (e.g., distance versus face-to-face) or between two media has dramatically decreased. This method has invariably shown no statistically significant difference between the two experimental treatments studied no matter which two phenomena were being investigated. The fact that no statistically significant difference were observed in almost all of the comparative studies indicated the inadequacy of the comparative method of inquiry in, at least, matters related to distance education.

Understanding the limitations of these types of studies, researchers have pursued the following strategies:

- They have adopted a wider variety of research methods in conducting their inquiries.

- They have embarked on conducting a series of quantitative studies to improve research techniques in distance education, thus making methods of inquiry in the field more appropriate to the questions at hand, as well as more precise and rigorous.

- They have developed a deeper understanding of the relationship between quantitative and qualitative data when more than one method of inquiry was applied in a study. Through triangulation, researchers have increased the level of certainty that the results they obtain will be valid and reliable and not a mere effect of how data was collected, analyzed, or interpreted.

In addition, the application of system dynamics to distance education as a research method provided the means to develop testable models of constructs: It combined qualitative data collected in explicating basic assumptions in modelling a theoretical construct (such as transactional distance made by major stake-holders in an organization or a program) with quantitative data to test the validity and reliability of a model.

Purpose and Method

This chapter offers a critical examination of issues regarding methods of research in the field of distance education based on the following three different types of scholarly studies:

(1) Recent quantitative analyses of trends in research and methods of inquiry in the field by Shachar, (2008); Zawacki-Richter, Bäcker, and Vogt, (2009); Gokool-Ramdoo, (2009); Davies, Howell, and Petrie,

(2010); de Oliveira Neto, and dos Santos, (2010); and Ritzhaupt, Stewart, Smith, and Barron, (2010).

(2) Selected individual research articles published in the English language between 2008 and mid-2011 in three leading journals:

   a. *The American Journal of Distance Education*, a print publication (http://www.ajde.com/)

   b. *The International Review of Research in Open and Distance Learning*, an open access publication (http://www.irrodl.org)

   c. *The Journal of Distance Education*, Canada, also an open access publication (http://www.jofde.ca)[1]

(3) Selected studies in application of system dynamics in distance education as a research method.

A critical review of these sources will focus on areas in which:

- progress has been made to adopt and use appropriate methods of inquiry for adding to the knowledge base of the field of distance education

- further work by researchers is needed to establish comprehensive methods of inquiry that would be responsive to myriad constructs in distance education

Early Signs of Maturity

The review of literature conducted for this chapter indicated an increase in the volume of research studies published, as well as noticeable improvement in their quality. Scholarship in the field is showing early signs of maturity. Researchers are using phenomenological methods to ascertain if specific constructs are operationally present in distance education

---

1 These journals were chosen for the leadership they have provided to support scholarship and disseminate research results in distance education during the contemporary conceptual growth of the field. The starting point of 2008 was chosen to coincide with the conclusion of the study of Zawacki-Richter, et al. (2009) in order to include selected articles, which were published from then until mid-2011.

programs and systems. Quantitative methods (sometimes mixed with qualitative methods) are also used to:

- reflect on how research is conducted in the field of distance education
- refine new research instruments
- conduct meta-analysis of extant studies
- analyze massive amounts of data that is generated in discussion forums or similar networked environments.

To test the assertion that the volume of research studies has dramatically increased we need only to look at the research being conducted and the contributions to the literature in the field being made by a new cadre of educators in different disciplines who teach courses at a distance, design instructional systems for distance teaching and learning, or manage distance education organizations, systems, and programs—in addition to those scholars who specialize in distance education.

In http://Distance-Educator.com, a website that I established in 1995, and have edited since then to reflect news and information about the field, I have listed 40 scholarly journals that are directly related to the field or a subfield of distance education. In addition, journals that are totally unrelated to distance education and specialize in specific disciplines, such as *Journal of Nursing Education*, have also published respectable studies concerning issues related to distance education. In fact, as the practice of distance education has expanded dramatically in the last 10 years, one may see an article about distance education in the current issue of journals in fields of study that are not associated with distance education at all. A quick search in Google Scholar showed several publications in this category ranging from *Educational Psychology* to *Nature and Science*, just to name two, to illustrate how scholarship about distance education has extended to other fields.

The following table shows a compilation of different research methods used in distance education as gleaned from the review of recent literature in the field, particularly the studies of Shachar (2008); Zawacki-Richter, et al. (2009); Gokool-Ramdoo (2009); Davies, et al. (2010); de Oliveira Neto, et al. (2010); and Ritzhaupt, et al. (2010).

Table 5.1 Compilation of different research methods used in distance education.

Quantitative	Qualitative	Theoretical/ Analytical	Historical
Statistical descriptive, comparative, regression, and factor analysis	Case study	In this line of inquiry several quantitative and/or qualitative methods are mixed depending on the objective of the critical analysis or theory building. In studies that both methods are used, quantitative and qualitative data are often triangulated to examine the reliability and validity of the results, thus adding more rigor to studies.	Historical research generally depends on examination of archived documents, and other similar artifacts in the time period of the study. There is a dearth of historical research in distance education, therefore, methodology in this category in the field is not well articulated yet.
Meta analysis	Semi structured interviews		
Survey	Focus gropus		
Cost effectiveness			
Analysis of online dialog	Analysis of online dialog		
Experimental and quasi-experimental	Grounded theory		
	Ethnographic study		
	Phenomeno-logical analysis		

A Quick Review of the Past

To understand the extent and importance of progress in adopting a wide range of research methods in the last 10 years as shown in the above table, a quick review of recent history is in order. A criticism of the field in the past has been the dearth of scholarly articles that are data-driven and theory-based (Saba, 2000). With the exception of a few articles, literature about distance education in each periodical before the turn of the century reflected the following:

(1) Descriptions of programs in various institutions with no discernible methodology in developing a descriptive account that indicated their validity or reliability as well as their appropriateness for generalizability. Purely descriptive studies of systems and programs have all but disappeared from the leading journals. However, researchers still continue to present elaborate descriptions of the institutions or settings in which they have conducted their research studies without explaining the direct relationship of the unique characteristics or special features of such settings with the purpose, method, or results of their studies.

(2) General surveys of learners' attitudes towards a program or a course of study offered by a specific institution. Similar to descriptive studies, results of these surveys were not generalizable to other institutions because the instruments used to collect the data were not standardized nor were they based on basic theoretical constructs of distance education. Researchers continue to use survey studies; however, an increasing number of data collection instruments in recent studies are validated and their results are more reliable and generalizable.

(3) Comparisons of various dimensions of distance education with "traditional" (e.g. face-to-face, brick and mortar, and so on) education, which invariably showed "statistically no significant difference" between the two modalities compared. Recent examples of comparative studies in Donkor, (2010); Ferguson, and DeFelice, (2010); Ward, Peters, and Shelley, (2010); Bassili, (2008); Carter, (2008); and Cragg, Dunning, and Ellis, (2008) used variations of the experimental method (e.g., quasi-experimental or mixed experimental methods with interviewing subjects). These studies confirmed the inadequacy of comparative quantitative studies as they also resulted in no statistically significant difference between the experimental group and the control group of subjects in relation to the experimental variables.

Failure of the Experimental Comparative Method and its Consequences

Use of the quantitative method to compare two modes of education, which was the predominant form of inquiry for many years before the turn of the century, requires further elaboration. Analysis of this method's failure illustrates important points that may pave the way for adopting a systems-dynamic approach to research in distance education, an approach that combines qualitative and quantitative data for understanding complex systems, such as distance education.

Fundamental flaws of the comparative experimental or quasi-experimental methods of inquiry include:

- Distance education is not examined on the basis of its own merits. In contrast, it is looked at in comparison to other forms of education, such as face-to-face classroom instruction, on-campus education, and so forth.

- Modes of education characterized as "traditional," "face-to-face," and "brick and mortar" are predominantly craft-oriented and are not designed to follow a standard set of procedures for presenting instruction or managing a program or system; therefore, the constructs that are measured comparatively are not truly comparable.

- The effect of experimental variable(s) on learning or other similar constructs are measured when aggregate quantitative data collected from the control group is compared with that of the experimental group in a research design that leaves out individual differences of group members. It is no surprise that looking for differences where they have been eliminated by the experimental design or the statistical procedure has revealed no significant difference time after time over the last five decades!

- The learner or other subjects are often removed from their normal environment and put in a laboratory condition to control for experimental variables—a practice that can cast doubt on the reliability and validity of research results when they are applied to educational institutions for improving educational practices outside of the laboratory environment.

- Data collected reflects a moment in time. Emergent qualities of learners, managers, or other key players over time are not taken into account in studies that take a snapshot of the data that is collected for the study.

Ascendance of the Qualitative Methods

The shortcomings of the comparative statistical methods to move research forward shifted the attention of researchers in the field to qualitative forms of inquiry in distance education, as well as in other related fields, such as educational technology. Using qualitative approaches, researchers in distance education have produced exploratory studies that are most appropriate for theory building by identifying new constructs or examining their operational presence in distance education programs. Researchers have succeeded in adopting qualitative methods of inquiry that, unlike descriptive and comparative studies, actually offer new knowledge about which constructs are operational in a distance education system and how such constructs can be analyzed and studied further in future research projects.

Results presented in a new genre of studies, which focussed on trends in research in distance education (Shachar, 2008; Zawacki-Richter, et al. 2009; Gokool-Ramdoo, 2009; Davies, et al., 2010; de Oliveira Neto, et al., 2010; Ritzhaupt, et al., 2010) as well as individual selected research articles for this chapter that were published between 2008 and mid-2011 showed that in the past decade researchers have expanded their use of phenomenological methods. A few examples include the following:

- Scripture (2008) explored the application of problem-based learning for distributed systems.
- Barbour and Hill (2011) focussed on the experiences of Canadian rural students enrolled in virtual schools.
- Dolan (2011) examined the experience of the isolated adjunct online faculty.

These and other similar phenomenological studies expand the theoretical base of distance education if their results are subjected to tests of validity, reliability, and generalizability. In other words, an important source for formulating hypotheses for empirical quantitative studies is the outcome of qualitative and analytical exploratory inquiry. Qualitative explorations of this kind must lead to formulating new hypotheses that can be tested in experimental studies using methods other than the traditional comparative statistical analysis, which has proven to be of limited use in understanding distance education. An example of an optimal method is the systems dynamic method (described further below), which combines qualitative and quantitative methods to study complex systems while taking into consideration assumptions, viewpoints, and opinions of major players in an organization, such as students, teachers, administrators, policy makers, and other stakeholders.

Improving Quantitative Methods

For conducting more refined and complex research projects, scholars have published data-based studies to improve research methods that are essential to the field. Examples of these lines of inquiry include:

- Hill, Song, and West (2009), who focussed on research constructs used in Web-based learning environments
- Oriogun (2009), who conducted a study to validate a new method of analyzing online message transcripts
- Buraphadeja and Dawson (2008), who analyzed models for assessing critical thinking using content analysis of computer-mediated communication
- Zhang, Koehler, and Spatariu (2009), who developed a research instrument consisting of an inventory that measures students' motivation to engage in critical reasoning in online discussions

Researchers have also demonstrated how quantitative methodologies can harvest and analyze data from a wide range of individual studies in order to glean new information from them. Of particular interest in this line of inquiry are Ritzhaupt, et al. (2010) who presented co-word analysis for examining the increasing volume of research studies in the field, as well as, Shachar (2008) who suggested using meta-analysis, "a collection of systematic techniques for resolving apparent contradictions in research findings" (p. 3) in multiple studies.

Use of Theory

The critical review conducted for this chapter indicated that very few studies were grounded directly on a particular formal theory of distance education. The use of theory is important to the study of research methods when the appropriateness of a method of inquiry in researching specific constructs in distance education is in question. As explained before, researchers are interested in phenomenological studies to explore and eventually ascertain if specific constructs are operational in distance education systems. This would be either to expand extant theories of distance education or propose new ones. This line of inquiry for theory building is not surprising given the relative youth of distance education as a field of study and its enormous complexity as a field of practice. As Saba (2003, 2007) demonstrated, distance education is a general systems concept with myriad components that affect each other and are affected by each other.

System Dynamics Method of Inquiry

In studying complex phenomena, such as distance education, it is not enough to understand the effect of one variable on another. The researcher must look at the relationships among myriad components that dynamically affect each other and are affected by each other *over a period of time*. In such systems, one variable could be the cause in a subsystem of a larger system and at the same time be the effect in another subsystem of the same larger system during the same time period. In other words, isolating one system component and studying it separately may shed light on the behaviour of that particular component, but it cannot provide any new knowledge about how that component behaves in relation to other components of a system of which it is a member. Studying experimental variables isolated from the entire system cannot inform us about the behaviour of the entire system as whole.

System dynamics provides a method of inquiry for the researcher to look at the entire operation of a distance education system, such as a single or dual mode institution, or the training department of a corporation that is involved in distance teaching and learning, or any subset of these larger systems. In order to understand distance education as a complex system of instructors, learners, administrators, instructional designers, as well as many other professionals who work together to facilitate the learners' learning, system dynamics offers the following affordances:

- It combines qualitative data in the form of assumptions made for the initial states of each system variable with quantitative data collected on how system variables may behave under certain conditions.

- It preserves the integrity of data collected from single subjects that show the effects of the interaction of their individual traits on myriad experimental variables. That is, data points on each subject in such studies are not aggregated to erase the effects, if any, of individual differences among subjects. This is a crucial methodological issue as future distance education systems will become more responsive to the individual interests, needs, and traits of learners by adopting learning systems that can adapt to the learners' preferences, traits, and prior knowledge.

- It allows for empirical observation of how multiple variables affect each other and are affected by each other *over time.*

- It provides for observing emergent qualities of system variables over a period of time including learners' cognition, behaviour, and emotive states; management practices in a system; or other system components.

- It offers the possibility to conduct experiments in normal settings. A laboratory is not required to control for variables that are always present in ordinary conditions for learners, managers, or other players. For a more comprehensive explanation of systems as a method of study in distance education see Saba (2003, 2007).

A hierarchical model of the field presented by Saba (2003) and refined in Saba (in print) depicted the complexity of system variables involved in various nested levels of distance education organizations and programs. These levels range from hardware systems to global systems, each performing a specific role in relation to other levels to make such programs and organizations function.

Figure 5.1 System variables involved in various levels of distance education programs.

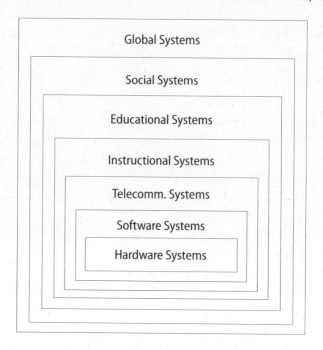

Global Systems

Social Systems

Educational Systems

Instructional Systems

Telecomm. Systems

Software Systems

Hardware Systems

Hardware systems are the necessary equipment needed to produce instructional materials, establish and maintain communication between the instructor and learner and among learners. Professionals who work in this system level are engineers and technicians who design, install, and repair different hardware components.

Software systems consist of the array of computer programs needed to convey instructional messages to students or to maintain synchronous communication between instructor and learner and among students. These systems range from e-mail to more complex programs such as Web-based video conferencing systems (e.g., Adobe Connect, Blackboard Collaborate), learning and content management systems (e.g., Moodle, Blackboard, WordPress, and so on) as well as student information management systems (SIMS), and customer relation management (CRM) applications. Professionals who work at this level are software engineers, programmers, videographers, audio engineers, graphic artists, as well as writers, editors, typesetters, proofreaders, and many others in similar professions.

Telecommunication systems are necessary to connect the instructor with learners and to provide connection among learners. A variety of such systems are used today in distance education that range from broadcast and cable television to telecommunications satellites and the Internet.

Instructional systems are courses, modules, learning objects, and supporting elements, such as databases, that include the instructional strategy and content for each subject, knowledge domain, skill set, and competency taught and learned. Professionals who work at this system level are instructors, instructional designers, subject matter experts (SMES), and evaluators. They work closely with those who are in the software systems to produce instructional materials. As complex adaptive learning systems will emerge and provide for personalized learning, the learner may also be added to the list of such professionals since many decisions previously predetermined by instructional systems will be made by the learner dynamically as the learning process progresses over time.

Educational systems represent a collection of courses that form a discipline, usually placed in an academic department or the training division of corporations or government agencies. Professionals at this system level consist of school principals, department chairs, training managers, chief learning officers, academic deans, and vice presidents of human resource development or academic affairs officers.

Societal systems consist of individuals who work in government agencies or private organizations that create the legal and financial basis for distance education to function. Laws governing accreditation, telecommunication, copyright, and public and private allocation of funding to distance education are outputs of this system level. Professionals in this level include legislators, lobbyists, government agency administrators, regulators and rule makers, attorneys, grant administrators in the public and the private sector, as well as members of state and national distance education associations.

Global systems consist of a network of institutions and international associations that make distance education viable throughout the world. Professionals at this level include officers and members of international bodies such as the World Bank, UNESCO, International Council for Open and Distance Education, European Distance and e-Learning Network and similar organizations that support projects and hold conferences and meetings in different countries of the world.

Research in Each System Level

One of the major characteristics of hierarchical complex systems is that each higher level subsumes the lower levels and is affected by the higher levels, directly or indirectly. For example, an increase in the level of regulations at the societal system level affects how instruction may be designed at the instructional and software system levels. Exploratory phenomenological research has primarily focussed on the following areas:

- Role or characteristics of learners and professionals, such as instructors; components that are generally related to the instructional systems level

- Variables, such as, motivation, satisfaction, retention, and so on, that are involved in the instructional systems level

- Roles or characteristics of systems manager in the educational system level.

Research in the field has, therefore, concentrated on instructional or educational systems levels and has not considered other levels that are very much part of the normal practice of distance education. This observation raises the following questions:

- Has distance education theory been articulated optimally to include the myriad constructs in which researchers are interested? An example is the extent to which theories of distance education have been examined in terms of emerging learning theory of connectivism. Bell (2011) suggested that connectivism is a learning theory for the digital age and presented a comprehensive analysis of its application in theory-driven research. Another example is the extent to which the relationship of established methods of teaching and learning, such as problem-based learning, to distance education theory has been examined.

- To what extent should methods of research in distance education be directly derived from the extant or emerging comprehensive theories of distance education? For example, Gokool-Ramdoo (2009) extended the application of *transactional distance theory* to develop an evidence-based model of policy analysis and development. Also, Boitshwarelo, (2011) suggested *design research* as a method to understand *social networked learning* as a construct in the comprehensive emerging theory of connectivism.

- As the practice of distance teaching has gained more popularity in various fields of sciences and humanities, to what extent will teachers and scholars who are in disciplines other than distance education influence the future theory building and selection of research methodologies in the field of distance education? Such theories and methods may be derived from the particular fields of instructors, such as engineering, literature or nursing, to name a few, and not necessarily from distance education.

- To what extent are teachers and scholars who are in disciplines other than distance education aware of the theoretical foundations and research methodologies of the field?

This last question is particularly important in the sense that it can significantly impact the methods and types of inquiry in the field in the future. Therefore, it needs further elaboration here. Over the long history of the practice of distance education until recent years, researchers who focussed on distance education also specialized in the field as their primary academic discipline, or came from disciplines and practices, such as educational technology or extended and adult education that were closely affiliated with distance education. As we move into the second decade of the current century, the review of literature conducted for this study made it clear that many other professionals have joined the ranks of distance education scholars who conduct research in the field. These professionals include:

- instructors who are engaged in teaching at a distance in a variety of subjects other than distance education

- instructional designers who design distance education courses and programs for many subjects areas

- administrators of organizations in K–12 or higher education who are actively engaged in managing distance education systems and programs.

These professionals are posing legitimate questions in their studies to add to the knowledge base of the field because such questions may pertain to their particular interests as practitioners who teach, manage systems, or design instruction for distance learning and teaching. Questions they pose may range from adoption of certain hardware and software systems, to cultural considerations, among myriad other issues that practitioners may face during a typical day. While this is a welcome development for adding to the knowledge base of the field, very few researchers who do not focus on distance education as their primary area of scholarship seem to be aware of the history, theory, and literature of distance education as lack of reference to the established literature of the field in their articles indicate. The majority of the articles written by this group of professionals examine theoretical constructs in their own primary area of study. Left out of their consideration are the theories and constructs that are native to the field of distance education. Since there will always be many more researchers who do not specialize in distance education as compared to those who select the field as the primary area of their scholarship, the emergence of this cadre of researchers will have far-reaching effects on the future direction of scholarship in distance education if they continue to ignore the literature of the field in the coming years.

The field requires a set of commonly agreed upon theories, principles, constructs, and rules to guide research projects. At this point, studies that highlight the common background of the field of distance education are lacking. An important example of this type of study is historical research. As Moore (2008) indicated, a dearth of studies in how the field has developed historically is lamentable in itself. However, lack of such studies have also led to the current conceptual confusion in the field—a problem that has become one of the most challenging methodological issues in research in distance education. For example, it is not always clear if researchers refer to seemingly the same referents with different names, such as Web-based learning, online learning, eLearning, and so on. Therefore, a core set of commonly agreed upon constructs is lacking today to move research in distance education to its next level of development.

FOUNDATIONAL CONCEPTS

Moore, Dickson-Deane, and Galyen (2010) conducted a survey study in which respondents were asked to define selected terms, such as, *distance education, e-learning* and *online learning* and describe their attributes. The study confirmed "conflicting responses," as well as "great differences" about the meaning of these terms. The study concluded that such lack of common understanding of foundational concepts has implications for classifying research results and collaborating among scholars internationally.

Guri-Rosenblit and Gros (2011) conducted a thorough analysis of the term *e-learning* and its different connotations in the literature. Their study concluded that *e-learning* is a confusing term given that the current technologies vary greatly in their abilities and affordances. It does not seem possible, at this stage, to aggregate technologies into one term that is used by all practitioners and researchers in this field, as e-learning may include a range of technologies in which electrons are active, from the telephone to satellites and the Internet. In another study Guri-Rosenblit (2009) demonstrated that authors have fundamental misconceptions about how distance education is defined, and why e-learning can be a subset of distance education, but it cannot supplant it as a research construct.

Construct Validity

Currently, very few studies attempt to verify experimentally the validity of concepts, such as e-learning or online learning, similar to the study conducted by Saba & Shearer (1994) to verify the validity of the concept of *distance* in *education* by experimentally examining the theory of *transactional distance*. As Moore (1993) posited and Saba & Shearer (1994) experimentally demonstrated, distance in education or transactional distance is determined by the dynamic interplay of key variables of structure and dialogue as these variables can be measured in the frequency of certain utterances of speech acts of the learner and the instructor. In other words, while physical distance between the learner and the instructor can be determined in miles or kilometers, speech acts as well as other units of measurement, such as indicators of social presence, determine psychological and social distance in education. As it was tentatively demonstrated in a systems dynamic model (Saba & Shearer 1994), when structure increases—as measured by speech acts attributed to the instructor or the instructional agency (e.g., the university)—transactional distance increases. Also, as dialogue measured by speech acts attributed to the learner increases, structure and transactional distance decrease. Further, since structure and dialogue are highly dependent on the individual characteristics of the learner, transactional distance may differ greatly in each moment of instruction for each individual learner (Saba 2003, 2007). As embryonic as this Saba & Shearer's study of 1994 was and as tentative its findings remain to be, similar demonstrations of verification and establishment of validity is necessary for terms, such as e-learning or online learning, if they are to be taken as serious theoretical constructs.

A more recent example of such an analysis is the discussion of the concept of *openness* presented by Wiley and Hilton (2009). The authors in this article analyzed the concept of openness by specifying its dimensions as compared to the predominantly closed systems of the brick and mortar higher education. This analytical article needs to be augmented with a method of measuring the openness of educational institutions to determine their openness quotient.

SUMMARY AND CONCLUSION

In the last few years, researchers in distance education have favoured the use of phenomenological methods of inquiry to explore constructs that may be operational in distance education systems. Such exploratory studies, however, must be augmented with quantitative data-based and theory-driven studies to verify the validity of constructs and concepts that have surfaced in these studies. Also, triangulating quantitative and qualitative data offers a method to make the validation of constructs, as well as determining the extent of the effect of experimental variables, a more rigorous process.

Systems dynamic, which combines the use of qualitative and quantitative data, offers an optimal means of studying complex systems, such as distance education. Applying this research method is lacking in the field to study the effect of myriad constructs (or system components) on each other as time progresses in an instructional session or in an organization as a whole. Research studies using single subjects is also possible when systems dynamic is used, without compromising the data points of each subject by aggregating them. For example, the concept of e-learning and online learning must be subjected to the same systems analysis as the concept of transactional distance was in Saba and Shearer (1994).

REFERENCES

Barbour, M. K., & Hill, J. (2011). What are they doing and how are they doing it? Rural student experiences in virtual schooling. *The Journal of Distance Education, 25*(1) Retrieved from http://www.jofde.ca/index.php/jde/article/view/725/1248

Bassili, J. N. (2008). Motivation and cognitive strategies in the choice to attend lectures or watch them online. *The Journal of Distance Education, 22*, 129–48. Retrieved from http://www.jofde.ca/index.php/jde/article/view/50/708

Bell, F. (2011). Connectivism: Its place in theory-informed research and innovation in technology-enabled learning. *International Review of Research in Open and Distance Learning, 12*, 98–118. Retrieved from http://www.irrodl.org/index.php/irrodl/issue/view/44

Boitshwarelo, B. (2011). Proposing an integrated research framework for connectivism: Utilising theoretical synergies. *International Review of Research in Open and Distance Learning, 12*, 161–79. Retrieved from http://www.irrodl.org/index.php/irrodl/issue/view/44

Buraphadeja, V., & Dawson, K. (2008). Content analysis in computer mediated communication: Analyzing models for assessing critical thinking through the lens of social constructivism. *American Journal of Distance Education, 22*, 130–145. Retrieved from http://www.tandfonline.com/doi/full/10.1080/08923640802224568

Carter, L. M. (2008). Critical thinking dispositions in online nursing education. *The Journal of Distance Education, 22*, 89–114. Retrieved from http://www.jofde.ca/index.php/jde/article/view/454/706

Cragg, C. E. B., Dunning, J., & Ellis, J. (2008). Teacher and student behaviours in face-to-face and online courses: Dealing with complex concepts. *The Journal of Distance Education, 22*, 115–128. Retrieved from http://www.jofde.ca/index.php/jde/article/view/45/707

Davies, R. S., Howell, S. L., & Petrie, J. A. (2010). A review of trends in distance education scholarship at research universities in North America, 1998–2007. *International Review of Research in Open and Distance Learning, 11*(3). Retrieved from http://www.irrodl.org/index.php/irrodl/article/view/876/1602

de Oliveira Neto, J. D., & dos Santos, E. M. (2010). Analysis of the methods and research topics in a sample of the Brazilian distance education publications, 1992 to 2007. *American Journal of Distance Education, 24*, 119–134. Retrieved from http://www.tandfonline.com/doi/abs/10.1080/08923647.2010.497325

Dolan, V. (2011). The isolation of online adjunct faculty and its impact on their performance. *The International Review of Research in Open and Distance Learning, 12*, 62–27. Retrieved from http://www.irrodl.org/index.php/irrodl/issue/view/45

Donkor, F. (2010). The comparative instructional effectiveness of print-based and video-based instructional materials for teaching practical skills at a distance. *International Review of Research in Open and Distance Learning, 11*, 96–116. Retrieved from http://www.irrodl.org/index.php/irrodl/issue/view/40

Ferguson, J. M., DeFelice, A. E. (2010). Length of online course and student satisfaction, perceived learning, and academic performance. *International Review of Research in Open and Distance Learning, 11*, 73–84. Retrieved from http://www.irrodl.org/index.php/irrodl/article/view/772/1547

Gokool-Ramdoo, S. (2009). Policy deficit in distance education: A transactional distance. *International Review of Research in Open and Distance Learning, 10*(4). Retrieved from http://www.irrodl.org/index.php/irrodl/article/view/702/1326

Guri-Rosenblit, S. (2009). Distance education in the digital age: common misconceptions and challenging tasks. *The Journal of Distance Education, 23*, 105–122. Retrieved from http://www.jofde.ca/index.php/jde/article/view/627/887

Guri-Rosenblit, S., & Gros, B. (2011). E-learning: Confusing terminology, research gaps and inherent challenges. *The Journal of Distance Education, 25*(1). Retrieved from http://www.jofde.ca/index.php/jde/article/view/729/1206

Hill, J. R., Song, L., & West, R. E. (2009). Social learning theory and web-based learning environments: A review of research and discussion of implications. *American Journal of Distance Education, 23*, 88–103. Retrieved from http://www.tandfonline.com/doi/abs/10.1080/08923640902857713

Moore, J. L., Dickson-Deane, C., & Galyen, K. (2010). E-learning, online learning, and distance learning environments: Are they the same? *Internet and Higher Education, 14*, 129–.

Moore, M. G. (1993). Theory of transactional distance. In D. Keegan (Ed.), *Theoretical principles of distance education* (pp. 22–39). London, UK: Routledge.

Moore, M. G. (2008). Where is the historical research? *American Journal of Distance Education, 22*, 67–71. Retrieved from http://www.tandfonline.com/doi/abs/10.1080/08923640802035014

Oriogun, P. K. (2009). Detecting aspects of critical thinking by cleaning online message transcript through code-recode. *American Journal of Distance Education, 23*, 34–50. Retrieved from http://www.tandfonline.com/doi/abs/10.1080/08923640802661694

Ritzhaupt, A. D., Stewart, M., Smith, P., & Barron, A. E. (2010). An investigation of distance education in North American research literature using co-word analysis. *International Review of Research in Open and Distance Learning, 11*, 37–60. Retrieved from http://www.irrodl.org/index.php/irrodl/issue/view/40

Saba, F. (2000). Research in distance education: A status report. *The International Review of Research in Open and Distance Learning, 1*(1). Retrieved from http://www.irrodl.org/index.php/irrodl/article/view/4/337

Saba, F. (2003). Distance education theory, methodology, and epistemology: A pragmatic paradigm. In M. G. Moore & W. G. Anderson (Eds.), *Handbook of distance education* (pp. 3–20). Mahwah, NJ: Lawrence Erlbaum.

Saba, F. (2007). A systems approach in theory building. In M. G. Moore (Ed.), *Handbook of distance education* (pp.43–57). Mahwah, NJ: Lawrence Erlbaum.

Saba, F. (in print). Building the future: A theoretical perspective. In M. G. Moore (Ed.), *Handbook of distance education.*

Saba, F., & Shearer, R. L. (1994). Verifying key theoretical concepts in a dynamic model of distance education. American Journal of Distance Education, 8, 36–59. Retrieved from http://www.tandfonline.com/doi/abs/10.1080/08923649409526844

Scripture, J. D. (2008). Recommendations for designing and implementing distributed problem-based learning. *American Journal of Distance Education, 22*, 207–221. Retrieved from http://www.tandfonline.com/doi/abs/10.1080/08923640802430462

Shachar, M. (2008). Meta-Analysis: The preferred method of choice for the assessment of distance learning quality factors. *International Review of Research in Open and Distance Learning, 9*(3), 1–15.

Ward, M. E., Peters, G., and Shelley, K. (2010). Student and faculty perceptions of the quality of online learning experiences. *The International Review of Research in Open and Distance Learning, 11*, 57–77. Retrieved from http://www.irrodl.org/index.php/irrodl/article/view/867/1610

Wiley, D. and Hilton III, J. (2009). Openness, dynamic specialization, and the disaggregated future of higher education. *International Review of Research in Open and Distance Learning, 10*(5). Retrieved from http://www.irrodl.org/index.php/irrodl/article/view/768/1414

Zawacki-Richter, O. (2009). Research in distance education: A Delphi study. *The International Review of Research in Open and Distance Learning, 10*(3). Retrieved from http://www.irrodl.org/index.php/irrodl/article/view/674/1260

Zawacki-Richter, O., Anderson, T., & Tuncay, N. (2010). The growing impact of open access distance education journals: A bibliometric analysis. *The Journal of Distance Education, 24*(3). Retrieved from http://www.jofde.ca/index.php/jde/article/view/661/1210

Zawacki-Richter, O., Bäcker, E. M., & Vogt, S. (2009). Review of distance education research (2000 to 2008): Analysis of research areas, methods, and authorship patterns. *International Review of Research in Open and Distance Learning, 10*, 21–50. Retrieved from http://www.irrodl.org/index.php/irrodl/article/view/741/1433

Zhang, T., Koehler, M. J., & Spatariu, A. (2009). The development of the motivation for critical reasoning in online discussions inventory (MCRODI). *American Journal of Distance Education, 23*, 194–211. Retrieved from http://www.tandfonline.com/doi/abs/10.1080/08923640903294411

Part II

MESO-LEVEL RESEARCH: MANAGEMENT, ORGANIZATION, AND TECHNOLOGY

Organization and Management of Online and Distance Learning

Ross Paul

The rapidity of technological change and the related explosion of interest and use of online learning in the past decade have resulted in a significant lag between practice and research in its management and administration. This is not a new phenomenon. Writing as recently as 2004, Michael Beaudoin (2004, p. 79) found only four book titles dedicated to open and distance education leadership and management published between 1990 and 2001. Taking into account the escalating rapidity of technological change and the usual publication lag, this paper focusses on research published since 2005.

This chapter addresses issues of research into management and organization, strategic planning and leadership, educational policy, and intellectual property and copyright. Other subjects and issues that pertain directly to effective management of online and distance learning are addressed elsewhere in this volume, notably professional development and faculty support, costs and finance, the management of educational technology, innovation and change, learner support, and quality assurance.

The discussion is limited to two kinds of institution: campus-based colleges and universities and post-secondary institutions dedicated to open and distance learning[1] and does not address corporate training and development of traditional or virtual elementary and secondary schools.

While they share significant similarities, there are important differences between the introduction of online learning into campus-based institutions and the impact of technology on open universities. The former seek ways to integrate online learning into an institution built around face-to-face teaching while open universities are struggling to adjust often dated technological processes in a rapidly changing environment.

After the completion of a literature review, three strong themes emerged: the ongoing need for more and better research into the area of organization and managment in ODEL institutions, the critical importance of taking account of institutional cultures in the management of change, and the tendency for newcomers to the field to ignore its established literature.

One challenge for a review of this sort is confusion in the literature among various terms in and around online distance education. For example, the concept of *learning* is variously modified as distance, online, e-, technology enhanced, Web-based, Web 2.0, mixed-mode, networked, mobile, technology enhanced, hybrid, blended, or flexible. While some authors take considerable pains to define the terms in their own papers (for example, Pachler and Daly, 2011), many others take their own terminology for granted. Given that new terms are being coined regularly in this fast-growing field, it is important that researchers define their terms precisely from the outset. Guri-Rosenblit and Gros (2011) provide a useful overview of this concern.

MANAGEMENT AND ORGANIZATION

The influential British writer, Gilly Salmon (2010) sets the context for an interest in research into the organization and management of distance education and online learning.

> University leaders already know much about learners' needs, changing
> demographics, and the challenges of the complex relationships

---

1 As almost all of these are open universities, that term will be used throughout the paper to refer to such institutions in general.

between technologies and pedagogies. However, they know less about how to prepare for changes in learners' expectations, including what, in the range of opportunities, is significant and what is not. (p. 28)

The challenge goes well beyond learner expectations to include those of employers, consumers, and government in a context where higher education is much more publicly accountable and far less protected by the traditional ivory tower.

There has been a paucity of research into the organization and management of distance learning, and much of the literature, such as it is, is anecdotal and reflective rather than experimental or inquiry based. Perhaps the most popular approach is the institutional case study, either written by someone reflecting on his or her own leadership or by a more dispassionate researcher with interest in organizational issues. Hannum (2009), among others, has suggested that, while case studies were useful during the early stages of distance education, their application is limited to their specific context. He advocates for "optimization studies that look beyond technology as the variable that matters and instead look to those variables that directly influence learning outcomes" (p. 173). It is this sort of research he believes to be sorely lacking in the field.

This view is consistent with that of Christensen, Horn, and Johnson (2011, pp. 196–97) who push for a major paradigm shift in educational research, emphasizing randomized control trials and learner-specific studies over more traditional descriptive approaches and correlation studies which they claim have little impact on improving learning outcomes.

There is a compelling case for a much stronger research orientation among practitioners in online learning, especially surrounding its introduction into traditional college and university programs. The past decade has seen a veritable explosion in online course offerings and enrolments in campus-based institutions, dramatically increasing the need to ensure the integration of these approaches into the mainstream of the institution. While researchers have been slow to respond, there is some indication that more are recognizing the importance of carefully designed, outcome-based studies intended to optimize the effectiveness of online teaching and learning.

As one example, Meyer and Barefield (2010) evaluated the availability and effectiveness of administrative support for online teaching faculty in a premier medical university in the US. They developed the Online Teaching Infrastructure Matrix and tested it with faculty in the university. The matrix is divided into three parts: the foundation stage (six elements), the developmental stage (nine), and the maintenance stage (six). The matrix approach provides a good overview of the issues involved in introducing online teaching to a campus-based institution.

A significant number of authors decry the haphazard and random way that online learning has been introduced in so many colleges and universities (see, for example, Pachler and Daly, 2011, p. 6). Many, such as Vasser (2010), speak to the importance of instructional design, which was so instrumental in the development of the Open University (OUUK) and its many imitators around the world, an issue covered by Campbell and Schwier in Chapter 13 of this volume. Others advocate not only for course and program design but also for strategic planning, evaluation, and attention to the sustainability of distance learning courses.

Chaney, Chaney, and Eddy (2010) take the latter approach, suggesting five assumptions that can be used by program planners of distance learning courses and programs. The assumptions are based on self-assessments of the successes and failures in the authors' collective 57 years of program design at six different American distance learning universities. They conclude their analysis with a lengthy list of performance indicators for quality assurance in distance education.

Paolucci and Gambescia (2007) identified the range of general administrative structures employed by universities offering online degree programs by surveying 239 American universities that offer at least one completely online graduate degree. They found that 90% of the institutions were delivering their online degree programs with an internally-based administrative arrangement, but noted a trend for the distance education unit to succeed the academic department as the chosen administrative structure (External administrative structuring, paras. 3, 4, & 10).

Conducting a case study of Indiana University's Kelly Direct online degree program, Magjuka, Shi, and Bonk (2005) offered 10 critical design and administrative issues for online program success. Schauer, Rockwell, Fritz, and Marx (2005) similarly used a modified Delphi study to assist an expert panel to identify 62 concepts organized in 8 issue categories important to implementing distance education courses and programs. Not surprisingly, the most important concepts were faculty commitment and skill development. They concluded that implementing distance education must be a collaborative effort among the department, college, and central administration with the departmental chair as the pivotal point in the entire process (Summary, para. 1).

Pina (2008) looked at 30 factors found in the literature that influence the institutionalization of innovations. One hundred and seventy distance-learning professionals rated the implementation success of each factor. The most highly-rated components were course management systems, and online registration and library resources, while the lowest ratings were given to professional and financial incentives to faculty and recruiting faculty participation. It is also interesting to note that administrators rated their institutions more successful than did faculty (Results, paras. 1–2). It would be useful to conduct further research comparing overall college and university performance according to which components were seen to be successfully integrated in each case.

Pachler and Daly (2011) worry that in the current economic climate e-learning will be seen as a way of cutting higher education budgets rather than encouraging research-informed pedagogical development (p. 132). Citing the work of Laurillard (2008), they lament research that distorts the coherence of the overall educational environment while giving technology disproportionate impact.

One of the most prolific and influential writers about the management of technology and education is Tony Bates. His most recent book, written in conjunction with Albert Sangrà (2011), is based on empirical studies of e-learning practice in over 20 universities worldwide and in-depth case studies of 11 universities and colleges, 6 in Europe and 5 in North America. Written primarily for senior academic administrators, the book uniquely addresses the integration of technology not only into campus-based universities and colleges but also into open universities. Using nine criteria to judge the extent of technological integration, Bates and Sangrà found a discouraging gap between hope and reality in their research. They found no evidence, either in the case studies or the literature, to show that the investment in technology was leading to improved learning. Instead of saving money, there was evidence that technology costs were rising, particularly in the areas of faculty workload, learning management systems, and learning technology support. Like many writers, they emphasize the importance of strategic planning and holistic thinking. They propose specific and sometimes radical changes necessary to improve learner performance and to reduce costs, and they encourage reader responses to their ideas.

Bates and Sangrà recognize that the biggest challenges facing academic change are cultural, not technological. This is consistent with much writing on leadership and change in higher education (Paul, 2011, pp. 49–71, Bergquist & Pawlak, 2008, and Schein, 2010). While those seeking to integrate technology into any form of post-secondary institution will look first to the specific studies on open and distance learning referred to in this paper, they will also find value in the broader literature of change and academic culture. As one example, the quadrant approach to learning innovation promoted by Salmon (2010, pp. 33–36) can also be understood through the cultures of the academy identified by Bergquist and Pawlak.

In advocating a Web 2.0 strategy for online learning students, Lee and McLoughlin (2010) address the needs and concerns of students studying at a distance. Rather than following "the widespread practice of incorporating traditional classroom pedagogical strategies into the Web-based delivery of courses," they advocate developing "authentic and relevant learning spaces and experiences for students through Web 2.0"(p. 66).

Every year the Western Interstate Commission for Higher Education and the Campus Computing Project collaboratively conduct a survey to obtain data on the instructional, operational, and technology infrastructure of online programs in higher education in the US. Their November 2010 report found significant increased investment in faculty training programs for online and distance education programs, with more than half of its surveyed institutions making such training mandatory. Notwithstanding rapidly growing online enrolments, almost three-quarters of respondents identified faculty resistance to teaching online courses as a significant barrier to their expansion and success. Another significant finding was that most of the institutions surveyed had either reorganized the management of their online education programs within the past two years or expected to do so in the next two. Budget issues and the need to coordinate instructional resources were primary reasons for the reorganizational efforts (Green, 2010).

The rapid development of new technology has posed equally significant challenges to open universities, which have evolved from correspondence models to the kind of course team/instructional design/student support approach first developed at the Open University of the United Kingdom (OUUK) and subsequently mimicked by open universities around the world.

A fascinating case study is the Al-Quds Open University (QOU), which serves more than 50,000 students in Palestine, the majority of whom have no other options for higher education. Matheos, Rogoza, and Hamayil (2009) examined QOU's efforts to redesign its existing model to a blended learning model that would offer a wide variety of delivery options and open resources. This was a direct challenge to the epistemology of its traditional distance offerings and the limitations of using only one resource, the course text (para. 6). Through faculty and student surveys, the authors deemed the associated extra work for both groups a worthwhile investment (Discussions and Conclusion, para. 1), however their paper somewhat glosses over the challenges of changing the prevailing delivery model as well as the associated cost and workload increases. No matter the positive impacts, introducing and trying to integrate new modes of delivery can render courses less cost-effective. It will be fascinating to track the institution's ongoing wrestling with such an ambitious change agenda.

One of the world's largest universities, with over one million off-campus students, the Anadolu University in Turkey has also undergone significant change to its primary distance education technology in recent years. Through the use of surveys, Akbulut, Kuzu, Latchem, and Odabasi (2007, p. 348) found only a minority of the faculty involved in innovation, research, and diffusion in open, distance, or e-learning. The authors noted a widespread need for professional staff development outside the Education and Open Education faculties. A concomitant concern is that faculty will focus less on specialized research into distance education, one of the supposed advantages of institutions dedicated to it.

Even though apparently operating independently of the literature and experience of open universities, some American advocates for improvements to online learning on traditional campuses are proposing models that nevertheless emulate the structures and processes of single-mode institutions. For example, Lowenthal and White (2009) propose centralized administration and oversight, collaborative and standardized course design, and faculty assessment and training—concepts all too familiar to experienced practitioners in open universities outside America. It will be interesting to see if practitioners can find an approach that avoids the worst pitfalls of both the creative but inefficient "craft" model of course production and the mass production, industrial model of single delivery mode universities.

Whether in the context of corporate change (Wasyluk & Berge, 2007) or traditional colleges and universities (Keaster, 2005; McFarlane, 2011; Portugal, 2006; Tipple, 2010), strong leadership is an important element in bringing about the necessary changes and support for an effective online learning strategy. Following Beaudoin (2002), Portugal (2006) emphasizes the importance of leadership as distance learning becomes part of the academic mainstream. Through the presentation of a wide-ranging review of the literature, she indicates the need for leaders in the field to be aware of the relevant research and to develop a variety of skills across all facets of distance education.

McFarlane (2011) examined the leadership roles of distance learning administrators in light of the demand for value and quality in educational distance learning programs and institutions. Applying Mintzberg's (1989) theory of informational, interpersonal, and decisional managerial roles and activities, he identifies three key challenge areas: quality of instruction, misuse of technology, and cost effectiveness, and he envisions the responses in terms of 12 leadership functions.

In his study of a traditional academic department in a public American university, Keaster (2005) looks at the case of his own department, which evolved from no online courses in 1999 to a robust online element a few years later. The department made a number of changes in policies and processes to adapt to the new reality. Keaster notes that adaptation was aided by its ability to hire new, young faculty members who were significantly less resistant to change than some of their longer-serving colleagues.

Given that so much of online learning has come to campus-based institutions through the efforts of individual faculty members, often without initial institutional support, it is not surprising that a number of writers have identified the importance of formal strategic planning for online learning, a crucial management tool that is too frequently overlooked. For example, Pisel (2008) developed a 10-phase planning model for distance education using the informed opinion from a panel of peer-nominated experts via iterative Delphi questionnaires.

Tipple (2010) stresses the need for effective leadership of online adjunct faculty who are increasingly playing a key role in the delivery of online courses. He documents the startling growth of the percentage of part-time faculty in American colleges and universities from less than a quarter of faculty ranks in 1970 to about half today, and, hence, the importance both of integrating them into academic ranks and helping them develop the requisite teaching skills. He draws parallels between the needs of online adjunct faculty members and online students for effective systems and personal support.

Tipple's work is supported by Bedford (2009) who did a qualitative analysis of the role of the adjunct in five American universities, three online and two traditional campuses. Suggesting that the resistance of tenured faculty to teaching online in the face of continuing growth of online programs and enrolments will continue to result in the demand for adjuncts to fill the void, she advocates managing adjunct faculty members in ways that respect their unique professional position. Puzzifero-Schnitzer (2005) also is concerned about the management of adjunct faculty, suggests adoption of Chickering and Gamson's (1987) well-known seven principles of good practice in this context.

Leadership in distance learning is not confined to those directly responsibility for online courses and programs in a campus-based university. The attitudes, knowledge, and support of chairs, deans, and provosts are also critical. Olson and Hale (2007) surveyed these groups in five American universities, first in 2000 and again in 2006 to assess the impact of the explosion of Web-based courses over that time period. While they found administrators to be positive about Web-based courses and supportive of increasing their numbers, they were concerned about their impact on faculty time as well as issues of academic dishonesty and student self-discipline. Olson and Hale offer four potential explanations for the disparity between generally positive faculty attitudes towards online learning and their overwhelming preference for traditional classroom teaching and analyze each in turn (Discussion, para. 1).

While most of the work listed above is American, there are strong similarities with the materials prepared for senior administrators in New Zealand by Ako Aotearoa, the National Centre for Tertiary Teaching Excellence. The project, Taking the Lead: Strategic Management for e-Learning (www. akoaotearoa.ac.nz), sets out six primary areas for senior managers to consider: strategy, structures, resourcing, decision-making, collaborating and outsourcing, and selecting technologies. The regularly updated project includes key questions for senior executives in the tertiary sector and a very useful set of case studies.

As an advocate for understanding institutional culture as a prerequisite to effective organizational change (Paul, 2011, pp. 69–71), I am particularly drawn to the analysis by Cowie and Nichols (2010) that depicts hybrid learning course development as a clash of cultures. In a study of New Zealand's Laidlaw College, they found significantly different perceptions of the chosen project management model between faculty members and instructional designers. It was only after this clash of cultures was recognized and addressed and the project management model altered accordingly that the college progressed effectively within a new, shared culture.

Similarly, an Australian study at the University of Sydney focussed on using project management to align the personal and pedagogical goals of academics and instructional designers as a key to integrating e-learning practices (Ward, West, Peat, & Atkinson, 2010), while Doherty (2010) underlined the importance to project success of ensuring that processes meshed with the collegial nature of the University of Auckland. The importance of such project management approaches to e-learning is underlined by the recent dedication of an entire number of the *Journal of Distance Education* to the topic (Pasian, 2010).

The pace and complexity of technological change increasingly demands that leaders know about and understand the most recent technologies and how they might be effective in assisting the institution to achieve its goals. Chester (2006) suggests the value of seeing chief information officers (CIOs) as advocates for and champions of technologies best aligned with institutional missions and mandates. This approach puts less emphasis on the technology itself, placing the CIO more in the forefront of decision making and strategic planning.

The rapid evolution of online learning is pushing leaders of open universities to rethink their entire academic model as they are increasingly forced to compete with more nimble and responsive uses of the Internet that make traditional approaches to distance education (course teams comprised of subject matter experts, instructional and visual designers, editors) look cumbersome and expensive in comparison. Many advocate directed planning strategies for open universities. Using examples from India, South Africa, Canada, and Hong Kong among others, Panda (2008) argues for both the necessity of strategic planning and sensitivity to its shortcomings and limitations.

Ironically, a significant planning and leadership challenge for today's open universities is the rapid rise of interest in open educational resources

(OER). When MIT launched its OpenCourseWare (OCW) project in 2001, making almost all of its course materials freely available online, it could do so without threatening its core mission because it was not entering the world of distance education. It offers no credit for the OCW courses: they are not a path to an MIT degree (Walsh, 2011, p. 63). The result has been a worldwide public relations coup for the university as individuals see the quality of its course materials and other institutions adopt and adapt them for their own use.[2]

For an open university, on the other hand, making courses freely available is to threaten their lifeblood because the courses are already designed for independent study at a distance. Its leaders fear a devastating loss of enrolments—why would students pay for a course that they can already get for free? There have been a number of interesting responses: the OUUK's OpenLearn (www.openlearn.open.ac.uk), and the collaboration among a number of universities to establish the Open Educational Resources University (http://wikieducator.org/OER_university). There are obvious parallels with music, movie, and, most recently, book-publishing industries are also dramatically confronted with the commercial challenges of openness.

A fear of losing enrolments spurred current research being conducted by the Open Universiteit of the Netherlands (Shuwer & Janssen, 2011). Students were surveyed on three different applications of OER to their institution's courses: offering short courses, 10% of course materials, or 100% of course materials for free, in the latter case charging fees for all related tutoring, services, and examinations. First indications are that the students responded positively to all alternatives with a slight preference for the third. To the researchers' surprise, there were no significant differences among age groups. An unpublished follow-up qualitative analysis reaffirms their earlier findings (Shuwer, Janssen, & Mulder, 2012).

Decrying the lack of research on leadership in distance education, Tait (2008) presents a compelling case for leadership development in the field and outlines its central components, both in terms of values and skill development. Given the challenges currently facing open universities, strong institutional leadership is critical to the continuing success of such institutions in a much more competitive, agile, and fast-moving post-secondary environment.

---

2 It will be interesting to follow the impact of the very recent MITx initiative, which gives students the opportunity (at no cost) to obtain a diploma (but not a degree) from the university.

Wallace and Young (2010) examined the types of policy and process issues that arose during a pilot project to redesign a single graduate program using blended learning at the University of Manitoba in Canada. They were particularly interested in the gradual transition from individual instructors' initiatives to institutionalized practice, noting that such change usually results from initiatives challenging existing policies and practices rather than as a single, comprehensive institutional response. Given the early stages of adopting blended learning into the institution, many of the issues raised had not been previously extensively examined, let alone resolved. The most important policy issues included course approval and equivalency, faculty workload, and resources (Discussion, para. 1).

A related study by Wallace (2010) goes into more details about the specific policies, academic and administrative, that had to be addressed with the rapid development of e-learning. With the blurring of distinctions between traditional and online teaching and learning, she found an increasing need for academic policy that addressed both contexts (p. 97).

Pachler and Daly (2011, p. 49) note how difficult it is to embed e-learning into a campus-based university. Technologies are often oversold and underused, leading to policy tensions with current researchers. They suggest there is strong evidence that innovation suffers when practitioners experience pressures to work with multiple initiatives of a complex nature, so that they can even be counter-productive in the long term (p. 50).

Based on a study of written distance education policies in four land grant universities in the us, Irele (2005) challenges the notion that distance education is being accepted and integrated into the mainstream of higher education. Direct references in institutional policies tended to be add-ons, so that, while they co-existed, "the overwhelming evidence from the study is that, as they accommodate distance education, the universities are showing signs they consider it to be a foreign body within their system" (Integrating the Distance Education System, para. 3). It would be interesting to repeat Irele's review today to see if policies are significantly more integrated, given the explosion in enrolments and programs since 2005.

Litto (2008) recounts recent attempts in Brazil to update educational policies even though there is a continuing tendency to treat distance learning "as a shadow of conventional learning" (p. 681). A more detailed, institutional case study looks at the policy issues and strategic planning at the University of the West Indies that culminated in the establishment of its Open Campus (Kuboni, 2008).

Thompson and Vidal (2011) give a useful overview of the chapters contained in the second edition of Moore's *Handbook of Distance Education* (2007), which respectively addresses policies, administration, and management.

It is unfortunate that the implications of moving to blended or fully online course delivery in so many campus-based institutions are dealt with only when it becomes highly evident that current policies are inadequate. Effective online education requires a full-scale overhaul not only of teaching and learning practices and academic policy, but of all the institution's services to students as well. That is why educational policy review and revision is an important component of effective strategic planning for online learning.

INTELLECTUAL PROPERTY AND COPYRIGHT

Significant copyright issues are associated with the ease with which faculty and students can acquire digital content for online courses. Sweeney (2006) found that, aside from a small percentage of academics with web design or copyright training, very few were aware of their institution's specific copyright and fair use policies. Given that such ignorance can lead to costly legal infringements, it follows that institutions must make compliance information more accessible to faculty.

Sweeney (2007) examined the impact of online course materials on copyright issues between faculty members and the administration in public and private doctoral research-intensive universities in the US. Her findings emphasize the importance of faculty–administration cooperation on intellectual property—its absence can significantly hamper the institution's ability to respond to student demand for distance education courses. Kranch (2008) reinforces this conclusion after reviewing both faculty and administrative viewpoints on copyright matters. Johnson (2006) stresses the importance of establishing an institutional protocol for the management of intellectual property for distance learning. Nemire (2007) offers a useful review of copyright rules and regulations and the outcomes of several court cases around the issue of fair use for distance educators. Many countries are in heated legislative battles between copyright owners and consumers; effective college and university leaders will do everything they can to ensure that the needs and concerns of their students and faculty are in the forefront of the debate.

A confounding factor in understanding copyright is the importance of national context and the specific legalities that apply in a given jurisdiction. Notwithstanding the efforts of organizations like the Creative Commons to develop one approach across all nations (Bissell, 2009, p. 100), it is important to look at specific national cases to understand fully the issues filtered through their particular legal provisions. Examples include Dooley, Lindner, and Dooley (2005) and DeVary (2008) for the United States; Geist (2010) in Canada; Vuori and Gururajan (2002) in Australia; and Davies (2011) and Secker (2010) in the UK. The latter is of particular interest because she discusses copyright issues and fair dealing provisions for e-learning in several English-speaking contexts, including the UK, Ireland, Australia, New Zealand, Canada, and the US (pp. 7–24). Secker's article gives a comprehensive overview of e-learning and copyright in the United Kingdom, including a case study at Brunel University to illustrate how one institution seeks to respond to the challenges posed by the increased use of e-learning environments and e-resources (pp. 17–20).

TWO SOLITUDES IN RESEARCH?

The relatively recent American *Online Journal of Distance Learning Administration* (OJDLA) is one of the very few peer-reviewed journals dedicated to the management side of online learning. Counting from 2005 forward to the most recent edition in the fall of 2011, almost 20% of the 199 articles are of direct interest to this paper: organization and management (21); leadership (5); institutional case studies (5); strategic planning (3); policy (2); and copyright (1). Other related subjects covered in this collection include faculty perceptions of online learning and associated rewards, development and support (28 articles), student perceptions and success factors (18), quality assurance (17), technological applications to teaching and learning (15), student retention and support (15), financial issues and sustainability (8), instructional design (8), marketing and communications (8), knowledge and course management systems (6), comparisons with face-to-face learning (5), academic dishonesty (4), and the use of adjunct professors (4). Almost all concern higher education with an overwhelming emphasis on the challenges of integrating online learning into campus-based institutions.

At the Barcelona research workshop of the European Distance Education Network (EDEN) in 2006, during a panel discussion among three giants in the field—Börje Holmberg, Otto Peters, and Michael Moore—there was speculation about whether those interested in bringing distance education to campus-based universities would look first to the literature of open and distance learning or whether they would proceed almost independently of it. The fear was expressed that most newcomers to the field would ignore several decades of research and practice.

These fears seem to have been well founded. At least for those writing in the OJDLA, the context is overwhelmingly American and there is almost no acknowledgement of earlier distance education literature. Even a couple of specific references to the history and context of distance education make no mention of any of its known theorists—the above trio plus perhaps Desmond Keegan and Greville Rumble. The only exception is the OJDLA paper by Irele (2005) of Penn State University who cites all five!

A tendency for newcomers to distance education and online learning to publish research without consulting the established literature in the field is not confined to a single journal or country. Based on her experience as a reviewer for Canadian, American, British, and Australian journals, Conrad (2007) offers thoughtful reflections on the current state of research in distance education and on the tendency for new entrants to the field, whose background is in another discipline, to ignore its established literature.

Those familiar with the literature of open and distance learning, as represented in the top five journals identified by Zawacki-Richter, Bäcker, and Vogt (2009), will tend to agree with Conrad, but, since most practitioners in traditional universities around the world will probably never read the journal in which her comments are published, it is difficult to see how the situation will change, in the near future at least. This is an important issue for further consideration.

CONCLUSIONS AND SUGGESTIONS FOR FURTHER RESEARCH

Three primary challenges for research into the organization and management of online and distance learning arise from the above review:

research-based leadership, the critical importance of institutional culture, and the need to break down the two research solitudes.

Research-Based Leadership

Leadership of higher educational institutions has become much more intensive and complex in recent years and senior management needs all the help it can get. While there will always be an intuitive aspect to the art, institutional heads cannot afford to make decisions without the best available information about the probable outcomes of competing strategies.

Pachler and Daly (2011) argue for a different way of conceptualizing e-learning research to address the integration of temporal and contextual issues and to be inclusive of the possibility of multiple distinct themes and the complex linkages across them.

There is an acknowledged gap between the growing research base and much policy-making in educational institutions regarding adoption, course design, and, crucially, practitioner development (p. 134).

Institutional leaders must be research oriented in their approaches to the management and organization of online and distance learning. Referring to the earlier examples, research should be learner driven (Salmon) and outcome-based (Hannum), not technologically driven (Pachler and Daly).

It is also vital to recognize that the rapid changes in our society are challenging fundamental assumptions about what constitutes knowledge and how it is created and applied. This is a subject that should be of primary importance to faculty and senior management alike. As Bates (2010) expresses it:

> This epistemological issue is a direct challenge to the primacy of
> academic knowledge and has specific relevance to how or whether
> universities should address the issue of lifelong learning and applied
> knowledge. It raises questions about the role of scientific thinking, the
> power and nature of collective intelligence, the extent to which know-
> ledge can be created independently of individuals, and how innovation
> occurs. The response to such questions will affect not only the content
> of the curriculum, but also how learning should be structured and
> where it will be delivered. (p. 20)

The pace of change is not going to slow down as ICTs increasingly dominate our lives. While institutional leaders are wrestling with the challenges of blending online learning into their institutions, students are increasingly preoccupied with social media, which have the capacity to change the learning paradigm much more dramatically than any technological change has made to date. As has so often been the case in the past, the new communication technologies will be incredibly disruptive but they can also be harnessed for learning and communications of unprecedented effectiveness. It will be up to institutional leaders to make sure that it is the latter, not the former, that prevails.

Our established colleges and universities will continue both to embrace and resist change. The opportunity and need for first-rate research into how institutions plan for and implement change is greater than ever.

The Critical Importance of Institutional Culture

While some aspects of research into online and distance learning in either traditional institutions or open universities are unique to the field, change-oriented leaders will ignore the broader literature on institutional culture at their peril.

In his book, *The Decentring of the Traditional University*, Francis (2010) is interested in educational research that has "started to map out and describe the ways participatory cultures support the emergence of self-directed learning activities beyond formal educational contexts" (p. 21). For him, the implications for educational policy and practice are profound as learners, not administrators, drive change. He has a very useful section on directions for further research, including learner as designer; using a variety of digital tools for creative appropriation; understanding better how individuals cultivate, nurture and mobilize globally distributed funds of living knowledge; learning through serious play in virtually figured worlds; and "development work research" helping teams become more aware of the mediated nature of their own collective activities (pp. 124–28).

There is ripe opportunity for innovative research of this sort that will be of immense value to institutional leaders in the field.

The Need to Break Down the Two Research Solitudes

It is one thing to acknowledge the research solitudes between campus-based and open universities, and quite another to redress the problem. The burgeoning interest in research on online and e-learning, especially in

America, is to be welcomed but it would be even more useful if it were more strongly based in theory.

The argument here, then, is less about what research needs to be done than how it should be dispersed and shared, so that the two solitudes recognize the lessons eachother has to offer. The litmus test would be much more cross-over writing in the various journals so that each is read by a broader cross-section of the higher education communities around the world.

As campus-based and online institutions evolve towards each other, their leaders could benefit immeasurably from the experiences, successes, and failures of each.

REFERENCES

Akbulut, Y., Kuzu, A., Latchem, C., & Odabasi, F. (2007). Change readiness among teaching staff at Anadolu University, Turkey. *Distance Education, 28*(3), 335–350.

Bates, A. W. (2000). *Managing technological change: Strategies for college and university leaders.* San Francisco, CA: Jossey-Bass.

Bates, A. W. (2010). New challenges for universities: Why the must change. In U-D. Ehlers, & D. Schneckenberg, (Eds.), *Changing cultures in higher education: Moving ahead to future learning* (pp. 15–25). Heidelberg, Germany: Springer.

Bates, A. W., & Sangrà, A. (2011). *Managing technology in higher education.* San Francisco, CA: Jossey-Bass.

Beaudoin, M. F. (2002). Distance education leadership: An essential role for the new century. *Journal of Leadership Studies, 8*(3), 131–145.

Beaudoin, M. F. (2004). *Reflections on research, faculty and leadership in distance education.* Oldenburg, Germany: Carl von Ossietzky Universität.

Bedford, L. A. (2009). The professional adjunct: An emerging trend in online instruction. *Online Journal of Distance Learning Administration, 12*(3).

Bergquist, W. H., & Pawlak, K. (2008). *Engaging the six cultures of the academy.* San Francisco, CA: Jossey-Bass.

Bissell, A. N. (2009). Permission granted: Open licensing for educational resources. *Open Learning, 24*:1 (February), 97–106.

Chaney, D., Chaney, E., & Eddy, J. (2010). The context of distance learning programs in higher education: Five enabling assumptions. *Online Journal of Distance Learning Administration, 13*(4).

Chester, T. M. (2006). A roadmap for IT leadership and the next ten years. *Educause Quarterly, 29*(2).

Chickering, A.W., & Gamson, Z. F. (1987). Seven principles for good practice in undergraduate education. *American Association of Higher Education Bulletin. 39*(7), 3–7 (online version).

Christensen, C. M., Horn, M. B., & Johnson, C. W. (2011). *Disrupting class: How disruptive innovation will change the way the world learns.* New York: McGraw-Hill.

Conrad, D. (2007). Quo vadis? Reflections on the current state of research in distance education. *Distance Education, 28*(1), 111–116.

Cowie, P., & Nichols, M. (2010). The clash of cultures: Hybrid learning course development as management of tension. *Journal of Distance Education, 24*(1), 77–90.

Davies G. (2011) General guidelines on copyright. In Davies G. (Ed.), *Information and communications technology for language teachers* (ICT4LT), Slough, UK: Thames Valley University [Online]. Retrieved from http://www.ict4lt.org/en/en_copyright. htm [Accessed 28/10/2011]

DeVary, S. (2008). National distance education trends and issues: Intellectual property. *Distance Learning, 5*(1).

Doherty, I. (2010). Agile project management for e-learning developments. *Journal of Distance Education, 24*(1), 91–106.

Dooley, K. E., Lindner, J. R., & Dooley, L. M. (2005). *Advanced methods in distance education: Applications and practices for educators, administrators and learners* (203–229). Hershey, PA: Information Science Publishing.

Francis, R. (2010). *The decentring of the traditional university: The future of (self) education in virtually figured worlds.* London, UK: Routledge.

Geist, M. (2010). *From "radical extremism" to "balanced copyright": Canadian copyright and the digital agenda.* Toronto, ON: Irwin Law.

Green, K. C. (2010, November). *Managing online education 2010.* Paper presented at the WICHE Cooperative for Educational Telecommunications (WCET) conference, La Jolla, CA. Retrieved from www.campuscomputing.net/2010-managing-online-education

Gueverra, J. (2007). Repositioning for a virtual culture. *On the Horizon, 15*(3), 139–44.

Guri-Rosenblit, S., & Gros, B. (2011). E-learning: Confusing terminology, research gaps and inherent challenges. *Journal of Distance Education, 25*(1).

Hannum, W. (2009). Moving distance education research forward. *Distance Education, 30*(1), 171–173.

Irele, M. E. (2005). Can distance education be mainstreamed? *Online Journal of Distance Learning Administration, 8*(2).

Johnson, L. (2006). Managing intellectual property for distance learning. *Educause Quarterly, 2*, 66–70.

Keaster, R. (2005). Distance education and the academic department: The change process. *Educause Quarterly, 28*(3).

Kranch, D. A. (2008). Who owns online course intellectual property? *The Quarterly Review of Distance Education, 9*(4), 349–356.

Kuboni, O. (2008). Transnational policies and local implementation: The University of the West Indies Distance Education Centre. In T. Evans, M. Haughey, & D. Murphy (Eds.), *International handbook of distance education* (pp. 686–705). Bradford, UK: Emerald.

Laurillard, D. (2008). The teacher as action researcher: Using technology to capture pedagogic form. *Studies in Higher Education, 3*(2), 139–54.

Lee, M. J. W., & McLoughlin, C. (2010). Beyond distance and time constraints: Applying social networking tools and web 2.0 approaches in distance education. In G. Veletsianos (Ed.), *Emerging technologies in distance education* (pp. 61–87). Edmonton, AB: Athabasca University Press.

Litto, F. M. (2008). Public policy and distance education in Brazil. In Evans, T., Haughey, M., & Murphy, D. (Eds.), *International handbook of distance education* (pp. 671–683). Bradford, UK: Emerald.

Lowenthal, P. R., & White, J. W. (2009). Enterprise model. In P. Rogers, G. Berg, J. Boettcher, C. Howard, L. Justice, & K. Schwenk (Eds.), *Encyclopedia of distance and online learning* (2nd ed.), (923–936). Hersey, PA: IGI Global.

Magjuka, R. J., Shi, M., & Bonk, C. J. (2005). Critical design and administrative issues in online education. *Online Journal of Distance Learning Administration, 8*(4).

Matheos, K., Rogoza, C., & Hamayil, M. (2009). Leapfrogging across generations of open and distance learning at Al-Quds Open University: A case study. *Online Journal of Distance Learning Administration, 12*(4).

McFarlane, D. (2011). The leadership role of distance learning administrators (DLAs) in increasing educational value and quality. *Online Journal of Distance Learning Administration, 14*(1).

Meyer, J. D., & Barefield, A. C. (2010). Intrastructure and administrative support for online programs. *Online Journal of Distance Learning Administration, 13*(3).

Mintzberg, H. (1989). *Mintzberg on management: Inside our strange world of organizations.* New York: Free Press.

Moore, M. G. (Ed.). (2007). *Handbook of distance education* (2nd ed.). New York: Routledge.

Nemire, R. E. (2007). Intellectual property development and use for distance education courses: A review of law, organizations, and resources for faculty. *College Teaching, 55*(1), 26–30.

Olson, J. N., & Hale, D. F. (2007). Administrators' attitudes toward web-based instruction across the UT system. *Online Journal of Distance Learning Administration, 10*(4).

Pachler, N., & Daly, C. (2011). *Key issues in e-learning: Research and practice.* London, UK: Continuum.

Panda, S. (2008). Strategic planning and distance education. In T. Evans, M. Haughey, & D. Murphy (Eds.), *International handbook of distance education* (pp. 477–98). Bradford, UK: Emerald.

Paolucci, R., & Gambescia, S. F. (2007). Current administrative structures used for online degree program offerings in higher education. *Online Journal of Distance Learning Administration, 10*(3).

Pasian, B. L. (2010). "In this issue." In *Journal of Distance Education, 24*(1), i–vi.

Paul, R. H. (2011). *Leadership under fire: The challenging role of next Canadian university president.* Montréal and Kingston: McGill-Queen's University Press.

Paul, R. H., & Brindley, J. E. (2008). New technology, new learners, and new challenges: Leading our universities in times of change. In T. Evans, M. Haughey, & D. Murphy (Eds.), *International handbook of distance education* (pp. 435–51). Bradford, UK: Emerald.

Pina, A. A. (2008). How institutionalized is distance learning? A study of institutional role, locale and academic level. *Online Journal of Distance Learning Administration, 11*(1).

Pisel, K. (2008). A strategic planning process model for distance education. *Online Journal of Distance Learning Administration, 11*(2).

Portugal, L. M. (2006). Emerging leadership roles in distance education: Current state of affairs and forecasting future trends. *Online Journal of Distance Learning Administration, 9*(3).

Puzziferro-Schnitzer, M. (2005). Managing virtual adjunct faculty: Applying the seven principles of good practice. Online Journal of Distance Learning Administration, 8(2).

Salmon, G. (2010). Learning innovation for the twenty-first century. In U-D. Ehlers & D. Schneckenberg (Eds.), *Changing cultures in higher education: Moving ahead to future learning* (pp. 27–41). New York, NY: Springer.

Schauer, J., Rockway, S. K., Fritz, S. M., & Marx, D. B. (2005). Implementing distance education: Issues impacting administration. *Online Journal of Distance Administration, 8*(3).

Schein, E. H. (2010). *Organizational culture and leadership* (4th ed.). San Francisco, CA: Jossey-Bass.

Secker, J. (2010). *Copyright and e-learning: A guide for practitioners.* London, UK: Facet.

Shuwer, R., & Janssen, B. (2011). *Towards a sustainable model for OER at Open Universiteit.* Paper presented at 2011 Open Education Conference, Park City, UT, October 27, 2011.

Shuwer, J., Janssen, B., & Mulder, F. (2012). *Towards a sustainable OER business model: A scenario study.* Paper presented at Cambridge 2012, Queen's College, Cambridge, April 17, 2012.

Sweeney, P. C. (2006). Faculty, copyright law and online course materials. *Online Journal of Distance Learning Administration, 9*(1).

Sweeney, P. (2007). Intellectual property and online courses: Policies at major research universities. *Quarterly Review of Distance Education, 8*(2), 109–25, 187–90.

Tait, A. (2008). Leadership development for distance and e-learning. In T. Evans, M. Haughey, & D. Murphy (Eds.), *International handbook of distance education* (pp. 435–51). Bradford, UK: Emerald.

Thompson, M. M. & Vidal, M. (2011). Policies, administration and management. *American Journal of Distance Education, 25*(1), 33–49.

Tipple, R. (2010). Effective leadership of online adjunct faculty. *Online Journal of Distance Learning Administration, 13*(1).

Vasser, N. (2010). Instructional design processes and traditional colleges. *Online Journal of Distance Learning Administration, 13*(4).

Vuori, T., & Gururajan, R. (2002). Impact of copyright laws on the flexible delivery of university education. Paper presented at 2002 Conference on Instructional Technology and Universities in Asia (ITUA), 3–5 April, Thailand. Retrieved from www.stc.arts.chula.ac.th/ITUA/Papers_for_ITUA_Proceedings/Timocopyright4

Wallace, L. (2010). Online teaching and university policy: Investigating the disconnect. *Journal of Distance Education, 22*(1), 87–100.

Wallace, L., & Young, J. (2010). Implementing blended learning: Policy implications for universities. *Online Journal of Distance Learning Administration, 13*(4).

Walsh, T. (2011). *Unlocking the gates: How and why leading universities are opening up access to their courses.* Princeton, NJ: Princeton University Press.

Ward, M-H., West, S., Peat, M., & Atkinson, S. (2010). Making it real: Project management strategic e-learning development processes in a large, campus-based university. *Journal of Distance Education, 24*(1), 21–42.

Wasyluk, O. and Berge, Z.L. (2007). Leadership influence on corporate change involving distance training. *Online Journal of Distance Learning Administration, 10*(1).

Zawacki-Richter, O., Bäcker, E.M., and Vogt, S. (2009). Review of distance education research (2000 to 2008): Analysis of research areas, methods, and authorship patterns. *The International Review of Research in Open and Distance Learning, 10*(6), 21–50.

The Costs and Economics of Online Distance Education

7

Greville Rumble

Education, is and has always been, an economic activity. The provision of education consumes resources—not only financial (the cost of schools and the facilities they house), but, above all, in the form of the labour involved in transmitting knowledge, skills, and understandings to each generation of learners. In addition, learners incur certain opportunity costs: they spend both time and money on education. Moreover, while education has traditionally been viewed as a good in itself, it has increasingly come to be understood as an investment in the future productivity of those receiving the education, as measured by the value of the work they do for their employers, as well as the remuneration they receive over the course of their lives, and the taxes they contribute to the state. Behind the costs and benefits of education lie a complex web of choices that are determined, at least in the minds of economists, by answers to such questions as: How much will the provision of education cost? What financial benefits accrue to those who spend money on education? How good a rate of return does education offer in comparison to other forms of investment? Are there ways of reducing the cost of provision, so that the same education can be delivered less expensively? Is there a basic level of entitlement to education the cost of which should be met by the state? How should people and society pay for education—through general taxation, or out of their own pockets? Should payment be deferred through state loans?

The economics of education emerged as a distinct field of study in the late 1950s and early 1960s with the publication in the UK of work by Vaizey (1958) and Wiseman (1959) and with the delivery in 1960 of Theodore Schultz's lecture (Schultz, 1961) to the American Economic Association on investment on human capital (Johnes, 1993). Vaizey focussed on the costs and funding of public and private education in the United Kingdom; Schultz paved the way for the development of human capital theory which lead to Becker's seminal work on human capital (Becker, 1964). Becker's work was extended by Psacharopoulos, who looked at the rates of return on education at primary, secondary, and post-secondary education levels across 78 countries (Psacharopoulos, 1994), work that was subsequently updated by Psacharopoulos and Patrinos (2004). This analysis led the World Bank to conclude that in many countries public spending on education was being misallocated in view of the evidence "derived from the effect of schooling on earnings and productivity, that in many countries the average dollar invested in primary education returns twice as much as one invested in higher education" (World Bank, 1986, p. 1). Such thinking led to specific recommendations to favour expenditures on primary education (World Bank, 1988, 1995) and influenced the thinking behind the 1990 Jomtien Conference on Education for All.

Meanwhile, other work looked at the extent to which the level of education within a population is related to rates of economic growth (Blaug, 1972; Stevens & Weale, 2004) and at the social benefits to be derived from investment in higher education (Task Force, 2000; World Bank, 2002). While such studies initially supported the case for public investment in education, the trend in recent years has been to argue that because students pursuing post-secondary education directly benefit from it through a higher earnings capacity, they should be responsible for a greater share of the cost of such education (see for example, Johnstone, 1986; UKDES, 1988; World Bank, 1986; Wran Committee, 1988). How such cost-sharing should be accomplished—options include higher up-front fees, higher fees coupled with increased bursaries for the disadvantaged, repayable loans, income-contingent repayable loans, and graduate taxes—has occasioned much debates, as have questions concerning how to protect the interests of disadvantaged students (e.g., Woodhall, 2006), how to ensure the viability of loan schemes, and how appropriate such schemes are in countries with underdeveloped administrative systems (e.g., Barr & Crawford, 2005; Chapman 2005; Chapman & Ryan, 2002; Ziderman & Albrecht, 1995).

WHY DID THE ECONOMICS OF EDUCATION BECOME AN IMPORTANT FIELD OF INQUIRY?

Interest in the economics of education developed in an environment in which the demand for education was increasing as individuals recognized that education was a passport both to a job (the more educated one is the less likely one is to be unemployed) and to a higher level of earnings (the more educated one is, the more one is likely to earn). These private benefits sit alongside public benefits—in particular the belief held by many that an educated labour force is one of the engines of national economic growth. This latter point led governments and development agencies to see spending on education as an investment in achieving and maintaining national prosperity. In addition, in the aftermath of World War II there was an increased emphasis on social justice and equality of opportunity in many countries—with the expectation that those who had at an earlier age been denied educational opportunities would now be given a chance to access education.

In response to these pressures two things happened. Firstly, the age at which compulsory initial education ended was raised throughout the developed and developing world. The pressure has been to move from universal primary education (roughly 6 years of schooling), through universal basic education (9 years), towards universal secondary education (13 years of schooling). Second, the rate of participation in education beyond that which is compulsory has increased at both secondary and tertiary levels. In higher education, the trend has been away from the provision of education to an elite (up to 15% of the relevant age group) towards mass education (participation by anywhere from 16% to 50% of the group) and ultimately to "universal" access (defined as participation by more than 50% of the group) (Trow, 1974; see also Trow, 2006). As a result, the proportion of those being educated has risen at the same time that a massive increase in population has occurred, which has seen the mid-year world population grow from 2.56 billion in 1950 to 3.04 billion in 1960 to 6.96 billion in 2011 (US Census Bureau, 2012). The global education sector is consequently huge and continuing to grow as the world population moves towards a projected 9.38

billion in 2050, according to the US Census Bureau (2012), which presages yet further growth in the sector.

THE COSTS OF EDUCATIONAL PROVISION

Traditional education is a labour intensive business. With expansion, the public sector's ability to pay for education has been severely tested, and as a result the financing of education has become a major public policy issue. Generally, governments look for ways of reducing or at least containing costs. One strategy is to pass some or all of the cost on to the consumer—so-called cost-sharing. This approach has been especially popular at the post-secondary level but has also been advocated in connection with secondary and, particularly, upper secondary education. Another strategy is to reduce the unit cost of education. Within traditional classroom-based institutions of higher education, in particular, efforts to reduce unit costs have included:

- A move away from an overly simplistic reliance on increasing the student-staff ratio to a more sophisticated costing model that unpacks the relationship between staffing levels, class hours, and student numbers, thus making the specific cost drivers more transparent (Sheehan & Gulko, 1976)

- A shift from teaching models based on dialogue within small groups to large-scale lectures, in some cases using closed-circuit television to narrowcast the lectures into overflow classrooms (a technique taken to its logical conclusion in the Central Broadcasting and Television University in China);

- Reducing staff hours through a greater degree of independent, resource-based learning—an approach that ties in well with media-intensive distance teaching methods;

- Reducing the faculty costs by hiring cheaper adjunct staff who work on service contracts;

- Most recently, a greater reliance on peer-supported learning, in place of direct teacher-student interaction (see, for example, Daniel, Kanwar, & Uvalić-Trumbić, 2008).

The search for more cost-efficient methods has also extended to secondary education where there is a much greater interest in independent, resource-based learning.

For many years distance education, in its earliest technological guise of correspondence education, had been provided by commercial correspondence schools where the prime motivations were, with a few exceptions, to make a profit from fees by maximizing enrolments and minimizing costs; by governments providing an alternative form of public schooling to isolated rural populations (where cost was not the major concern); and by universities wanting to meet the needs of individuals who were unable to attend a campus full-time. Provided that such ventures were relatively cheap or—within the commercial and university sectors—covered their costs, there was no systematic exploration of their costs.

Then, beginning in 1975, in response to the paucity of cost studies available (Klees, Orivel, & Wells, 1977), and given the high absolute costs of the large-scale educational television (ETV) projects, UNESCO led the way in promoting both the discussion of methods of cost analysis for new educational media, and the dissemination of cost studies (see Eicher, Hawkridge, McAnany, Mariet, & Orivel, 1982; Jamison, 1977; Jamison, Klees, & Wells, 1978; UNESCO, 1977; UNESCO, 1978; Wagner, 1982). These studies not only established a methodology for analyzing the costs of media-based educational systems, but also saw the development of cost functions that described in broad terms the way in which the costs of such systems would behave given changes in the breadth of the curriculum offered by, and in the number of students enrolled on, particular projects. In parallel, and using a somewhat different approach, a group of researchers began to look at the costs of the British Open University (OUUK) where the escalating absolute costs of the project, and the apparently open-ended nature of the commitment to the project, were beginning to raise concerns within its funding body (Laidlaw & Layard, 1974; Smith, 1975; Wagner, 1972; Wagner, 1977). These studies, along with others undertaken between the mid-1970s and early 1980s (for example, Oliveira & Rumble, 1992; Perraton, 1982; Perraton,

1993), showed that distance education could bring the average cost per full-time equivalent (FTE) student/learner and/or per hour of instruction down to a unit cost that was lower than that achieved in traditional face-to-face educational settings. As a result, the application of mass communications technology and distance learning approaches came to be seen as a way of lowering the unit costs of education (Eicher, Hawkridge, McAnany, Mariet, & Orivel, 1982, p. 40; Jamison, Suppes, & Wells, 1974, p. 57;).

By the early 1980s, education economists understood the cost elements involved in technology-intensive educational projects, the cost structure of such projects (Jamison, Klees, & Wells, 1978; Wagner, 1977), as well as the fundamental difference between the cost structure of face-to-face teaching (low fixed costs, high variable costs, apparently limited scope for economies of scale within a model based on teacher–student interaction) and distance education (high fixed costs, low variable costs, very considerable scope for economies of scale arising from the mass use of pre-prepared learning materials coupled with no or little face-to-face support). The factors affecting costs also became clearer over time. These include the following:

- the number of learners or students enrolled (which affects both the absolute costs and the degree to which economies of scale can be achieved)

- the relative degree to which a course relies on materials prepared by the instructor specifically for use in the course, in contrast to preexisting materials (such as books available through libraries) and/or assignments that do not require the use of materials

- the number of courses on offer (the more courses the greater the volume of learning materials needed)

- the number of years that courses once designed are presented, and hence the frequency with which materials have to be remade or replaced

- the technology used. Each technology has its own cost structure—basically the mix of variable and fixed costs, and the nature of the cost drivers underlying the variable costs (see Bates, 1995; Hülsmann, 2000).

- the local cost of technology. Institutions that rely on imported technology paid for in foreign exchange may find that the cost per learner per hour of such technology is greater than the corresponding cost per learner per hour of face-to-face teaching, particularly in countries where labour is cheap. In countries where labour costs are high, the reverse may be the case, with the cost per learner per hour of a given technology being less than the labour costs of classroom teaching (Orivel, 2000).

- the level of student support provided by the institution (for example, tuition however offered, assignment marking), as opposed to unpaid peer support arranged between students
- the organizational structure (including the extent to which technologies and services are supported from within the institution, or bought-in from external suppliers)
- working practices (for example, whether course material writers are expected to do their own editing, or whether all texts are edited professionally)
- the nature of the internal labour market and the nature of the contracts of employment (and particularly the difference between contracts of service where staff are paid a salary or wage to do a particular job full- or part-time, and contracts for service where free-lance contractors are paid an agreed amount to do a particular task such as write a course book, edit a text, take a tutorial, or mark a script).

By the mid-1990s, the major lessons had been learned—at least with respect to the technologies then in use. However, there were some fundamental weaknesses behind the research (Rumble, 1998). Firstly, cost studies were based on data derived from standard approaches to cost accounting developed in the early 1900s. These did not accurately link overhead costs back to specific products, services, and activities (Johnson & Kaplan, 1987). Indeed, few distance-teaching institutions bothered to allocate teaching and support staff costs to courses, with the result that the costs of courses using differing mixes of technologies could not be established with any degree of accuracy. This failure was also true of dual-mode institutions (Rumble, 2012). Only with the development of activity-based costing around spreadsheets has it become possible to move beyond simplistic cost functions to identify cost drivers and track costs more closely to the activities (products, services, customers, business sustaining activities) that give rise to those costs (Rumble, 2012).

In the absence of activity-based costing, those working in the field relied on a broad brush approach to analyze the behaviour of fixed and variable costs. Smith (1975) and Wagner (1977), for example, assigned Open University costs to just three drivers: overheads (deemed to be fixed), courses, and students. Similarly, broad brush approaches were used to model the costs of ETV projects (Jamison, Klees, & Wells, 1978). The cost functions developed to model costs thus failed to identify "the fundamental variables, which affect costs, in sufficient detail to be of practical value to people who are trying to prepare an operating budget for an institution" (Rumble, Neil, & Tout, 1981, p. 235).

EARLY RESEARCH FINDINGS AND THEIR LIMITATIONS

Research in the 1970s and 1980s showed that the unit cost per student of teaching at a distance could be significantly less than that of face-to-face education but this was by no means always the case. Sometimes the unit cost of a distance education system was higher. Also, the tendency for distance education systems to have higher dropout rates meant that the same level of cost advantage was not carried through to comparisons in the cost per graduate (Rumble, 1997). However, these findings were all too often based on an analysis of operating costs alone, with the capital costs of projects being ignored. This was a fundamental weakness. So at best it was only possible to conclude with Perraton (1993) that in the *right* circumstances distance education might be cheaper than face-to-face education.

There was also an assumption that the cost structures of both types of institutions were optimized. Mace (1978), for example, queried the extent to which OUUK was internally cost-efficient. Could not, he asked, the same output be achieved at less cost? Was broadcasting, a hugely expensive element of the OU's costs at that time, really necessary to OU's teaching system? There was enormous reluctance to answer such questions at the time.

The 1980s and 1990s also saw significant budgetary cuts in traditional universities as higher education systems shifted from elite to mass coverage. Unit costs fell as student enrolments increased without a proportionate increase in staff numbers, student class hours were reduced, and the use of cheaper adjunct staff on contracts for service proliferated. Budgets continued to shrink during the following decade, even as institutions of higher education moved in the direction of universal coverage. Moreover, the concomitant shift to teacher-moderated e-learning may actually have increased the costs in distance education by introducing a more labour-intensive form of teaching. The problem with these changes is that we do not know what affect they have had on the relative costs of distance and face-to-face teaching because the comparative cost studies are not being done.

There have also been changes in the cost of technologies: technology costs are relatively high when a technology is at an early stage of development but fall as the technology and the industry around it develops. When an institution adopts a technology at an early stage in its development, it may well have to provide its students with equipment to run the technology—as the OUUK did when it first experimented with computer-mediated communication within a course. What it gained was interaction—at a cost (Rumble, 1989). Once a technology becomes embedded in a society, one can assume that almost all students will have access to it at which point it is reasonable to expect the students to equip themselves with the technology so that they can participate in the learning. But while this may be reasonable in a rich country, it may not be so in a poor country.

In spite of all these caveats, in the 1990s it was possible to say that the costs and economics of distance education were relatively well-understood. It was clear that the cost structure of distance education differed significantly with that of face-to-face education, and that whatever the caveats about the quality and range of the cost studies available, distance education systems had the potential to be cheaper per equivalent student and per hour of instruction than traditional forms of education.

In conjunction with the work discussed above, some research has been conducted on the relative cost-effectiveness of distance education but most of this work has assumed, without any objective foundation for the assumption, that the quality of a graduate produced by distance education is the same as that of a comparable graduate from a face-to-face setting. An exception to this was provided by those studies that compared the performance of distance- and face-to-face-taught students sitting exactly the same examinations (see Rumble, 1997, for a summary of studies), and by studies that have sought to compare the post-qualification performance in similar jobs of persons whose training was undertaken by different means (Nielsen & Tatto, 1993).

Although the basic cost structure had been mapped by 1980, the models used to explicate the costs were both crude and subject to serious caveats, and they tended to be based on an idealized either/or distinction: either one was dealing with a pure distance education system, or one was dealing with a classroom-based system. Yet in practice few institutional models were like this (Rumble, 1998). The OUUK had always incorporated some face-to-face teaching at tutorial centres and summer school. By the 1990s, however, it was not unusual to meet Open University students who thought that they got more face-to-face teaching within the distance-teaching Open University than they did in campus-based UK universities, where students were increasingly expected to study independently. By then, too, blended learning approaches were beginning to erode the old distinctions.

RESEARCH INTO THE COSTS AND ECONOMICS OF ONLINE LEARNING

The effective and widespread use of computer-assisted instruction emerged in distance education following the development of personal computers (PCs); the replacement of analogue by digital technologies followed by the digitalization of text, audio, and video; and the linking of PCs through the Internet. The first two developments allowed distance education systems to create and distribute educational software supporting a variety of Computer Assisted Instruction (CAI) or Computer-Based Teaching (CBT) programs of increasing sophistication—enabling computer-mediated teacher-student communication and interaction among students.

Within this context what constitutes online learning varies enormously. Typologies have their dangers, but they can also be useful in sorting out one's thinking. The following typology was offered by Hülsmann (2004) based on ideas put forward by Rumble (2001a):

a. Type-i models of e-education offer internally developed *information* resources involving text, audio, and video in electronic format. No student support is involved.

b. Type-c models of e-education offer *computer-mediated communications* (CMC) supporting tutor–student and student–student interaction around course structures and pre-existing learning materials that involve minimal cost. Interactive support may be offered in synchronous (Type-c1) or asynchronous mode (Type-c2).

c. Type-i/c systems, which combine both approaches.

The cost elements of online learning have been explored (see Rumble, 2001b). There have been a number of studies of the costs of Type-i systems, all of which demonstrate the very wide spread of costs depending on the nature of the actual materials developed (e.g., Arizona Learning Systems, 1998). Simple web pages with a course outline and linked webliography/bibliography can be provided at very little cost. However, a virtual reality environment within which students can immerse themselves is very costly indeed. The very range of costs makes any generalization difficult, and in fact most online systems actually conform to Type-c2 systems with students accessing publicly available text, audio, and video resources electronically through webliographies, digitalized course "libraries," and their own research. Here again, there are few detailed cost studies of particular systems (a notable exception being Hülsmann, 2003). The cost structure of such systems is much closer to face-to-face education than it is to mass-media distance education programs although there is in fact considerable evidence that academic staff spend more time teaching online courses than face-to-face courses (Rumble, 2001a; Seaman, 2009; McCarthy & Samors, 2009).

In response to this situation, Neely & Tucker (2010, p. 20) have argued that "college decision makers need to consider the full range of cost implications associated with . . . online offerings" (and, by extension, with other types of distance programs). Managers who wish to contain the costs of online learning will therefore encourage independent (non-supported) and peer-supported learning (see, for example, Daniel, Kanwar, & Uvalić-Trumbić, 2008) from open source materials (such as, MIT's OpenCourseware, the OUUK OpenLearn projects, and the Commonwealth of Learning's WikiEducator program).

As with the earlier generation of cost studies, there are relatively few well-founded cost studies available, and even where they exist the complex mix of cost elements and cost drivers in a single program make it difficult to transfer lessons from one system to another. This is especially so where the aim is to transfer a socio-technological mix involving technologies that attract developed country price levels into a developing country where the costs of imported technologies are high and labour costs low (Orivel, 2000). In this connection it is worth bearing in mind that, while in developed societies access to the Internet is increasingly taken to be the norm (although even here there may be disparities between rich and poor, old and young, and members of different ethnic groups), in developing countries the situation may be very different. In a book biased towards the use of ICTs in Asian distance education, Latchem and Jung (2010) admit that "for reasons of cost, access, and equity, most ODL institutions *still* make *extensive* use of the traditional technologies dating back to the days of correspondence education" and that "audiovisual media, radio and TV" remain valuable especially where literacy is low. In addition, they note that "*wherever possible*, ODL providers also employ face-to-face teaching and learning" (2010, pp. 1–2 , my emphasis).

There is, as Unwin et al. (2010) comment in respect of a survey of the use of learning management systems (LMS) in Africa, an enormous gap between rhetoric and reality on the ground. The fact is that in poor countries, many of the students who would most benefit from access to e-learning simply cannot afford it.

THE RESEARCH AGENDA

From what has been said it should be clear that there is now a reasonably solid understanding of the *cost elements* involved in distance and online education and in the way in which such costs can be influenced. But against this, there are very few comparative studies that allow one to say with any degree of certainty what the cost implications of a particular socio-technological design will be. There is also almost no understanding of the private and social benefits of distance and online education in comparison with those of face-to-face education, nor has any consideration been given to the way in which the costs of providing such education should be met in different contexts. The need to look more seriously at the relationship between the costs of distance and online education, and the price charged to accessing such education, has been raised by Rumble (1997) and Rumble and Litto (2005). Where prices go up, standard economic theory suggests that willingness to pay will be reflected in a demand curve for the product, and that if or when the price is increased the level of demand will change (elasticity of demand).

When first set up, the OUUK—while always believing that students should pay something towards their course—kept course fees as low as it could in order to ensure that the University was accessible to even the poorest of students. In response to this, the government, which met most of the cost of studying at the University, fixed a maximum quota on the number of students admitted each year in order to limit its financial exposure. The result was that levels of frustrated demand increased. In the 1990s, however, the University agreed to raise its fees in order to remove its waiting list, while introducing a greatly increased bursary scheme for those students who were financially disadvantaged. More recently, the UK government has changed the way in which higher education is funded in England (although conditions in Scotland, Wales, and Northern Ireland where national assemblies and parliaments have devolved powers are different). For Open University students resident in England, the modular tuition fees rose from roughly £ 1,300 per full-time, full-year equivalent study in 2010–2011 (Rogers, 2010) to £ 5,000 in September 2012 (Open University, 2011a). It has yet to be seen how this will affect the University's market, particularly in England, where the fee for the Science entry-level course rose to £2,500 in October 2012 (although it remained just £735 in Scotland, where Scottish students are still subsidized).

More generally, the entry costs of study can be considerable, particularly where students have to equip themselves with computers and printers, fund their own access to the Internet, and buy learning materials and study consumables. Latchem and Jung's comment referenced above then becomes an important consideration (Latchem & Jung, 2010). Policy makers and providers need to take into account the extent to which target audiences can afford to meet the costs of study when designing institutions and pricing courses (Rumble & Litto, 2005).

What students are prepared to pay may, of course, depend on the benefits that they think they will attain in terms of employment, pay, and future job security. No research has been done here comparing the private and social costs and benefits of distance and online education on the one hand, and face-to-face education on the other. The OUUK carried out some surveys that consistently showed that Open University graduates felt that their studies had benefited them, with nearly half of Open University graduates reporting some kind of occupational benefit (Woodley, 1995), while an early study by Lee, Futagami, and Braithwaite (1982) calculated that the private rate of return to students of the Korean Air Correspondence High School was about 27%, compared with about 10% for those attending a regular high school.

One of the benefits enjoyed by OUUK students is that the flexible nature of distance study allowed them to study while they remained in employment. In 2009–2010 over 70% of Open University students were employed full-time (Open University, 2011b). But the expansion of part-time higher education in the UK (where full-time study was once the norm) means that this is no longer an advantage available mainly to Open University students. In other societies more used to the concept of students working their way through college, such an advantage would be less apparent. Another factor is the age of individuals when they graduate.

In the early years of Open University almost all students were over the age of 21, whereas those entering the traditional universities were predominantly school leavers. Mace (1978) found that in 1975 Open University graduates were on average 37 years old as compared to an average age of 22 for graduates of traditional universities. Assuming retirement at age 65 this meant that they had a working life of about 28 years to enjoy any earnings' boost they derived from their studies, compared with some 43 years for traditional graduates. By age 37, too, their careers were more likely to be mapped out, with powerful institutional forces within the labour market that would inhibit mobility. This led Mace to conclude that the economic value of an open university degree would necessarily be less than that of a degree from a traditional college. However, although the average age of new undergraduate students at the Open University is 32 (Open University, 2011b), even before the sharp rise in the cost of university study, Murray (2010) reported that some 25% of new Open University students are aged 17 to 25 (up from 15% in 2009–2010 (Open University, 2011b). Many of these young students aim to complete their studies rapidly—they could graduate within three years, a rate equivalent to full-time study. With many universities in the UK charging the maximum tuition fee, students are allowed to levy GBP 9,000 per annum (the average fee is GBP 8,678, according to Shepherd & Vasagar, 2011), the financial attraction for students resident in England wishing to study in the OUUK is significant.

Against this, there is the related question of the credentialing power of distance teaching compared with face-to-face universities. In the mid-1970s Carnoy and Levin (1975) argued that "to assume the value of an Open University degree will be similar to one from Oxbridge [i.e., Oxford or Cambridge] or the 'Red bricks' [the large civic universities founded in the 19th and early 20th centuries, such as the universities of Birmingham, Manchester, and Leeds] . . . simply ignores the credentialing effect of higher education institutions." An Open University's graduate, they argued, "is not likely to receive either consumption or income benefits from his education that are as high as those of a person from the more conventional university setting" (pp. 390–96).

No doubt further case studies on the costs of particular institutions and technology applications would be useful—especially if they also look at the capital as well as the operating costs of such systems. It would also be interesting to see detailed studies, comparable to Laidlaw and Layard (1974), looking at the relative costs of distance, online, and face-to-face courses. Such studies, which could usefully be conducted across a number of national educational systems, are much needed given the changes in technology costs and the very considerable efficiencies that have been achieved in both distance and face-to-face provision. Given the interest in using distance and online education to expand the provision of places at secondary as well as at higher education level, it would be important for the studies to look at the costs of open schooling (Daniel, 2010) as well as at the costs of distance higher education. With so many institutions now engaged in various blended learning approaches, it would be important for such studies to unpack institutional costs at course level (see Rumble 2012 for an example of the methodological approach that needs to be adopted). More specifically, there is also a need for further studies on the way in which online education impacts on teacher time.

However, valuable though such studies might be, they pale in significance in relation to some of the wider issues that need to be researched. There is very considerable scope for a series of studies to look at the private rates of return of distance and online education, relative to the rates achieved by students who have studied by traditional means. Such studies should also look at the credentialing power of various approaches to learning, and in particular seek to unpack whether what is really important is not so much what one learns and where one learns, but who one gets to know in the process. Within this context, and against the background of the recent research by Brown, Lauder and Ashton (2011) that highlights the global production of graduates destined for high-skill, low-paid jobs, the role of technology in education may well be to bring down the costs of upper secondary and higher education so that the costs that fall on the individual and the state are more commensurate with the earnings and benefits open to an increasingly impoverished middle class.

REFERENCES

Arizona Learning Systems. (1998). Preliminary cost methodology for distance learning. Phoenix, AZ: Arizona Learning Systems and the State Board of Directors for Community Colleges of Arizona.

Barr, N., & Crawford, I. (2005). *Financing higher education: Answers from the UK.* London, UK: Routledge. Retrieved from http://public.eblib.com/EBLPublic/ PublicView.do?ptiID=199511

Bates, T. (1995). *Technology, open learning, and distance education.* London, UK: Routledge.

Becker, G. S. (1964). *Human capital.* New York, NY: Columbia University Press.

Blaug, M. (1972). *An introduction to the economics of education.* Harmondsworth, UK: Penguin Books.

Brown, P., Lauder, H., & Ashton, D. N. (2011). *The global auction: The broken promises of education, jobs and incomes.* New York, NY: Oxford University Press.

Carnoy, M., & Levin, H. M. (1975). Evaluation of educational media: Some issues. *Instructional Science, 4*(2), 385–406.

Chapman, B. (2005). *Income contingent loans for higher education: International reform. (Discussion Paper No. 491).* Acton, AU: Australian National University, Centre for Economic Policy Research. Retrieved from http://econrsss.anu.edu.au/ pdf/DP491.pdf

Chapman, B., & Ryan, C. (2002). Income-contingent financing of student charges for higher education: Assessing the Australian innovation. *The Welsh Journal of Education, 11*(1), 64–81.

Daniel, J., Kanwar, A., & Uvalić-Trumbić, S. (2008). The right to education: A model for making higher education equally accessible to all on the basis of merit. *Asian Journal of Distance Education, 6*(2), 5–11.

Daniel, J. S. (2010). *Mega-schools, technology, and teachers: Achieving education for all.* New York, NY: Routledge.

Eicher, J.-C., Hawkridge, D., McAnany, E., Mariet, F., & Orivel, F. (1982). *The economics of the new educational media, Vol. 3: Cost and effectiveness overview and synthesis.* Paris: UNESCO.

Hülsmann, T. (2000). *The costs of open learning: A handbook.* Oldenburg, Germany: Bibliotheks-und Informationssystem der Carl von Ossietsky Universität Oldenburg.

Hülsmann, T. (2003). Costs without camouflage: A cost-analysis of Oldenburg University's two graduate certificate programs offered as part of the online Master of Distance Education (MDE): A case study. In U. Bernath & E. Rubin, (Eds.), *Reflections on teaching and learning in an online program: A case study.* Oldenburg, Germany: Bibliothecks-und Informationssystem der Carl von Ossietsky Universität Oldenburg.

Hülsmann, T. (2004). Low cost distance education strategies: The use of appropriate information and communication technologies. *International Review of Research in Open and Distance Learning, 5*(1), 1–14.

Jamison, D. T. (1977). *Cost factors in planning educational technology systems.* Paris: UNESCO.

Jamison, D. T., Klees, S. J., & Wells, S. J. (1978). *The costs of educational media: Guidelines for planning and evaluation.* Beverly Hills, CA: Sage.

Jamison, D. T., Suppes, P., & Wells, S. (1974). The effectiveness of alternative media: A survey. *Review of Educational Research, 44*(1), 1–67.

Johnes, G. (1993). *The economics of education.* Basingstoke, UK: Macmillan.

Johnson, H. T., & Kaplan, R. S. (1991). *Relevance lost: The rise and fall of management accounting.* Boston, MA: Harvard Business School Press.

Johnstone, D. B. (1986). *Sharing the costs of higher education: Student financial assistance in the United Kingdom, the Federal Republic of Germany, France, Sweden, and the United States.* New York: College Entrance Examination Board.

Klees, S., Orivel, F., & Wells S. (1977). *Economic analysis of educational media. Final report of the Washington Conference.* Paris/Washington: UNESCO, US AID, ICEM, EDUTEL.

Laidlaw, B., & Layard, R. (1974). Traditional versus open university teaching methods: A cost comparison. *Higher Education, 3*(4), 439–68.

Latchem, C. R., & Jung, I. (2010). *Distance and blended learning: Opening up Asian education and training.* Abingdon, UK: Routledge.

Lee, K., Futagami, S., & Braithwaite, B. (1982). The Korean air-correspondence high school. In H. Perraton (Ed.), *Alternative routes to formal education: Distance teaching for school equivalency.* Baltimore, MD: John Hopkins University Press.

Mace, J. (1978). Mythology in the making: Is the open university really cost-effective? *Higher Education, 7*(3), 295–309.

McCarthy, S. A., & Samors, R. J. (2009). *Online learning as a strategic asset. Vol. 1: A resource for campus leaders.* Association of Public and Land-Grant Universities. Retrieved January, 2011, from http://www.aplu.org/NetCommunity/Document. Doc?id=1877

Murray, J. (2010). Young students flock to the OU. *The Guardian.* Retrieved September 6, 2011, from http://www.guardian.co.uk/education/2010/jun/29/open-university-young-students

Neely, P. W., & Tucker, J. P. (2010). Unbundling faculty roles in online distance education programs. *International Review of Research in Open and Distance Learning, 11*(2), 20–32.

Nielsen, H. D., & Tatto, M. T. (1993). Teacher upgrading in Sri Lanka and Indonesia. In H. Perraton (Ed.), *Distance education for teacher training.* London. Routledge.

OECD. (2011). Education at a Glance 2011: OECD Indicators. OECD Publishing. Retrieved from http://www.oecd.org/dataoecd/61/2/48631582.pdf

Oliveira, J. B., & Rumble, G. (Eds.). (1992). E*ducación a distancia en América Latina: Análisis de costo-efectividad.* Washington, D.C.: World Bank.

Open University. (2011a). *Fees 2012.* Retrieved from http://www8.open.ac.uk/study/explained/fees-2012/new-to-study

Open University. (2011b). *Facts and figures 2009/2010*. Retrieved from http://www8.
open.ac.uk/about/main/the-ou-explained/facts-and-figures and http://www.
open.ac.uk/about/documents/about-facts-figures-0910.pdf

Orivel, F. (2000). Finance, costs and economics. In J. Bradley & C. Yates (Eds.), *Basic
education at a distance*, 2. London; New York: Routledge/Falmer.

Perraton, H. D. (1984). *Alternative routes to formal education: Distance teaching for
school equivalency*. Baltimore, MD: Johns Hopkins University Press.

Perraton, H. D. (1993). *Distance education for teacher training*. London: Routledge.

Psacharopoulos, G. (1994). Returns to education: A global update. *World Development*,
22(9), 1325–43.

Psacharopoulos, G., & Patrinos, H. A. (2004). Returns to investment in education: A
further update. *Education Economics*, 12(2), 111–34.

Rogers, S. (2010). Tuition fees 2010/11: find out how much each university charges.
The Guardian. Retrieved September 5, 2010, from http://guardian.co.uk/news/
datablog/2010/oct/12/tuition-fees-universities

Rumble, G. (1989). On-line costs: Interactivity at a price. In R. Mason & A. Kaye
(Eds.), *Mindweave: Communication, computers, and distance education*. Oxford:
Pergamon Press.

Rumble, G. (1997). *The costs and economics of open and distance learning*. London:
Kogan Page.

Rumble, G. (1998). *The costs and economics of open and distance learning:
Methodological and policy issues*. Vol. 1. Thesis submitted for the Degree of Doctor
of Philosophy by Published Work. Milton Keynes: Open University.

Rumble, G. (2001a). "The costs of providing online student services", in Student
Services. In The Open University (Ed.), *Student services at the UK Open University:
Papers and debates on the economics and costs of distance education and
e-learning*, (pp. 72–82). Paper presented to the 20th World Conference of the
International Council for Open and Distance Education, Düsseldorf, Germany.

Rumble, G. (2001b). The costs and costing of networked learning. Journal of
Asynchronous Learning Networks, 5(2), 75–96.

Rumble, G. (2012). Financial management of distance learning in dual mode
institutions. *Open Learning*, 27(1), 37–51.

Rumble, G., & Litto, F. (2005). Approaches to funding. In C. McIntosh (Ed.),
Perspectives on distance education: Lifelong learning and distance education.
Vancouver and Paris: Commonwealth of Learning and UNESCO.

Rumble, G., Neil, M., & Tout A. (1981). Budgetary and resource forecasting. In A. Kaye
& G. Rumble (Eds.), *Distance teaching for higher and adult education*. London:
Croom Helm, Open University Press.

Schultz, T. (1961). Investment in human capital. *American Economic Review*, 51, 1–17.

Seaman, J. (2009). *Online learning as a strategic asset, Vol. 2: The paradox of faculty
voices: Views and experiences with online learning*. Association of Public and
Land-Grant Universities. Retrieved September, 2009, from http://www.aplu.org/
NetCommunity/Document.Doc?id=1879

Sheehan, B. S., Gulko, W. W., & Mason, T. (1976). The fundamental cost model. *New directions for institutional research: Assessing computer-based systems models.* San Francisco: Jossey-Bass.

Shepherd, J., & Vasagar, J. (2011). Tuition fees reach £8,678.36 average among universities posting price lists. *The Guardian.* Retrieved September 6, 2011, from http://www.guardian.co.uk/education/2011/apr/18/tuition-fees-universities-maximum-charge

Smith, R. C. (1975). A proposed formula for Open University expenditure in a plateau situation. Internal paper, June. In *Review of academic staff working group: Report of a group to Department of Education and Science and to the Council of the Open University.* Milton Keynes, UK: Open University.

Stevens, P., & Weale, M. (2004). Education and economic growth. In Geraint Johnes & J. Johnes (Eds.), *International handbook on the economics of education.* Cheltenham, UK; Northampton, MA: Edward Elgar.

The Task Force on Higher Education and Society. (2000). *Higher education in developing countries: Peril and promise.* Washington, DC: World Bank.

Trow, M. (1974). Problems in the transition from elite to mass higher education. *Policies for Higher Education* (pp. 55–101). Presented at the General Report on the Conference on Future Structures of Post-Secondary Education, Paris: OECD. Retrieved from http://cshe.berkeley.edu/publications/docs/PP.Trow.MassHE.1.00.pdf

Trow, M. (2006). Reflections on the transition from elite to mass to universal access: Forms and phases of higher education. In J. Forest & P. Altbach (Eds.), *International handbook of higher education* (pp. 243-80). New York: Springer.

UK Department of Education and Science. (1988). *Top-up loans for students.* London: H.M.S.O.

UNESCO. (1977). *The economics of new educational media.* Paris: UNESCO.

UNESCO. (1980). *The economics of new educational media. Volume 2: Cost and effectiveness.* Paris: UNESCO.

Unwin, T., Kleessen, B., Hollow, D., Williams, J. B., Oloo, L. M., Alwala, J., Mutimucuio, I., Eduardo, F., & Muianga, X. (2010, 21 Jan.). Digital learning management systems in Africa: Myths and realities. *Open Learning, 25*(1), 5–23.

US Census Bureau. (n.d.). Total midyear population for the world, 1950–2050. Retrieved September 25, 2012, from http://www.census.gov/ipc/www/idb/worldpop.php

Vaizey, J. (1958). *The costs of education.* London, UK: Allen & Unwin.

Wagner, L. (1959). The economics of education. *Scottish Journal of Political Economy, 6,* 48–58.

Wagner, L. (1972). The economics of the Open University. *Higher Education, 1*(2), 159–83.

Wagner, L. (1977). The economics of the Open University revisited. *Higher Education, 6*(3), 359–81.

Wagner, L. (1982). *The economics of educational media.* London, UK: Macmillan.

Woodhall, M. (2006). Financing higher education: The role of tuition fees and student support. In *Higher education in the world 2006: The financing of universities* (pp. 122–30). Basingstoke and New York: Palgrave Macmillan and GUNI.

Woodley, A. (1995). The experience of older graduates from the British Open University. *International Journal of University Adult Education, 34*(1), 37–48.

World Bank. (1986). *Financing education in developing countries: An exploration of policy options.* Washington D.C.: World Bank.

World Bank. (1988). *Education in Sub-Saharan Africa: Policies for adjustment, revitalization and expansion.* Washington D.C.: World Bank.

World Bank. (1995). *Priorities and strategies for education.* Washington D.C.: World Bank.

World Bank. (2002). *Constructing knowledge societies: New challenges for tertiary education.* Washington D.C.: World Bank.

Wran Committee. (1988). R*eport of the committee on higher education funding (under the chairmanship of Neville).* Canberra: Australian Government Publishing Service.

Ziderman, A., & Albrecht, D. (1995). *Financing universities in developing countries.* Washington, D.C.: Falmer.

8 The Use of Technology in Distance Education

Gráinne Conole

Electronic technology has been used in earnest in education for over 40 years, from the development of interactive multimedia resources through to the use of the Internet, and mobile and augmented technologies in recent years (Spector, Merrill, van Merrienboer, & Driscoll, 2008). This chapter provides a review of the area and reflects on the promises and challenges of trying to incorporate technologies into education. Research in the field has matured; now a vibrant sub-set of different research areas, such as exploring learners' perceptions of the use of technologies, practitioners' practices, the use of Open Educational Resources, and more broadly open approaches to the design and delivery of educational offerings, help guide the use of pedagogical patterns and learning design as a methodology to enable teachers to make informed decisions about using technologies.

THE EMERGENCE OF THE FIELD

Educational technology as a field can be traced to the beginning of the 19th century, however, significant investment in the field dates back to the 20th century, specifically the sixties with the development and use of teaching machines and the emergence of multimedia software in the eighties. In parallel, there was a shift from a focus on behaviourist approaches to learning (with a focus on the individual and stimulus and response approaches) to more constructivist (building on prior knowledge) and social situative (learning with others and in a context) approaches (Thorpe, 2002; Mayes & de Freitas, 2004) to recent focus on connectivist pedagogies (Dron & Anderson, 2012) with a focus on personal network development.

New technologies appeared to offer much to support these new pedagogies, particularly through new social and participatory media that have emerged in the last five years or so. Molenda (2008) states that educational technology as a field has developed through a series of phases as new technologies have emerged. Its origins are in the use of visual and audiovisual systems; then radio, television, teaching machines; the design of instructional systems; computers; and ultimately the use of the Internet for both storage and processing of information and communication.

In addition to educational technology, over the years different terms have been used with respect to researching the use of technologies for learning and teaching. These include: *e-learning, learning technology, networked learning,* and *technology-enhanced learning.* Each term has a subtle nuance, for example: Kehrwald (2010) citing Steeples and Jones (2002) argues that, "networked learning, by definition, involves the use of information and communication technologies to create connections" (p. 2). By utilizing those connections, learners have opportunities for interpersonal interaction and more complex social activity. Thus, networked learning is an active, social endeavour in which the mediating technologies provide an infrastructure for social activity.

Educational technology suggests the emphasis is on formal learning, however it is important that the term covers the tools and techniques of non-formal and informal learning as well. Conole and Oliver (2007, p. 4) favour the term *e-learning* and make the following distinctions:

- *E-learning* is the term most commonly used to represent the broader domain of development and research activities on the application of technologies to education.

- *Information and communication technologies* (ICT) refer to the broad range of technologies used in education.

- When both terms are used in the context of their use in learning and teaching we tend to use the term *learning technologies.*

For some, the term *e-learning* has become too closely tied in with a particular subset of technologies, namely learning management systems, and the term *technology-enhanced learning* (TEL) has been favoured in many European contexts, as it is thought that TEL emphasizes the support of learning by technologies. For the purpose of this chapter the term *e-learning* will be used as I think it most adequately encapsulates the nature of the field, which is, researching the use of technologies (covering Internet-based technologies as well as mobile and other devices) to support learning and teaching.

THEORY AND METHODOLOGY

E-learning as a field is inherently applied and interdisciplinary. Researchers come from a wide range of disciplines and bring with them a rich set of theoretical perspectives and methodologies.

A group of influential thinkers were identified in a series of interviews with key researchers in the field (Conole, Scanlon, Mundin, & Farrow, 2010). There appears to be a common shared discourse underpinning the field. Socio-cultural approaches—in particular the work of Vygotsky (1978), Engeström and others around cultural–historical activity theory (CHAT) (Engeström, Miettinen, & Punamäki, 1999) , Laurillard's theory on rethinking university teaching and learning (Laurillard, 2002), and Mason (Mason & Kaye, 1989). Other theoretical perspectives these researchers are drawing on include the following: Alan Collins on design-based research (Collins, 1992); Michael Patton on utilization-focussed evaluation (Patton 2008); Barbara Rogoff on cultural psychology (Rogoff, 2003); Maggie Boden on artificial intelligence and psychology (Boden 1989); Lave and Wenger on communities of practice (Lave & Wenger 1998); Alan Blackwell and others on inter-disciplinarity (Blackwell, Wilson, Street, Boulton, & Knell, 2009); Howard Gardner on multiple intelligences (Gardener, 1993); James Wertsch on mediating artifacts (Wertsch, 1991); and Michael Cole (Cole, Engeström, & Vasquez, 1997).

Looking at some of the specific texts that were cited as influences is also insightful. These included *Educating the Reflective Practitioner* (Schön, 1987), *Academic Tribes and Territories: Intellectual Enquiry and the Cultures of Discipline* (Becher & Trowler 2001), *Distributed Cognition* (Salomon

1997), *Plans and Situated Actions: The Problem of Human-Machine Communication* (Suchman, 1987), *A Dynamic Medium for Creative Thought* (Kay, 1972), *Doing Research/Reading Research Re-interrogating Education* (Dowling & Brown, 2010) and *Commons and Border Lands* (Strathern, 2004).

In the same interviews the following were cited as the methodologies that were most frequently used: socio-cultural research, activity theory, qualitative research methodology, design research methodology and grounded theory. It should be noted that these researchers were primarily European and, arguably, more quantitative approaches are evident in other parts of the world, such as North America.

Therefore, these texts and methodologies give us a rich insight into the nature of the field and how it is being researched, as well as an indication of the key areas of research focus.

TODAY'S TECHNOLOGIES

This section will provide a review of the current spectrum of technologies that are available to support learning and will consider some of the ways in which they are being used to support different pedagogical approaches. An emphasis will be placed on types of technologies and their associated characteristics and how these can support different pedagogical approaches and mechanisms for learners to communicate and collaborate with peers and tutors in an online learning context.

Conole, Smith, and White (2007) provide a timeline of technologies in education from the sixties to 2000. They describe the emergence and influence of the following: mainframe computers, desktop computers, graphical interfaces, the Internet, virtual learning environments (VLEs),[1] managed learning environments (MLEs), and mobile and wireless devices. Use of these tools included the creation of interactive multimedia materials and e-assessment, the creation of departmental web pages to store course materials, the use of e-mail and discussion forums to support communication between tutors and learners, and the creation of holistic online learning environments using VLEs.

Since 2000 we have seen the emergence of new technologies that provide a plethora of ways in which teachers and learners can interact and

---

1 Also termed learning management systems (LMSs)

communicate. These include new social and participatory media, which O'Reilly referred to as *Web 2.0 technologies* (O'Reilly 2004; O'Reilly 2005), virtual worlds such as Second Life, game-based technologies, and, more recently, augmented and gesture technologies. The *2011 Horizon Report* lists the technologies that a group of experts believe are most likely to have an impact within a one-, three-, and five-year timeframe. For 2011, these were: e-books and mobile devices, augmented and gesture technologies, and, within five years, learning analytics (Elias, 2011). Siemens (2010, para. 2) defines *learning analytics* as "the use of intelligent data, learner-produced data, and analysis models to discover information and social connections, and to predict and advise on learning."

In a review of social and participatory media, Conole and Alevizou (2010) categorize them as follows: media sharing (such as YouTube and Flickr), media manipulation and mash ups, instant messaging, online games and virtual worlds, social networking, blogs, social bookmarking, recommender systems, wikis and collaborative editors, and syndication tools. In addition, they identified a number of important affordances (Gibson, 1979) that these technologies offer to support learning. De Freitas and Conole (2010) list the following as key technological trends that have emerged in recent years:

(1) A shift towards ubiquitous and networked technologies.

(2) The emergence of context and location aware devices.

(3) The increasingly rich and diverse different forms of representation and stimulatory environments possible.

(4) The trend towards more mobile and adaptive devices.

(5) A technical infrastructure that is global, distributed, and interoperable.

Conole (2013a, p. 48) notes the following trends:

(1) A shift from the Web as a content repository and information mechanism to a Web that enables more social mediation and user-generated of content.

(2) New practices of sharing (for example, Flickr for images, YouTube for videos, and SlideShare for presentations) and mechanisms for content production, communication, and collaboration (through blogs, wikis, and micro-blogging services such as Twitter). Social

networking sites provide a mechanism for connecting people and supporting different communities of practice (such as Facebook, Elgg[2] and Ning).[3]

(3) A scale, or "network effect," is emerging as a result of the quantity of information available on the Web, the multiplicity of connectivity, and the scale of user participation. As a result, new possibilities for sharing and harnessing these network effects are occurring.

Conole goes on to argue that these trends point to new ways in which users are behaving in online spaces and provide a range of opportunities for supporting learning and teaching practices. Through these new technologies the Web is more participatory and user-centred, supporting more open practices. A number of characteristics define social and participatory media and demonstrate the ways in which they enable these more participatory approaches. First, the ability to peer critique on the work of others is now common practice in the blogosphere. Second, tools that enable users (both students and teachers) to generate their own content. Third, these technologies enable collective aggregation on a global scale, which refers both to the ways in which individuals can collate and order content to suit their individual needs and personal preferences, as well as the ways individual content can be enriched. Fourth, a rich ecology of community formations have now emerged, from tightly defined communities of practice (Wenger, 1998) through to looser networks and collectives (Dron & Anderson, 2007). Lastly, new forms of digital identity are emerging; individuals need to define their digital identity and how they "present" themselves across these spaces (Keen, 2007). The avatars we choose to represent ourselves, the style of language we use, and the degree to which we are open (both professionally and personally) within these spaces, give a collective picture of how we are viewed by others.

In addition to social and participatory media, we have seen the emergence of smart phones, tablets, and e-book devices in recent years, which provide learners with access to a rich range of learning materials. Many of these devices enable some degree of interactivity, for example, the ability to annotate resources or share and discuss them with others. The affordances of mobile learning include the ability to learn anywhere and anytime and

---

2 http://elgg.org

3 http://www.ning.com

being able to bridge between formal, informal, and non-formal learning. In the MyArtSpace project, Sharples, Lonsdale, Meek, Rudman, and Vavoula (2007) explored the use of mobile devices between schools and museums. The students were able to view multimedia presentations of museum exhibits, take photos, make voice recordings, write notes, and see who else has viewed the exhibit. Mobile devices are particular powerful when combined with location-aware functionality and can be used to promote activities such as geocaching. Clough (2010) defines *geocaching* as a leisure activity in which participants use a global positioning system (GPS) mobile device to locate a hidden cache. The cache is usually a physical container concealed somewhere in the landscape. Participants are given a starting location (a car park or other easily identifiable spot) and then use the GPS coordinates to guide them to the cache. Geocaching involves exercise and getting about outdoors. Clough reports on a study on the use of GPS with social technologies. The study aimed to consider whether these technologies can provide an effective focus for community activities and, if so, whether this combination of location-awareness, mobile, and Web 2.0 technology results in the creation of novel informal learning opportunities (Clough, 2010).

An active area of research is the exploratory use of games and virtual worlds to support learning. These can be particularly useful in fostering situative pedagogies such as authentic and role-based learning. A JISC briefing paper (2007) refers to this technology as game-based learning (GBL), which ranges from rich immersive virtual worlds, such as Second Life, to simple interactive and quiz-based games. The paper argues that serious games, services, and applications have a role to play in relation to their potential to provide greater opportunities for personalizing learning experiences (O'Donoghue, 2010). The report goes on to cite a number of benefits of GBL, which include motivation, integrating a range of tools, and the spontaneous formation of social networks. Games such as World of WarCraft have a vibrant and extensive network of online gamers distributed worldwide, supporting and peer-critiquing each other as they develop their gaming competences. Gros (2010) lists the following as some of the benefits of games-based learning: games as a powerful context, immersive learning, development of soft skills, and the ability to support complex learning. Virtual worlds, such as Second Life, can promote authentic and role-based learning. For example, they can be used to create art galleries and museums, to support virtual exhibitions, to simulate medical wards or law courtroom role plays (EDUCAUSE, 2008). The power of Second Life is that it provides an authentic virtual environment acting as a proxy for the real world and allows users to inhabit personas and situations that might otherwise be unavailable to them. The SWIFT project[4] has created a virtual genetics laboratory that is being used with students at the University of Leicester to provide them with an authentic environment to get accustomed to working in a laboratory—from learning basic safety rules through to the use of virtual equipment such as microscopes and centrifuges (Rudman, Lavelle, Salmon, & Cashmore, 2010).

Haptic technologies, which involve the sense of touch, are increasingly being used, particularly in vocational and applied learning contexts, primarily for robotic, medicine, and space industries. Their development, like previous technologies, often spins down to valuable application in education. For example, Tse et al. (2010) describe a virtual dental training system (hapTEL), that allows dental students to learn and practice procedures such as dental drilling, caries removal, and cavity prevention for tooth restoration.

One of the key affordance of many new technologies, particularly social and participatory technologies, is the way in which they can promote more open approaches to practice. Conole considers what adopting more open practices might mean in terms of the design and delivery of educational interventions and in terms of digital scholarship and more open approaches to research (Conole, 2013a).

Learning design and pedagogical patterns have emerged in recent years as more open approaches to the design of learning interventions. Conole (2013a) introduces a new learning design methodology, which aims to help practitioners make more informed design decisions that are pedagogically effective and make innovative use of technologies. The methodology aims to shift teacher practice from an inherent and belief-based approach to one that is explicit and design-based. The aspiration is that such an approach will guide teacher design practice and help make the design process more explicit and hence sharable. The methodology includes a range of conceptual visual design tools, as well as approaches for fostering the sharing and discussing of learning and teaching design, through structured real events and via specialized social networking tools, such as Cloudworks.[5]

---

4 http://www2.le.ac.uk/departments/genetics/genie/projects/swift
5 http://cloudworks.ac.uk

In parallel, there has been significant interest in the area of pedagogical patterns (Goodyear, 2005; Goodyear & Retalis, 2010). The concept of pedagogical patterns is derived from the work of Alexander et al. (1977). They define a pattern as something that:

> describes a problem which occurs over and over again in our environment, and then describes the core of the solution to that problem, in such a way that you can use this solution a million times over, without ever doing it the same way twice. (1977, p. x)

Bergin states that a pattern is supposed to capture best practice in some domain. Pedagogical patterns try to capture expert knowledge of the practice of teaching (Bergin, 2002). A number of projects have now developed libraries of pedagogical patterns to support different types of pedagogy (see for example, the design patterns in the e-learning Pointer Project,[6] the E-LEN project,[7] the TELL project[8] and the Pedagogical Patterns Project (PPP)[9]).

In terms of open delivery, an area of interest that has emerged in recent years is the development and promotion of open educational resources (OER). The OER movement is based on the premise that educational resources should be freely available. It has been promoted by organizations such as the Hewlett Foundation and UNESCO. Early work focussed on the creation and population of OER repositories, and there was perhaps a naïve assumption that if these resources were made available learners and teachers would use and repurpose them. However evaluation of the use of this repositories showed that this was not the case (Petrides & Jimes, 2006; McAndrew, et al., 2009). As a result, research effort has now shifted to identifying the practices around the design, use and repurposing of OER. The OPAL initiative[10] analyzed over 60 case studies of OER initiatives and from this derived a set of OER practices, namely: strategy and policy, staff development and support, tools and tool practices, and enablers and barriers (Conole, 2013a). These have now being incorporated into a set of guidelines for key stakeholders

---

6 http://www.comp.lancs.as.uk/computing/research/cseg/projects/pointer/pointer,html

7 http://www2.tisip.no/E-LEN

8 http://cosy.ted.unipi/gr/tell

9 http://www.pedagogicalpatterns.org/

10 http://oer-quality.org/

(learners, teachers, institutional managers, and policy makers). Individuals or organizations can use the guidelines to benchmark their existing OER practices and then as a guide to the creation of a vision and implementation plan. The hope is that practical use of these guidelines will result in better uptake and use of OER.

In addition to free resources, we have also seen the emergence of free courses, often referred to as *massive online open courses* (MOOCs). The *New York Times* referred to 2012 as the Year of the MOOC[11]. Daniel (2012) overviews many of the challenges and promises of this format—most notably the affordance of offering educational programming to large number of students at almost no cost to the students. For example, Siemens and Downes developed and delivered a twelve-week online course on connectivism called Connectivism and Connective Knowledge.[12] This course provided a nice example of an extension of the open movement, moving beyond the OER movement to providing a totally free course. Not only were the tools and resources free that they used in the course, but so was the expertise. An impressive 2,400 students joined the first course in 2008, although ultimately the number of active participants was only about 200. Recently, private for-profit companies have emerged to partner with prestigious universities to cover MOOCs with registrations in the hundreds of thousands of students (Rodriguez, 2012). However, these free resources and courses are challenging existing educational institutions: in a context where expertise, tools, and resources are free, what is the role of traditional institutions? In addition, we are seeing new business models emerging as a result, such as the Peer-to-Peer University,[13] which provides a peer-accredited, "badging," scheme for competences and the OER University,[14] which is an international consortium of institutions. With the OER University, learners can work through any materials they want and when they are ready can choose to be accredited through one of the consortium member institutions.

Weller discusses what it might mean to adopt more open approaches to scholarship and research (Weller, 2011). He argues that there are three interrelated characteristics: open, digital, and networked. He argues that new

---

11 http://www.nytimes.com/2012/11/04/education/edlife/massive-open-online-courses-are-multiplying-at-a-rapid-pace.html?_r=0

12 http://ltc.umanitoba.ca/connectivism/?p=189

13 http://p2pu.org/en/

14 http://wikieducator.org/OER_university/Home

technologies mean we can do things differently. He cites the way in which Twitter, for example, can enable researchers to have access to immediate expertise. We have also seen how the social networking site, Cloudworks,[15] which was developed for academics, can be used as a means to promote the sharing and discussion of learning and teaching ideas. Academics are increasingly using a range of social tools (such as Twitter, blogs, wikis, social networking sites, social bookmarking sites, etc.) to support their academic practice and to be part of a global network of peers.

Finally, two relatively new areas of inquiry are the work on learning spaces and learning analytics. The Spaces for Knowledge Generation (SKG) project,[16] which aimed to inform, guide, and support sustainable development of learning and teaching spaces and practices (Keppell, Souter, & Riddle, 2011). It explored what new forms of learning spaces might be needed to use new technologies effectively in a blended learning context. The project developed seven principles for designing learning spaces:

- *Comfort.* A space that creates a physical and mental sense of ease and well-being.

- *Aesthetics.* Pleasure that includes the recognition of symmetry, harmony, simplicity, and fitness for purpose.

- *Flow.* The state of mind felt by a learner when totally involved in the learning experience

- *Equity.* The consideration of needs as defined by cultural and physical differences

- *Blending.* A mixture of technological and face-to-face pedagogical resources.

- *Affordances.* The 'action possibilities' that the learning environment provides the users, including such things as kitchens, natural light, WiFi, private spaces, writing surfaces, sofas, and so on.

- *Repurposing.* The potential the space has for multiple uses.

Learning analytics is an emerging field—the first international conference was held in Banff in 2011. In the *2011 Horizon Report* (Johnson, Smith,

---

15 http://cloudworks.ac.uk

16 http://www.skgproject.com/

Willis, Levine, & Haywood, 2011), learning analytics was listed as the technology most likely to have the greatest influence on education within a five-year timeframe. Learning analytics can be used as a tool to understand learning behaviour, to provide evidence to support design of more effective learning environments, and to make effective use of social and participatory media.

CHALLENGES OF THE FIELD

Despite the clear potential of technologies to promote and foster different pedagogical approaches, a number of challenges remain. Five main challenges are outlined below:

- the slow uptake of technologies
- the lack of a theoretical foundation for the field application of research findings to policy and practice
- the need to better integrate research, policy, and practice
- the changing existing cultures
- the challenges faced by developing countries

Despite the rhetoric and significant investment in the field, technologies are not being used extensively to support learning and teaching (Cuban, 1986). The reasons for this are complex and multifaceted (technical, organizational, and pedagogical). Molenda (2008) observes that the barriers cited for the lack of use of audiovisual tools in the 1940s and 1950s are similar to those cited for lack of use of computers in the 1990s, namely: accessibility issues, lack of training, unreliability of equipment, limited budgets, and the difficulty of integrating technologies into the curriculum. Despite the promise of technology, we have not seen it revolutionize education (Beabout, et al., 2008). Cuban reviewed the use of technology from the 1920s onwards. His central argument was that despite the policy directives on more use of technologies in classrooms, technologies have not had a significant impact on classroom practice. It seems that, although the technologies may change, the barriers and reasons for lack of uptake remain much the same. Teachers lack the appropriate digital literacy skills (Jenkins, 2009) to make effective use of new technologies to support their teaching.

Bennett and Oliver (2011) argue for the importance of theory to underpin e-learning research. They suggest that the focus of much of the research in the field tends to be on practical implementations and that it is not adequately grounded in theory. They conclude by stating that this lack of theoretical underpinning,

> risks turning the field into a narrow and derivative area of work: at best, only able to draw from other areas; and at worst, only of relevance to those with a vested interest in the specific practical situation currently under study. (p. 187)

Conole (2010) has argued that there is a disconnect between research findings in the field and their impact on policy and practice. She describes a technology intervention framework that can be used to enable a closer integration of research, policy, and practice (see figure 8.1). In related work, she describes how this framework is applied in the OPAL initiative to promote and foster the uptake of open educational resources (OER) (Conole, 2013a).

Figure 8.1 A framework for policy intervention.

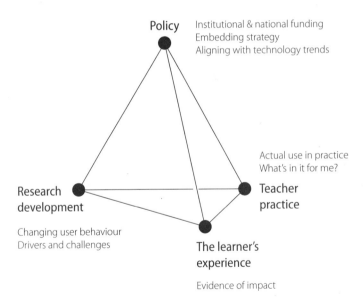

Policy
Institutional & national funding
Embedding strategy
Aligning with technology trends

Actual use in practice
What's in it for me?

Research development

Teacher practice

Changing user behaviour
Drivers and challenges

The learner's experience

Evidence of impact

Shifting teacher practice away from a focus on content to an emphasis on activity and the learner experience is a real challenge, particularly for distance education institutions, which are predominantly built on a Fordist industrial model. This modern economic model is largely based around a social system that utilizes an industrialised and standardised form of mass production, in this case centered on the provision of printed materials. Such a structure is inadequate in terms of the provision of digital materials, making effect use of the affordances of new technologies. Much more agile approaches are needed to meet the needs of today's learners.

Developing countries face additional challenges. Many do not have mature technical infrastructures or adequate Internet provision. Indeed, for some countries even electricity is in limited supply. In such cases, clearly online learning is more of a dream than a reality. However, these countries are finding makeshift solutions, for example, the use of mobile devices (with longer battery lives) rather than computers, as well as making materials available on smart devices rather than online and use of free resources, such as open educational resources.

CONCLUSION

The new technologies described in this chapter clearly have significant potential to transform learning and teaching. The emergence of these technologies has shifted practice on the Internet away from passive information provision to active user engagement. They offer learners and teachers a plethora of ways to communicate and collaborate, to connect with a distributed network of peers, and to find and manipulate information. We are beginning to see ways in which teacher and learner practice and experience is changing as a result; however, we are only beginning to understand how to utilize these effectively.

These technologies also raise challenging questions: What are the implications for traditional educational institutions in a world where content and expertise is increasingly free? What is the appropriate balance of institutional learning management systems versus cloud-based computing? How are roles and identities changing? What are the implications of the increased blurred context of formal/informal learning, and teaching/learning?

Conole argues that a number of shifts in practice are evident (Conole, 2013a). First, researchers are increasingly adopting more open practices in how they disseminate and communicate their research findings. Many researchers now keep blogs as a means of publishing ideas in progress, which complement more traditional forms of publication through journals and books. In addition, many institutions now have open research repositories and require researchers to deposit their research outputs. Second, we are beginning to see the collective wisdom of the crowd (Surowiecki, 2005) by using an individual's Twitter network to ask questions and provide answers and harnessing the collective mass to address large-scale research questions and data collection.[17] Thirdly, digital scholarship is becoming increasingly important and is challenging traditional metrics for measuring academic impact. Fourthly, open resources and courses are challenging traditional educational offerings; we are seeing the emergence of new alliances and business models as a result. Fifthly, learners are now technologically immersed and see technologies as a core learning tool. They are adopting more just-in-time approaches to learning and, increasingly, working more collaboratively (Sharpe & Beetham, 2010). Finally, the surfeit of tools now available is bewildering and institutions and individuals increasingly need to make informed choices of which technologies to use in which contexts, mixing institutional systems with freely available, cloud-based services. All raise direct or indirect challenges to policy, funding, individual and collective rights, privacy, and responsibility.

Thus, potential topics for future research in the field include:

(1) What might a coherent learning design language look like and how might it be shared?

(2) What other mediating artefacts do we need to develop so that learners and teachers can make more effective use of technologies to support learning? What are the different ways in which learning interventions can be represented?

(3) How can we foster a global network and communities/networks of practice to enable learners and teachers to share and discuss learning and teaching ideas? How can social networking and other dialogic tools be used to enable teachers to share and discuss their learning and teaching practices, ideas and designs?

(4) What tools do we need to guide design practice, visualize designs, and provide a digital environment for learners and teachers to share and discuss?

(5) What are the implications and likely impact of social and participatory media for education and how can they be harnessed more effectively to support learning?

---

17 See for example http://www.ispot.org.uk/ and http://www.galaxyzoo.org/

(6) What will be the impact of new emergent technologies on the stakeholders involved in education?

(7) What new pedagogies are emerging as a result of these new technologies?

(8) What are the implications for learners, teachers, and institutions of new social and participatory media?

(9) How will the processes of supporting learning (design, delivery, support, and assessment) change as a result of new technologies?

(10) What social exclusion issues are arising with the increased use of new technologies? How can we promote more socially inclusive practices?

(11) How are Open Educational Resources being design, used, and repurposed?

(12) What are the implications for formal institutions of the increasingly availability of free resources, tools and even total educational offerings, such as Massive Online Open Courses (MOOCS)?

(13) What digital literacy skills do learners and teachers need to make effective use of these technologies and resources? To what extent are they evident and how can they be developed?

(14) How are the ways in which learners and teachers communicate and collaborate changing with the use of these technologies?

(15) How can we create effective new digital learning environments to promote the use of social and participatory media and OER?

(16) How can informal learning using OER be assessed and accredited?

(17) What kinds of policy directives are in place to promote social inclusion through the use of OER and how effective are they?

(18) What new methodologies and theoretical perspectives will be needed to address these research questions and to interpret the findings?

This is an exciting but challenging time for education, where we operate within an increasingly networked society (Castells, 2000) and under increasing financial constraints. Industrial modes of learning are no longer appropriate and do not meet the needs of an individual in today's society. Learning needs to be contextualized, relevant, social, and just-in-time. New technologies provide an important part of the solution in terms of addressing this, but teachers and learners need support, guidance, challenge, and opportunities to make informed decisions on how to harness these technologies for their particular needs.

REFERENCES

Alexander, C., Ishikawa, S., Silverstein, M., Jacobsen, M., Fiksdahl-King, I., & Angel, S. (1977). *A pattern language: Towns, buildings, construction.* New York, NY: Oxford University Press.

Beabout, B., Carr-Chellman, A. A., Alkandari, K. A., Almeida, L. C., Gursoy, H. T., Ma, Z., & Modak, R. S. (2008). The perceptions of New Orleans educators on the process of rebuilding the New Orleans school system after Katrina. *Journal of Education for Students Placed at Risk (JESPAR), 13*(2–3), 212–37.

Becher, T., & Trowler, P. (2001). *Academic tribes and territories: Intellectual enquiry and the cultures of discipline* (2nd rev. ed.). Buckingham, UK: Open University Press.

Bennett, S., & Oliver, M. (2011). Talking back to theory: The missed opportunities in learning technology research. *Research in Learning Technology, 19*(3), 179–89.

Bergin, J. (2002). *Some pedagogical patterns.* Retrieved from http://csis.pace. edu/~bergin/patterns/fewpedpats.html

Blackwell, A. F., Wilson, L., Street, A., Boulton, C., & Knell, J. (2009). *Radical innovation: Crossing knowledge boundaries with interdisciplinary teams.* [Technical Report No. 7670]. Cambridge, UK: University of Cambridge. Retrieved from http://www.cl.cam.ac.uk/techreports/UCAM-CL-TR-760.pdf

Boden, M. A. (1989). *Artificial intelligence in psychology: Interdisciplinary essays.* Cambridge, MA: MIT Press.

Castells, M. (2000). *The rise of the network society: The information age: Economy, society and culture, Vol. 1.* Hoboken, NJ: Wiley.

Clough, G. (2010). Geolearners: Location-based informal learning with mobile and social technologies. *IEEE Transactions on Learning Technologies, 3*(1), 33–44. doi:10.1109/TLT.2009.39.

Cole, M., Engeström, Y., & Vasquez, O. A. (1997). *Mind, culture, and activity: Seminal papers from the Laboratory of Comparative Human Cognition.* Cambridge, UK: Cambridge University Press.

Collins, A. (1992). Towards a design science of education, In E. Scanlon & T. O'Shea (Eds.), *New directions in educational technology* (pp. 15–22). Berlin: Springer-Verlag.

Conole, G. (2010). Bridging the gap between policy and practice: A framework for technological intervention. *Journal of e-Learning and Knowledge Society,* (Vol. 6), 13–27.

Conole, G. (2013a). *Designing for learning in an open world.* Berlin: Springer Verlag.

Conole, G. (2013b). *A technology intervention framework for promoting OER: Lessons from the OPAL initiative.* Vancouver, BC: UNESCO/Commonwealth of Learning.

Conole, G., & Alevizou, P. (2010). *A literature review of the use of Web 2.0 tools in higher education*. Milton Keynes, UK: The Open University.

Conole, G., & Oliver, M. (2007). *Contemporary perspectives in e-learning research: Themes, methods and impact on practice*. London, UK: Routledge.

Conole, G., Scanlon, G., Mundin, P., & Farrow, R. (2010). *Technology-enhanced learning as an site for interdisciplinary research*. Milton Keynes, UK: The Open University, Institute of Educational Technology. Retrieved from http://cloudworks. ac.uk/cloud/view/3419

Conole, G., Smith, J., & White, S. (2007). A critique of the impact of policy and funding on practice. In G. Conole & M. Oliver (Eds.), *Contemporary perspective in e-learning research: Themes, methods and impact on practice*. Oxford, UK: Routledge.

Cuban, L. (1986). *Teachers and machines: The classroom use of technology since 1920*. Amsterdam: Teachers College Press.

Dowling, P., & Brown, A. (2009). *Doing research/reading research: A mode of interrogation for education*. New York: Routledge.

Dron, J., & Anderson, T. (2007). Collectives, networks and groups in social software for e-Learning. *Proceedings of World Conference on E-Learning in Corporate, Goverment, Healthcare, and Higher Education, Québec*.

EDUCAUSE. (2008). *7 things you should know about second life*. Retrieved from http:// net.educase.edu/ir/ libary/pdf/ELI7038.pdf

Elias, T. (2011). *Learning analytics: Definitions, processes and potential*. Retrieved from http://learninganalytics.net/LearningAnalyticsDefinitionsProcessesPotential.pdf

Engestrom, Y., Miettinen, R., & Punamäki, R.-L. (1999). *Perspectives of activity theory*. Cambridge, UK: Cambridge University Press.

De Freitas, S., & Conole, G. (2010). Learners experiences: How pervasive and integrative tools influence expectations of study. In R. Sharpe, H. Beetham, & S. de Freitas (Eds.), *Rethinking learning for a digital age: How learners are shaping their own experiences*. New York: Routledge.

Gardner, H. (1993). *Frames of mind: The theory of multiple intelligences*. New York, NY: Basic Books.

Gibson, J. J. (1979). *The ecological approach to visual perception*. Hillsdale, NJ: Lawrence Erlbaum.

Goodyear, P. (2005). Educational design and networked learning: patterns, pattern languages and design practice. *Australasian Journal of Educational Technology*, *21*(1), 82–101. Retrieved from http://www.ascilite.org.au/ajet/ajet21/goodyear.html

Goodyear, P., & Retalis, J. (2010). *Technology-enhanced learning: Design patterns and pattern languages*. Rotterdam: Sense Publishers.

Gros, B. (2010). Game-based learning: A strategy to integrate digital games in schools. In J. Yamamoto, J. C. Kush, R. Lombard, & C. J. Hertzog (Eds.), *Technology implementation and teacher education: Reflective models* (pp. 365–79). Hershey, PA: Information Science Reference.

Jenkins, H. (2009). *Confronting the challenges of participatory culture media education for the 21st century*. Cambridge, MA: MIT Press.

JISC. (2007). *Game-based Learning: A JISC briefing paper*. London, UK. Retrieved from http://www.jisc.ac.uk/publications/briefingpapers/2007/pub_gamebasedlearningBP/pub_gamebasedlearningBP_content.aspx

Kay, A. C. (1972). *A dynamic medium for creative thought*. Minneapolis, MI: The National Council of Teachers of English.

Keen, A. (2007). *The cult of the amateur: How today's Internet is killing our culture and assaulting our economy*. London, UK: Nicholas Brealey.

Kehrwald, B. A. (2010). Democratic rationalisation on the network: Social presence and human agency in networked learning. *Proceedings of the 7th International Conference on Networked Learning, Aalborg, Denmark*.

Keppell, M., Souter, K., & Riddle, M. (2011). *Physical and virtual learning spaces in higher education: Concepts for the modern learning environment*. Hershey, PA: IGI Global.

Laurillard, D. (2002). *Rethinking university teaching: A conversational framework for the effective use of learning technologies*. London, UK: RoutledgeFalmer.

Lave, J., & Wenger, E. (1998). *Communities of practice: Learning, meaning and identity*. Cambridge, UK: Cambridge University Press.

Mason, R., & Kaye, A. (1989). *Mindweave: Communication, computers, and distance education*. Oxford, UK: Pergamon Press.

Mayes, T., & de Freitas, S. (2004). *Review of e-learning theories, frameworks and models*. JISC e-learning models desk study. Retrieved from http://www.jisc.ac.uk/uploaded_documents/Stage%202%20Learning%20Models%20(Version%201).pdf

Mc Andrew, P., Inamorato dos Santos, A., Lane, A., Godwin, S., Okada, A., Wilson, T., Connolly, T. (2009). *OpenLearn research report 2006-2008*. The Open University. Retrieved from http://www3.open.ac.uk/events/6/2009727_62936_01.pdf

Molenda, M. (2008). Historical foundations. In J. M. Spector, M. D. Merrill, J. van Merrienboer, & M. P. Driscoll (Eds.), *Handbook of research on educational communications and technology*. (3rd ed.), (pp. 3-20). New York: Springer.

Johnson, L., Smith, R., Willis, H., Levine, A., and Haywood, K., (2011). *The 2011 Horizon Report*. Austin, TX: The New Media Consortium.

O'Donoghue, J. (2010). *Technology-supported environments for personalized learning methods and case studies*. Hershey, Pa.: IGI Global.

O'Reilly, T. (2004). *The architecture of participation*. Retrieved from http://www.oreillynet.com/pub/a/oreilly/tim/articles/architecture_of_participation.html

O'Reilly, T. (2005). *What is Web 2.0: Design patterns and business models for the next generation of software*. Retrieved June 11, 2012, from http://oreilly.com/web2/archive/what-is-web-20.html

Patton, M. Q. (2008). *Utilization-focussed evaluation*. Los Angeles, CA: Sage.

Petrides, L., & Jimes, C. (2006, October). Open educational resources: Toward a new educational paradigm. *iJournal*, (4), 1-5.

Rudman, P. D., Lavelle, S. P., Salmon, G., & Cashmore, A. (2010). SWIFT-ly enhancing laboratory learning: Genetics in the virtual world. *Gehalten auf der ALT-C 2010 Conference Proceedings.*

Salomon, G. (Ed.). (1996). *Distributed cognitions:Psychological and educational considerations* (reprint ed.). Cambridge, UK: Cambridge University Press.

Schön, D. A. (1987). *Educating the reflective practitioner: Toward a new design for teaching and learning in the professions.* San Francisco, CA: Jossey-Bass.

Sharpe, R., Beetham, H., & de Freitas, S. (2010). *Rethinking learning for a digital age: How learners are shaping their own experiences.* New York: Routledge.

Sharples, M., Lonsdale, P., Meek, J., Rudman, P., & Vavoula, G. (2007). An evaluation of MyArtSpace: A mobile learning service for school museum trips. *Proceedings of 6th Annual Conference on Mobile Learning,* Melbourne: mLearn.

Siemens, G. (2010). *What are learning analytics? E-Learningspace: learning, networks, knowledge, technology, community.* Retrieved from http://www.elearnspace.org/blog/2010/08/25/what-are-learning-analytics/

Spector, J. M., Merrill, M. D., van Merrienboer, J. & Driscoll, M. P. (2008). *Handbook of research on educational communications and technology.* New York: Springer.

Steeples, C., & Jones, C. (2002). *Networked learning: Perspectives and issues.* New York: Springer.

Strathern, M. (2004). *Commons and borderlands: Working papers on interdisciplinarity, accountability and the flow of knowledge.* Herefordshire, UK: Sean Kingston.

Suchman, L. A. (1987). *Plans and situated actions: The problem of human-machine communication* (2nd ed.). Cambridge, UK: Cambridge University Press.

Surowiecki, J. (2005). *The wisdom of crowds: Why the many are smarter than the few and how collective wisdom shapes business, economies, societies and nations.* London: Abacus.

Thorpe. M. (2002). From independent learning to collaborative learning: New communities of practice in open, distance and distributed learning. In M. R. Lea & K. Nicoll (Eds.), *Distributed learning: Social and cultural approaches to practice* (pp. 131–51). New York: Routledge.

Tse, B., Harwin, W., Barrow, A., Quinn, B., San Diego, J. and Cox, M. (2010). Design and development of a haptic dental training system: hapTEL, EuroHaptics'10. *Proceedings of the 2010 International Conference on Haptics – Generating and perceiving tangible sensations* (Part II), (pp. 101–8). Springer-Verlag: Berlin.

Vygotsky, L. S. (1978). *Mind in society: The development of higher psychological processes.* Cambridge, MA: Harvard University Press.

Weller, M. (2011). *The digital scholar: How technology is transforming scholarly practice.* London: Bloomsbury Academic.

Wenger, E. (1998). *Communities of practice: Learning, meaning, and identity.* Cambridge, UK; Cambridge University Press.

Wertsch, J. V. (1991). *Voices of the mind: A sociocultural approach to mediated action.* Cambridge, MA.: Harvard University Press.

9 Innovation and Change: Changing How we Change

Jon Dron

Distance education is defined not so much by the geographical distance that the label implies as by the technologies, both soft and hard, that are used to reduce that distance. Along with the technologies come processes that relate to their use, pedagogies that are made to fit with those tools and processes, and a demographic that is defined in some large part by its ability to access the information and communication technologies (ICTs) used in the process. When considering change and innovation in distance education, our focus will, inevitably, be on those technologies, their implementation, invention, meaning, diffusion, and acceptance.

This chapter addresses the following main questions:

- What changes and innovations have occurred in distance education?
- How does such change come about? What are its drivers, what are the obstacles to change?
- How should change be managed in a distance environment?

Change in distance education comes about due to a range of factors, none of which may be seen in isolation, all of which combine and interact to form a complex set of conditions. These include, non-exclusively:

- the opportunities afforded by new technologies, including pedagogies

- the constraints of available technologies, including pedagogies
- path dependencies caused by earlier decisions
- the desires and expectations of learners
- the constraints of learners, notably geographical isolation, the need to live and work somewhere else while learning, the need to access learning opportunities not available at their own location
- constraints due to external contextual factors such as competitors, government legislation, funding models, and relationships with prior learning
- changes in theoretical models of learning
- trends, fashions, and attitudes to learning and to technology

Some of these aspects are common to all education. For the sake of economy, by and large we will only focus on those that are notably different in distance education. There are many theories of innovation and many theories of change that account for diversity, creativity, adoption, and design. To avoid a massive creep in scope, in this chapter we deliberately limit our focus to those that are distinctive to distance education.

MAJOR THEORY

Generations of Distance Education

If we are to understand change as it relates to distance education, then it is important to clearly identify those aspects of distance education that are susceptible to forces of change and that are distinctive in distance education. To do this, it seems logical to look at the history of distance education and what kinds of change have occurred. Traditionally, the history of distance education has been divided according to the kinds of ICT it employs, which, given that the field is largely defined by ICTs, makes some sense. Bates (Bates, 2005) for example, follows Kaufman and Nipper in identifying three generations: single-mode (such as print or radio), mixed mode with tuition (an industrial model typified by CD-ROMs, high production values, and telephone tutors) and social modes (typified by forums and learning management systems). Similarly, Gunawardena and McIsaac trace its history in terms of ICTs, from early print models, radio, television and networked technologies to the present day (Gunawardena & McIsaac, 2004). Anderson and Dron take a somewhat different tack by considering generations in terms of dominant pedagogies of the period (Anderson & Dron, 2011). This perspective helps to maintain a focus on the distinctive features that make those technologies educational rather than simple information and communication tools, and thus distinguishes them from other uses of similar tools outside an educational context.

The first generation of distance pedagogies uses the behaviourist/cognitivist model. This model includes cognitive–constructivist approaches such as those of Piaget as well as behaviourist and cognitivist approaches such as those of Skinner, Bruner, and Gagne. The model is based on a learner-centric view in which the focus is on how individuals learn. The second generation is the social constructivist model, following such theorists as Dewey and Vygotsky. This model is informed by the notion that knowledge is socially constructed and emphasizes the importance of others in developing and refining understanding. The third generation is the connectivist model. In this model, knowledge is in the network, both human and non-human, and learning lies in wayfinding and making sense of the network. There is an emerging fourth generation that Dron and Anderson suggest should be described as holist, which recognises that, learning and teaching are deformed by context and that no pedagogy has primacy. It is important to note, however, that pedagogies are no less technologies than the ICTs with which they are combined to form a specific learning technology. Given, therefore, that distance education is essentially about technology, if we are to understand what it is and how change occurs within it, we need to explore the meaning of *technology*.

Technologies

Almost every aspect of distance education is enacted and defined through technology, from organizational processes to communication tools, from production methods to pedagogies. To understand technology and how it changes is thus by far the most important foundation for understanding change in distance education.

Unfortunately, *technology* is a slippery and evolving concept. Its modern usage emerged in the early part of the 19th century (Kelly, 2010) but has often been seen as an elusive abstraction (Nye, 2006) that has led some to abandon it altogether and replace it with something more precisely defined, such as *technics* (Mumford, 1934) or *technique* (Ellul, 1970). Technologies predate scientific methods by at least tens of millennia (Kelly, 2010; Taylor,

2010; Zhouying, 2004) but are often associated with science. Guangbi's useful distinction, quoted in Zhouying (2004), is that science is theoretical knowledge that is concerned with discovery and cognition, while technology is operable knowledge that is concerned with invention and practice. Much science is made possible only because of technology and much technology is made possible only because of science (Rosen, 2010). There are numerous alternative definitions of *technology*. Bessant and Francis (2005) call technologies the "ways that people get complicated things done" (p.97). Nye (2006) sees technologies as a combination of tools and purpose; Papert (1987) suggests that technologies are tools with a context. For Kelly, technology is "a force: a vital spirit that throws us forward or pushes against us. Not a thing but a verb" (2010, p. 56). S. Johnson (2010) describes technologies in terms of the jobs they do for us. The highly persuasive definition that we will use here comes from Arthur (2009) who argues that technologies are the "orchestration of phenomena to some purpose" (p. 51). This makes sense of Franklin's discussion of the technologies of prayer (Franklin, 1999) and Dron's identification of pedagogies as educational technologies (Dron, 2012). Phenomena may be natural or artificial, physical, mental, or abstract —from the effects of rubbing carbon on paper to the interaction of different aspects of legislation, from understanding how people learn to the quantum behaviour of subatomic particles.

Technological Evolution and Change

Technologies evolve and change in fairly predictable patterns. McLuhan's suggestion that humans might be the "sex organs of the machine world" (1964, p. 56) hints at a teleological view of a technological ecology. Technologies appear to involve a dynamic of their own that is not designed from the top down nor intended by their creators. By treating what he calls the *technium* as a richly intertwined ecology in which patterns of evolutionary change emerge with similar retrospective inevitability as those in nature, Kelly shows that our technological ecosystems are evolving in a manner that approaches natural systems in complexity (Kelly, 2010). This does not mean that technological and natural evolution are identical. Technologies are designed. This means that they are subject to fewer constraints than natural systems; new types can emerge without local constraint and almost *ex nihilo*: designed systems do not need to move through intermediate working forms (Page, 2011). None the less, there is a trajectory to technological evolution that is strongly determined by history. Ideas and developments occur in relation to what came before, building on and nearly always incorporating earlier forms. Johnson (2010) makes use of Kauffman's construct of the adjacent possible (Kauffman, 2000) to explain how, as complex ecosystems develop, they open up new possibilities that were not formerly available, thereby leading to creative opportunities for further possibilities to emerge.

Kauffman formalizes the concept to show how, whether in natural or designed systems, it inevitably leads to an efflorescence of forms. Arthur builds on this to demonstrate that technology evolves not through genetically mediated reproduction with variation but with variation arising through assembly and recombination (Arthur, 2009). As more technologies are available to combine and recombine, so they experience accelerating rates of evolution, and increasing diversity (Page, 2011). This constant expansion of the adjacent possible helps to explain how patterns of growth in numbers and ranges of technologies used in all education, not just that at a distance, have exploded over recent decades after hundreds or perhaps thousands of years of slow change (Bates, 2005).

Hard and Soft Technologies

In order to understand how innovation can occur in technologies, it is necessary to understand the ways that technologies may be changed. Technologies are not equally malleable. They can be *softer* (implying greater malleability) or *harder* (implying less flexibility). While there are many competing and overlapping definitions of what this means (e.g., McDonough & Kahn, 1997; Norman, 1993; Zhouying, 2004) we take the view in this chapter that, building on Arthur's definition of technology, softness comes when humans actively enact the orchestration of phenomena to some use (Arthur, 2009). By contrast, hardness occurs when the orchestration is built into the technologies. This means that softer technologies require more effort, are less consistent, and are mostly slower to produce results than harder technologies, but they offer greater flexibility and opportunities for creativity, innovation, and change. The minimal definition of a learning technology is that it must incorporate, as part of its orchestration, pedagogy or pedagogies, whether implicit or explicit. Simply put, learning technologies must do something to enable people to learn, which implies that they employ some method for bringing about learning. Pedagogies, on the whole, are rather soft technologies, adapted, contextualized, and reified by teachers in response to beliefs, activities, and feedback about phenomena that are orchestrated to achieve learning.

When technologies, be they hard or soft, are assembled with others by addition they make the original softer. Generally speaking, when hard technologies are assembled to replace those that already exist, technologies become harder. For example, if a learning management system is too restrictive in requiring a particular form or date for submission, then it may be softened (made more flexible) by asking students to submit work via e-mail instead. Conversely, if e-mail submission proves inefficient or unreliable, the process may be replaced with a more automated system employing a learning management system.

What makes a technology softer or harder is the degree to which humans are compelled to, may, or should make creative choices. For example, licence conditions that prevent end-users from adapting software for their own needs are a hard technology that is enacted in law rather than software or hardware, making most proprietary learning technologies harder in at least one respect than their open-source equivalents. Conversely, a computer, because it is the universal tool, medium, and environment, is among the softest of technologies ever created. However, the degree of hardness/softness of a technology is partially determined by the end users and their competencies. A computer may be a very soft technology for a competent programmer, but a very hard one for the operator of a sales terminal. It is important to note that, though they are using the same machine, the assembly is quite different in each case, utilizing different phenomena for different purposes: the tool that is labelled "computer" can thus be infinitely many technologies. This is also true of even humble tools like the screwdriver, which is a quite different technology when it is used to stir paint than when it is used to turn screws, demonstrating the technology often orchestrates different phenomena for different purposes. Because it has many uses (Kauffman, 2008), a screwdriver is thus a part of many very soft technologies.

The more we embed processes and techniques in our tools, be they pedagogies or machine tools, the fewer choices are left to humans. The price we pay for the efficiencies and capabilities offered by hardening our technologies is therefore the loss of capacity to make changes, but the price we pay for softening our technologies is in effort, speed, and potential for error. A central theme in the evolution of distance learning is thus a tension between creativity and efficiency. It is usually easier to adopt a soft technology in the short term, but more difficult to sustain it in the longer term. For example, open source software may be more flexible, but the skills and effort needed to maintain it could make it a costlier and far more complex alternative than an off-the-shelf product. A course based on soft and malleable dialogue is quicker to design than one based on cognitivist–behaviourist principles, but takes much more effort to sustain and to scale. A learning management system that makes some pedagogical decisions on behalf of the teacher may be easier to use, but constrains the range of pedagogies that may be employed. Hard technologies are resistant to change and embody the status quo. Soft technologies enable creativity and change: where change occurs in distance education it is thus because, to the creator of a technology, it was soft. The harder the technology, the more resistant it will be to change.

Technological Acceptance and Use

It is not enough for technologies to change in order for change to occur in distance education. Those technologies need to be used, integrated, and absorbed into the educational system. Rogers's innovation diffusion theory (Rogers, 1995) has been highly influential as a means of describing how new technologies are taken up within a group or society. The pattern of acceptance by innovators, early adopters, early majority, late majority, and laggards has entered into popular vocabulary as a means of identifying or asserting identity in an individual's relationships with technology.

As well as describing the ways that technologies are taken up within a community, Rogers identified a characteristic S-curve for adoption that was influenced by five main factors: relative advantage, compatibility, trialability, observability, and complexity. While the S-curve is broadly accepted as a fair empirical description of the ways that identifiable groups of people approach innovative technologies, there is considerably less agreement about the factors relating to technologies that influence their success or failure. Rogers's factors were based more on inductive reasoning than empirical observation. Several competing models that provide a more solid foundation for exploring the ways that technologies diffuse through a society or community have been developed, the most popular of which is the technology acceptance model (TAM), based on the theory of reasoned action (Davis, 1989). The essence of the TAM model is that the success or failure of a new instance of (information) technology is determined by interplay between its perceived usefulness and its perceived ease of use. While it offers a compelling model, TAM has been criticized in recent years as providing an idealized and empirically naïve view that provides little predictive power and only some help with managing the process when applied in the real world (Bagozzi, 2007).

The uptake of technology is not simply a matter of whether people choose to use a technology but whether that technology actually has any real value. TAM has been developed and refined by Venkatash and others to incorporate more of these factors, leading to the Unified Theory of Acceptance and Use of Technology (UTAUT), which has become widely used over the past decade (Venkatesh, Morris, Davis, & Davis, 2003). UTAUT attempts to place more emphasis on empirical findings as a means of prediction as well as to provide a broad description of how technologies are accepted by a given population. UTAUT extends the two main constructs of TAM to include social influences and other facilitating conditions. Overlaid on these, various authors have added a host of other factors including gender, age, experience, voluntariness, playfulness, self-efficacy, and much more. As Bagozzi (2007) observes, the combination of many (at least 8) independent variables for predicting behaviour and at least 41 independent variables for predicting intention makes the model seem very cumbersome, to say the least, as well as highly culturally determined.

The Task-Technology Fit (TTF) model provides an alternative concerned primarily with the performance of a technology. It is a common-sense idea that, simply put, implies that one will achieve good performance when a technology provides features and support that fit the task (Goodhue & Thompson, 1995). Goodhue and Thompson's version of the TTF model includes a range of factors that lead to utilization, to create the Technology to Performance Chain (TPC) model. This considers task characteristics, individual user characteristics, technology characteristics, and an assortment of precursors such as beliefs, habits, norms, and facilitating conditions that, together with TTF, can be used to predict or explain performance impacts. Of course, any technology acceptance model has to work within a distance education setting to be of use. For this, it is useful to apply a domain-specific quality model. The most successful of these in recent years is the SLOAN-C five-pillar model (Moore, 2005) which considers five dimensions of quality: learning effectiveness, scale (cost-effectiveness and commitment), access, faculty satisfaction, and student satisfaction. While subject to many interpretations, the breadth of the five pillars provides a useful framework for evaluation of innovation.

Disruptive Technologies

Perrow offers a model of technology divided into the routine and the non-routine, with the latter finding their application in unanalyzable, problem-solving areas, with many exceptions to rules (Perrow, 1986). In the behaviourist/cognitivist years, the technological assemblies that constituted distance education were notably fixed in the area of the routine: to create learning sequences was to follow a series of formalized steps, typified by Gagne's nine events of instruction (Gagne, 1985). To support such developments, models such as ADDIE and Dick and Carey's systematic design methods (Dick & Cary, 1990) attempted to turn loose, craft-based methods into reliable and repeatable mechanical design methods. It is notable that, as distance education has become more social and grounded in the construction of knowledge; the technologies that support it have become softer, more yielding and more open to uncertainty in form and function. This tension between soft and hard technologies has been and remains an ongoing feature of distance education over the past decades. Softness opens up opportunities for change and increasing creativity, in which teacher-invented technologies are overlaid on top of the electronic and organizational tools. This makes fertile ground for the non-routine or disruptive technologies.

Christensen distinguishes between routine and non-routine kinds of technologies, differentiating between those that sustain and those that disrupt, for which Christensen coined the term *disruptive technologies* (1997). As the ever-increasing changes wrought, as the adjacent possible expand, some technologies have the capacity to change the way we behave or work, whether they are at the high end of discontinuous revolution or the low end of improving efficiency. There are significant differences in how we adopt each kind of technology. Arthur notes that most technologies grow by a process of assembly, and radical discontinuities are as rare, for much the same reasons, as Kuhnian scientific revolutions (Arthur, 2009). One reason for this is that disruptive technologies are innovations that at first may result in worse product performance than what came previously (Christensen, 2008). It is an almost universal feature of truly innovative technologies that they tend to be less able when they first make an appearance than the technologies that they replace. For example, propeller-driven aircraft outperformed jet engines for around two decades before jet engines developed to a point where they were clearly superior to their forebears (Arthur, 2009).

This initial worsening can act as a brake on initial uptake, especially for hard technologies that lack innate flexibility, and may be part of the reason that, though there are many inventions, only a few take root.

Systems Theories

An alternative way of understanding technology diffusion in distance education relates to systems theory, in which the various components of an educational technology system are examined in relation to one another and their broader context. Systems theories create dynamic models in which actors are viewed in terms of their connections with others, a principle followed to its logical conclusion in actor-network-theory, where the human and the non-human are all treated as *actants* in an interconnected and co-dependent network (Latour, 2005). Thanks to their deep connectedness with almost all systems in society, from government to commerce, as well as path dependencies that stretch back into medieval times, educational systems are unusually impervious to change, a feature that masks the effects of disruption at first (Christensen, Horn, & Johnson, 2008). This is echoed by Blin and Munro (2008) who, looking at technological change through the lens of activity theory, make the important observation that technologies are a part of an overall socio-technical system and that their success or failure is highly dependent on how they integrate with the existing processes and technical forms within an institution as well as in a broader context. Importantly, they often fail to fit. Dron (2012) similarly suggests that there is no innate primacy in the roles of technologies (including pedagogies) within an educational system but that all must work together as part of the technological assembly. Something radically new is unlikely to fit as easily as something that is an incremental evolution of old technologies.

This is an unequal assembly in which some parts are more equal than others. As Brand (1997) observes, slower moving, larger scale agents play a more important role in determining the shape of a system than smaller, faster changing technologies. This means that the path dependencies of history that have led to large-scale structures, such as universities, schools, classrooms, libraries, and so on, will tend to force smaller innovations and changes into a mould that may be a poor fit, and thus such technologies may fail to gain a significant foothold or be mutated so that their usefulness is considerably diminished.

A complete systems view suggests that to make big changes the changes should therefore be made across the system, concentrating on the larger slow-moving parts. Such changes are, thankfully, rare, or we would spend our lives running to stay in the same place like the Red Queen in *Alice Through the Looking Glass*. That said, disruptive technologies could be the lever for such a change. Christensen describes how innovative change spreads in a technological system, typically through small footholds that work their way through the system once established in niches (Christensen, 2008). It is notable that the spread of distance technologies to face-to-face institutions, where the LMS is virtually ubiquitous and increasingly large parts of programs are available in distance formats, shows very much this pattern. Dron (2002) explains how, in distance education, open universities provided relatively secluded spaces that were fertile breeding grounds for innovation; these spaces were able to develop fairly fully before spreading to the broader ecosystem. This is a distinctly Darwinian evolutionary pattern. Like the species of finch evolving on different Galapagos Islands, parcellation enables a higher rate of evolution that may then spread to the broader population as links and isthmuses form. This is not limited to changes across the educational system. For such changes to spread in a similar way within an organization, an organizational hierarchy that is either relatively flat or that distributes significant autonomy to the branches of the hierarchy can provide the levels of parcellation needed for innovations to gain a foothold. Allowing many flowers to bloom requires new varieties to be at least partially sheltered from each other at first, so that those that might be weaker in their initial stages of development have a chance to reach maturity.

OPEN QUESTIONS

Behaviourist/Cognitivist Solutions and Open Questions

The behaviourist/cognitivist approach to distance education has traditionally led to a slow process of change to or within a course. For those following a pattern of large-scale industrialization, as suggested by Peters (1994), huge amounts of effort and time are delivered up-front in the production of learning resources, designs, and materials, with reduced costs emerging only when courses and learning materials are re-used over a period of, typically, years (Bates, 2005). This makes them extremely unresponsive to changes occurring around them: topical courses are difficult to produce, and it is hard to adapt a course to any social context much less for an individual. They are archetypally hard technologies, especially when presented as monolithic packages.

One response to these problems has been attempts to employ reusable learning objects (RLOS). The theoretical advantage of RLOS lies in the ability to reuse and recombine objects to create new learning resources with relatively little effort. This allows creative flexibility because of the softening effects of aggregation. RLOS were popular among their creators in the 1990s and early 2000s but, in most contexts, failed to gain much foothold. A variety of reasons for this failure have been proposed (McGreal, 2004; Polsani, 2003) and they may all play a role. A proliferation of incompatible and committee-driven standards, issues around ownership, licensing and copyright, a failure to define appropriate granularities for RLOS, inflexibility in options or tools to modify, assemble and customize objects, a focus that failed to take into account the ways that people actually construct courses, and weaknesses in a conceptual model that claimed benefits derived from object-oriented software design but only delivered minimal benefits of poorly fitting Lego bricks might have played a role (Dron, 2007).

However, where it is possible to enforce more rigid adherence to standards and methods, such as in large private education companies and military organizations, RLOS have had a good deal of success. In recent years, a more flexible approach has been employed that rechristens RLOS as *open educational resources* (OERS), a more generic term that embraces the ambiguities inherent in the original concept (Friesen, 2009). What makes OERS distinctive is not their technical implementation so much as the fact that they are open and softer, so may be freely adapted and changed, rather than simply assembled in limited ways, as was the case with RLOS. They benefit both from the innate softening power of assembly as well as the capacity to be changed, modified, and adapted at a fine level of granularity. OERS present a far more powerful approach to reuse than RLOS, which re-establishes context, adaptability, and ownership for those seeking to use them. Economic models for sustainability of such resources remain an issue, but in practical terms, the availability of countless millions of high-quality OERS from reputable sources, including many of the world's top universities, makes this a moot point. Unfortunately, as such content becomes more prevalent, it becomes increasingly difficult to find the most effective and relevant OERS.

Collaborative filtering provides a potential solution as it has proven to be a highly effective means of recommending books (Amazon), videos (YouTube) and other resources, while Google's PageRank, an adaptive algorithm, makes it perhaps the most successful example of online learning on the planet today. However, recommendations based on explicit or implicit preferences are of far more limited value in an educational context, where needs are highly discontinuous, where current needs seldom predict future requirements, and where there are many dimensions of value apart from simple preference (Drachsler, Hummel, & Koper, 2007; Dron, Mitchell, Siviter, & Boyne, 2000). Some attempts have been made to marry semantic web ontologies to recommendations (e.g., Karampiperis & Sampson, 2004), but these are complex to produce and maintain, and the ontologies are nearly always driven by rigid subject taxonomies rather than pedagogical value that shifts to suit learner and contextual differences. Few if any effective solutions yet exist that adapt well to context or that provide a pedagogically driven map that can supply a program of learning rather than just resource recommendations. There are also risks of unnecessary hardening if recommendations become too strong and the development of sub-optimal fitness (Page, 2011) and filter bubbles—an echo chamber effect in which novelty and diversity is suppressed (Pariser, 2011).

One solution to the problem of adaptation and diversity is the use of adaptive hypermedia (AH), in which a single set of resources can be adapted to many different user needs (Brusilovsky, 2001). While this continues to flourish as an area of research, few benefits have seeped into the mainstream, at least partly because AH is difficult to produce. This is not just because of having to model potential paths but also because the provision of more material is more work, which makes production even slower than in the traditional non-adaptive model. Also, there are limited authoring tools (Cristea & Verschoor, 2004) and learner models are often quite primitive and inflexible, but it is difficult to improve flexibility without also increasing difficulties or at least complexity for learners (Kay, 2006). Some success has been achieved in looser forms of adaptation, especially those employing social methods, and some attempts have been made at establishing standards for inter-operability of user and content models, but the fact that adaptivity means that there must be more content also means that cost and complexity of AH remains high. Whether or not such methods result in learning improvements, their cost effectiveness remains open to question. Some forms of AH, especially those that present a filtered view rather than emphasizing or de-emphasizing content, also run the risk of hardening.

Social-Constructivist Solutions and Open Questions

Social models of learning are effective and, in principle, soft and flexible, requiring relatively few resources to create and relatively little time to make changes and implement innovations. However, in keeping with the maxim that soft is "hard," they are very expensive to run and they scale very badly (Annand, 2007; Bates, 2005). For small cohorts, flexibility is easy to achieve and innovations can be implemented quickly and easily. For large cohorts, the only plausible method of teaching is to split students into small groups, often led by cheaper trainee or student facilitators, whose expertise and experience may lead to variable standards and quality. This in turn raises issues of quality control and management, which means that costs are not only high in terms of tutoring time but also in management. Unless standards are allowed to drift, this introduces a harder layer of management technology, which means that many of the benefits of softness and flexibility for change are lost.

Few effective generalizable solutions to this quandary have been proposed, though there are methods that can work in limited cases. Pedagogical techniques such as peer teaching, for example, offer some reduction in the need for tutoring time and can increase the number of students that may be accommodated by a single academic facilitator (Goodlad & Hirst, 1989). This is a very soft technology that generally requires skill and creativity to implement effectively, although intelligent crowd-powered ICTs can help to guide the process (Gutiérrez, Pardo, & Kloos, 2006; Vassileva, 2004) and there are great pedagogical benefits from teachback (having students demonstrate their knowledge by simulating or actually teaching someone else) (Pask & Lewis, 1972).

Connectivist Solutions and Open Questions

One of the most compelling arguments for the use of connectivist approaches in distance learning is their innate capacity for and valorization of change. The major foundations of connectivism include the principles that currency is critical for all connectivist learning, that learning is a knowledge creation process, and the learning happens in many different ways and rests in a diversity of opinions (Siemens, 2005). This makes connectivist approaches innately extremely soft. The methods and technologies used in a connectivist approach to learning and teaching thus embrace change at a fundamental level and provide fertile ground for diversity and innovation. Connectivist approaches are seldom bound to any but the broadest of intended learning outcomes, seldom involve the need for large amounts of planning or structure, and seldom require the use of specific tools. This does not make the management of change in a connectivist model unproblematic. In fact, the chaos that ensues swings notably away from a Stalinist regime of excessive control to one where it is commonplace for there to be insufficient control, a chaotic Red Queen regime in which learners are left lost in social space, running to stay in the same spot, and moving through sub-optimal paths. Once again, we see that soft technologies are hard to use.

The enormous drop-out rate from such courses is, partly, the consequence of such problems, though other factors such as lack of need for commitment, lack of accreditation, and lack of formal support have also contributed to challenges of early connectivist learning experiments. This is a fast-evolving and developing problem space where solutions ranging from simple organizational procedures to complex mashup, analytic, and visualization tools vie to provide solutions that are, as yet, poorly developed, and the balance between soft flexibility and hard structure remains problematic.

IMPLICATIONS FOR PRACTICE

The braiding of technologies that defines and characterizes distance education presents both threats and opportunities. As technologies evolve, they open up new adjacent possibles, but they do so in an environment of constraint full of ossified paths and histories that cannot easily be rewritten. In this section we look at approaches to facilitating innovation and assembling systems for distance education that are flexible and reliable.

Conditions and Cultures for Innovation

If it is assumed that change is a good (or at least a necessary) thing, then it is important that an organization designs the processes and procedures to support it. In an organizational context, this is about building processes and organizational forms that provide space for innovation to occur. Organizational approaches include the use of a variant on Skunk Works (a term derived from Lockheed Martin's separate entity for innovation, who own the trademark in most countries), time to play (such as Google's famous day-a-week on innovative projects that interest their workers), and policies that valorize diversity and experimentation. Florida (2005) has found that the most creative and innovative cities thrive because of tolerance of and cultivation of diversity, and very similar principles apply within organizations (Seely Brown & Duguid, 2000).

Importantly, such initiatives should not be separated from the rest of the organization, nor should they separate those who are innovating from those who perform more mundane work. Brown has found that organizations that take people out of their working context in order to foster innovation do indeed encourage people to innovate, but their innovations do not seep into and spread through the organization unless such a process is embedded in the workplace (Brown, 2009). There is a fine balance between providing the space and time to innovate and the need to integrate: It is easy for demands of everyday work to reduce the capacity to innovate, but separation of people from their context in time and/or space reduces the chances that innovative thinking will spread through the organization. The same digital technologies that have come to dominate distance learning, especially those that are inherently social, can, of course, help to fill this gap by enabling communities to overlap and blend (Dron, Anderson, & Siemens, 2011).

Conditions and Cultures for Adoption

Hew and Brush (2006) identify a range of barriers to adoption of technologies: resources, institution, subject culture, attitudes/beliefs, knowledge/skills, and assessment. The grocery-type list seems a little arbitrary and full of overlaps but is useful as an instrument for discovering areas of difficulty. The researchers found that the overwhelming number of reported barriers (in this case for K–12 teachers but the principle is transferable) related to resources and knowledge/skills. If change is to be enabled and passed through the system, it is vital that sufficient resources, including time, tools, and opportunities to learn are provided.

Classic divisions within academia and commerce, where hierarchical levels of organization effectively separate disciplines and administrative areas, are a poor means for innovation to occur and disseminate (Becher & Trowler, 2001). Hierarchies make it difficult for connections between branches of the tree to be made and encourage a monoculture where diversity is throttled (S. Johnson, 2012). An institution that is built on hierarchical lines is a harder technology than one that is more distributed. Innovation and change tend to happen at the edges between communities when people are able to shift between systems, communities, and disciplines (Wenger, 1998). It is also important in any system to ensure that the organizational technologies are not too hard: as Brand observes of buildings, "high-road" magazine architecture tends to be beautiful but inflexible, failing to adapt to changing needs and circumstances.

The most effective designs for change are those that may most easily be extended and modified (Brand, 1997). This primarily means building systems from smaller pieces by assembly, following Arthur's observation that technologies evolve through a process of assembly (2009). An ecological approach can help evolve diversity and thus innovation (Brown, 2009). In ecological terms, parcellation plays a central role in accelerating evolution, but must be tempered by a mechanism for innovation to pass out of small islands and isolated spaces into the larger savannahs and spaces (Calvin, 1997). The message is clear, there should be fuzzy, permeable, and changeable borders between isolated organizational spaces, where innovation can emerge and seep through the organization, without the bottlenecks and filtering of artificially imposed hierarchical layers (Seely Brown & Duguid, 2000).

Approaches to Design for Change

Soft technologies enable and usually demand creativity, adaptation, and change, while hard technologies actively militate against it with regard to the phenomena that such technologies orchestrate. Constraints can form a stable base from which creativity might stem, but only if they do not replace the creative process. If those constraints are the result of hardening and replacing, say, pedagogies then they prevent innovation.

Given that distance education is defined by technologies, if we are seeking to enable change our technologies should be at least somewhat soft with regard to pedagogies, or at least capable of being softened. This creates a complex tension because the price to be paid is usually in terms of ease of use, efficiency, freedom from error, and speed. There is at least a partial solution to this dilemma. Arthur's (2009) insight that technology evolves through a process of assembly provides the key to building distance education systems that are adaptable and evolvable.

Physical assembly has historically required a high degree of skill but, now that the majority of distance learning involves digital platforms and virtual technologies, the means to assemble rich learning spaces for distance education is now affordable, available, and within reach. When it was necessary to understand complex tools such as programming languages to create dynamic content and interactive designs for learning, making changes was a technically complex process. Building from pre-assembled components makes it simple, though does demand that teachers and learning designers need proficiency or the means to become proficient or call on the proficiency of others. The principle of making change through assembly applies to both content and the processes needed to create the technologies of distance education. Assembly of components allows softer technologies to be built out of smaller, harder technologies and, where it is necessary to make adjustments, narrows the range of adjustments that need to be made to smaller, more easily managed components.

In general, the softer a system is to begin with, the easier it will be to change. Because humans are the orchestrators of phenomena, they are part of the technology and can therefore influence it to become whatever they wish simply by deciding to do things differently, notwithstanding the affordances and limitation of change inherent in the surrounding technologies with which it is assembled. However, the effort needed by both teachers and students in softer systems can make it uneconomical and unnecessarily difficult for both parties, so it is often useful to replace softer processes with harder technology pieces. To give an extreme example, the softest pedagogy for a course might be to simply tell students the topic to be covered and to tell them to go and find out for themselves. This might be seen as a very flexible approach, but for most learners it would be far too soft and would leave many feeling unsupported and confused. Increasing the hardness by adding more structure to the process, based on knowledge of cultural standards, prerequisite knowledge, and how people learn, would make it easier for most students. However, beyond a certain point, the reduced flexibility and reduced opportunities for change and adaptation as increasingly hard elements replaced the softer processes would be counter-productive for those who need more personal control.

Content Re-Use Process

In the cognitivist/behaviourist model of distance education, the use of OERS as part of the learning technology assembly can make an industrial approach far more adaptable and agile, reducing the time from planning to implementation of courses from years to weeks, and enabling the fairly rapid adaptation of courses that are already running. It can also allow for the development of different paths that may be more suited to different learners, a process that was, in the past, unfeasibly expensive for all but the largest scale of course implementation. This means that older cascading waterfall design methodologies that take a step-wise project management approach of the sort championed by Dick and Carey or embedded in the ADDIE process need to be modified, accelerated, or abandoned to enable faster development cycles, easier learner and teacher customization, and richer feedback loops. There are lessons to be drawn here from the software development world using methodologies such as Scrum or Extreme Programming (XP) (Johnson, 2006).

For those adopting a social–constructivist model, OERS can provide vital resources to help scaffold a problem-based approach, providing raw materials to be used in the co-construction of knowledge. OERS, in the loosest sense, are also a necessary basis for connectivist models of learning: They offer important nodes to be connected in the knowledge that exists out in the network.

Whatever pedagogies underpin the use of external content, difficulties remain in finding OERS that are appropriate and adaptable to specific needs and the Not-Invented-Here syndrome, though lessened by the capacity to adapt some resources (Laurillard, Swift, & Darby, 1993).

Learning Environment Design Process

Beyond OERS, the use of components is also crucial to the creation of technically mediated processes that may be easily changed so that, for example, technologies for communication, sharing, discovery, connection, and organization may be used and customized by those who are relatively unskilled in the use of these technologies. To support cognitivist/behaviourist and social–constructivist models, variations on the LMS have become the normal supporting technology. Unfortunately, they have proven to be hard technologies, brittle and inflexible, creating a strong set of path dependencies and proprietary lock-in, even when implemented through open source tools (Lane, 2009).

Much of the value of the LMS is that it reduces choices for the designer of learning spaces, offering a pre-built structure where the system designers have already made smaller decisions. However, this makes it significantly complex to make changes that are not easily accommodated by the system. There are various levels of technology support based on assembly of components that can overcome this problem, again softening through the process of assembly. At its simplest, a plugin-based architecture, enabling the development of learning environments that are customised to their context, can provide a flexible and easily extended basis for learning at a distance. Moodle (flexible through plugin modules) or Blackboard (flexible through plugin Building Blocks) are popular examples of this genre, each offering a monolithic core that can be modified or extended with extra blocks of code created by IT departments, the community, or commercial providers.

A more flexible framework, OKI, was initially designed as an ambitious attempt to provide a system built almost entirely around plugin-like components but it was over-complex and its flagship product, Sakai, largely ossified this framework into what is essentially just another LMS like its more monolithic competitors. The problem with plugin-based approaches is that they tend to be run at an organizational level, with plugins determined and installed centrally. The larger the organization, the higher the hierarchical top-down level at which this happens, which means that the most well-meaning centralized IT departments are bound by the need to cater for everyone to produce something that is, inevitably, a compromise for some, if not all, who wish to use it. They are soft for the system administrators but can remain hard for those who use them to create learning experiences. The more that component-based assembly can be devolved to the creators of learning spaces, the greater the opportunities for innovation and change because it makes the technologies as used by those individuals softer.

At the opposite extreme to the managed spaces of institutional and commercial learning environments, for those following a connectivist approach there are countless sites and systems that may be found and/or configured to suit almost any conceivable learning need. Larger social sites offer a wide range of means for individuals to assemble a variety of technologies in a single space, in a manner that is not dissimilar to the process of adding plugins but that, crucially, is under the control of the teacher or learning designer rather than the administrators of ICTs. Facebook and OpenSocial apps, or widget-based interfaces such as those used by Wookie, or social application assembly kits such as those provided by Ning allow teachers and learners to construct very highly customized learning technologies.

For those following a connectivist model, the emphasis on sense-making, filtering, and assembly means that any and all technologies for sharing, communication, and connection are valid means of acquiring knowledge. To a large extent, control over not just the content and process but also the technological means of managing that process is what makes it a connectivist approach in the first place. The big downside of the total freedom implied by a connectivist approach is the skill needed and the relatively unstructured and unguided dispersal of knowledge across the network. With virtually limitless choices, making any intelligent choices becomes difficult and thus reduces rather than increases control (Schwartz, 2004). As Baynton (1992) suggests, control is not just about having choice but also having the power to make those choices, which means knowing enough to distinguish between them. A number of solutions can make this easier, most of which involve some form of further assembly: in essence, to make systems from larger pieces. Lightweight APIs (application programming interfaces) as well as interchange formats such as RSS make it possible to link most modern social systems more or less richly in the form of mashups. This is especially useful when combined with templates, whereby designers do not need to build systems from scratch but may use partially assembled systems as a starting point.

Bearing in mind that change is a learning process, templates provide the scaffolding to help less experienced learners to become competent and effective experts. Unlike the guided process of the LMS, templates that are constructed from components do not present an insuperable barrier for those who need something not provided by the system. Component-based designs may always be softened by adding new technologies to augment the old, or hardened by replacing flexible, softer components with less flexible, harder components.

There is one notable dark side to an assembly approach to enabling change in learning environments: managing many small pieces that are required to interoperate can be significantly harder for ICT managers than managing a monolith, where a single team of creators helps to assure consistency and interoperability between the pieces. There are no simple answers to this problem apart from careful adherence to standards (as they emerge) for interfaces, coding, and design.

Approaches to Selecting Learning Technologies

While a combination of objects and templates that can be assembled is effective for building distance education systems with flexibility for change, it is also necessary to be able to select the right pieces in the first place. Tony Bates (2005) has devised the ACTIONS model for selecting technologies for use in a distance education context, which includes, in approximate order of importance:

- *Access.* No technology will have any value unless learners may access it. This is not quite as simple as whether, say, a device is available, but also how it is available; a shared computer in a house, for example, is less valuable to learners than one to which they have exclusive use.

- *Cost.* It is at least as much to do with cost-effectiveness as actual price of delivery.

- *Teaching and learning.* How good is the support provided for intended or implicit pedagogies and methods? While the technology should minimally provide the necessary medium for the intended practices, some will be a better fit than others.

- *Interactivity and user friendliness.* Does it enable learners to interact with content, teachers, and one another?

- *Organizational issues.* What are the requirements and barriers within an organization? For Bates, this covers a multitude of contextual and system factors.

- *Novelty.* How new is it?

- *Speed.* How quickly can it be used to create and change courses?

While access is probably the first thing to consider in most cases in distance education contexts, the order of significance of the other factors will vary. The author has participated in many developments where speed is far more significant than the other factors and drives the choice of technology, for example, but has never come across a situation where novelty is more important than any other factor on the list. Although one suspects that the order of the factors is more to do with creating a snappy acronym, and Bates plays down the huge range of interdependencies between them, his ACTIONS model offers a viable framework for technology selection and specification that can greatly increase the potential for successful change.

Consideration of all of these factors does not assure successful uptake. For this it is necessary to turn to models of technology acceptance and task–technology fit but, as we have seen, these are best seen as guides for reflective practice than formulae for success. It is also notable that Bates's model underplays the dependencies between novel technologies and those that are already available, relegating the problem to a minor aspect of organizational issues. This is not just important but, one could argue, it is paramount. If, as we have seen throughout this chapter, technologies are assemblies, then it is crucial that they should work well together. This is not only true of the electronic elements, where things like standards and APIS can help, but in the pedagogies and organizational systems of which it will be a part. To give a trivial but telling example, a technology in which the word *course* is hard-coded to mean what North Americans recognise as a certain kind of learning unit will fit poorly with an educational system such as that found in the UK where such units are more commonly described as *modules*, or *papers* in New Zealand, and where *course* has a quite different meaning, more akin to that of *program* in North America.

Following from this, an important aspect of managing change is not just selecting but in deselecting technologies. Path dependencies, locked-in databases of content and interaction, and the inevitable intertwining of technologies into other technologies and systems means that this is often significantly more difficult than selecting them in the first place. Few have the luxury of reinventing systems from the ground up and the costs of moving from something as deeply entwined as, say, a learning management system, are extremely high, almost always leading to resistance and resentment. Once again, being able to assemble technologies from small components in the first place can mitigate many of these problems, allowing components to be replaced with relatively little disruption to the whole system.

CONCLUSION

The rapid and radical changes in teaching and learning technologies during the past decade show little or no sign of abating in the future. Disruptive non-routine technologies change the rules again and then again. Increasing affordability and sophistication of extraordinarily useful and convenient machines—such as 3D printers—means that the ability to easily assemble technologies for learning will soon no longer be limited to virtual objects. The merging of physical and virtual spaces through ubiquitous computing, where devices are embedded in our surroundings in ever-greater densities, from shirt buttons to furniture, from intelligent cloth to smart dust, will open vistas of opportunity and threat. Augmented reality, where virtual information is overlaid on real spaces so that we can know more about our surroundings when we need to know it, will open up adjacent possibles that we can only begin to guess at and change the things we need to know and how we need to know them. These, and others like them, will be and are becoming truly disruptive technologies that will radically alter the ways that we can enable learning and that will, no doubt, lead to new and enhanced pedagogies that are not yet conceivable. This is not because we cannot imagine the tools and their affordances (we can), nor that the pedagogies that will emerge will be completely new to the world (they won't), but because we cannot reliably infer the effects that they will have in a large system, nor the roles they will play when they work together, nor the adjacent possibles that will emerge through those assemblies.

The shared characteristics of these emerging systems are their capabilities for assembly and integration at a depth of sophistication that we have never seen before. This means that they will be remarkably soft, malleable and open to creative uses. If such changes are not to overwhelm us or to channel us in directions we do not wish to go, we need models and conceptual tools to deal with them and their interactions, of which we have hinted in this chapter.

However, we also need to be mindful that change is, for the most part, not a wave so much as a diverse rippling tide that fills in gaps very unevenly. Resistance to change is only a small factor when compared with the massive economic, cultural, and social inequalities that exist worldwide, where there are innumerable places that the Internet has barely touched, places it is controlled with vigour, places where clean water, let alone electricity, has yet to arrive, places where cultural mores, exploitive elites, and religious prohibitions actively resist change. Learning technologies, be they pedagogies, programs, or pedestals, are codetermined by their surrounding ethics, socio-economic circumstance, legislation, belief systems, histories, and desires. They are not, and have never been, neutral agents. As well as being value laden in their inception and acceptance, they are co-determinants of what we do, what we are and how we behave (Feenberg & Callon, 2010). We shape our buildings and afterwards our buildings shape us (Churchill, 1943). We shape our tools and then our tools shape us (McLuhan, 1994, p.xxi). While change will surely come, it will be uneven and take many forms. The great softness of the new opportunities for assembly might make such tools bend easily to fit the larger whole, perhaps (at least at first) even reinforcing rather than disrupting educational norms and rituals.

What binds all aspects of change is the process of learning. To learn is to change and the changes wrought by and wrought in distance education are, by and large, virtually all manifestations of learning: a process of growth that incorporates earlier knowledge and builds upon it to create new knowledge. To learn is also to learn to learn, and learning to learn is thus, more often than not, to change how we go about changing. If we can learn new ways of changing, then we can begin a rich evolutionary process where the rules of evolution themselves evolve (Kelly, 1994), thus enabling more change and continuous evolution towards a peak of fitness that forever moves as we approach it. This process of change and learning defines all of our educational systems, albeit sometimes it seems as if the change happens in almost geological timescales. It is therefore quite important to understand it, not as a simple process of cause and effect but as a richly dynamic, interconnected, and human system in which we are at once the actors and the acted-upon, simultaneously subject and object, caught in a never-ending dance where no one knows the steps but from which a marvellous order emerges.

REFERENCES

Anderson, T., & Dron, J. (2011). Three generations of distance education pedagogy. *International Review of Research in Open and Distance Learning, 12*(3). Retrieved from http://www.irrodl.org/index.php/irrodl/article/view/890

Annand, D. (2007). Re-organizing universities for the information age. *International Review of Research in Open and Distance Learning, 8*(3).

Arthur, W. B. (2009). *The nature of technology: What it is and how it evolves.* New York: Free Press.

Bagozzi, R. P. (2007). The legacy of the technology acceptance model and a proposal for a paradigm shift. *Journal of the Association for Information Systems, 8*(4). Retrieved from http://aisel.aisnet.org/jais/vol8/iss4/12

Bates, A. W. (2005). *Technology, e-learning and distance education.* London, UK: Routledge. Retrieved from http://books.google.co.uk/books?id=Qc4_UAtJDKwC

Baynton, M. (1992). Dimensions of "control" in distance education: A factor analysis. *The American Journal of Distance Education, 6*(2), 17–31.

Becher, T., & Trowler, P. R. (2001). *Academic tribes and territories* (2nd ed.) Buckingham, UK: Open University Press.

Bessant, J., & Francis, D. (2005). Transferring soft technologies: Exploring adaptive theory. *International Journal of Technology Management & Sustainable Development, 4*(2), 93–112. Intellect Ltd. doi:10.1386/ijtm.4.2.93/1

Blin, F., & Munro, M. (2008). Why hasn't technology disrupted academics' teaching practices: Understanding resistance to change through the lens of activity theory. *Computers & Education, 50*(2), 475–490. Retrieved from http://www.sciencedirect.com/science/article/B6VCJ-4R4DFSW-2/2/195270ba14481199ef7da5eb03bc1ae3

Brand, S. (1997). *How buildings learn.* London: Phoenix Illustrated.

Brown, T. (2009). *Change by design: How design thinking transforms organizations and inspires innovation.* London: HarperCollins. Retrieved from http://books.google.co.uk/books?id=8ZRpPgAACAAJ

Brusilovsky, P. (2001). Adaptive hypermedia. *User Modelling and User-Adapted Interaction,* (11), 87–110.

Calvin, W. H. (1997). The six essentials? Minimal requirements for the darwinian bootstrapping of quality. *Journal of Memetics, 1.*

Christensen, C. (1997). *The innovator's dilemma: When new technologies cause great firms to fail.* Cambridge, MA: Harvard University Press.

Christensen, C. (2008). Disruptive innovation and catalytic change in higher education. *Forum Futures,* 2008, 43–46. Retrieved from http://net.educause.edu/ir/library/pdf/ff0810s.pdf.

Christensen, C., Horn, M., & Johnson, C. (2008). *Disrupting class: How disruptive innovation will change the way the world learns.* New York: McGraw Hill.

Churchill, W. (1943). H. C. Deb. 28 October 1943, Vol 393 c403.

Cristea, A., & Verschoor, M. (2004). The LAG grammar for authoring the adaptive web. *International Conference on Information Technology: Coding and Computing,* Vol. 1, (pp. 382–386). Las Vegas, NV: IEEE.

Davis, F. D. (1989). Perceived usefulness, perceived ease of use, and user acceptance of information technology. *MIS Quarterly, 13*(3), 319–340. Retrieved from http://www.jstor.org/stable/249008

Dick, W., & Cary, L. (1990). *The systematic design of instruction* (3rd ed.). New York: Harper Collins.

Drachsler, H., Hummel, H., & Koper, R. (2007). Recommendations for learners are different: Applying memory-based recommender system techniques to lifelong learning. In E. Duval, R. Klamma, & M. Wolpers (Eds.), *SIRTEL workshop at the EC-TEL 2007 Conference* (pp. 17–20), Crete, Greece. New York: Springer Verlag.

Dron, J. (2002). *Achieving self-organization in network-based learning environments.* Brighton, UK: University of Brighton, School of Computing, Mathematical & Information Sciences. Retrieved from http://www.cmis.brighton.ac.uk/staff/jd29/thesisorrectedfinaldraft.pdf

Dron, J. (2007). *Control and constraint in e-learning: Choosing when to choose.* Hershey, PA: Idea Group International.

Dron, J. (2012). The pedagogical–technological divide and the elephant in the room. *International Journal on E-Learning, 11*(1).

Dron, J., Anderson, T., & Siemens, G. (2011). Putting things in context: Designing social media for education. In S. Greener & A. Rospligliosi, Eds., *European Conference on E-Learning 2011.* Brighton, UK: ACI.

Dron, J., Mitchell, R., Siviter, P., & Boyne, C. (2000). CoFIND: An experiment in n-dimensional collaborative filtering. *Journal of Network and Computer Applications,* (23), 131–42.

Ellul, J. (1970). *The Technological Society.* (J. Wilkinson, trans.). New York: A.A. Knopf.

Feenberg, A., & Callon, M. (2010). *Between reason and experience: Essays in technology and modernity.* (Kindle ed.). MIT Press.

Florida, R. (2005). *Cities and the creative class.* New York: Routledge.

Franklin, U. M. (1999). *The real world of technology.* Concord, ON: House of Anansi.

Friesen, N. (2009). Open educational resources: New possibilities for change and sustainability. *International Review of Research in Open and Distance Learning, 10*(5). Retrieved from http://www.irrodl.org/index.php/irrodl/article/view/664

Gagne, R. (1985). *The Conditions of learning* (4th ed.). New York: Holt, Rhinehart & Winston.

Goodhue, D. L., & Thompson, R. L. (1995). Task-technology fit and individual performance. *MIS Quarterly, 19*(2), p. 213.

Goodlad, S., & Hirst, B. (1989). *Peer-tutoring: A guide to learning by teaching.* London, UK: Kogan Page.

Gunawardena, C. N., & McIsaac, M. S. (2004). Distance education. In D. H. Jonassen (Ed.), *Handbook of research for educational communications and technology* (2nd ed.), (pp. 355–96). Mahwah, NJ: LEA.

Gutiérrez, S., Pardo, A., & Kloos, C. D. (2006). Finding a learning path: Toward a swarm intelligence approach. In V. Uskov (Ed.), *5th IASTED international conference on Web-based education* (pp. 94–99). Puerto Vallarta, MX: ACTA Press.

Hew, K. F., & Brush, T. (2006). Integrating technology into K–12 teaching and learning: Current knowledge gaps and recommendations for future research. *Educational Technology Research and Development, 55*(3), 223–252. doi:10.1007/s11423-006-9022-5.

Johnson, D. L. (2006). *Designing to learn: Using agile software engineering methods for participatory instructional design.* Ann Arbor, MI: ProQuest.

Johnson, S. (2010). *Where good ideas come from: The natural history of innovation.* New York: Penguin.

Johnson, S. (2012). *Future perfect: The case for progress in a networked age.* New York: Riverhead/Penguin.

Karampiperis, P., & Sampson, D. (2004). Adaptive instructional planning using ontologies. In Kinshuk, C. K. Looi, E. Sutinen, D. Sampson, I. Aedo, L. Uden, & E. Kahkonen (Eds.), *ICALT 2004* (pp. 126–30). Joensuu, Finland: IEEE.

Kauffman, S. (2000). *Investigations*. New York: Oxford University Press.

Kauffman, S. (2008). *Reinventing the sacred: A new view of science, reason and religion*. Philadelphia, PA: Basic Books.

Kay, J. (2001). Learner Control. *User Modeling and User-Adapted Interaction, 11*(1-2), 111-27. Retrieved from http://www.springerlink.com/openurl.asp?genre=article&id=doi:10.1023/A:1011194803800

Kelly, K. (1994). *Out of control: The new biology of machines*. London, UK: Addison Wesley.

Kelly, K. (2010). *What technology wants*. New York: Viking.

Lane, L. M. (2009). Insidious pedagogy: How course management systems affect teaching. *First Monday, 14*(10). Retrieved from http://firstmonday.org/htbin/cgiwrap/bin/ojs/index.php/fm/article/view/2530/2303

Latour, B. (2005). *Reassembling the social: An introduction to actor-network-theory*. New York: Oxford University Press.

Laurillard, D., Swift, B., & Darby, J. (1993). Academics' use of courseware materials: A survey. *ALT-J, 1*(1), 4-14. doi:10.1080/0968776930010102.

McGreal, R. (2004). Learning objects: A practical definition. *International Journal of Instructional Technology and Distance Learning, 1*(9), 21-32. Retrieved from http://itdl.org/Journal/Sep_04/article02.htm

McLuhan, M. (1994). *Understanding media: The extensions of man*. Cambridge, Massachusetts: MIT Press.

McDonough, E. F., & Kahn, K. B. (1996). Using 'hard' and 'soft' technologies for global new product development. *R&D Management 26*(3) 1996), pp. 241-53. doi: 10.1111/j.1467-9310.1996.tb00959.x.

Moore, J. C. (2005). *The Sloan consortium quality framework and the five pillars*. Retrieved from http: //sloan consortium.org

Mumford, L. (1934). *Technics and civilization*. New York: Harcourt Brace. Retrieved from http://books.google.com/books?id=KupAAAAAIAAJ

Norman, D. A. (1993). *Things that make us smart: Defending human attributes in the age of the machine*. Cambridge, MA: Perseus.

Nye, D. E. (2006). *Technology Matters: Questions to Live With*. Cambridge, Massachusetts: MIT Press.

Page, S. E. (2011). *Diversity and complexity*. Princeton, NJ: Princeton University Press.

Papert, S. (1987). *A critique of technocentrism in thinking about the school of the future*. Retrieved from http://www.papert.org/articles/ACritiqueofTechnocentrism.html

Pariser, E. (2011). *The filter bubble: What the Internet is hiding from you*. New York: Penguin.

Pask, G., & Lewis, B. (1972). *Teaching strategies: A systems approach*. Bletchley, UK: Oxford University Press.

Perrow, C. (1986). Complex organizations: A critical essay. New York: Random House. Retrieved from http://books.google.com/books?id=19VkAAAAIAAJ

Peters, O. (1994). *Otto Peters on distance education: The industrialization of teaching and learning*. London: Routledge.

Polsani, P. (2003). Use and abuse of reusable learning objects. *Journal of Digital Information, 3*(4).

Rogers, E. M. (1995). *Diffusion of innovations.* New York: Free Press. Retrieved from http://books.google.ca/books?id=LpkPAQAAMAAJ

Rosen, W. (2010). *The most powerful idea in the world: A story of steam, industry, and invention.* New York: Random House. Retrieved from http://books.google.com/books?id=L1ZJToXrFZYC

Schwartz, B. (2004). *The paradox of choice: Why less is more.* New York: HarperCollins.

Seely Brown, J., & Duguid, P. (2000). *The social life of information.* Boston, MA: Harvard Business School.

Siemens, G. (2005). Connectivism: A learning theory for the digital age. *International Journal of Instructional Technology and Distance Learning, 2*(1). Retrieved from http://www.itdl.org/journal/jan_05/article01.htm

Taylor, T. (2010). *The artificial ape: How technology changed the course of human evolution.* New York: Palgrave Macmillan.

Vassileva, J. (2004). Harnessing P2P Power in the Classroom. *ITS 2004* (pp. 305–14).

Venkatesh, V., Morris, M. G., Davis, G. B., & Davis, F. D. (2003). User acceptance of information technology: Toward a unified view. *MIS Quarterly, 27*(3), 425–78. JSTOR. doi:10.2307/30036540

Wenger, E. (1998). *Communities of practice: Learning, meaning and identity.* New York: Cambridge University Press.

Zhouying, J. (2004). Technological progress in history: A survey of evolution and shift of research emphasis from "hard-tech" to "soft-tech" development. *International Journal of Technology Management & Sustainable Development, 3*(2), 133–48.

10 Professional Development and Faculty Support

Margaret Hicks

As higher education institutions around the world become more focussed on quality agendas and accountability, there is growing awareness of the critical function played by faculty[1] in creating, supporting, and assessing high-quality learning experiences (Hénard, 2010). Thus there is a need to ensure that all faculty are adequately prepared, motivated, and supported to carry out *all* aspects of academic practice including those that take place online or at a distance. We are moving into an era where all faculty need to have a level of competence with online learning and technologies. This is no longer optional but is *core* to the university learning environment. If this proposition is accepted then it raises the immediate question of how to best support faculty in both online and blended learning contexts.

As a learning modality there is a common understanding about the term *distance education* in contrast to on-campus teaching; however *online* and the use of different technologies in teaching and learning are blurring these

---

1 The term *faculty* is used throughout this chapter to refer to academic teaching staff in universities, as this was the term used in Zawacki-Richter's research (2009).

understandings and also the expectations of faculty. This is particularly evident in institutions where multi-modes of delivery are offered. Conflations of the terms are developing (Guri-Rosenblit and Gros, 2011) as elements of more hybrid, blended modes of delivery increase in popularity, where teaching includes a combination of face-to-face and virtual interactions with students. It is also important to acknowledge, as new technologies are being introduced to all modalities of teaching, the lessons that can be learned from distance education. As Bates observes:

> Distance education is now struggling to keep up with technological change, and as a result risks losing its unique identity and function. Nevertheless, distance education has developed procedures and practices that are valuable in ensuring the appropriate use of technology in teaching, and it would be a tragedy if this knowledge and experience were lost because of failure by distance and conventional educators to learn from one another. (2008, p. 233)

Significantly, we are now at a point in time where higher education institutions are enhancing their capacity technologically, and if the capabilities of faculty are also developed, it provides the ability to be more flexible and innovative in the ways that teaching and learning can be delivered and students can engage with learning. Universities are taking advantage of these developments to reach larger groups of students who may be remote and/or on campus but require or prefer more flexible learning modes. Increasingly, universities are using their learning management systems to deliver all services online and there is now less opportunity for faculty *not* to have some involvement in online teaching. It is therefore not surprising that professional development and faculty support was identified as an important area requiring more research (Zawacki-Richter, 2009).

SCOPING PROFESSIONAL DEVELOPMENT AND FACULTY SUPPORT

This chapter specifically addresses professional development and faculty support and, in doing so, the following considerations shape the discussion.

(1) Given the broadness of the topic, its complexities, and many
    contextual interpretations, some propositions relating to professional
    development and faculty needs are made. It is acknowledged that

these statements in themselves are contestable, and there is ongoing debate in the many communities of professional development about definitions, theoretical frameworks, perspectives, and practices. This in itself is an ongoing research project.

(2) Due to the complexities relating to a single understanding of professional development and the vast volume of literature on this and related topics, it is not possible to ensure that all the literature has been scoped. I have limited the search to recent literature (approximately the last five years) recognizing that what is presented is more a sample rather than a comprehensive review of this literature.

(3) Because of the nature of technologies, their developments and adoptions, their application in higher education teaching is a fast-moving and changing area of practice (Tynan & Lee, 2009). What may be a need at one point of time can very quickly move to the norm or be out-dated as a new technology or application is introduced.

(4) Importantly, I pose questions for further research. Again the number of questions and the level of specificity can be extensive and limitless, but I try to focus on key issues to be addressed.

UNDERSTANDING PROFESSIONAL DEVELOPMENT AND FACULTY SUPPORT

The need for faculty professional development is well documented and many state this in discussions about institutional engagement in technology and improved teaching and learning (Moore, 2006; Tanner, 2011). The most recent *ECAR National Study of Undergraduate Students and Information Technology* (EDUCAUSE, 2011) highlights that faculty need more assistance in their use of technologies in teaching, that students are wanting more online components as part of their learning experiences, and hence there is a need to provide more professional development opportunities.

The terms *professional development* and *faculty support* also have multiple meanings and different associations in different contexts. While others have debated and unpacked the meanings of these terms—*academic, staff, educational, faculty, instructional, organizational,* and *professional development* (Macdonald, 2009)—rather than repeat this discussion, I acknowledge the different interpretations and nuanced differences and will use *professional development* and *faculty support* in their broadest sense to encompass the terms.

Professional development in higher education is a young and emerging field of academic practice; a growing body of literature is developing with strengthening international links between countries, professional associations and colleagues in recognising similarities, differences, and research agendas in this work. Some recent discussions provide a good overview of the field, taking into account national differences and histories of this field of practice (Gosling, 2008; Hicks, 2006; Macdonald, 2009; Sorcinelli, Austin, Eddy, & Beach, 2006; Stefani, 2011). The *International Journal of Academic Development* (IJAD) provides a scholarly forum for discussion and research about this field of practice. It must also be acknowledged that some research on professional development is accessed from within the discipline or from particular modes of teaching, for example, engineering education or problem-based learning.

It is also important to recognise the distinction between formal and informal development opportunities. Discussions about professional development often and almost exclusively focus on formal development opportunities and activities. Informal development or *non-formal learning*, the term that Eraut (2000) prefers, is often under-recognized, but is a powerful and common way for knowledge to be developed and shared. Eraut's research focussed on how people learn, understanding the meaning of non-formal learning, and the development of a typology to conceptualize this type of learning. Although not evidenced-based, many recognize the value of informal interactions that occur between faculty in staff rooms, chat rooms, and other places. Yet little attention is given to non-formal learning when discussing professional development and faculty support for online distance education. This points to a significant area of further investigation.

- What is the role of non-formal learning in developing faculty?
- How can more non-formal learning opportunities be encouraged and valued?
- Are emerging teacher networks as found through social media, e-mail lists, and others providing new models of non-formal learning and support?

A distinction is often made between technical professional development and support for pedagogy. It is important that these are not separated and that professional development initiatives are integrated to include technical aspects, the pedagogy of learning, and their interactions (Koehler, Mishra, & Yahya, 2005). We increasingly understand the complex relationships between tools and the way they are used. As Kelly persuasively argues today, and Marshall McLuhan much earlier, "we are now symbiotic with technology" (Kelly, 2010, para. 3).

There are almost as many models of formal professional development as there are educational institutions. Fraser, Gosling, and Sorcinelli (2010) have attempted to conceptualize the different models within a framework that focusses on the individual, the institution, and the sector. Formal development can be organized and delivered by staff acting in defined roles as academic/faculty developers but can also be delivered by others both internal and external to the institution. Telg et al. (2005) raise the issue of the expertise of people delivering professional development. In their important report of the project, *A Roadmap to Effective Distance Education Instructional Design*, they focussed on the training of distance education trainers and highlighted the need to address the issue of the qualifications and training expertise of the people providing the professional development and faculty support. This poses the following questions:

- What are the qualifications, attributes, and level of expertise needed for delivering effective professional development for faculty?

- How important is it for developers or deliverers of faculty development to have discipline or academic credentials so as to be recognized by faculty for their expertise?

- Are there useful distinctions between training and development opportunities?

While the literature on professional development covers a wide range of areas, I want to make three observations that are particularly pertinent to this discussion:

- the link with the quality agendas
- the difficulty in demonstrating the impact of professional development
- the lack of empirical studies to evidence the field of professional development

Historically the organization of formal professional development activities for faculty, the establishment of units and centres, and the appointment of staff in dedicated roles to deliver these activities was largely due to an increasing focus on quality agendas in higher education—quality improvement and enhancement. More recently, as quality assurance agendas pervade the higher education environment, professional development has become aligned with initiatives and indicators to ensure *compliance*. Latchem provides an overview of the various approaches to quality assurance in online distance education in chapter 12 of this volume. While an increasing emphasis on quality provides both opportunities and challenges this has become a contested space within the professional development community and has influenced diverse individual o'rientations and institutional frameworks (Land, 2004; Hicks, 2006).

Higher education environments continue to change, as there is greater diversity in the student population, increased use of technology, increasing competition from the private sector, and more external accountability. As noted by Sorcinelli et al, (2006), "providing institutional support for faculty members facing changing contexts and new demands becomes an essential strategic choice" (p. xviii). It is well acknowledged that support for changing contexts, especially in the area of technology, is needed (Oblinger & Hawkins, 2006), but what are less clear are good models and methods to do this. Understanding where institutions position themselves in relation to quality agendas and the broader context is a critical consideration in any research into professional development and faculty support.

As accountability and standardization agendas become an increasing part of higher education experiences, being able to measure and demonstrate *impact* of professional development initiatives and interventions also attracts greater attention. Professional development and faculty support are not immune from this scrutiny. But how this is done and with what metrics and indicators is a topic that continues to be discussed and debated within the professional development community (Macdonald, 2009; Sorcellini et al, 2006). Framing the impact and evaluation of professional development for different learning modalities needs to be part of these discussions and inform future research agendas.

Although a strong need to investigate professional development and faculty support for online distance education has been identified, there continues to be a lack of empirical research to answer many critical questions, such as those raised earlier (Moore, 2006). There are however many case studies at an individual institutional level. While many of these cannot be generalized, they do offer insights into issues for further research. At another level, there is increasing commentary of a larger volume on areas of online education and professional development, and while I touch on some of this, again given that much of this is at the level of commentary and not evidenced based, I draw on them only to highlight some future areas of research. The area of technology-enhanced learning changes rapidly, thus impacting on the relevancy and currency of the research. A faculty needs analysis that is used as the basis for targeted professional development can very quickly be out-of-date.

RESEARCHING FACULTY PROFESSIONAL DEVELOPMENT AND
SUPPORT FOR ONLINE LEARNING

As mentioned above, while there is a growing literature on professional development, much of this is descriptive in nature and reflects the experience of individual authors rather than based on any large-scale empirical studies. As identified by many, little is known about how to best support staff to teach online (Taylor & McQuiggan, 2008). Moore identified that what is missing "is the perspective of the individual faculty members of their own development" (2006, p. 61).

The Sloan Consortium recently contributed to bridging this gap with a survey of over 10,000 faculty from 69 American colleges and universities in 2008 and 2009 (Seaman, 2009). This survey specifically sought the views and experiences of faculty with online teaching. Importantly and taking the position of online being part of all faculty experiences, the survey was targeted to all faculty members regardless of whether they were teaching fully online or not. Although only one-third of respondents had taught a fully online course, the responses concluded that all sectors of faculty are engaged in some level of online instruction, regardless of their employment type, full- or part-time employment, or age. This confirms some of the assumptions raised earlier, but also suggests that we need a more nuanced understanding of the profile and needs of faculty and their online engagement. Two other findings from this study are relevant to this discussion. The first relates to workload and the second to the quality of online learning. Both have implications for professional development.

The extra effort demanded to develop courses and teach online is often raised as an issue related to workload by faculty. The Sloan study (Seaman, 2009) confirmed these beliefs about effort on task with 64% of faculty stating that it takes more time and effort to teach online than face-to-face and more than 85% of faculty believing that online course development takes more time and effort. Others advocate that significant additional time is required to learn the technologies and then prepare teaching material (Tynan & Lee, 2009). Again, further investigation needs to made into whether this is a result of first-time engagement with technologies, the type of support and development provided and accessed, and the instructional strategies employed by teachers. Longitudinal data, tracking individual experiences over time, would be useful in assisting institutions in determining the right type and quantity of support to promote effective online teaching.

Quality agendas are at the forefront of attention for most institutions, and the Sloan survey tested the perception, held by many, that online courses do not have the same quality learning outcomes as face-to-face instruction. However these views are shifting with greater engagement with online learning. The majority of faculty with online teaching experience believed that "learning outcomes were as good as or better than face-to-face instruction" (Seaman, 2009, p. 7). This again demonstrates that an investigation into the alignment and assessment of effective measures of learning outcomes for online courses and the quality of the student experience is needed.

Two questions in the Sloan survey investigated barriers faculty see to teaching online and the quality of campus support structures. The greatest barriers to teaching online related to the perceived and/or real additions to workload required and the lack of institutional support and recognition for online teaching. Faculty were asked to rank eight areas of institutional support: technological infrastructure, support for online development, support for online delivery, support for online students, policy on intellectual property, recognition in tenure and promotion, incentives for developing online, and incentives for delivering online. The area with the highest ranking of satisfaction was technological infrastructure. This is sending a clear message that, while at an institutional level a focus on technical infrastructure and technical support can (and often does) dominate, institutional positioning that emphasizes quality, rewards, and recognition for online teaching is increasingly important and essential.

The Sloan survey provides the first and most recent large-scale research on faculty views and experience with online learning and provides some excellent base level data and observations for future research. In terms of future research, four areas have been identified across the literature and now shape the remaining discussion in this chapter both in relation to what has been done at an institutional/commentary level and in terms of future research. These include:

- institutional positioning, engagement, and support for online learning
- a more nuanced understanding of the profile of staff teaching online and their needs
- different types of professional development
- the impact of professional development and faculty support on student learning outcomes

While large-scale research studies on professional development and faculty support for online distance education are limited, there are a larger number of institutional case studies. Many offer some insightful perspectives into faculty support but there are great variations in the quality of these studies. Some authors employ a whole-of-institution perspective and others document the experiences of a few individuals at a department or school level. A comprehensive review of all institutional case studies on this topic is out of scope for this chapter, but a selection is reviewed to provide a sample of this work.

INSTITUTIONAL POSITIONING, RECOGNITION, AND INCENTIVES FOR TEACHING ONLINE

How an institution values and positions teaching and its different modes of delivery is a critical component of any professional development strategy. As already noted, we are going through a period of time where understandings of online distance education, online education and technology-enhanced learning are variable across higher education institutions. As a result, online education can be and is often treated separately from core teaching activities. The consequences are that activities associated with online teaching are often positioned outside of mainstream teaching activities in terms of workload recognition, promotion, professional development support, rewards, and incentives for online teaching.

Higher education institutions need to recognize effort and commitment to professional development that includes a focus on online distance education and technology-enhanced learning as part of the mainstream suite of incentives and rewards for good teaching practices and to be quite explicit about what is recognized. At an institutional level, Taylor and McQuiggan (2008) investigated institutional support in their survey of staff at Pennsylvania State University. Faculty were asked to identify the primary incentive that they would want to receive for participating in professional development. No single incentive that stood out against others, the highest percentage being given to recognition towards promotion and tenure (23%). In contrast to the findings of the Pennsylvania State University survey, Wang, Gould, and King (2009) report that Fort Hays State University has introduced financial payments for online course development, rewards for participating in professional development, and specifically recognized online teaching in their tenure criteria. While they report good faculty engagement with the range of initiatives that are offered, what has not been reported are any measures of impact on student learning outcomes.

Others also advocate for whole-of-institutional approaches for supporting faculty teaching online. Fang (2007), in his consideration of development for online faculty, stresses the move from a *training model* to one that involves greater commitment by the institution. He proposes a new model for performance improvement that is performance based and includes faculty training, communities of practice, performance support, formative evaluation, and knowledge sharing. He reports on the success of applying this model at his university and, while not comprehensive, it is another example of the need for a holistic, systematic institutional approach to professional development and faculty support. Forsyth, Pizzica, Laxton, and Mahony (2010), in the discussion of their university experience, also highlight university governance and organizational culture as one of the key elements in assuring quality online distance education offerings, and one that is often missing.

From an institutional perspective, Tynan and Lee (2009) completed in-depth interviews with a range of stakeholders across their university related to professional development and the integration of technologies in teaching and learning. They concluded with three propositions:

(1) Staff need to be afforded better access to information and strategies to raise their own desire and awareness of how to use ICTs to enhance student learning.

(2) Academics must be encouraged and empowered to approach the use of ICTs to enhance student learning with creativity and innovation.

(3) Institutional frameworks are still needed to provide academics with sufficient guidance and direction in the use of ICTs to enhance student learning. (2009, pp. 104–5)

Underlying each of these propositions are the importance of institutional commitment, the need for an articulated framework, and institutional support of change. Specifically relating to professional development, Tynan and Lee aptly argue, "The future of higher education depends on a holistic, research-informed, looking forward response to academic staff development, in a manner driven fundamentally by personal awareness, responsibility, ownership and agency" (2009, p. 106).

These studies, all focussed at a whole-of-institution level, indicate the importance of institutional support for formal professional development activities and that recognition and reward for online activities as part of campus-based or distance education teaching be mainstreamed with the support, recognition, and reward of good teaching practices. While there will be differences in institutional approaches, further investigation on how different models impact on improved student learning outcomes is needed.

UNDERSTANDING FACULTY NEEDS

If programs and interventions are going to be designed that are more faculty centred, there is a need at an institutional level to understand in more depth the needs of faculty. It is essential to have reliable and valid instruments to readily identify and understand the needs of faculty and the ability to benchmark these needs across the sector (Taylor & McQuiggan, 2008). A more rigorous methodology to collect information about the needs of both faculty and people in faculty development/training roles can only assist and inform the quality of this development and will be of great interest to institutions in their ability to provide more effective and targeted professional development.

The Australian Council of Open and Distance Education (ACODE) has moved in this direction through its benchmarking project. Using a collaborative process across multiple institutions at a national level, eight areas for benchmarking were identified and good practice statements, performance indicators, and measures for each one were developed. Two areas relate specifically to this discussion: professional/staff development for the effective use of technologies for teaching and learning (5) and staff support that makes a distinction between technical support and educational support (6). The benchmarking tools were piloted across seven Australian universities to focus the items and test their usefulness; subsequent reports have attested to their usefulness for institutions to focus on the quality of their practices and suggest strategies and interventions for improvement.

In contrast to using a survey instrument that can be administered to a large target group such as the Sloan survey or at an institutional level in the case of Penn State (Taylor & McQuiggan, 2008), Lackey (2011) has obtained a detailed understanding of the training needs of faculty who are going to teach online through semi-structured interviews using qualitative methodology. Lackey interviewed six faculty from three different institutions about how they prepared to teach online, what activities they accessed which were most beneficial, and areas for further development. Through a detailed analysis of the interview data, the key message is the need for just-in-time assistance, both pedagogical and technical, whether that be in person (formally or informally), via formal workshops or through independent resources. Every person interviewed was at a different level in terms of what support they required, hence they needed the ability to tailor their needs. Lackey concluded, "Going forward, informal and formal training programs should be thoughtfully balanced with technology and pedagogy using a progressive delivery method to provide faculty with the necessary skills to be successful in online teaching" (2011, p. 20).

These early investigative studies make important contributions to our understanding of faculty needs for online teaching; however, there is still considerably more research to be done at institutional levels and across the sector, at national levels and internationally, to better understand current faculty needs and to have validated instruments and methodologies to assess these needs. This again points to an important area of future research.

In addressing professional development and faculty support for online distance education, the discussion can be broad, leading from how development and support is framed and oriented, to specific types of development activities and how they are delivered. In this section I briefly cover some different frameworks, models, and approaches to professional development. Wilson (2011) recently reviewed current practice in faculty development for web-enhanced learning in university teaching. She identified five different perspectives that dominate faculty development practice: cognitive learning theory, constructivist learning theory, situated learning theory, distributed cognition, and distributed expertise. Based on these perspectives and the diversity of frameworks she reviewed, four frameworks through which professional development can be delivered are highlighted: technology-adoption, skills acquisition, scholarly engagement, and resource-based frameworks. This review of different frameworks provides a good overview of different practices and also a structure by which decisions can be made at an institutional level about how professional development is conceptualized and ultimately delivered.

Building on the survey reported by Taylor and McQuiggan (2008) and using adult learning theory as a guiding theoretical framework, McQuiggan (2011) developed twelve essential attributes of faculty professional development programs. This framework and attributes are being used to shape faculty support and they include a three-tier approach: faculty orientation to online education (an eight-week program), mentoring, and ongoing support. The program is being evaluated and, as reported, there are early indications of strong satisfaction from participants with this approach (McQuiggan, 2011).

Across the literature, a large number of individual institutional case studies have been reported and a few representative examples are included to give a sense of approaches that institutions are using. They include an example of an online module to deliver professional development to a dispersed faculty, a team approach to faculty support, and the use of social networking as an approach.

Macdonald and Poniatowska (2011) reported on the development of an online professional development module designed to help faculty at the

Open University in the United Kingdom understand how to support students using online tools. The Open University is the UK's largest provider of online distance education to over 250,000 students per annum with 12,000 faculty developing and teaching course modules. Offering professional development from this institution's perspective needs to overcome the major challenge of the sheer number of faculty engaged in teaching and the wide range and diversity of experiences and capabilities that they bring. An understanding of the working contexts of staff was an important driver in designing the module. Through the evaluation of the module they concluded, "community plays a central role in working practices . . . and is clearly of significance to many staff in supporting their professional development" (Macdonald & Poniatowska, 2011, p. 131). Given the profile of the Open University faculty (many geographically dispersed) the online module provides an opportunity to bring faculty together in a virtual way. This is truly an example of using an online distance education approach to providing professional development.

Unlike traditional professional development, which is often focussed at an individual level, there are others who strongly advocate that the development and delivery of online courses is more effective if done by teams (Oblinger & Hawkins, 2006). Wang, Gould and King (2009) report on a team approach to faculty support for the development of online education that they are focussing on at Fort Hays State University in the United States. Driven by a need for a stronger emphasis on the quality assurance of their courses, they have implemented an approach that is more collaborative and team-oriented. Beaumont, Stirling, and Percy (2009) have used a tutors' forum, to engage subject coordinators, tutors, and casual staff, who are dispersed geographically and time-wise, to develop as a team through an online discussion space. Ward, West, Peat, and Atkinson (2010) advocate a project management methodology with a mix of professional and academic staff in teams to support strategic e-learning development. All of these examples support the importance of communities of practice, a strong approach to professional development that has been adopted by many and well researched by Wenger (2010, 1998).

Given the increasing use of networks and Web 2.0 technologies in many sectors, it is not surprising to find advocates for professional development activities that use these emerging technologies. Anderson (2009, in Ostashewski & Reid, 2010) identifies a lack of research into the use or impact of online networks and collectives for professional development and learn-ing. Ostashewski and Reid (2010) note that there is little research into using social networking environments to both deliver professional development opportunities and facilitate online communities. One advantage of using these modes and environments for professional development is that they provide first-hand experience for faculty and teachers on how students are learning and engaging in a range of technologies. Ostashewski and Reid report on a study using design-based research that develops an interven-tion based on networked teacher professional development. They identify a model that supports a new kind of professional learning that combines both formal and informal activities and support. Through the practical applica-tion of the Networked Learning Framework, seven design principles have been identified for online professional development, making an important contribution to this discussion.

There is continued and further need to investigate the types, models, and approaches to professional development and faculty support, but the important question that still remains to be investigated is: What impact will different models of professional development have on enhanced learning experiences for students?

THE IMPACT OF PROFESSIONAL DEVELOPMENT AND FACULTY SUPPORT ON STUDENT LEARNING OUTCOMES

While identifying theoretical frameworks and reporting on individual case studies are important and add value to our understanding of professional development and faculty support in this space, it is critically important to understand the relationship between these initiatives and student learning outcomes. Having identified this focus and the need to use changes in stu-dent learning as an indicator of impact, it is important to acknowledge that, as professional development and faculty support focusses on the individ-ual teacher, these interventions and resources are one step removed from the direct student experience. Any evaluation of the impact professional development activities have on student learning needs to be mediated through faculty who are supported or engaged in these activities. This raises the question of how professional development work is evaluated; this has become one of the most significant areas of attention in the professional practice of professional development (Macdonald, 2009; Brew, 2011). As Stefani rightly acknowledges in the introduction to her book dedicated to this topic, evaluation continues to be a problematized and contested topic due to the "lack of an agreed framework for evaluation of the impact, added value and effectiveness of academic development" (2011, p. 4). Gray and Radloff (2011) rightly challenge the very use of the term *impact*. Yet, in a higher education world focussed on assuring quality and accountability being able to demonstrate these connections continues to be important. This raises further questions for investigation:

- Can effectiveness and impact be demonstrated, and how?

- Can the community involved in professional development and faculty support develop a culture of evaluation and some agreed approaches and tools to meet these needs?

Within this area of discussion Gunn (2011) focusses on evaluating digital environments. She supports an evidence-based approach and advocates for guidance in the areas of evaluation and e-learning, which are based on empirical evidence and multiple experiences rather than individual case studies. She outlines a design-based research approach to e-learning, which has been implemented at the University of Auckland. These approaches apply to any new teaching and learning innovations or initiatives, and yet significant gaps remain in understanding approaches or shared practices.

As has been demonstrated by the studies cited in this chapter, professional development for online teaching faculty is undeveloped and underresearched. It is very clear that more research is needed on the quality of professional development activities offered and, most importantly, on the "impact on institutional and individual performance" (Moore, 2006, p. 62). As Stefani succinctly summarizes, "Our practice should be research and evidence based; and that evaluation should focus on the processes by which developers effect change in attitudes and academic practice" (2011, p. 223). This, indeed, is a research agenda in itself. Conceptual discussions, methodologies of how to achieve this, and well theorised, larger scale studies are needed across institutional boundaries to make a substantial contribution to this discussion.

It is generally agreed that clear distinctions between online teaching, distance education, and campus-based teaching cannot and should not be made. With the increased use of technology in teaching, these modes of delivery have converged; the knowledge and skills of all faculty have blurred and, given their interdependence on technologies, continue to change. The need for professional development and faculty support is a critical element in assuring good teaching and learning practices through any delivery mode. However, what is not as clear is how best to do this. I have broadly categorized the discussion of a complex and multi-faceted area of professional practice into four broad areas: institutional positioning, faculty needs, types of professional development, and impact. These areas are not discrete. They draw from multiple disciplines; each is a major research project in its own right. As can be demonstrated throughout this discussion, there are almost as many individual approaches and practices as there are institutions, but having a clearly articulated institutional approach is necessary.

An institutional approach needs to be context specific, flexible, and multi-mode to address the differences in faculty needs and expertise. However, while a range of approaches and interventions are presented across the literature, many are not rigorously evaluated. Faculty satisfaction may be measured with an individual intervention, but taking this harder step further to determine if there has been any change in student learning outcomes is often absent. Critically, this is where the focus needs to be and where future research will be of most benefit for the sector, institutions, and individuals.

REFERENCES

ACODE (Australasian Council of Open, Distance and eLearning). (n.d.). *ACODE benchmarks*. Retrieved from http://www.acode.edu.au/resources/ACODE_ benchmarks.pdf

Bates, A. (2008). Transforming distance education through new technologies. In T. Evans, M. Haughey, & D. Murphy (Eds.), *The international handbook of distance education* (pp. 215-35). Bingley, UK: Emerald.

Beaumont, R., Stirling, J., & Percy, A. (2009). Tutors' forum: Engaging distributed communities of practice. *Open Learning, 24*(92), 141-54.

Brew, A. (2011). Forward. In L. Stefani (Ed), *Evaluating the effectiveness of academic development: Principles and practices,* New York: Routledge.

EDUCAUSE. (2011). E*CAR national study of undergraduate students and information technology.* Washington, DC: EDUCAUSE.

Eraut, M. (2000). Non-formal learning and tacit knowledge in professional work, *British Journal of Educational Psychology, 70,* 111–36.

Fang, B. (2007). A performance-based development model for online faculty, *Performance Improvement, 46*(5), 17–24.

Forsyth, H., Pizzica, J., Laxton, R., & Mahony, M. J. (2010). Distance education in an era of eLearning: Challenges and opportunities for a campus-focused institution. *Higher Education Research and Development, 29*(1), 15–28.

Fraser, K., Gosling, D., & Sorcinelli, M. D. (2010). Conceptualizing evolving models of educational development. In J. Mcdonald & D. Stockley (Eds.), *Pathways to the profession of educational development, 122,* (pp. 49–58). San Francisco: Jossey-Bass.

Gosling, D. (2008). *Educational development in the United Kingdom: Report for the heads of educational development group.* Retrieved from http://www.hedg.ac.uk/documents/HEDG_Report_final.pdf

Gray. K. & Radloff. A. (2011). Impact Evaluation and its Implications. In Stefani. L. *Evaluating the effectiveness of academic development: Principles and practices.* New York: Routledge. 209-220.

Gunn, C. (2011). Innovation and change: Responding to a digital environment. In Stefani, L. (Ed.), *Evaluating the effectiveness of academic development: Principles and practices* (73–86). New York: Routledge.

Guri-Rosenblit, S., & Gros, B. (2011). E-learning: Confusing terminology, research gaps and inherent challenges. *The Journal of Distance Education/Revue de l'Éducation à Distance, 25*(1).

Hénard, F. (2010). *Learning our lesson: Review of quality teaching in higher education.* Paris: Organization for Economic Cooperation and Development.

Hicks, M. (2007). *Positioning the professional practice of academic development: An institutional case study.* Unpublished doctoral dissertation, University of South Australia, Adelaide.

Kelly, K. (2010). *Domesticated cyborgs.* Retrieved from http://quietbabylon.com/2010/domesticated-cyborgs-kevin-kelly/

Koehler, M., Mishra, P., & Yahya, K. (2005). Tracing the development of teacher knowledge in a design seminar: Integrating content, pedagogy and technology. *Computers & Education 49,* 740–62.

Land, R. (2004). *Educational development: Discourse, identity and practice.* Buckingham, UK: SRHE and Open University Press.

Lackey, K. (2011). Faculty development: An analysis of current and effective training strategies for preparing faculty to teach online. *Online Journal of Distance Learning Administration, 14*(5).

Macdonald, J., & Poniatowska, B. (2011). Designing the professional development of staff for teaching online: An OU (UK) case study. *Distance Education, 32*(1), 119–34.

Macdonald, R. (2009). Academic development. In M. Tight, K. H. Mok, J. Huisman, & C. C. Morphew (Eds.), *The Routledge international handbook of higher education* (pp. 427–40). New York: Routledge.

Moore, M. G. (2006). Editorial: Faculty professional development. *The American Journal of Distance Education, 20*(2), 61–63.

Oblinger, D. G. & Hawkins, B. L. (2006). The myth about online course development. *EDUCAUSE 41*(1), 14–15.

Ostashewski, N., & Reid, D. (2010). Networked teacher professional development: Applying the networked learning framework to online teacher professional development. In *Proceedings of Edge Conference 2010: E-learning: The horizon and beyond*, 12–5 October, St. John's, Newfoundland & Labrador, Memorial University.

Seaman, J. (2009). *Online learning as a strategic asset: Vol. 2: The paradox of faculty voices: Views and experiences with online learning, APLU-Sloan National Commission on Online Learning.* Retrieved from http://sloanconsortium.org/ sites/default/files/APLU_online_strategic_asset_vol2-1.pdf

Sorcinelli, M. D., Austin, A. E., Eddy, P. L., & Beach, A. L. (2006). *Creating the future of faculty development.* Bolton, MA: Anker.

Stefani. L. (2011). *Evaluating the effectiveness of academic development: Principles and practices.* New York: Routledge.

Tanner, L. (2011). *Uni 2.0: Will the Internet kill universities?* Chancellor's Lecture Series. Melbourne, AUS: Victoria University. Retrieved from http://www.vu.edu.au/sites/ default/files/mcd/pdfs/LECTURE-Uni2.0-Will-The-Internet-Kil-Universties.pdf

Taylor, A., & McQuiggan, C., (2008). Faculty development programming: If we build it, will they come? *EDUCAUSE Quarterly*, 29–37.

Telg, R. W., Lundy, L., Irani, T., Bielema, C., Dooley, K. E., Anderson, E., & Raulerson, R. (2005). Distance education training for distance education trainers. *The Quarterly Review of Distance Education, 6*(4), 331–42.

Tynan, B., & Lee, M. J. W. (2009). Tales of adventure and change: Academic staff members' future visions of higher education and their professional development needs. *On the Horizon, 17*(2) 98–110.

Wang, H., Gould, L. V., & King, D, (2009). *Positioning faculty support as a strategy in assuring quality online education.* Retrieved from http://www.innovateonline. info/index.php?view=article&id=626

Ward, M., West, S., Peat, M., & Atkinson, S. (2010). Making it real: Project managing strategic e-learning development processes in a large, campus-based university. *Journal of Distance Education, 24*(1), 21–42.

Wenger, E. (1998). *Communities of practice: Learning, meaning, and identity.* New York: Cambridge University Press.

Wenger, E. (2010). Communities of practice and social learning systems: The career of a concept. In C. Blackmore (Ed.), *Social learning systems and communities of practice.* London: The Open University. doi 10.1007/978-1-84996-133-2_11, _c.

Wilson, G. (2011). Promoting web-enhanced learning in university teaching: Current practice in web-enhanced faculty development. In M. Repetto, & G. Trentin, G.

(Eds), *Faculty training for web-enhanced learning* (pp. 61–78). New York: Nova Science.

Zawacki-Richter, O. (2009). Research areas in distance education: A Delphi study. *International Review of Research in Open and Distance Learning, 10*(3), 117.

Learner Support in Online Distance Education: Essential and Evolving

Jane E. Brindley

Distance learners are expected to plan their academic programs, set their own study schedules, balance their studies with other responsibilities (work/family), communicate proficiently in writing, find and use learning resources well, and read and synthesize efficiently. Those distance learners studying in cohorts are expected to collaborate effectively with their peers in virtual groups, and those studying in self-paced courses are often expected to create their own learning networks. Accordingly, studying at a distance requires maturity, a high level of motivation, capacity to multi-task, goal-directedness, and the ability to work independently and cooperatively.

Obviously, not all students enter online studies with this set of aptitudes and skills. In response, post-secondary institutions dedicated to distance delivery of education usually have a comprehensive suite of services and resources to help learners become engaged with the institution and each other and develop the skills and motivation necessary to succeed in their studies and make a successful transition to the work place. These support services include the library, advising and counselling, academic skill assessment and development, community development, peer-to-peer support, and administrative services. These services support the learning process but do not include direct subject teaching and are the focus of this chapter.

In distance education, learner support services have been held up as critical to learner satisfaction, motivation, engagement, and success (LaPadula, 2003; Mills, 2003; Rekkedal, 2004; Ryan, 2004; Simpson, 2002; Tait, 2004). Although the literature has tended to be more speculative and descriptive than evidence-based in this regard, a great deal of attention has been paid to how to best help distance learners persist in their studies and meet their educational goals—despite the considerable demands of distance study.

Web-based technologies have opened up new opportunities and present new challenges. The use of the Internet in provision of learner support requires rethinking models of support to capitalize on the affordances of the Internet to provide new customized services and to automate services and interactions that can actually be more effectively delivered by computers than by humans (Anderson, 2004). Further, not only are institutions dedicated to distance teaching confronted by this challenge.

The availability and ease of access to essential services for the remote student may be the most challenging issue for institutions engaged in distance learning because of the significant cost involved in both developing new services and redesigning on-campus services for non-campus based students (SREB Distance Learning Policy Laboratory, 2002, p. 2–3).

Although not a significant topic in the literature, it is important to note the difference between providing support to distance learners who are in self-paced continuous enrolment courses compared to supporting learners in cohort-based virtual classrooms. Although all distance learners face some of the unique demands of studying independently and require similar kinds of support services, those who are not in paced groups studying the same subject are much more likely to experience isolation. Unlike their peers in virtual classrooms, self-paced students in continuous enrolment courses do not have prescribed opportunities for collaborative learning, for example, engaging in small group projects for course credit, or for spontaneous peer contact that frequently takes place in the virtual classroom in the form of same-time chat and subsequent e-mail contact. However, institutions with continuous enrolment and self-pacing can create opportunities for learning collaboratively by setting up shared virtual spaces for students and providing incentives for participation (Anderson, 2005). Some examples of this kind of initiative are described later in the chapter.

Despite lessons from earlier forms of distance education about the need for learner support services (Rekkedal, 2004, p. 90), institutions are generally much quicker to put curriculum online than to develop equally accessible support services. However, the progress in online learner support in the past few years is significant and the current literature is being generated from both campus-based (dual mode) and distance teaching institutions.

The first section of this chapter will consider the literature that has shaped the development of the field learner support including main theoretical insights derived from research, student satisfaction surveys and needs assessments, and models and guidelines for good practice. The following section of the chapter presents a sample of studies that address major topics of interest in the field. Finally, questions for future research are identified. Literature reviewed includes writing that has been most influential to practice, and more recent articles, and pertains only to post-secondary institutions.

THE EVOLUTION OF LEARNER SUPPORT: THE LITERATURE

The literature specifically addressing learner support services is limited relative to some other fields in distance education (Zawacki-Richter, Bäcker, & Vogt, 2009). However, if the net is more widely cast than distance education journals, there is a body of literature that has significantly influenced the field, provided a rationale for learner support models, and has led to guidelines for good practice. This literature tends to fall into three broad categories that do the following:

- provide theoretical insights (learning theories, attrition research)
- evaluate satisfaction with and/or assess need for support services
- provide guidance for learner support practice (models for learner support provision, good practices).

Theoretical Insights and Conceptualizations

Learning Theory
Early forms of learner support were course-content based and provided by an instructor or tutor, so it is natural that teaching and learning theories have

influenced the development of other types of support services. Holmberg (1989) offered the concept of *guided didactic conversation* that allowed the student to remain independent but be supported by an encouraging voice embodied in self-study materials and/or written feedback from the instructor. Within this humanistic model, he argues that the "conversation" enhances motivation and facilitates learning through the communication of empathy with the learner.

Sewart's (1993) concept of *continuity of concern*, a tenet of learner support at the Open University, United Kingdom (OUUK), also focussed on dialogue within the learner–tutor relationship. Sewart's primary innovation was to have the same tutor-counsellor address both non-academic and academic concerns with a given student over the student's entire term of studies at the university. Rumble (2000) confirmed that this broader conception of learner support was heavily influenced by adult education theory and practice (cf. Knowles, 1970) with its focus on development of independent learners.

By contrast, in North America the course related support (teaching) has traditionally been separated administratively from other learner support services and carried out by specialized staff (versus tutors). However, similar to the OUUK model, the development of the latter was significantly influenced by adult education theory and, except for delivery mode, support services for distance learners resembled those at conventional institutions, typically including inquiries, orientation, technical help, advising, counselling (career and personal), library services, study skills development, and student advocacy (McKinnis-Rankin & Brindley, 1986).

Adult learning theory continues to be a significant guiding framework as learner support has evolved toward using proactive contact and scaffolding when necessary as a means of helping learners gradually take control of their own learning process. Vygotsky's (1978) theory of shared discourse between learner and teacher, which results in a shift of control toward the learner, has been applied to other forms of support that help learners toward independence. Distance education library services have long been a model of this kind of support, not just providing access to resources but also teaching information literacy skills (George & Frank, 2004; Needham & Johnson, 2007).

Moore and Kearsley (2012), heavily influenced by adult learning principles, recognized that learners can exercise control over their learning, being more or less autonomous depending upon their readiness and the learning context. Their theory of transactional distance is one of the most researched and tested theories in distance education and has had a pervasive impact on the conceptualization of learner support as helping to reduce the transactional distance between learner and institution and assist learners in successfully developing the necessary skills to negotiate contexts where greater autonomy is required.

Web-based technologies have enabled a more open approach to teaching, with less reliance on a structured course package and more on interaction among students and with the instructor. Within this environment, learner support practitioners have embraced a constructivist model of learning that fully acknowledges the role of the learners as active and instrumental, relating content to their own experience and participating in constructing knowledge, individually and with their peers. Enabled by technology and a learning model that values collaboration and social learning, much more attention is now being directed toward finding ways to facilitate learner-to-learner support as a way of engaging and retaining students (cf. Boyle, Kwon, Ross, & Simpson, 2010).

Predictive Models based on Attrition and Retention Research
The heterogeneity of distance learners, together with the unique demands of studying at a distance, is seen to present some challenges with regard to persistence (Gibbs, 2004). Distance education institutions have responded to attrition by trying to untangle the complex reasons for dropout and by extrapolating from this research to design retention initiatives. Attrition and persistence research and theory have probably had more impact on the development of learner support practice and theory than any other area of investigation (Bajtelsmit, 1988; Billings, 1988; Brindley, 1987; Brown, 1996; Kember, 1990; Sweet, 1986; Tinto, 1993; Rekkedal, 2004). (See chapter 17 by Woodley and Simpson for further discussion of attrition.)

One approach to investigating dropout is to use post-hoc surveys of learners who leave their studies early (cf. Bartels & Rekkedal as cited in Rekkedal, 2004). Inevitably these studies identify reasons that are external to the institution such as insufficient time for study or a change in personal or work circumstances that interfered with study (Woodley, 2004). These reasons may reinforce the need for early anticipatory guidance for new students that would help them to better manage their time and be prepared to cope with unexpected circumstances. However, self-reports from dropouts considered in isolation from other factors often raise more questions than answers.

Brindley (1987) discovered that students who persisted experienced a similar type and number of hindering incidents (for example, a geographical move or a change in health, work, or family situation) as those who eventually dropped out. More recently, Kemp (2002) reports that, "For the most part, external commitments—in the form of personal, family, home, financial, and community commitments—were not found to be significant predictors of persistence . . . in distance education" (p. 75).

Although it is unlikely that post-hoc surveys can truly reflect the complex interplay of factors that result in a dropout decision, the results from these studies have occasionally been extrapolated to guide practice with some good result. For example, one reason that students frequently cite for dropping out is choosing the wrong course (Astin cited in Woodley, 2004). In response, Simpson (2004a) successfully demonstrated that retention can be improved when institutions are more proactive in using a combination of methods and resources to help students with course choice.

Another approach to attrition research is to develop multi-factorial predictive models that consider the complex set of learner and institutional variables that interact over time to produce a dropout decision. Early models based on undergraduates in traditional American universities have had enormous and enduring influence. Tinto's (1975) model, the one most frequently cited, describes the beginning student as having predisposing characteristics that determine entry level institutional and goal commitment. Over time, depending upon how successfully the student is socially and academically integrated into the institution, that commitment is weakened or strengthened eventually resulting in dropout or persistence. Tinto's model has been adapted for use with adult learners and for distance education with the predictive variables changed to match the circumstances of context and learner population (cf., Bajtelsmit, 1988; Bean & Metzner, 1985; Kember, 1995; Sweet, 1986).

Woodley (2004) concludes that the value of a "Tintoesque" framework is that it helps us to understand *persistence* as meaning the learner undertakes a longitudinal process of cost-benefit assessments for staying with a particular institution. According to Brindley (1987) all students meet with both hindering and facilitating incidents, some internal to themselves, some in their home or work environment, and some over which the institution has control. Woodley points out that the latter should be our primary concern in moving forward to action.

An advantage of having conventional institutions engaged in online learning is that they bring considerable new energy and resources to the field. A number of institutions have been experimenting with learner analytics, mining data from learning management and student information systems to find the most salient predictors of attrition and retention. WCET (the WICHE Cooperative for Educational Technologies) (2011), announced a project that combines the data sets from six institutions participating in the Predictive Analytics Reporting (PAR) Framework. The data set includes over 640,000 anonymized student records and over 3 million course level records, focussing on 34 common predictor variables for persistence/dropout. The data will be used to explore patterns that emerge when the data sets from considerably different institutions are analyzed as a single, unified sample.

The goal of the PAR Framework is to identify demographic, pedagogical, and institutional variables that influence student retention and progression, to consider how the factors affecting dropout might differ from indicators of completion, to use the findings to inform development of strategies to improve learner engagement and support (WCET, 2011), and to better target these to specific groups and individuals. This long-term study should fulfill the expressed need for large population and cross-institutional research to obtain more accurate predictors of academic persistence. In future, data from learner analytics (including an individual profile) can be shared directly with students, putting them in a better position to be self-directed in taking advantage of support services that will contribute to their success.

Although no silver bullet has been discovered, predictive modelling has revealed most dropout occurs early during the first distance education course and certain factors appear to contribute significantly to persistence and to attrition that an institution has the potential to influence. These include finding courses more rigorous than expected, adjusting to a self-directed approach and the online environment, acquiring academic skill sets, and experiencing satisfaction and a sense of belonging (cf. Bocchi, Eastman, & Owens-Swift, 2004; McGivney, 2004). As a result, learner support approaches have become much more purposeful, proactive, and timely, focussed on early intervention, anticipatory guidance, preparedness for online study, skill development, and social and academic engagement.

Student Satisfaction Surveys and Needs Assessment

Surveys of satisfaction with support services are most often used as a measure of quality and to identify any unmet needs. While the use of satisfaction as a quality measure is debatable, satisfaction surveys have had a significant influence on the development of learner support practice, reflecting a culture of customer service, and yielding important feedback from students about how well their expectations are being met, a factor that has been linked to retention (Gaskell, 2009).

In a survey at the New York Institute of Technology, online students indicated satisfaction with current services but expressed a desire for additional services such as clubs, a newspaper, online tutoring, development seminars, and access to an online psychologist (LaPadula, 2003). This study identifies three major areas of desired services: academic advising/career counselling, personal/mental health counselling, and "services that promote a sense of community" (p. 121–23). The third, while challenging for institutions to facilitate, speaks to the need for many distance learners to feel more connected to their institution and to each other.

Dare, Zapata, and Thomas (2005) conducted a large-scale survey at North Carolina State University, comparing on-campus and distance learners as to the importance of and satisfaction with aspects of support services. The results reveal that distance learners appear to be fairly pragmatic in placing greatest importance on registration and records, library services, and advising. However, like LaPadula (2003), these researchers found a desire for additional services such as counselling, orientation, health services, leadership development, and physical facilities. Dare et al. cite demographic trends that indicate a growing number of younger students who choose to study online or combine online studies with on-campus studies, likely resulting in a greater demand for support services that go beyond meeting basic needs.

Satisfaction surveys frequently reveal low usage and/or lack of awareness of support services by online learners (Cain, Marrara, Pitre, & Armour, 2003; Dare, Zapata, & Thomas, 2005; Simpson, 2004b). Cragg, Andrusyszyn, and Fraser (2005) found that many students, even though frustrated and in need of assistance, did not make use of counselling and advising services, indicating a need for institutions to be more proactive. Students on campus often learn about services and opportunities for engagement from their peers. The same may be true for online learners as they are provided with more opportunities to interact (Kretovics, 2003) through the use of customized portals and the development of virtual communities of students.

Guidance for Learner Support Practice

Models for Learner Support Provision

Distance teaching institutions have a history and culture of responsiveness to a diverse body of students. Good customer service has been recognized as a means toward student retention (Brindley, 1995; Gibbs, 2004). Rumble (2000) argues that in a competitive market, distance education institutions can capitalize on their expertise in service provision and systems approach to management to become exemplary service organizations. Hardy Cox and Belbin (2010) note that "students have come to expect higher levels of customer service: 24/7 online technical support, a twenty-four hour turnaround on e-mail inquiries, immediate response self-directed services, and an online 'two-click rule' to locate service and obtain a quick response" (p. 226). They point out, "often best practices in distance student services are grounded in a business model of customer service" (p. 231). Within a formalized educational program, customer service is still a negotiated process but in a learner-centred institution, learners are seen as active and instrumental, making choices about when, how, and with whom to seek support.

The development of integrated models for provision of online learner support that are learner-centred, use technology wisely, and offer benchmarks for evaluation demonstrates that the field is becoming more sophisticated in conceptualization of purpose. An effective learner support model is one that can be aligned to an institutional value system, goals and strategic priorities, approach to teaching and learning, and the unique and changing needs and goals of the learners served. It should provide a framework that facilitates planning, evaluation, and resource allocation.

Hülsmann (2004) addresses providing learner support in a model of education traditionally based on economies of scale. Offering more comprehensive support services adds to the cost per student, which must be justified by achievement of desired outcomes, including but not limited to improved retention. Simpson (2008) has developed a formula for calculating the cost versus benefit of learner support and demonstrates its use with a variety of specific interventions.

Tait (2004) describes a planning and management model of learner support with three primary domains (cognitive, affective, systemic), and identifies specific functions and services in each. The model is not prescriptive but rather adaptable depending upon learner characteristics and contextual factors such as geography, scale, management system, and technological infrastructure. In the 10 years since Tait's article, institutions have made enormous progress in applying technology to improve learner support in all three domains.

In dual mode institutions, integrated models of online support services designed for both on and off campus students are now seen as providing better service for all students and as being more efficient than maintaining separate systems for distance learners (Dare, Zapata, & Thomas, 2005; Kretovics, 2003). As a result, there is growing convergence between models of online learner support between distance teaching and conventional institutions that offer online study. Three examples follow.

The Western Cooperative for Educational Telecommunications (WCET) model (Shea & Armitage, 2002) is widely cited as a key resource that provides detailed guidelines for developing online learner support. "One very valuable outcome of the WCET project was the creation of a graphic, 'Web of Student Services', that displays the various student services recommended for online learners" (Kendall, 2005, p. 55). One student and a curriculum are at the centre of the web, representing the need to customize individual support. Five integrated suites of services for learners form the surrounding architecture of the web: an administrative core, communications and information, academic services, personal services, and student communities. There is an expandable boundary at the outer edge of the web representing the evolving nature of the field. (See graphic, Shea, 2005, p. 17.)

Ryan (2004) depicts a learner support framework as a table that lists the potential critical points of contact or need in the student life cycle and the corresponding desired response in the form of a resource or service. For each point of contact, Ryan identifies which of four types of interaction is involved (learner–content, learner–teacher, learner–learner, and learner–learning support specialist) (p. 127).

Floyd and Casey-Powell (2004) propose the Inclusive Student Services Process Model (ISSPM) to serve both online and on-campus students, based on student development through five phases of the learner life cycle. The authors identify the primary goal of the learner in each phase, the role support plays in reaching it, the specific services to be offered, and benchmarks for quality. It notably includes "environmental management" and "fostering sense of belonging" in the "learner support phase" (p. 59), which reinforces the importance of facilitating learner–learner interaction and creating communities that promote mutual peer to peer support as described by Kretovics (2003). As institutions grapple with how to continue to provide quality support to greater numbers of students, it is likely that peer support will become much more important.

Identification of Good Practices

The development of best practices in online support demonstrates that the field is maturing and recognized as being a specialized professional endeavour. *Online Student Support Services: A Best Practices Monograph* (http://www.onlinestudentsupport.org/Monograph/) is an open online publication providing strategies and best practices to help institutions make the transition to online learner support services. The monograph is presented as a well-organized website with links to a wide variety of exemplary services and is continually updated. A similar resource is the online Student Services found on the website of the Washington State Board for Community and Technical Colleges (http://www.sbctc.ctc.edu/college/s_index.aspx).

Some authors have drawn from the literature to identify characteristics of learner support services that exemplify good practice. Brindley and Paul (2004) identify six essential elements of effective learner support from distance learning practice that could be applied in any post-secondary setting (p. 45), and Shea (2005) proposes 10 desirable characteristics of online student services that should shape good practice (pp. 17–19).

An innovative development is the opening in 2005 of the Centre for Transforming Student Services (CENTSS, http://www.centss.org/), an American private/public partnership offering web-based resources on a fee for service basis. The focus of their work is helping higher education institutions assess the quality of their online student services with an audit tool designed from a learner's point of view (Shea, 2005, p. 20). The CENTSS audit covers 31 student service areas each of which is measured against benchmarks of increasingly customized and personalized levels, or generations, of service.

Preliminary findings indicate that the audit tool is useful for identifying gaps and overlaps in service. It reveals differences in levels of services across institutions and in quality among services within individual institutions. Comparisons among institutions reveal those that redesign their student services using cross-functional teams to develop a strategic plan and those with creative staff who are eager to adopt new practices (as opposed to those with the most resources) are more likely to exhibit best practices (Shea, 2005).

RESEARCH ARTICLES ON MAJOR TOPICS IN LEARNER SUPPORT

A sampling of current literature is presented to represent four emerging areas of interest in learner support that are being driven by the need to use resources effectively and demonstrate accountability, respond to the increasingly heterogeneous demographic of online learners, take advantage of the many opportunities offered by new technologies, and facilitate learner-to-learner support such as that offered through communities of learners.

Intervention Studies

Although attrition studies often conclude with recommendations for specific kinds of support interventions, relatively little evaluative research has been done to find out about their impact, particularly in comparison to the numerous studies of the effects of instructional design, teaching methods, and technology applied to teaching and learning.

To demonstrate a statistically significant effect from an intervention study, a controlled experimental design with large samples is needed—conditions difficult to achieve in single institution studies. Use of control groups is rare because institutions do not want to withhold services intentionally, and documented evaluation studies are rarely replicated, making it difficult to generalize from findings. However, the value of small intervention studies should not be underestimated. They yield useful information and, taken together, help build the field of knowledge and contribute to improvement of practice.

Some researchers are successful in employing larger samples and experimental designs and building a valuable body of work over time. Simpson (2004b) reports that OUUK students who received an early proactive supportive telephone call showed higher course completion rates at the halfway mark and at the end of the course than those who did not. In a cost-benefit analysis, he concludes that, based on the cost of the call per student versus the cost of replacing a dropout with a new student, proactive interventions are worth the investment.

Simpson (2004b) introduces the concept of "maximum possible increase in retention" (p. 82), and recommends using predictor variables to target interventions for students most likely to benefit. Although targeting interventions raises an ethical issue of withholding services from students without knowing for which student interventions will make a difference while also not informing students that they have been targeted because they are seen as vulnerable (Kelly & Mills, 1997). This line of research holds promise as learner analytics become more sophisticated and predictor variables more accurate.

Based on his work with proactive support, Simpson (2008) proposes a new theory, Proactive Motivational Support (PaMS), which applies concepts from motivational theory and positive psychology to proactive contact with learners that helps them identify and apply their strengths to learning. A similar study based on social support theory, using an experimental design to compare the effect of proactive contact on students new to distance learning, also found that the intervention had a positive effect on student satisfaction and intention to re-enrol (Brindley, 2000) but showed no significant difference for persistence.

Intervention studies indicate that students respond positively to proactive contact from institutional personnel but the nature of the mediating variable, if any, is not clear. Timing of contact is less ambiguous. Frydenberg (2007) found no differences in attrition and persistence rates between online and on-campus students, but a significant difference in the pattern of attrition with online students dropping out very early. This is consistent with many studies that reveal that when distance learners drop out, they usually do so early in their first course, indicating the need for early contact.

Learner Characteristics and Changing Demographics

Research on learner characteristics is covered in chapter 16. However, three trends that have significant implications for learner support are noted here.

First, many institutions with online courses and programs are enrolling students from beyond their borders and must be prepared to respond to cultural and language differences (Spronk, 2004). Bray, Aoki, and Dlugosh (2008) summarize the challenge for institutions with a global reach:

There is a greater need for understanding of the approaches to learning required to support students from other cultures in order to "get the mix right" and to avoid projecting false or stereotypical images onto them or ignoring important differences. (p. 2)

Secondly, pressure on public institutions to widen access has resulted in much greater diversity in the student body, challenging them to provide a wide variety of support to meet the needs of learners under-prepared for the rigour of online learning (Gibbs, 2004). Thirdly, a similar challenge is presented by the increasing number of young students who are choosing online study for its convenience and familiar and attractive technology but who may not have yet developed the self-directedness and maturity required for success (Kelly & Mills, 2007). The increasing use of assessments of readiness for online learning as self-help and advising and counselling tools (cf. Hall, 2011; Pillay, Irving, & Tones, 2007) reflect the growing concern about students embarking on online study without the prerequisite skills.

How much responsibility lies with the institution to help students succeed and how much lies with the student is an open question. However, given an intentional widening of access and that grants to institutions are dependent upon enrolments and graduates, there is pressure to minimize dropout and maximize success. Perhaps more importantly, institutions that value openness and social justice have an ethical obligation to ensure those who have been invited in are provided with the best opportunity to succeed (Kelly & Mills, 2007).

Using Technology Effectively

Anderson (2004) discusses the need to capitalize on the affordances of new technologies in rethinking how best to provide student support. Kvavik and Handberg (2000) provide a case study of how their institution redesigned their entire learner support system, automating straightforward transactions, and retraining staff to provide one-on-one service to students who require individualized service for complex interactions. Rethinking current practice is an important first step for any institution, but web-based and mobile technologies can also be used in innovative ways to accomplish what was not previously possible, such as providing customizable portals, creating dynamic virtual communities of learners, and helping students develop new skills and think in new ways.

Mobile applications work with web-based systems, making institutional information, administrative services, and even the library, portable. The North Carolina State University library now offers a mobile application that provides catalogue searches, information about computer availability in labs, and access to a reference librarian (http://www.lib.ncsu.edu/m/about.html). However, innovative use of technology can accomplish more than access. The critical transition is the one between making generic information available on web pages and providing information customized by the individual through a portal. Steele and Thurmond (2009) draw parallels among Bloom's taxonomy, the DIKW (data, information, knowledge, and wisdom) processing model from knowledge management, and the learner support conceptual model provided by CENTSS (described earlier) to demonstrate how web-based services with higher levels of performance can facilitate higher levels of cognitive processing by students. An example might be a student learning how to customize her portal so that data are gathered and synthesized for applications such as running a degree or financial aid audit. Learner analytics (using existing data sources to construct predictive models) not only inform institutions in the development of targeted interventions but can also help learners make more informed decisions about using support services. (See chapter 8 by Conole for further discussion of learner analytics.)

Steele and Thurmond (2009) point out that use of smart technologies allows students to self-serve. This, in turn, frees advisors to focus on direct interaction with students and the development of additional resources (such as interactive FAQ sites).

New technologies show promise for serving greater numbers of learners, offering more self-directed and customized services, providing service quickly when needed, and possibly assisting students to become more independent and self-aware. However, technologies are expensive and can also have unintended consequences. Strategic planning and research and evaluation are required in order to use technology most effectively.

LEARNING COMMUNITIES AND PEER-TO-PEER SUPPORT

Somewhat ironically, improved efficiency in the form of online administrative transactions and self-service probably contribute to a sense of anonymity, making efforts to create a social atmosphere for online learners that much more important. Web-based technologies offer unique opportunities to facilitate learner–learner contact (Dare, Zapata, & Thomas, 2005) that can provide the important social component of belonging to an academic community, facilitate peer-to-peer support, and teach critical skills of collaborative online learning (Anderson, 2003; Stodel, Thompson, & MacDonald, 2006, p.18). Kadirire (2007) reports that the instant messaging capability of various mobile devices that have been enhanced for interaction and collaboration makes these effective tools for online community building.

Kretovics (2003) argues that learner support staff have the expertise and responsibility to facilitate campus communities, whether in person or virtually. Student portals can be customized to "push" information according to individual interests and linked with social media to foster communities of common concern. Using a campus ecology model, he highlights the importance of including online learners in institutional life, pointing out that, "distance students are essentially commuter students who use a different vehicle" (p. 2).

Some institutions have student governments for distance learners (e.g., OUUK, Washington State University, Athabasca University) that help students identify with their institution and promote loyalty. Peer support and study partner programs, shared virtual spaces, and social networking sites such as blogs, message boards, and chat rooms, operate at a course, program, and institutional level. Excelsior College New York hosts the Electronic Peer Network as a way for students to interact on social and academic matters, and Washington State University has the Studio Café and the Speakeasy where students "can chat, work on assignments together, and get new insights about their ideas" (LaPadula, 2003, p. 123). Using ELGG, an open source social networking engine, Athabasca University (AU) created The Landing, a virtual space for students to share profiles, discuss ideas, blog, and create e-portfolios (Anderson, 2005). In the context of an institution such as AU, which has continuous enrolment and self-pacing in many programs (versus cohorts or classes), creating virtual spaces for learners is critical to facilitating spontaneous and student-initiated networks and study partners.

Boyle Kwon, Ross, and Simpson (2010) report on three studies using peer-to-peer mentoring support, two of which showed a higher rate of persistence of mentored over non-mentored students. Self-reports from students in the third study indicated that they found a mentor useful and helpful in numerous ways. The authors noted that there is significant staff time involved in setting up the matches between peers but that the cost per student for peer support is significantly lower than a staff member making a proactive telephone call (as per Simpson, 2004b), reinforcing the notion that peer-to-peer contact will be used increasingly as a cost-effective method of providing support.

For learners outside of formal institutions, such as those taking advantage of open courseware or joining a MOOC, peer support in the form of a study buddy or learning group can be critical to deepening the learning experience. Kamenetz (2011), in her guerrilla guide for those who wish to learn outside of an institution, recommends forming or joining a peer support group, noting that there are many active online learning communities for almost any subject area. Informal online study is becoming much more common and may offer models for developing and sustaining learning communities that can be used within institutional settings.

DIRECTIONS FOR FUTURE RESEARCH

The research agenda in learner support reflects current and future challenges as identified in the literature reviewed in this chapter. Four major areas for investigation are identified: targeting investment for greatest effect, capacity building, learner support as a professional practice, and fostering student to student support. These four areas are presented in the form of questions and sub-questions and address the most pressing issues.

(1) Which investments in learner support make the most difference?

Should the focus continue to be on skill building and community building to engage students and offer a sense of belonging? Which interventions make the most difference and with which learners? Which technologies are the best investments to meet learner support needs? How can learner support models be improved to provide frameworks adaptable to different contexts? Which theories hold the promise as frameworks for design of these models? How can learner analytics and other large data base studies (e.g., PARS, CENTSS) inform theory and practice? Are there ways to demonstrate the effectiveness of learner support interventions and use of technologies in meeting intended outcomes? To what extent it is possible to help students who are not ready for online learning become ready, and what are the most cost-effective methods for doing so?

(2) How can institutions build learner support capacity to address the diversity and volume of demands?

If only very large or very well resourced institutions have the human resource and technology capacity required to offer customized student portals, 24/7 library and technical support services, academic advising, and learner skills development such as a writing centre, what is the best way for medium and smaller institutions to serve their learners equally well? Can these services be cost effectively outsourced without loss of effectiveness? Is collaboration across institutions a good solution for service provision (Wang, 2005)? How can institutions collaborate to offer better service to their students without losing their unique identities? In the face of finite resources and students who lack the requisite skills and aptitudes for distance study, how much responsibility does an institution have for preparedness of their learners? Is this a pragmatic issue or an ethical issue (cf. Kelly & Mills, 2007; Needham & Johnson, 2007)? How can institutions calculate the maximum percentage of increase in retention in order to set realistic goals for what learner support can accomplish (Simpson, 2004b)?

(3) How can the field of online learner support be strengthened?

Can professions in learner support be better defined with specific required competencies and improved professional development programs (cf. Dunn, 2005; Mishra, 2005)? How can professional practices, research, literature, and open support resources for students across conventional and distance teaching institutions be developed and shared?

(4) What are the possibilities for building dynamic virtual communities of students?

What attracts and motivates students to engage critically with peers outside of the classroom? Can peer-to-peer support be part of the solution to capacity building? How can institutional enthusiasm for development of communities be balanced with students' needs for

independence and flexibility? Is there a way to build the social component of learning in a virtual environment? Are there ways to create
a sense of belonging, loyalty, and pride in one's institution through
creation of particular kinds of communities? What can institutions
learn about how to facilitate online social learning from activities that
are going outside their walls (cf. Kamenetz, 2011)?

CONCLUSION

Support systems for distance learners have become more proactive, more
purposeful, and more effective in helping learners succeed in their studies.
Learning theories, attrition and persistence research, service models and
guidelines for good practice, an increasingly diverse learner population, student feedback, evaluation of interventions, and new technologies have all
been powerful in shaping the field toward its current focus on learner preparedness, skill development, and learner engagement with the institution
and peers. The development of models of support that are learner-centred,
apply technology effectively, and offer benchmarks for evaluation, and the
investment in large studies such as the Predictive Analytics Reporting (PAR)
Framework and new initiatives such as the Centre for Transforming Student
Services (CENTSS) speak to the recognition of the essential role that learner
support has in a quality online educational experience. However, providing
learner support to those who study online is still a relatively young field and
the opportunities for research and development are many.

REFERENCES

Anderson, T. (2003). Getting the mix right again: An updated theoretical rationale for
interaction. *International Review of Research in Open and Distance Learning, 4*(2),
1–14.
Anderson, T. (2004). Student services in a networked world. In J. E. Brindley, C.
Walti, & O. Zawacki-Richter (Eds.), *Learner support in open, distance and online
learning environments* (pp. 39–50). Oldenburg, Germany: Bibliotheks- und
Informationssystem der Universität Oldenburg.
Anderson, T. (2005). *Distance learning: Social software's killer ap?* The Open &
Distance Learning Association of Australia. Retrieved from http://hdl.handle.
net/2149/2328

Bajtelsmit, J.W. (1988). *Predicting distance learning dropouts: Testing a conceptual model of attrition in distance education.* Report to the International Council for Distance Education Research Committee from a study conducted at The American College, Bryn Mawr, PA.

Bean, J. P., and Metzner, B. S. (1985). A conceptual model of non-traditional undergraduate student attrition. *Review of Educational Research, 55*(4), 485–540.

Billings, D. M. (1988). A conceptual model of correspondence course completion. *The American Journal of Distance Education, 6*(2), 17–31.

Bocchi, J., Eastman, J.K., & Owens-Swift, C. (2004). Retaining the online learner: Profile of students in an online MBA program and implications for teaching them. *Journal of Education for Business, 79*(4), 245–53.

Boyle, F., Kwon, J., Ross, C., & Simpson, O. (2010). Student–student mentoring for retention and engagement in distance education. *Open Learning, 25*(2), 115–30.

Bray, E., Aoki, K., & Dlugosh, L. (2008). Predictors of learning satisfaction in Japanese online distance learners. *International Review of Research in Open and Distance Learning, 9*(3), 1–18.

Brindley, J. E. (1987). *Attrition and completion in distance education.* Unpublished master's thesis, Vancouver, University of British Columbia.

Brindley, J. E. (1995). Learners and learner services: The key to the future in distance education. In J. M. Roberts & E. M. Keough (Eds.), *Why the information highway? Lessons from open and distance learning* (pp. 102–25). Toronto: Trifolium Books.

Brindley, J. E. (2000). *The effects of a social support intervention on distance learner behaviour.* Unpublished doctoral dissertation, University of Ottawa.

Brindley, J. E., & Paul, R. (2004). The role of learner support in institutional transformation: A case study in the making. In J. E. Brindley, C. Walti, & O. Zawacki-Richter (Eds.), *Learner support in open, distance and online learning environments* (pp. 39–50). Oldenburg, Germany: Bibliotheks- und Informationssystem der Universität Oldenburg.

Brown, K. (1996). The role of internal and external factors in the discontinuation of off-campus students. *Distance Education, 17*(1), 44–71.

Cain, D. L., Marrara, C., Pitre, P. E., & Armour, S. (2003). Support services that matter: An exploration of the experiences and needs of graduate students in a distance learning environment. *Journal of Distance Education, 18*(1), 42–56.

Cragg, B., Andrusyszyn, M., and Fraser, J. (2005). Sources of support for women taking professional programs by distance education. *Journal of Distance Education, 26*(1), 21–38.

Dare, L., Zapata, L., & Thomas, A. (2005). Assessing the needs of distance learners: A student affairs perspective. *New Directions for Student Services, 112*(Winter), 39–54.

Dunn, S. T. (2005). A place of transition: Directors' experiences of providing counselling and advising to distance students. *Journal of Distance Education, 20*(2), 40–57.

Floyd, D. L., & Casey-Powell, D. (2004). New roles for student support services in distance learning. *New Directions for Community Colleges, 128*, 55–64.

Frydenberg, J. (2007). Persistence in university continuing education online classes. *International Review of Research in Open and Distance Learning, 8*(3).

Gaskell, A. (2009). Student satisfaction and retention: Are they connected? *Open Learning, 24*(3), 193–96.

George, L., & Frank, I. (2004). Beyond books: Library services to distance education students. In J. E. Brindley, C. Walti, & O. Zawacki-Richter (Eds.), *Learner support in open, distance and online learning environments* (pp. 39–50). Oldenburg, Germany: Bibliotheks- und Informationssystem der Universität Oldenburg.

Gibbs, G. (2004). Editorial. *Open Learning, 19*(1), pp. 4–7.

Hall, M. (2011). A predictive validity study of the Revised Mcvay Readiness for Online Learning Questionnaire. *Online Journal of Distance Learning Administration, 14*(3), 1–5.

Hardy Cox, D., and Belbin, B. (2010). Student services at a distance. In D. Hardy Cox and C. Carney Strange (Eds.), *Achieving student success: Effective student services in Canadian higher education*, (pp. 221–34). Montréal and Kingston: McGill-Queen's University Press.

Holmberg, B. (1989). *Theory and practice of distance education*. London, UK: Routledge.

Hornak, A., Akweks, K., & Jeffs, M. (2010). Online student services at the community college. In R. L. Garza Mitchell (Ed.), *New directions for community colleges*, 150, (pp. 79–87). San Francisco, CA: Jossey-Bass.

Hülsmann, T. (2004). The two-pronged attack on learner support: Costs and the centrifugal forces of convergence. In J. E. Brindley, C. Walti, & O. Zawacki-Richter (Eds.), *Learner support in open, distance and online learning environments* (pp. 241–50). Oldenburg, Germany: Bibliotheks- und Informationssystem der Universität Oldenburg.

Kadirire, J. (2007). Instant messaging for creating interactive and collaborative m-learning environments. *International Review of Research in Open and Distance Learning, 8*(2), 1–14.

Kamenetz, A. (2011). *The edupunks' guide to a DIY credential*. Retrieved from http://www.smashwords.com/extreader/read/77938/1/the-edupunks-guide-to-a-diy-credential

Kelly, P., & Mills, R. (2007). The ethical dimensions of learner support. *Open Learning, 22*(2), 149–157.

Kember, D. (1990). The use of a model to derive interventions which might reduce drop-out from distance education courses. *Higher Education, 20*(1), 11–24.

Kemp, W. (2002). Persistence of adult learners in distance education. *The American Journal of Distance Education, 16*(2), 65–81.

Kendall, J. R. (2005). Implementing the web of student services. *New Directions for Student Services*, 112, 55–68.

Knowles, M. S. (1970). *The modern practice of adult education*. New York: Association Press.

Kretovics, M. (2003). The role of student affairs in distance education: Cyber-services or virtual communities. *Online Journal of Distance Learning Administration*, 6(3). Retrieved from http://www.westga.edu/~distance/ojdla/fall63/kretovics63.html

Kvavik, R. B., & Handberg, M. N. (2000). Transforming student services: The University of Minnesota takes a fresh look at client/institution interaction. *EDUCAUSE Quarterly*, 23(2), 30–37.

LaPadula, M. (2003). A comprehensive look at online student support services. *American Journal of Distance Education*, 17(2), 119–28.

McGivney, V. (2004). Understanding persistence in adult learning. *Open Learning*, 19(1), 33–46.

McInnis-Rankin, E., & Brindley, J. E. (1986). Student support services. In I. Mugridge & D. Kaufman (Eds.), *Distance education in Canada* (pp. 60–80). London, UK: Croom Helm.

Mills, R. (2003). The centrality of learner support in open and distance learning. In A. Tait, & R. Mills (Eds.), *Rethinking learner support in distance education* (pp. 102–13). London, UK: RoutledgeFalmer.

Mishra, S. (2005) Roles and competencies of academic counsellors in distance education. *Open Learning*, 20(2), 147–59.

Moore, M. G., & Kearsley, G. (2012). *Distance education: A systems view of online learning* (3rd ed.). Belmont, CA: Wadsworth.

Needham, G., & Johnson, K. (2007). Ethical issues in providing library services to distance learners. *Open Learning*, 22(2), p. 117–128.

Pillay, H., Irving, K., & Tones, M. (2007). Validation of the diagnostic tool for assessing tertiary students' readiness for online learning. *Higher Education Research & Development*, 26(2), 217–34.

Rekkedal, T. (2004). Internet based e-learning, pedagogy and support systems. In J. E. Brindley, C. Walti, & O. Zawacki-Richter (Eds.), *Learner support in open, distance and online learning environments* (pp. 71–93). Oldenburg, Germany: Bibliotheks- und Informationssystem der Universität Oldenburg.

Rumble, G. (2000). Student support in distance education in the 21st century: Learning from service management. *Distance Education*, 21(2), 216–35.

Ryan, Y. (2004). Pushing the boundaries with online learner support. In J. E. Brindley, C. Walti, & O. Zawacki- Richter (Eds.), *Learner support in open, distance and online learning environments* (pp. 125–34). Oldenburg, Germany: Bibliotheks- und Informationssystem der Universität Oldenburg.

Sewart, D. (1993). Student support systems in distance education. *Open Learning*, 8(3), 3–12.

Shea, P. (2005). Serving students online: Enhancing their learning experience. *New Directions for Student Services*, 112(Winter), 15–24.

Shea, P., & Armitage, S. (2002). *Beyond the administrative core: Creating web-based student services for online learners: Guidelines for creating student services online.* Retrieved from http://wcet.wiche.edu/wcet/docs/beyond/overview.pdf

Simpson, O. (2002). *Supporting students in online, open and distance learning* (2nd ed.). London, UK: Kogan Page.

Simpson, O. (2004a). Retention and course choice in distance learning. In U. Bernath & A. Szücs (Eds.), *Proceedings of the 3rd EDEN Research Workshop, Oldenburg*, March 4–6, 2004, (pp. 381–87). Oldenburg, Germany: Bibliotheks- und Informationssystem der Universität Oldenburg.

Simpson, O. (2004b). The impact on retention of interventions to support distance learning students. *Open Learning, 19*(1), 79–95.

Simpson, O. (2006). Predicting student success in open and distance learning. *Open Learning, 21*(2), 125–38.

Simpson. O. (2008). Cost benefits of student retention policies and practices. In W. Bramble and S. Panda (Eds.), *Economics of distance and online learning* (pp. 162–78). London, UK: Routledge.

Spronk, B. (2004). Addressing cultural diversity through learner support. In J. E. Brindley, C. Walti, & O. Zawacki-Richter (Eds.), *Learner support in open, distance and online learning environments* (pp. 283–93). Oldenburg, Germany: Bibliotheks- und Informationssystem der Universität Oldenburg.

SREB Distance Learning Policy Laboratory Student Services Subcommittee. (2002, June). *Anytime, anyplace services for the 21st century student*. Atlanta, GA: Distance Learning Policy Laboratory. Retrieved from http://www.sreb.org/uploads/documents/2009/10/2009101508465545/Student_services_Final_5.31.02_USE.pdf

Steele, G. E., & Thurmond, K. C. (2009). Academic advising in a virtual university. *New Directions for Higher Education, 146*, 85–95.

Stodel, E. J., Thompson, T. L., & MacDonald, C. J. (2006). Learners' perspectives on what is missing from online learning: Interpretations through the community of inquiry framework. *International Review of Research in Open and Distance Learning, 7*(3), 1–24.

Sweet, R. (1986). Student dropout in distance education: An application of Tinto's model. *Distance Education, 7*(2), 201–13.

Tait, A. (2004). On institutional models and concepts of student support services: The case of the Open University UK. In J. E. Brindley, C. Walti, & O. Zawacki-Richter (Eds.), *Learner support in open, distance and online learning environments* (pp. 205–17). Oldenburg, Germany: Bibliotheks- und Informationssystem der Universität Oldenburg.

Tinto, V. (1975). Dropout from higher education: A theoretical synthesis of recent research. *Review of Educational Research, 45*(1), 89–125.

Tinto, V. (1993). *Leaving college: Rethinking the causes and cures of student attrition.* Chicago: University of Chicago Press.

Vygotsky, L. S. (1978). *Mind in society: The development of higher psychological processes*. Cambridge, MA: Harvard University Press.

Wang. T. (2005). Tension in learner support and tutor support in tertiary web-based English language education in China. *International Review of Research in Open and Distance Learning, 6*(3), 1–18.

WCET. (2011). *WCET receives grant for groundbreaking higher education research.* Retrieved from http://www.prweb.com/releases/2011/5/prweb8429528.htm

Woodley, A. (2004). Conceptualizing student dropout in part-time distance education: Pathologizing the normal? *Open Learning, 19*(1), February, 47–63.

Zawacki-Richter, O., Bäcker, E., & Vogt, S. (2009). Review of distance education research (2000 to 2008): Analysis of research areas, methods, and authorship. *International Review of Research in Open and Distance Learning, 10*(6), 21–50.

Quality Assurance in Online Distance Education

12

Colin Latchem

Whenever English philosopher and broadcaster Professor C. E. M. Joad had to answer a question put to him on the BBC's *The Brains Trust*, his first response was always, "It all depends on what you mean by . . ." This certainly applies to online distance education with its wide range of pedagogical methods and technology applications. At one end of the continuum, online learning comprises didactic texts translated into digital form or live or recorded tele-lectures with little or no opportunities for interaction and largely assessed by multiple-choice methods. At the other end is Downes's (2005) e-learning 2.0, in which, as Ehlers (2012) explains, online learning ceases to be the mere delivery of digital learning products for the students' consumption and becomes a platform whereupon knowledge and learning are created by students through interaction, collaboration, and inquiry. Between these two points lie an infinite number of forms of provision. So, in discussing quality assurance (QA) in online distance education, we must be mindful that these forms of provision have may have different quality indicators and may require evaluation to occur in different settings and at various stages of e-learning readiness.

The second point to be considered is that extravagant claims can be made for online distance learning, especially by technophiles who regard technology positively, adopt it enthusiastically, and see it as the solution to every education problem. However, not everyone is convinced of its quality. This is partly because, as Thierer (2010) observes, every technological revolution brings out a fresh crop of techno-pessimists and techno-Pollyannas. Even Socrates, in Plato's *Phaedrus*, disparaged the then-new technology of writing claiming that it disrupted social relationships and caused its users to imagine that they were learning a great deal when in fact they were learning nothing of value. There is nothing new about techno-pessimism!

The view that technologically delivered education is just as good as face-to-face instruction is far from universal. Daniel (2010) remarks on the hostility to online distance education shown by the Chinese government by permitting the Open University of China only to offer two- or three-year junior college degree programs rather than the higher-status four-year bachelor degree programs provided by the conventional universities; another example is legislation by the Brazilian, Japanese, and Malaysian governments that stipulates the percentage of degree courses to be provided face-to-face. Even some of those teaching online question the quality of their courses. Seaman (2009) reported that 48 percent of faculty in the US public and land-grant universities with experience teaching online courses concluded that they were "inferior or somewhat inferior" to their face-to-face equivalents, and only 15 percent rated themselves as "somewhat superior or superior." Two years later, Allen and Seaman (2011) still found that one-third of the senior management in these same universities believed that the learning outcomes of online education were inferior to those of face-to-face instruction, and less than one-third believed that their faculty accepted the value and legitimacy of online education. This explains why Shrock (2009; 2010) reports that not only are there increasing numbers of "We do not accept online coursework" statements appearing on university websites but that some of these institutions reject applications from academics with online degrees—even those they themselves offer!

Such distrust of online learning by academics derives partially from the fact that online distance education is often adopted for reasons of commercial gain or economy or by private for-profit providers, some of whom fall seriously short on quality. For the year 2010, Cohen and Winch (2011, pp. 23-25) reported a 48 percent increase worldwide in the number of online degree or diploma "mills" (organizations offering bogus credentials for sale). There had been a 20 percent increase in known diploma mills in the US (from 810 to 1,008) and a 31 percent increase in Europe as a whole, where a total of 603 mills now operated. Over half (56.2 percent) of these European mills claimed to be based in the UK, which now had a total of 339, up from 271 in the previous year.

Power and Gould-Morven (2011) characterize online learning as having a "head of gold," providing the key to better higher education and serving large numbers of low unit-cost enrolments, but "feet of clay," with low levels of uptake in mainstream academia owing to concerns over quality. Researching US employers' perceptions of online education, Seibold (2007) found that while they recognized its advantages, they did not think it was equivalent to traditional study because it lacked interactivity and a sense of community. Surveying the current state of development and future perspectives of online learning in European education and training and its contribution to achieving the EU objectives for growth and innovation, Aceto et al. (2007) concluded that online learning still had some way to go in ensuring quality and that the excessive hype and expectations meant that the risk of a bubble burst was high.

The concerns that educational quality can be compromised in online learning point to the need for policy-makers, planners, managers, practitioners, and researchers to provide evidence that online distance education is as good as—and, preferably, superior to—the traditional forms of delivery. A lot of money, time, and effort is being expended on online learning, so it needs to be shown that this is achieving quality educational outcomes.

QUALITY

Writers such as Juran and DeFeo (2010) define *quality* as "fitness for purpose." However, this is a corporate perspective and presupposes that it is always possible to foresee how products and services will be used and to ensure that all of the stakeholders have the same needs and expectations. Exploring the nature and usage of the term *quality* in the higher education context, Harvey and Green (1993) posited that it can be defined not as "fitness for purpose," but as "exceptional," as "perfection" (zero defects), as "value for money," or as "transformative." This last definition aligns with that of Pirsig (1974), who suggested that quality was an indefinable but fundamental driver that causes everything to achieve ever-higher quality, and when quality becomes habitual or customary things become static and moribund. Such observations take us beyond QA as a mere box-ticking process of assessing predetermined standards towards a culture of continuous improvement.

ACCREDITATION

Many countries have now established national accreditation and QA agencies. Their regulatory and quality review arrangements may vary according to the kinds of provider (private, public sector, or overseas), types of provision (face-to-face, blended, or distance learning), and levels of provision (institutional, program, or educational service), and they are generally tailored to the individual countries' particular circumstances. However, Middlehurst and Woodfield (2004) and Jung, Wong, Li, Baigaltugs, and Belawati (2011) find commonalities of culture and practice underpinning these different approaches. All of the agencies aim to assure students that institutions and programs meet endorsed academic and professional standards and to enable educators, peak bodies, professional accreditation bodies, and others to reach agreement upon these standards. The granting of accreditation or the assurance of quality typically relates to:

- student outcomes
- curriculum, courses, and courseware
- teaching and learning
- student and faculty support
- assessment, evaluation, and internal QA systems
- management
- staff
- resourcing
- returns on investment and benefits to the national economy and society

However, Gallagher (2010) claims that determining the performance indicators and measures for these is often contentious, with the more powerful stakeholders' perspectives prevailing. The agencies also tend to be more concerned with the easily measurable inputs (such as the number of teachers, library provision, and student attrition rates) rather than the outputs, outcomes, and impacts (the benefits to the graduates, economies, and society as a whole). They may also apply minimum standards and soften the pass/fail nature of accreditation by providing probationary periods and opportunities to reapply (Chalmers & Johnson, 2012).

Two notable exceptions to national regulatory bodies overseeing the quality of higher education are Canada and the US. As federal systems, they both have a complicated mix of licensing requirements and accreditation standards. These confront and often confound providers wishing to operate beyond their own provincial or state borders and can create tensions between national and local systems and institutions striving to maintain their long-held local or regional autonomy and competitive market positions. They also enable rogue operators to take advantage of the regulatory gaps, having a negative impact on the reputation of online learning as a whole (Parker, 2012).

Mutual trust and recognition agreements among accreditation and QA organizations are an indispensable element in assuring that institutions, courses, and programs meet the required standards. The strongest political basis for such mutual accreditation is the 1999 Bologna Declaration. This declaration proposed a European higher education area in which students and graduates could use prior qualifications in one country as acceptable entry requirements for further study in another and led to the establishment of the European Credit Transfer and Accumulation System. In 2003, the ministers of the signatory states charged the European Network for Quality Assurance in Higher Education (ENQA) with developing an agreed set of standards, procedures, and guidelines on QA for higher education. The resultant *Standards and Guidelines for Quality Assurance in the European Higher Education Area* dealt with the issues of institutional QA, external QA, and the external QA agencies themselves. However, ENQA stressed that the prime responsibility for QA must remain with the universities and that this called for the creation of an institutional culture that focusses on quality.

Countries attach great importance to sovereignty over their higher education systems, and the differences in their accreditation systems stand in the way of comprehensive QA frameworks for transnational higher education and attempts to protect students against substandard international distance education providers. The OECD's 2005 *Guidelines for Quality Provision in Cross-Border Higher Education*, developed in collaboration with UNESCO and 30 member countries and expert bodies, set out how governments, higher education and other providers, student bodies, QA and accreditation agencies, and academic and professional recognition bodies can share responsibility in the sending and receiving countries.

The OECD guidelines are not legally binding, and again, mindful of the diversity of national higher education systems, they leave the member countries to assume responsibility for their own QA frameworks. However, they have been endorsed by the American Council of Education, the International Association of Universities, and the Association of Colleges and Universities of Canada and form the basis for the QA and accreditation systems of the regional networks responsible for transnational higher education in Arab, Association of Southeast Asian Nations (ASEAN), Asian-Pacific, Caribbean, Central and Eastern European, Ibero-American, and African countries. All of these regional associations have signed memorandums of understanding with the International Network for Quality Assurance Agencies in Higher Education (INQAAHE), a worldwide association of 200 or so organizations involved in QA in higher education. INQAAHE has also published *Guidelines of Good Practice for Higher Education Quality Assurance Agencies* (for a critical review, see Blackmur [2008]). However, there is, as yet, no overall agreement on the standards and accountability measures to be applied to transnational online distance education and on whether these should be the same as those for conventional higher education.

ONLINE DISTANCE EDUCATION

QA in online distance education is a more contentious issue than it is in campus-based education. Some writers, such as Woodhouse (2006), hold that the criteria for judging inputs and processes and their correlation with quality outcomes are similar in both face-to-face and online distance education; however, because teachers, students, and resources are dispersed, online, and possibly in different countries, assessing quality may require different questions and enquiry methods. By contrast, writers such as Jara and Mellar (2009) argue that the QA arrangements for e-learning should be different from those applied to traditional distance learning and on-campus delivery. Among the elements they see as distinctive to online distance learning are:

- *Distributed teams.* Academics may work in collaboration with other professionals in developing and delivering courses and support systems without necessarily being in the same location.

- *Disaggregated processes.* The design, teaching, and assessment may be carried out by different people or teams (and may sometimes be outsourced).

- *Distant location of students.* Staff members have limited opportunities to interact with students and are dependent upon students' willingness to log in and respond to their requests.

- *Openness to review.* Because content, resources, and communications are mainly text-based and usually archived in electronic form, they can be subject to more in-depth, continuous, and unobtrusive monitoring of participants' activities.

Other factors have an impact on quality in the case of open institutions. Conventional schools, colleges, and universities operate on a *quality-in* model, carefully managing the qualifications and numbers of the entrants. By contrast, open providers such as India's National Institute of Open Schooling or the UK's Open University operate on a *quality-out* model. They believe that it is never too late to learn and accept entrants with no or lesser formal qualifications and whose strengths and talents are less easy to identify. Achieving the necessary completion and graduation rates with such students places enormous demands upon staff and resources. Moreover, different performance indicators may be needed to assess the value-adding dimensions of the teaching and learning, the extent to which the learners improve on their earlier performance or exceed what they might reasonably have been expected to achieve, and the long-term benefits of their education, to themselves and to society.

Many open and distance students across the globe are in rural, remote, or marginalized communities. They lack any tradition of formal education, role models, or access to the kinds of knowledge and resources taken for granted in more privileged settings. The curricula, teaching styles, delivery and assessment methods, and support systems need to be designed so as to help these learners find pathways out of their disadvantage, and there is call for special effort and, arguably, special performance indicators.

Many open and distance institutions also serve huge numbers of learners, and, as Daniel (2010) observes, it is easy to lose a culture of quality customer service in institutions swamped by demand. India's Indira Gandhi National Open University serves around 3.5 million students in India and 40 other countries. The Open University of China has over 2.5 million students. Turkey's Anadolu University has an enrolment of over 1 million off-campus students in Turkey, the Turkish Republic of Northern Cyprus, and Western European countries. Providing teaching, learning, and support for such large numbers is costly and challenging. Stripped-down, low-overhead provision may appeal to the many learners anxious to obtain qualifications for reasons of employment and to governments and private providers, but they certainly present enormous challenges in terms of quality.

Then again, many online distance education providers are not only challenged by the tyranny of distance but also by the requirement to operate across geo-political boundaries. Transnational institutions such as the University of the South Pacific and the University of the West Indies must meet the expectations of the governments of their member countries. The Spanish National University of Distance Education provides distance education for its more than 180,000 students in Bata, Berlin, Berne, Brussels, Buenos Aires, Caracas, Lima, London, Malabo, Mexico City, Paris, and São Paulo. The Virtual University for the Small States of the Commonwealth provides online professional, vocational, and technical distance courses within a transnational qualifications framework that can be readily adapted to the national contexts and crediting systems of 30 small nations. India's National Institute of Open Schooling, serving 1.9 million students with only 251 full-time staff, relies upon thousands of managers, teachers, facilitators, and other personnel in a network of regional centres, study centres, schools, vocational institutions, and non-governmental organizations across the subcontinent. How effectively and efficiently such partnerships and networks are coordinated and managed clearly affects the quality of the educational services.

QUALITY STANDARDS FOR ONLINE DISTANCE EDUCATION

Quality standards aim to represent agreed levels of service or organizational performance that should be met each and every time. In regard to quality standards for e-learning, Bates (2010) expresses surprise at how often academic colleagues argue that there are none. Among those that he commends are:

- FuturEd and Canadian Association for Community Education,

Canadian Recommended E-learning Guidelines (CanREGS) and *Open eQuality Learning Standards*

- Quality Matters Program (US)

- JISC Innovation Group, *Effective Practice in a Digital Age: A Guide to Technology-Enhanced Learning and Teaching* (UK)

- QAA's amplified *Code of Practice for the Assurance of Academic Quality and Standards in Higher Education: Section 2, Collaborative Provision and Flexible and Distributed Learning (Including e-Learning)* (UK)

- Swedish National Agency for Higher Education E-learning Quality

- European Association of Distance Teaching Universities, *Quality Manual for E-learning in Higher Education*

- E-Learning Maturity Model (New Zealand)

- Australian Flexible Learning Framework Toolboxes (Quality e-Learning Resources)

- Australasian Council on Open, Distance and E-Learning, *ACODE Benchmarks*

- *ISO/IEC 19796-1:2005 Information Technology – Learning, Education and Training – Quality Management, Assurance and Metrics – Part 1: General Approach.*

Universities can also assure quality by comparing their processes and performance metrics to best practice in other institutions, nationally or internationally. Benchmarking e-learning is extensively described by Bacsich (2005; 2009a; 2009b). Examples include the Higher Education Academy/JISC Benchmarking of E-learning Exercise in the UK; EU projects such as Benchmarking of Virtual Campuses (BEN VIC); MASSIVE; European University Quality in eLearning (UNIQUe); Re.ViCa and the E-xcellence scheme; Quality Matters (QM), used by many US universities; Pick&Mix (Bacsich, 2005) in the UK, now used commercially in the EU and Canada; the e-learning Maturity Model (eMM), developed by Marshall and Mitchell (2004) in New Zealand and also used in the UK, Australia, and the US; and the Australian Council on Open, Distance and E-Learning (ACODE) benchmarks.

Lucent Technologies (1999) suggest that three approaches are commonly adopted in applying QA to online distance education:

- a service model that focusses on providers' embedding quality in distance delivery methods, courseware, and support services

- a stakeholder analysis model that involves more than the learning providers in defining quality and setting the benchmarks

- a quality improvement model that involves continually assessing stakeholder expectations and addressing indicators of quality and areas of concern

However, it is clear that there is no "one size fits all" model. Some online distance education QA frameworks—for example, the European Foundation for Management Development Certification of E-learning (EFMD CEL)—concern program accreditation. Others focus on institutional accreditation, such as the European UNIQUE. Some focus primarily on product. For example, Nichols (2002), citing Garvin (1988), suggests that online learning standards should concern:

- *Performance.* The finished product should operate in an effective way, as determined by the enduser.

- *Features.* The "bells and whistles" incorporated into the finished product should be appropriate and not detract from the overall objectives of the project.

- *Reliability.* The finished product should not be subject to malfunction.

- *Conformance.* The finished product should comply with industry standards, using standard technologies (although those technologies can be pushed to their utmost), and reflect established education theory.

- *Durability.* The finished product should be relevant and either timeless (in the case of teaching established principles) or easily updated.

- *Serviceability.* It should be easy to repair or adjust the finished product as required.

- *Aesthetics.* The overall "feel" of the finished product should be professional and user-friendly.

- *Perceived quality.* The finished product should enhance the reputation of [the institution] as a quality. (p. 2)

The UK Quality Assurance Agency's earlier *Guidelines on the Quality Assurance of Distance Learning* (1999) were concerned with adapting and extending standard QA procedures for the approval, monitoring, and review of programs to cover non-traditional modes of delivery and learning based on ICT, whether delivered on campus or at a distance. The guidelines covered:

- system design
- program design, approval and review
- management of program delivery
- student development and support
- student communication and representation
- student assessment

The QAA *Code of Practice for the Assurance of Academic Quality and Standards in Higher Education, Section 2: Collaborative Provision and Flexible and Distributed Learning (Including e-Learning)—Amplified Version* (QAA, 2010) covers on-campus as well as distance provision. Part B of this code considers the outcomes expected of such provision, including the e-modes. Expressed from a student's point of view, these are grouped according to delivery, learner support, and assessment and are supported by explanations of the reasoning behind them.

The QAA code also refers to relevant British Standards Institution (BSI) publications regarding QA of e-learning. For example, BS 8426:2003 (BSI, 2003) concerns e-support in all forms of e-learning, whether human tutors are involved or the e-support is automated, whether the learners work individually or in groups, and whether the pedagogy involves learners in constructing their own understanding or in committing content to memory. These standards include the procurement, design, benchmarking, development, evaluation, and communication of information about e-learning courses, learning materials, and e-support services, including online tutorials and intelligent system performance aids.

Barker (2007) states that the FuturEd Open eQuality Learning Standards developed, sponsored, and endorsed by a number of national and international organizations stipulated that these standards should be:

- *Consumer-oriented* – developed with particular attention to return on investment in e-learning for learners

- *Consensus based* – developed through consultation with a balance of provider and consumer groups

- *Comprehensive* – inclusive of all elements of the learning system: outcomes and outputs, processes and practices, inputs and resources

- *Recommended only* – using persuasion and market forces rather than legislation to ratchet up the quality of e-learning

- *Futuristic* – describing a preferred future rather than the present circumstances for design and delivery

- *Adaptable* – best used for adult and post-secondary education and training but adaptable to other levels of learning services (p. 110)

Bates (2007) observes that criticisms of the quality standards applied to e-learning may reflect the dominance of technical standards and external assurance standards over more pedagogically directed quality issues.

Ehlers (2004; 2012) argues that e-learning 2.0 requires different questions to be asked, different objects and processes to be evaluated, different quality criteria to be applied, and different approaches to be adopted. He posits that QA should progress from being primarily concerned with input variables, evaluating pre-determined objectives, learning environments and content developed by faculty, to assuring and assessing outcomes. He suggests that quality should be measured in terms of the extent to which particular learning scenarios stimulate the learners, motivate them to find, remix, and repurpose content to accord with their own intentions, and share their content and ideas with others—not necessarily in the same institution or the same country.

Ehlers (2012) also suggests that there should be a greater emphasis on learners' perspectives on quality. He finds that online learners judge quality in online provision in terms of:

- communication and interaction between tutors and learners

- communication and collaboration with other learners, experts, or tutors

- the expected technical standards

- the cost and effort involved in the learning experience in relation to the benefits and outcomes

- the provision of standard information and individualised counselling on course content, learning methodologies, and technical matters

- a sense of "presence" in the lessons (although this is more highly valued by some groups of learners than others)
- the didactics (content, learning goals, methods, and materials)

Jung (2012) observes that while customer focus is a tenet of QA, very few online learning QA frameworks take serious heed of students' needs and expectations. Two exceptions are Canada's Open eQuality Standards and the European Commission–funded Sustainable Environment for the Evaluation of Quality in e-Learning (SEEQUEL). She suggests that for quality to be assured it is important to consult with students to determine the following:

- The extent to which students with different learning styles, motivations, and technological competencies differ in their perceptions of quality in e-learning
- The extent to which learners with different prior learning experiences perceive the quality of e-learning
- The extent to which learners' perspectives of e-learning quality is culturally determined
- The extent to which providers' and learners' perceptions of e-learning quality coincide or are complementary or in conflict
- How findings on learners' perceptions of e-learning quality can be applied to improve the quality of QA frameworks for e-learning and help to develop the culture of learning

Grifoll et al. (2009) suggest that new QA indicators may be needed with the evolution of new teaching and learning technologies that enable the establishment of new and diversified educational communities and redefinition of student's roles, from that of learner to that of explorer.

TRANSNATIONAL ONLINE DISTANCE EDUCATION

Harry and Perraton (1999) observe that, while distance learning widens access, it can be culturally laden and threaten time-honoured educational practices. Wong (2007) warns of cultural bias in programs derived from

Western cultures. Talalakina (2010) observes that teachers and learners in cultures at the collectivistic end of the value spectrum, who are more accustomed to teacher-centred environments, may have problems with Western-style programs embodying an individualistic value system. Western education is concerned with encouraging students to thoughtfully examine and debate ideas and issues. It originates in the Socratic method (Rud, 1997) and in the approaches of such educational pioneers as the English abbot Ælfric of Eynsham (c. 955–c. 1010), who assigned each pupil a role and invited him to engage in spontaneous, individual, and inventive philosophical debate (Watkins, n.d.).

In Asian societies, such humanistic, progressive, analytical, and radical approaches may conflict with the Confucian legacy wherein the central theme is order, the teacher is responsible for transmitting the knowledge, the learners' duty is to absorb and reiterate whatever the teacher teaches, and the examination system is designed to test this transmitted knowledge. Wang (2006) describes how in People's Republic of China the authorities deny teachers the freedom to teach as they wish, and so they must grapple with two competing sets of requirements: the need to conform to the administrators' expectations and the need to respond to the diverse needs of their students.

Similar issues can arise in the Islamic countries. *Islam* means "voluntary surrender to the will of Allah," and the Qur'an is considered the literal word of God. Gursoy (2005) observes that the time-honoured responsibility of teachers in Islamic countries has been to preach the text, and the students' duty has been to memorize the text. Khafagi (2004) suggests that in Middle Eastern countries the Internet is regarded as a source of information and entertainment rather than as a learning tool and that this, plus the tradition of oral learning in Arabic cultures, lead to different patterns of learning. The World Bank (2008) notes that in Arab countries, teacher-led, face-to-face instruction is considered quality education and ICT is primarily used for information transmission and passive learning. Studying Arab distance education students in the US, Al-Harthi (2005) found that, while students liked the anonymity of online learning, they still depended on their tutors to define the rules and procedures and initiate communications, were reluctant to make uninvited contributions or ask for clarification, and, in the absence of oversight from their teachers, tended to procrastinate. Culture also affects the nature of organizations and relationships. (Gunawardena provides a detailed overview of cross-cultural issues in global online distance education in chapter 2 of this volume.)

Hofstede's (1990) Power Distance (PD) index indicates the extent to which different cultures expect power to be distributed. High PD countries have centralized political power, hierarchical organizations, and large differences in status and income. Low PD countries have flatter organizations and greater equality. Asian countries score highly on the PD index, which again explains why many Asian learners regard their teachers or set texts as the principle authoritative sources of knowledge, regard themselves as inferiors, and prefer to learn passively rather than interact with their teachers in person or online (Wang, 2007). By contrast, most teachers and learners in Western universities regard themselves more as partners in learning. PD not only has ramifications in pedagogy, but it can also affect the openness and accountability in QA systems.

Latchem and Jung (2010) show that e-learning can mean different things in different cultures. In Asia, for example, e-learning often involves telelecturing by streamed video/audio or videoconferencing, instructional packages, and multiple-choice testing rather than the self-paced, socially constructed Web 2.0 learning of the West. In Japan, 82 percent of university classes are lecture-based, with the expectation that students will recall what they are taught, rather than engage in critical, independent enquiry and in articulating and defending viewpoints. And one of the reasons for the inability of the Open University of Japan to move into e-learning is that it is bound by a law declaring that it "shall offer educational services through broadcasting and face-to-face classes at local study centres," which is why it is still known as *Hoso Daigaku* (broadcasting university) (Aoki, 2009; 2010).

To summarize, QA in transnational online distance education needs to take account of the degree of e-learning readiness in the populace and institutions (Kapp, 2005), the cultural differences between countries and institutions in terms of QA procedures, definitions of *quality* and *standards* (Billing, 2004), PD factors (Hofstede, 1990), and ways of communicating (Hall, 2000). Thus, in judging the quality of transnational programs, special performance measures are required, for example, in regard to:

- the nature and extent of collaboration with the overseas partners in course development and delivery

- allowance for different states of e-learning readiness, language competency, and teaching and learning styles

- inclusion of intercultural case studies, role plays, and experiential learning

- opportunities for interaction, reflection, and conceptual and practical understanding of how people differ across cultures.

QUALITY ASSURANCE AND OPEN EDUCATIONAL RESOURCES

In 2001, in an unprecedented move, the Massachusetts Institute of Technology announced the release of nearly all its courses on the Internet for free access. Since then, the number of institutions offering open educational resources (OERs) has increased, and the emergence of Web 2.0 and open content licensing of learning materials has led to the concept of the Open Educational Resource University (OERu) (Stacey, 2011; Taylor, 2011). The OERu is a partnership of accredited universities, colleges, and polytechnics across five continents that enables learners to study online, for free, anywhere in the world. Should students wish to gain academic credit, they can also pay reduced fees when they feel ready for assessment.

Andrade et al. (2011) express concern that, while educational institutions, teachers, students, and self-directed learners may find it easy to access OERs, they may find it more difficult to be sure of their quality. Hylén (2006) observes that some users may be persuaded by the reputation of a particular provider. For example, users can be confident of the academic and pedagogical standards of the MIT OpenCourseWare and of the courses and materials from such institutions as the Carnegie Mellon University, Rice University, or the Open University. Or the resources may have been peer-reviewed. For example, most of the free and open collection of online teaching and learning resources listed by the Multimedia Educational Resource for Learning and Online Teaching (MERLOT) have been peer-reviewed in terms of quality of content, teaching and learning potential, and ease of use by teachers and students. However, not all of the OERs in this repository have been reviewed. Another approach can be letting the users themselves rate and/or comment on OERs and how they have used them. Other users could check the evaluations and the number of downloads for particular OERs and then decide for themselves whether the OERs are useable, reusable, repurposeable, and of high quality. However, peer review is time consuming, so it may be advisable for some organizations to develop a quality checklist for

OERs, focussing on trustworthiness of content, quality of pedagogy, legality, accessibility, technical interoperability, and other issues.

Hylén concludes that one can predict a growing debate on the new cultural and economic, as well as educational, realities of OERs. If their use is to take hold in education, some form(s) of QA will be needed to ensure that they conform to best practice. The same argument holds for the more recent learning phenomenon of Massive Open Online Courses (MOOCs), which are attracting so much interest among governments, institutions, and philanthropic and corporate agencies. Some MOOCs are designed to enable anyone, anywhere, to study at the university level for free or test their learning readiness by taking "taster courses." Some MOOCs are "digital storefronts," designed to market providers' brands globally. Some providers see massification as a way of increasing openness and access; others see it as a means of economizing or profiteering. Some providers are elite institutions, while others are for-profit start-ups. The so-called CMOOCs use constructivist principles, whereas XMOOCs employ a knowledge transmission model. Advocates regard MOOCs as a "disruptive technology," developing new markets and new models. Bates (2012) sees them as retrograde, arguing that MOOC supporters talk as if distance learning had just been invented and nothing was known about the need for quality in instructional design and for learner support. In view of the high non-completion rates being reported, Yuan and Powell (2013) suggest that the issues of quality (including the awarding for degree credit , sustainability, pedagogy, as well as the awarding of credit for MOOCs, are of major concern for higher education.

THE COSTS OF QA IN ONLINE DISTANCE EDUCATION

Academic resistance to managerialism (Anderson, 2008) must be acknowledged. And burdensome, overly costly, and bureaucratic QA procedures must be avoided at all costs.

Kaner (1996) recommends consulting those directly involved (students, teachers, administrative support staff, technical support staff, etc.) in order to hear their complaints about the time, costs, and inconvenience of any quality failures in systems, programs, and services and then using this feedback as evidence of the cost benefits of QA. Campanella (1999) argues for calculating the "total quality costs" of avoiding defects at the outset. This can be done by first establishing the costs of gaining stakeholder consensus on the needs for QA, the development of QA policies and procedures, the provision of training in QA, and the formative and summative evaluation of products and services to ensure that these conform to the required standards—and then by setting these against the internal and external failure costs and the opportunity costs. *Internal failure costs* are incurred when programs need to be revised, replaced, or abandoned before they are delivered to the public. The later this occurs, the higher the costs. *External failure costs* arise once programs are being delivered and, for example, an unanticipated need arises to deal with learners' problems and complaints, or dropout and failures rates are higher than estimated, or there is adverse publicity and loss of trust or morale, and so on. The costs of remediation at this stage are typically far higher than internal failure costs. *Opportunity costs* are the benefits that can be achieved if failure costs are not incurred.

Highly developed QA systems ensure that quality products and services are quickly and efficiently delivered and gain user satisfaction with, and stakeholder confidence in, the systems, programs, and services. On the other hand, the prevention and appraisal costs of zero-defect systems can be high. So, as Nguyen and Pirozzi (2006) advise, it is important to calculate what form of QA will provide the best return on investment. To keep quality costs in balance, Laurillard (2007) suggests determining the critical benefits and their related costs as follows:

- clarify the purpose of a technology-enhanced learning innovation
- identify the key parameters that confer learning benefits
- compare old, new, and blended methods
- model alternative plans
- support an iterative approach to designing a plan against the cost it generates
- capture the planning in a form that can be communicated and revised
- define the staff resources needed to realize a plan
- assess the per student cost of the teaching time for a course (p. 24)

IS ONLINE DISTANCE EDUCATION YET GOOD ENOUGH?

Unfortunately, as Ryan and Brown (2012) have found, with a market-driven philosophy and the abandonment of centralized online distance education support, many of the lessons learned over the years regarding quality in off-campus and technology-based provision are now being disregarded. They instance the audits of two institutions with long and honourable traditions in distance education conducted by the Australian Universities Quality Agency (whose operations have now transferred to the Tertiary Education Quality and Standards Agency). Despite one university's professed commitment to the ACODE benchmarks and the other's claim to be "at the forefront of online learning," these audits showed the quality of these two institutions' online distance provision to be very much in question. These AUQA reports serve to identify the gap than can exist between the rhetoric and reality of quality, and they reinforce Reid's (2005, p. 4) conclusion that the current pervasive social ideology is "constructing Australian universities as entrepreneurial businesses in an education marketplace."

James Joyce once described errors as "portals of discovery," but Romiszowski (2004) observes that it is extremely difficult to identify specific reasons why online distance education projects fail or exhibit serious problems. He sees this as a limitation but also an opportunity for a research agenda that builds on what has been established in the field and verifies what has not. He suggests that the factors that most strongly affect the ultimate success or failure of online applications have less to do with the technologies and technicalities of course design and more to do with the broader and more general factors that influence the success or failure of any innovation. He provides a timely reminder that educational technology involves the design, development, application, and evaluation of systems, methods, and media for learning, not simply the hardware and software.

AN OUTCOMES APPROACH TO QA

Many claims are made for online distance learning. For example, UCL (n.d.) suggests that it

- widens access and equity
- permits study at any time and location
- places the responsibility for learning with the students, which equips them for lifelong learning
- increases motivation by engaging students in interaction

- provides contiguous feedback so that students can reflect on their mistakes

- provides staff and faculty with more time for teaching development and research as a result of the automation of repetitive teaching and administration duties

- improves teaching quality through the review and update of teaching practices and the introduction of new technology

- saves time and money, thus unlocking further resources that can be used for enhancing teaching and so forth

It is essential to collect evidence that support these claims for the following groups:

- governments, institutions, and others, to help them envision, define objectives, and prioritize the responsible and effective provision of funds and resources for online distance education

- providers, who require evidence of the impact and benefits of their programs

- e-learners, who require assurance of the economic value and standards of provision and qualifications

- other stakeholders eager to see online distance education receive greater recognition and support

However, many online distance education QA systems are essentially concerned with measuring inputs such as management, funding, staffing, technology, infrastructure, and instructional design. To meet the various stakeholders' needs and expectations, it could be argued that QA measures should be more concerned with:

- *Outputs.* The immediate educational effects of online distance provision.

- *Outcomes.* The short- to medium-term individual, institutional, and societal consequences of these outputs.

- *Impacts.* The longer-term, significant, and sustained improvements in national socio-economic circumstances, institutions, and graduates.

Kirkpatrick's (1994) widely used model for teaching, learning, and training measures four levels of outcomes:

(1) what the learners thought and felt about the learning experience

(2) the resultant increase in knowledge or capability

(3) the extent of behaviour and capability improvement and implementation/application

(4) the cost-effectiveness of the methods and their effects on the learner's environment

It is difficult to find an example of this from higher education. But let us consider the QA of a non-formal online distance education program: the Commonwealth of Learning's Lifelong Learning for Farmers (L3F) program in Tamil Nadu, India.

When this program was originally conceived in 2004, the aim was to evolve a self-replicating and self-sustaining program in lifelong learning for farmers, using modern ICTs to build capacity in developing value-added farming, ensuring food and livelihood security, and encouraging the more sustainable use of natural resources. Two years into the project, Speirs (2008) could report that 500 villagers regularly attended the ICT-based learning sessions; that learning materials, CDs, newsletters, and Internet/intranet presentations were available; that ICT kiosks had been established; that the number of bank loans to farmers (60 percent of whom were women) had increased; that goat-rearing methods, market options and prices, and family circumstances had improved; and that other NGOs and villages were becoming involved. Achieving these outcomes cost the Commonwealth of Learning (COL) less than USD 80,000, most of which was spent on local consultancies. All the other resources came from local partners, extension agencies, and banks, as well as a telecom provider attracted by the business prospects.

A year later, Spaven (2009) reported that COL had found partners willing to transfer the model to Sri Lanka, Mauritius, Papua New Guinea, and Uganda. And two years after this, Thamizoli, Francis, Soundari, Kamaraj, and Balasubramanian (2011) were able to report that, in the previous two years, 5,000 women farmers had studied dairy methods, goat rearing, horticulture, finance, business, credit management, and law and human rights by means of m-learning, multimedia, local television, and face-to-face training. The total credit to the L3F farmers and total turnover of their enterprises had increased markedly; the L3F farmers had significantly higher value assets, income, and household infrastructure than the other farmers; their learning behaviour was significantly different; and they had stronger cognitive social capital and a higher level of empowerment. These farmers had also created their own website for m-learning in the Tamil language for other farmers, featuring multimedia agricultural learning materials, regional agricultural news, and daily weather and market information. Would that there were more such longitudinal impact and outcomes studies being conducted in all sectors to provide evidence of the quality of online distance education.

Quality of outcomes is receiving increasing attention at the governmental, institutional, and academic program levels. Adamson et al. (2010) argue that clear statements and evidence of learning outcomes make qualifications more transparent for students; help employers better understand the knowledge, skills, and competencies of applicants; increase transparency and comparability between qualification standards (for example, within the Bologna Process); and inform course design.

The Commonwealth of Learning (Latchem, 2012) offers a practical guide on how to measure outputs, outcomes, and impacts in online distance education applications in the non-formal sector. This model could be extended and adapted to other sectors.

The OECD has been conducting a Feasibility Study for the Assessment of Higher Education Learning Outcomes (AHELO), the purpose of which to see whether it is practically and scientifically feasible to assess both the inputs (what the students bring to their degree studies) and the outputs (what they graduate with) across different cultures, language groups, and institutions. It was envisaged that this could help universities assess and improve their teaching, aid students in making better informed choices in selecting institutions, help policy-makers to ensure that the considerable amounts spent on higher education are well spent, and enable employers to know whether the skills of the graduates entering the job market matched their needs. The feasibility study has focussed on generic skills (critical thinking, analytic reasoning, problem-solving, and written communication); discipline-specific skills in economics and engineering; and contextual information to link these data to the students' backgrounds and learning environments. The issues of value-adding analysis and value-adding models have also been considered. While it has been found that much of AHELO is workable, and while the study has provided lessons and stimulated reflection on how learning outcomes might be more effectively measured in the future, at the time of writing no decision has been made to undertake a main study (OECD, 2012; 2013).

Arguably, such an outcomes-based approach to QA could be applied in judging the quality of all forms of technology-based learning in conventional classrooms, open schooling, workplace-based training, and formal and non-formal education. The number and calibre of student enrolments and retention rates, the participation of those from low socio-economic or geographically disadvantaged communities, and the number of credits achieved could be measures of quality. And where e-learning 2.0 methods are employed, with knowledge being created, negotiated, shared, remixed, repurposed, and applied in new contexts, rather than simply taught, learners' capacities could be measured in these terms:

- acquisition of the knowledge, skills, and attitudes required for employment, lifelong learning, and best thinking in the learners' particular fields
- self-directed learning and constructing and applying new knowledge
- interacting and collaborating with others in creating and discussing knowledge rather than always being dependent upon ready-made content and viewpoints
- recognizing, reflecting on, and responding to personal learning needs, strategies, and progress
- using information retrieval, communication, and creative tools effectively and efficiently
- monitoring and documenting progress in portfolios and developing reports and presentations in various media
- critically reflecting on and developing personal conclusions about the role, ethics, and use of technology in society

It follows from this that the *quality of faculty* could be judged in terms of:

- leading and innovating in the adoption of learner-centred methods and technology applications
- serving diverse talents and opening up new opportunities for learning through online distance learning

- devising and managing relevant and purposeful assessment and feedback strategies
- researching and improving knowledge and practice in online distance education

The *quality of institutional and partnership management* could be assessed in terms of:

- responding to the forces driving the online distance education agenda
- developing and implementing visions and plans
- understanding and continually improving the learning experiences of students
- encouraging, supporting, and rewarding staffs' roles and activities
- determining critical success factors that will improve institutional performance and outcomes
- ensuring quality in online distance education

In addition, evidence would also be needed to demonstrate that online distance education course credits or credentials are recognized locally and internationally as having the same value and transferability as those of conventionally delivered programs and that both learners and providers are receiving adequate returns on their investments of time and resources.

CONCLUDING REMARKS

This chapter has raised a number of critical questions about QA in online distance education, all of which call for further research. For example:

- Should online distance learning be accredited and judged by the same measures and standards as conventional teaching and training, or do its distinctive attributes warrant special consideration?
- Should such learning be judged in terms of inputs or outputs, outcomes, and impacts?
- What systematic QA mechanisms are needed to demonstrate the quality of OERS?
- How do different cultures interpret and measure the quality of online

distance education, and are different quality standards needed to match these cultural differences?

Finding answers to these questions calls for a move beyond advocacy, rhetoric, and small-scale studies to undertaking long-term studies that demonstrate whether and how online learning can help schools, colleges, and universities produce students with the generic attributes and internationally competitive standards required for the 21st century by achieving: excellence (superior, exceptional, and distinctive education), consistency (quality for all learners in all situations), fitness for purpose (meeting all stakeholders' needs and expectations), value for money (achieving the same educational outcomes at a lower cost or better educational outcome at the same cost), and transformation (significant, systematic, and sustained improvement and innovation).

As Bates (2011) reminds us, it is critical to ask where the decision to move into e-learning originates. Is it simply the brainchild of some senior manager who believes that online learning should be adopted for purely strategic or financial reasons? Or is it adopted because some department head or individual thinks, "Build it and they will come"? Or does it come from an institution that has carefully thought through how and why it should use online distance learning, has established a student need best met by online learning, has determined which courses should be delivered online and which through blended learning, and has identified what training, time, and resources will be needed? As Bates observes, all but the last of these are bound to fail the quality tests.

Bates (2010) notes that because online distance education is still often under a cloud of suspicion, it can be subject to more demanding forms of QA than conventional teaching and learning. So QA needs to be approached with due care.

Chalmers and Johnson (2012) observe that minimum standards often apply in accreditation and QA. For online distance education to demonstrate its worth and capacity to transform education, minimum standards are not good enough. Rigorous and critical self-, peer-, and institutional reviews are required to pursue the ideal of ever-higher quality. And QA should not simply be mandatory, external, and concerned with accountability, but voluntary, internal, and concerned with developing a culture of quality. Ultimately, governments, institutions, and other funding bodies will be prepared to fund and support only those systems and methods that achieve outstanding outcomes and are likely to have a major impact in the future.

REFERENCES

Aceto, S., Delrio, C., Dondi, C. Fischer, T., Kastis, N., Klein, R., Kugemann . . . Szûcs, A. (2007). HELIOS *Report: e-Learning for Innovation in Europe.* The Horizontal E-Learning Integrated Observation System project co-funded by the European Commission. Brussels: MENON Network EEIG. Retrieved from http://www. menon.org/publications/HELIOS%20thematic%20report-%20Access.pdf

Adamson, L., Becerro, M., Cullen, P., González-Vega, L., Sobrino, J. J., & Ryan, N. (2010). *Quality assurance and learning outcomes.* Helsinki: European Association for Quality Assurance in Higher Education. Retrieved from http://www.enqa.eu/files/WSR%2017%20-%20Final.pdf

Al-Harthi, A. S. (2005). Distance higher education experiences of Arab Gulf students in the United States: A cultural perspective. *The International Review of Research in Open and Distance Learning, 6*(3). Retrieved from http://www.irrodl.org/index.php/irrodl/article/view/263/406

Allen, I. E., & Seaman, J. (2011). *Going the distance: Online education in the United States, 2011.* Retrieved from http://www.onlinelearningsurvey.com/reports/goingthedistance.pdf

Anderson, G. (2008). Mapping academic resistance in the managerial university. *Organization, 15*(2), 251–70. Retrieved from http://org.sagepub.com/content/15/2/251.short

Andrade, A., Ehlers, U-D., Caine, E., Carneiro, R., Conole, G., Kairamo, A-K., . . . Holmberg, C. (2011). *Beyond OER: Shifting focus from resources to practices.* OPAL Report 2011. Duisburg-Essen, Germany: University of Duisburg-Essen, Open Educational Quality Initiative.

Aoki, K. (2009). *E-Learning in the fantasyland: Myths and reality of education in Japan.* Paper presented at ICL2009, September 26–28, 2009, Villach, Austria.

Aoki, K. (2010). Challenges of transforming the Open University of Japan into the third generation distance education institution. *Proceedings of IODL & ICEM: International Joint Conference and Media Days* (pp. 79–92), October 6–8, 2010, Anadolu University, Turkey.

Bacsich, P. (2005). *Theory of benchmarking for e-learning: A top-level literature review* (p. 40). Sheffield: UK. Retrieved from http://www.matic-media.co.uk/benchmarking/Bacsich-benchmarking-2005-04.doc

Bacsich, P. (2009a). *Benchmarking e-learning in UK universities: Lessons from and for the international context.* Paper presented at the 23rd ICDE World Conference on Open Learning and Distance Education, Maastricht, Netherlands, 7–10 June 2009. Retrieved from http://www.openhogeschoolnetwerk.com/Docs/Campagnes/ICDE2009/Papers/Final_Paper_338Bacsich.pdf

Bacsich, P. (2009b). Benchmarking e-learning in UK universities: The methodologies. In T. Mayes, D. Morrison, H. Mellar, P. Bullen, and M. Oliver (Eds.), *Transforming higher education through technology-enhanced learning* (pp. 90–106). York, UK: The Higher Education Academy. Retrieved from http://www.heacademy.ac.uk/assets/documents/learningandtech/Transforming-07.pdf

Barker, K. C. (2007). E-learning quality standards for consumer protection and consumer confidence: A Canadian case study in e-learning quality assurance. *Educational Technology & Society, 10*(2),109–19.

Bates, T. (2010, August 15). E-learning quality assurance standards, organizations and research. [Blog]. Retrieved November 9, 2013, from http://www.tonybates.ca/2010/08/15/e-learning-quality-assurance-standards-organizations-and-research

Bates, T. (2011, October 30). Why you need an e-learning plan. [Blog]. Retrieved November 9, 2013, from http://www.tonybates.ca/2011/10/30/why-you-need-an-e-learning-plan/

Bates, T. (2012). What's right and what's wrong about Coursera-style MOOCs. *Online learning and distance education resources*, moderated by Tony Bates, August 5, 2012. http://www.tonybates.ca/2012/08/05/whats-right-and-whats-wrong-about-coursera-style-moocs/

Billing, D. (2004). International comparisons and trends in external quality assurance of higher education: Commonality or diversity? *Higher Education* (47), 113–37.

Blackmur, D. (2008). A critical analysis of the INQAAHE Guidelines of Good Practice for higher education quality assurance agencies. *Higher Education, 56*(6), 723–34.

British Standards Institution. (2003, August). *BS 8426:2003: A code of practice for e-support in e-learning systems.* London, UK: British Standards Institution.

Campanella, J. (Ed.). (1999). *Principles of quality costs: Principles, implementation, and use* (3rd ed.). Milwaukee, WI: ASQ Quality Press.

Chalmers, D., & Johnson, S. (2012). Quality assurance and accreditation in higher education. In I. Jung & C. Latchem (Eds.), *Quality assurance and accreditation in distance education and e-learning,* (pp.1–12). New York: Routledge.

Cohen, E. B., & Winch, R. (2011). *Diploma and accreditation mills: New trends in credential abuse.* Bedford, UK: Verifile Accredibase. Retrieved from http://www.accredibase.com/upload/documents/accredibase_accredibasereport.pdf

Daniel, J. (2010, October). *Distance education under threat: An opportunity?* Keynote address at the IDOL & ICEM 2010 Joint Conference and Media Days, Eskisehir, Turkey. Retrieved November 21, 2013, from http://www.col.org/resources/speeches/2010presentation/Pages/2010-10-06.aspx

Downes, S. (2005, October 16). E-Learning 2.0. *eLearn Magazine*. Retrieved from http://www.downes.ca/post/31741

Ehlers, U-D. (2004). *Quality in e-learning from a learner's perspective.* Paper presented at the Third EDEN Research Workshop 2004, Oldenburg, Germany. Retrieved from http://www.eurodl.org/materials/contrib/2004/Online_Master_COPs.html

Ehlers, U-D. (2012). Quality assurance policies and guidelines in European distance, and e-learning. In I. Jung & C. Latchem (Eds.), *Quality assurance and accreditation in distance education and e-learning*, pp.79–90. New York: Routledge.

Gallagher, M. (2010). *The accountability for quality agenda in higher education.* Canberra, AU: Group of Eight Australia. Retrieved from http://www.go8.edu.au/ government-_and_-business/go8-policy-_and_-analysis/2010/the-accountability-for-quality-agenda-in-higher-education

Garvin, D. (1988). *Managing quality.* New York: Macmillan.

Grifoll, J., Huertas, E., Prades, A., Rodríguez, S., Rubin, Y., Mulder, F., and Ossiannilsson, E. (2009). *Quality assurance of e-learning. ENQA Workshop Report 14.* Helsinki: European Association for Quality Assurance in Higher Education. Retrieved from http://www.enqa.eu/indirme/papers-and-reports/workshop-and-seminar/ENQA_wr_14.pdf

Gursoy, H. (2005). A critical look at distance education in Turkey. In A. A. Carr-Chellman (Ed.), *Global perspectives on e-learning: Rhetoric and reality,* (pp. 116–126). Thousand Oaks, CA: Sage.

Hall, E. T. (2000). Context and meaning. In L. A. Samovar & R. E. Porter (Eds.), *Intercultural communication: A reader* (9th ed.), (pp. 34–43). Belmont, CA: Wadsworth.

Harry, K., & Perraton, H. (1999). Open and distance learning for the new society. In K. Harry (Ed.), *Higher education through open and distance learning,* (pp. 1–12). New York/Vancouver: Routledge/The Commonwealth of Learning.

Harvey, L., & Green, D. (1993). Defining quality. *Assessment and Evaluation in Higher Education, 18*(1), 9–34.

Hofstede, G. (1990). *Cultures and organizations: Software of the mind.* Maidenhead, UK: McGraw-Hill.

Hylén, J. (2006). Open educational resources: Opportunities and challenges. *Proceedings of Open Education 2006: Community, culture and content,* September 27–29, Utah State University (pp. 49–63). Retrieved from http://cosl.usu.edu/conferences/opened2006/docs/opened2006-proceedings.pdf

Jara, M., & Mellar, H. (2009). Factors affecting quality enhancement procedures for e-learning courses. *Quality Assurance in Education, 17*(3), 220–32.

Jung, I. (2012). Learners' perceptions and opinions of quality assurance. In I. Jung & C. Latchem (Eds.), *Quality assurance and accreditation in distance education and e-learning* (pp. 244–54). New York: Routledge.

Jung, I., Wong, T. M., Li, C., Baigaltugs, S., & Belawati, T. (2011). Quality assurance in Asian distance education: Diverse approaches and common culture. *The International Review of Research in Open and Distance Learning, 12*(6). Retrieved from http://www.irrodl.org/index.php/irrodl/article/view/991/1953

Juran, J. M., & DeFeo, J. A. (2010). *Juran's quality handbook: The complete guide to performance excellence* (6th ed.). Columbus, OH: McGraw-Hill.

Kaner, C. (1996). Quality cost analysis: Benefits and risks. *Software QA, 3*(1), 23. Retrieved from http://www.badsoftware.com/qualcost.htm

Kapp, K. M. (2005). *Are you ready for e-learning?* Alexandria, VA: American Society for Training & Development. Retrieved from http://www.astd.org/LC/2005/0405_kapp.htm

Khafagi, B. (2004). *Education is the key: Middle Eastern countries invest in the future: Interview with Dr. Bassem Khafagi by Beate Kleessen.* University of Anadolu, Turkey. Retrieved from http://tojde.anadolu.edu.tr/tojde19/news/interview.htm

Kirkpatrick, D.L. (1994). *Evaluating training programs: The four levels.* San Francisco: Berrett-Koehler.

Latchem, C. (2012). *Quality assurance toolkit for open and distance non-formal education.* Vancouver: The Commonwealth of Learning.

Latchem, C., & Jung, I. (2010). *Distance and blended learning in Asia.* New York: Routledge.

Laurillard, D. (2007). Modelling benefits-oriented costs for technology enhanced learning. *Higher Education, 54*(1), 21–39.

Lucent Technologies. (1999). *A summary of quality issues in distance education.* Chicago, IL: Bell Labs.

Marshall, S. (2004). E-learning standards: Open enablers of learning or compliance strait jackets? [Keynote address.] *Proceedings of the 21st ASCILITE Conference,* December 5–8, 2004, Perth, Australia. Retrieved from http://www.ascilite.org.au/conferences/perth04/procs/marshall.html

Marshall, S., & Mitchell, G. (2007). *Benchmarking international e-learning capability with the e-learning maturity model.* Retrieved from http://www.caudit.edu.au/educauseaustralasia07/authors_papers/Marshall-103.pdf

Middlehurst, R., & Woodfield, S. (2004). *International quality review and distance learning: Lessons from five countries.* Washington DC: Council for Higher Education Accreditation. Retrieved from http://cshe.berkeley.edu/research/regulation/documents/IQR_DistLearning_Dec04.pdf

Nguyen, H. Q. & Pirozzi, R. (2006, November). *Understanding quality cost.* Retrieved from http://www.logigear.com/newsletter-2006/298-understanding-quality-cost.html

Nichols, M. (2002). *Development of a quality assurance system for elearning projects.* Paper presented at the Australian Society for Computers in Tertiary Education (ASCILITE) Conference 2002, Auckland, New Zealand. Retrieved from http://www.ascilite.org.au/conferences/auckland02/proceedings/papers/004.pdf

Organisation for Economic Co-operation and Development (OECD). (2012). *AHELO interim feasibility study report: Highlights: What have we learned so far?* Paris: OECD. Retrieved from http://search.oecd.org/officialdocuments/displaydocumentpdf/?cote=edu/imhe/ahelo/gne(2012)6&doclanguage=en

Organisation for Economic Co-operation and Development (OECD). (2013). *Assessment of higher education learning outcomes: Feasibility study report, volume 3--Further insights.* Paris: OECD. Retrieved from http://www.oecd.org/education/skills-beyond-school/AHELOFSReportVolume3.pdf

Office for Standards in Education, Children's Services and Skills (Ofsted). (2009). *Virtual learning environments: An evaluation of their development in a sample of educational settings*. London, UK: Ofsted. Retrieved from http://www.ofsted.gov. uk/resources/virtual-learning-environments-evaluation-of-their-development-sample-of-educational-settings

Parker, N. (2012). Quality assurance and accreditation in the United States and Canada. In I. Jung & C. Latchem (Eds.), *Quality assurance and accreditation in distance education and e-learning* (pp. 58–68). New York: Routledge.

Pirsig, R. M. (1974). *Zen and the art of motorcycle maintenance*. New York: William Morrow.

Power, M., & Gould-Morven, A. (2011), Head of gold, feet of clay: The online learning paradox. *International Review of Research in Open and Distance Learning, 12*(2). Retrieved from http://www.irrodl.org/index.php/irrodl/article/view/916Cached

Quality Assurance Agency for Higher Education. (2010). *Code of practice for the assurance of academic quality and standards in higher education: Section 2: Collaborative provision and flexible and distributed learning (including e-learning)*. Gloucester, UK: Author. Retrieved from http://www.qaa.ac.uk/ Publications/InformationAndGuidance/Documents/collab2010.pdf

Reid, I. (2005). Quality assurance, open and distance learning, and Australian universities. *International Review of Research in Open and Distance Learning, 6*(1), 1–12.

Romiszowski, A. J. (2004). How's the e-learning baby? Factors leading to success or failure of an educational technology innovation. *Educational Technology, 44*(1), 5–27. Retrieved from http://asianvu.com/digital-library/elearning/elearning_ failure_study-romiszowsky.pdf

Rud, A. G. (1997). The use and abuse of Socrates in teaching. *Education Policy Analysis Archives, 5*(20). Retrieved from http://epaa.asu.edu/ojs/article/view/621/743

Ryan, Y., & Brown, M. (2012); National quality assurance guidelines and policies for distance education in Australia and New Zealand. In I. Jung & C. Latchem (Eds.), *Quality Assurance and Accreditation in Distance Education and e-Learning*, pp. 91–101. New York: Routledge.

Seaman, J. (2009). *Online learning as a strategic asset. Volume II: The paradox of faculty voices: Views and experiences with online learning*. New York: Association of Public and Land-grant Universities/Babson Survey Research Group. Retrieved from http://www.aplu.org/document.doc?id=1879

Seibold, K. N. (2007). *Employers' perceptions of online education*. Unpublished doctoral thesis, Oklahoma State University, Stillwater, Oklahoma. Retrieved from http://digital.library.okstate.edu/etd/umi-okstate-2378.pdf

Shrock, J. R. (2009, May 10). US: No job if you only have an online degree. *University World News*, 75. Retrieved November 9, 2013, from http://www. universityworldnews.com/article.php?story=20090508115810625

Shrock, J. R. (2010). *US: Marks from online courses being rejected. University World News*, 142. Retrieved November 9, 2013, from http://www.universityworldnews. com/article.php?story=20101002100346835

Spaven, P. (2009, March). *Evaluation of the Commonwealth of Learning 2006–2009 plan: Final report.* Vancouver, BC: The Commonwealth of Learning. http://www.col.org/PublicationDocuments/External%20Evaluation_0609.pdf

Speirs, K. (2008, March 6). Lifelong learning for farmers. *Commonwealth Quarterly.* Retrieved from http://www.thecommonwealth.org/EZInformation/176131/060803life/

Stacey, P. (2011, February 22). Open Educational Resource University (OERU). [Blog]. Retrieved November 9, 2013, from http://edtechfrontier.com/2011/02/22/open-educational-resource-university-oeru/

Talalakina, E.V. (2010). Fostering cross-cultural understanding through e-learning: Russian-American forum case-study. *International Journal of Emerging Technologies in Learning, 5*(3). Retrieved from http://online-journals.org/i-jet/article/viewArticle/1290

Taylor, J. (2011). The OER university: From logic model to action plan. [Keynote Address]. Paper presented at *Open Planning Meeting for the OER for Assessment and Credit for Students Project*, Otago Polytechnic, 23 February 2011, Dunedin, New Zealand.

Thamizoli, P., Francis, H., Soundari, H., Kamaraj, K., & Balasubramanian, K. (2011). *Learning for farming initiative: Longitudinal study tracing the lifelong learning for farmers' activities in Tamil Nadu, India 2011.* Vancouver, BC: Commonwealth of Learning.

The Chronicle of Higher Education. (2010, October 31). *Faculty views about online learning.* Retrieved from http://chronicle.com/article/Faculty-Views-About-Online/125200//

The OPAL Report 2011. *Open Education Resources Initiative* (OPAL) http://duepublico.uni-duisburg-essen.de/servlets/DerivateServlet/Derivate-25907/OPALReport2011-Beyond-OER.pdf

Thierer, A. (2010, January 31). Are you an Internet optimist or pessimist? The great debate over technology's impact on society. The Technology Liberation Front. [Blog]. Retrieved from http://techliberation.com/2010/01/31/are-you-an-internet-optimist-or-pessimist-the-great-debate-over-technology%E2%80%99s-impact-on-society/

UCL Centre for the Advancement of Learning and Teaching. (n.d.). *Activity: Claims about e-learning: CPD4HE: Open Resources on HE Teaching and Learning.* London: Author. Retrieved from http://www.ucl.ac.uk/calt/cpd4he/resources/learning-technology/activity_2

Wang, M. J. (2007). Designing online courses that effectively engage learners from diverse cultural backgrounds, *British Journal of Educational Technology, 38*(2), 294–311.

Wang, V. (2006). The instructional patterns of Chinese online educators in China. *Asian Journal of Distance Education, 4*(1). Retrieved from http://www.asianjde.org/2006v4.1.Wang.pdf

Watkins, A. E. (n.d.). *Aelfric's colloquy: Translated from the Latin.* [Paper 016]. Retrieved from http://www.kentarchaeology.ac/authors/016.pdf

Wong, A. L. (2007). Cross-cultural delivery of e-learning programs: Perspectives from Hong Kong. *The International Review of Research in Open and Distance Learning, 8*(3). Retrieved from http://www.irrodl.org/index.php/irrodl/article/view/426/937

Woodhouse, D. (2006, May). *The quality of transnational education: A provider view.* INQAAHE Workshop. Retrieved from www.nvao-event.net

World Bank. (2008). *The road not travelled: Education reform in the Middle East and North Africa.* Washington, DC: World Bank.

Yuan, L & Powell, S. (2013, March). *MOOCs and open education: Implications for higher education—a white paper.* JISC Centre for Educational Technology and Interoperability Standards (CETIS) and the University of Bolton, UK. http://publications.cetis.ac.uk/wp-content/uploads/2013/03/MOOCs-and-Open-Education.pdf

Part III

MICRO-LEVEL RESEARCH: LEARNING AND TEACHING IN DISTANCE EDUCATION

Major Movements in Instructional Design

Katy Campbell and
Richard A. Schwier

More and more, the Internet is creating a "paranational culture that combines global connectivity with local specificity, a 'glocal' phenomenon that seems to resist national political agendas" (Poster, 1999, p. 236). If true, the online community might operate both as a social homogenizer and at the same time as an agent of social change that transcends strictly local concerns. If we need evidence of how powerful the Internet and social media can be, we need look no further than the Arab Spring. Cell phone images of political protesters accompanied by blogs and tweets were distributed around the world, resulting in "glocal" pressure on autocratic leaders to be transparent, and accountable to local citizens. Online learning has the capacity to span and challenge diverse online communities, organized communities, and exclusionary in-groups because it allows us to explore alternatives to social, cultural, and political boundaries. The design of these online environments helps shape the identities of these virtual communities (Adria & Campbell, 2006). In other words, instructional designers can be agents of glocal social change.

That's the promise. However, most cyber or online universities are created as cultural institutions that reflect the sociocultural values of their existing communities, often based on traditional, and sometimes antiquated, university assumptions and practices. These institutions are encouraged to recruit international students with a goal of increasing plurality. But there are issues: a review of learning design and program delivery suggests that many online institutions do not take advantage of multiple sociocultural perspectives and uncritically reflect a (Western) dominant-culture curricula design (Collis & Remmers, 1997; Hongladarom, 2001; Kenny, Zhang, Schwier, & Campbell, 2005; Stewart, Shields & Sen, 2001; Rogers, Graham, & Mayes, 2007; Young, 2007). As a result, most of these environments reflect little understanding of cultural intelligence. As local problems become glocal issues, learning organizations around the world share the challenges and opportunities of professional, mid-career learners. Is it realistic or even possible that uncritical Western ideals of economic and social progress can adequately define life, politics, and education across a diversified world? Programs in which adult learners work collaboratively to confront social issues strongly support the imperative to design the learning experience as "one of facilitated constructivist learning through dialogue, or an open-ended, non-dogmatic, and emancipatory discourse" that respects cultural differences and realities (Harris, 2000, p. 39).

Are instructional designers taught to engage through their practice in an emancipatory discourse? Is change agency addressed in the academic preparation of instructional designers? This is not how instructional design (ID) has been traditionally approached or portrayed in higher education, in North America at least, and North America has long been the locus of development of instructional design research and the source of over 100 related graduate programs (Kenny, Zhang, Schwier, & Campbell, 2005). Although the "objective" scientific paradigm (i.e., cognitive science) has dominated research and preparation of instructional design(ers), not to mention ID discourse, through the decades theory and practice has consistently reflected the sociocultural and political conditions and contexts in which they have occurred. For example, in distance education instructional designers work directly with faculty to help them think more critically about the needs of all learners about, issues of access, the social and cultural implications of the use of information technologies, alternative learning environments, and related policy development. As such they are important participants in shaping interpersonal, institutional, and societal agendas for change.

Instructional design is not simply a technical methodology to be applied to design situations. Instructional design, like all sciences (Kuhn, 1962) has always been a situated practice, although it has not usually been explored or described in this way. Hongladarom (2001) argued that because the Internet bears the stamp of American cultural values (liberalism, egalitarianism, individualism, exceptionalism, and competitiveness) these values are well embedded in both the technology and the nature of the communication enabled by it. In effect, the Internet is the "outcome of an international, cosmopolitan culture where participants share little in common in terms of historical backgrounds" (p. 316); certainly MOOCS can be a manifestation of this phenomenon. In this chapter and elsewhere (Campbell, Schwier, & Kenny, 2009; Schwier, Campbell, & Kenny, 2004) we challenge one of the grand narratives of instructional design theory: instructional design is a scientific domain immune to the sociocultural, geopolitical, and economic contexts in which its temporal research, education, and practice are situated. On the contrary, we show that instructional design has always been informed and shaped by the social movements in which it has been situated.

A BRIEF HISTORICAL OVERVIEW OF ID RESEARCH AND PRACTICE

The roots of instructional design can be traced back to the 1920s, when a behaviourist approach to educational psychology emerged, represented by Edward Thorndike's (1874–1949) theory of connectionism—the stimulus-response (S-R) model. Two decades later, Hull (1884–1952) developed the concept of *drive reduction*, a motivational model of behaviour that emphasizes learners' wants, attention, and activities. Challenges during this time, related to military–industrial productivity, led to the development of applied mechanized technology to increase the efficiency of the learning process. Thus, behavioural models, teaching machines, and the interest in standardized instruction contributed to the instructional media research and training development needs of World War II (Leigh, 1998).

Early attempts to apply general systems theory and systems analysis, and Robert Gagné's (1965) seminal work on the conditions of learning, occurred soon after World War II (Banathy, 1987). By 1980 over 60 published ID models, conceptualized around the "standard" stages of analysis, design, development, implementation, and evaluation (ADDIE) were available and became the standard model of instructional design practice (Andrews & Goodsen, 1980/1991; Gustafson & Branch, 2002). The majority of ID models (Dick, Carey, & Carey, 2005) are process-based although some models, such as those of Gagné and Briggs (Gagné, Briggs, & Wager, 1988), were theory-based as well; they were developed on the basis, first, of behavioural learning theory and, later, on cognitive theories of learning that dominated the field for over 40 years (Willis, 1998).

Such models, modified to be less descriptive, continue to thrive in various portrayals (cf. Morrison, Ross, & Kemp, 2004; Seels & Glasgow, 1998) and have been taught to thousands of graduate students. At present, the role of the instructional designer ranges from consultation on educational and instructional video; to development of computer-based instruction, printed media, curriculum, and online courses; to mentor and facilitator of faculty development, and a host of other diverse responsibilities (Ritzhaupt, Martin, & Daniels, 2010; Schwier & Wilson, 2010). While there is evidence that instructional designers have been pivotal to the growth and success of online offerings in higher education (Bates, 2005), critical theorists have described their products and environments as prescriptive, restrictive, and reductionist, due in no small way to the culture they have acquired within their areas of study that include behavioural systems and cognitivist views of learning (e.g., de Castell, Bryson, & Jenson, 2002; Garrison, 1993; Vrasidas, 2001).

However, a discourse is beginning to emerge about the actual practice of instructional designers, characterizing it as situated and embedded in context (Cox & Osguthorpe, 2003; Kenny, Zhang, Schwier, & Campbell, 2004; Visscher-Voerman & Gustafson, 2004). For example, our own research among Canadian instructional designers suggests that clients (i.e., faculty members in higher education) working with instructional designers in development projects are actually engaging, as learners, in a process of professional and personal transformation that has the potential to transform the institution and the broader society. As a situated practice, ID requires us to establish common ground-embracing interests, personal values, and sociopolitical awareness, especially in a global economy with its cross-national development projects.

In the remainder of this chapter, we tell a different story about the history and practice of instructional design in the 20th and 21st centuries. In this story we place research on learning and theory building, applications of instructional design theory and development of models, and implications for distance education practice, on a temporal and sociopolitical timeline that illustrates how reflective of social, cultural, political, and economic currents ID has always been. We argue that designers of distance education environments should be familiar with the history that has shaped their field and, going forward, should be able to critically design within relevant sociocultural frameworks. The organizing contexts are 1) the war years and the birth of instructional design, 2) multiculturalism and the identity movements, and 3) globalization, neo-liberalism, and lifelong learning.

THE WAR YEARS AND THE BIRTH OF INSTRUCTIONAL DESIGN

In the United States, comprehensive professionalization and standardization of modern military education largely began during the interwar years (1918–1940) in partial response to the challenges faced during World War I. The technological advancements of WWI signalled a need for new strategies and training protocols (Odom, 2000). The Army Industrial College was established in 1924, later becoming the Army–Navy Staff College in World War II, and now the Industrial College of the Armed Forces (Yeager, 2005).

With the advent of the World War II the American military was required to train hundreds of thousands of military personnel rapidly. Behavioural psychologists such as Thorndike, Hull, and, later, Tyler (1902–1994), who was called the father of behavioural objectives, laid the groundwork. With the experience of creating standardized methods of instructional delivery using teaching machines, military researchers developed "a bevy of training films and other mediated materials" (Leigh, 1998, p.1) for instructional purposes. The American military realized that educational technology had significant implications for military training, mostly in the form of instructional media such as films, slides, handbooks, and "realistic" models (Saettler, 1990). Specialized groups that included civilian educators, artists, communications specialists, advertisers, and personnel from theatre and motion pictures combined to develop a "military technology of instruction" (p. 184); the current multidisciplinary design team reflects this approach. According to Hoban (1946), "Behind the developments in Army films was a broad concept of the dynamics of human behaviour, an empirical understanding of the reasons why people behave as they do, and a positive approach to the direction and control of human behaviour" (Saettler, 1990, p. 184).

Foundational Learning Theories: Behaviourism and Cognitivism

Beginning with the overall aim of predicting and controlling (human) behaviour through observable and measurable scientific methods, the behaviourist school holds that all behaviour can be explained as a product of learning. On this basis, appropriate stimuli will condition an individual's behaviour, thereby producing particular outcomes. Adhering closely to the scientific method, and extrapolating from the work of evolutionary theorists Darwin and Galton, behaviourist methods reflected, as well, the growing social and industrial impetus of *scientific management*. Derived from the writings of Frederick W. Taylor (1856–1915), the practices of Taylorism emerged from the factory systems of the industrial revolution. Taylor's approaches separated manual from mental labour and instrumentally divided work processes into discrete parts, for example, the assembly line theories and practices of Henry Ford (aka Fordism). For the behaviourists, behaviour and human emotion, like work, could be understood systematically and through a mechanistic lens.

Midcentury, B. F. Skinner's work on operant conditioning and positive and negative reinforcement advanced *neo-behaviourism* even further. Focussed on rewarding particular behaviours in particular environments, Skinner suggested that all we can know are "the external causes of behaviour and the observable results of that behaviour" (Hunt, 2007, p. 305). He outlined an ideal scientifically controlled utopian society in *Walden Two* (1948), detailing his belief that behavioural engineering would produce good individuals conditioned to behave in a good society. Skinner's work was highly influential in fields such as education and instructional design (Hunt, 2007). Behaviourist approaches are still in use today as with controlled laboratory practices of experimental psychology and the quantitative methodologies that underpin much scientific and social scientific research.

In the 1960s Robert Gagné demonstrated concern for the different domains of learning. His book *Military Training and Principles of Learning* differentiated psychomotor skills, verbal information, intellectual skills, cognitive strategies, and attitudes, aligning with Bloom's six cognitive domains of learning. This thinking later extended to Gagné's nine instructional events, or activities necessary for learning. These events continue today to be used for the basis for the design of instruction and are treated as global constructs that can be applied to many different instructional media. Cognitive theories still inform much of what we think of as newer learning technologies, for example, in the design of learning management systems that assign different locations for various learning activities, and that feature well-crafted and scaffold-learning modules.

The Rise of Individualism

The rationalization of society, of science, seen in the application of cognitive science to learning, followed from the Enlightenment's premise of absolute knowledge or *truth*. Truths could be determined through the use of objective methodological procedures and the separation of the subject from the object of study (e.g., Descartes, 1596–1650). This methodological empiricism assumes that the investigator, or *knower*, can separate him- or herself from objects of study, can divest him- or herself of prior knowledge, and thus can be a detached observer of the social and natural worlds. These principles underpin the modern scientific method: the separation of human from nature enabled the articulation of concepts such as empiricism and objectivity. With this went the notion of the model human as rational, independent, and free of interference, which we have seen articulated above in the search for a way to program learning that is based on value-free science. However, the political theories of the Enlightenment largely failed to address questions of difference. That is, as a product of dominant European societies, these theories replicated gender-, race- and class-based essentialism (Mill, 2008).

Enlightenment dualisms such as nurture/nature, male/female, public/private, white/black, which underpinned the scientific method and articulated through cultures of science and gender, reflected absolute divisions in the natural and social order and are core to objectivism (Merchant, 2001). Jordanova (1999) and others argue that dualisms must be understood within a cultural matrix of meaning but, historically, the metaphorical linkages between them follow certain patterns and can come to shape reality. In other words, they reflect cultural statements about an idealized (moralistic), perspective on the social and natural world. These statements come to serve a normative role intended to shape social relations and thinking. For example, in the history of instructional design, *praxis* ("evidence-based practice") has derived from the scientific method in the form of experimental or quasi-experimental research design that seek to control human variables and learning conditions. Qualitative methods, that we argue explore the social/cultural world of ID research and practice, have only recently been accepted as legitimate research in the field.

The Open and Distance Learning Organization

As we have seen, Fordism, while not a learning theory, is closely aligned with systems thinking and has influenced the structure of many distance organizations. Achieving economies of scale in most open and distance learning institutions (ODLs) are necessary to ensure cost-effective access for students experiencing time, place, and/or situational barriers to formal and credentialed education (Bates, 2005; Moore & Kearsley, 2005). Many ODLs have effectively achieved economies of scale by adopting an industrialized model of distance education (Peters, 1967, 1998). In fact, in *Distance Education at Universities and Higher Education Institutions: Didactical Structure and Comparative Analysis—A Contribution to the Theory of Distance Education* (1967) Peters conceives of distance education as the *most* industrialized form of teaching and learning. This model requires a separation of the preparation of materials and resources for teaching and learning from the interaction of students with those materials and with their instructor. In the industrialized model, in which the large-scale production and delivery of learning resources may resemble an assembly line approach, the focus is on the construction of the learning and teaching materials, i.e., instructional design. In this model, instructional designers gained influence and authority, as their specialized expertise was valued on much the same level as the subject matter expertise of faculty. Lockwood (in Peters, 2004) is persuasive that "our aim should not be for teacher dominated, goal directed behaviour [that perpetuates] previous teaching and learning practices in the new environment but to consider a whole array of possibilities that are open to us" (p. 9).

The Optimal Blueprint

Advocating a mastery approach to learning, Bloom (1956) endorsed instructional techniques that reflected learner requirements, providing instructional developers a means by which to match subject matter and instructional methods. However, Bloom's taxonomy was not in and of itself "capable of satisfying the desire of large organizations to relate resources and processes to the performances of individuals" (Leigh, 1998). Systems thinking began to emerge when Bloom's taxonomy was combined with Ludwig von Bertalanffy's general systems theory, which was based on the integrative nature of biological interactions (Leigh, 1998). This work encouraged matching the content and delivery of instruction in the context of a whole organization, as well as groups and individuals within the organization. The advances of Skinner, Bloom, and von Bertalanffy (1901–1972) were usually employed to develop instruction in what was only *assumed* to be an effective and efficient manner. The formalization of a standardized design process still had yet to be devised.

In the turbulent decade of the Vietnam War, Grant Venn (1970) argued that the current educational system was only serving the advantaged minority of schoolchildren, while those not attending college were conscripted to a war in Asia. Critical theorists such as Paulo Friere and Michael Apple were taking up related concerns; the *hidden curriculum* became a metaphor for the socialization of students through the experience of being in school; it was "an approach to living and an attitude to learning" (Meighan, p. 314, 1986). Concerned with a low achievement rate in public schools, Robert Morgan proposed an experiment with an *organic curriculum*, which would incorporate into the educational system the best instructional practices identified through research. One of the researchers involved in the large-scale project was Leslie Briggs, who had demonstrated that an instructionally designed course could double achievement, reduce variance, and reduce time-to-completion; the effect size of the treatment was four times that of the control group, who received no training (Silber & Foshay, 2010). The search for the optimal blueprint for learning became a Holy Grail for instructional designers.

As we have seen, the systems view is based on the assumption that using an instructional systems design model that is based on learning theories closely tied to behaviourism and systems theory (Banathy, 1987; Merrill, 1983) is necessary for effective learning transactions. Specifically, the use of an instructional systems design model will identify what is to be taught, determine how it will be taught, and evaluate the instruction to determine what is necessary. It is a linear and cyclic, systematic and prescriptive approach to instructional design. These elements are essential if learning is to be effective under all conditions. Hence, when instruction is designed based on a systems instructional design model, the end result is effective instruction—regardless of who is teaching. Or, stated more directly: education that is teacher-proof.

Implications for Instructional Design

Educational technology came of age during World War II (Saettler, 1990), although ironically the training push did not include systematic evaluation of learning or performance. However, during this time visual instruction converged with educational technology; educators generally grew more sensitive to the consideration of scientific theory to the practical problems of instruction (Saettler, 1990; Reiser, 2001).

Instructional Technology and the Structure of ODL

Duncan (2005) outlines the close historical relationship between military training and distance education, while acknowledging the contentiousness of distance learning practices in military circles. Beginning with correspondence education offered to both soldiers and civilians, distance learning expanded in part due to economic concerns but simultaneously raised concerns over the loss of traditional (classroom) learning programs and lack of adequate instructional strategies. However, the US Department of Defense, today considered one of the "most prominent leaders for modern day technology-based distance education" (p. 397), is credited with the development of ARPSNET (a forerunner to the Internet) and is identified as a key developer of cutting-edge instructional technologies. American investment in military training and R&D was, and remains, foundational to the research in learning, cognition, instruction, and performance. Reiser (2001) defined two practices emerging from the war years as core to the field of ID: the use of media for instructional purposes and the use of systematic instructional design procedures.

Simulations and Gaming

Simulation training, precursors to today's virtual worlds and gaming, went beyond pure battlefield applications in the post-war period. For example, the 1960s and 1970s saw the development of intercultural simulation exercises—often based on what was called the *university model*—designed to modify soldiers' attitudes, communications skills, and cross-cultural sensitivity, and often as part of military briefings and overseas postings (Fowler & Pusch, 2010). At the same time, intercultural simulations were being developed in other branches of government and the corporate sector. The US Peace Corps, for example, developed similar training modules in the 1960s that combined academic and experiential learning with physical fitness training (Fowler & Pusch, 2010); the American Foreign Service, medical institutes, and universities, among others, adopted similar diversity training programs in the following decades.

MULTICULTURALISM AND SOCIAL IDENTITY MOVEMENTS

The years after World War II saw the rise of counterculture movements, reflected in the American civil rights movement of the 1950s and 1960s. The new radical politics also spawned the antiwar movement/peace movement, the human rights movement (Canada), the gay rights movement, the re-emergence of feminism in the mid-20th century (alongside the sexual revolution), and the rise of the New Left. Following our thesis that instructional design research and practice is socially and culturally situated, we have organized this section to reflect the identity movements of the 1970s through the 1990s that followed from these paradigmatic shifts in social and cultural values. In other words, how did instructional design research, education, and professional practice change to reflect the sociocultural values of diversity, democratization, inclusion, the American melting pot versus Canadian pluralism, the politics of difference, integration, citizenship, and community cohesion?

Theories and policies of multiculturalism emerged from the cultural paradigms shifts of the 1960s and, in particular, in relation to the cultural needs of non-Europeans who were immigrating to North America in response to the social and political challenges resulting from civil wars (e.g., Vietnam), religious conflicts (e.g., Irish Protestants and Catholics) economic pressures and opportunities (e.g., repatriation of Hong Kong to the PRC), the rise of extremism (e.g., terrorism), and shifting of geopolitical boundaries (e.g., the dismantling of the Berlin Wall). The term *multiculturalism* now generally refers to accommodations made by state and/or dominant cultural groups of a diverse range of marginalized (or minority) cultures. These marginalized groups are defined in relation to race or ethnicity, nationality, indigeneity, and religion. While equal opportunity legislation and improved human rights protections formalized these views in most Anglophone and/or industrialized countries, a backlash against concepts of diversity and multiculturalism have arisen in the past decade, particularly since the events of 9/11.

Multicultural policies sought to balance the push for assimilation into dominant cultural values (for example, the American melting pot) with the more pluralistic notions associated with diversity. Pluralism—cultural, political, and social—closely associated with postmodern social theory of the 1970s, 1980s and 1990s, recognizes the multiplicity of identity while also accounting for the power-laden practices that enable identity. Strategies of inclusion included various methods of egalitarianism, such as revaluing forgotten or excluded histories and experiences (for example, the recovery of oral histories, the rewriting of curricula to include diverse examples, the inclusion of personal narratives in research). Strategies also included specificity and contextualization in an effort to challenge the universalist/essentialist, gendered, and raced dualisms of the Enlightenment (McLaren, 1997).

In the education world during this time the women's liberation movement, in particular, initiated women's increasing participation in postsecondary education and the workforce. While the egalitarian principles of the New Left opened up new opportunities for marginalized groups, such opportunities were greatly advanced by emancipatory pedagogical theories (Freire, 1970; Giroux, 1983; Collins, 1986; hooks, 1994; West, 1997). Gender and technology research informed the deficit myth and generated interest in the social contexts in which technology was used (e.g., "the chilly climate"). Curriculum and instructional design researchers began to examine issues of authority, challenging the origins of truth and knowledge and the agency of the learner to participate in their construction. The social and cultural origins of curriculum and theories of learning came under scrutiny through a nuanced lens that permitted multiple and sometimes conflicting perspectives; constructivism began to frame discussions of pedagogy and design. More complex and contextualized understandings of identity, in which aspects of identity are seen to be socially- and culturally-specific and constructed, are outcomes of this period.

These perspectives suggest that concepts such as citizenship or equality, as well as government policies and practices, for instance, cannot be objective or colour-blind, and that no such policies or belief systems are politically neutral, even instructional design theory and models such as the instructional systems design (ISD), or ADDIE. For example, we have shown that ISD emerged from a period of time during which large groups had to be quickly trained in procedures that relied on repeated and accurate actions (e.g., soldiers): behaviourist notions of learning prevailed in such contexts.

Also during this time computer-based learning and the rise of the Internet extended the reach of designers and distance educators to populations in different geopolitical areas and to learners from different sociocultural backgrounds learning in North American or Western settings. The androcentric, Western design of computer-based learning was challenged (Chegwidden, 2000). The term *digital divide* was coined to describe geographical inequalities in access to computer technologies, but it was soon expanded to include questions about gender, socioeconomic circumstances, accessibility, and cultures of learning (Bowers, 1988). Distance educators began to consider the design requirements for online learning communities that included participants from different cultures and in different time zones, with a wide range of reliability in technology connections; a spectrum of dominant languages while the language of instruction was predominantly English; and expectations for instructor and peer interaction, learning assessment, individual versus group activities, and appropriateness of content. Cultural theories such as Hofstadter's cultural dimensions (1997) and Nielsen and colleagues' work on internationalization and localization of interface design (Nielson, 1990; del Galdo & Nielson, 1996) were adapted to learning design in attempts to respect the diverse life experiences and memberships in multiple cultures of (i.e., identities) learners. Entire issues of learned journals were devoted to considerations of culture and design (British Journal of Educational Technology, July 1999).

Implications for Instructional Design

Why does distance education need instructional designers who are socially, culturally, and politically aware? Rogers, Graham, and Mayes (2007) argued that, while the interest in cross-cultural learning markets has been increasing, "the initial high hopes for international e-learning have not been fully met" (p. 198) and have resulted in disillusionment, perhaps evidenced by the relatively few e-learning initiatives that have reached across geographic, political, and cultural borders. The authors wonder whether this may be partly attributable to the influence of "their own cultural blinders" to which instructional designers are not "immune" (p. 198). Burnham (2005) also questioned whether the expression of instructional design, grounded as it is in Western cultural presuppositions, was of inherently less value to non-Western learners using those designs. Their concern reinforced the call for adding cultural considerations to models of instructional design as an attempt to more fully contextualize the practice of instructional design (McLaughlin & Oliver, 2000). The specific expression of culture in instructional design is elusive but important. It ranges from consideration of culturally appropriate visual design elements such as layout and colour (Misanchuk, Schwier, & Boling, 2000), to attention to epistemological and pedagogical emphases in cultures (Young, 2007), to consideration of cross-cultural design and exposure to pluralistic learning environments (Collis & Remmers, 1997).

The need to design for plural cultures is at odds with the need to design for a specific culture. User-centred principles of instructional design suggest that a precise and narrow articulation of an audience can lead to optimal learning designs, a proposition that seems axiomatic. At the same time, learning products are easily shared, often without regard to the audience for which they were originally designed. Designers need to be sensitive to the global implications of their work. In many cases, the products of ID are exposed to a wide array of disparate cultures, and in fewer cases they are intentionally designed for cross-cultural settings. Supporting a community of online lifelong learners raises questions of identity. Each participant brings membership in multiple and interdependent communities and, so, possesses a fluid identity. Specific learning communities could then become part of a distinctive culture of learners and extend notions and assumptions of what national culture and identity can be. This is an opportunity for the cyber-university to host and contribute to the development of more active and critical global citizens who participate in and help shape the tolerant, diverse, and inclusive communities that "stimulate creativity and innovation" (Piper, 2002, p. 5), and contribute to regional and global knowledge economies.

Learning theories: Constructivism

The work of Dewey (1859–1952), Montessori (1870–1952), Piaget (1896–1980), Bruner (1915–), and Vygotsky (1896–1934), among others, is generally credited with the historical precedents for constructivist learning theory.

Constructivism describes learning theory and epistemology. Constructivists design based on their beliefs that each learner individually constructs meaning during a learning process that is socially contextualized: No knowledge is independent of the meaning attributed to experience, or constructed by the learner, or community of learners. In other words, learning consists both of constructing meaning and constructing systems of meaning that are tested against past and current social experience. When designing from a constructivist perspective, the focus is on the learner rather than on the content. This is in contrast to behaviourism, which focusses on intelligence, domains of objectives, levels of knowledge, and reinforcement. Fosnot (1996) presents four epistemological assumptions at the heart of what we refer to as *constructivist learning*, that is, knowledge: 1) is physically constructed by learners who are involved in active learning; 2) is symbolically constructed by learners who are making their own representations of action; 3) is socially constructed by learners who convey their meaning making to others; and 4) is theoretically constructed by learners who try to explain things they don't completely understand (Gagnon & Collay, n.d.).

Instructional designs representative of constructivism place the instructor in a different role and relationship with learners. The responsibility for learning rests with the learner, rather than with the teacher. The teacher's role is to aid the learner in coming to his or her own understanding. As a facilitator or coach, the instructor is continually in conversation with the learner, asking questions that encourage the learner to elaborate, challenging him or her to use personal experience as a starting point for making sense of the world (Teachnology, 2012).

Research in the past decade emphasized the role of well-designed online discussions in the forms described above in the development of social capital in a learning community, while some research is challenging the cognitive benefits of these activities in terms of increased levels of critical thinking (Cleveland-Innes & Garrison, 2005; Kanuka & Garrison, 2004; Kanuka, Rourke & Picard, 2005). A number of emerging learning design heuristics to increase the value of these activities include an enhanced and highly structured role for the facilitator, structured response guidelines such as those developed by Scardamalia and Bereiter (1994) in their work with computer-supported collaborative learning, and meaningful, relevant conversation in which members have a personal stake in contributing to cultural identity and either virtual or regionalized community action.

The notion, then, that knowledge is a dialectic process shifts attention from the mastery of content to the sociocultural setting and the activities of the people in a learning environment. That is, if knowledge emerges from lived social practices it can only be fully understood and assessed in relation to those activities (Luppicini, 2002). As illustration, Luppicini cites the example of an online course involving participants in Mexico and the United States (described by Gunawardena, et al., 2001) in which the two cultural groups differed significantly in "perceptions of language, power distance, gender differences, collectivist vs. individualist tendencies, conflict, social presence, time frame, and technical skills" (p. 90).

With increasing internationalization in higher education, and as more institutions consider shared credentials, we will encounter an increasing diversity of learners from different experiential, educational, social, cultural, economic, and language backgrounds in online classrooms. This places an impressive set of demands on instructional designers who are engaged in the process of designing online learning environments that can satisfy, or at least not disenfranchise, an increasingly diverse population of learners. As the boundaries between physical, geographical, and sociocultural environments become more permeable, assessment must be responsive to diversity and reflect critical and inclusive practices. While culture, age, gender, and life situation influence all aspects of the teaching/learning context, nowhere are the stakes and student interest more focussed than on assessment.

Assessment

The right-answer environments of behaviourism and, to an extent, cognitivism foster a culture of competitiveness rather than collaboration, in which the instructors assume the power to distribute success and failure. We argue that this approach reflects a set of values about the sources of knowledge: who holds it, who shapes it, and who has the right to it. This dialogue emanates from critical theory and is central in terms of a global curriculum. Proponents of this approach argue that the assessment of learning reflects fairness, however constructivists argue that "fairness does not exist when assessment is uniform, standardized, impersonal and absolute; rather it exists when it is appropriate. . . ." (Funderstanding.com, para. 3).

In constructivist environments learners play a more active role in the assessment of their own learning through the use of tools and activities such as reflective exercises, self-evaluations in tandem with peer assessments, collaborative projects, semantic mapping, and e-portfolios. Through reflection they can identify gaps in their learning and strategize how to improve (Wiggins, 1990). The instructional designer, encourages and guides the instructor to design a situation or problem, make resources available, use simple assessments as a bridge to prior knowledge and experience, develop guiding questions or probes, group learners to maximize sharing multiple perspectives in a social milieu, and create opportunities for critical reflection of learning and the learning process.

Most distance learners live and learn in the world of work. Relevant and productive assessment is authentic; it as closely as possible replicates the task or process being assessed, or illustrates the learning in daily practice. An instructor who assesses for authenticity either creates natural or real-life settings and activities or contextualizes learning in the settings that already exist in order to understand and document how learners think and behave over an extended period of time. In other words, the instructor uses multiple sources for gathering information that would reveal a more accurate picture of learning progress as well as emphasizing the process of learning, not just the final product. In fact, "situating assessment and evaluation as essentially social activities, influenced by unique affordances and constraints of a particular educational context, is a critical pedagogical component when designing and teaching online courses" (Matuga, 2006, p. 317).

GLOBALIZATION, NEO-LIBERALISM, AND LIFELONG LEARNING

In contrast to the pluralistic and inclusive politics of multiculturalism, the current neo-liberal emphasis on market demand is shaping the academic planning and curriculum design strategies of higher and distance education and disproportionately impacting marginalized individuals. Many nations link lifelong learning with skills enhancement and employability; funding models tend to follow. In both the UK and Canada the industry sectors considered most promising for global competitiveness (for example management education, or specialized technology education) are often targeted for envelope funding for research and education (SSHRC's Leadership, Innovation and Prosperity competition, http://www.sshrc-crsh.gc.ca/funding). This model includes bursaries and scholarships, tax credits, industry partnerships, and social policy such as relaxed immigration requirements for foreign workers. However, these policies have the tendency to exclude particular communities of learners, including single parents, early school-leavers, the retired and semi-retired, residents of economically-stressed rural communities, immigrants who need to re-credentialize in their new culture, and women. A global examination reveals that males tend to dominate in the vocational, technical and work-based realms, which tend to receive more political attention and resources, while females are found more in community education and the caring disciplines (Leathwood & Francis, 2006). As Kamler (2006) protests, a focus on the economic or developmental approach to lifelong learning is "at odds with more inclusive goals, such as widening participation to . . . [those] previously excluded from taking up learning opportunities due to social, economic or geographical constraints" (p. 154).

Neo-liberal political and fiscal policy emerged with the decline of the welfare state in the 1960s–1970s, marked by Margaret Thatcher's conservative policy reform in the UK, emulated by Ronald Reagan in the US, and taken up globally by industrialized nations. Economic and social policy shifts quickly followed in many European and North American countries. Expanding on early liberal principles, the neo-liberalism emphasis on individual responsibility largely eroded the 1960s and 1970s advances of the New Left.

Brodie (2005) identifies principles of decentralization, privatization, individualization, and the elevation of the market over the public sector as central components neo-liberalism. Brodie argues that,

> the emergence of the neoliberal state in Canada and elsewhere has
> been marked by a growing income polarization between the rich and
> the poor . . . and acceleration and intensification of the feminization of
> poverty, and the marginalization of already marginalized groups, espe-
> cially, mothers, persons with disabilities, and visible minority women,
> to the fringes of the labour market and society. (pp. 87–88)

Neo-liberal policies have greatly affected the structure of labour forces in industrialized countries as well as the social experience of working. A shift to part-time, cyclical, and poorly paid work, in part explains the changing career trajectory of numerous Gen-Xers and their younger counterparts: With more individuals unemployed, under-employed, or reliant on unstable employment, more are returning to formal education to retrain or upgrade their skills. Often occurring during midlife and alongside other adult responsibilities of family and work, lifelong learners alter what the "standard" student looks like.

Lifelong learning has economic, political, and sociocultural dimensions. World organizations such as UNESCO, the World Bank, the Organization for Economic Co-operation and Development (OECD) have made lifelong learning a high priority agenda item. For example, the OECD (1996) described the value of lifelong learning to create a society of individuals motivated to continue learning throughout their lives, both formally and informally. Broadly defined, this landscape includes adult and community education, vocational education and training, and work-based and distance learning at public, private, and corporate institutions.

Canadian political rhetoric reflects the neo-liberal perspective, casting lifelong learning as increasingly important in a knowledge-based society and contributing directly to Canada's economic competitiveness. The Education and Lifelong Learning Group within the Conference Board of Canada commissioned a report (2001) on workplace learning that linked lifelong learning directly with productivity, and emphasized e-learning as the transformative agent, "by improving Canada's skills, innovation and knowledge base and by leveraging our capacity in information and communications technologies, e-learning will be a key to productivity, competitiveness and prosperity" (p. i). Since employer-funded training often takes place in the work context, professional men are likely have wider access to formal and credentialed lifelong learning by virtue of their socioeconomic circumstances, while women and other marginalized populations continue to be excluded from these tools of socioeconomic mobility (Kamler, 2006).

Lifelong learning can be more profoundly associated with global wellbeing on sociocultural dimensions. Global and pluralistic communities of lifelong learners may be best positioned to take on the wicked and ill-defined problems of sustainability, including human health, peace and conflict, food security, climate change, and other shared challenges. For example, ScenarioThinking.org (2006) from Korea identifies e-democracy as one of the most promising fields in lifetime learning; others (Im & Bautista, 2009) propose a key global role for cyber-universities in educating for sustainable development.

Distance education offers the higher education community an opportunity to rethink the role of education at many levels and to leverage this opportunity in positive social ways (Zemsky & Massy, 2004). Morgan and O'Reilly (2006) compellingly describe the potency of the online learning community as being "about the drama of the multiple meaning, the contrary viewpoint, the search for credible sources, and the elusive nature of 'truth' in a postmodern world" (p. 87). The transition from face-to-face teaching to e-learning has the potential to appeal to those learners and their instructors who are interested in the capacity of this community to contribute to social change. At its best, the virtual learning environment has the potential to be socially transformative in its power to be inclusive, which is, to support diverse cultures, languages, work contexts, learning needs and styles, prior experiences, generations, economic circumstances, social contexts, and geographic locations. The learner in this emerging context is a member of an international community of learners, and it is by addressing this potential that instructors and administrators can in part enable the transition from face-to-face learning to e-learning. "In other words, the formation of a learning community through which knowledge is imparted and meaning is co-created sets the stage for successful learning outcomes" (Palloff & Pratt, 1999, p. 5).

Implications of Globalization, Neo-Liberalism, and Lifelong Learning for Instructional Design

As local problems become global issues, learning organizations around the world share the challenges and opportunities of the lifelong or life-wide learner—longer life spans, longer workdays, work intensification, increasing urbanization, national and transnational mobility, diversity in communities, restructured work worlds that require multiple sequential career changes, accelerating technological innovation, and global networks.

All institutions of higher education must respond to these learners by widening access and increasing flexibility, becoming more publicly accountable, building necessary partnerships with public and private organizations, acknowledging funding pressures and diversifying portfolios, and supporting formal and informal communities of learning. Instructional designers, through their expression of social agency, are uniquely positioned to help cyber-universities, in particular, re-engage their communities. Peters and Boer (2000) suggest that the engaged institution facilitate lifelong, rather than selective, learning; require faculty to refocus their commitment to the improvement of teaching as a primary activity with as much academic currency as research; increase access of the majority to affordable education through diversity, heterogeneity, and social equity; lead initiatives based on social intervention; and accept and encourage a paradigm shift from what is taught to what is learned. Online universities are uniquely positioned to develop environments and supports that embed learning in social contexts and engage diverse communities in authentic problem solving, as long as they respond to the inequality of access of marginalized learning communities.

Virtual Learning Communities and MOOCs

Learning design and learning outcomes within the framework of learner engagement are dependent on conversation. Conversations between and among instructional designers, experts, instructors, learners, the community, and the institution invoke multidirectional collaborations that extend learning for all who are involved in the process. The notion of conversation, and its fundamental importance to learning and the design of learning spaces, is central to the notion of virtual learning communities—those online learning spaces where participants engage each other to learn socially.

Distributed communities of practice and virtual learning communities are two structures that have importance to instructional designers who are building online learning environments that emphasize conversation. A *virtual learning community* (VLC) is a group of people who gather online with the intention of pursuing learning goals, while a *distributed community of practice* (DCOP) refers to a group of geographically distributed individuals who are informally bound together by shared expertise and shared interests or work (Daniel, O'Brien, & Sarkar, 2003). So, simply speaking, VLC environments are focussed on pursuing shared learning that also has individual importance; DCOP environments emphasize shared work and shared expertise. In both cases individuals depend on information and communication technologies to connect to each other, and conversation is at the core of learning.

An important feature for instructional designers to consider if they are trying to build an online learning community is the community's level of formality. Although most manifestations of community have an element of learning in them, not every community can be referred to as a *formal learning community*. A formal learning community implies that members have explicit and shared goals for their learning, and they are typically defined externally and delivered as a course. This manifestation of VLC dominates the higher education landscape, as institutions have devoted considerable resources to moving traditional curricula into online settings.

But learning in an informal virtual learning community typically includes knowledgeable or experienced individuals who voluntarily join those who are less knowledgeable, contributing to the growth of others and, by extension, to the community itself.

Some of the important affordances of virtual learning communities, whether formal or informal include:

- sharing data, information, and knowledge

- connecting people-to-people, people-to-systems, and systems-to-systems to help people do their work more efficiently and effectively regardless of time and space

- creating individual and organizational awareness of members' identities, members' knowledge, and members' awareness of which members possess valuable knowledge

- facilitating the creation of a community knowledge repository and tools for engagement, knowledge deliberations, and negotiation, and stimulating the generation of new ideas and locating information

- helping individuals build useful social networks with others in their fields of interest

- linking isolated geographic, political, organizational, professional, and linguistic cultures

- ensuring that knowledge is accessible to those who need it and can act on it to benefit learning

Of course, the ubiquity of social media and the range of communication applications available to users are contributing to the dynamic social and informal learning we see cropping up everywhere online, and it is challenging instructional designers to build learning environments that take advantage of a wide range of new affordances. Instructional designers need to recognize that they are designing social spaces, and that bounded learning models, analogous to classrooms with walls and closed doors, are not sufficient to address the needs of learners. Opening online learning environments to incorporate informal and diverse social learning spaces offers fresh opportunities to instructional designers, and also challenges the dominant discourse of what is considered "legitimate" learning, based on institutional control of accreditation and certification.

Foundational Learning Theories: Connectivism

This challenge is illustrated by *connectivism,* an emerging learning theory that is important to how instructional designers think about the learning spaces they design (Bell, 2011). Connectivism emphasizes the importance of social and networked learning, suggesting that much that we consider learning is actually embedded in the nodes of a learning network (Siemens, 2005; 2010). The theory suggests that learning is a process that occurs within imprecisely defined and shifting environments that are not entirely under the control of the individual. It suggests that learning can reside outside of individuals and within an organization or a database, and takes the position that the connections that enable us to learn are more important than any static knowledge a learner might have.

Recently, there have been a number of open learning initiatives that exhibit features of both bounded and unbounded VLCs. For example, Couros (2009) developed a course that offers layers of participation to "thin" the walls of the traditional university classroom. Students can register and participate in comparatively conventional ways using videoconferencing technologies, collaboration with online mentors, and completing assignments. But an informal audience can observe and participate in the course without restriction, and engage with each other and with the registered participants and instructor. This creates a dynamic learning environment, and one that contravenes the typical higher education definition of a *course.*

Stephen Downes credits Dave Cormier with coining the acronym MOOC, for massive open online course, to describe the structure and intention of this kind of course (Downes, 2009). As an application of the MOOC framework, George Siemens and Stephen Downes offered an online course on connectivism theory as a credit course for a small number of students, but as a non-formal learning platform it has attracted more than 2,000 students worldwide each time it has been offered. The course has featured daily updates, networks of bloggers discussing topics in the course, videoconferencing sessions, a course wiki, and discussion groups using a variety of technologies such as Second Life to participate in the course, but a fundamental design consideration is that students are expected to build their own experiences from a rather chaotic array of opportunities that are provided and from those they construct.

These courses, and others that will inevitably follow, signal important shifts in the design of learning spaces, and it appears that open approaches to designing learning experiences are scalable. They also point to a philosophical shift from closed and bounded learning systems to open, transparent, and egalitarian beliefs about learning. Learners are not only responding to their own personal epistemologies to make their own learning, they are responding to environmental opportunities to make their own learning environments. In this way, they are not just making meaning, they are fashioning the environments in which their learnings/meanings will continue to be recreated. And this begs the question of how instructional designers can shape the environments in ways that support this level of freedom to explore and learn. There is no model for designing MOOCs, nor should there be. At a professional level, these kinds of environments require instructional designers to move far beyond the prescriptive and utilitarian approaches that marked earlier historical trends.

Design

The introduction of virtual learning communities, MOOCs, and other connectivist learning environments afford exciting opportunities to instructional designers, as they challenge some of the fundamental pedagogies and beliefs about learning that seem to dominate higher education. Connected and social learning challenges faculty to think about learners as self-directed and capable of building and controlling their own personal learning environments. They ask faculty to shed layers of identity based on content expertise in favour of becoming wise advisors who can guide and connect learners to the resources and social networks they need. There are strong headwinds in institutions of higher education that oppose this kind of movement. Forces such as tradition, authority, competition, and accountability, among other things, reinforce the inertia in higher education, and this presents unique challenges to instructional designers. In order to capitalize on the affordances offered by connected self-directed learning, instructional designers need to see themselves as change agents who are capable of influencing their institutions and higher education at a fundamental level.

Another important implication for instructional designers is that they need to become connected learners themselves. They need to experience first-hand what it means to be a self-directed learner and to build a rich personal learning network. Becoming familiar with the tools of social networking will be helpful, but more importantly, learning to leverage social networks for learning will allow instructional designers to advise faculty intelligently on how to integrate emerging environments.

CONCLUSION: CHALLENGES, OPPORTUNITIES, RESPONSIBILITIES

The development of engaged, online, lifelong learners occurs in a relational process of conversation that challenges instructors, learners, instructional designers, the institution, and the community to address—and contribute to the deconstruction of—real social problems. Personal knowledge based on prior experiences and belief systems is available and evolves through the social interaction inherent in sharing stories of practice in which colleagues attempt to make their perspectives clear and meaningful to others, and to understand the perspectives they offer in return. This process of social construction and deconstruction, leading to social action, challenges those of us in these socially evolving cyber-institutions to evaluate the taken-for-granted and traditional infrastructure on which they have likely been (virtually) built.

We also argue that the goals of identity development have historical roots in social, cultural, and political systems, artifacts, language, and behaviour, and that these can be used to manage the transition, critically and reflectively, from face-to-face learning to an e-learning community that is paranational, creative, socially active, and designed for inclusion.

Technologies critically influence the work of instructional designers in distance learning. In particular, social media and distance learning technologies have fundamentally changed the models of instructional delivery available to instructional designers in distributed environments. They have afforded learning that is learner-centred, individualized, and interactive, but of course, designers have not always taken advantage of these affordances. We still seem to encounter (and create) distance learning programs that seem to be little more than a direct translation of correspondence courses to Web-based environments. We still find instructors and designers who invest only modest amounts of energy in distributed learning environments. We still know of institutions that promote distance learning as a method of attracting a fresh revenue stream, where the provision of online resources (with an absence of community) is considered innovative and sufficient for learners.

Instructional designers and other influential contributors involved in the design and development of distributed learning programs must challenge and push boundaries of traditional practices if higher education is to maintain its relevance to students and society. Instructional designers in particular will need to engage practice at several levels to bring the kinds of societal and institutional transformation necessary for higher education adapt to its environment. Among other things, this means moving beyond the design of courses and academic programs into the design and development of policies.

At the institutional level, instructional designers can analyze market behaviours, forecast economic success and make recommendations, link financial needs to learning and performance programs, develop appropriate intervention approaches, interact with and determine various interests of stakeholders, and implement desirable change strategy within an institution.

At the societal level, instructional designers can work together with stakeholders in government and corporate organizations and with individuals to identify and influence emergent socio-political policies outside their institutions and develop appropriate responses. Further, IDS can analyze and understand institutional capacities to respond to emerging needs and opportunities and to promote cultural sensitivity. They can work with institutions to articulate needs for professional development and help organizations to build the capacity to respond to needs and opportunities. The agency roles played by instructional designers are capable of transforming society and institutions, and an agency perspective invites fresh research challenges and questions.

But in the end, it is important for instructional designers, particularly those involved in distance learning, to realize that no set of roles or questions can fully embrace the issues of identity and change agency. In order to be effective, instructional designers need to develop a connoisseur's appreciation for the broad cultural forces in play when instructional design is done, the ways in which instructional design work interacts with sweeping societal change, and the social ramifications of new communication technologies and the affordances they offer. At the same time, the connoisseur instructional designer must attend to the nuances of the work, continuing the longstanding focus of creating effective learning resources and environments, but appreciating that being effective is a very elusive, very context-based, and very value-laden goal.

The War Years and The Birth of Instructional Design

Representative Publications 1920–1965

Tyler, R. W. (1949). *Basic principles of curriculum and instruction*. Chicago, IL: The University of Chicago Press.

Skinner, B. F. (1953). *Science and human behaviour*. New York: Macmillan.

Flanagan, J. C. (1954). The critical incident technique. *Psychological Bulletin, 51,* 327–58.

Bloom, B. S., Engethart, M. D., Furst, E. J., Hill, W. H., & Krathwohl, D. R. (1956). *Taxonomy of educational objectives, The classification of educational goals. Handbook I: Cognitive domain.* New York: David McKay.

Gagné, R. M. (1962). *Psychological principles in system development.* New York: Holt, Rinehart & Winston.

Glaser, R. (1962). Psychology and instructional technology. In R. Glaser (Ed.), *Training research and education*. Pittsburgh, PA: University of Pittsburgh Press.

Gagné, R. M. (1965). *The conditions of learning* (1st ed.). New York: Holt, Rinehart & Winston.

Multiculturalism and Social Identity Movements

Representative Publications 1970–2011

Knowles, M. (1975). *Self-directed learning.* Chicago: Follet.

Clark, R. (1983). Reconsidering research on learning from media. *Review of Educational Research, 53*(4), 445–59.

Haraway, D. (1985). A manifesto for cyborgs: Science, technology, and socialist feminism in the 1980s. *Socialist Review, 15*(80), 65–107.

Beckwith, D. (1987). Group problem-solving via computer conferencing: The realizable potential. *Canadian Journal of Educational Communication, 16*(2), 89–106.

Apple, M., & Jungck, S. (1990). You don't have to be a teacher to teach this unit: Teaching, technology, and gender in the classroom. *American Educational Research Journal, 27,* 227–51.

Acker, S., & Oatley, K. (1993). Gender issues in education for science and technology: Current situation and prospects for change. *Canadian Journal of Education, 18*(3), 255–72.

Inkpen, K., Upitis, R., Klawe, M., Lawry, J., Anderson, A., Ndubda, M., . . . Hsu, D. (1994). 'We have never-forgetful flowers in our garden': Girls' responses to electronic games. *Journal of Computers in Mathematics and Science Teaching, 13*(4), 383–403.

MacCann, A. (1996). Designing accessible learning materials for learners with disabilities and learning difficulties. *Australian Journal of Educational Technology, 12*(2), 109–20.

Culture and new technologies. (1999). *British Journal of Educational Technology, 30*(3) [Special issue].

United States Department of Agriculture Higher Education Challenge Grant. (2002–04). *Learning differences in gender and culture: Roadmap to effective distance education instructional design.* Retrieved Nov 11, 2011, from www.umsl.edu/services/ctl/DEID

Kidd, T. T., & Chen, I. (2008). *Social information technology: Connecting society and cultural issues.* Hershey, PA: IGI Global.

DuCharme-Hansen, B. A., & Dupin-Bryant, P. A. (2004). *Web-based distance education for adults.* Malabar, FL: Krieger.

Scale, J. (2006). The rainbow bridge metaphor as a tool for developing accessible e-learning practices in higher education. *Canadian Journal of Learning & Technology, 32*(2), 79–98.

Globalization, Neo-liberalism, and Lifelong Learning

Representative Publications 1990–2011

Norman, D. (1993). *Things that make us smart: Defending human attributes in the age of the machine.* Saddle River, NJ: Addison Wesley.

Wenger, E. (1998). *Communities of practice. Learning meaning and identity.* Cambridge, UK: Cambridge University Press.

Garrison, D. R., Anderson, T., & Archer, W. (2003). A theory of critical inquiry in online distance education. In M. G. Moore & W. G. Anderson (Eds.), *Handbook of distance education* (pp. 113–27). Mahwah, NJ: Lawrence Erlbaum.

Rogers, E. (2003). *Diffusion of innovations* (5th ed.). New York: The Free Press.

Siemens, G. (2005). *Connectivism: A learning theory for the digital age.* Elearnspace. Retrieved from http://www.elearnspace.org/Articles/connectivism.htm

Role of distance learning in the right to education. (2008). *International Review of Research on Open and Distance Learning, 9*(1) [Special Issue].

Bonk, C. (2010). *The world is open: How web technology is revolutionizing education.* San Francisco, CA: Jossey-Bass.

Jonassen, D. H., Howland, J., Moore, J., & Marra, R. M. (2010). *Learning to solve problems with technology: A constructionist perspective*. Florence, KY: Routledge.

De Waard, I., Abajian, S., Gallagher, M. S., Hogue, R., Keskin, N., & Koutropoulodriguez, A. C. (2011). Using mLearning and MOOCs to understand chaos, emergence, and complexity in education. *International Review of Research on Open and Distance Learning, 12*(7), 94–115.

REFERENCES

Adria, M., & Campbell, K. (2006). E-learning as nation-building. In M. Bullen & D. Janes (Eds.), *Making the transition to e-learning: Strategies and issues* (pp. 1–16). Hershey, PA: Idea Group.

Allen, C. W. (2002). Wright military training at College Park in 1901. *Air power history 49*(2), 12–21.

Andrews, D. H., & Goodson, L. A. (1991). A comparative analysis of models of instructional design. In G. J. Anglin (Ed.), *Instructional technology, past, present, and future* (pp. 133–55). Eaglewood, CO: Libraries Unlimited. (Reprinted from the *Journal of Instructional Development, 3*(4), 2–16).

Aronowitz, S., & De Fazio, W. (1997). The new knowledge work. In A. H. Halsy, H. Lauder, P. Brown, & A. Stuart Wells (Eds.), *Education: Culture, economy, and society* (pp. 193–206). Oxford: Oxford University Press.

Banathy, B. H. (1987). Instructional systems design. In R. M. Gagné (Ed.), *Instructional technology: Foundations* (pp. 85–112). Hillsdale, NJ: Lawrence Erlbaum.

Bannan-Ritland, B., Dabbagh, N., & Murphy, K. (2001). *Learning object systems as constructivist learning environments: Related assumptions, theories and applications*. Retrieved from http://www.reusability.org/read/

Bates, A. W. (2005). *Technology, e-learning and distance education* (2nd ed.). New York: RoutledgeFalmer.

Bell, F. (2011). Connectivism: Its place in theory-informed research and innovation in technology-enabled learning. *The International Review of Research in Open and Distance Learning, 12*(3). Retrieved from http://www.irrodl.org/index.php/irrodl/article/view/902

Bloom, B. S. (1956). *Taxonomy of educational objectives*. Boston, MA: Allyn and Bacon.

Bowers, C. A. (1988). *The cultural dimensions of educational computing: Understanding the non-neutrality of technology*. New York: Teachers College Press.

Brodie, J. (2005). The great undoing: State formation, gender politics, and social policy in Canada. In B. A. Crow & L. Gotell (Eds.), *Open boundaries: A Canadian women's studies reader* (pp. 87–96). Toronto: Pearson Education Canada.

Burnham, B. (2005). *The adult learner and implications for the craft of instructional design*. Paper presented at the 9th annual Global Conference on Computers in Chinese Education, Laie, HI.

Campbell, K., Schwier, R. A., & Kenny, R. F. (2009). The critical, relational practice of instructional design in higher education: An emerging model of change agency. *Educational Technology Research and Development* (57)5, 645–661.

Chegwidden, P. (2000). Feminist pedagogy and the laptop computer. In E. Balka & R. Smith (Eds.), *Women, work and computerization: Charting a course to the future.* Vancouver, BC: Kluwer Academic Publishers.

Cleveland-Innes, M., & Garrison, R. (2005, May). *Online learning: Interaction is not enough.* Paper presented at the annual meeting of the Canadian Association of Distance Education, Vancouver, BC.

Cohen, D., & Prusak, L. (2001). *In good company: How social capital makes organizations work.* Boston, MA: Harvard Business School.

Collins, P. H. (1986). Learning from the outsider within: The sociological significance of black feminist thought. *Social Problems, 33*(6), 14–32.

Collis, B., & Remmers, E. (1997). The World Wide Web in education: Issues related to cross cultural communication and interaction. In B. Khan (Ed.), *Web-based instruction* (pp. 85–92). Englewood Cliffs, NJ: Educational Technology.

Conference Board of Canada. (2001). *E-learning for the workplace: Creating Canada's lifelong learners.*

Cooper, J. B., and Taqueti, V. R. (2008). A brief history of the development of mannequin simulators for clinical education and training. *Postgraduate Medical Journal, 84,* 563–70.

Couros, A. V. (2009). Open, connected, social: Implications for educational design. *Campus-Wide Information Systems, 26*(3), 232–39.

Cox, S. & Osguthorpe, R.T. (2003, May / June). How do instructional design professionals spend their time? *TechTrends, 47*(3), 45–7, 29.

Daniel, B. K., O' Brien, D., & Sarkar, A. (2003). A design approach for a Canadian distributed community of practice on governance and international development: A preliminary report. In R. M. Verburg & J. A. De Ridder (Eds.), *Knowledge sharing under distributed circumstances* (pp. 19–24). The Hague: NWO-MES.

de Castell, S., Bryson, S., & Jenson, J. (2002). Object lessons: Towards an educational theory of technology. *First Monday, 7*(1). Retrieved November 11, 2013, from http://www.firstmonday.org/issues/issue7_1/castell/

del Galdo, J. E., & Nielsen, J. (Eds.). (1996). *International user interfaces.* New York: Wiley.

Dick, W., Carey, L., & Carey, J. O. (2005). *The systematic design of instruction* (6th ed.). New York: Allyn and Bacon.

Dikshit, H. P. (2002, February). *Re-engineering social transformation through ICT-enabled education: IGNOU perspective.* Proceedings of UNESCO-LEARNTEC 2002 Conference, Karlsruher Messe – und Kongress-GmbH.

Downes, S. (2009). *MOOC and mookies: The connectivism & connective knowledge online course.* [Slides.] Retrieved from http://www.slideshare.net/Downes/mooc-and-mookiesthe-connectivism-connective-knowledge-online-course-presentation

Fosnot, C. (1996). *Constructivism: Theory, perspectives, and practice.* New York: Teachers College Press.

Fowler, S. M., &. Pusch, M. D. (2010). Intercultural simulation games: A review (of the United States and beyond). *Simulation Gaming, 41*(1), 94–115.

Freire, P. (1970). *Pedagogy of the oppressed.* New York: Continuum.

Funderstanding.com. (2011, April). Authentic assessment. Retrieved November 11, 2013, from http://www.funderstanding.com/v2/

Gagné, R. M. (1965). *The conditions of learning* (1st ed.). New York: Holt, Reinhart and Winston.

Gagné, R. M., Briggs, L. J., & Wager, W. W. (1988). *Principles of instructional design* (3rd ed.). New York: Holt, Reinhart and Winston.

Gagnon, G. W., Jr., & Collay, M. (n.d.). *Constructivist learning design.* Retrieved from http://www.prainbow.com/cld/cldp.html

Game On. (2004). I*ndustrial Engineer: Engineering and Management Solutions at Work, 36*(9), 29.

Garrison, D. R. (1993). A cognitivist constructivist view of distance education: An analysis of teaching-learning assumptions. *Distance Education, 14*(2), 199–211.

Giroux, H., & Purpel, J. (1983). *The hidden curriculum and moral education: Deception or discovery?* Berkeley, CA: McCutchan.

Gunawardena, C. N., Nolla, A. C., Wilson, P. L., Lopez-Islas, J. R., Ramírez-Angel, N., & Megchun-Alpízar, R. M. (2001). A cross-cultural study of group process and development in online conferences. *Distance Education, 22*(1), 85–121.

Gustafson, K. L., & Branch, R. M. (2002). What is instructional design? In R. A. Reiser & J. V. Dempsey (Eds.), *Trends and issues in instructional design and technology* (pp. 16–25). Upper Saddle River, NJ: Merrill Prentice Hall.

Harris, B. (1979). Whatever happened to little Albert? *American Psychologist 34*, 151–60.

Harris, D. (2000). Knowledge and networks. In T. Evans & D. Nation (Eds.), *Changing university teaching: Reflections on creating educational technologies* (pp. 34–44). London: Kogan Page.

Hoban, C. F. (1946). *Movies that teach.* New York: Dryden.

Hock, R. R. (2009). *Forty studies that changed psychology: Explorations into the history of psychological research* (6th ed.). Upper Saddle River, NJ: Pearson Prentice Hall.

Hofstede, G. (1997). *Cultures and organizations: Software of the mind.* New York: McGraw-Hill.

Hongladarom, S. (2001). Global culture, local cultures, and the Internet: The Thai example. In C. Ess & F. Sudweeks (Eds.), *Culture, technology, communication: Towards an intercultural global village* (pp. 307–24). Albany, NY: SUNY Press.

hooks, b. (1994). *Teaching to transgress: Education as the practice of freedom.* New York: Routledge.

Hunt, M. (2007). *The story of psychology.* New York: Anchor Books.

Im, Y., & Bautista, D. (2009). Conceptualizing a cyber university model in support of effective ESD. *Asia-Pacific Collaborative Education Journal, 5*(1), 13–28.

Jordanova, L. (1999). *Nature displayed: Gender, science and medicine, 1760–1820.* London: Longman.

Kamler, B. (2006). Older women as lifelong learners. In C. Leithwood & B. Francis, (Eds.), *Gender and lifelong learning: Critical feminist engagements* (pp. 153–63). Routledge: London.

Kanuka, H. & Garrison, D. R. (2004). Cognitive presence in online learning. *Journal of Computing in Higher Education, 15*(2), 19–30.

Kanuka, H., Rourke, L., & Picard, J. (2005, May). *Moving beyond online discussions.* Paper presented at the annual meeting of the Canadian Association of Distance Education, Vancouver, BC.

Kenny, R. F., Zhang Z., Schwier, R. A., & Campbell, K. (2005). A review of what instructional designers do: Questions answered and questions not asked. *Canadian Journal of Learning and Technology, 31*(1), 9–26.

Kuhn, T. S. (1962). *The structure of scientific revolutions.* Chicago, IL: University of Chicago Press.

Leathwood, C., & Francis, B. (Eds.). (2006). *Gender and lifelong learning: Critical feminist engagements.* New York: Taylor and Francis.

Leigh, D. (1998). *A brief history of instructional design.* Retrieved from http://www.docstoc.com/docs/42431373/A-Brief-History-of-Instructional-Design

Luppicini, R. J. (2002). Toward a conversation system modelling research methodology for studying computer-mediated learning communities. *Journal of Distance Education, 17*(2), 87–101.

Matuga, J. M (2006). The role of assessment and evaluation in context: Pedagogical alignment, constraints, and affordances in online courses. In D. D. Williams, S. L. Howell, & M. Hricko (Eds.), *Online assessment, measurement and evaluation: Emerging practices* (pp. 316–30). Hershey, PA: Idea Group.

McGreal, R. (Ed.). (2004). *Online education using learning objects. Open and Distance Learning Series.* London: RoutledgeFalmer.

McLaren, P. (1997). Multiculturalism and postmodern critique: Toward a pedagogy of resistance and transformation. In A. H. Halsy, H. Lauder, P. Brown & A. S. Wells (Eds.), *Education: Culture, economy, and society* (pp. 520–40). Oxford, UK: Oxford University Press.

McLoughlin, C. (1999, June) *Culture on-line: Development of a culturally supportive web environment for indigenous Australian students.* Paper presented at EdMedia99, Seattle, WA.

McLoughlin, C. & Oliver, R. (2000). Designing learning environments for cultural inclusivity: A case study of indigenous online learning at tertiary level. *Australian Journal of Educational Technology, 16*(1), 58–72.

Meighan, R. (1986). *A sociology of educating.* San Diego, CA: Saunders College Publishing/Harcourt Brace.

Merchant, Carolyn. (2001). Dominion over nature. In M. Lederman (Ed.). *Gender and Science Reader* (pp. 68–81). London: Routledge.

Merrill, M. D. (1983). Component display theory. In C. M. Reigeluth (Ed.), *Instructional-design theories and models: An overview of their current status* (pp. 279–333). Hillsdale, NJ: Lawrence Erlbaum.

Mill, J. S. (2008). *On the subjection of women.* London: Hesperus.

Misanchuk, E. R., Schwier, R. A., & Boling, E. (2000). *Visual design for instructional multimedia.* Retrieved from http://rickscafe.wordpress.com/2009/01/13/visual-design-for-instructional-multimedia/

Moore, M. G., & Kearsley, G. (2005). *Distance education: A systems view* (2nd ed.). Belmont, CA: Wadsworth.

Morgan, C., & O'Reilly, M. (2006). Ten key qualities of assessment online. In M. Hricko & S. L. Howell (Eds.), *Online assessment and measurement: Foundations and challenges* (pp. 86–101). Hershey, PA: Idea Group.

Morrison, G. R., Ross, S. M., & Kemp, J. E. (2004). *Designing effective instruction.* Hoboken, NJ: John Wiley.

Napoli, D. S. (1981). *Architects of adjustment: The history of the psychological profession in the United States.* Port Washington, NY: Kennikat.

Nielsen, J. (Ed.). (1990). *Designing user interfaces for international use.* Amsterdam: Elsevier Science.

Odom, W. O. (2000). Under the gun: Training the American Expeditionary Forces, 1917–1918. *Military Review, 80*(4), 100–6.

Organization for Economic Cooperation and Development. (1996). *Lifelong learning for all.* Paris: OECD.

Palloff, R. M., & Pratt, K. (1999). *Building learning communities in cyberspace: Effective strategies for the online classroom.* San Francisco, CA: Jossey-Bass.

Peters, O. (1967, 1994). Distance education and industrial production: A comparative interpretation in outline. In Keegan & Desmond, (Eds.), *Otto Peters on distance education: The industrialization of teaching and learning* (pp. 107–27). New York: Routledge.

Peters, O. (1998). *Learning and teaching in distance education: Analysis and interpretations from an international perspective.* London, UK: Kogan Page.

Peters, O. (2004). *Distance education in transition: New trends and challenges* (4th ed.). Oldenburg, GER: Bibliotheks- und Informationssystem der Universität Oldenburg. Retrieved from http://www.uni-oldenburg.de/zef//mde/series

Peters, O., & de Boer, W. F. (2000). New didactics for WWW-based Learning Environments: Examples of good practice at the University of Twente. In F. Scheuermann (Ed.), *Campus 2000: Lernen in neuen Organizationsformen* (pp. 289–98). Münster, Germany: Waxmann.

Piper, M. C. (2002, October). *Building a civil society: A new role for the human sciences.* Killam Annual Lecture. Dalhousie, NS: Trustees of the Killam Trusts. Retrieved from http://www.killamtrusts.ca

Poster, M. (1999). National identities and communications technologies. *The Information Society, 15* (4), 235–40.

Powell, G. (1997). On being a culturally sensitive instructional designer and educator. *Educational Technology, 37*(2), 6–14.

Reiser, R. A. (2001). A history of instructional design and technology, Part 1: A history of instructional media. *Educational Technology Research & Development, 49*(1), 53–64.

Ritzhaupt, A., Martin, F., & Daniels, K. (2010). Multimedia competencies for an educational technologist: A survey of professionals and job announcement analysis. *Journal of Educational Multimedia and Hypermedia, 19*(4), 421–49.

Rogers, P., Graham, C., & Mayes, C. (2007). Cultural competence and instructional design: Exploration research into the delivery of online instruction cross-culturally. *Educational Technology Research & Development, 55*(2), 197–217.

Saettler, P. (1990). *The evolution of American educational technology.* Englewood, CO: Libraries Unlimited.

Scardamalia, M., & Bereiter, C. (1994). Computer support for knowledge-building communities. *The Journal of the Learning Sciences, 3*(3), 265–83.

Scenario Thinking.org (2006). The future of e-learning in Korea 2020. Retrieved from www.scenariothinking.org/wiki/index.php/The_Future_of_E-learning_in_Korea_2020

Schwier, R. A., Campbell, K., & Kenny, R. F. (2004). Instructional designers' observations about identity, communities of practice and change agency. *Australasian Journal of Educational Technology, 20*(1), 69–100.

Schwier, R. A., Campbell, K., & Kenny, R. F. (2007). Instructional designers' perceptions of their agency: Tales of change and community. In M. Keppell (Ed.), *Instructional design: Case studies in communities of practice* (pp. 1–18). Hershey, PA: Idea Group.

Schwier, R. A., & Wilson, J. R. (2010). Unconventional roles and activities identified by instructional designers. *Contemporary Educational Technology, 1*(2), 134–47. Retrieved from http://www.cedtech.net/articles/123.pdf

Seels, B., & Glasgow, Z. (1998). *Making instructional design decisions* (2nd ed.). Upper Saddle River, NJ: Merrill Prentice Hall.

Self, K. L., Stinnette, M. F., Loeben, M. L., & Muli, R. J. (2010). The United States Air Force Expeditionary Centre: Airpower from the ground up. *Air and Space Power Journal, 24*(1), 6–15.

Siemens, G. (2004). *Connectivism: A learning theory for the digital age.* Retrieved from http://www.elearnspace.org/Articles/connectivism.htm

Siemens, G. (2010). *What is the unique idea in connectivism?* Retrieved from http://www.connectivism.ca/?p=116

Silber, K. H., & Foshay, W. R. (2010). *Handbook of improving performance in the workplace: Instructional design and training.* San Francisco, CA: Pfeiffer.

Skinner, B. F. (1948). *Walden Two.* Indianapolis, IN: Hackett.

Stewart, C. M., Shields, S. F., & Sen, N. (2001). Diversity in on-line discussions: A study of cultural and gender differences in listservs. In C. Ess & F. Sudweeks (Eds.),

Culture, technology, communication: Towards an intercultural global village (pp. 161–86). Albany, NY: SUNY Press.

Teachnology. (2012). *Constructivism learning theory.* Retrieved November 11, 2013, from http://www.teach-nology.com/currenttrends/constructivism/

Venn, G. (1970). *Man, education and manpower.* Alexandria, VA: American Association of School Administrators.

Visscher-Voerman, I., & Gustafson, K. L. (2004). Paradigms in the theory and practice of education and training design. *Educational Technology Research and Development, 52*(2), 69–89.

Vrasidas, C. (2001). Constructivism versus objectivism: Implications for interaction, course design, and evaluation in distance education. *International Journal of Educational Telecommunications, 6*(4), 339–62.

Weingarten, N. C. (2005). History of in-flight simulation at General Dynamics. *Journal of Aircraft, 42*(4), 290–98.

West, C. (1997). The new cultural politics of difference. In A. H. Halsy, H. Lauder, P. Brown & A. S. Wells. (Eds.), *Education: Culture, economy, and society* (pp. 509–19). Oxford: Oxford University Press.

Wiggins, G. (1990). The case for authentic assessment. *Practical Assessment, Research & Evaluation, 2*(2). Retrieved from http://PAREonline.net/getvn.asp?v=2&n=2

Willis, J. (1998). Alternative instructional design paradigms: What's worth discussing and what isn't? *Educational Technology, 38*(3), 5–16.

Yaeger, J. W. (2005). The origins of joint professional military education. *JFQ: Joint Forces Quarterly, 37,* 74–82.

Young, P. A. (2007). Culture and the design of information and communication technologies. In C. Montgomerie & J. Seale (Eds.), *ED-MEDIA 2007: World conference on educational multimedia, hypermedia & telecommunications* (pp. 833–36). Vancouver, BC: Association for the Advancement of Computing in Education.

Zemsky, R., & Massy, W. (2004). *Thwarted innovation: What happened to e-learning and why. A Final Report for The Weatherstation Project of The Learning Alliance at the University of Pennsylvania in cooperation with the Thomson Corporation.* Philadelphia: University of Pennsylvania.

Zuckerman, D. W., & Horn, R. E. (1970). *The guide to simulation games for education and training.* Cambridge, MA: Information Resources.

Interaction and Communication in Online Learning Communities: Toward an Engaged and Flexible Future

Dianne Conrad

The character of online distance learning, if viewed from space, could be identified by several outstanding and very visible conceptual centres. As well-known scholar Robin Mason noted two decades ago, "No concept so characterizes educational thinking in the 1990s as does interactivity" (1994, p. 26). Mason's observation holds true today. Accepting as its basic premise that interaction and communication—the hallmarks of learning communities—are necessary, positive structures that enhance our well-being and health as learners, this chapter will elaborate on the nature of these related concepts, outlining their historical evolution and their contribution to our current understanding of online distance learning, as well as to contemporary practice. This discussion will culminate in a consideration of what's next. Where will our current practice and research interests in interaction and communication in learning communities take us?

Scholars and writers spanning all aspects of the sciences and humanities have long been intrigued by Zola's *condition humaine*. Not surprisingly, therefore, the stunning development of Internet technologies over the past several decades has been accompanied by explorations into the human condition by psychologists, sociologists, philosophers, educators, and technologists. Within our field of distance education, an early body of literature sought to make sense out of the dramatic leap to computer technologies, labelled at the time as the fourth or fifth generation of distance education, following on the earlier delivery formats of print-based correspondence education, broadcast technologies, audio and video teleconferencing, and limited forays into pioneering computer-mediated communication formats (Collins & Berge, 1995; De Kerckhove, 1997; Eastmond, 1995; Gackenbach, 1998; Palloff & Pratt, 1999; Rheingold,1993; Turkle, 1995; Wallace, 1999).

The seductive combination of technological innovation and the recognition of a universal need for increased learning focussed early interest on the potential for online interaction among learners and their teachers. In 1994 Wagner described interaction this way: "Interactions are reciprocal events that require at least two objects and two actions. Interactions occur when these objects and events mutually influence one another" (p. 8). She also distinguished between human interaction and the term *interactivity*, which she saw as a characteristic of the technology itself, arguing that "interactivity may eventually be viewed as a machine attribute, while interaction may be perceived as an outcome of using interactive instructional delivery systems" (p. 26). Interaction is considered here to fall within the broader term *communication*, which embraces not only Wagner's "reciprocal events" between at least two actors but also issues of language, rhetoric, immediacy, literacy, and culture—and a resulting array of analytic strategies and devices that is beyond the purview of this chapter.

In 1995, in an early but seminal investigation into distance learning, Eastmond raised issues around the tensions of interaction in his theme of "alone but together"; Turkle, in *Alone Together: Why We Expect More from Technology and Less from Each Other* (2011), echoes that theme as she follows up on her earlier investigations into society's fascination with computers and technology while moving us into 21st century considerations. Turkle explains our changing relationship with technology in this way:

> I once described the computer as a second self, a mirror of mind. Now the metaphor no longer goes far enough. Our new devices provide space for the emergence of a new state of the self, itself, split between the screen and the physical real, wired into existence through technology. (p. 16)

Indeed, the metaphors describing past human–computer interaction are no longer adequate. Turkle's realization parallels the evolution of the distance education field away from its initial fascination with the magic of technology to a more substantial interest in the human dimension. In the educational realm, that evolution was evidenced by the shift from what *technology* could do to what *learners* could do, to how they would enable their learning through the technology available to them—in other words, a shift from a technology orientation to a pedagogical orientation (Blanton, Moorman, & Trathen, 1998). Several key pieces of literature marked this important shift in thinking, which became more prominent as the distance education field became more comfortable with, and practiced in, online learning.

INTERACTION AND COMMUNICATION IN LEARNING COMMUNITIES

An examination of relevant literature will focus on related twin themes that centre on learning communities, communication, and interaction. Those themes could be described this way: communication and its resultant interaction are key to online learning success; healthy learning communities engender appropriate and relevant levels of interaction.

Following on early theorizing on the nature of distance education, Moore (1989), Wagner (1997), and Anderson and Garrison (1998) first provided important early insights into the nature of interaction in computer-enhanced learning. Moore's initial categorization of three types of interaction (learner-learner, learner-content, and learner-instructor) was expanded into all six possible types of interaction by Anderson and Garrison, who first broached the possibility of content interacting with content, foreshadowing semantic web developments (1998). Subsequently, discussions of the quality and quantities of interactive modes included typologies of types of interactions, domains of interactions (cognitive, affective), frequencies of interaction, gender-specific interactions, and cultural-specific interactions (Conrad,

2009; Garrison, Anderson, & Archer, 2000; Jeong, 2007; McLoughlin & Oliver, 2000).

In 1998, Wenger's seminal work on communities of practice (CoP) laid the current foundation for the consideration of community-based inter-action and communication in work settings. At about the same time, and building on the concept of community, Garrison, Anderson, Archer, and Rourke's research on online presence initially brought forward a new schema for understanding the online dynamic in terms of cognitive, instructional, and social domains (Garrison, Anderson, & Archer, 2000). From that research evolved the equally important theory of a Community of Inquiry (CoI), defined as "a process of creating a deep and meaningful (col-laborative-constructivist) learning experience through the development of three interdependent elements—social, cognitive and teaching presence" (CoI website). The CoI model has subsequently launched another stream of investigative research into the effects and relationships of its respective parts (Akyol & Garrison, 2008; Cleveland-Innis, 2010).

A parallel and not-unrelated research stream, also dependent on Wenger (1998), Wilson, Ludwig-Hardman, Thornam, and Dunlap (2000), Stacey (1999), Bullen (1998), and Wegerif (1998) and some of the early work of Gundawardena and her colleagues (1995; 1997), drew at the same time on adult education and learning theory literature to discuss community not as a learning laboratory per se but as an affective, social landscape. Tied most closely with Garrison, Anderson, and Archer's social presence literature (2000), this study of community focussed on relationship-based interaction, in which "like-minded groups of people share goals or special occasions" (Conrad, 2002). This approach to understanding commun-ity, taken from schools of social learning theory (Bandura, 1986; Vygotsky, 1978), moved the communication and interaction discourse closer to Garton, Haythornthwaite and Wellman's (1997) prescient work on online social networking and also capitalized on adult learning theories from the works of adult educators Cross (1981), Dewey (1938), Knowles (1970), and Wlodkowski (1999).

From the intersections of these discourses, there developed a body of literature concerned with the study of interaction within online learning communities. The evolution from online learning's initial technology-based curiosity to a pedagogically-based concern with the nature of learners' exchanges with one another and with instructors has benefited from two recent theoretical centres—constructivism and blended learning—fuelled also by the fact of ever-developing Web 2.0++ technologies. Building on those foundational pieces, scholars from around the world have contributed to our current appreciation and understanding of the importance of interaction and communication in the teaching-learning exchange (Akyol & Garrison, 2008; Dron, 2007; Kirschner, Strijbos & Kreijns, 2004; Mayes, 2006; Shih & Swan, 2005; Swan, 2002; Wilson, Ludwig-Hardman, Thornam & Dunlap, 2004).

LEARNING COMMUNITIES AND INTERACTION: THEORIES TO FRAME BY

Online learning communities comprise learners and their instructors who share purpose and virtual time-on-task. Learning communities nest within Web-based frameworks and are fuelled and sustained not only by the energy of the individuals who populate them but also by the many learning resources and objects that are brought to the community by both learners and instructors.

Recent theories that purport to explain qualitatively the online teaching-learning dynamic will focus on a number of key aspects in order to understand the nature and texture of online interaction. Issues of control, autonomy, content, learning styles, culture, and gender complement the general understanding of the Community of Inquiry's three domain presences—cognitive, social, and instructional. What follows is a discussion of current theories and the issues that bind them to the central questions that direct this chapter: What is the nature of communication and interaction in online learning communities? What is its current state, and what is its future role in the continued quest for successful online learning strategies?

The field of open and distance education leans heavily on several prominent theorists. Ally (2008) traces the field's debt, historically, to cognitive and behavioural theory, and, more recently, to constructivist and connectivist theories. In recent years, positivist approaches to education and learning that objectified learning have ceded place to constructivist views.

The constructivist paradigm, drawing on the works of Dewey (1938) and Vygotsky (1978), among others, focusses on individuals making sense of their lived experiences. Social constructivism emphasizes the importance of culture, language, and the social environment in learning. Online learning platforms enable constructivist practice through their facilitation of communicative and interactive activities and the resultant building of community (Conrad, 2002; Rovai, 2002; Swan, 2002). As Garrison and Anderson argue, "The value of e-learning is in its capacity to facilitate communication and thinking and thereby construct meaning and knowledge" (2003, p. 6).

While constructivist thought firmly underpins our thinking in the here and now, other theories played substantially into our early understandings of distance education—notably Peters' industrial theory and Simonsen's equivalency theory (Simonsen, Smaldino, Albright, & Zvacek, 2009)—although it can be argued that our explanations of today's open and distance learning have moved well past these theoretical bases. Moore's theory of transactional distance, however, formulated in the early 1970s, continues to serve as a base for our current understanding of interaction and communication and their attendant issues.

Moore's theory rests on the foundational concept that the separation of teacher from learner creates *transactional distance*, "the interplay among the environment, the individuals and the patterns of behaviours in a situation" (Moore, 2007, p. 91). On the basis of this prmise, Moore highlighted the relativity of the transactional exchange, emphasizing structure, dialogue, and autonomy as key elements in the communication equation that resulted. His focus on learner autonomy within transactional distance became a centrepiece for Garrison's early work on distance education (1989), in which he postulated a triad of control, autonomy, and responsibility to explain the range of communication possibilities among learners and teachers at a distance.

Garrison, in subsequent work alone (2000) and with others (Garrison & Baynton, 1987; Garrison, Anderson & Archer, 2000), continued to examine the interplay of communication factors centred on the elements of autonomy and control within the framework of distance learning. Ancillary factors of independence and interdependence, support, and power also played into the mix and were recognized for their ability to create shifts in the negotiation between content and activity, and to enhance autonomy and control (Anderson, 2004). Following on the constructs of autonomy and control, Dron (2007) moved the conversation forward theoretically and broached issues of communication and interaction in an example such as this: "A message on a discussion forum is not just the information that it contains, but contributes materially to the way that the environment is presented to all other participants" (p. 14). Dron's observation on the interplay of form and content bridges Garrison, Anderson, and Archer's (2000) Community of Inquiry framework to McLuhan's early famous reflections on the nature of medium and message.

The Community of Inquiry framework, presented earlier in this chapter as an important link in the connection of workplace-based Community of Practice theory and online learning theory, highlights a structured educational environment that brings together the core elements of social, cognitive, and teaching presence for the purposes of critical reflection and discourse (Garrison, Anderson, & Archer, 2000). In so doing, it places communication and interaction functions into the crux of the learning process and permits their viewing through the key lenses of social exchange, cognitive process, and instructional presence.

Meanwhile, in 1986, in his theory of interaction and communication, Holmberg had highlighted seven broad assumptions, which he later expanded in 1995 into eight equally-broad parts. The seed of Holmberg's initial thinking, however, is this: "The medium used to bring about empathy is normally friendly conversation. This is the very simple background of my theory of teaching-learning conversations in distance education" (Holmberg, 2006). Holmberg expanded on this humanistic-oriented concept contained in the 1995 revision, by explaining:

> Personal relations, study pleasure, and empathy between students and those supporting them (tutors, counsellors, etc.) are central to learning in distance education. Feelings of empathy and belonging promote students' motivation to learn and influence the learning favourably. Such feelings are conveyed by students being engaged in decision-making; by lucid, problem-oriented, conversation-like presentations of learning matter that may be anchored in existing knowledge; by friendly, non-continuous interaction between students and tutors, counsellors, and others supporting them. (Simonsen, Smaldino, Albright, & Zvacek, 2009, p. 48)

Holmberg's additional theoretical principles also encompassed cognition ("deep learning"), lifelong learning, societal benefits, and flexible delivery formats—in short, the whole spectrum of factors necessary to explain the phenomenon of learning online. His emphasis on the importance of communication and interaction has been highlighted here to illustrate his contribution to the model of online interaction—the Community of Inquiry —that holds most sway in our current thinking. Holmberg also noted the role of the media in at least partially creating empathic motivation for learning through the use of a conversational tone that he referred to as *guided didactic interaction.*

That said, theorists have put forward other models to explain the phenomena of online interaction and communication, which is not surprising given their prominence in the learning dynamic; in fact, Mayes concluded a 2006 article by asking if interactivity could be interpreted as a synonym for learning. From Europe, Kirschner, Strijbos, and Kreijns (2004) suggested a model for "integrated electronic collaborative learning environments (IECLES)" (p. 24), in which they featured a "unique combination of the technological, social and educational contexts" (p. 26) and stressed the importance of designing learning environments around what they defined as the important features of the collaborative learning environment: "task ownership, task character, and task control" (p. 31). Although a complicated model, it nonetheless does not add much to our understanding of interaction and communication as viewed through the CoI model.

Blended learning, however, described as "the thoughtful fusion of face-to-face and online learning experiences" by Garrison and Vaughan (2008. p. 5), is purported to represent an important intersection of engaged face-to-face learners with Internet potential. The trajectory of blended learning has resulted from educational queries regarding the imposition of new technology on old paradigms as well as from economic and social pressure on institutions to adapt and change to meet 21st century higher education learning needs. For the purposes of this chapter, the trend toward blended learning serves as a catalyst and an aid, not specifically in the interests of redesign, as outlined by Garrison and Vaughan (2008), but in the search for understanding the current positioning and meaning of interaction and communication in online communities. If blended learning represents the best possible marriage of face-to-face classroom learning with online learning, it is important to recognize the strengths of both and to thus create innovative opportunities for learning. The blended learning approach, therefore, in maximizing interaction and communication among learners to an optimal, collaborative, and accessible state, underpins 21st century innovation and future potential in defining community, presence, and all notions of space-and-place. However, it should be noted that blended learning restricts access through geographic constraint and obligation—precisely the challenge met by earlier generations of distance education to expand access.

WHERE TO, NOW? NEXT?

Our 21st century romance with technology and with the educational processes that depend on technology has been well documented. From pioneers in education (Eastmond, 1995; Garrison, 1989; Rheingold, 1993) to those exploring facets of communication (de Kerckhove, 1997; Rose, 2000; Wallace, 1999) and even those who have looked more broadly at society's attempt to deal with and understand itself during changing times (Menzies, 2005; Rheingold, 2002), we have studied our progress with varying degrees of interest and alarm. Turkle's 2011 exploration of our societal relationship with digital technology and its effect on how we understand community and each other notches the conversation one step further as she explores the questions raised by interaction and communication issues as a metaphorical structure of two stories, naming them as

> today's story of the network, with its promise to give us more control over human relationships, and tomorrow's story of sociable robots, which promise relationships where we will be in control, even if that means not being in relationships at all. (p. 17)

Turkle's look to the future circles back to foundational issues of community, control, and communication. We understand, conceptually and theoretically, the interplay and dynamic of those critical factors. Garrison and Anderson, almost a decade ago (2003), called for more quantitative measures to establish the validity of online formats as sound pedagogical structures. Since then, the field has recognized online learning's potential with numbers (Jeong 2007; Jeong & Frazier, 2008); we recognize and celebrate its successes; and we understand more fully how online technologies can integrate with face-to-face options to create multi-dimensional blended models (Garrison & Vaughan, 2008). While the purview of this chapter does not include a discussion of technological innovations, software, hardware, or Web 2.0++ developments, it does need to address—having upheld the place of interaction and communication in online learning communities from historical and conceptual perspectives—its ongoing and potential role as a critically important learning condition.

There is no evidence, at the time of writing, that academic support of and interest in interaction and communication is not thriving; in fact, on the contrary, the literature indicates a healthy state. A random review of journal articles published in the world's most widely-read online ODL journal—*The International Review of Research in Open and Distance Learning (IRRODL)*—shows that in a recent issue (Vol.12, No. 6, 2011), 4 of 10 research articles examined interaction and communication from various perspectives (hearing-challenged learners; social media collaboration; applying the CoI framework; applying constructionist principles). Three of four book reviews addressed Web 2.0 teaching-learning-engagement topics. *IRRODL*'s issue Vol. 12, No. 5, 2011, addressed issues of communication and interaction in three of its nine research articles; and a special issue (Vol. 12, No. 3, 2011) concerned itself exclusively with the design and delivery of social-networked learning (Zawacki-Richter, Bäcker, & Vogt, 2009).

Communications guru Marshall McLuhan fairly accurately predicted the cyber-future in statements such as this: "each form of transport not only carries, but translates and transforms the sender, the receiver, and the message" (1995, p. 90). How will online learning address and accommodate the implications of change given recent advancements and additions to its forms of transport? In consideration of this question, the following discussion will consider several elements of current practice, including open educational resources (OERs), social media and networking, and mobile learning.

Open Education Resources

Open educational resources (OERs) are learning materials that are made freely available for use. OERs can include entire courses or parts of courses—course materials, modules, tests, and videos, to name a few. As resource objects, their presence and the anticipated increase in their use among online and traditional learners give rise to speculation about changed expectations or realities in online interaction, exchange, and communication. In the online medium—where instructors encourage interaction, where communication among learners and between learners and instructor is valued and nurtured, and where social presence and community serve as the glue cementing the learning environment across time and space—could the availability of disparate or discrete OERs potentially lessen the volume or quality of communication among learning groups? If, as the newly-formed

Open Educational Resource University (OERU)[1] envisions, global learners are able to select resources from myriad providers and cobble together their own learning packages, which will either be granted credit by an accrediting body or made available for assessment by an accrediting body or an assessment service, could the expectation of community-oriented communication and the CoI model that has developed over the past two decades lose prominence? Early questions about the structure of OERU have so far concerned issues of organization, administration, funding, and the fact of OERs' potential challenges to open and distance institutions (Bates, 2011).

Although there has not been much formally published literature on OERU pedagogy, learning, and communication, there has been considerable discussion about these important issues among early adopters (private correspondence with OERU Foundation, 2011) and plentiful informal discussion on blogs and other online venues. In considering communication, OERU partners, for example, have used the interaction typology of student–student, student–teacher, and student–content to formulate workable avenues for communication using peer-support models, design, and technology to ensure the inclusion of appropriate levels of interaction and communication among learners, and between learners and instructors.

Within the OER movement, the increasing popularity and presence of Massive Open Online Courses (MOOCs) again raises issues of interaction. MOOCs, by definition, may potentially enrol thousands of learners. Is any level of interaction or useful communication possible? These are early days with no solid empirical evidence yet available. Postings of comments on *Chronicle of Higher Education* articles, however, offer the following views (Carey, 2012):

"[these courses] strike against teaching as an intimate process . . ."

"The pedagogy reported here . . . is probably higher education at its worst."

---

1 The Open Educational Resource University (OERU) is a loose consortium of 30 (at time of writing) partner institutions. OERU aims to "provide a route to formal accreditation through the study of free open educational resources" (Bates, 2011) developed by accredited institutions around the world. OERU will not confer degrees but will collaborate with accredited institutions that will provide assessment services for a fee. Athabasca University is a founding member of OERU.

"It's the old sage on the stage, passive learning, parrot it back on a few tests, forget it, and on to the next cycle."

To many educators, this writer included, the interactive pedagogical model described in this chapter is of key importance to the academic validity of MOOCs. Currently, however, higher education as a field is more focussed on the potential of the accreditation of MOOC learning to learners' degree programs at recognized institutions.

Social Media as Engagement Tools: Crossing Boundaries

In the face of proliferating social media such as Facebook and Twitter, is in-class interaction among learners in peril? In fact, the opposite appears to be true, according to recent college-level studies investigating learners' use of social media such as Facebook and Twitter (Davidson, 2011; Rice, 2011a, 2011b). Research findings indicate that learners are incorporating course work questions into social media-hosted interactions with other learners, advantaging themselves of instant and continual access to their peers. Davidson (2011) described a 2003 Duke University initiative with iPods that demonstrated "students who had grown up connected digitally gravitated to ways that the iPod could be used for collective learning. They turned iPods into social media and networked their learning in ways we did not anticipate." From the same experiment, Davidson celebrated multi-tasking as "the ideal mode of the 21st century, not just because of information overload but also because . . . [on] the Internet, everything links to everything, and all of it is available all the time." Duke's experiment illustrates the changing nature of learning in a connected world that increasingly demands and values sustainability, flexibility, and openness. Creativity and access, two more qualities that underpin the popularity of social media, are also complementary to the continued facilitation of interactive activities in online learning.

The boundaries, however virtual, that have separated in-course learning from the rest of the world have become increasing blurred by social media. Online learners' blogs and wikis, for example, once lodged within their courses, are making their way out of courses onto the Internet. In a recent presentation in which she explored these movements toward new forms of open, social, and participatory learning, Conole (2010) restated the importance of immediacy and community in communication while demonstrating ways in which new digital media can be personalized and made interactive and collaborative. In other words, the core values of interaction and communication as humanizing factors, central to distance education's theoretical base, beginning with Moore and Holmberg and ranging forward to Garrison and Anderson, continue to be recognized for their importance although, in McLuhan's words, their forms of transport are evolving.

Mobile Learning: A New Form of Transport

Mobile learning (m-learning) "through the use of wireless technology, allows anyone to access information and learning materials from anywhere and at any time" (Ally, 2009, p. 1). A subset of both open and flexible learning and e-learning, m-learning personalizes the learning process to a "just enough, just in time, just for me" (Peters, 2009, p. 116) model of learning.

As blended learning blurred—deliberately—the lines between online and face-to-face modes of delivery (Garrison & Vaughan, 2008), so too does mobile learning blur the lines not only between *here* and *there* but also between social networking, educational discourse, and content-driven learning. In other words, traditional understandings of formal and informal learning are increasingly muddied. Garrison, Anderson, & Archer's *presences* (2000)—social, instructional, and cognitive—while still constituting a viable model for analyzing online and blended learning in formal contexts, have the potential to exhibit themselves in new ways. "Technology is unbundling the university. In five years, students will mix online and in-person courses, professors will rely on new course formats and modules from multiple colleges, and the library will be dispersed" (Parry, 2011). Parry's predictions have already, to some degree, come to pass.

Recent examples of this blurring of formal and informal abound. Students are encouraged to use Twitter to pass notes in class as *idea-sharing* and to continue to share their thoughts outside class. In-class blogs are interconnected by a *mother blog,* and blogs both inside and outside class are linked. "The commenting and linking are crucial," a Baylor University professor recently observed, "as those activities are essential parts of being in the real blogosphere" (Gardner Campbell, qtd. in Young, 2011). The notion of a *real blogosphere* itself speaks to the exporting of community, communication, and interaction to a realm not only outside the classroom, whether bricks-and-mortar or virtual, but also outside the purview of formalized or organized learning. Like the cloud, the blogosphere exists *out there* and is available upon demand in a mobile and connected society.

The fluidity and instant accessibility of communications networks work both ways, however. Educators have long since become accustomed to being critiqued and rated online. Recently, teachers have taken to publicly critiquing their students using the same media—Twitter, Facebook, blogs. This newfound interactivity harks back to earlier calls for both caution and etiquette in the tweeting-posting world that remind us of the fundamental values underlying communication modes and urge users to strive for the creation of an online presence that is positive and professional (Posner, Varner, & Croxall, 2011).

INTO THE FUTURE, SECURELY CONNECTED

Just as we can expect and hope that civility will not vanish as interactive potential increases, we can assume that neither will courses nor curriculum will disappear in the face of technological and social innovation. (One recalls the sky-is-falling predictions that teachers would disappear with the advent of broadband capabilities and video-conferencing.) The changes that we are seeing—changes in who does what, how, and when—are changes that reinforce what we have learned about learning, namely, that in fast-moving and rapidly evolving societies, communication is essential, connection and interaction are both necessary and valued, and the need for flexibility is imperative (Menzies, 2005). Researchers report that, as a means of addressing these demands, mobile learning devices offer "unique educational affordances" (Peters, 2009, p. 117) of portability, social interactivity, and an unprecedented degree of connectivity, while still permitting scope for individual choice in designing customized and personal routes to desired information.

As educators and researchers still toiling within institutions, with eyes both on the present and the future, we ask ourselves: How can we accommodate current learning needs and preferences using new media and course design? And what should we investigate to better understand or create the future? In spite of futurists who decry barely observable rates of change in traditional educational systems, innovative educators and researchers are cognizant both of the positive potential of change and the challenges levelled by the voices such as Turkle (2011) and Arina (2011). We understand Arina's call for moving "from static and pre-defined learning environments to dynamic and self-organizing informal learning environments"—to what he calls *serendipic* learning (para. 7). The movement toward OERS will call upon the self-directed energy necessary to such learning, while the proliferation of mobile learning devices will facilitate that transition.

The trend toward both OERS and mobile learning converges with social media on the axis of interaction and communication. Describing the relationship and impact of technology on scholarly practice, Weller (2011) examines the role of a scholar's traditional commitment to public engagement in the convergence of audiences through new digital media. In the definition of the Higher Education Funding Council for England, *public engagement* consists in "specialists in higher education listening to, developing their understanding of, and interacting with non-specialists," the public including "individuals and groups who do not currently have a formal relationship with an HEI [Higher Education Institution] through teaching, research or knowledge transfer " (qtd. in Weller, 2011, para. 2). As Weller points out, "much of what we currently aim to achieve through specific public engagement projects can be realised by producing digital artefacts as a by-product of typical scholarly activity" (para. 31).

Within open and distance classrooms, there is continued innovation in ways of communicating and interacting. One such innovation, termed *pedagogical podcasting*, is reported to improve learner engagement, as well as to offer support, to reduce learners' feelings of isolation, and to enhance mobility, personalization, and relationship-building. Audio-streaming is not new, but Salmon reports encouraging research results in both cognitive and affective domains from the integration of more sophisticated and organized podcasts using Wimba voice boards. As an example, she sites the case of a professor who, given his other responsibilities, was not able to meet with his students on a weekly basis—or even at all. Nonetheless, as a result of his systematic and strategic use of podcasts, he was perceived by his students to be a "wonderful guy" who was very supportive and "gave great feedback" (Salmon, 2010). "He really helps you to understand things," enthused his students, and the course attracted double registration numbers the next time it was offered. This endorsement of the positive effects of voice-contact reaffirms learners' need for and appreciation of connection.

As the popularity of e-books soars, independent booksellers, like so many other retailers and service-providers in our society, are examining their strengths in order to determine the viability of their future positions in the scheme of things. They have decided that community is key (*National Post*, 2011). They have decided (or at least they hope) that by providing the opportunity for communication and interaction among customers, and with the helpf of a knowledgeable staff and a solid customer base, they can survive the e-juggernaut. Similarly, the continued creation and sustaining of a sense of community—the ability of online learners to engage with one another and interact personally and meaningfully with and within that community—will be central to the continued success and development of online learning. Over a decade ago, Rose (1999) declared that the concept of interactivity "has become so firmly entrenched within the discourse of educational computing that it is a truism to say that instructional software is interactive and that interactivity promotes learning, and a kind of heresy to dispute it" (p. 44). As it was then, it is now: we cannot dispute the value of interaction and communication as a critical facet of learning. Leading educational voices, including those calling for change in order to confront the problems besetting higher education in an economically stressful climate, hold to the importance of interaction and communication as sound online teaching strategies, maintaining that "continuous connectivity provides authentic collaborative learning experiences congruent with the development of critical and creative thinkers in a rapidly evolving knowledge society" (Garrison & Vaughan, 2008, p. 154).

From another perspective, futurist Marc Prensky created a simple metaphor to describe *his* vision for the type of change that he feels is necessary in order for educators to contribute to, and assist in developing, a productive 21st century learning society. In his nouns versus verbs metaphor, the verbs are the "unchanging *skills* of education, such as thinking critically, communicating effectively, presenting logically, and calculating correctly" (2011, p.7). The nouns are the *tools* of education, "the technologies that students use to learn and practice the skills" (Prensky, 2011, p. 7). Prensky points out that, while the nouns are changing—currently they include items such as Twitter, e-mail, blogs, Wikipedia, cloud computing, OERs, podcasts— the underlying *verb* concepts will not change. In fact, their importance is such that our focus must remain on them in spite of the kaleidoscope of new nouns, or tools, that serve as vehicles for the implementation of verb actions, or concepts. It's a simple, almost childish, metaphor that effectively captures, nonetheless, the wisdom of both change and stasis; of McLuhan's medium and message, and of theoretical notions of interaction and communication as stated over the years by open and distance learning theorists.

REFERENCES

Akyol, Z., & Garrison, D. R. (2008). The development of a community of inquiry over time in an online course: Understanding the progression and integration of social, cognitive and teaching presence. *Journal of Asynchronous Learning Networks (JALN)*, *12*(3).

Ally, M. (2008). Foundations of educational theory for online learning. In T. Anderson (Ed.), *The theory and practice of online learning* (pp. 15–44). Edmonton, AB: Athabasca University Press.

Ally, M. (Ed.). (2009). *Mobile learning: Transforming the delivery of education and training*. Edmonton, AB: Athabasca University Press.

Anderson, T. (2003). Getting the mix right again: An updated and theoretical rationale for interaction. *International Review of Research in Open and Distance Learning (IRRODL)*, *4*(2). Retrieved from hhttp://www.irrodl.org/index.php/irrodl/article/view/149/

Anderson, T. (2004). Teaching in an online learning context. In T. Anderson & F. Elloumi (Eds.), *The theory and practice of online learning*. Retrieved from http://cde.athabascau.ca/online_book/ch11.html

Anderson, T., & Garrison, D. R. (1998). Learning in a networked world: New roles and responsibilities. In C. Gibson (Ed.), *Distance learners in higher education: Institutional responses for quality outcomes* (pp. 97–112). Madison, WI: Atwood.

Arina, T. (2011). *Concepts*. [Blog]. Available at: http://tarina.blogging.fi/concepts/

Bandura, A. (1986). *Social foundations of thought and actions*. Englewood Cliffs, NJ: Prentice-Hall.

Bates, A. W. (2011). *Introducing the OERu—and some questions*. [Blog]. Available at: http://www.tonybates.ca/2011/10/05/introducing-the-oeru-and-some-questions/

Blanton, W. E., Moorman, G., & Trathen, W. (1998). Telecommunications and teacher education: A social constructivist review. *Review of Research in Education*, *23*, 235–75.

Bullen, M. (1998). Participation and critical thinking in online university distance education. *Journal of Distance Education*, *13*(2), 1–32.

Carey, K. (2012). Into the future with MOOCs. T*he Chronicle of Higher Education*. Retrieved from http://chronicle.com/article/Into-the-Future-With-MOOCs/134080

Cleveland-Innis, M. (2010). *Back to the future: What's next for the online Community of Inquiry model?* Retrieved from http://auspace.athabascau.ca:8080/dspace/handle/2149/2585

Collins, M. P., & Berge, Z. L. (1995). Introduction to Volume Two. In Z. L. Berge & M. P. Collins (Eds.), *Computer mediated communication and the on-line classroom* (Vol. 2, pp. 1–10). Cresskill, NJ: Hampton Press.

Community of Inquiry website. Retrieved November 12, 2013 from http://communitiesofinquiry.com/model

Conole, G. (2010). *Toward new forms of open, social and participatory learning.* [Video]. Paper presented at NADE-NFF Conference 18 November 2010. Retrieved from http://vimeo.com/17433104

Conrad, D. (2002). Deep in the hearts of learners: Insights into the nature of online community. *Journal of Distance Education, 17*(1), 1–19.

Conrad, D. (2009). Cognitive, instructional, and social presence as factors in learners' negotiation of planned absences from online study. *International Review of Research in Open and Distance learning (IRRODL), 10*(3). Retrieved from http://www.irrodl.org/index.php/irrodl/article/viewArticle/630/1261

Cross, K. P. (1981). *Adults as learners.* San Francisco, CA: Jossey-Bass.

Davidson, C. N. (August, 2011). Collaborative learning for the digital age. *The Chronicle of Higher Education.* Retrieved from http://chronicle.com/article/Collaborative-Learning-for-the/128789/

De Kerckhove, D. (1997). *Connected intelligence: The arrival of the web society.* Toronto: Somerville House.

Dewey, J. (1938). *Experience and education.* New York: MacMillan.

Dron, J. (2007). *Control and constraint in e-learning: Choosing when to choose.* Hershey, PA: Idea Group.

Eastmond, D. (1995). *Alone but together: Adult distance study through computer conferencing.* Cresskill, NJ: Hampton Press.

Gackenbach, J. (Ed.). (1998). *Psychology and the Internet.* San Diego: Academic Press.

Garrison, D. R. (1989). *Understanding distance education: A framework for the future.* London, UK: Routledge.

Garrison, D. R. (2000). Theoretical challenges for distance education in the 21st century: A shift from structural to transactional issues. *International Review of Research in Open and Distance Learning (IRRODL), 1*(1). Retrieved from http://www.irrodl.org/index.php/irrodl/article/view/2/333

Garrison, D. R., & Anderson, T. (2003). *E-learning in the 21st Century: A framework for research and practice.* London, UK: RoutledgeFalmer.

Garrison, D. R., Anderson, T., & Archer, W. (2000). Critical inquiry in a text-based environment: Computer conferencing in higher education. *The Internet and Higher Education, 2* (2–3), 87–105.

Garrison, D. R., & Baynton, M. (1987). Beyond independence in distance education: The concept of control. *American Journal of Distance Education, 1*(3), 3–15.

Garrison, D. R., & Vaughan, N. (2008). *Blended learning in higher education: Framework, principles, and guidelines*. San Francisco, CA: Jossey-Bass.

Garton, L., Haythornthwaite, C., & Wellman, B. (1997). Studying online social networks. *CJMC, 3*(1). Retrieved from http://onlinelibrary.wiley.com/doi/10.1111/j.1083-6101.1997.tb00062.x/full

Gunawardena, C. N. (1995). Social presence theory and implications for interaction and collaborative learning in computer conferences. *International Journal of Educational Telecommunications, 1*(2/3), 147–166.

Gunawardena, C. N., & Zittle, F. (1997). Social presence as a predictor of satisfaction within a computer mediated conferencing environment. *American Journal of Distance Education, 11*(3), 8–26.

Holmberg, B. (1986). *Growth and structure of distance education.* (3rd ed.). London: Croom Helm.

Holmberg, B. (2006). *The Peters-Moore-Holmberg debate theory.* Retrieved from http://www.eden-online.org/contents/conferences/research/barcelona/Borje_Holmberg.pdf

Jeong, A. (2007). The effects of intellectual openness and gender on critical thinking processes in computer-supported collaborative argumentation. *Journal of Distance Education, 22*(1), 1–18.

Jeong, A., & Frazier, S. (2008). How a day of posting affects growth patterns of asynchronous discussion threads and computer-supported collaborative argumentation. *British Journal of Educational Technology, 39*(5), 875–87.

Kirschner, P., Strijbos, J-W., & Kreijns, S. (2004). Designing integrated, collaborative e-learning. In W. Jochems, J. van Merrienboer, & R. Koper (Eds.), *Integrated e-learning: Implications for pedagogy, technology & organization.* London, UK: RoutledgeFalmer.

Knowles, M. (1970). *The modern practice of adult education.* Chicago, Ill: Follett.

Mason, R. (1994). *Using communications in open and flexible learning.* London: Kogan Page.

Mayes, T. (2006). Theoretical perspectives on interactivity in e-learning. In C. Juwah (Ed.), *Interactions in online education* (pp. 9–26). London, UK: Routledge.

McLoughlin, C., & Oliver, R. (2000). Designing learning environments for cultural inclusivity: A case study of indigenous online learning at tertiary level. *Australian Journal of Educational Technology, 16*(1), 58–72. Retrieved from http://www.ascilite.org.au/ajet/ajet16/mcloughlin.html

McLuhan, M. (1995). *Understanding media: The extensions of man.* Cambridge, MA: MIT Press.

Menzies, H. (2005). *No time: Stress and the crisis of modern life.* Vancouver, BC: Douglas & McIntyre.

Moore, M. G. (1989). *Three modes of interaction. A presentation of the NUCEA forum: Issues in instructional interactivity.* NUCEA Conference, Salt Lake. American *Journal of Distance Education, 3*(2), 1–7.

Moore, M. G. (2007). The theory of transactional distance. In M. G. Moore (Ed.), *Handbook of distance education* (2nd ed.). Mahwah, NJ: Erlbaum.

National Post. (June 2, 2011). The end of bookstores? Retrieved from http://arts.nationalpost.com/2011/06/02/culture-club-the-end-of-bookstores/

Palloff, R. M., & Pratt, K. (1999). *Building learning communities in cyberspace*. San Francisco, CA: Jossey-Bass.

Parry, M. (October, 2011). *A Chronicle Educause panel: Challenges for the 'unbundled' university*. Retrieved from http://chronicle.com/blogs/wiredcampus/a-chronicle-educause-panel-challenges-for-the-unbundled-university/33812?sid=wc&utm_source=wc&utm_medium=en

Peters, K. (2009). M-learning: Positioning learners for a mobile, connected future. In M. Ally (Ed.), *Mobile learning: Transforming the delivery of education and training* (pp. 113–34). Edmonton, AB: Athabasca University Press.

Posner, M., Varner, S., & Croxall, B. (February, 2011). Creating your web presence: A primer for academics. *Chronicle of Higher Education*. Retrieved from http://chronicle.com/blogs/profhacker/creating-your-web-presence-a-primer-for-academics/30458

Prensky, M. (2011). The reformers are leaving our schools in the 20th century: Why most U.S. school reformers are on the wrong track, and how to get our kids' education right for the future. *SNS Newsletter*. Retrieved from http://www.marcprensky.com/blog/archives/000077.html

Rheingold, H. (2002). *Smart mobs: The next social revolution*. Cambridge, MA: MIT Press.

Rheingold, H. (1993). *The virtual community: Homesteading on the electronic frontier*. New York: Harper Perennial.

Rice, A. (October, 2011a). Use of mobile apps grows on campuses, but 'cloud' services are slow to catch on. *Chronicle of Higher Education*. Retrieved from http://chronicle.com/blogs/wiredcampus/use-of-mobile-apps-grows-on-campus-but-cloud-services-are-slow-to-catch-on/33777?sid=wc&utm_source=wc&utm_medium=en

Rice, A. (October, 2011b). Students push their Facebook use further into course work. *Chronicle of Higher Education*. Retrieved from http://chronicle.com/blogs/wiredcampus/students-push-their-facebook-use-further-into-academics/33947?sid=wc&utm_source=wc&utm_medium=en

Rose, E. (1999). Deconstructing interactivity in educational computing. *Educational Technology*, 39(1), 43–49.

Rose, E. (2000). *Hypertexts: The language and culture of educational computing*. London, ON: Althouse.

Rovai, A. F. (2002). Building sense of community at a distance. *International Review of Open and Distance Learning (IRRODL)*, 3(1). Retrieved from http://www.irrodl.org/index.php/irrodl/article/view/79/152

Salmon, G. (2010). *The renaissance for voice: Transforming learning.* [Video]. Retrieved from http://norgesuniversitetet.no/video/the-renaissance-voice-transforming-learning

Shih, L., & Swan, K. (2005). Fostering social presence in asynchronous online class discussions. Learning 2005: The next 10 years. *Proceedings of the 2005 conference on Computer Support for Collaborative Learning,* (pp. 602–606).

Simonsen, M., Smaldino, S., Albright, M., & Zvacek, S. (2009). *Teaching and learning at a distance: Foundations of distance education* (4th ed.). Boston: Allyn Bacon.

Stacey, E. (1999). Collaborative learning in an online environment. *Journal of Distance Education, 14*(2), 14–33.

Suler, J. (1996). *The psychology of cyberspace.* Retrieved January 30, 2014, from http://truecenterpublishing.com/psycyber/psycyber.html

Swan, K. (2001). Virtual interaction: Design factors affecting student satisfaction and perceived learning in asynchronous online courses. *Distance Education, 22*(2), 306–331.

Swan, K. (2002) Building communities in online courses: The importance of interaction. *Education, Communication and Information, 2*(1), 23–49.

Turkle, S. (2011). *Alone together: Why we expect more from technology and less from each other.* New York: Basic Books.

Turkle, S. (1995). *Life on the screen: Identity in the age of the Internet.* New York: Simon and Schuster.

Vygotsky, L. (1978). *Mind in society.* Cambridge, MA: Harvard University Press.

Wagner, E. (1994). In support of a functional definition of interaction. *The American Journal of Distance Education, 8*(2), 6–29.

Wagner, E. (1997). Interactivity: From agents to outcome. In Thomas E. Cyrs (Ed.), *Teaching and learning at a distance: What it takes to effectively design, deliver, and evaluate programs* (pp. 19–26). San Francisco: CA: Jossey-Bass.

Wallace, P. (1999). *The psychology of the Internet.* Cambridge: Cambridge University Press.

Wegerif, R. (1998). The social dimension of asynchronous learning networks. *Journal of Asynchronous Learning Networks, 2*(1), 34-49.

Weller, M. (2011). *The digital scholar: How technology is transforming scholarly practice.* Retrieved from http://www.bloomsburyacademic.com/view/DigitalScholar_9781849666275/chapter-ba-9781849666275-chapter-007.xml

Wenger, E. (1998). *Communities of practice: Learning, meaning and identity.* New York: Cambridge University Press.

Wilson, B. G., Ludwig-Hardman, S., Thornam, C. L., & Dunlap, J. C. (2004). Bounded community: Designing and facilitating learning communities in formal courses. *The International Review of Research in Open and distance Learning (IRRODL), 5*(3). Retrieved from http://www.irrodl.org/index.php/irrodl/article/ViewArticle/204/286

Wlodkowski, R. (1999). *Enhancing adult motivation to learn* (2nd ed.). San Francisco, CA: Jossey-Bass.

Woods, R. H., & Baker, J. D. (2004). Interaction and immediacy in online learning. *International Review of Research in Open and Distance Learning (IRRODL)*, 5(2). Retrieved from http://www.irrodl.org/index.php/irrodl/article/view/186/268

Young, J. R. (February, 2011). Actually going to class, for a specific course? How 20th-century. *Chronicle of Higher Education*. Retrieved from http://chronicle.com/article/Actually-Going-to-Class-How/126519/

Zawacki-Richter, O., Bäcker, E. M., & Vogt, S. (2009). Review of distance education research (2000 to 2008): Analysis of research areas, methods, and authorship patterns. *International Review of Research in Open and Distance Learning*, 10(6), 21–50. Retrieved from http://www.irrodl.org/index.php/irrodl/article/view/741/1461

15 Quantitative Analysis of Interaction Patterns in Online Distance Education

Allan Jeong

With increased reliance on student-student interactions in distance education, computer-mediated communication has been the focus of much research over the last few decades. In this area of research, content analysis is commonly used to identify and classify students' utterances into specific categories, followed by an analysis of the frequencies of utterances observed within each category (Rourke, Anderson, Garrison, & Archer, 2001). However, this approach generates results that are mainly descriptive rather than prescriptive in nature, reporting for example the frequencies of arguments, challenges, and explanations observed in a discussion. Message frequencies alone provide little information to explain or predict how participants respond to given types of messages, how response patterns are influenced by latent variables (for example, message function, content, communication style, response latency) and exogenous variables (such as, gender, personality traits, discussion protocols, type of task), and how particular response patterns improve the quality of discussions and assist groups in achieving the desired learning outcomes (Jeong, 2005).

At the heart of this issue is the question of *what* to examine and code in online discourse (examples include cognitive, meta-cognitive, social behaviours; individual versus group; message versus sentence units) and *how* to analyze the discourse data (such as, frequency counts, response probabilities, Markov chains) in ways that provide findings that are meaningful, insightful, and are of predictive and strategic value. A myriad of models and approaches have been developed and used to elucidate, make more explicit, and operationally measure the form, function, and the dynamic and interactive nature of online discourse. As a result, the following sections present brief descriptions of some of the quantitative methods developed and used by researchers to study online communication at a micro-analytic level. Key authors and articles are cited in this section to highlight and illustrate specific methods. These methods include quantitative content analysis (Rourke et al., 2001), social network analysis, sequential analysis (Jeong, 2005), hidden Markov modelling with multidimensional scaling (Soller, 2004), structural equation modelling (Garrison, Cleveland-Innes, & Fun, 2010), and path analysis (Jeong, Lee, & Kim, 2011). The section begins with a review of the quantitative content analysis method on which many if not all the subsequent and more sophisticated analytic methods are based in varying degrees. Immediately following the descriptions and analysis of each analytic method will be a listing of their major limitations along with suggested directions for future research.

QUANTITATIVE CONTENT ANALYSIS (QCA)

QCA is the foundational method on which many if not most other quantitative methods are based. It is used extensively in computer-mediated communication (CMC) research to determine the nature, function, and quality of messages in relation to a specific task or cognitive function such in critical thinking and argumentation. Rourke et al. (2001) describe the procedures in detail and identify some of its methodological challenges and issues. To conduct QCA, researchers: 1) identify representative samples of the communication they wish to study; 2) create a coding scheme and protocol for identifying and classifying each unit of meaning into a specific category and train coders to use this protocol; 3) compare codes between coders to test for inter-rater reliability; and 4) analyze the frequencies of units observed within the categories and/or test for relationships between categories, outcomes, and other variables to produce either a descriptive or experimental study.

Researchers have used these procedures to examine the latent content (as opposed to the surface-level content such as number of words or misspellings) in order to determine the frequency of utterances that serve a specific social or cognitive function (e.g., make a claim, question the claim). For example, Gunawardena, Lowe, and Anderson's (1997) interaction analysis model was used to classify student postings in online debates. Their model was designed specifically to capture the social knowledge construction process. It consisted of 21 categories (e.g., statement of opinion, disagreement, clarifying meaning, testing against personal experience, and summarizing of agreements) organized sequentially into five main phases that identify the main stages of the knowledge construction process. After coding the discussion transcripts with their interaction model, they identified and described specific moments in the discussions where students progressed from one phase to the next phase to validate their five-phase model of the knowledge construction process. Overall, this and other proposed interaction models serve as useful tools for measuring and providing quantitative descriptions of the sorts of behaviours (or speech acts) that take place in many online discussions.

One of the main challenges in using QCA, as noted by Rourke et al. (2001), is that students' online postings often addresses multiple functions. As a result, researchers often struggle in their attempts to establish a reliable and consistent way to parse each posting into meaningful units prior to coding each unit. One single unit of meaning can be found either within a phrase, a sentence, or an entire paragraph. Studies that have used QCA rarely if ever report any measure of inter-rater reliability to establish the extent to which the postings are similarly and consistently parsed into units of meaning. The second challenge is that the more codes that exist within a coding scheme, the more likely the level of inter-rater reliability will decrease. As a result, the process of coding discussion transcripts is often a very time- and resource-intensive task. The following approaches, computer-scripted discussions and auto-coding with machine-based learning, have been used to address some of these issues.

Computer-Scripted Discussions

Computer-scripted discussion systems have been designed specifically to scaffold and by default code or tag each student's postings. Numerous text-based communication tools have been developed to support, for example, collaborative argumentation by presenting students with various response options/prompts and rules of argumentation within the discussion environment. For example, Loll, Pinkwart, Scheuer, and McLaren (2011) have recently developed a threaded discussion tool called LASAD (Learning to Argue: Generalized Support Across Domains) that helps students to classify the function of their messages (e.g., claim, supporting evidence, rebuttal) prior to posting a message to the discussion. When a message is posted, the category that the student assigns to the message (e.g., argument, challenge, explanation) is explicitly displayed in the message subject heading. In ShadowPD forum (Jonassen & Remidez, 2002), constraints can also be placed on message–response sequences such that messages are attached to responses by a set of constrained links so that, for example, claims can only be linked to supporting evidence, and counter claims can only be linked to rebuttals. The technique of placing constraints on what types of messages can be posted to a discussion, and the use of labels to mark the function of each message, has been applied in other asynchronous discussion environments such as Fle3 (Leinonen Virtanen, & Hakkarainen, 2002), Ntool (Beers, Boshuizen, & Kirschner, 2004), and in live chats such as AcademicTalk (McAlister, Ravenscroft, & Scanlon, 2004).

One advantage of using computer-scripted discussions is that each posting is intended to serve one and only one function at a time. As a result, the unit of meaning or speech act that each student intends to convey/execute within a posting is explicitly identified and classified by the student. Another potential advantage is that the codes that are assigned to each posting are determined by the intentions of the discussion participants, and not by the experimenter. This might suggest that inter-rater reliability is of a lesser concern or issue, but that is not necessarily the case. Jeong and Juong (2007) implemented five message categories (argument, explanation, evidence, critique, other) to support collaborative argumentation and found that students classified their postings only 51% of the time with Cohen's Kappa = .31 (Cohen, 1960). In contrast, a comparison of two coders' classifications of the students' postings using the same coding scheme produced a Cohen's Kappa of .87. As a result, future research on these computer systems will need to focus attention on testing and reporting the accuracy of students' codes and finding ways to increase accuracy. In addition to this potential problem with inter-rater reliability is that the discussion protocol in itself is likely to influence how students interact with one another. As a result, it cannot be determined to what extent the interactions observed within these types of computer systems can be generalized to discussions produced in non-scripted discussion environments.

Machine-Based Learning Systems

Machine-based learning systems use computational linguistics to classify online discourse automatically. For example, Rosé et al. (2008) developed a suite of tools called TagHelper that automatically implements a number of different algorithms to segment and classify a student's utterances into speech acts. Using a combination of strategies that include analysis of text features and the sequential relationship of one speech act to another speech act, TagHelper was able to produce acceptable levels of reliability (ranging from Cohen Kappa values of .60 to .96) in coding discussions across multiple dimensions defined in a coding scheme developed by Weinburger and Fischer (2006). Cohen Kappa of .60 was achieved in coding micro-level argumentation, and .70 for coding macro-level argumentation. See Rosé et al. (2008) for complete details about the various methods and measures of effectiveness.

One benefit of using machine learning systems to code group discussions is that the discussions need not be coded by the experimenter or the students, thus making it possible to code and analyze a larger corpus of data while avoiding the use of discussion protocols and message tagging schemes that might have unintended effects on the way students interact with one another. Furthermore, this approach can be incorporated into a discussion environment, as it has in the ARGUNAUT system (McLaren et al., 2007), to analyze online discourse automatically in real-time to help instructors moderate discussions more effectively. One of the requirements of using machine-based learning is that the experimenter must manually code an initial corpus of data to provide data that can be used to train the system. Furthermore, this process must be repeated when analyzing different types of discourse using different coding schemes that address different instructional goals and task demands.

Regardless of what methods are used to code student discourse in online environments, the QCA method of classifying and observing discourse move frequencies is limited in its ability to identify stable and meaningful patterns in student behaviours—patterns that can be generalized across different student groups, discussion topics, task structures/demands, and domains. By relying simply on observed frequencies, one study might in theory find that one group posted a significantly larger number of questions but significantly fewer explanations than another group. Or, the study finds that the first group posted proportionately more questions than explanations than the second group. Examining these types of patterns might shed some light, for example, on how a particular intervention helped to encourage more questions from students. However, there is no basis on which to establish what proportion of questions-to-explanations is to be considered an acceptable level and to be established as the norm. Furthermore, the observed frequencies do not help to explain the immediate context and discourse moves that elicit students' questions or to determine the extent to which students' questions elicit explanatory responses. In other words, simple frequencies do not provide insights into the sequential relationships between dialog moves to fully capture the action–reaction dynamics between discussion participants. To examine the relationships between discourse moves and discussion participants, and in order to build on the frequency counts produced from using QCA, researchers are using the methods of social network analysis, Markov chain analysis, and sequential analysis.

SOCIAL NETWORK ANALYSIS (SNA)

This method examines interactions between participants by producing quantitative measures that are conveyed visually via network graphs or sociograms. Coloured nodes in the graphs represent individual participants or a subset of participants. The edges that link the nodes identify participants who produced at least one response to the messages of another participant (out-degree values). Alternatively, the edges can also be used to identify individual participants who received at least one or more responses from certain participants (in-degree values). The distance between the nodes conveys how often one participant responded to or received responses from a certain participant. The shorter the distance between two participants, the greater number of responses exchanged between the two participants. When using SNA to analyze the observed frequency of exchanges between individual participants, one can, for example, measure density (how often the participants overall respond to one another's postings) and centrality (to what extent certain discussants play a central role across multiple conversational threads (Scott, 2000). As a result, *density* describes the general level of cohesion between the participants, and *centralization* describes the extent to which this cohesion is organized around particular participants.

Using the SNA method, de Laat, Lally, & Lipponen (2007) conducted a study to determine how interaction patterns between students in a collaborative project changed over time. In figure 15.1 are three sociograms produced from the analysis of out-degree values (number of times a student posted responses to certain students) observed at the beginning, middle, and final phases of the group project. The findings revealed that group cohesion in the middle remained mostly the same while out-degree centralization went up. While decreases occurred in both level of cohesion and centrality near the end of the project, certain members in the group continued to communicate actively with most if not all of the other group members. Students were interviewed (using the critical event recall method) to identify the factors that contributed to these changes in interaction patterns (e.g., socializing and group norming at the beginning, breaking into small work groups, taking on the role of group moderator, and so forth).

Overall, this case study demonstrates that SNA can be used as a descriptive tool to identify interaction patterns between certain students and reveal how interactions patterns change over time. SNA can then be used in combination with other methods to determine the underlying factors (e.g., what, why and how students are communicating with other students) that contribute to observed changes in interaction patterns and whether certain changes in interaction patterns lead to better group learning and group performance. A limitation of using SNA in this manner is that it remains to be seen if group cohesion and centrality is a reliable predictor of group performance and learning given the various ways in which groups structure and coordinate tasks over the course of a group project. In addition, SNA graphs only reveal information on who is interacting with whom and not on the nature and function of the interactions that take place between participants. As a result, research can be conducted to see if predictive validity can be improved by comparing graphs that convey the relationships between students within a subset of exchanges, such as exchanges with opposing viewpoints (claim→disagree, claim→counter-evidence) versus exchanges with supporting viewpoints (claim→agree, claim→supporting evidence).

Figure 15.1 Change in group interaction patterns in a collaborative group project (de Laat, Lally, & Lipponen, 2007).

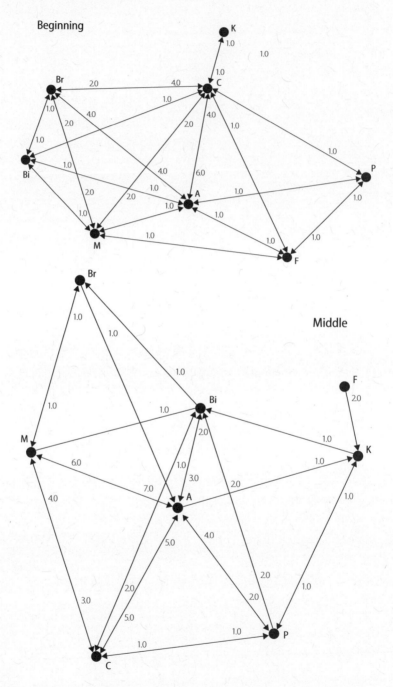

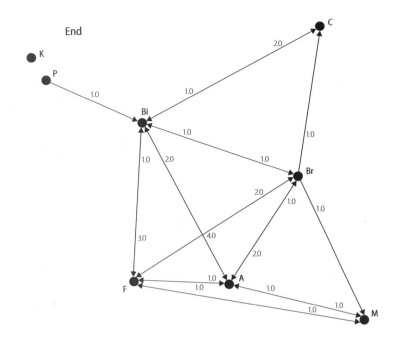

MARKOV CHAIN ANALYSIS

To examine the functional relationships between messages and responses, attempts have been made to identify patterns in the relationships between messages (Levin, Kim, & Riel, 1990; Newman, Webb, & Cochrane 1995; Gunawardena, Lowe, & Anderson 1997; Sudweeks & Simoff 1999; Fahy, Crawford, & Ally 2001). Levin, Kim, and Reil (1990) attempted to map and analyze message flow. Sudweeks and Simoff (1999) applied neural network analysis by assigning numerical values to the strength of interrelations between messages. Gunawardena, Lowe, and Anderson examined transitions between phases of critical thinking to illustrate the social construction of knowledge. All of these studies however fall short of providing a robust, more precise, and process-oriented method to measure and visualize student interactions in ways that can enable researchers to determine how specific dialog sequences trigger deeper discussions, cognitive processing, and learning.

Given the complexity and dynamic nature of discourse, dialog-move sequences do not always unfold in orderly and predictable ways. Soller (2004) believed that this is a reason the simple frequencies of each dialog move performed by learners did not distinguish learners who scored high versus low on a post-test measuring knowledge acquisition. As a result, Soller incorporated a process-oriented approach that examined how interactions unfold over time by producing transitional state diagrams to convey how likely (or the probability) one dialog move was followed by another dialog move (e.g., inform, acknowledge, request information, discuss with doubt, agree). This interaction data (sometimes referred to as Markov chains), combined with post-test scores, were analyzed using multidimensional scaling to reveal clusters of three- to four-event chains that were observed among high performing groups (for example, request info→explain→agree; request info→explain→request clarification→provide clarification) and low performing groups (such as, propose→explain→acknowledge; propose→express doubt).

This particular application of Markov chain analysis produced findings to reveal two, three, and four dialog-move sequences that were associated with and were believed to help students achieve superior learning. These findings reveal the types of interactions to be encouraged and discouraged either by the instructor or by discourse systems that incorporate machine learning and natural language processors for automated gauging and monitoring of student discourse. Further understanding as to how these longer chains of dialog moves develop requires an even closer micro-genetic examination of the transitional probabilities between dialog-move pairs and the factors that positively and adversely affect the probabilities that result in improvements and breakdowns in the group communication and group learning.

SEQUENTIAL ANALYSIS

To conduct a finer-grain micro-analysis of the transitional probabilities between specific dialog moves, Jeong (2006) used sequential analysis to determine: a) how the use of conversational language (e.g., making references to participants by name, saying thank you, and use of greetings and emoticons) affected the probabilities of certain responses elicited by arguments, challenges, explanations, and presentation of supporting evidence; and b) to what extent the observed probabilities are significantly higher and lower than the expected probabilities based on z-scores (Bakeman &

Gottman, 1997). The findings revealed that the (argument→challenge→exp lanation) interaction was more likely to emerge from students' interactions when students used more conversational language when presenting arguments, challenges, and explanations.

Figure 15.2 Response patterns produced from messages with or without conversational language.

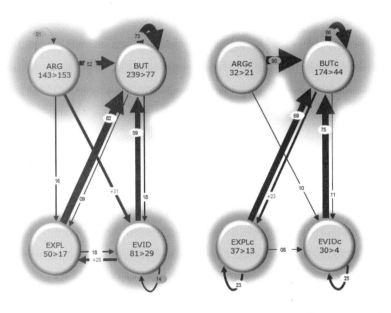

Without conversational language   With conversational language

ARG = argument, BUT = challenge, EVID = supporting evidence, EXPL = explanation, c denotes messages presented in a conversational style, + denotes transitional probabilities significantly higher than expected based on z-scores at p < .01; the size of glow surrounding each dialog move conveys the number of times the dialog move was observed; first digit in node conveys number of times dialog move was observed, and second digit following the > symbol is the total number of messages posted in response to the dialog move. State diagram produced with DAT software (Jeong, 2011).

For example, figure 15.2 shows that arguments presented without conversational language elicited challenges in 52% of responses, compared to 90% when arguments were presented with conversational language. In addition, challenges presented without conversational language elicited explanations in only 9% of responses compared to 23% when presented with conversational language.

Although similar analysis can be conducted with SNA software by replacing the nodes with dialog moves (instead of the names of individual participants), figure 15.2 demonstrates that comparing and identifying differences in patterns between groups can be conducted more effectively by: 1) keeping the positions of each dialog move identical in both diagrams; and 2) varying the thickness (instead of the length) of the edges connecting dialog moves in direct proportion to the observed transitional probabilities between dialog moves. Further clarity can be achieved by varying the saturation of the edges (e.g., solid black or light gray edges) in relation to the observed probabilities or to z-scores that determine whether the observed probabilities are significantly higher or lower than the expected probabilities. To identify patterns that convey how dialog moves emanate from prior dialog moves in order to provide a historical perspective, historical state diagrams can be produced (Jeong, 2011) to convey how likely each dialog move elicited the dialog move of interest. Overall, sequential analysis and these particular methods for increasing precision in pattern identification should enable future studies to: 1) determine to what extent differences in discourse patterns/processes (particularly patterns among message–response pairs or first order chains as opposed to longer higher order chains) account for variance in group performance and learning outcomes; and 2) better predict how particular dialog moves under certain conditions influence response behaviours in ways that help to produce dialog move-sequences/chains that lead to significant gains in group performance and learning.

STRUCTURAL EQUATION MODELLING AND PATH ANALYSIS

Structural equation modelling and path analysis are two other methods used to examine the dynamic and emergent nature of interactions between participants. Using structural equation modelling (SEM), Chen and Chiu (2008) examined how earlier messages affected later messages along five dimensions: (1) evaluations (agreement, disagreement, or unresponsive actions); (2) knowledge content (contribution, repetition, or null content); (3) social cues (positive and negative acknowledgments); (4) personal information; and (5) elicitation (eliciting response or not). By analyzing 131 messages across seven topics in a university mathematics discussion forum, this study generated a SEM model that conveyed the causal relationships between these five categories of messages. The study found that: a) a disagreement or contribution in the previous message increased the likelihoods of disagreements and social cue displays in the current message; and b) online discussion messages that disagreed with an earlier message were more likely to elicit responses. Like the findings generated with sequential analysis (Jeong, 2006) presented above, Chen and Chiu's findings suggest that instructors can monitor online discussions at the message level to promote critical thinking, facilitate discussion of controversial topics, and reduce status effects.

Jeong and Lee (2010) used path analysis (a variation of SEM where only one indicator is needed to measure each variable/behaviour) to determine how five particular online behaviours are directly and indirectly related to the quality of students' postings in online debates—five behaviours that online instructors might use to set minimum participation requirements. The five behaviours were: 1) messages posted to initiate a new discussion thread; 2) different days in which the student made one or more postings; 3) messages posted in reply to another students' posting; 4) replies elicited from each student's posting; and 5) reciprocated replies (or uptakes) posted by each student. The path analysis produced a model that suggested that: a) requiring students to post a certain number of replies to other students' postings could have an adverse effect on the quality of students' postings; and b) instructors can set requirements on number of opening arguments/threads posted and number of different posting days to increase directly the number of responses elicited by each student's messages and number of reciprocal replies in order to increase the quality of students' postings.

Both SEM and path analysis provide useful tools to determine the possible direct and indirect cause–effect relationships between particular student behaviours and outcomes in online discussions. Using these two methods to distinguish behaviours that have direct from indirect effect on any given target behaviour enables researchers to determine strategically which one or two behaviours online instructors can key on, monitor, and promote to achieve the desired target behaviours. By identifying and promoting just a few key behaviours, online instructors can avoid imposing on students with too many posting requirements and still elicit the target behaviours. At the same time, one of the limitations of these two methods is that they cannot be used to test the causal direction between behaviours. The direction of the arrows in a structural equation or path analysis model represents only the researcher's hypotheses as to how one behaviour affects another. Furthermore, there is always the possibility that several alternative models also fit the data equally well. Nevertheless, these two approaches are effective means to improving our structural understanding of the causal relationships within a complex system of behaviours observed in online discussions.

IMPLICATIONS FOR FUTURE RESEARCH

The methods presented above provide just a sample of the quantitative methods that researchers have developed and used to achieve a more precise and in-depth understanding of discourse in online environments. To refine these methods and to establish the validity of the findings produced with these methods, further research is needed to determine what interaction models and typologies will produce the most useful findings when used to conduct a micro-genetic analysis of online discourse. To achieve this, researchers will need to develop and articulate more precise models and theories of collaborative knowledge construction (across different task-demand structures). The detailed model of collaborative knowledge construction articulated by Stahl (2004), for example, can be used to frame the identification, selection, and operation of collaborative interactions to build interaction models that are coherent, complete, and conceptually sound. At this time, a large number of interaction models exist that are similar in many ways while possessing their own set of nuances and idiosyncrasies (Marra, Moore, & Klimczak, 2004). Establishing a theoretical framework will help researchers synthesize and integrate existing interaction models and use these models to conduct more systematic body of research.

In addition, the interaction models that have been proposed by researchers differ widely in the dimensions of group interaction represented in the models that serve as the focal points of the analysis. For example, Henri's (1992) model of interactivity consists of three categories (explicit interaction, implicit interaction, and independent statement) that identify structural relationships in terms of how a student's message is related to the previous messages of other students. Rourke's (2001) social presence model consists of three categories in which its first category (interactive) is also structural in nature. This category is then combined with the cohesive category that addresses processes related to group building/processing, and the affective category that addresses the emotional dimension of group discourse. In contrast, Gunawardena, Lowe, and, Anderson's (1997) model consists of five main categories that represent solely the cognitive operations that group members must perform to construct shared meaning and knowledge. Studies that use these models often examine each dimension in isolation, and those that do examine the inter-relationships between dimensions often report descriptive findings that are of little or no strategic value.

To conduct the research needed to help achieve a full understanding of how discourse leads to improvements in group learning/performance, particular attention must be focussed foremost on the *cognitive* operations exhibited in dialog move and move sequences. The assumption here is that the cognitive processes that learners perform is the primary determinant of student learning. With the cognitive dimension as the central focus of the discourse analysis, researchers can systematically examine how changes across other dimensions (e.g., social, emotional, meta-cognitive) affect changes in discourse processes. For example, Garrison, Cleveland-Innes, & Fung (2010) used structural equation analysis to reveal the extent to which learners' social interactions and interactions with instructors impacted the cognitive processes performed by learners. Furthermore, Jeong (2006) used sequential analysis to examine how conversational language (a social dimension) affected positive changes in discourse patterns observed in online group debates.

Finally, future research is needed to determine if and to what extent the integration of existing interaction models is even possible or desirable. Researchers who use qualitative methods to study online discourse often argue that each learning community possesses its own unique set of practices that reflect and are situated within a social-cultural context. Each learning community's set of practices thereby shapes and constrains the discourse and discourse process. As a result, it may not be theoretically possible or even desirable to develop interaction models that can be generalized across multiple contexts.

Future research can be conducted by applying the quantitative methods described above to determine: a) to what extent interaction models can be developed and applied across contexts; b) if such models only work when the typologies articulate the discourse processes at the macro- versus the micro-level; and c) if differences in discourse between different learning communities stem from differences in dialog move typologies, or differences in dialog sequences/processes. All three of these issues can be addressed by examining which models and approaches reveal discourse patterns that best predict learning and performance. The extent to which researchers are able to develop and disseminate software tools for building interaction models, classifying and micro-analyzing discourse, and conveying the findings to other researchers and practitioners will likely determine future success in addressing these fundamental questions.

REFERENCES

Bakeman, R., & Gottman, J. (1997). *Observing interaction: An introduction to sequential analysis*. Cambridge, UK: Cambridge University Press.

Beers, P. J., Boshuizen, E., & Kirschner, P. (2004). *Computer support for knowledge construction in collaborative learning environments*. Paper presented at the American Educational Research Association Conference, San Diego, CA.

Chen, G., & Chiu, M. (2008). Online discussion processes: Effects of earlier messages' evaluations, knowledge content, social cues and personal information on later messages. *Computers & Education, 50*(3), 678–92.

Cohen, J. A. (1960). Coefficient of agreement for nominal scales. *Educational and Psychological Measurement, 20*, 37–46.

de Laat, M., Lally, V., & Lipponen, L. (2007). Investigating patterns of interaction in networked learning and computer-supported collaborative learning: A role for social network analysis. *International Journal of Computer-Supported Collaborative Learning, 2*, 87–103.

Fahy, P. J., Crawford, G., & Ally, M. (2001). Patterns of interaction in a computer conference transcript. *International Review of Research in Open and Distance Learning, 2*(1), 1–24.

Garrison, D. R., Cleveland-Innes, M., & Fung, T. S. (2010). Exploring causal relationships among teaching, cognitive and social presence: Student perceptions of the community of inquiry framework. *Internet and Higher Education, 13*(1–2), 31–36.

Gunawardena, C., Lowe, C., and Anderson, T. 1997. Analysis of global online debate and the development of an interaction analysis model for examining social construction of knowledge in computer conferencing. *Journal of Educational Computing Research, 17*(4), 397–431.

Henri, F. (1992). Computer conferencing and content analysis. In O'Malley, C. (Ed.), *Computer Supported Collaborative Learning*, (pp. 117–36). Heidelberg: Springer-Verlag.

Jeong, A. (2005). A guide to analyzing message-response sequences and group interaction patterns in computer-mediated communication. *Distance Education*, 26(3), 367–83.

Jeong, A. (2006). The effects of conversational styles of communication on group interaction patterns and argumentation in online discussions. *Instructional Science, 34*(5), 367-97.

Jeong, A. (2012). *Discussion analysis tool.* Retrieved November 14, 2013 from http://myweb.fsu.edu/ajeong/dat

Jeong, A., & Juong, S. (2007). Scaffolding collaborative argumentation in asynchronous discussions with message constraints and message labels. *Computers & Education*, 48, 427–45.

Jeong, A., & Lee, W. (2010). *A path analysis of online discussion behaviours and their impact on quality of posting in online debates.* Paper presented at the American Educational Research Association conference, New Orleans, LA.

Jeong, A., Lee, W. J., & Kim, H.Y. (2011). *A path analysis of online discussion behaviours and their impact on quality of posting in online debates.* Paper presented at the American Educational Research Association conference, New Orleans, LA.

Jonassen, D., & Remidez, H. (2002). *Mapping alternative discourse structures onto computer conference.* Paper presented at Computer Support for Collaborative Learning 2002 conference: Foundations for a CSCL Community, Boulder, CO.

Leinonen, T., Virtanen, O., & Hakkarainen, K. (2002). Collaborative discovering of key ideas in knowledge building. In *Proceedings of the Computer Support for Collaborative Learning 2002 Conference*, Boulder, CO. Retrieved November 14, 2013 from http://fle3.uiah.fi

Levin, J., Kim, H. & Riel, M. (1990). Analyzing instructional interactions on electronic message networks. In L. Harasim (ed.), *Online Education* (pp. 185-213), Praeger, New York.

Loll, F., Pinkwart, N., Scheuer, O., McLaren, B. M. (2011). Developing collaborative argumentation systems: What advice do the experts have? In H. Spada, G. Stahl, N. Miyake, & N. Law (Eds.), *Connecting computer-supported collaborative learning to policy and practice: CSCL2011 Conference Proceedings, Vol. II – Short Papers & Posters*, pp. 980-81. International Society of the Learning Sciences.

Marra, R. M., Moore, J., & Klimczak, A. (2004). Content analysis of online discussion forums: A comparative analysis of protocols. *Educational Technology Research & Development, 52*(2), 23-40.

McAlister, S., Ravenscroft, A., & Scanlon, E. (2004). Combining interaction and context design to support collaborative argumentation using a tool for synchronous CMC. *Journal of Computer Assisted Learning, 20*(3), 194-204.

McLaren, B. M., Scheuer, O., De Laat, M., Hever, R., De Groot, R., & Rose, C. P. (2007). Using machine learning techniques to analyze and support mediation of student e-discussions. In R. Luckin, K. Koedinger & J. Greer (Eds.), *Frontiers in artificial intelligence and applications, Vol. 158, Artificial intelligence in education: Building technology-rich learning contexts that work*, (pp. 331-38), Amsterdam: IOS Press.

Newman, R., Webb, B., & Cochran, C. (1995). A content analysis method to measure critical thinking in face-to-face and computer supported group learning. *Interpersonal Computing and Technology, 3*(2), 56-77.

Olson, G., Olson, J., Carter, M., & Storrosten, M. (1992). Small group design meetings: An analysis of collaboration. *Human-Computer Interaction, 7*(4), 347-74.

Rosé, C., Wang, Y-C., Cui, Y., Arguello, J., Stegmann, K., Weinberger, A., & Fischer, F. (2008). Analyzing collaborative learning processes automatically: Exploiting the advances of computational linguistics in computer-supported collaborative learning. *Computer-Supported Collaborative Learning, 3*, 237-71.

Rourke, L., Anderson, T., Garrison, D. R., & Archer, W. (2001). Methodological issues in the content analysis of computer conference transcripts. *International Journal of Artificial Intelligence in Education, 12*, 8-22.

Scott, J. (2000). Social network analysis: A handbook. Thousand Oaks, CA: Sage.

Soller, A. (2004). Computational modelling and analysis of knowledge sharing in collaborative distance learning. *The Journal of Personalization Research, 14*(4), 351-81.

Stahl, G. (2004) Building collaborative knowing: Elements of a social theory of CSCL. In J.-W. Strijbos, P. Kirschner, & R. Martens (Eds.), *What we know about CSCL: And Implementing it in higher education* (pp. 53-86). Boston, MA: Kluwer Academic Publishers. Retrieved November 14, 2013 from http://gerrystahl.net/cscl/papers/ch16.pdf

Sudweeks, F. & Simoff, S. J. (1999). Complementary explorative data analysis. In S. Jones (Ed.), *Doing Internet research: Critical issues and methods for examining the net* (pp. 29-55). Thousand Oaks, CA: Sage.

Weinberger, A., & Fischer, F. (2006). A framework to analyze argumentative knowledge construction in computer-supported collaborative learning. *Computers & Education, 46*(1), 71-95.

From the Back Door into the Mainstream: The Characteristics of Lifelong Learners

Joachim Stöter, Mark Bullen,
Olaf Zawacki-Richter, and
Christine von Prümmer

Yesterday's non-traditional students [are] tomorrow's lifelong learners.

Schuetze & Slowey

KNOW YOUR LEARNERS!

Access to a university education used to be the privilege of a few. In industrialized countries of the 1950s an average of barely 5% of a particular age group took up academic studies (Teichler & Wolter, 2004, p. 64). The traditional student profile was that of a person under 25 years of age, male, financially independent, who studied full-time and went directly from school to university (Garz, 2004). What has changed? At the beginning of the 21st century, about 50% of a particular age group enrols for studies at a tertiary education institution in OECD countries (OECD, 2010). Surprisingly, this enormous expansion in numbers has been overshadowed by other changes, for example, large changes in the structure of the higher education system, the substance of programs offered, and the function of higher education itself.

Contemporary higher education is characterized by increasing divers-ification, away from the traditional student profile. Forty-five per cent of the current post-secondary population in America comprises adult stu-dents (Ke, 2010). According to figures presented by the National Centre for Education Statistics in the United States, 39% of the 21 million undergradu-ate and graduate students in the US are over 25 years of age, and 11% are 40 years of age or older. The percentage of part-time students increases with age. While only 22% of students aged 18 to 24 are enrolled part-time, 67% of adult students of 40 years or more choose this mode of study (Knapp, Kelly-Reid, & Ginder, 2011). Gender balance is also changing. For example, in Canada the percentage of female university graduates grew from 34% in 1971 to over 60% in 2006 (Frenette & Zeman, 2007). Additionally, more and more young people are enrolling in online programs —a trend that indicates a change in the clientele of distance learning universities. Nick Allen (2004) former vice-president of University of Maryland University College, an insti-tution focussing on part time and distance education programs, writes:

> Our student body is quite diverse. In age, the biggest segment is from 25 to 44; but increasingly the age group under 25 is growing. These are traditional students who usually go to residential campuses. However, in the United States, those campuses are becoming more and more expensive, and many students have to work and go to school part-time. So increasingly they come to us. (p. 274)

In the 1960s and 1970s, political interest in "non-traditional studies" (cf. Gould & Cross, 1977) was awakened because society began to acknowledge education as the basis for wealth and the creation of value. Universities began to open their doors to non-traditional target groups to enable "mass higher education." This was the beginning of the open learning movement and the establishment of open universities as distance education institu-tions. In his book *Learning at the Back Door: Reflections on Non-Traditional Learning in the Lifespan,* Charles Wedemeyer (1981) emphasizes the import-ance of open and distance learning for widening access to diverse groups of non-traditional students: "The new urgency respecting learning, to cope with societal behavioural problems (health, energy, crime, human rights, resources, peaceful co-existence, population, pollution, etc.), signals the need for educational approaches that recognize and acknowledge the sig-nificance of non-traditional learning throughout life" (p. 206).

The open universities experiment was probably the most important and innovative higher education reform initiative of the 1960s and 1970s (MacKenzie, Postgate, & Scupham, 1975). Peters (2008) highlights the success of the Open University UK: "The Open University [. . .] became famous for its open entrance policy, its focus on teaching adults, and for its extraordinary success in producing more graduates than all other universities of the country put together" (p. 227). He concludes that "distance education paves the way from elitist education to mass education" (p. 229). Tait (2008) emphasizes that a major function of open universities is to provide "individual opportunity and social justice that the higher education system cannot or will not satisfy because of its own interests or limited vision" (p. 92). In addition to these reasons, the cost-effectiveness of these models as compared to traditional campus-based education allows for the growth of open universities in the developing world.

Over the last decade, e-learning and distance education has developed rapidly in the higher education sector. Tait noted in 1999:

> The secret garden of open and distance learning has become public, and many institutions are moving from single conventional mode activity to dual mode activity, that is to say offering a range of modes of study from the full-/part-time and conventional/distance spectrum. (p. 141)

Today, there is almost no higher education institution that does not utilize e-learning in blended learning programs or at least in addition to on-campus lectures and labs. Thus, online distance education has moved from the periphery into mainstream higher education.

Furthermore, the development of online distance learning is speeding up the globalization of the education market (Amirault & Visser, 2010). Higher education institutions use modern information and communication technologies to reach new target groups and to export entire transnational programs (cf. McBurnie & Ziguras, 2007; Simonis & Walter, 2006). The growth of international cooperation brings together learners with diverse cultural backgrounds (cf. chapter 2 by Gundawardena in this volume). Mason (1998) describes the potential and opportunities of global distance education: the possibility that participants can learn alongside classmates from all over the world; access to high quality education programs no matter where you live; worldwide access to the expertise of international experts; access to a broad curriculum that a single institution could never offer; and the possibility of generating new financial gains in the global education market through the acquisition of new target groups.

Since the globalization of the education market leads to further divers-ification of the student body, the instructional design of international pro-grams should take into account intercultural aspects (cf. chapters 2 and 12 in this volume, and Zawacki-Richter, Bäcker, & Bartmann, 2010). The cultural context of a target group should be incorporate into the critical review and adjustment of existing programs. Experts who emphasize the importance of a culturally balanced curriculum warn that the internationalization of education programs is often driven by technology and serves mainly mar-keting and commercial purposes (Lauzon, 2000). The economic power of selling international degrees becomes clear when considering the example of Australia: after raw materials, higher education programs are the main export goods of the country[1].

The increased diversity in student profiles represents a challenge for many conventional universities whose curricula, delivery modes, and stu-dent support systems are often not able to respond to the diverse needs of "non-traditional" students (Kerres & Lahne, 2011). It is essential to give atten-tion to the context, characteristics, motivation, abilities, prior knowledge, experience, and so forth of the learners to design appropriate and successful learning opportunities and to avoid failure and drop-out. Therefore, learner and context analysis are the first fundamental steps in the instructional design process: "As designers, we need to understand the relevant charac-teristics of our learners and how those characteristics provide either oppor-tunities or constraints on our designs" (Morrison, Ross, & Kemp, 2007, p. 52).

THEORETICAL CONSIDERATIONS

Lifelong Learning and Distance Education

The theory and practice of adult learning is one of the main topics within the concept and political agenda of lifelong learning (LLL) in Europe. The integration of formal, non-formal, and informal education (cf. Foley, 2004) to enable continuous lifelong and personal development is partially in response to the OECD lifelong learning discourse, and has also been

---

1 Australian Bureau of Statistics: http://www.abs.gov.au [23.02.2012]

influenced by various scholars and theorists striving to articulate a systematic approach to lifelong education (e.g., Adiseshiah, 1973; Ahmed, 1982; Bélanger, 1994; Cropley, 1980; Dave, 1976; Gelpi, 1984; Giere, 1994; Husén, 1974; Knoll, 1974; Lengrand, 1970; Suchodolski, 1976). The OECD report *Recurrent Education: A Strategy for Lifelong Learning* (Kallen & Bengtsson, 1973) focusses mainly on aspects of employability, nevertheless, that discussion had a great impact on the field of education itself. Wedemeyer (1981) points out that the term *lifelong* could suggest that learning is a step-by-step process based upon add-ons after the formal learning time in school, while the integration of non-formal and informal, as well as non-traditional learning could rather be described as *lifespan* learning. In fact, LLL connects all learning throughout one's whole life and should therefore be seen as a holistic approach to learning.

A definition of the concept of LLL was developed by Dave (1976), who suggests that education is a process during one's lifespan, which aims at the "fullest possible development in different stages and domains of life" (Dave, 1976, p. 34). Even though Dave (1976) points out that "lifelong education is not confined to adult education" (p. 51), the development of LLL greatly influenced the field of adult education and has become a major area for policy making. Various related associations, institutions, and networks were founded to focus on the topic (e.g., International Council for Adult Education (ICAE), UNESCO Institute for Lifelong Learning (UIL) and the European Association for the Education of Adults (EAEA)). The EAEA overview of adult education and LLL within different European countries[2] shows that each country follows its own unique policy for LLL. Nevertheless, member states of the European Union have developed similarly while other countries have expanded their formal adult education system (Tuijnman & Boström, 2002). However an international study on policy issues in ten different countries (Australia, Brazil, Côte d'Ivoire, Hungary, India, Morocco, The Philippines, Switzerland, England and Wales, and the US) revealed that still huge dissimilarities exist among countries with regard to their LLL strategies, laws, and policies, which hinder the effective establishment of adult learning opportunities (Haddad, 1996). These findings raise the question of how best to offer educational opportunities to adults in terms of LLL, and

---

2 EAEA, Country Presentations: http://www.eaea.org/country [22.01.2012]

how to define a consistent research approach to adult education, particularly for online distance education.

As Daniel (2005, p. 9) points out, distance education "will be a powerful tool for supporting lifelong learning" (Daniel, 2005, p. 9). The instructional foundation of most models of distance education supports self-directed and autonomous learning (see Evans, Haughey, & Murphy, 2008), and such self-management skills are essential to LLL. Not only does distance education encourage the concept of lifespan learning, but it equips students with the tools they need to develop a self-regulated learning appoach, thereby enabling their success (Peters, 2008).

In order to respond to the needs of adult students, it is important to consider their characteristics and profiles. With regard to LLL, Dave (1976) emphasizes that: "Lifelong education is characterized by its *flexibility* and *diversity* in *content, learning tools* and *techniques,* and *time* of learning" (pp. 51–52). These aspects need to be taken into account when programs are developed for adults. Since most adults have to juggle various commitments like work or care of children or family members, they require more flexible ways to learn (Kember, 1995). Thus, online distance education is an appropriate mode of delivery to respond to the needs of adult learners.

NON-TRADITIONAL STUDENTS IN HIGHER EDUCATION

The distinction between traditional, distance and so-called non-traditional students (NTS) is becoming blurred (Thompson, 1998; Teacher & Welter, 2004; Kerri's & Lane, 2009). Traditional students are using more and more tools developed in the context of distance education, and NTS are a dynamically growing group amongst on-campus students, while distance learning is also expanding in terms of enrolled students at the growing open universities. Further, traditional students are beginning to develop similarities with NTS in terms of everyday life commitments (Wilkesmann, Virgillito, Bröcker, & Knopp, 2012).

The traditional student model began to change as far back as the early seventies and to a lesser extent, even before that (Gould & Cross, 1972). Between 1972 and 1974, the number of part-time students began to surpass the number of full-time students in the United States, and for the year 1980 Wedemeyer observed student groups were differentiated into more and more sub-groups (Wedemeyer, 1981). This new, yet diverse, group of learners was denoted in various different ways: adult student, re-entry student, returning student, adult learner, new majority, under-represented, working-class, widening participation students, first-generation entrants, and more (e.g. Ely, 1997; Stuart, 2006). Although *non-traditional student* is now a frequently used term, a widely accepted definition does not exist. Ely described non-traditional students in just a few sentences: "I am your adult student, age 25 or older, who has returned to school either full-time or part-time. While attending school I also maintain additional adult life responsibilities such as employment, family, and financial commitments. [...] I am your non-traditional student" (Ely, 1997, p. 1).

Such an attempt is only a first step in defining this group of students, and many countries apply different definitions. For example, the National Centre for Education Statistics (NCES) in the United States refers to seven different aspects in defining NTS: "delayed enrollment into post-secondary education, attended part time, financially independent, worked full time while enrolled, had dependents other than a spouse, was a single parent, did not obtain a standard high school diploma" (Horn & Carroll, 1996, p. 2). To fulfill even one of these criteria is enough to be classified as NTS in US statistics. A widely applied German definition uses three categories: mode of study (part-time, distance, or parallel with paid work), alternative ways to access higher education (without formal entrance qualifications), and recurrent learners who come to university at a later point in life (Teichler & Wolter, 2004). Another definition of NTS was implemented by the European Union Targeted Socio-Economic Research Program Project (1998–2001) on adult access to higher education (HE): "A new mature student entrant (by age in respective countries) with no previous HE qualifications whose participation in HE is constrained by structural factors additional to age" (Johnston et al., 2002, p. 5).

An international study about student retention in higher education named five different groups of NTS: "low income or economic status groups, people with disabilities, students who are first in their family to participate in higher education, mature age students, and people from minority groups and refugees" (Fleming, 2009, p. 9). Despite these various definitions of NTS, it remains challenging to describe exactly what kinds of characteristics define these students. It becomes even more difficult from the perspective of international comparison (Wolter, 2012), particularly in attempting to compare different national proportions of NTS.

Varying national definitions of NTS can lead to widespread differences in recorded numbers. The 2008 Eurostudent analysis (Orr, Schnitzer, & Frackmann, 2008) indicates percentages of this group for different European countries. While Germany, for example, exhibits only about 4% of non-traditional students among its total student population, the figure for Sweden is almost 40%. It is not only different definitions that explain these varying percentages. For example, the structure of German higher education itself creates a problem, because the mode of full-time and on-site studies, together with curricular inflexibility, restricts the opportunities of NTS for parallel work and study (Wolter, 2012). In addition, European-funded research projects such as PRILHE (Koivista & Jokinen, 2007) indicate that national classifications of low income, social class, and ethnicity cannot be used in international comparative studies without further explanations (RANLHE, 2009).

The most recent definition, provided by Schuetze and Slowey (2012) identified seven types of lifelong learners in an international comparison study, which could be useful as a starting point:

- second chance learners
- equity groups (from under-represented groups in HE)
- deferrers (who start their study years after they have completed formal entrance qualifications to access higher education)
- recurrent learners (who return to university for another academic degree)
- returners (for example, drop-out students)
- refreshers (who upgrade their knowledge)
- learners in later life

CHARACTERISTICS OF ADULT LEARNERS IN HIGHER EDUCATION

In order to address the needs of adult students—and NTS are one rapidly growing group within these students—their distinctive characteristics need to be taken into account. Thompson (1998) records that demographic and situational variables like gender, age, location, life roles, ethnic background, and disabilities emerged as key aspects in various studies. Research often focusses on some of these aspects and reveals that these elements are linked to the concept of open and distance learning (Chao & Good, 2004), because open learning demands more intrinsically motivated students and removes barriers to learning opportunities for adults.

Adult education requires different approaches compared to teaching children or undergraduate students. Adults accumulate knowledge and experience during their lifetime, due to the influence of experience, adult learning is more practical, life orientated, and problem based (Wlodkowski, 2008). According to Ke, high-quality online learning for adults is characterized by: "1) social interaction and collaboration with peers, 2) connecting new knowledge to past experience, 3) immediacy in application, 4) a climate of self-reflection, and 5) self-regulated learning" (2010, p. 808). Such an approach to adult learning is characterized by deep learning (Fink, 2003). However, these findings are not only true for adults but for learners of all ages, which supports the need for a precise description of distance learners' characteristics in order to work out their specific learning needs.

While being employed or being older than 24 years seem to be comprehensible criteria for the description of adult students, instructional designers need to know more than this about their target groups. Various authors and studies (to be discussed on the following pages), indicate several characteristics that have a direct influence on the instructional design of a course—whether online or face-to-face—in order to tailor it to the needs of the target group.

While entry characteristics such as educational qualifications, family situation, employment (amongst others) have been well examined, Kember emphasizes that for open learning courses most studies do not notably analyze such characteristics as predictors for learning outcomes. Nevertheless, these variables do influence student behaviour in open learning scenarios: "Background information on students is important as a starting point" (Kember, 1995, p. 77).

Personality variables can explain success or the extent of participation in online distance education. Biner, Bink, Huffman, & Dean (1995) widen the list of variables to include cognition, emotions and behaviour, while other authors (Willis, 1994; Eastmond, 1995) emphasize flexibility, autonomy, and tolerance of ambiguity as being influencing factors. What is known as the Big Five general categories of personality traits (openness, conscientiousness, extraversion, agreeableness, and neuroticism), could be included in this consideration as a meaningful way to develop an empirical research approach to investigate personality factors of students (McRae & Costa, 1987, 1997; McCrae & Terracciano, 2005). Another well-known personality scale, the sixteen personality factor questionnaire (16PF Questionnaire) may be used to predict academic achievement and characteristics of college dropouts (Cattell & Mead, 2008).

Another aspect that affects learners' success is the concept of *self-directedness*. The idea that learners who are separated from their teachers need to demonstrate a greater capacity for autonomous learning has led to a scale to measure this variable, the Self-Directed Learning Readiness Scale (SDLRS) (Durr, Guglielmino, & Guglielmino, 1996; Fisher, King & Tague, 2001), but Thompson (1998) concludes that the results of various studies are inconsistent.

Motivation is another variable that has been the subject of various studies. Not only does learning itself require ongoing motivation, but also the decision to enrol as a distance learner is influenced by motivational and volitional factors. However, conflicting evidence is reported for the impact of motivation on learning progress. For example, Sankaran and Bui (2001) found that higher motivation can lead to better performance—in web-based as well as on-campus settings—and that students with equal motivation levels perform comparably, regardless of the learning format. A study by Hochholdinger, Meister, and Schaper (2008) about learning and performance goal orientations as special aspects of learning motivation revealed no significant influence on learning success. While distance education students are often described as highly motivated adult learners, Qureshi, Morton, and Antosz (2002) found that distance learners were less motivated than on-campus students.

Time (in terms of both availability and flexibility) and space (in terms of vicinity) are essential attributes that influence one's choice of where to enrol. Willis (1994) introduced the learning environment as another aspect, which focusses on the technical facet of open and distance learning (ODL) and seems to be a key reason that students join online programs. Other reasons for enrolling in online programs are many and often individual. Some students prefer technological settings, some may have had bad experiences with traditional learning environments, or some have decided to study independently (Eastmond, 1995). But more likely they require flexibility.

The mode of interaction between learner, instructions, learning tools, teachers, and other learners influenced the development of a wide array of models to measure different learning styles: Kolb's model, Honey and

Mumford's model, Gregorc's model, the Sudbury model of democratic education, Fleming's VAK/VARK model, the Myers Briggs Type Indicator (MBTI) and the DISC assessment (cf. Thompson, 1998; Cassidy, 2004). The neuropsychological hybrid model of learning (Jackson, 2009) has recently received attention and is supported by empirical evidence.

While all these concepts sound good on paper, the implementation into the daily work of educators is at least questionable. Studies about learning styles are indeed widespread but a growing number of critics argue against the validity of these studies. Regarding the methodological approach of learning style research, Curry describes the problem very accurately: "Like the blind men in the fable about the elephant, learning styles researchers tend to investigate only a part of the whole and thus have yet to provide a definitive picture of matter before them" (Curry, 1990, p. 50). Reviews about learning style theories and studies revealed that no effect due to the style of learning alone could be found (cf. Cohen, Hyman, Ashcroft, & Loveless 1989; Coffield, Moseley, Hall, & Ecclestone, 2004; Massa & Mayer, 2006; Wallace, 2011). As Coffield and colleagues point out, there are over 70 different models about learning styles, and the mainstream use of these models has somehow lead to an unreflective adoption of some measurement tools. Something that was mentioned in an earlier context by Richardson (2000), who points out that, for example, distance education borrows concepts from other education fields—such as learning style research—and does not question the methods or research literature itself.

Riener and Willingham (2010) summarize the major review about learning styles quite accurately by mentioning that while students differ in terms of interests, knowledge and abilities, there is no evidence that they have different learning styles. Students have different preferences for how to learn, but the empirical proof that these preferences will positively influence learning results, has yet to be provided.

THE EMERGENCE OF THE DIGITAL LEARNER

One of the more recent developments related to discussions of learner characteristics has been the emergence of the concept of *digital literacy* and, more specifically, the *digital learner*. The discourse around young people and their technological fluency was popularized by futurists and pundits such as Prensky (2001a), who coined the terms *digital natives* and *digital immigrants*, and Tapscott (1997, 2009), who coined the term *net generation*. According to this discourse, the generation born roughly between 1980 and 2000 has been profoundly influenced by the advent of digital technologies and the immersion in a digital and networked world to the point where, it is argued, they have developed unique characteristics that have a profound impact on how they learn. As a consequence, educators are urged to develop new approaches to teaching and learning and to make radical changes to our educational systems to accommodate these unique learners.

While Prensky and Tapscott have probably done the most to popularize this notion, many others have taken up the idea that we have a generation of learners who behave differently; they have different social characteristics, ways of using and making sense of information, ways of learning, and expectations about life and learning, all due to their exposure to digital technology (Howe & Strauss, 2000; Oblinger & Oblinger, 2005; Palfrey & Gasser, 2008; Prensky, 2001b, 2005). This discourse is particularly relevant to distance educators because, if one accepts the notion of the digital native, two of its most obvious implications are that we should be integrating more technology into our teaching and that the digital learner prefers online learning to traditional face-to-face teaching. However, the digital natives discourse is not supported by sound research and does not help explain learner preferences for modes of delivery nor their comfort or skills in using digital technologies for learning.

While there is no doubt that the use of ICTs is growing and that younger people tend to use digital technologies more than older people, there is a troubling lack of empirical support for the claims about the impact of this growing ICT use. The discourse around learners and digital technology is dominated by claims that emerge from non-scholarly literature. Some appear in the popular or lay press; others are found in proprietary research funded by and conducted for private business. Still others are in quasi-academic publications that have the appearance of academic or scholarly quality but are not informed by empirical research. More recently, a growing body of sound empirical research has developed that contradicts the key claims of the digital natives discourse.

Prensky (2001a, 2001b, 2005), Tapscott (1998, 2009) and, to a lesser extent, Palfrey and Gasser (2008) have all claimed that the ubiquity of digital technologies and young peoples' intensive use of these technologies is affecting how they think, interact, and make sense of the world. The following assertion is typical of the claims in popular literature:

> [T]oday's students think and process information fundamentally differently from their predecessors. These differences go far further and deeper than most educators suspect or realize. . . . They like to parallel process and multi-task. They prefer their graphics before their text rather than the opposite. They prefer random access (like hypertext). They function best when networked. They thrive on instant gratification and frequent rewards. They prefer games to "serious" work. (Prensky, 2001a, pp. 1-2)

One of the more widely cited references in support of the claims about the distinct characteristics of digital natives is Howe and Strauss' *Millennials Rising: The Next Great Generation* (2000). In it they state: "Over the next decade, the Millennial Generation will entirely recast the image of youth from downbeat and alienated to upbeat and engaged—with potentially seismic consequences for America" (p. 4).

Tapscott (2009) also makes some sweeping statements about digital natives and coined the term the *net generation*. He proposes what he calls his eight net generation norms: freedom, customization, integrity, scrutiny, collaboration, entertainment, innovation, and speed. Oblinger & Oblinger (2005) have probably done the most to legitimize the notion that this generation has unique personal and behavioural characteristics because their book was published by the well-known EDUCAUSE organization and made available as a free download. They echo much of what Howe & Strauss (2000) say about this generation. Drawing on the work of Prensky (2001a, b), Tapscott (1998), Seely-Brown (2002), and Howe & Strauss (2000), they argue that the net generation is digitally literate, connected, social, and has a preference for experiential learning and immediate feedback.

Until recently, there has been a largely uncritical acceptance of the discourse on digital natives. Other researchers, writers, and commentators have repeated the claims, which has helped to give the discourse a sense of legitimacy. Even researchers who acknowledge the lack of empirical support for the generational argument continue to either frame the issue in generational terms or give prominence to the unfounded generational claims, which further entrenches the digital natives discourse (Bates & Sangrà, 2011; Corrin, Lockyer, & Bennett, 2011).

IMPLICATIONS FOR TEACHING, LEARNING, AND DISTANCE EDUCATION

There is a distinctly prescriptive thread to the digital natives discourse. Tapscott (2009), for example, argues that we need to move away from what he claims is the dominant broadcast mode of education and incorporate more interactive, collaborative, and constructivist pedagogies and instructional designs. Prensky (2001a, 2001b) argues for greater use of gaming and game-based designs. Palfrey & Gasser (2008) take a more cautious line and urge educators to resist the temptation to implement radical changes. At the same time, however, they suggest that digital learners want more team-based, collaborative, and game-based learning. Oblinger & Oblinger (2005) also argue for this but go further and recommend structured learning experiences that are socially meaningful and use visual and kinesthetic approaches. The dominant theme in all these prescriptions for change driven by the digital generation is the need for greater use of digital technology and a rejection of traditional face-to-face modes of teaching.

There is something intuitively appealing about these prescriptions for educational change. It does seem to make sense that being immersed in digital technology almost from birth should have some impact, and that if today's students are indeed learning differently then we should consider new approaches to teaching and learning. However, in order to accept the calls for change we have to accept the underlying assumption that there has been a generational change in learners and, to date, there is no convincing evidence to support that.

DIGITAL LEARNER RESEARCH

Bennett, Maton, and Kervin (2008) conducted one of the first comprehensive reviews of the research on digital learners and concluded the issue is much more complex than is being portrayed in the popular media:

> While technology is embedded in their lives, young people's use and
> skills are not uniform. There is no evidence of widespread and universal
> disaffection, or of a distinctly different learning style the like of which
> has never been seen before. We may live in a highly technologized
> world, but it is conceivable that it has become so through evolution,
> rather than revolution. Young people may do things differently, but there
> are no grounds to consider them alien to us. Education may be under
> challenge to change, but it is not clear that it is being rejected. (p. 783)

More recently, after reviewing the literature and conducting a study at the
BC Institute of Technology in Canada, Bullen, Morgan, and Qayyum (2011)
concluded that generation is not the issue:

> While our study found that the use of some ICTs was ubiquitous (e.g.,
> mobile phones, e-mail, and instant messaging) we did not find any
> evidence to support claims that digital literacy, connectedness, a need
> for immediacy, and a preference for experiential learning were charac-
> teristics of a particular generation of learners. (p. 18)

These are just two of many studies that reach conclusions that are at odds
with the dominant discourse around young people and their technology skills and what this means for education. Others studies and reviews
include Bekebrede, Warmelink, and Mayer, (2011); Hargittai (2010); Jones
and Cross (2009); Kennedy et al. (2007); Kennedy et al. (2009); Margaryan,
Littlejohn, and Vojt (2011); Pedró (2009); Reeves and Oh (2007); Romero,
Guitert, Bullen, and Morgan (2011); van den Beemt, Akkerman, and Simons
(2010), and Friesen (2012). The common theme to all these studies is that
it would be unwise to assume that learners of a particular age all possess
sophisticated digital technology skills, are demanding an end to face-to-
face teaching, and want more technology and online learning. Selwyn
(2009) highlights the significance of this clear disconnect:

> The onus perhaps now falls on academic communities of information
> scholars and other social scientists to better promote empirically-
> grounded and socially-aware portrayals of the complexities of young
> people's uses of technology—thus providing realistic alternatives to the

discourse of the digital native and the attendant public and political concerns that surround it. (p. 376)

What does this mean for distance educators? It reinforces the point made earlier in this chapter about the importance of context and of doing a proper analysis of the needs and characteristics of learners and avoiding the temptation to rely on generalizations. Pratt (1988) provided a powerful response against the prevailing orthodoxy about adult learners and argued persuasively that andragogy is a relational construct. The same can be said about digital fluency. Bennett, Maton, and Kervin (2008) aptly put it this way:

> Research . . . shows that students change their approach to learning depending on their perception of what a task requires and their previous success with a particular approach. . . . To attribute a particular learning style or even general preferences to a whole generation is thus questionable. (p. 780)

PREVIOUS EMPIRICAL STUDIES

As early as 1987, Börje Holmberg recommended in his seminal article "The Development of Distance Education Research," that research was required to better understand the characteristics of distance students, their motivation to study, their milieu and their needs, in terms of clarifying the research agenda for the field of open and distance learning (Simonson, Schlosser, & Orellana, 2011).

Investigating distance learners in terms of their characteristics, the relationships between these above-mentioned factors, and their impact on student achievement in distance learning programs has developed into a major focus of study (Thompson, 1998). A literature review by Zawacki-Richter, Bäcker, and Vogt (2009), covering the many aspects of distance education revealed that 16% of the papers included in the review (N=695) examined learner characteristics. These results are relevant because, in the wide field of distance education, learner characteristics will be an even more important topic for the future, since today there are not only more students, but they are indeed more heterogeneous than ever (Schuetze & Slowey, 2002; Wolter, 2012; Guri-Rosenblit, 2011). Thus, we need more research efforts to help us develop more effective distance education programs.

Demographic, socio-economic, and other learner characteristics are closely linked to student success. Since the early 1990s numerous researchers have reported a positive correlation between achievement and the age of students (e.g., Dille & Mezack, 1991; Souder, 1994); distance learners and non-traditional students tend to be more intrinsically motivated (Thompson, 1998); more autonomous learners (Johnston et al., 2002); more self-efficient and more organized (Harlow, 2006); and their work commitment strengthens their persistence (Kemp, 2002). Motteram and Forrester (2005) investigated the experiences of online students in distance learning programs and concluded that a broad support approach (e.g., technical, personal, and motivational) is needed to address their diverse needs.

Barriers for successful students often cannot be attributed to a single factor and even self-directed learners experience many barriers (Grace & Smith, 2001). Flexible off-campus learning is only effective if learners are disciplined and consistent in their learning methods (Samarawickrema, 2005). According to Richardson and Newby (2006), the main variables related to student motivation and learning strategies are: gender, age, prior online learning experiences, and program focus. Personality traits such as being introverted or extroverted can have an important impact on the instructional design of study programs, for example, extroverts are negatively influenced through lack of contact with a teacher, while introverts are not (Offir, Bezalel, & Barth, 2007).

Although there are differences in the composition of the student body in different countries and distance teaching institutions, distance learners in tertiary education still share some characteristics that set them apart from students in conventional higher education. The most obvious of these are age, family, and socio-economic situation. Table 16.1 shows some of the published data from three single-mode distance teaching universities, the British Open University (OUUK)[3], the German FernUniversität (FeU)[4], and the Canadian Athabasca University (AU).[5]

---

3 http://www.open.ac.uk/about/documents/about-facts-figures-0910.pdf [16.1.2012]

4 http://www.fernuni-hagen.de/universitaet/profil/zahlen/index.shtml
   http://www.fernuni-hagen.de/arbeiten/statistik/open_m/studstat/2010/20102_13_Alter.pdf [16.1.2012]

5 http://www2.athabascau.ca/aboutau/glance.php [16.1.2012]

Table 16.1 Distance learner profile data from three open universities.

	OUUK			FeU		AU
Age	31 (median)				29–35 (main age group)	29 (average) 37 (average)
	age groups OUUK	under- graduate	graduate	age groups FeU		
	17 and under	3%	0%	17 and under	0.2%	
	18–24	14%	4%	18–24	9.5%	
	25–34	29%	31%	25–31	34.4%	
				32–38	25.8%	
	35–44	28%	36%	39–45	17.2%	
	45–54	16%	21%	46–52	8.7%	
	55–64	7%	6%	53–59	2.8%	
	65 and over	3%	2%	60 and over	1.5%	
Paid work	> 70%				ca. 80%	81%
Gender	proportion of women	61% (u) / 50% (g)			46%	67%

In order to illustrate the profiles and socio-economic background of distance learners in more detail, the following section draws upon recent survey data collected at the German FernUniversity in Hagen as part of a research project on the situation of students enrolled in their third term in the winter semester 2010/11 (von Prümmer, 2012). The survey replicates a study carried out in 1986 as an internationally comparative project on the situation of women and men in distance education (cf. Kirkup & von Prümmer, 1990; von Prümmer, 2000).

Of the 1,681 students who participated in the online survey, 56% were female, i.e. women were over-represented compared with all FeU students (46%). At the time of the survey the average age of the students was 35.4 years with a range from 22 to 73 years. Women on average were slightly younger (34.8 years) than their male counterparts (36.1 years). With a mean age of 34.8 years undergraduate students were one year younger than students in master and doctoral programs (35.7 years).

Family Situation and Social Selectivity

Students' family situation reflects the fact that predominantly these are not young people entering university directly after completing their secondary schooling. Thirty-four per cent of the women and 26% of the men are parents, and most of these live as a family with their partner and one or more children. Most of the single parents (n=74) are women (89%). A total of 493 parents (29%) provided information about the number of children in their household: forty per cent have one child, 43% have two children, and 17% have three or more children. A multiple response question about the age of the children shows that four out of ten were under school age, 18% babies and toddlers up to 3 years of age, 20% from 3 to under 6 years old. Forty-seven per cent of the children were of school age, 31% from 6 to under 14 years, 16% from 14 to under 18 years. Fourteen per cent of the children living with their distance education parent(s) were 18 years and older at the time of the survey.

It is a well-established fact that access to higher education is "socially selective, i.e., certain groups are over-represented or under-represented" in the student population (Orr, Schnitzer & Frackmann, 2008, p. 56) and research has shown that "fundamental social disparities have proven to be relatively stable" (Isserstedt, Middendorf, Kandulla, Borchert, & Leszczensky, 2010, p. 9). Open universities were established with the explicit aim of improving equity of access by making it possible to pursue a degree later in life. For instance, according to its mission statement, AU "is dedicated to the removal of barriers that restrict access to and success in university-level study and to increasing equality of educational opportunity for adult learners worldwide"[6] and the OUUK's mission is to "promote educational opportunity and social justice by providing high-quality university education to all who wish to realise their ambitions and fulfil their potential."[7]

One would expect that the social composition of the student population should therefore yield a higher proportion of students from backgrounds usually under-represented in tertiary education institutions. In fact, this was shown to be true for students of the (West) German FeU 25 years ago, documented both in the student statistics and from a survey of women and men studying at a distance. Although students from a working class background

---

6 http://www2.athabascau.ca/aboutau/mission.php [17.01.2012]

7 http://www8.open.ac.uk/about/main/the-ou-explained/the-ous-mission [17.01.2012]

were under-represented compared to the general population, their percentage was higher at the FeU than at traditional German universities (von Prümmer, 1997).

Figure 16.1 Socio-economic status of distance education students (FeU, 2011; N=1,681) compared with students at conventional universities (HIS, 2009; N=16,370).

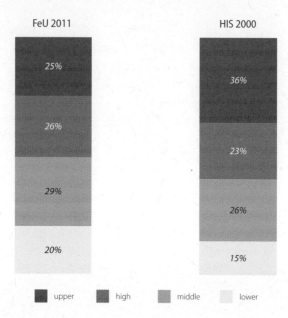

The construct of the social background was introduced in 1982 for the German social census and is an indicator that measures correlations between economic situation, educational background of the family, and student behaviour. According to this point of view, the educational attainment and occupation of students' parents can be seen as a measure of the social make-up of the student body (Orr, Gwosć & Netz, 2011).

Figure 16.1 indicates the differences between students from the FeU and campus-based traditional university students from the 2009 HIS survey (Isserstedt, Middendorf, Kandulla, Borchert, & Leszczensky, 2010). While the mid-tier of the high- and middle-status groups seems quite similar, in the upper and lower groups the differences become clearer. While 36% of the regular students share an upper socio-economic family background, only 25% of the FeU students do. It is almost trivial to say that universities recruit their students largely from academic backgrounds where at least one parent has completed tertiary education. The 2009 HIS survey confirms "stability over time" of the selective participation rates according to educational background (Isserstedt et al., p. 124). Half the student population in the survey (51%) comes from families where at least one parent has a degree. A quarter of the students (24%) come from families where both parents have completed tertiary education. Again, the FeU survey shows a lower proportion of students from such highly educated family backgrounds. 41% of FeU students come from an academically educated family background where at least one parent has obtained a degree.

Employment

As is usual for distance students, the majority of survey participants are in paid work, either full-time (57%) or part-time (26%). Again, the answers show familiar gender patterns as 72% of the men but only 45% of the women are in full-time paid work. The students who are not earning a salary are registered as unemployed (2.7%), pensioners (1.7%), on parenting leave (2.7%), or doing unpaid family work (4.0%). Women are by far more likely to take parenting leave and to take care of their families and homes full-time without pay, making up 93% of each of these groups.

Most distance students encounter problems in their studies because of the demands of their paid work. A multiple-response question shows that only one quarter of the respondents in paid work (24%) can claim to spend as much time on the job as their contract requires. Eighteen per cent have to put in significantly more hours always, and 22% have to do this at foreseeable intervals. Thirty-eight per cent face additional expenditure of time at irregular and often unexpected intervals. A few respondents occasionally encounter situations where they have to spend less time on their paid work than expected (4.0%) and an even smaller group always works fewer hours (0.8%). This means that the majority of distance students must expect to deal with situations where the demands of their paid work interfere with their study schedules and affect their ability to meet deadlines.

Enrolment Data and Motivation to Study

The majority of the survey participants (74%) are not newcomers to tertiary education. Three out of ten (29%) have previous study experience without gaining a degree and 45% came to their distance studies already having earned a college or university degree. Considering Bachelor and Masters students only we find expected differences as nearly all (97%) of the students in a Master's program but less than one third (30%) of the Bachelor students had already completed a degree. Two thirds (64%) of the respondents pursue their distance studies part-time, one fifth (21%) do so full-time. The others are enrolled as continuing education students (3.4%) or as visiting students (11.5%) who are registered in a degree course at another university.

Students were asked to rate, on a scale of 1 (=very important) to 5 (=unimportant), a list of 21 study goals with respect to the relevance these had for their decision to enrol. The highest ratings went to work and career-related items and to items reflecting a wish for personal development. With a mean of $\emptyset = 1.70$ the most important study goal is the opening of "new occupational perspectives" followed by an "enjoyment of new areas of knowledge" ($\emptyset = 1.79$), gaining a "higher qualification for my job" ($\emptyset = 1.82$) and a "wider knowledge in my area of speciality" ($\emptyset = 1.88$). A factor analysis sorted the study goals into four areas: Factor 1 comprises items related to career and employment; Factor 2 items related to acquiring knowledge. These two factors comprise 15 of the 21 items, which underlines the important role these considerations played in students' decisions to study. Factor 3 deals with issues of (self) esteem; and Factor 4—in the broadest sense— with making a new start.

Different answering patterns are found by comparing first-time students with students who had already gained a degree before enrolling. All but two items are rated more highly by students without previous study experience. Not surprisingly, the differences are greatest with respect to Factor 4 as the items here are less important for people who already possess a degree. First-time students are more in need of gaining their "initial professional qualification" ($\emptyset = 2.66$ vs. 2.91) and making use of distance studying for "testing my ability to study," something that the postgraduates have obviously already succeeded in doing ($\emptyset = 2.65$ vs. 3.45).

The study goals that lead students to embark on tertiary education at a time in their lives when most of them are gainfully employed (83%), in their mid-thirties ($\emptyset = 34.8$ years), and living with a partner or in a family situation (71%) are linked with their decision to enrol. The most often-quoted reason is the freedom from classroom schedules and flexibility of time. Eighty-four per cent of the respondents agreed that this was a consideration in their decision to enrol at the FeU. While this reason is a fairly sweeping statement, which could refer to any aspect of a student's life, the next most-often chosen items refer specifically to work-related aspects. Three quarters of the FeU students cannot afford to give up their job in order to study at a traditional university but "must continue to earn money" (75%) or to fulfil their "work commitments" (75%). Just over half of the respondents became distance students because they did not want their part-time studies to interfere with their job, which was their "first priority" (53%), or feared that an interruption of their career would jeopardize their future prospects (52%).

Figure 16.2 Student reported reasons for studying at a distance at FernUniversität.

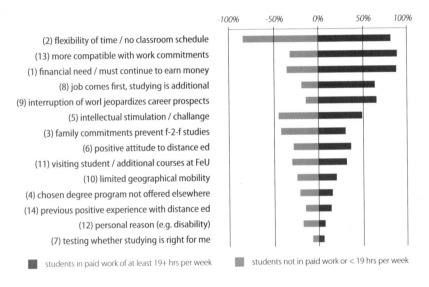

Other reasons for studying at a distance are directly tied to students' private lives. Considering household composition we find—as might have been expected—that 83% of respondents with children were prevented by family commitments from attending a traditional university, and that the percentage is higher among mothers (88%) than fathers (79%).

CHANGING STUDENT PROFILES AT CAMPUS-BASED UNIVERSITIES

In order to investigate the hypothesis that the profiles of traditional students at campus-based universities have become more and more diverse and might now be comparable to non-traditional students such as those described above who study at the FernUniversität, students at three conventional German universities—the Universities of Oldenburg (UOL), Duisburg-Essen (UDE), and Dortmund (TUD)—were surveyed during the winter term 2009/2010. Major findings with regard to the student profiles, their family and employment situation are summarized in table 16.2.

Table 16.2 Survey of undergraduate students at three conventional German universities (N=3,687).

	Total N=3,687	UDE N=1,300	TUD N=1,397	UOL N=990
age	22.9	22.8	22.7	23.4
proportion of women	47%	40%	45%	61%
migration background	27%	32%	31%	16%
parents without higher education degree	63%	63%	62%	66%
second chance education	10%	10%	8%	12%
without general qualification for university entrance	5%	6%	3%	8%
own children	3%	3%	3%	4%
caring for family members	7%	9%	6%	5%
apprenticeship + work experience	16% 40%	12% 36%	13% 33%	26% 53%
employed >15 hrs/week	60% 12%	62% 15%	60% 10%	58% 8%
de-facto part-time student (< 25 hrs/week)	24%	29%	22%	18%
wish for part-time study	19%	22%	18%	15%

From "Abweichungen vom Bild der Normalstudierenden – was erwarten Studierende?" by U. Wilkesmann, A. Virgillito, T. Bröcker, & L. Knopp, (2012). In M. Kerres, A. Hanft, U. Wilkesmann, & K. Wolff-Bendik (Ed.s), *Studium 2020 Positionen und Perspektiven zum lebenslangen Lernen an Hochschulen* (p. 64). Münster: Waxmann.

The authors also investigated the differences between the actual study conditions and the expectations about these conditions. On a Likert scale ranging from 1 (not important at all) to 5 (very important), students were asked to rate different aspects of the study conditions. The variance analysis depicted in figure 16.3 shows the specific areas in which major differences between the actual and the expected study conditions were found (i.e., the difference between demand and provision).

Figure 16.3 Scatterplot for the dimensions of student expectations (current state vs. target state).

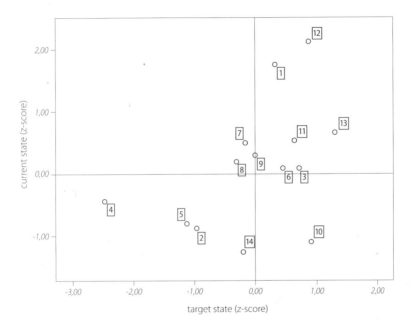

In the top right corner of figure 16.3 we find aspects with a high demand that are fulfilled to a high degree (e.g., 12=approachability of faculty). Those areas at the bottom of that figure are interesting, showing high expectations that the students perceive as not being met to a great extent by the campus-based institution: 2=integration of practical knowledge, 3=appropriate number of students per class, 5=application of work-related experience, 6=opportunities for part-time work, 7=independent work, 8=self-directed learning, 9=project work, 10=flexible assessment, 14=recognition of prior learning. The detailed results of the variance analysis can be found in table 16.3.

Table 16.3 Dimensions of student expectations.

Dimension	Target Sate	Current State
1. open access	3.96	3.51
2. integration of practical knowledge	3.26	2.47
3. appropriate number of students per class	4.16	2.85
4. unusual hours	2.45	2.65
5. application of work-related experience	3.18	2.50
6. opportunities for part-time work	4.03	2.85
7. independent work	3.70	3.02
8. self-directed learning	3.62	2.90
9. project work	3.78	2.93
10. flexible assessment	4.27	2.39
11. contact person	4.13	3.03
12. availability of lecturers	4.26	3.66
13. info study organisation	4.49	3.08
14. recognition of prior learning	3.67	2.32

These articulated needs and demands are those we would usually expect from non-traditional students, which supports the hypothesis that the profiles of traditional and non-traditional are increasingly converging—in other words, the previously clear boundaries between traditional and non-traditional are now becoming blurred.

CONCLUSION AND PERSPECTIVES FOR FUTURE RESEARCH

Access to education and flexible learning opportunities are the key to life-long learning. Distance education and educational technologies provide powerful tools for fostering participation in formal, informal, and non-formal educational settings. The traditional distance education student who needs to juggle various job and family commitments is moving from the back door into the mainstream. It is a political goal to further increase participation of so-called non-traditional adult students in order to serve the needs of disadvantaged groups. This is a matter of social justice, equity, and ethics (cf. chapter 1). Committed to this goal, educational institutions must respond to the needs of an increasingly diverse student body. A prerequisite for being able to design appropriate student support systems (cf. chapter 11) is to be well informed about the multiple profiles, characteristics, and needs of this diverse student body.

Since the target groups will become more and more heterogeneous, a widespread research approach is needed to embrace their diverse needs. It is not only about new student groups like the non-traditional students mentioned, but also about how to implement lifelong learning in higher education and society itself. It remains challenging to describe exactly what if any distinctive characteristics can be generalized to all characteristics that define non-traditional students. This becomes even more difficult when considering internationally comparative perceptions (Wolter, 2012), particularly in order to compare various national proportions of non-traditional students. Regarding the definition of lifelong learners a widely accepted approach seems to be essential in order to enable international comparisons.

Other aspects that should be taken into account are the various educational qualifications, skills and competencies that lifelong learners bring to their studies. Therefore, the recognition and accreditation of prior learning and skills is an important pathway in widening access to higher education (cf. Conrad, 2011). The improvement of the quality, permeability, and effectiveness of systems of education and training is a key priority within the European Union's Copenhagen Declaration (2002), which advocates common principles for the recognition and accreditation of learning outcomes, especially for informal and non-formal learning. In response to this process a decision by the German Conference of Education Ministers (KMK, 2002; 2008) addressed the recognition of non-academic learning outcomes in higher education.

This decision laid the foundations for the accreditation of vocational learning outcomes by stipulating that "knowledge and skills acquired outside the higher education system can be accredited for a higher education program on the basis of a . . . level assessment when their content and level is equivalent to the part of the study program that is to be replaced." According to the KMK decision, a maximum of 50% of a higher education program can be replaced with knowledge and skills acquired elsewhere. However, in order to implement prior learning accreditation and recognition to improve permeability, it is very important to develop and apply validated instruments that comply with academic standards (Müskens, Tutschner, & Wittig, 2009).

Regarding the question about learning styles as a part of a distance learning research agenda, Coffield, Moseley, Hall, and Ecclestone (2004) highlight the following implications for rigorous research on that topic:

> [T]he research field of learning styles needs independent, critical, longi-
> tudinal and large-scale studies with experimental and control groups to
> test the claims for pedagogy made by the test developers. The investiga-
> tors need to be independent—that is, without any commitment to a
> particular approach—so that they can test, for instance, the magnitude
> of the impact made by the innovation, how long the purported gains
> last, and employ a research design which controls for the Hawthorne
> Effect. (p. 143)

A closer look at the relationship between motivation and the learning setting, whether online or on-campus, should also be addressed: "To be able
to reap the full benefits of distance education, it is important for educators
to match technology with the background and needs of the learners if education is to be effective" (Sankaran & Bui, 2001, "Conclusion", para. 5–6).

We also know that, increasingly, learners will be coming to distance education with experience and skills in using digital technologies. As we cau-
tioned earlier, however, we should not assume that all younger students are
fluent in the use of these technologies, particularly in using them for educational purposes. Research shows this not the case and that defining learner
characteristics based on generation is not helpful. Instead we need further
research that seeks to understand how learners are using digital technologies in different aspects of their lives and if and how academic and social
uses are related.

Current research discussed in this chapter supports the hypothesis that
in some ways traditional and non-traditional students are beginning to converge in terms of their expectations and needs regarding their study, and
that the old dichotomy of traditional/non-traditional students is no longer
valid (Maschwitz & Vajna, 2011). However in other ways the student body
is diverging. Students with diverse backgrounds, competencies, needs, and
expectations are today's and tomorrow's lifelong learners: "Should this
group stay within the focus of education politics—and this is the explicit
goal of the European education efforts—it will become necessary to develop

institutions of distance education" (Alheit, Rheinländer, & Wastermann, 2008, p. 599) and these distance education institutions must learn to cope with students from diverse backgrounds, expectations, and work habits.

REFERENCES

Adiseshiah, M. S. (1973). Lifelong education. In R. H. Dave & N. Stiermerling (Eds.), *Lifelong learning and the school.* Hamburg: UNESCO Institute for Education.

Ahmed, M. (1982). Editorial introduction: Putting into practice the perspective of lifelong recurrent learning. *International Review of Education, 28*(2), 133–41.

Alheit, P., Rheinländer, K., & Watermann, R. (2008). Zwischen Bildungsaufstieg und Karriere Studienperspektiven, nicht-traditioneller Studierender. *Zeitschrift für Erziehungswissenschaft, 11*(4), 577–606.

Allen, N. H. (2004). The University of Maryland University College: Institutional models and concepts of student support. In J. E. Brindley, C. Wälti, & O. Zawacki-Richter (Eds.), *Learner support in open, online and distance learning environments* (pp. 273–81). Oldenburg, Ger: Bibliotheks- und Informationssystem der Universität Oldenburg.

Amirault, R. J., & Visser, Y. L. (2010). The impact of e-learning programs on the internationalization of the university. New York: Nova Science Publishers.

Athabasca University. (2012a). Athabasca University at a glance. Retrieved from http://www2.athabascau.ca/aboutau/glance.php

Athabasca University. (2012b). Mission statement. Retrieved from http://www2.athabascau.ca/aboutau/mission.php

Bates, A. W., & Sangrà, A. (2011). Managing technology in higher education: Strategies for transforming teaching and learning. San Francisco: Jossey-Bass.

Bekebrede, G., Warmelink, H. J. G., & Mayer, I. S. (2011). Reviewing the need for gaming in education to accommodate the next generation. *Computers & Education, 57*(3), 1521–29.

Bélanger, P. (1994). The dialectics of lifelong educations. *International Review of Education, 20*(3–5), 353–81.

Bennett, S., Maton, K., & Kervin, L. (2008). The 'digital natives' debate: A critical review of the evidence. *British Journal of Educational Technology, 39*(5), 775–86.

Biner, P., Bink, M. L., Huffman, M. L., & Dean, R. S. (1995). Personality characteristics differentiating and predicting the achievement of televised-course students and traditional-course students. *The American Journal of Distance Education, 9*(2), 46–60.

Bullen, M., Morgan, T., & Qayyum, A. (2011). Digital learners in higher education: Generation is not the issue. *Canadian Journal of Learning Technology, 37*(1).

Cassidy, S. (2004). Learning Styles: An overview of theories, models, and measures. Educational Psychology, 24(4), 419–44. doi:10.1080/0144341042000228834

Cattell, H. E. P., & Mead, A. D. (2008). The sixteen personality factor questionnaire (16PF). In G. Boyle, G. Matthews, & H. D. Saklofske (Eds.), *The SAGE handbook of personality theory and assessment; Vol 2 Personality measurement and testing* (p. 135-78). Los Angeles, CA: Sage.

Chao, R., & Good, G. E. (2004). Nontraditional students' perspectives on college education: A qualitative study. *Journal of College Counseling, 7*(1), 5.

Coffield, F., Moseley, D., Hall, E., & Ecclestone, K. (2004). *Learning styles and pedagogy in post-16 learning: A systematic and critical review.* London, UK: Learning & Skills Research Centre, London. Retrieved from http://lerenleren.nu/bronnen/Learning%20styles%20oby%20Coffield%20e.a..pdf

Cohen, S. A., Hyman, S., Ashcroft, L., & Loveless, D. (1989). *Mastery learning versus learning styles versus metacognition: What do we tell the practitioners?* Paper presented at the annual meeting of the American Educational Research Association, San Francisco.

Conrad, D. (2011). The landscape of prior learning assessment: A sampling from a diverse field. *International Review of Research in Open and Distance Learning, 12*(1), 1-4.

Corrin, L., Lockyer, L., & Bennett, S. (2010). Technological diversity: An investigation of students' technology use in everyday life and academic study. *Learning, Media & Technology, 35*(4), 387-401.

Cropley, A. J. (Ed.). (1980). *Towards a system of lifelong education: Some practical considerations.* Hamburg, Oxford: UNESCO Institute for Education, Pergamon Press.

Curry, L. (1990). A critique of the research on learning styles. *Educational Leadership, 48*(2), 50-52, 54-56.

Daniel, J. (2005). Preface. In C. McIntosh (Ed.), *Lifelong learning and distance higher education.* Paris: Commonwealth of Learning, UNESCO Publishing.

Dave, R. H. (1976). *Foundations of lifelong education.* Hamburg, Oxford: UNESCO Institute for Education, Pergamon Press.

Declaration of the European Ministers of Vocational Education and Training, and the European Commission, convened in Copenhagen on 29 and 30 November 2002, on enhanced European cooperation in vocational education and training (The Copenhagen Declaration). Retrieved from ec.europa.eu/education/pdf/doc125_en.pdf

Dille, B., & Mezack, M. (1991). Identifying predictors of high risk among community college telecourse students. *The American Journal of Distance Education, 5*(1), 24-35.

Durr, R., Guglielmino, L. M., & Guglielmino, P. J. (1996). Self-directed learning readiness and occupational categories. *Human Resource Development Quarterly, 7*(4), 349-58. doi:10.1002/hrdq.3920070406

Eastmond, D. V. (1995). *Alone but together: Adult distance study through computer conferencing.* Cresskill, NJ: Hampton Press.

Ely, E. E. (1997). The non-traditional student. Paper presented at the 77th American Association of Community Colleges Annual Conference, Anaheim, CA.

Evans, T., Haughey, M., & Murphy, D. (2008). *International handbook of distance education.* Bingley, UK: Emerald.

FernUniversität in Hagen. (2012a). Zahlen und daten. Retrieved November 18, 2013 from http://www.fernuni-hagen.de/universitaet/profil/zahlen/index.shtml

FernUniversität in Hagen. (2012b). Studierende nach altersgruppen. Retrieved November 18, 2013 from http://www.fernuni-hagen.de/arbeiten/statistik/open_m/studstat/2010/20102_13_Alter.pdf

Fink, L. D. (2003). *Creating significant learning experiences: An integrated approach to designing college courses.* San Francisco: Jossey-Bass.

Fisher, M., King, J., & Tague, G. (2001). Development of a self-directed learning readiness scale for nursing education. *Nurse Education Today, 21,* 516–25.

Fleming, T. (2009). *Access and retention: Experiences of non-traditional learners in HE: A literature review. European Lifelong Learning Project 2008-10.* Retrieved Feb. 18, 2012, from http://e prints.nuim.ie/2427/

Foley, G. (2004). *Dimensions of adult learning: adult education and training in a global era.* New York: McGraw-Hill International.

Frenette, M., & Zeman, K. (2007). *Why are most university students women? Evidence based on academic performance, study habits and parental influences.* Ottawa: Statistics Canada.

Friesen, N. (2012). Critical theory and the mythology of learning with technology. In S. B. Fee & B. Belland (Eds.) *The role of criticism in understanding problem solving: Essays in memory of John C. Beland.* (pp. 69–86). New York: Springer. doi 10.1007/978-1-4614-3540-2_6

Garz, D. (2004). Studium als biographische Entwicklungschance [Academic studies as a chance of biographical development]. *Sozialer sinn: Zeitschrift für hermeneutische sozialforschung,* (3), 387–412.

Gelpi, E. (1984). Lifelong education: Opportunities and obstacles. *International Journal of Lifelong Education, 3*(2), 79–87.

Giere, U. (1994). Lifelong learners in the literature: A bibliographical survey. *International Review of Education, 40*(3–5), 383–93.

Gould, S. B., & Cross, K. P. (Eds.). (1972). *Explorations in non-traditional study.* The Jossey-Bass series in higher education (2. Aufl.). San Francisco: Jossey-Bass.

Grace, L., & Smith, P. (2001). Flexible delivery in the Australian vocational education and training sector: Barrier to success identified in cases studies of four adult learners. *Distance Education: An International Journal, 22*(2), 196–211.

Guri-Rosenblit, S. (n.d.). *Opening Up Access to Higher Education: Implications and Challenges. The Open University of Israel - Working paper series,* (11-2011). Retrieved from http://www.openu.ac.il/policy/download/maamar-11.pdf

Haddad, S. (1996). Adult education: The legislative and policy environment. Special section of the International Review of Education. *International Review of Education, 42*(1–3).

Hargittai, E. (2010). Digital na(t)ives? Variation in Internet skills and uses among members of the "Net Generation". *Sociological Inquiry, 80*(1), 92–113.

Harlow, J. E. (2006). *Social integration, motivational orientation, and self-regulated learning strategies of online versus face-to-face theological seminary biblical language students.* Greensboro, SC: University of South Carolina. Retrieved November 18, 2013 from http://libres.uncg.edu/ir/uncg/listing.aspx?id=952

Hochholdinger, S., Meister, D. M., & Schaper, N. (2008). Die bedeutung der lernmotivation für den lern- und transfererfolg betrieblichen e-learnings. *Zeitschrift für E-learning, Lernkultur und Bildungstechnologie, 3*(1), 8–18.

Holmberg, B. (1987). The development of distance education research. *American Journal of Distance Education, 1*(3), 16–23.

Horn, L. J., & Carroll, C. D. (1996). *Nontraditional undergraduates: Trends in enrollment from 1986 to 1992 and persistence and attainment among 1989-90 beginning postsecondary students. Postsecondary education descriptive analysis reports.* Statistical analysis report. Washington DC: National Centre for Education Statistics.

Howe, N., & Strauss, W. (2000). *Millennials rising: The next great generation.* New York: Random House.

Husén, T. (1974). *The learning society.* London, UK: Methuen.

Isserstedt, W., Middendorf, E., Kandulla, M., Borchert, L., and Leszczensky, M.(2010). *The economic and social conditions of student life in the Federal Republic of Germany in 2009. 19th social survey of the Deutsche studentenwerk conducted by his hochschul-informations-system – selected results.* Berlin: Federal Ministry of Education and Research.

Jackson, C. J. (2009). Using the hybrid model of learning in personality to predict performance in the workplace. In *Proceedings of 8th IOP Conference,* (pp. 75–79), Sydney, Australia. Retrieved from http://www.allworthjuniper.com.au/8th_IOP_Conference_Proceedings.pdf#page=76

Johnston, R., Merrill, B., Correia, A. M. R., Sarmento, A., Kanervo, K., CREA, Lönnheden, C., Bron, A., Alheit, P., Henze, A., & Greer, P. (2002). *Enriching higher education: learning and teaching with non-traditional adult students (LIHE-Learning in HE: Improving practice for non-traditional adult students).* Coventry, UK: University of Warwick.

Jones, C., & Cross, S. (2009). Is there a net generation coming to university? In *Proceedings of ALT-C 2009 "In dreams begins responsibility": Choice, evidence and change,* 8–10 September 2009, Manchester, UK.

Kallen, D., & Bengtsson, J. (1973). *Recurrent education: A strategy for lifelong learning.* Washington, DC: OECD. Retrieved March 5, 2012 from http://www.eric.ed.gov/ERICWebPortal/contentdelivery/servlet/ERICServlet?accno=ED083365

Ke, F. (2010). Examining online teaching, cognitive, and social presence for adult students. *Computers & Education, 55*(2), 808–20.

Kember, D. (1995). *Open learning courses for adults.* Englewood Cliffs, NJ: Educational Technology Publications.

Kemp, W. C. (2002). Persistence of adult learners in distance education. *American Journal of Distance Education, 16*(2), 65–81.

Kennedy, G., Dalgarnot, B., Bennett, S., Gray, K., Waycott, J., Judd, T., Bishop, A., Maton, K., Krause, K., & Chang, R. (2009). *Educating the net generation: A handbook of findings for practice and policy.* Melbourne, AU: University of Melbourne.

Kennedy, G., Dalgarnot, B., Gray, K., Judd, T., Waycott, J., Bennett, S., Maton, K., Krause, K., Bishop, A. , Chang, R., & Churchward, R. (2007). *The net generation are not big users of Web 2.0 technologies: Preliminary findings.* Paper presented at the ASCILITE conference, Singapore.

Kerres, M., & Lahne, M. (2009). Chancen von e-learning als beitrag zur umsetzung einer lifelong-learning-perspektive an hochschulen. In N. Apostolopoulos, H. Hoffmann, V. Mansmann, & A. Schwill (Eds.), *E-Learning 200: Lernen im digitalen Zeitalter* (p. 347–57). Münster, GER: Waxmann.

Kirkup, G., & von Prümmer, C. (1990). Support and connectedness: The needs of women distance education students. *Journal of Distance Education, 5*(2), 9–31.

KMK. (2002). *Anrechnung von außerhalb des Hochschulwesens erworbenen Kenntnissen und Fähigkeiten auf ein Hochschulstudium (I).* Bonn: KMK - Kultusministerkonferenz [The Standing Conference of the Ministers of Education and Cultural Affairs of the Länder in the Federal Republic of Germany].

KMK. (2008). *Anrechnung von außerhalb des Hochschulwesens erworbenen Kenntnissen und Fähigkeiten auf ein Hochschulstudium (II).* Bon: KMK - Kultusministerkonferenz [The Standing Conference of the Ministers of Education and Cultural Affairs of the Länder in the Federal Republic of Germany].

Knapp, L. G., Kelly-Reid, J. E., & Ginder, S. A. (2011). *Enrollment in postsecondary institutions, fall 2009: Graduation rates, 2003 & 2006 cohorts, and financial statistics, fiscal year 2009.* Washington, DC: National Centre for Education Statistics.

Knoll, J. (1974). *Lebenslanges lernen.* Hamburg: UNESCO Institute for Education.

Köhler, T., & Gapski, J. (1997). *Studentische lebenswelt: Analyzen zum Alltag und Milieu, zu Bildungs- und Studienstilen, zur Lebensphase Studium bei Studierenden der Universität Hannover.* Hannover: Agis.

Koivista, M., & Jokinen, L. (Eds.). (2007). *PRILHE: Promoting reflective independent learning in HE: Student handbook: Becoming a more critical, autonomous, reflective learner.* Coventry, UK: University of Warwick.

Lauzon, A. (2000). Distance education and diversity: Are they compatible? *American Journal of Distance Education, 14*(2), 61–70.

Lengrand, P. (1970). *An introduction to lifelong education.* Paris: UNESCO.

MacKenzie, N., Postgate, R., & Scupham, J. (1975). *Open learning systems and problems in post-secondary education.* Paris: UNESCO.

Margaryan, A., Littlejohn, A. & Vojt, G. (2011). Are digital natives a myth or reality? University students' use of digital technologies. *Computers & Education, 56*(2), 429–40.

Maschwitz, A., & Vajna, C. (2011). Berufstätige Studierende – Studierende Berufstätige. Veränderte Studierendenpräferenzen und Öffnung der Hochschulen für neue Zielgruppen. *Tagungsband zur Jahrestagung 2010 der DGWF* (272–281). Bielefeld: Deutsche Gesellschaft für wissenschaftliche Weiterbildung und Fernstudium e.V. (DGWF).

Mason, R. (1998). *Globalising education: Trends and applications.* London: Routledge.

Massa, L. J., & Mayer, R. E. (2006). Testing the ATI hypothesis: Should multimedia instruction accommodate verbalizer-visualizer cognitive style? *Learning and Individual Differences, 16*(4), 321–35

McBurnie, G., & Ziguras, C. (2007). *Transnational education: Issues and trends in offshore higher education.* Milton Park, NY: Routledge.

McCrae, R. R., & Costa, P. T. (1987). Validation of the five-factor model of personality across instruments and observers. *Journal of Personality and Social Psychology, 52*(1), 81–90.

McCrae, R. R., & Costa Jr., P. T. (1997). Personality trait structure as a human universal. *American Psychologist, 52*(5), 509–16.

McCrae, R. R., & Terracciano, A. (2005). Universal features of personality traits from the observer's perspective: Data from 50 cultures. *Journal of Personality and Social Psychology, 88*(3), 547–561. doi:10.1037/0022-3514.88.3.547

Morrison, G. R., Ross, S. M., & Kemp, J. E. (2007). *Designing effective instruction.* Hoboken, NJ: Wiley.

Motteram, G., & Forrester, G. (2005). Becoming an online distance learner: What can be learned from students' experiences of induction to distance programs? *Distance Education, 26*(3), 281–98.

Müskens, W., Tutschner, R., & Wittig, W. (2009). Improving permeability through equivalence checks: An example from mechanical engineering in Germany. In R. Tutschner, W. Wittig, & J. Rami (Eds.), *Accreditation of vocational learning outcomes: European approaches to enhance permeability between vocational and higher education* (pp. 10–33). Bonn: Nationale Agentur Bildung für Europa beim Bundesinstitut für Berufsbildung (NA beim BIBB).

Oblinger, D. G., & Oblinger, J. L. (2005). *Educating the net generation.* Boulder, CO: Educause.

OECD. (2010). *Education at a glance.* Paris: OECD Publications.

Offir, B., Bezalel, R., & Barth, I. (2007). Introverts, extroverts, and achievement in a distance learning environment. *American Journal of Distance Education, 21*(1), 3–19.

Open University. (2012a). *Facts and figures 2009/2010.* Retrieved January 16, 2012 from http://www.open.ac.uk/about/documents/about-facts-figures-0910.pdf

Open University. (2012b). *The OU's mission.* Retrieved January 17, 2012 from http://www8.open.ac.uk/about/main/the-ou-explained/the-ous-mission

Orr, D., Gwosć, C., & Netz, N. (2011). *Social and economic conditions of student life in Europe. Synopsis of indicators. Final report. Eurostudent IV 2008–2011.* Bielefeld, Ger.: W. Bertelsmann Verlag.

Orr, D., Schnitzer, K., & Frackmann, E. (2008). *Social and economic conditions of student life in Europe: Synopsis of indicators, Final report. Eurostudent III 2005-2008.* (HIS, Ed.). Bielefeld, Ger.: Bertelsmann, W. Verlag.

Palfrey, J., & Gasser, U. (2008). B*orn digital: Understanding the first generation of digital natives.* New York: Basic Books.

Pedró, F. (2009). *New millennium learners in higher education: Evidence and policy implications.* Paris: OECD-CERI.

Peters, O. (2008). The contribution of open and distance education to lifelong learning. In P. Jarvis (Ed.), *The Routledge international handbook of lifelong learning* (pp. 223-237). Milton Park, NY: Routledge.

Pratt, D. D. (1988). Andragogy as a Relational Construct. *Adult Education Quarterly, 38*(3). 160-172.

Prensky, M. (2001a). Digital natives, digital immigrant, part I: Do they really think differently? *On the Horizon, 9*(6).

Prensky, M. (2001b). Digital natives, digital immigrants, part II: The scientific evidence behind the digital native's thinking changes, and the evidence that digital native-style learning works! *On the Horizon, 9*(6).

Prensky, M. (2005). Listen to the Natives. *Educational Leadership, 63*(4), 8-13.

Qureshi, E., Morton, L. L., & Antosz, E. (2002). An interesting profile: University students who take distance education courses show weaker motivation than on-campus students. *Online Journal of Distance Learning Administration, 5*(4). Retrieved April 25, 2012 from http://www.westga.edu/~distance/ojdla/winter54/Quershi54.htm

RANLHE. (2009). European lifelong learning project 2008-10: Access and retention: Experiences of non-traditional learners in HE. *An overview of national statistics on retention and withdrawal.* Retrieved February 19, 2014 from http://www.dsw.edu.pl/fileadmin/www-ranlhe/files/national_stat.pdf

Reeves, T., & Oh, E. (2007). Generational differences. In J. M. Spector, M. D. Merrill, J. van Merrienboer, & M. P. Driscoll (Eds.), *Handbook of research on educational communications and technology,* (pp. 295-303).

Richardson, J. C., & Newby, T. (2006). The role of students' cognitive engagement in online learning. *American Journal of Distance Education, 20*(1), 23-37.

Richardson, J. T. E. (2000). *Researching student learning: Approaches to studying in campus-based and distance education.* Maidenhead, UK: Open University Press.

Riener, C., & Willingham, D. (2010). The myth of learning styles. *Change: The Magazine of Higher Learning, 42*(5), 32-35.

Romero, M., Guitert, M., Bullen, M., & Morgan, T. (2011, September 30). Learning in digital: an approach to digital learners in the UOC scenario. *European Journal of Open & Distance Learning.* Retrieved November 18, 2013 from http://www.eurodl.org/index.php?article=440

Samarawickrema, G. R. (2005). Determinants of student readiness for flexible learning: Some preliminary findings. *Distance Education, 26*(1), 49-66.

Sankaran, S. R., & Bui, T. (2001). Impact of learning strategies and motivation on performance: A study in web-based instruction. *Journal of Instructional Psychology, 28*(3), 191–98.

Schuetze, H. G., & Slowey, M. (2002). Participation and exclusion: A comparative analysis of non-traditional students and lifelong learners in higher education. *Higher Education, 44*(3-4), 309–27.

Schuetze H. & M. Slowey (Eds.). (2012). *Global perspectives on higher education and lifelong learners*. Oxon, UK: Routledge Chapman & Hall.

Seely-Brown, J. (2002). Growing up digital. *USDLA Journal, 16*(2).

Selwyn, N. (2009). The digital native: Myth and reality. *Aslib Proceedings: New Information Perspectives, 61*(4), 364–379.

Simonis, G., & Walter, T. (Eds.). (2006). *Lernort Universität: Umbruch durch internationalisierung und multimedia*. Wiesbaden, Ger.: Verlag für Sozialwissenschaften.

Simonson, M., Schlosser, C., & Orellana, A. (2011). Distance education research: A review of the literature. *Journal of Computing in Higher Education, 23*(2-3), 124–142.

Souder, W. E. (1994). The effectiveness of traditional vs. satellite delivery in three management of technology master's degree programs. *The American Journal of Distance Education, 7*(1), 37–53.

Stuart, M. (2006). 'My friends made all the difference': Getting into and succeeding at university for first-generation entrants. *Journal of Access, Policy and Practice, 3*(2), 162–184.

Suchodolski, B. (1976). Lifelong education: Some philosophical aspects. In R. H. Dave (Ed.), *Foundations of lifelong education*. Oxford, UK: UNESCO Institute for Education/Pergamon.

Tait, A. (2008). What are open universities for? *Open Learning, 23*(2), 85–93.

Tait, A. (1999). The convergence of distance and conventional education. In R. Mills & A. Tait (Eds.), *The convergence of distance and conventional education: Patterns of flexibility for the individual learner* (pp. 141–148). London: Routledge.

Tapscott, D. (1997). *Growing up digital: The rise of the net generation*. New York: McGraw-Hill.

Tapscott, D. (1998). *Growing up digital: The rise of the net generation*. Toronto: McGraw-Hill.

Tapscott, D. (2009). *Grown up digital: How the net generation is changing our world*. Toronto: McGraw-Hill.

Teichler, U., & Wolter, A. (2004). *Studierchancen und Studienangebote für Studierende außerhalb des Mainstreams in Deutschland: Eine Bestandsaufnahme anlässlich der Diskussion über die Zukunft der HWP. (Vizepräsident für Lehre, Studium, Prüfungen und Weiterbildung, Ed.). HWP – Hamburg Universität für Wirtschaft und Politik*. Retrieved Feb. 14, 2012, from http://www.wiso.uni-hamburg.de/fileadmin/sozialoekonomie/fachbereich/Forschung/GutachtenWolterTeichler_01.pdf

Thompson, M. M. (1998). Distance learners in higher education. In C. C. Gibson (Ed.), *Distance learners in higher education* (pp. 9–24). Madison, WI: Atwood.

Tuijnman, A., & Boström, A.-K. (2002). Changing notions of lifelong education and lifelong learning. *International Review of Education, 48*(1–2), 93–110.

van den Beemt, A., Akkerman, S., & Simons, P. R. (2010). Pathways in interactive media practices among youth. *Learning, Media & Technology, 35*(4), 419–434.

von Prümmer, C. (1997). *Frauen im Fernstudium: Bildungsaufstieg für Töchter aus Arbeiterfamilien.* Frankfurt: Campus Verlag.

von Prümmer, C. (2000). *Women and distance education: Challenges and opportunities.* London: RoutledgeFalmer.

von Prümmer, C. (2012). "Das ist die einzige Möglichkeit für mich überhaupt zu studieren..." Eine Untersuchung zur Situation von Studentinnen und Studenten im Fernstudium. *Befragung der Drittsemester im WS 2010/2011.* Hagen, Germany: FernUniversität.

Wallace, G. W. (2011, November). *Wisdom from this crowd. Why is the research on learning styles still being dismissed by some learning leaders and practitioners?* Retrieved April 18, 2012, from http://elearnmag.acm.org/archive.cfm?aid=2070611

Wedemeyer, C. A. (1981). *Learning at the back door: Reflections on non-traditional learning in the lifespan.* Madison, WI: University of Wisconsin Press.

Wilkesmann, U., Virgillito, A., Bröcker, T., & Knopp, L. (2012). Abweichungen vom Bild der Normalstudierenden – was erwarten Studierende? In M. Kerres, A. Hanft, U. Wilkesmann, & K. Wolff-Bendik (Eds.), *Studium 2020 Positionen und perspektiven zum lebenslangen lernen an hochschulen* (pp. 59–82). Münster, Ger.: Waxmann.

Willis, B. (1994). *Distance education: Strategies and tools.* Englewood Cliffs, NJ: Educational Technology Publications.

Wlodkowski, R. J. (2008). *Enhancing adult motivation to learn: A comprehensive guide for teaching all adults.* Hoboken, NJ: John Wiley.

Wolter, A. (2012). From individual talent to institutional permeability: Changing policies for non-traditional access routes in German higher education. In H. Schuetze & M. Slowey (Eds.), *Global perspectives on higher education and lifelong learners* (S. 280). Oxford, UK: Routledge Chapman & Hall.

Zawacki-Richter, O., Bäcker, E. M., & Bartmann, S. (2010). *Lernen in beweglichen Horizonten...: Internationalisierung und interkulturelle Aspekte des E-Learning. Handbuch E-Learning,* (32. Ergänzungslieferung), 1–20.

Zawacki-Richter, O., Bäcker, E. M., & Vogt, S. (2009). Review of distance education research (2000 to 2008): Analysis of research areas, methods, and authorship patterns. *International Review of Research in Open and Distance Learning, 10*(6), 21–50.

Student Dropout: The Elephant in the Room

17

Alan Woodley and
Ormond Simpson

This chapter is a little different from other chapters in this book. It is in the form of a dialogue between two educational researchers, both partly retired, who have between them spent more than 70 years in distance education. The chapter is not an academic treatise—it does not contain an argument supported by references. It is unashamedly polemical and reflects the authors' contention that there is an issue often (and indeed even scandalously) neglected in the hype about distance education: student dropout.

ORMOND SIMPSON:

Dear Alan,

When I joined the United Kingdom Open University (UKOU) in 1974 one of the first things I read was an excellent article by you about retention. Naïvely I thought that everyone shared your own view as to the importance of student retention in distance learning. It seemed so obvious that what happened to its students would be the ultimate test of an institution. But since then I've watched as retention became or remained the ultimate invisible elephant in the room, the statistic to which everyone gives lip service but apparently no serious thought.

Now the UKOU's graduation rate (the simplest measure of student retention) is 22%—only one in five of its new students ever end up with a degree from the UKOU. That compares with a graduation rate of 82% for full-time students and 39% for part-time students at UK universities (HEFCE, 2009. Note these rates are calculated over 11 years after entry in 1997).

And the UKOU is better than most. Where the data are available (and not surprisingly they're hard to find) the graduation rates in international distance education are often around 10% or less (Simpson, 2011a)—see figure 17.1. (Note that the London University International Program is in effect a mix of distance and face-to-face.)

Figure 17.1 Graduation rates at distance education and conventional institutions.

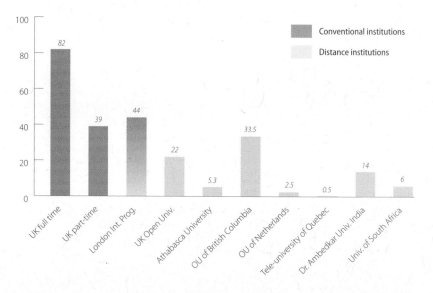

Now, these figures are disputable. They are derived from a variety of sources (see the reference), some may be unreliable, and they take no account of the way distance students can transfer to other institutions, decide that they only want an intermediate qualification and so on. Some institutions including those above may well have high transfer-out rates. On the other hand, we know that much dropout occurs very heavily in the first few weeks of a first module (up to 40% in the case of the UKOU), and the data suggests that such students do not return, so it seems unlikely that they later transfer elsewhere. There is also unsubstantiated evidence that other distance institutions also have low graduation rates (the University of Phoenix at 5%, the University of South Africa at 6%, and so on).

Clearly we need far more research into what happens to distance students. But for the moment it seems safe to assume that average graduation rates in distance education are lower than those in conventional education by a considerable fraction.

In addition where we have good historical data there are signs that graduation rates may be actually decreasing. The UKOU graduation rate has declined from around 59% in its first year to its current level of 22% (Simpson, 2011b)—see figure 17.2.

Figure 17.2 Cumulative UKOU graduation rates (%) by year of enrolment.

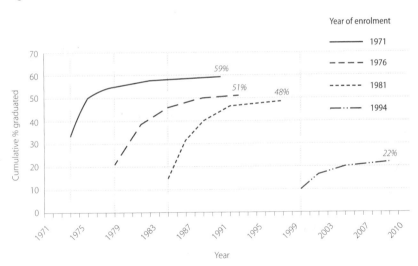

Since it can take up to 11 years for graduation figures to become more or less constant, it is difficult to establish the latest graduation data for any institution. However, in the case of the UKOU the number of graduates each year still appears to be decreasing (see figure 17.3) despite increasing enrolments.

Figure 17.3 UKOU degrees awarded annually.

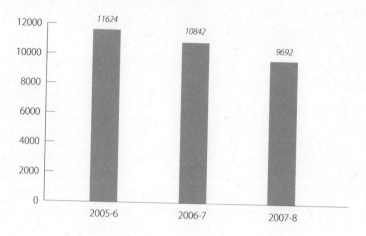

We cannot extrapolate from UKOU figures to other institutions. But if this is the case for an institution widely held to be an international cynosure of distance education, then other institutions' dropout rates may well follow similar trends. Why is this and do you think it can ever be changed?

ALAN WOODLEY:

Retention is indeed the elephant in the room that is distance education. You ask why is this and can it be changed?

In answer to your first question, I would suggest that few people care as long as the lights are off and the elephant behaves itself.

The paper that you mentioned had been written because somebody at the Open University had noticed that drop-out rates on higher level modules had been increasing year on year *(Editor's note: in UKOU parlance a module is a short—often one year—course of study that combines with other modules—up to ten or so—to form a degree course or program)*. On the basis of our research, Malcolm Parlett and I (Woodley & Parlett, 1983) advanced various reasons for this, but before we could publish, the trend was reversed (almost certainly due to the increase in fees, which seem to inspire increased effort and higher completion). Interest in the topic immediately diminished.

Can it be changed? Of course! In my book only death precludes intervention. All we need is an appreciation of the complexity of the phenomenon, recognition of cost-effective strategies, and the motivation to act.

To extend your metaphor, can/should we poke the elephant with a pointed stick?

ORMOND:

Thanks, Alan. Poking the education distance elephant with a sharp stick is not likely to be a career-enhancing move—as perhaps our careers illustrate.

But I take the point about the motivation to act. It seems to me that distance institutions have very little motivation to act on retention. They resemble the old correspondence colleges who made their money off the students who enrolled and then promptly dropped out, thus requiring no more costly services. As there was never a shortage of new students, this policy worked well—I think you pointed this out in your recent vividly entitled article "Plenty of Saps."

Part of the problem is that distance institutions don't seem to be required to publish their retention data. If they did, potential students might be charier of investing their money. After all, if you were going to buy a bus ticket and the driver said, "Morning sir, you do realize that there's only a 20% chance that this bus will reach its destination?" Would you get on board?

Instead, in the UK institutions rely on quoting from the National Student Survey in their publicity material. The UKOU always gets glowing reports from that survey. But of course the survey only goes to roughly 30% of students—those who are well on the way to graduation. Any bus company would get a good report if they were careful to only ask the passengers who arrived on time, despite the fact that such people were probably only a fraction of their passengers overall.

So what stick would you suggest for poking and what part of the elephant?

ALAN:

I think there might be a bit of a stick shortage! In an ideal world, of course, protest would arise among the consumers/students who have been failed by the system. Singly or collectively they would make their displeasure known to the institution and improvements would be made. This seems unlikely to happen for a number of reasons.

In my experience, students who withdraw ignore Dylan Thomas's plea and *do* "go gentle into that good night." They just fade away back into their safe havens. When provoked by surveys they blame themselves or their life circumstances. The University itself is usually singled out for praise, apart possibly from workload problems. It seems unlikely that they will even tell their friends not to partake.

There is a students' union that is massively subsidized by the University, has representatives on all committees, and all students belong to it. Why is the improvement of student retention not its key policy aim every year? Is it because the union representatives are usually battle-hardened successful students? Or have they too been beguiled by the University's public relations campaigns with its picturesque graduation ceremonies and case studies of former chip shop workers who are now professional design engineers?

ORMOND:

Alan, sadly I suspect you're right about the self-blame capacity of students who drop out. And, of course, the successful students can point to the high dropout rates and say, "Look, see how tough it is, and yet I succeeded."

But I suspect it's not just the students who are affected by that feeling but distance education staff as well. I think staff can have two approaches to students:

(1) "We're here to weed out the unfit—we're here to set the standards and if some students don't reach them then that's all to the good." I think of this as the Darwinista approach.

(2) "Students are doomed to pass or fail and there's not much we can do about it—we'll provide the highest quality learning experiences we can but it's up to the students to use them." I call this the Fatalista approach.

I'm not saying either attitude is completely wrong, but that they can be and often are carried too far. Yes, we have to set standards but that's not the same as weeding people out. And Fatalistas have to remember that the highest quality learning experience you can give students is *to pass their course.* Just talking about high-quality learning experiences may be to let ourselves off the hook.

I was at a conference recently where most of the speakers were talking about their new podcasts, video clips, podcasts, computer forum techniques, and so on. I tried to remind colleagues of Anderson's comment that most students drop out because of reduced motivation, and that the first thing students do when they are losing motivation is to stop visiting websites, watching podcasts, and so on. Concentrating on providing elegant teaching materials is like focussing on how to ice a cake, forgetting that you have to bake it first. Or, more pejoratively perhaps, visiting a battlefield site and offering the survivors manicures—half your combatant learners have already gone. And, by and large, lost learners do not speak—yet.

The hope is that students will be engaged and motivated by technology and stay on course as a result. But the evidence for that happening is still rather thin and it's relatively rare to find research that tries to find such evidence. For example, a recent study that I recently approved in refereeing tried to measure the retention effect of social networking in computer forums in a course and found no increase (Anon, 2012). And anyone who has spent any time on a computer will know that technology can have a deterrent effect as well.

So if we can't rely on students or staff to put pressure on about retention, is there anyone else? There is increasing competition in distance education from providers worldwide—the biggest growth in distance education at the moment is apparently from for-profit providers such as the University of Phoenix and many Asian for-profit universities, as well as corporate training arms such as the "Coca-Cola University," with sovereign providers such as China not far behind. Will any of them try to compete on the basis of increased retention for their students?

ALAN:

That might happen but I'm doubtful. For example I think that UKOU academics are not all that bothered about drop-out rates on the modules they produce because there are no real penalties attached and because they are too distant from the "coal-face" to see the human impact. By the time the modules are running, the academics are writing new courses and it is the tutors who have to pick up the pieces. I fear that this distance between students and course creators, a feature of many industrial model forms of distance education, may be an unfortunate bi-product of this model.

The majority of OU students don't graduate. Dropping out is the norm and the graduate is the "deviant." So researchers should be thinking of dropping out as normal behaviour. They should not be looking for personality flaws in the "failures."

As you know very well, we can predict a person's chance of OU study success with a fair degree of accuracy. So, should we tell a black 23-year-old with no educational qualifications that his chances of passing are virtually zero?

ORMOND:

Thanks, Alan. We should just explain the UKOU's *predicted probability of success* system briefly for people who've not come across it. Using a statistical binary regression analysis of previous students' success linked with their entry characteristics, such as previous education, gender, age and so on; we can attach a predicted probability of success to every new student entering the University. Figure 17.4 shows the number of students in each probability of success band for the approximately 50,000 students entering a few years ago and shows, for example, that around 3,000 students had between a 20 to 30% chance of completing their module that year (Simpson, 2006).

This prediction is surprisingly accurate (Simpson, 2006)—see figure 17.5. This predictive model is a simple example of the newish field of learning analytics—the collection of data about learners, partly in order to identify the conditions that might cause them to disengage before they actually do (Siemens, 2011). It's possible that such systems may enable tutors to intervene and reduce dropout, but given the fact that much dropout is *before* learners have fully engaged in the first place and that the level of intervention may need to be at a level that is unlikely to be fundable, I'm doubtful that it will make a difference. As Schum (2011) asks, (playing devil's advocate) "surely data analytics have nothing to say about intrinsic disposition to learn, emotional resilience in the face of adversity. . . . " We must see.

So returning to your question Alan—this is such a tricky ethical issue you've sneaked in! If we don't tell him, then we might be guilty at the least of letting him waste his time and money and simply adding to what might be a sense of on-going failure. On the other hand if we do tell him, will that demoralize him right from the outset so that prediction becomes self-fulfilling? After all, even if he's in the 10% probability of success band that still means he might be the one in ten who would have succeeded—if only we hadn't told him.

Figure 17.4 Predicted probability of success rates for new UKOU students.

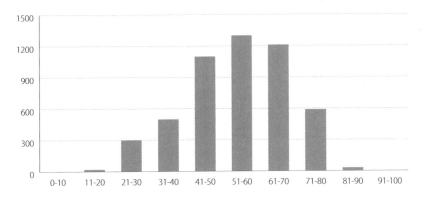

Figure 17.5 Predicted probability of success versus actual success rates.

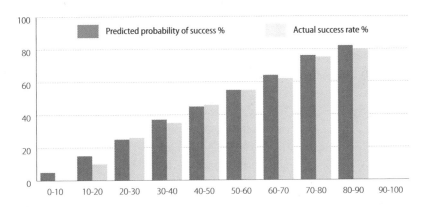

There may be a way out of this dilemma if, instead of telling him, we let him find out in such a way that enables him to change that probability. Let him take a self-assessed diagnostic test that tells him privately his chances of success, but also tells him how he could increase those chances—for example, by taking a different module, improving his entry qualifications, and so on. I'd have liked to experiment along those lines in the UKOU but never quite had the courage.

But this may be a straw elephant: a colleague of mine at the University of South Africa ran a small-scale experiment in which he did tell students their chances of success (Pretorius & Prinsloo, 2010). He found that retention actually improved in the group he told. This was too small a scale experiment to draw conclusions from but fascinating just the same. However we're getting off the topic a little. Tell me in one paragraph what your personal recipe for retention would be.

ALAN:

How would I reduce dropout?

(1) Make it harder to get in. Not through selection but with brutal honesty about what the students will be getting into and make them think carefully about it.

(2) Make it harder to get out. Don't let them drift off into the void.

ORMOND:

I think you've probably summed it up in two phrases! I might try to be a bit less than "brutal" about letting students in—I'd be wary of the danger of deterring potential students who would succeed but who lack the confidence to start. We all have stories of the truck driver with no qualifications that got a first in maths, the housewife who was told by her teachers that she'd never amount to anything who ended up with a master's in literature, and so on. So I think I might reword your suggestion to say we should be very much clearer about what students should expect in a module—after all the second most common reason UKOU students give for dropping out is that they were on the wrong module.

But again, you're right about making it harder to get out. Some years ago a UKOU colleague and I tried to work out just how many ways there were of "escaping" from the University. We came up with 14 exit points: failing to register on a module after an offer, dropping out without telling the University, formally withdrawing, failing to pay a fee on time, failing to attend a summer school, failing to accept a re-sit exam offer—the list went on and on. We tried to set up a response from the University to each point—we felt like the apocryphal little Dutch boy—with 14 fingers in the dike. We did have some very modest success with formal withdrawals where we did manage to retrieve around 4% of them—usually they had withdrawn because they'd misunderstood some aspect of the regulations or the University's quite unnecessarily complex assessment system.

ALAN:

Reasons for dropping out are many and various. So a single theory that attempts to explain all dropouts will be so general as to be vacuous. It will be like saying that death is caused by people stopping breathing!

ORMOND:

Well yes, we know that the reason students give for dropping out are often rationalizations, and that taking them seriously is often a great way of letting ourselves off the hook (again) as they are often things we could do nothing about—illness, job changes, and so on. Personally I think there's one overwhelming reason why students dropout—I go with Professor Edward Anderson's comment: "The best predictor of student retention is motivation. Retention services need to clarify and build on motivation and address motivation-reducing issues. Most students drop out because of reduced motivation." (Anderson, 2006)

But "being on the wrong module" occurs sufficiently often as a reason to be worth doing something about. We've experimented in the past with several ways of giving students course choice advice (Simpson, 2004). Three in particular I thought could be effective. These were:

- *Diagnostic quizzes.* These are most useful for maths, science, and technology-based modules.

- *Students' course reviews.* Students who have completed a module would post advice on the web for new students contemplating that module. Such user ratings are becoming very popular on social networks and may carry more weight with new students than the descriptions provided by the institution, which, owing to the increasing desperation of the marketing people to recruit, seem to become more of a hard sell every year. (For examples of student course reviews see http://www3.open.ac.uk/study/undergraduate/course/aa100.htm)

- *Taster packs.* These would provide samples of the module content and assessment material including student assignments with tutors comments and would be designed to give students a kind of test drive of a module. Or perhaps, even bolder, release the whole student package as an open educational resource, so that students are fully aware of the content, activities, and expectations of the unit.

It's very difficult to design experiments that assess if such materials actually help students make better course choices. And I remember getting criticized by some OU faculty for using taster packs, as they said seeing course materials would deter some students from registering. In fact we found students said they were actually more motivated to study the module when they could see more exactly what kind of challenge it would be. It's often fear of the unknown that's the greatest fear. But going back a bit when you said, "Make it harder to get out. Don't let them drift off into the void"—what did you have in mind?

ALAN:

If I had to advocate a single strategy to reduce dropout rate, I would phone up the students on a regular basis and ask them how they are doing.

ORMOND:

Again, I think you've hit the nail on the head very precisely. I'd include e-mailing students regularly as well, but in the end retention is mostly a function of *proactive* contact from institution to student. So much of the effort in institutions goes into *reactive* contact—waiting for students to contact the institution and ask for help. I'm reminded of another of Professor Edward Anderson's comments: "Student self-referral does not work as a mode of promoting persistence. Students who need services the most refer themselves the least. Effective retention services take the initiative in outreach and timely interventions with those students" (Anderson, 2006).

We even have evidence for your strategy in the UKOU's PaSS (Proactive Student Support) Project. In this project new students were divided into a control and experimental group so that both groups had identical average predicted probability of success. The experimental group then received a short (about 10 minutes long) pre-module phone call. The results showed a consistent 5% increase in retention at the end of the module (Gibbs, Regan, & Simpson, 2007)—see table 17.1.

Table 17.1 Results of the UKOU PaSS Project.

Year	Number of students in trial	Increase in retention of experimental group over control
2002	2,866	3.9%
2003	1,354	5.1%
2004	931	4.2%
2005	10,131	7.6%
Totals 2002–2004	5,151	5.04%

Five percent doesn't sound like very much, but it was rather more than any other project had achieved and it was the result of just one proactive intervention. Also, and very importantly, it was cost-effective—the cost of the intervention per student was less than increase in the government grant for module completion. That's worth exploring later.

We also used a learning motivational model for the content of the phone call. One of my contentions about distance learning is that it is sometimes too self-centred and doesn't look outside itself for useful research findings. I believe that there's interesting work being done by psychologists, such as Dweck, Seligman, Keller, and others, on what motivates students to learn that we can use. Our phone call used a melange of their approaches, which we called *proactive motivational support*, and I increasingly believe that the role of the teacher in distance education is less to teach and very much more to motivate students to learn (Simpson, 2008a).

There's other data about the retention effects of proactive contact using e-mail (Rekkedahl, 1982; Case and Elliot, 1997; Chyung, 2001; Visser, 1998), including some recent research by myself (2010), Twyford (2007), and Huett, Kalinowski, Moller, and Huett (2008)—see table 17.2.

It's possible that such proactive contact could be made by other media such as text messages, tweets, or Facebook notifications. The advantage of using texts in developing countries is the much wider access to mobile phones than the Internet. But Facebook, Twitter, and other schemes may have the same disadvantage as all Internet-based contact systems—the first thing a student does when they are becoming de-motivated is to stop visiting sites and following feeds. I suspect the same may be true for social networking—students using Facebook and other social networking sites to communicate, although I think you differ from me on this!

Table 17.2 Retention increases using proactive motivational support methods.

Study	Method	Finding
Rekkedahl (1982, Norway)	Postcards	46% increase in retention
Case & Elliot (1997, US)	Phone calls	15-20% increase in retention
Visser (1990, UK)	Postcards	27% increase in retention
Chyung (2001, US)	Phone calls	Dropout reduced from 44% to 22%
Mager (2003, US)	'Telecounselling'	5% increase in retention
Simpson (2006, UK)	Phone call before course starts	5.04%
Twyford (2007, Aus)	Motivational emails	11.7% increase over control
Huett (2008, US)	Motivational emails	23.4% increase over control
Simpson (2001, UK)	Phone calls plus motivational emails	18.9% increase over control

I wonder if you want to comment here about using other media as well—from text messages as they do in Africa to Tweets and Facebook notifications. We find that students rarely phone anymore and are even less likely to answer the phone.

I think your comment also illustrates another important point about retention: the need to focus very tightly on a very few cost-effective strategies rather than trying to do everything that might have some effect (I think of this as the "retention goulash" approach). As Veronique Johnston of Napier University writes, "Trying everything that works doesn't work" (Johnston, 2002).

We will both remember the UKOU's retention project, which we worked on some twelve years ago, that produced—was it?—38 recommendations. When we went back a few years later it was very hard to see if any of them had actually happened. I remember at a conference in Bogota a couple of years ago, Vincent Tinto—the doyen of full-time student retention—saying that in his extensive experience many retention projects had simply faded out after a few years (Tinto, 2009). It seems to me that without that clear focus on one or two retention strategies that's bound to happen.

Veronique's comment reminds me of a similar statement from Professor John Hattie from his famous meta-survey of teaching methods: "Almost everything works" (Hattie, 2008). The difficulty then is finding what works most cost-effectively. Because you don't have unlimited resources to spend on student retention, and if you spread it too thinly you're in danger of getting no effects at all. And of course if you're lucky enough to get a retention increase you have no idea which of your many initiatives had the most effect. So you don't find out what the cost-benefits of them were.

Talking of costs and benefits, what do you think of the recent changes in the UK on university funding? The UK government is withdrawing substantial amounts of direct university funding and developing a student loan scheme so students will pay much increased tuition fees.

ALAN:

The UKOU has probably stumbled on the best way to reduce dropout. As a result of the UK government's new fee policy, UKOU has announced a massive hike in fees (from around £500 for a 60-credit point module to £2500). Previous findings have shown that people will think twice about withdrawing when they have made a large financial commitment. However, the downside is that registrations will also drop!

ORMOND:

This feels like a massive enforced gamble on UKOU's part. It will be hoping that students will compare its fees of £5000 per year equivalent favourably with the £9000 per year that full-time students have to invest. But thinking back to our earlier discussion, UK full-time students have only a risk of 18% of losing that investment through dropping out, whereas UKOU part-time students face a nearly 80% risk of loss. A financial adviser who recommended that investment would be up before an ethics committee, wouldn't he? In fact investing in distance education is riskier than investing in wildcat oil well drilling, where there's generally only a 10% risk of losing your money!

ALAN:

Well maybe we should approach dropout from a different perspective. It's true that the majority of OU students don't graduate. So dropping out is the norm and the graduate is the "deviant." So researchers should be thinking of dropping out as normal behaviour. They should not be looking for personality flaws in the "failures."

ORMOND:

I like your concept of dropping out as normal behaviour! But that raises another issue that worries me about distance education's sanguine approach to student retention. Given that the main output of distance institutions is dropped-out students (up to 90% in some cases) what is the effect on those people of dropping out? There's some evidence from John Bynner of the University of London Institute of Education that dropping out of full-time higher education is bad for you (Bynner & Edgerton, 2001). As you can see, figure 17.6 shows the relative probability of experiencing depression, unemployment, and (for women) violence from partners, according to educational experience.

Students that drop out of full-time higher education appear to have a higher probability of negative effects than either successful completers (which might be expected) but also than people who never went to university in the first place. Now it could be argued that people drop out (for example) because they become depressed, rather than become depressed because they've dropped out. This is arguable, although it seems inherently more likely that people become depressed as a result of an action (dropping out) rather than spontaneously becoming depressed and then dropping out. And after all they were not too depressed to get into university in the first place. Professor Sir John Layard suggests that depression is the biggest health issue in the UK and costs the nation many millions of pounds in lost production and treatment. So if this data is in any way an accurate representation of the reality, then the subsequent cost to UK society of treating dropout-related depression and paying for unemployment must be in the billions of pounds.

Figure 17.6 Probability of suffering depression, unemployment, and (for women) partner violence according to educational experience (adapted from Bynner & Edgerton, 2001).

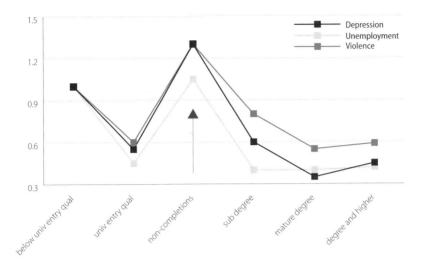

But does this apply in any way to distance education? Given that distance students are often studying part-time, are working or running a home, and are consequently less involved in their studies, can we hope that dropping out of distance education has much less serious effects than dropping out of full-time education. But do we know that? Has anyone researched this? Since dropout students are our main output, we really ought to know what effect we are having on them. At the least there should be a distance education version of the Hippocratic oath (which doctors still swear in some form) that we should do no harm.

My suspicion is that many distance education students are already partial casualties of our education systems and are studying to try to overcome the consequences of their previous education. So dropping out may actually add to their negative learning experiences and view of themselves. Of course as distance educators we are probably fortunate that dropout students tend to blame themselves rather than us. But if—as you suggest—students begin to pay considerably more for their courses will that attitude change? Might they demand a more secure investment return for their course fees? Let's hope so!

Now, so far you and I have talked almost exclusively about the role of student support as a way of reducing dropout. Your suggestion that supporting students by phoning them up is the best way to increase their retention I'm sure is absolutely right. I heard this put in its most succinct form when I was at an academic board meeting of the Open Polytechnic of New Zealand where there were some student representatives. One of them was asked what was the most important single thing that kept her going on her course. She immediately replied (imagine this in a Kiwi accent), "Well, if a tutor phones me, I love them already."

But there is another aspect to reducing dropout and that's the distance course itself. The way a distance education course is structured, its workload, its assessment strategies and its style of writing, must all affect its retention rate. I know you did some work on comparing courses for retention very early in the life of the UKOU—what were your conclusions then, and are they still relevant today?

ALAN:

In 1981 the highest dropout rate for a UKOU module was 71 percent and the lowest 17 percent, a range of 54 percent! (Woodley & Parlett, 1983). This variation was almost certainly related to the aspects of course design you mention. But these aspects are hard to quantify and all we were able to do was to look at certain more concrete course features. For example, we showed that dropout was higher on maths modules, on 30- (rather than 60-) credit point modules, on modules with no residential summer school, on modules with few students, and on modules that had been running for a number of years.

However, our conclusions were extremely cautious. It was not simply a case of recommending that new courses should avoid the negative features we had identified. It was debatable whether the relationships we had found were simply causal ones, what would be the knock-on effects of such changes, whether the relationship was strong enough to warrant action, and whether the UKOU could actually make these change.

When faced with a module with a high dropout rate, academics usually have a story about why it was a disaster. They are less good at identifying and implementing good design principles, and I would have to say that research has not helped them much. The pre-testing of new courses has been of limited value, and replacement versions of old courses tend to be different rather than demonstrably better.

ORMOND:

I believe that the variation in dropout rates between courses is still going on in the UKOU at least. Just a few years ago another UKOU colleague and I created a scattergram for modules where we plotted the percentage of students actually getting to the module final exam against the percentage passing the exam—see figure 17.7.

Figure 17.7 Variations in course module dropout rates as related to attending and passing exams.

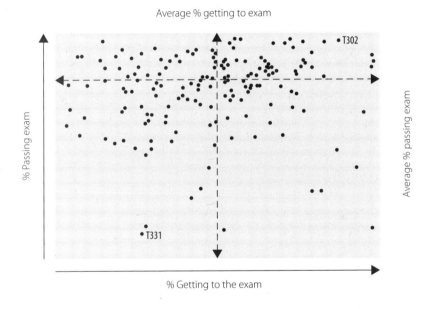

Average % getting to exam

% Getting to the exam

Each point represents a module and as you can see there are huge variations in both getting to the exam and passing the exam rates. The dotted crosshairs are at the average rates and divide the scattergram into four quadrants. The modules that concerned me most were the ones in the lower right quadrant—modules where a large number of students got to the exam but then failed it. This seemed to me to be breaking a contract we have with students: if they put in the work and pass the continuous assessment part of the module, they should have a good chance of passing the exam.

You can also see that following on from the variations in getting and passing rates, there are even larger variations in overall completion rates since they are the product of getting and passing rates. The highest course module at the top right-hand of the chart (T302) has an overall completion rate of more than 80% compared with the lowest at the bottom left (T331) which is in the region of 40%, despite, in this case, both modules being at the same level in the same faculty.

My colleague, a man of more courage than I, approached the course module team saying, "We notice that the success rates on your module are rather low compared with others in the same faculty. Can we help in some way?" To which the inevitable reply was, "No thanks. We know the rates are low, it's a difficult module." A truly Darwinista response.

But let me move on to a different topic. What about e-learning? Most of the articles I see in journals these days are about some aspect of e-learning, often about some novel way of presenting material. But I don't seem to see anything much that relates to increasing student retention. E-learning seems to me to be the classic case of the Fatalista approach to teaching: We'll put all our effort into doing lovely podcasts rather than doing what would actually increase retention—contacting students.

ALAN:

I am a bit more optimistic than you, Ormond. For one thing I was always a fan of student self-help groups and the ability of students in them to support and motivate each other. E-learning and especially the recent developments in social networking, such as the use of Facebook, means that these groups can be formed electronically and can operate across any distance. Also, e-learning can provide a great variety of study activities and break up the monotony of endless reading. However, just as with TV broadcasts in the early days, if these activities are not made integral to the course and assessable, then time-pressed students will omit them.

It is early days, but when I looked at the retention rates on UKOU courses that use e-learning they are very similar to those that do not. In fact, a good hypothesis in distance education seems to be that whatever you do, retention rates seem to stay much the same!

ORMOND:

That's a depressing thought! But in the absence of dedicated research efforts to change distance education retention rates I wonder if that's really true. I'm a Marxist in that context. As he said: "Philosophers have interpreted the world; the point, however, is to change it". Following that train of thought I suspect in the end it comes down to finance. I've been trying to follow the advice of Deep Throat in the Watergate saga, "Follow the Money." It seems to me that there is a fundamental misapprehension that retention is a pure cost to institutions. But in fact it's not difficult to show that spending money on retention can actually make an institutional profit if it's done properly (Simpson, 2008b). Maybe a wider acknowledgement of that fact would be the ultimate key to persuading distance educators that retention is not just important but the single most important concept in distance education?

ALAN:

I certainly think that it would be instructive to highlight just how much it costs to recruit each new OU student. Like you, I suspect that it is far more than the cost of retaining a current student. Apart from anything else, it seems that UKOU's strategy of throwing more and more marketing resources at the task of recruiting vast numbers of new students is unsustainable in the long run.

ORMOND:

Lastly, I wonder if there's an issue about distance education research itself. Am I getting more cantankerous or is the quality of the research I see sometimes not very good? There certainly have been recent criticisms of distance education research such as Zawacki-Richter, Bäcker, & Vogt (2009). But what I mean is that time and time again I see a report of some initiative—usually some novel e-learning software—that is then evaluated by a questionnaire that finds that students thought the initiative was helpful. The report then concludes that the initiative or software enhanced the student learning experience. Very seldom is there any acknowledgement that the questionnaire only went to the survivors of the initiative or any hard evidence of increased retention.

OK. I understand that educational research is not easy. Finding a way to emulate the medical research model, with its randomized controlled studies comparing experimental and control groups is particularly difficult. But it's not wholly impossible, there are some good examples and I think we need to demand more of researchers and reports.

ALAN:

If distance education institutions want to become a true *learning organization* then they have to become systematic in designing, implementing, and evaluating innovations in the general area of teaching and learning, and particularly with regard to retention. Previous attempts to improve retention have tended to be small local interventions that have been impossible to evaluate and have not been scaled up.

In the UKOU, for example, other large-scale changes to the student support system have been introduced across the board on little or no evidence. However difficult it might be, distance institutions should bite the bullet and go for the medical research model and randomized controlled studies. Only then can we decide which strategies are sustainable and worthwhile.

ORMOND:

I think we can clearly agree on that! And despite the fact that many of our examples are drawn from the UKOU I guess we can also agree that the elephant (distance education dropout) is still in the room of all distance institutions. And it needs to be shot. . . .

CONCLUSION: ALAN AND ORMOND

We hope that we have made ourselves sufficiently clear about the purpose of our chapter. As far as we are concerned, the issue of retention in distance education is not one out of a dozen interesting topics for academics to wrangle enjoyably over but the central issue that affects real live people—our students—and quite possibly negatively in a majority of cases. It should be at the heart of any activity and reportage on distance education. Much of the academic discourse in distance education feels peripheral. It's as if car manufacturers spent all their time arguing over the shape of their cars' interior mirrors whilst ignoring the fact that 80% of their production is unsafe at any speed.

As it is, retention is barely mentioned as an issue in the literature—as exemplified in the otherwise admirable article reviewing distance education research (Zawacki-Richter, Bäcker, & Vogt, 2009), where it only gets a passing mention in a sub-heading.

In any case, retention should not be a topic for dissection of the nine-and-sixty ways in which it might just be possible to effect slight changes in it. As with the global financial crisis, we know what has to be done—the interesting question is why we don't do it.

Future research needs to focus on institutional attitudes to retention—what the psychosocial and attitudinal barriers are to increasing retention, not so much amongst students but amongst distance education staff. It also needs to learn from the new developments outside distance education in learning psychology—in particular what motivates students to learn and what sustains their motivation.

There also needs to be research into the cost-benefits of retention and to examine Daniel's *iron triangle* of accessibility, quality, and cost, where he maintains that changes in any one of those sides usually changes the other sides in undesirable ways (Daniel, West, & Mackintosh, 2006). It may be that the reality is that there is a "plastic triangle" where investment into retention improves students' graduation rates, thereby increasing students' and governments' willingness to pay more, which can then be re-invested back into retention.

We accept that this is a radical message. But as it stands, we believe distance education is essentially dysfunctional—we need to make retention the main thing, and then to keep the main thing the main thing.

REFERENCES

Anderson, E. (2006). *Retention for rookies*. Paper presented at the National Conference on Student Retention, San Diego, California.

Anon. (2012). *Collaborative learning amongst distance learners of mathematics*. Unpublished manuscript.

Buckingham Schum, S. (2011). *Learning analytics: Dream, nightmare, or fairydust?* Keynote paper presented at Ascilite 2011, December 6, 2011, Wrest Point, Hobart,

Tasmania. Abstract retrieved from http://people.kmi.open.ac.uk/sbs/2011/12/
learning-analytics-ascilite2011-keynote/

Bynner, J., & Edgerton, M. (2001). *The wider benefits of higher education: Report by
the Institute of Education, University of London, sponsored by the HEFCE and the
Smith Institute*. Retrieved from http://www.hefce.ac.uk/pubs/hefce/2001/01_46.
htm

Case, P., & Elliot, B. (1997). Attrition and retention in distance learning programs,
problems, strategies, and solutions. *Open Praxis, 1*, 30–33.

Chyung, S. Y. (2001). Systematic and systemic approaches to reducing attrition rates in
online higher education. *American Journal of Distance Education, 15*(3), 36–49.

Daniel, J., West, P., & Mackintosh, W. (2006). eLearning in open learning: Sacred cow,
Trojan horse, scapegoat or Easter bunny? Retrieved from http://www.col.org/
resources/speeches/2006presentations/Pages/2006-12-11a.aspx

Gibbs, G., Regan, P., & Simpson, O. (2007). Improving student retention through
evidence based proactive systems at the Open University (UK). *Journal of College
Student Retention, 8*(3).

Hattie, J. (2008). *Visible learning: A synthesis of over 800 meta-analyses relating to
achievement*. Retrieved from http://www.visiblelearning.biz/uploadedfiles/asttle/
VisibleLearning1ov4.pdf

HEFCE (Higher Education Funding Council for England and Wales). (2009). *Part-time
first degree study: Entry and completion*. Retrieved from http://www.hefce.ac.uk/
pubs/year/2009/200918/

Huett, J., Kalinowski, K., Moller, L., & Huett, K. (2008). Improving the motivation and
retention of online students through the use of ARCS-based e-mails. *The American
Journal of Distance Education, 22*, 159–76.

Johnston, V. (2002). *What works in student retention*. Paper resented at the Holistic
Student Support, University of Central Lancashire, Preston, UK.

Johnston, V., & Simpson, O. (2006). Retentioneering higher education in the UK:
Attitudinal barriers to addressing student retention in universities. *Widening
Participation, 8*(3).

Powell, R. (2009). *Openness and dropout: A study of four open distance education
universities*. Retrieved from http://www.ou.nl/Docs/Campagnes/ICDE2009/
Papers/Final_paper_262powell.pdf

Pretorius, A., & Prinsloo, P. (2010). *Exploring the impact of raising students' risk
awareness in introductory microeconomics at an African open and distance
learning institution*. Unpublished manuscript, University of South Africa.

Rekkedahl, T. (1982). The dropout problem and what to do about it. In J. Daniel,
M. Stroud, & J. Thompson (Eds.). *Learning at a Distance—a world perspective*.
Edmonton, Athabasca University, International Council for Correspondence
Education

Schum, B. S. (2012) *Learning Analytics: Dream, Nightmare, or Fairydust?* Retrieved
from http://galaslearninganalytics.blogspot.co.uk/2012/03/la-dream-nightmare-
or-fairydust-s.html

Simpson, O. (2004). Student retention and the course choice process: The UK Open University experience. *Journal of Access Policy and Practice, 2*(1), 44–58.

Simpson, O. (2006). Predicting Student Success. *Open Learning, 21*(2), 125–138.

Simpson, O. (2008a). Motivating learners in open and distance learning: Do we need a new theory of learner support? *Open Learning, 23*(3).

Simpson, O. (2008b). Cost benefits of student retention policies and practices. In W. J. Bramble & S. K. Panda (Eds.), *Economics of distance and online learning: Theory, practice, and research.* New York: Routledge.

Simpson, O. (2011a). *Higher Education Funding Council for England and Wales.* Retrieved from http://www.hefce.ac.uk/pubs/hefce/2009/09_18/

Simpson, O. (2011b). *Open University Facts and Figures 2007/2008.* UK Open University.

Simpson, O. (2011c). *Distance Education: Are we failing our students?* Paper presented at the University of South Africa Festival of Teaching and Learning.

Tinto, V. (2009). *Main characteristics of student drop out trends.* Presentation at the International Forum on Student Retention in Higher Education, Bogota 17th-18th September 2009.

Twyford, K. (2007). *Student Retention in Distance Education using Online Communication.* Unpublished doctoral thesis submitted to the OTEN, Austria.

Venkiah, V., & Salawu, I. (2009). Student attrition in Dr. B. R. Ambedkar Open University. *Indian Journal of Open Learning, 18*(3), 139–148.

Visser, L. (1998). *The development of motivational communication in distance education support.* Unpublished doctoral thesis submitted to the University of Twente, Enschede, The Netherlands.

Woodley, A. (1995). A string of pearls?: A broader approach to course evaluation. In F. Lockwood (Ed.), *Open and distance learning today.* New York: Routledge.

Woodley, A. (2011). Browne sky thinking: Estimating the impact of proposed changes to the fees system on part-time higher education students. *Widening Participation and Lifelong Learning, 13*(1), 27–38.

Woodley, A. (2012). "Plenty of saps". In E. J. Burge, C. C. Gibson, & T. Gibson (Eds.), *Flexible pedagogy, flexible practice: Notes from the trenches of distance education* (pp. 299–312). Athabasca: AU Press.

Woodley, A., & Parlett, M. (1983). Student drop-out. *Teaching at a Distance, 24*, 2–23.

Woodley, A., & Simpson, O. (2001). Learning and earning: Measuring "rates of return" among mature graduates from part-time distance courses. *Higher Education Quarterly, 55*(1), 28–41.

Zawacki-Richter, O., Bäcker, E., & Vogt, S. (2009). Review of distance education research (2000 to 2008): Analysis of research areas, methods, and authorship patterns. *International Review of Research in Open and Distance Learning, 10*(6).

Conclusion: Towards a Research Agenda

Terry Anderson and
Olaf Zawacki-Richter

TOWARDS A RESEARCH AGENDA

We hope this book serves as a modest contribution to advance the research agenda of distance education. A primary goal of this volume is to inform a vibrant international research initiative and to solicit support and collaborative partnerships for undertaking research into online distance education. A secondary goal is to improve the efficiency and effectiveness of such research by providing a summary chapter for each of the major research domains, such that it is easier for us to see further when standing upon the shoulders of our many international colleagues who have published in this area.

We define the term *research agenda* as a collective effort designed by and for researchers so as to provide guidance, coherence, and support for the collective products of that research. In order to plan and direct research and evaluate its outcomes, a research agenda must be more than simply descriptive, it must also be prescriptive and visionary. In its simplest form, a prescriptive research agenda sets out a list of proposed research activities based on some rationale and illustrates the interrelationships between these component parts. Furthermore, a broad discipline research agenda must also be more than a prescriptive list of the research priorities of any one group, institution, or funding agency; it must address the discipline as a whole. Finally, the research agenda should create a chart that both directs and guides researchers (and potential funders), at the same time as it inspires and energizes them.

Thus, in our introduction, we outlined a framework of research areas for the whole field of distance education with three major strands of research at the system, institutional, and individual level (macro-, meso-, and micro-) covering 15 research areas. In contrast to often arbitrary selection and aggregation of research topics, our approach is built upon a validated framework that emerged from a Delphi study (Zawacki-Richter, 2009) and a classification of the work published in the major journals over the past decade (Zawacki-Richter, Bäcker, & Vogt, 2009). This structure helps us to organize knowledge in the field and to identify research gaps and opportunities.

With respect to the development of a research agenda for online distance education, we must address the biases inherent in such an enterprise. It must be emphasized that we do not mean bias in a negative sense, but only in the sense that we must acknowledge the disciplinary, methodological, institutional, and national interests at play in such an undertaking. These include that (online) distance education:

- is a discipline in its own right.

- may apply a broad social sciences-based research methodology, and although it is most appropriate, the field is eclectic and should allow for, and value, a multiplicity of research paradigms including positivist, interpretive, critical, and pragmatic research paradigms.

- is relevant to both distance learning and information and communication technology-mediated campus-based learning.

- despite the global context in which it is practiced, is deeply embedded in cultural, national ,and bureaucratic institutions that greatly impact its function.

- that enough issues remain unresolved as to warrant the creation of such a research agenda.

We also propose that a research agenda, in any given discipline, can be defined as an ongoing, iterative process consisting of six interdependent activities:

(1) Quantify what research has previously been done.

(2) Review and evaluate that research.

(3) Describe new research needs on the basis of the quantification and evaluation.

(4) Prioritize the research needs in a research agenda.

(5) Perform and evaluate the new research, and by doing so . . .

(6) Redefine the research agenda.

The authors of each chapter were challenged to complete the first three tasks. They were chosen because they have world-class qualifications and experience in the research domain that they have reviewed. It would perhaps be nice if we had the resources or even the mandate to prioritize and commission a new research agenda (as prescribed the fourth directive listed above), unfortunately, the disparate nature of online researchers and the divergent contexts in which educational research must operate preclude such a global research agenda at this time. It is our hope that individual researchers, institutional groups, and regional, national, and international agencies, associations, and networks will take up the challenge of drafting research agendas based upon the chapters in this book. And perhaps more importantly, we hope these organizations will fund, coordinate, and disseminate the results and then recursively generate new research agendas. This task is large, but the reward and benefits from improving the quality and quantity of research and ultimately the quality and quantity of online distance education warrants this effort.

One example is an initiative in Australia where a research consortium in Australia between the University of New England (UNE), Charles Sturt University (CSU), Central Queensland University (CQUniversity), the University of Southern Queensland (USQ), and Massey University in New Zealand was established funded by the Australian government—the Distance Education Hub (DEHub). In this project the universities developed a research program for 2011–2021 and the research themes were categorized using the main research levels (macro-, meso-, micro-) and the 15 research areas identified in the Delphi study (Zawacki-Richter, 2009), which are the foundation for the structure of research areas we used for this book as well.[1]

Maintaining a research agenda is an organic and ongoing activity. It can also be described as a continual feedback loop. The amount of activity and

---

1 http://wikieducator.org/DEHub/Research_Themes

continuous evolution of a research agenda is an index of the robustness and maturity of the discipline. It is important that a research agenda is embedded into a clear-cut framework of research areas that accurately describes the profile of the discipline. This book builds upon such a validated structure and a quantitative analysis of previous research published in major distance education journals with a ranking of the most often addressed issues and neglected research areas (see Introduction).

The invited international authors of this volume bring in their expert knowledge and professional experience to give an overview of the state of the art in each research area and derive research needs based on that. Our goal is not to present a general research agenda with ranked priorities for online distance education that can be regarded as universally valid in all contexts. As mentioned above, an individual scientist or scholar, an institution or research centre, a national or international research agency, initiative or consortium may pursue their own research plans and strategies and set their own priorities. We hope, however, that the proposed research framework with the associated research issues and open questions will be regarded as our common ground in the community of distance education researchers, scholars, and reflective practitioners. From this common knowledge, we are confident that more integrated and thus effective research and of course practice will emerge.

* * *

Those who cannot remember the past are condemned to repeat it.

George Santayana

It would be convenient if research in online distance education could be described and proscribed by a tightly fitting research agenda that clearly identifies all of the relevant variables and the best method to uncover the relationships among these variables.

As the readers have seen as they progress through the chapters in this volume, online distance learning is a field that attracts and demands researchers with different paradigmatic outlooks, from multiple discipline perspectives. As systems operating in a global context, researchers must also both support and encourage research filtered through multiple cultural lenses. Nonetheless, we hope that the chapters serve as an initial starting point for professional researchers, practitioners, academics, and graduate students who wish to help us unravel the challenges and unknowns while we collaboratively and continually create and recreate effective online learning systems. Finally, we hope this volume aids each reader and researcher in doing so from an informed and evidence-based perspective.

As experienced distance education researchers, we echo the words of many veteran distance educators and emphasize that online learning has much more in common with older forms of distance education than many of the recent e-learning zealots and evangelists give credit. A quick review of the titles of the 17 chapters in this book bares evidence that each has been a focus of study for distance education researchers over many years, yet at the same time each research domain is greatly influenced by the rapidly changing online learning culture and tools of net-based education. Given the way in which we chose the topics for investigation (their importance within the distance education research literature base, and the distinguished and long-term research records of the authors chosen to write these chapters), it is no surprise that all acknowledge the importance of this research heritage. Thus, online distance education shares roots and many of the characteristics of older distance education and yet it is also profoundly changed, as illustrated by long-time distance education researchers Terry Evans and Margaret Haughey whose chapter focusses on new learning theories—many of which were and could not have been invented prior to the Web. Online education is about pedagogical, technical, and institutional change, but it also retains a rich heritage that both cannot and should not be ignored.

Online learning is by definition a form of education that is always mediated and heavily influenced by the technologies that support its use. Thus, there is a degree of technological determination as aptly expressed by Marshall McLuhan's colleague John Culkin who summarized McLuhan's ideas on the mutual reciprocal interdependence between humans and technologies: "We shape our alphabet and thereafter our alphabets shape us" (Culkin, 1967, p. 42). However, in the context of online learning, Culkin's quote could as easily have been, "We shape our schools and then our schools shape us."

Formal education is profoundly influenced by the attitudes and past experiences of teachers, learners, and administrators—most of which were acquired in face-to-face classrooms. Thus, there is a great deal of model transference in which older activities are replicated using new means of production or communication. Thus, we saw that the first audio and video-conference modes of distance education from the late 1980s were designed to mimic the face-to-face classroom; researchers even created an *equivalency theory* to argue, "The more equivalent the learning experiences of distant learners are to those of local learners, the more equivalent will be the outcomes of the educational experiences for all learners" (Simonson, Schlosser, & Hanson, 1999). Twenty years later we see the ubiquitous integration of asynchronous text and voice, immersive online environments, and distributed Web 2.0 collaboration tools that provide levels of connectivity and learning opportunity that have never and perhaps can never exist in the classroom. To quote McLuhan yet again, "A new medium is never an addition to an old one, nor does it leave the old one in peace. It never ceases to oppress the older media until it finds new shapes and positions for them," or further, "the message of any medium is the change of scale or pace or pattern that it introduces into human affairs" (McLuhan, 1964, p. 23). Thus, we see that online learning shares a profound, yet an uncomfortable, lineage with distance education. For some an emphasis on the new and flash is critical to attract new funding and support, to others the rich heritage from its distance education routes provides the legitimacy and necessary theoretical and empirical research base needed for academic acceptance. We hope that the chapters in this book have served both appetites.

Online distance education can be considered as the natural extension of distance education into another medium. Such extensions have been common throughout the decades since distance education was first developed based on text-based correspondence models. Thus, online distance education is both a revolution and an evolution.

Ironically this evolution is turning back upon itself with the recent flurry of activity providing online courses for campus-based students; the many (current majority?) courses that are "blended" and thus attempt to match the affordances of information and communications technologies with the immediacy of face-to-face education and the millions of students enrolling in massive open online courses (MOOCs). This creates opportunities for campus-based researchers and practitioners to benefit from the multi-decade-long research undertaken in earlier modes and models of distance education. Conversely, this convergence, as well as the arrival of media-rich online contexts such as immersive environments and high fidelity video conferencing allows exploitation and application of results from the centuries of research undertaken in face-to-face classroom. Each will be the richer for the experience.

Corresponding to this dual nature, it follows that researchers can productively take the tools, procedures, methods, and paradigms associated with these earlier models of distance education and apply these same tools today—to create an evolutionary path. Alternatively, new net-based research models can be used as platforms for radically new models of teaching and learning. Recently, interesting MOOCs have been run in which the roles of teacher, student, and content interaction has been radically alerted to place the learners more clearly in command of their learning and the expression and activity of that learning (Fini, 2009). MOOCs offer profoundly different economic models with enrolments often rising into the hundreds or even thousands of students, with much of the traditional student–teacher interaction of online distance education courses being substituted with student initiated student–content and student–student interaction. These MOOCs may offer profoundly different economic models and increase access to education at unprecedented scale. Yet, despite the radical economics and designs of MOOCs, they too will have to face each of the macro-, meso-, and micro- issues overviewed in the chapters of this book. And though the solutions may be resolved differently, the issues remain.

Finally, our hope is that online distance education researchers in the coming years will use each of these chapters as a springboard for propelling their own work forward. The chapter authors have each highlighted issues that remain unsolved and challenges yet unmet, but at the same time they document the considerable progress and knowledge gained over the past 50 years of distance education research. Besides serving to inspire and propel research effort, we hope that researchers will use the chapters as convenient summaries of what has already been studied and in some cases resolved. There are many opportunities for research, but funds and time are always limited. Thus, it is our hope that this collection of research summaries helps improve the quality of research undertaken and decreases the time and effort required to produce meaningful and helpful results.

REFERENCES

Culkin, J. (1967). Each culture develops its own sense-ratio to meet the demands of its environment. In G. Stearn (Ed.), *McLuhan hot and cool* (pp. 49–57). New York: Dial Press.

Fini, A. (2009). The technological dimension of a Massive Open Online Coouse: The case of the CCK08 course tools. *International Review of Research in Open and Distance Learning, 10*(5), 1–26.

McLuhan, M. (1964). *Understanding media: The extensions of man.* Toronto: McGraw-Hill.

Simonson, M., Schlosser, C., & Hanson, D. (1999). Theory and distance education: A new discussion. *American Journal of Distance Education, 13*(1), 60–75.

Simonson, M., Schlosser, C., & Orellana, A. (2011). Distance education research: A review of the literature. *Journal of Computing in Higher Education,* (23), 124–42.

Zawacki-Richter, O. (2009). Research Areas in Distance education: A Delphi study. *The International Review of Research in Open and Distance Learning, 10*(3). Retrieved from http://www.irrodl.org/index.php/irrodl/article/view/674/126

Zawacki-Richter , O., Baecker, E., & Vogt, S. (2009). Review of distance education research (2000 to 2008): Analysis of research areas, methods and authorship patterns. *International Review of Research on Distance and Open Learning, 10*(6). Retrieved from http://www.irrodl.org/index.php/irrodl/article/view/741/1433

Contributors

Terry Anderson is Professor and researcher in the Technology Enhanced Knowledge Research Centre at Athabasca University—Canada's Open University. He has published widely in the area of distance education and educational technology and has co-authored or edited seven books and numerous papers. Terry is active in provincial, national, and international distance education associations and a regular presenter at professional conferences. He teaches educational technology courses in Athabasca University Masters and Doctorate of Distance Education programs. His research interests focus on interaction and social media in educational contexts. Terry is the director of CIDER, the Canadian Institute for Distance Education Research (http://cider.athabascau.ca), and the editor of the *International Review of Research on Distance and Open Learning* (IRRODL, http://www.irrodl.org). The complete text of his edited book *The Theory and Practice of Online Learning* (2nd edition) is available as an Open Access resource at http://www.aupress.ca/books/Terry_Anderson.php. This text was the winner of the 2009 Charles E. Wedemeyer Award for the outstanding book of 2008 awarded by the University Continuing Education Association. His homepage is at https://landing.athabascau.ca/pg/profile/terrya and his blog, *Virtual Canuck*, is accessible at terrya.edublogs.org.

Jane E. Brindley is a clinical psychologist who specializes in the development, delivery, and evaluation of support services for adult learners using alternate delivery modes. She is a course author and faculty member in an online Masters of Distance Education program and has worked as a consultant and trainer in distance education in Canada, England, New Zealand, Scandinavia, India, China, and South and Central America. She is author of numerous articles as well as *Researching Tutoring and Learner Support* (an open source research methods manual for practitioners), co-author of *Learning on the Information Highway: A Learner's Guide to the Technologies*, and lead editor and chapter author for *Learner Support in Open, Distance and Online Learning*. She lives in Vancouver, Canada.

Mark Bullen (http://www.markbullen.ca) is the Dean of the Learning & Teaching Centre at the British Columbia Institute of Technology (BCIT) in Vancouver, Canada. Before joining BCIT in 2005, Dr. Bullen was involved in managing, developing, and researching distance education at the University of British Columbia, where he held the positions of Director of the Centre for Managing & Planning E-Learning (MAPLE) and Associate and Acting Director of the Distance Education & Technology department. He leads the international research project Digital Learners in Higher Education (http://digitallearners.ca) and is the editor of *The Journal of Distance Education*. (http://www.jofde.ca). He has extensive international consulting experience related to e-learning, including work in Australia, Bhutan, Croatia, Indonesia, Korea, Malaysia, Mexico, Mongolia, and Taiwan. He is an adjunct Professor in the UBC Master of Educational Technology program, the Athabasca University Master Distance Education, and the Master in Informatics at the Universidad de Alcalá in Spain.

Katy Campbell was born and raised in Edmonton and received her PhD (1994) in Instructional Studies from the University of Alberta. She joined the Faculty of Extension in 1996, was appointed Dean in 2009, and facilitated the development of a new academic plan emphasizing university–community engagement and the scholarship of engagement. Working with narrative and autoethnography within a feminist, poststructural, theoretical framework Dr. Campbell examines the socially constructed nature of instructional design in higher education and, more recently, in cross-cultural settings. She is primarily interested in questions of cultural identity (especially gender), agency, and social change. Dr. Campbell has held offices in numerous scholarly, professional, and community organizations, including Canadian Network for Innovation in Education (CNIE), IMS Global Learning Consortium Learning Design Working Group, the University of Alberta's Employment and Equity Committee, Racism Free Edmonton, Edmonton Region Immigrant Employment Council, and Equal Voice (Alberta North).

Gráinne Conole is Professor of Learning Innovation and Director of the Beyond Distance Research Alliance at the University of Leicester. She was previously Professor of E-Learning in the Institute of Educational Technology at the Open University, UK. Her research interests include the use, integration, and evaluation of information and communication technologies and e-learning and the impact of technologies on organizational change. Two of her current areas of interest are how learning design can help in creating more engaging learning activities and on open educational resources research. She has extensive research, development, and project management experience across the educational and technical domains; funding sources have included the EU, HEFCE, ESRC, JISC, and commercial sponsors. She serves on and chairs a number of national and international advisory boards, steering groups, committees, and international conference programs. She has published and presented nearly 1000 conference proceedings, workshops, and articles.

Dianne Conrad, a practising adult and distance educator for over 30 years, is currently the Director of the Centre for Learning Accreditation (CLA) and the Director of the Bachelor of General Studies program at Canada's Athabasca University as well as an Adjunct Professor in AU's Centre for Distance Education. Her research interests span both the fields of prior learning and adult and distance education, with a special focus on language and communication in both areas. In 2003, she was awarded the Wedemeyer Award for Excellence in Research in distance education and more recently received the 2010 Canadian Association for Prior Learning Assessment (CAPLA) award for institutional excellence of practice.

Jon Dron is an Associate Professor in the School of Computing and Information Systems and member of the Technology Enhanced Knowledge Research Institute (TEKRI) at Athabasca University, Canada. He is also an Honorary Faculty Fellow in the Faculty of Education & Sport, University of Brighton, UK. Straddling the technology/education divide, his research interests broadly centre on social aspects of learning technologies, with a particular emphasis on discovering, designing, and employing methods and technologies to enable learners to help each other to learn. He is the author of the book *Control and Constraint in E-Learning: Choosing When to Choose*. He has been a keynote speaker at many international workshops and conferences, and is author of scores of papers in journals, books, and conference proceedings, several of which have received top paper awards at international conferences. He is a National Teaching Fellow of the UK Higher Education Academy.

Terry Evans is a Professor in the School of Education at Deakin University in Geelong, Australia. He is recognized internationally for his publications, research, and scholarship in open and distance education, and in doctoral education and policy. He is a member of 10 editorial boards of international journals and is the editor or co-editor of 14 books including: *International Handbook of Distance Education* (with M. Haughey and D. Murphy, Bingley, UK, Emerald Publishing); *Doctorates Downunder: Key to successful doctoral study in Australia and New Zealand* (2nd ed.) (with C. Denholm, Melbourne, ACER, 2012); *Supervising Doctorates Downunder: Keys to successful supervision in Australia and New Zealand* (with C. Denholm, Melbourne, ACER, 2007).

Charlotte Nirmalani (Lani) Gunawardena, is Regents' Professor of Distance Education and Instructional Technology in the Organizational Learning and Instructional Technology Program, at the University of New Mexico, USA. She received her doctorate and master's degree from the University of Kansas, USA, and her bachelor's degree from the University of Sri Lanka, Kelaniya. She has published and presented on distance education for over 20 years and currently researches e-learning design, e-mentoring, and the sociocultural context and social construction of knowledge in online learning communities. She has directed US Department of Education distance education evaluation projects, conducted research on corporate distance learning, and consulted internationally on distance education for the World Bank and the Asian Development Bank.

Sarah Guri-Rosenblit is the Dean of Technology and Development at the Open University of Israel and a member of the Higher Education Reform Experts (HERE) committee in the Israeli Council for Higher Education. She received her PhD from Stanford University in 1984 in education and political science. Her areas of expertise are focussed on comparative research of higher education systems, distance education, and e-learning. She published books and dozens of articles in these fields. She was selected in 2005/6 as one of the 30 New Century Scholars in the Fulbright Program on Higher Education in the 21st Century: Global Challenge and National Response.

From 2003 until 2009 she was a member of the Scientific Committee of Europe and North America in the UNESCO Forum of Higher Education, Research and Knowledge. She is currently a member of the Scientific Committee of Doctoral Studies at the E-Learn Centre of Universidad Oberta de Catalunya, and in expert evaluations panels of HESC (Higher Education and Social Change) under the auspices of the European Science Foundation and the Bellagio Conference Centre of the Rockefeller Foundation.

Margaret Haughey, former Vice-President, Academic, Athabasca University, Canada, has been involved in research and administration of distance education for many years. Previously she was a Professor and Associate Dean, Graduate Studies, University of Alberta, where she taught research methods and supervised over 40 doctoral students' dissertations in the Department of Educational Policy Studies. She has also been a long-time editor of *The Journal of Distance Education*. Her own research has focussed on designs for learning and organizational aspects of distance education provision in both the k–12 and postsecondary sectors. She has collaborated with Terry Evans on a number of initiatives including the Emerald publication, *International Handbook of Distance Education* (2008).

Margaret Hicks, Director, Learning and Teaching, University of South Australia. Professor Margaret Hicks is Director of the University of South Australia's Learning and Teaching Unit. Margaret has worked in higher education for over 20 years and her research interests include academic development in higher education, student learning in higher education, and preparing teachers for university teaching. She has led the University's approach to integrated staff and student service provision, and provided leadership in major initiatives such as the foundation to university teaching course (Teaching @ UniSA), the Graduate Certificate in Education (University Teaching), UniSA's approach to academic integrity and English language proficiency. She is currently co-sponsor of the University's implementation of its new Learning Management System. She has recently led a national ALTC project on Preparing Academics to Teach in Higher Education and is also a member of HERDSA and CADAD, having served on both of their executives.

Allan Jeong, an Associate Professor in Instructional Systems at Florida State University, teaches courses in instructional technology and distance education. His research focusses on methods and tools for visualizing, modelling, and sequentially analyzing socio-cognitive learning processes in technology-mediated environments. He developed the Discussion Analysis Tool to generate transitional state diagrams that reveal the most frequent action sequences exhibited by low- versus high-performing students. He also developed JMAP, a software program that: a) visually superimposes, aggregates, compares, and assesses students' causal diagrams in relation to the maps of an expert, another student, or the collective maps of two or more students; and b) sequentially analyzes the actions students exhibit while creating causal diagrams to determine which processes help to create more versus less accurate causal diagrams. His overall goal is to better understand how different variables change the learning process, and how the resulting process directly affects learning outcomes.

Colin Latchem was formerly Head of the Teaching Learning Group at Curtin University, Perth, Western Australia and President of the Open and Distance Learning Association of Australasia. Since retiring, he has been a visiting professor / researcher at Japan's National Institute of Multimedia Education, the Korea National Open University, the UK Open University's Institute of Educational Technology and Turkey's Anadolu University. He has consulted for such organizations as the Commonwealth Secretariat, Commonwealth of Learning and AusAID and been a keynote speaker at international conferences in Australia, Asia, the Middle East, the US and the Caribbean. He is Asia-Pacific Corresponding Editor of the *British Journal of Educational Technology* and a board member of other international journals. His most recent books are *Distance and Blended Learning in Asia* (Routledge) and *Quality Assurance and Accreditation in Distance Education and E-learning* (Routledge), co-authored with Professor Insung Jung of ICU, Tokyo, and *Quality Assurance Toolkit for Open and Distance Non-formal Education* (Commonwealth of Learning).

Jennifer O'Rourke has taken on many different roles in open and distance learning in academic, professional development and community learning contexts: these include instructional design, course authorship, administration, tutoring, and research. Her recent work with WHO, ILO and UNHCR involves developing appropriate learning resources for staff in challenging contexts with limited technology access in widely dispersed locations throughout the world. Research interests include the intersection of values, organizational dynamics, and provision of effective, responsive and accessible learning programs.

Ross Paul is an Adjunct Professor at the University of British Columbia. He spent almost 40 years in leadership positions in higher education, at Bishop's University and Dawson College in Québec, Athabasca University in Alberta, and Laurentian University and the University of Windsor in Ontario, notably as President of the latter two institutions. He is the author of two books, *Leadership Under Fire: The Challenging Role of the Canadian University President* (2011) and *Open Learning and Open Management: Leadership and Integrity in Distance Education* (1990). He has travelled extensively as a consultant and is a frequent contributor to books and journals on open learning and the management of higher education. He was named a member of the Order of Canada in 2010 and received the Queen's Diamond Jubilee Medal in 2012.

Christine von Prümmer holds degrees from Smith College/USA (B.A.), Konstanz University (M.A.) and Dortmund University (Ph.D). She was Senior Researcher and Head of the Evaluation Unit at the German FernUniversität, a single-mode distance teaching university. For 34 years—from 1978 until her retirement in 2011—her institutional research spanned a wide range of issues such as access and exclusion, choice of subject areas, use of technologies, learning styles and the evaluation of courses and curricula. Since the early 1980s, her research and writing have focussed on gender in distance education and gender issues in virtual, open, and distance learning environments and has done comparative research on the situation of women in distance education in Germany and Britain. She is coauthor of the seminal paper *Support and Connectedness. The Needs of Women Distance Education Students* (1990) and the author of *Women and Distance Education: Challenges and Opportunities* (2000). Currently she is analyzing the data of a large-scale survey on the situation of women and men studying at the FernUniversität which she conducted in 2011. She continues to work as a consultant on distance education research and on gender issues in ODL and e-learning.

Greville Rumble was educated in Ecuador, Switzerland and England and has bachelor's degrees in History and Art History, a research master's degree in de facto theories of government in seventeenth-century England, and a PhD in the costs and economics of distance education. He worked (1970–2001) at the Open University in the UK in a number of capacities including corporate planner, regional director, and Professor of Distance Education Management. Since the 1970s he has written and consulted widely on the management, planning, costs and financing of distance education projects at national, institutional, and departmental levels.

Farhad Saba is Professor Emeritus of Educational Technology at San Diego State University where he focussed his research and teaching on distance education. His current research, scholarly writing and consulting continue to be focussed on key theoretical concepts in the field and application of systems approach to developing the theoretical foundations of distance education. Saba received the Wedemeyer award for his contribution to the literature of distance education in 1987 and was inducted to the United States Distance Learning Association Hall of Fame in 2010. He has published extensively in scholarly journals and books and his consulting work includes major universities, and corporations as well as several state and federal agencies. He is the founder and editor of http://distance-educator. com/.

Richard A. Schwier is a Professor of Educational Technology and Design and Head of the Department of Curriculum Studies at the University of Saskatchewan, where he teaches graduate courses in learning theory and instructional design. He is the principal investigator in the Virtual Learning Communities Research Laboratory, which investigates the characteristics of non-formal and informal online learning communities. Dr. Schwier's other research interests include instructional design, authentic learning design and social change agency.

Ormond Simpson is a consultant in distance education, currently working for the UK Open University, and the London University International Programme where he is a visiting fellow. His most recent post was at the Open Polytechnic of New Zealand where he was visiting professor. Prior to that he worked at the UK Open University in student support and institutional research, and ran workshops and seminars in South Africa, Ghana, China, the West Indies, Colombia, Brazil, South Korea, The Gambia and Papua New Guinea. His distance education interests are in student support and retention, cost-benefits, ethical issues, learning motivation, e-learning and staff development. He has written two books *Supporting Students in Online Open and Distance Learning* and *Student Retention in Online Open and Distance Learning* as well as ten book chapters and more than thirty journal articles. He has a website www.ormondsimpson.com where some of his most recent work can be freely downloaded.

Joachim Stöter studied psychology with a focus in the areas of educational, legal and organizational psychology at the University of Osnabrück, Bremen and Vienna. From February 2008 until January 2011 he was a research assistant in the field of citizenship education at University of Oldenburg and from December 2009 to January 2011 at the University of Hannover. Joachim worked on various Comenius projects in the European lifelong learning programme (MIRACLE, VOICE, etc.). Since 2011 he is a research assistant and Ph. D. student in the field of educational technology in the Faculty of Education and Social Sciences at Oldenburg University. The main foci of his research are learner characteristics, student profiles and the integration of new media in educational settings.

Alan Tait is Pro-Vice Chancellor for Curriculum and Awards at the Open University UK and was formerly Dean of the Faculty of Education and Language Studies. He is Professor of Distance Education and Development and has a long record of professional practice, publication and the support of professional development in distance and e-learning. He is editor in chief of the *European Journal of Distance and E-Learning* (EURODL), was from 1989-1998 editor of *Open Learning*, was President of the European Distance and E-Learning Network (EDEN) from 2007–2010, and was Co-Director of the Cambridge International Conference on Open and Distance Learning and a senior member of St Edmunds College, University of Cambridge. In 2012 he was awarded an Honorary Doctorate by Moscow State University for Economics, Statistics and Informatics. He has worked widely in developing countries for international organisations such as UNESCO, the European Commission and the Commonwealth of Learning.

Alan Woodley worked for the British Open University for over forty years, carrying out research into topics such as retention, widening participation and graduate outcomes. He has now retired and devotes his time to his grandchildren and his garden. He finds these activities more productive but it is still difficult to get his voice heard!

Olaf Zawacki-Richter is Professor of Educational Technology at the University of Oldenburg (Germany), Faculty of Education and Social Sciences, Center for Lifelong Learning. Between 2008 and 2010 Dr. Zawacki-Richter hold a fixed term professorship in educational technology at the Fern University in Hagen, Germany's Open University. He is a member of the editorial board of the Canadian *International Review of Research in Open and Distance Learning* (IRRODL), the British journal *Open Learning,* the US-American *eLearn Magazine,* and the Australian journal *Distance Education.* Olaf served as invited keynote speaker, chair and reviewer at international conferences. He is a faculty member in the MBA in Educational Management at Oldenburg University and he is also teaching in the Online Master of Distance Education and E-Learning program, jointly offered by the University of Maryland University College (USA) and Oldenburg University.

Index

McGreal, Rory, 121
mentoring, 89, 95–96, 302–3
mobile learning (m-learning), 222–23, 393–94
mobile phones, 118
MOOCs. See massive open online courses
Mulder, Fred, 121
multiculturalism, 355–56
Multimedia Educational Resource for Learning and Online Teaching (MERLOT), 326

National Institute of Open Schooling, 318
neo-liberalism, 361–62
non-formal learning, 218, 223, 270–71
non-traditional students (NTS), 426–28

OERs. See open educational resources
online distance learning (ODL) (see also massive open online courses): benefits of felt by students, 209–11; demand for, 75–76; ideas for research on, 141–45; industrialized form of, 352–53; models for, 134–41; research into cost of, 206–8; suggestions for research into economics of, 208–11; and teaching models, 138–41
Online Journal of Distance Learning Administration (OJDLA), 188–89
Online Teaching Infrastructure Matrix, 177–78
OpenCourseWare (OCW), 185
open educational resources (OERs): adaptability of, 255; and collaboration, 121; cost of, 207; described, 184–85; development of, 225–26; and drop-out rate, 470; extent of, 17; implications of, 230–31; and interaction, 390–92; and quality assurance, 326–27; and reusable learning objects, 248; suggestions for further research on, 230–31
Open Educational Resource University (OERU), 226, 326, 391
Open Universiteit of the Netherlands, 185
open universities, 181, 422–23, 439–40, 446–47. See also specific universities
Open University (Japan), 325
Open University of China, 115, 312, 317
Open University of United Kingdom (OUUK): access policy, 46, 185, 208–9, 439; cost efficiency of, 204; drop-out rate at, 465–66, 476–78; graduation rate, 460–62; and learner support, 298–99; perceived

benefits of education at, 19, 209–10; professional development at, 280; profile of students at, 437–38; retention at, 463, 464, 470–73; revised model for, 133; success of, 423; tuition increase at, 473–74; in US, 117
OUUK. See Open University of United Kingdom

participatory evaluation, 51–54
partnerships, 120–22
path analysis, 415–16
pedagogical patterns, 225
pedagogical podcasting, 395
peer teaching, 250
peer-to-peer support, 301–3
Peer-to-Peer University, 226
Phoenix University, 117
pluralism, 356
podcasting, 395
privacy issues, 93
private-for-profit education, 50–51
professional development, 267–83; clarification of terms, 269–73; ideas for future research on, 283; impact on student outcomes, 281–82; importance of, 267–69; institutional support for, 275–77; lack of, at open universities, 181; overview, 21–23; survey of general research on, 273–75; types of, 279–81; understanding needs of faculty, 277–78

quality assurance, 311–35; assessment of, in online distance education, 328–29; cost of, 327–28; and dealing with pessimism about online education, 311–13; defined, 313–14; of distance education providers, 120, 121–22, 125; effect of culture on, 323–25; as factor of social justice, 55, 57–59, 65, 68–70; ideas for future research on, 334; of online courses, 274; of open educational resources, 326–27; outcomes approach to, 329–33; overview, 24–26; and professional development, 272; special challenges of online distance education, 316–18; standards for, 318–23, 334–35; standards for in face-to-face education, 314–16
quantitative content analysis (QCA), 404–8
Al-Quds Open University (QUO), 180–81

radio, 45
retention, 31–32, 463, 464, 470–73, 478–81
reusable learning objects (RLOs), 248

Second Life, 224, 367
self-pacing, 288
sequential analysis, 412–14
Skinner, B. F., 350
social contract, 56, 60, 66, 70
social environment, 92–96
social justice: and capabilities, 41–43; and
    e-learning, 363–64; factors involved in
    decision to implement, 44–45, 46–50;
    framework for audit on, 51–63; and growth
    of open universities, 422–23; guiding
    questions for audit on, 64–70; ideas for
    research on, 141–42; individual/societal
    concepts of, 39–44; and learner support,
    300; and measuring outcomes, 60–62;
    at open universities, 439–40, 446–47;
    overview, 10–12; participatory evaluation
    of, 51–54; review of policy on, 54–56, 66;
    strategies for, 56–60
social media, 221–22, 227, 257, 280–81, 391–94,
    471–72, 478
social network analysis (SNA), 408–11, 414
social networking, 280–81, 478
social presence, 93–94, 98, 416–17
software tools, 136–41, 143–44
Spaces for Knowledge Generation (SKG), 227
Spanish National University, 318
strategic planning, 182–85
structural equation modelling (SEM), 414–16,
    417
student course reviews, 469
sustainability, 55, 57, 59–60, 65, 69–70
systems dynamic method, 159, 160–63, 168
systems thinking, 352–53

Taylor, Frederick W., 350
teaching presence, 134–36, 359, 360–61
technology (see also specific technology),
    217–33: approaches for selecting, 258–59;
    approaches to innovation, 251–54;
    challenges in implementing, 228–30; cost
    of, 179, 202–3, 205, 206–8, 209, 258; current
    range of, 220–28; and definition of culture,
    84; design process of LMSs, 255–58; and
    digital divide, 117–18, 125; and digital

learners, 431–36; disruptive, 245–46, 247,
    260; and drop-out rates, 464–65, 471–72;
    effect on instructional design, 48, 223–27,
    356–57, 365–66; effect on research, 226–27;
    as focus of e-learning, 113, 115, 117, 133,
    430; as focus of professional development,
    267–68, 273–82; hard and soft, 241–43, 245,
    253–54; history of, 217–18, 220, 238–39,
    354–55; and history of interaction, 382–83,
    389–94; implications for, 230–31, 259–61;
    and instructional support, 227–28, 254;
    and learner support, 300–301, 302; and
    management, 179–80, 184; and mobile
    learning, 222–23; models for assessing,
    243–44; nature of evolutionary change
    in, 240–41; overview, 19–21; research
    studies into, 114, 116; selecting for learning
    resources, 247–51, 258–59; and social
    justice, 44–45, 67–68; and software
    tools, 136–41; suggestions for further
    research, 143–44, 228–32; and systems
    theories, 246–47; terminology of, 218–19;
    understanding the meaning of, 239–40;
    and virtual learning communities, 365–68;
    weaknesses of, 79, 312
technology-enhanced learning (TEL), 219
television, 117
Twitter, 227, 392, 393, 394

UKOU. See Open University of United
    Kingdom
UNESCO, 120, 121, 201
United Kingdom Open University. See Open
    University of United Kingdom (OUUK)
University of Maryland University College
    (UMUC), 120
University of Phoenix, 47

virtual learning communities (VLC), 365–66,
    367
Virtual University for the Small States of the
    Commonwealth, 318
virtual worlds, 223–24

Washington State University, 302
Web 2.0, 180, 280–81
WebCT, 136
World of WarCraft, 223